Treat this book with care and respect.

*It should become part of your personal
and professional library. It will
serve you well at any number
of points during your
professional career.*

SMALL BUSINESS MANAGEMENT

FOURTH EDITION

H. N. Broom, Ph.D.
Professor of Management and Statistics
Baylor University

Justin G. Longenecker, Ph.D.
Professor of Management
Baylor University

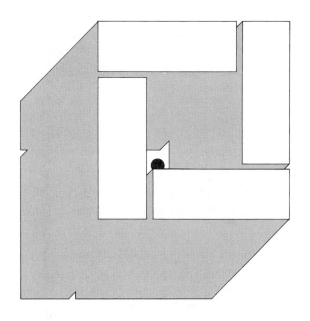

Published by

G23 **SOUTH-WESTERN PUBLISHING CO.**

CINCINNATI   WEST CHICAGO, ILL.   DALLAS   PELHAM MANOR, N.Y.
PALO ALTO. CALIF.   BRIGHTON, ENGLAND

Library of Congress Catalog
Card Number: 74-76898

ISBN No.: 0-538-07230-X

456**K**987

Printed in the United States of America

PREFACE

Small business firms constitute an important part of today's business system. The role of small business in our economic history, moreover, has been one of distinction and contribution. Although its relative importance has declined with the growth of big business, small firms in the 1970s are still making a major contribution to American economic life.

In a rapidly changing economic and social environment, managers of small business firms must anticipate and adjust promptly to significant shifts in customers' demands, competitors' actions, and public expectations. The issues of business strategy and social responsibility are crucial, therefore, in the management of a small enterprise. Although environmental change creates problems, it also creates opportunities. In every community, well-managed small firms are following strategies that enable them both to prosper and to contribute to the public welfare.

Improving the quality of small firm management will strengthen an important sector of the economy and also contribute to the success of individual firms. It is for this reason that the primary focus of this book is upon effective management of small business firms. The management process includes not only strategy determination but also the varied activities necessary in planning, organizing, actuating, and controlling small business operations. In each area the emphasis is placed upon those aspects of management that are uniquely important to small firms.

Text material has been updated and rewritten in this fourth edition. As one example, the text now includes an expanded treatment of business strategy and the process of strategic planning for small firms. This new edition also reflects current pressures of environmentalism, consumerism, and other issues of social responsibility. Fourteen new cases provide additional opportunities for student analysis of current problems and experience in decision making. The cases are diversified in character and portray a variety of administrative problems in many different business contexts.

Some chapters have been rearranged to provide a more orderly coverage of subject matter. In Part A we take a broad view of small business by considering its role in the American economy and the general patterns of success and failure. We then examine the basic management and business functions of small firms in Part B, and in Part C we deal with the processes involved in initiating new ventures. In Parts D and E we focus upon the areas of marketing management and financial management of the small firm; then we discuss its legal and governmental relationships in Part F. In the concluding section, Part G, we treat the problems involved in managing specific fields of small business such as a retail store, a franchise, a service firm, and a production plant.

In preparing the Fourth Edition, the authors have been aided by both students and colleagues. Small business owners have likewise been generous in providing raw materials for case problems. Among those assisting in supplying and interpreting case materials were J. R. Closs, Homer I. Longenecker, Mike McNamara, Parnell McNamara, Jr., Greg Smith, Johnnie R. Stewart, Nelson H. Sullivan, and Clair D. Weller. Credit lines on a number of cases show that they were prepared by other writers; we are indebted to them for permission to use these cases. In particular, we appreciate the opportunity of using cases prepared by our Baylor colleagues: Dr. Alan N. Cook, Professor Carlos W. Moore, Dr. Curtis C. Reierson, Professor John E. Schoen, Dr. Richard C. Scott, and Dr. J. Clifton Williams. Dr. Burke A. Parsons, Director of Business and Economic Research, Baylor University, helped us locate sources of current business data; and Dr. Emerson O. Henke, our Dean, extended cooperation in various ways. Thanks are also due to our student assistant, Cindy Childs, who helped in typing and editing the manuscript. Finally, we gratefully acknowledge the understanding, cooperation, and contributions of our wives, Norma and Frances, to the completion of this book.

H. N. Broom

Justin G. Longenecker

January, 1975
Waco, Texas

CONTENTS

v

PART B

MANAGERIAL FUNCTIONS, RELATIONS, AND PRACTICES IN SMALL BUSINESS

PART C
INITIAL PROBLEMS IN STARTING A SMALL BUSINESS

PART D

SELLING AND MARKETING RESEARCH IN SMALL BUSINESS

PART E

FINANCIAL AND ADMINISTRATIVE CONTROLS IN SMALL BUSINESS

PART F

LEGAL AND GOVERNMENTAL CONTROLS IN SMALL BUSINESS

PART G

OPERATING CERTAIN TYPES OF SMALL BUSINESS

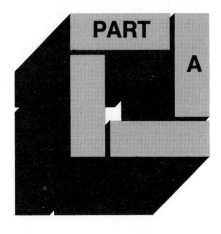

PART A

The Environment for Small Business Entrepreneurs

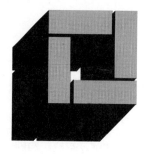

1

Small Business
in the American
Economy

Business in the United States today includes a mixture of both large and small firms. In many industrial areas, big business is clearly dominant. Small business institutions are dwarfed by such giants as General Motors with three-fourths million employees; Bank of America with deposits of $29 billion; Sears, Roebuck with sales of $10 billion; Prudential Insurance Company with $168 billion life insurance in force; and American Telephone and Telegraph Company with an annual profit in excess of $2 billion. Because of the greater visibility of big business, we tend to overestimate its importance and to underestimate the contributions of the less conspicuous small firms which are indispensable to the functioning of our economy.

Before we assess the significance of small business in various segments of our economy, let us look at the various criteria set forth in an attempt to arrive at an explicit definition of small business.

STANDARDS USED IN DEFINING SMALL BUSINESS

The same business may be described as "small" when compared to larger institutions and as "large" when compared to smaller firms. What is "small" depends upon one's point of view. Most observers would classify an independently-owned service station, restaurant, or retail store as a small business. Similarly, most would agree that the major automobile manufacturers are big businesses.[1] In between, however, are firms that may be considered large or small depending upon one's criteria and point of view. An explicit definition of small business is necessary for inclusion in legislation, for research purposes, and for reasoning intelligently concerning problems of the economy.

This raises the question, then, as to what yardsticks should be applied to determine business size. For example, is independent ownership a critical factor? Is either sales volume or number of employees a logical guide in describing smallness? Can a small business be described accurately in the same manner in both manufacturing and retailing? Can a business properly be described as small because its competitors are much larger? These and many other questions

---

[1] In 1966, the Small Business Administration classified American Motors, the nation's 63rd largest company with more than 28,000 employees, as small business. This permitted American Motors to enjoy special advantages in bidding on government contracts. The decision illustrated the arbitrary nature of such definitions and the unusual classifications that are possible.

come to mind as an attempt is made to introduce some precision into the concept of small business.

The number of employees on the firm's payroll is perhaps the most widely-used criterion, with 100 employees constituting a typical line of demarcation between small and large business. As a practical matter, however, many quite different standards have been applied at one time or another. There has been little consistency even from one piece of legislation to another. In fact, guides adopted for one purpose have often seemed impractical for use elsewhere.

Small Business Administration Standards

The Small Business Act of 1953 provides that a small business concern is "one which is independently owned and operated and not dominant in its field of operation." The Act also authorized the Small Business Administration, in making a more detailed definition, to use such criteria as number of employees and sales volume.[2]

In its lending programs the Small Business Administration has established upper limits for small firms as follows:[3]

Retailing and Service	$1 million to $5 million annual sales, depending on the industry
Wholesaling	$5 million to $15 million annual sales, depending on the industry
Manufacturing	250 or fewer employees (If employment is between 250 and 1,500, a size standard for the particular industry is used.)

Committee for Economic Development Standards

An examination of quantitative standards provides some conception of the nature of small business. In fact, these standards are both useful and necessary for some purposes. It seems likely, however, that certain qualitative measurements may be more practical as the primary approach to an analysis of managerial problems peculiar to the small business. Perhaps the best outline of qualitative characteristics is that prepared by the Committee for Economic Development.[4] In the view of this organization, any small business is characterized by at least two of the following key features:

1. Management is independent. Usually the managers are also owners.
2. Capital is supplied and ownership is held by an individual or a small group.
3. The area of operations is mainly local. Workers and owners are in one home community. Markets need not be local.
4. The business is small when compared to the biggest units in its field. The size of the top bracket varies greatly, so that what might seem large in one field would be definitely small in another.

---

[2] *Public Statement of Loan Policy* (Washington, D.C.: Small Business Administration, September, 1954), p. 1.

[3] *SBA Business Loans* (Washington, D.C.: Small Business Administration, 1973).

[4] *Meeting the Special Problems of Small Business* (New York: Committee for Economic Development, 1947), p. 14.

These characteristics vary in significance depending upon the particular problem involved. The factors of ownership and independence of management, for example, are much more important in financial management than in plant layout consideration. In general, the discussion of management concepts in this book is aimed at the type of concern that closely fits the C.E.D. pattern. More explicitly, the discussion will be directed toward independently controlled firms that offer both job and investment opportunities to entrepreneurs.

SCOPE AND TREND OF SMALL BUSINESS

In determining the importance of small business in the United States, two questions must be answered. The first concerns the amount or proportion of small business, and the second relates to the trend in small business volume. Expressed otherwise, how much business is "small," and is small business growing or declining?

Relative Importance of Small Business

An evaluation of the position of small business requires a comparison of small versus large concerns. A number of different measures might be used for this purpose. Based on the number of business units, for example, small business is of overwhelming importance. According to Table 1-1, about 95 percent of the firms have fewer than 20 employees, while fewer than 1 percent have more than 100 employees. This comparison is not completely realistic, however, because of the greater importance of large corporations.

Table 1-1
DISTRIBUTION OF FIRMS AND PAID EMPLOYMENT BY SIZE OF FIRM, 1967*

Size Class (Number of Employees)	Percent of Firms in Operation	Percent of Paid Employment	Cumulative Percent of Paid Employment
All size classes	100.0	100.0	
1- 19	94.7	21.7	21.7
20- 99	4.5	18.2	39.9
100-499	0.7	13.2	53.1
500 or more	0.1	46.8	99.9**

*Includes data for construction, manufacturing, mineral, retail trade, selected services, and wholesale trade industries.
** Total does not equal 100% because of rounding.
Source: U.S. Bureau of the Census, *Enterprise Statistics, 1967*, Part 1—General Report on Industrial Organization, Table 3-1 (Washington: U.S. Government Printing Office, 1972).

To correct this distortion, employment data can be used to show the distribution of personnel among businesses of various sizes. Even on this basis, small business accounts for a substantial portion of total employment. According to Table 1-1, firms with fewer than 100 employees account for about 40 percent of all paid employment;[5] those with fewer than 500 employees have about 53 percent. Regardless of the exact point at which one draws the line between large and small business, it is apparent that much—perhaps close to one half—of American business must be classed as small.

It is equally clear that small business is relatively more important in certain sectors of the economy than in others. Figure 1-1 presents a breakdown of paid employment by type of industry and size of firm. As might be expected, big business is strongest in manufacturing and mining. In contrast, small business predominates in service industries, wholesale trade, and retail trade. In the service industries, for example, only 35 percent of the employees in the industry are on the payroll of firms with 100 or more employees.

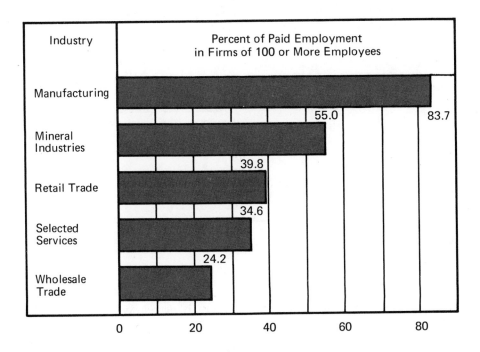

Figure 1-1
DISTRIBUTION OF PAID EMPLOYMENT BY INDUSTRY AND SIZE OF FIRM, 1967

Source: U.S. Bureau of the Census, *Enterprise Statistics, 1967*, Part I—General Report on Industrial Organization, Table 3-1 (Washington: U.S. Government Printing Office, 1972).

Vitality of Small Business

Political oratory might easily lead one to conclude that small business is vanishing and will soon be extinct. The champion of small business often

---

[5] Paid employment constitutes a simple and convenient criterion for an analysis of this type. One weakness is its tendency to understate small business volume by omitting proprietors, partners, and unpaid family help.

pictures small firms as powerless victims of big business corporations that are gradually taking over the economy. To understand the truth or error of these views, it in necessary to examine the trend of small business in recent decades.

Even though small business concerns have continued to survive, a question remains as to the business volume and importance of these units. Firms with a substantial volume may have been replaced by units of insignificant size. It is desirable, therefore, to examine changes in the structure of the economy with respect to the relative importance of different sized units.

Historical data for three industries (manufacturing, retail trade, and wholesale trade) indicate that the small business segment of the United States economy has grown less rapidly than the big business segment. Table 1-2 shows that, between 1947 and 1967, value added by the 200 largest manufacturing companies jumped from 30 percent to 42 percent of the total value added by manufacturing.

Table 1-2
PROPORTION OF MANUFACTURING ACTIVITY ACCOUNTED FOR BY THE LARGEST MANUFACTURING COMPANIES, 1947-1967

Year	Percent of Total Value Added	
	By 50 Largest Companies	By 200 Largest Companies
1947	17	30
1954	23	37
1958	23	38
1963	25	41
1967	25	42

Source: *Statistical Abstract of the United States*, 1972, p. 703.

In retailing, Table 1-3 shows that chains with 101 or more units increased their percent of sales from 12 percent to almost 19 percent of the industry total between 1948 and 1967.

Table 1-3
DISTRIBUTION OF SALES IN RETAIL TRADE BY SIZE OF FIRM, 1948-1967

Number of Units in Firm	Percent of Total Sales				
	1948	1954	1958	1963	1967
Single units	70.4	69.9	66.3	63.4	60.2
2 to 3 units	6.9	6.4	6.9	6.5	5.8
4 to 25 units	7.1	7.1	7.1	7.7	8.3
26 to 100 units	3.3	4.0	5.4	6.7	7.0
101 or more units	12.3	12.6	14.3	15.8	18.6

Source: U.S. Bureau of the Census, *Census of Business, 1967*, Vol. I, p. xxv; and *Census of Business, 1963*, Vol. I, p. 4-3.

Table 1-4 shows that the largest wholesalers—those with six or more units —increased their percentage of industry sales from 35 percent to 47 percent between 1939 and 1967.

Table 1-4
DISTRIBUTION OF SALES IN WHOLESALE TRADE BY SIZE OF FIRM, 1939-1967

Number of Establishments Operated by Firm	Percent of Sales			
	1939	1948	1963	1967
Single units	52.1	49.7	43.4	40.9
2 units	5.2	5.2	5.9	4.8
3 to 5 units	7.9	7.8	6.6	7.2
6 or more units	34.8	37.4	44.2	47.1

Source: U.S. Bureau of the Census, *Census of Business, 1963*, p. xxxii; and *Census of Business, 1967*, Vol. III, p. xx.

In each of the three industries above, it is evident that the shift has been in the direction of big business. While proponents of small business may be disturbed by this trend, the fact remains that small business is far from extinct. Even though there has been a shift of volume to larger concerns, small firms still account for a substantial portion of total business. The final section of this chapter will therefore explore the major areas of business to discover the variety and extent of small business opportunities.

FIELDS OF SMALL BUSINESS

In every major industry there are successful small firms. Small business entrepreneurs operate manufacturing plants, retail stores, florist shops, coal mines, radio stations, wholesale drug companies, construction firms, and hundreds of other types of businesses. Although the fields of small business are thus similar to the fields of business in general, smaller firms are relatively more important in some areas of the economy than in others—for example, in retailing than in manufacturing. The various business fields considered here are arbitrarily classified in the interest of providing a framework for discussion.

Production of Basic Raw Materials

Small-scale mining constitutes one major area of industry involving production of basic raw materials. Individual prospectors may become miners when they "make a strike," and the mine often continues to operate as a small business for many years. The mineral in question might be coal, gold, silver, copper, iron ore, zinc, uranium, or many others. There are thousands of small bituminous coal mines, for example, some of them strip mines that are operated with only a few employees. Similarly, wildcatters operating on a shoestring have brought in many an oil well. Some quarries and sand and gravel companies might also be classified in this area.

Mining provides opportunities for thousands of small entrepreneurs even though big business has considerable strength in this area. As Figure 1-2 shows, companies with fewer than 100 employees account for 45 percent of the total employment in this industry.

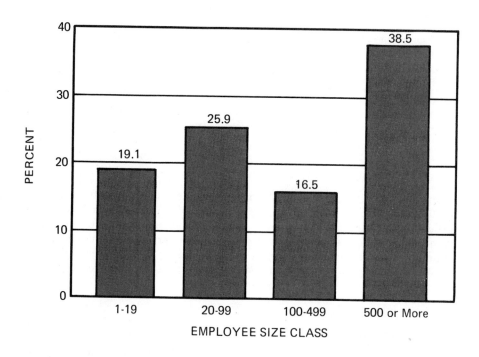

Figure 1-2
SIZE OF FIRM IN MINERAL INDUSTRIES
(DISTRIBUTION OF PAID EMPLOYMENT, 1967)

Source: U.S. Bureau of the Census, *Enterprise Statistics, 1967*, Part 1—General Report on Industrial Organization, Table 3-1 (Washington: U.S. Government Printing Office, 1972).

In the agricultural category are found such producers as the vegetable farmer of the Rio Grande Valley, the corn and grain farmers of the Middle West, the wheat ranchers of Kansas, the owner-operator of California and Florida orange groves, and the rice farmers and beet sugar producers of Louisiana. Chicken and turkey hatcheries and small-scale cattle ranches are also examples of original, agricultural producers.

Certain natural-product producers defy precise classification in either of the above categories. Examples include the salmon fisherman of the Columbia River region, among other river, lake, and deep-sea fishermen; small-scale loggers; and harvesters of moss in the bayous of Louisiana.

Although agriculture and forest products are fields of raw material production, as exemplified above, their operating and management problems are considerably different from those of other industrial fields. Many of the management concepts apply to enterprises of this nature, but the primary emphasis is on concerns in the nonagricultural field.

Manufacturing

Although big business overshadows small business in manufacturing, there are nonetheless hundreds of thousands of small concerns in this area. Small enterprises of this type include bakeries, sawmills, toy factories, job printing shops, shoe factories, bookbinding plants, ice cream plants, and soft drink bottling works. Small machine shops, ironworks, ready-mixed concrete plants,

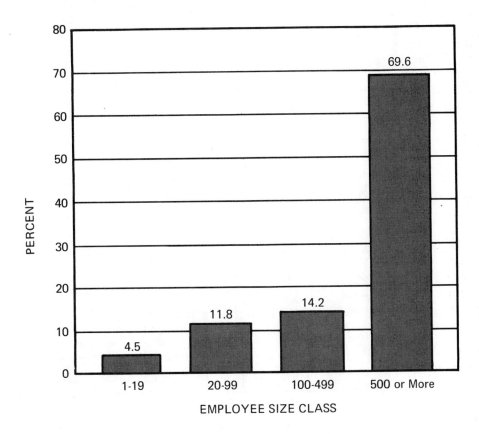

Figure 1-3
SIZE OF FIRM IN MANUFACTURING INDUSTRIES
(DISTRIBUTION OF PAID EMPLOYMENT, 1967)

Source: U.S. Bureau of the Census, *Enterprise Statistics, 1967*, Part 1—General Report on Industrial Organization, Table 3-1 (Washington: U.S. Government Printing Office, 1972).

cabinet shops, furniture manufacturing plants, and clothing manufacturing plants also fit this category. The list could be expanded indefinitely.

Manufacturing involves the conversion of basic raw materials into useful products needed and wanted by society. Manufacturing production requires a man-designed, machine-assisted process in which the component machines process or transport the materials. It is the larger investment required for production facilities that causes the average firm size to be greater in manufacturing than in most other areas. According to Figure 1-3 on page 9, almost 70 percent of manufacturing employment is concentrated in firms with more than 500 employees.

Wholesaling

Without question, wholesale trade is basically a small business area. Figure 1-4 shows that firms with fewer than 100 employees are responsible for more than 75 percent of the industry's paid employment. Even very small firms—those with fewer than 20 employees—have 41 percent of the total employment.

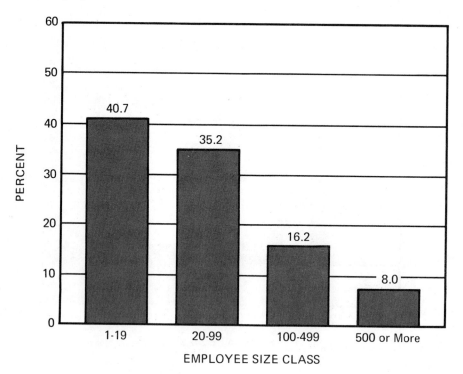

Figure 1-4
SIZE OF FIRM IN WHOLESALE TRADE
(DISTRIBUTION OF PAID EMPLOYMENT, 1967)

Source: U.S. Bureau of the Census, *Enterprise Statistics, 1967*, Part 1—General Report on Industrial Organization, Table 3-1 (Washington: U.S. Government Printing Office, 1972).

Small wholesale firms sell a wide range of products, such as drugs, groceries, hardware, fruits and vegetables, grain and farm produce, farm implements and supplies, machinery, industrial supplies, and electrical appliances. Petroleum bulk stations are also considered wholesale businesses, as are agents and brokers who buy or sell raw materials or manufactured products for the account of others. The wholesaler's function is primarily that of acting as middleman between manufacturers and retailers or industrial users—assembling, storing, and distributing the products.

Retailing

Retailers are merchants who sell goods to ultimate consumers, that is, to the customer who buys for individual or family use.

Small business examples abound. Among these are corner drugstores, independent grocery and meat markets, clothing stores, shoe stores, millinery shops, variety stores, auto accessories dealers, vendors of electrical appliances, bookstores, music stores, service stations, restaurants and other eating establishments, and general stores. Other examples include jewelry stores, hardware

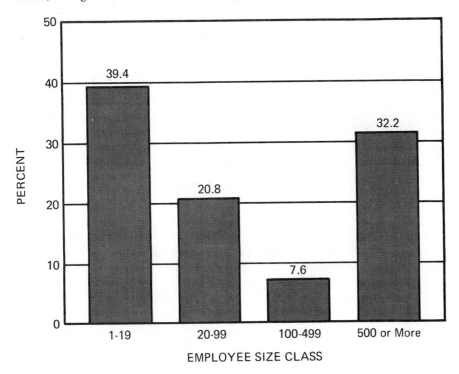

Figure 1-5
SIZE OF FIRM IN RETAIL TRADE
(DISTRIBUTION OF PAID EMPLOYMENT, 1967)

Source: U.S. Bureau of the Census, *Enterprise Statistics, 1967*, Part 1—General Report on Industrial Organization, Table 3-1 (Washington: U.S. Government Printing Office, 1972).

stores, record shops, sporting goods stores, toy stores, ice cream stands, furniture stores, and vending machine businesses. The range of small retailing extends even to small supermarkets, department stores, and mail-order houses.

Retail trade is an area in which small business predominates. Even though there are many chain stores, department stores, and mail-order firms that are business giants, the typical retailer is a small businessman. In fact, Figure 1-5 on page 11 indicates that 60 percent of the paid employees in retail trade are with firms having fewer than 100 employees.

Service Industries

Any attempt to catalog service businesses immediately impresses one with the diversity of these firms; there are far more than the famed 57 varieties. It may be helpful to note several broad classifications into which most service concerns can be fitted.[6]

Business Services. Business concerns of this type render service to other business organizations. Firms in this area include accounting firms, advertising agencies, public relations counselors, collection services, private employment agencies, blueprint services, tax consultants, management consultants, addressing services, and a host of others.

Personal Services. In the personal service group are found such concerns as barber and beauty shops, shoeshine stands, cleaning-pressing shops, laundries, coin laundries, funeral homes, photographic studios, travel agencies, and business colleges. Other examples include baby-sitting services, piano teachers and tuners, and public stenographers.

Automobile and Repair Services. The repair services include automobile repair, shoe repair, jewelry repair, upholstery and furniture repair, electrical repair, and blacksmith shops. In addition, automobile parking garages, parking lots, automobile and truck rental services, and car-wash establishments may be classified in this group.

Entertainment and Recreation Services. These include not only sports promoters and owners of professional athletic organizations, but also bowling alleys, swimming pools, racetracks, motion picture theaters, theatrical presentations, amusement parks, dance bands, orchestras, and the like.

Hotels and Motels. The operation of hotels, motels, tourist courts, and automobile trailer camps constitutes still another type of service provided by small business establishments.

Perhaps the outstanding characteristic of the service trade industries is their smallness. Even in nonservice industries—for example, retailing and

---

[6] It would be possible to classify members of the recognized professions, such as attorneys, architects, doctors, and dentists, as service businesses. They are excluded from the groups discussed, however, for reasons of expediency. Even though principles of business management are pertinent to certain of their operations, their activities are for the most part beyond the scope of this book. Of course, certified public accountants and others supplying business services are often regarded as professions, but they are included in the business services group.

wholesaling—service is a strong asset of the small entrepreneurs. It is the one point at which small entrepreneurs can often get the better of larger competitors. In a business that is exclusively service, therefore, an impressive advantage rests with the smaller operators.

According to Figure 1-6, 65 percent of the paid employees in service businesses are in firms of fewer than 100 employees. There is some variation in the relative importance of small firms in the different service fields. The hotel and motel group, for example, has more large concerns than any of the other groups. In fact, about 50 percent of the hotel and motel employees work in organizations with 100 or more employees. At the other extreme, only three or four percent of the employees of automobile repair shops work for companies that have 100 or more employees.[7]

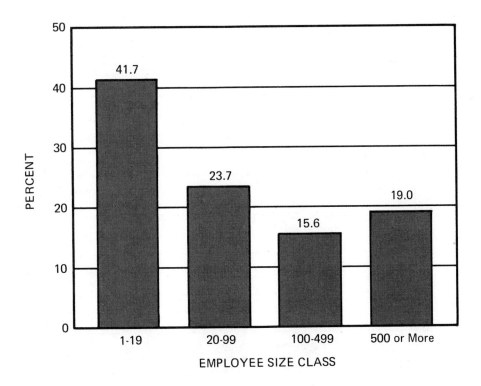

Figure 1-6
SIZE OF FIRM IN SERVICE INDUSTRIES
(DISTRIBUTION OF PAID EMPLOYMENT, 1967)

Source: U.S. Bureau of the Census, *Enterprise Statistics, 1967*, Part 1—General Report on Industrial Organization, Table 3-1 (Washington: U.S. Government Printing Office, 1972).

---

[7] U.S. Bureau of the Census, *Enterprise Statistics, 1967*, Part 1—General Report on U.S. Industrial Organization, Table 3-2 (Washington: U.S. Government Printing Office, 1972).

Finance, Insurance, and Real Estate

The best-known example of small financial institutions is the country bank, which means simply a commercial bank of relatively small size in a small town. In addition to commercial banks, other financial institutions include loan companies, pawnbrokers, sales finance companies, savings banks, building and loan associations, and credit unions.

Insurance agencies and real estate brokerage firms are two types of concerns in which small business predominates. The insurance agent is an independent businessman who represents and sells insurance policies for insurance companies. Most of the insurance companies themselves are sufficiently large to require classification as big business. The typical real estate brokerage firm employs only a few brokers. Insurance and real estate often are combined in the same organization.

Figure 1-7 portrays the relative importance of the small entrepreneur in the entire field of finance, insurance, and real estate. The importance of small firms is evident from this chart, which shows that 11 percent of the total receipts is in firms with less than $1 million in total assets and that 25 percent of the total receipts is in firms with less than $25 million in total assets.

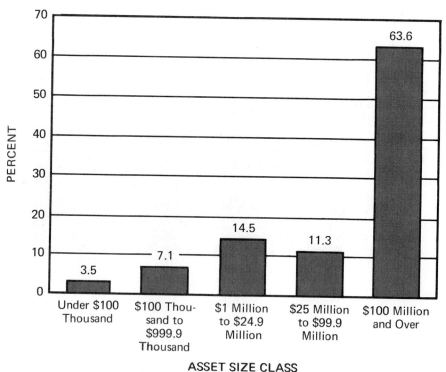

ASSET SIZE CLASS

Figure 1-7
SIZE OF FIRM IN FINANCE, INSURANCE, AND REAL ESTATE
(DISTRIBUTION OF TOTAL RECEIPTS OF CORPORATIONS, 1969)

Source: *Statistical Abstract of the United States, 1972,* p. 480.

Contract Construction

Although the general contractors who erect skyscrapers and mammoth factory buildings are big business concerns, there are thousands of small firms serving as general contractors on a more modest scale. In addition to general contracting, small firms play an important role in such specialized fields as electrical, plumbing, and painting contracting. Even public construction contractors such as those building streets, bridges, and sewers many times are small concerns.

It might seem to the layman that huge construction companies are responsible for most building, but the opposite is true. It is the small businessman who is the major builder in this country.

Figure 1-8 shows that 69 percent of the total employment of corporations engaged in contract construction was in firms with fewer than 100 employees. Only 13.5 percent of the industry's employment was in firms with 500 or more employees.

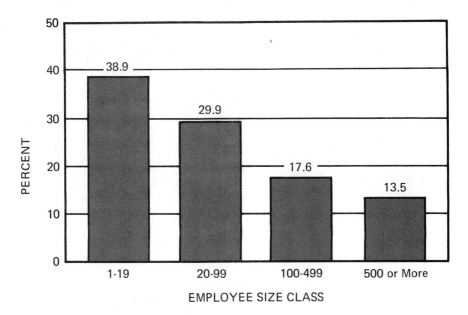

Figure 1-8
SIZE OF FIRM IN CONTRACT CONSTRUCTION
(DISTRIBUTION OF PAID EMPLOYMENT, 1967)

Source: U.S. Bureau of the Census, *Enterprise Statistics, 1967*, Part 1—General Report on Industrial Organization, Table 3-1 (Washington: U.S. Government Printing Office, 1972).

Transportation, Communication, and Public Utilities

In the field of transportation, communication, and public utilities, the investment in physical facilities is generally so great that only large firms can operate profitably.

As described in Figure 1-9, 72 percent of the corporate receipts in this industry is in very large firms—those with $100 million or more in total assets.

To be sure, there are successful small firms in this field even though they
account for a relatively small proportion of total output. Examples of such
concerns are taxicab companies; local bus lines; privately owned water systems; chartered flight services; radio and television stations; and publishers of
newspapers, books, and periodicals. It can be seen that, in certain specific fields,
small firms are much more important for the economy as a whole.

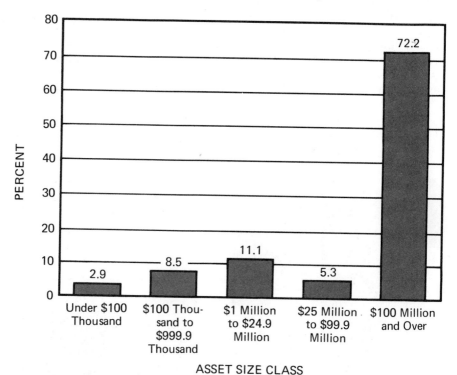

Figure 1-9
**SIZE OF FIRM IN TRANSPORTATION, COMMUNICATION, ELECTRIC, GAS, AND
SANITARY SERVICES
(DISTRIBUTION OF TOTAL RECEIPTS OF CORPORATIONS, 1969)**

Source: *Statistical Abstract of the United States, 1972,* p. 480.

 # Summary

1. Business firms may be described as large or small depending upon one's criteria
   and point of view. A number of quantitative yardsticks are available for the purpose of classifying firms on the basis of size. Although some of these are useful for

particular purposes, the characteristics suggested by the Committee for Economic Development describe quite well the independently owned and managed concern which is of primary interest in this book.

2. Although the overwhelming proportion of business firms is small, these firms account for a much lower proportion of production and employment. Perhaps close to one half of all business might be classified as small. In certain sectors of the economy—wholesale trade, retail trade, and service industries—small business predominates.

3. In the last two decades there has been an increase in the relative importance of large firms. This trend is discernible in manufacturing, wholesale trade, and retail trade.

4. There is a marked difference in the relative importance of small business in the various business and industrial fields. Small firms show their greatest strength relative to big business in wholesaling, retailing, service industries, contract construction, and mining.

5. Small concerns are overshadowed by large business in the fields of manufacturing; transportation, communication, and public utilities; and finance, insurance, and real estate.

 Discussion Questions

1. Is there any logical reason for the numerous different definitions of small business?

2. What virtues are there in the definition of small business proposed by the Committee for Economic Development?

3. (a) Of the businesses with which you are acquainted, which is the largest that you consider to be in the small business category? (b) Does it conform to any or all of the definitions given in this chapter?

4. What generalizations can you make about the relative importance of large and small business in the United States?

5. (a) In which sectors of the economy is small business most important? (b) What accounts for its strength in these areas?

6. What evidence is there of the increasing or decreasing importance of small business in this country?

7. In what fields of business are small firms less important than large concerns?

8. What accounts for the greater relative strength of large business (a) in manufacturing, (b) in transportation, and (c) in communication and public utilities?

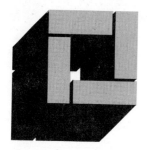

2

The Strengths and Weaknesses of Small Business

A free society such as ours gives business firms the right to exist and to function because they produce material goods and services for the use and enjoyment of its citizens. All legitimate business concerns presumably create such social values, but small firms provide a number of unique benefits. At the same time, small firms encounter their share of problems, some of which are directly related to their smallness. Similarly, their smallness endows them with a number of potential competitive strengths. This chapter treats these three aspects of the social role of small business—its special values, unique problems, and competitive strengths. The chapter concludes with an assessment of the impact of these various factors on small business in the future.

VALUES IN SMALL BUSINESS

The quantitative significance of small business has been noted in Chapter 1. To understand its full importance, however, it is necessary to recognize the virtues inherent in an economic structure in which small business plays an important role.

Freedom of Opportunity

One basic tenet of the American economic system is freedom of opportunity. Fortunately, our economic institutions have been such as to give broad scope to this concept of freedom. It has meant not only the right to select one's employer, but also the right to launch a new business enterprise.

Few barriers have been placed before the individual aspiring to business entrepreneurship. Little except ambition and beginning capital are required, and a few who try even succeed with ambition alone. As some have pointed out, this failure to screen prospective business owners permits entry by the unqualified as well as by the able. This means that freedom of opportunity may be a freedom to fail as well as to earn a profit. Freedom of opportunity does not guarantee success.

To the millions who are entrepreneurs, this particular freedom is one of the most cherished features of American life. To countless others, there is deep appreciation of the possibility of entering business if and when desired. Because these rights are meaningful and valuable to so many Americans, the five million small business institutions constitute a desirable aspect of the economic system in this country.

Areas of Small Business Superiority

One occasionally encounters the idea that big business is uniformly more efficient than small business. According to this idea, small business exists because of a charitable attitude or because big business has not yet entered a particular field of endeavor. The principal protection of small business is thought by those who hold this concept to be through government aid in one form or another. Such an extreme position, however, is unsupported by the facts. Analysis of the structure of American business reveals many areas in which the optimum-size establishment is not large.

It is true that technological considerations justify big business institutions in some industries. In steel and auto manufacturing, for example, production facilities must be sizable, requiring the accumulation of large amounts of capital. The factor of technology, however, does not apply with equal force to all industries. To illustrate, the production facilities and the capital investment required in most toy manufacturing plants, grocery stores, and shoe repair shops are relatively small. In many areas of the American economy, then, there is little advantage to be gained by big business from technology.

Mass production requires mass markets. In contrast, a limited or specialized market may be best served by a small business. One does not load a cannon to shoot a sparrow. Geography and product specialization both provide special, limited markets effectively served by small business concerns.

In the trailer manufacturing industry, for example, most of the emphasis is upon production of mobile homes or house trailers.[1] Sales of commercial and industrial trailers—which can be used for offices, labs, machine shops, and classrooms—are relatively small, estimated at less than 5 percent of total sales. Because of the small volume, many larger producers decline to engage in custom manufacturing of commercial and industrial trailers unless they can get large orders for 40 or more units. Specifically, they object to processing small orders that interfere with regular assembly operations. Reluctance of larger producers to compete vigorously for custom business permits smaller manufacturers, with annual sales volume running as low as $1,000,000, to secure much of this business.

Aside from considerations of market size and technology, small business generally can boast of several advantages. For example, small firms are able to resist the snowballing of overhead costs that plagues many large concerns. Flexibility and adaptability are virtues of many small businesses, contrasting sharply with cumbersome procedures of large organizations. The small business entrepreneur is also close to customers and employees, and this closeness provides a potential superiority.

There is economic justification, then, for the continued existence of small business concerns. They prosper and contribute to a higher standard of living by performing many tasks more efficiently than big business is able to do.

---

[1] "Offices That Can Hit the Road," *Business Week* (September 22, 1962), pp. 68-70.

Interdependence of Business

The interdependence of all kinds of business is one of the basic realities of our economic life. The fact that some functions are more expertly performed by small business enables the small firm to contribute to the success of larger business concerns. If small business were suddenly removed from the contemporary scene, big business would find itself saddled with a myriad of activities that could be only inefficiently performed.

Consider, for example, the process of distribution. Few manufacturers of consumer products find it desirable to own all of their wholesale and retail outlets. Chain stores and other big business retailing institutions are business giants, but they account for less than one half of retail sales. This fact of small business dominance in retailing clearly shows the vital role of small business in distributing the products of both large and small manufacturers.

Service as suppliers and subcontractors for larger concerns constitutes another significant role of small business. General Motors, for example, purchases goods and services from more than 37,000 smaller businesses, over three-fourths of whom employ fewer than 100 persons.[2] In addition, General Motors depends upon some 14,000 dealerships and 128,000 other retail outlets.

In national defense efforts this task of supplying prime contractors of governmental defense agencies becomes of critical importance. By means of subcontracting, large manufacturers are able to expand production facilities rapidly, thus contributing to a more effective defense effort.

Although distribution and supply functions constitute major aids of small firms to big business, this is not the limit of their contribution. Small business purchases raw materials, equipment, and supplies from larger concerns. In addition, a variety of services are offered to large concerns as illustrated by machine shop work, trucking service, and catering service. Professional services to big business are rendered also by accountants, lawyers, doctors, and other professional men who might be classed as small businessmen. Big business also gains through the services small firms render to purchasers of products made by large manufacturers. Electrical and other repair services are typical of such service firms.

Sources of Innovation

In the American economy there are approximately five million nonfarm business concerns. This means that experimentation and innovation may originate in five million different business institutions. It is true, of course, that innovation may come from individuals as well as from business units; but the primary emphasis here is upon innovation originating within industry or leading to formation of new firms. The question is whether many small units are more productive of discoveries and developments than a smaller number of larger units would be. If small business were largely replaced by big business, what would be the effect upon progress in producing new or better products, in rendering superior service, or in devising more efficient methods of production or distribution?

---

[2] James M. Roche, "Understanding: The Key to Business-Government Cooperation," *Michigan Business Review*, Vol. 21, No. 2 (March, 1969), p. 9.

The discoveries and the developments of industrial research laboratories must be recorded to the credit of the large business corporations supporting them. There is no question as to the considerable value of their contributions to the American standard of living. There is question, however, as to whether innovations would be maximized by concentrating industrial research in organizations of this type.

There is a tendency for the research of big business to emphasize the improvement of existing products. The thinking and the energies of personnel are channeled in this direction. It is quite likely, in fact, that some ideas are sidetracked because of their not being related to existing products or because of their unusual nature. Preoccupation with an existing product can sometimes blind one to the value of a novel idea. The jet engine, for example, had difficulty securing consideration by those who had been accustomed to internal combustion engines.

Revolutionary ideas often originate outside large business organizations. Some studies of patent records, in fact, show that the majority of major innovations originate with the individual or the small business. In a study of 61 major inventions of the twentieth century, Jewkes, Sawers, and Stillerman concluded that more than one half can be ranked as individual inventions.[3] These include such well-known examples as air conditioning, automatic transmission, ballpoint pen, cellophane, cinerama, helicopter, insulin, jet engine, kodachrome, power steering, and the zip fastener. It is also noteworthy that two revolutionary product developments in the photographic industry—copying machines and instant photography—are associated with newcomers like Xerox and Polaroid rather than with Eastman Kodak.

Moreover, new services are often inaugurated by small business entrepreneurs who perceive the need for such services. Consequently, the presence in the economy of millions of small business units tends to stimulate progress by providing many centers of initiative and sources of innovation.

Encouraging Competition

Many economists, beginning with Adam Smith, have expounded the values inherent in economic competition. In a competitive situation the entrepreneur is motivated to act in a socially desirable manner by the drive of individual self-interest. "It is not from the benevolence of the butcher, the brewer, or the baker that we expect our dinner," wrote Adam Smith, "but from their regard to their self-interest. We address ourselves, not to their humanity, but to their self-love, and never talk to them of our necessities, but of their advantages." It is competition that acts as the regulator to transform selfishness into service.

When monopoly replaces competition, the customer is at the mercy of the monopolist. The monopolist may set an exorbitant price, withhold a technological development, exclude new competitors, or otherwise abuse his position of power. To be sure, there are few absolute monopolies, but concentration in a number of industries approximates this condition. The administered price has replaced the market-determined price in many areas of the economy.

---

[3] John Jewkes, David Sawers, and Richard Stillerman, *The Sources of Invention* (London: Macmillan and Co., Ltd., 1958), p. 82. By permission.

There is no guarantee of competition in numbers alone. Many tiny concerns may be no match for one large firm or even several firms that dominate an industry. Generally speaking, however, the existence of many healthy small business firms in an industry constitutes a barrier against monopoly. The five million small business units may thus be viewed as a desirable bulwark of the American capitalistic system.

Other Socially Desirable Virtues

The factors already discussed do not exhaust the values inherent in small business. Among others that are important are the following:

1. Small business operation is a means of self-employment for older persons, physically handicapped persons, and minority groups who find it difficult to obtain gainful employment elsewhere.
2. Individual entrepreneurs profit from the management experience and the practice in the art of leadership gained as entrepreneurs whether they remain such or take jobs in big business later on.
3. Large business concerns, except via mergers, do not ordinarily start big. Nearly all industrial giants of today, such as Ford, Du Pont, and International Harvester Company, started as small businesses owned and operated as sole proprietorships. Small business, thus, is the progenitor of big business.

PROBLEMS OF SMALL BUSINESS

All business firms face problems, and small firms enjoy no special immunity. Surveys have from time to time verified the existence and, to some extent, discovered the nature of such problems.[4] Although researchers have established no "official list" or uniformly-recognized group of difficulties, they have detected a number of recurring themes. An effort has been made in this section to touch upon entrepreneurial concerns that are rather generally troublesome to small business. The first step toward positive management is the identification and understanding of these problem areas.

Lack of Management Ability and Management Depth

Perhaps the greatest problem of small business management is the lack of necessary skills in the management group. In a very small business the entrepreneur is a one-person management team. Even with the assistance of a small management staff, the entrepreneur must "spread himself thin." Top-level decisions, together with all the lesser tasks of management that the assistants cannot accomplish, devolve on the entrepreneur. Unfortunately this requires a diversity of talents—and no individual has superior ability in all areas of management. In fact, a merchant or an industrialist may have only one area of special ability. Perhaps this individual is a superior salesperson, a shrewd buyer, or a creative inventor. It may be that this individual is a production

---

[4] For example, a survey of small business problems was authorized by a presidentially-appointed task force and reported in "Improving the Prospects of Small Business," Report of the President's Task Force on Improving the Prospects of Small Business (Washington: U.S. Government Printing Office, 1970).

specialist of superior ability. But no one person possesses all of these abilities to a high degree. Hence, the small entrepreneur who must perform these functions with little or no managerial help faces a problem of serious proportions.

The management process is hampered not only by a lack of diversified talents but also by the manager's frequently casual or superficial approach to management problems. The manager often does not understand the intricacies of maintaining adequate business records or of preparing financial statements. Or, if financial data are available, the manager may lack the necessary knowledge or appreciation of their value to interpret and use them effectively. Big business managers either know how to use the records and statements properly to guide decision making, or they employ experts to do so for them. Small businesses alone are plagued by inadequacy and serious misuse of business records and business information.

Small business managers also fail to exercise the highest quality of management insofar as they are bound by tradition and are insensitive to need for change in policies and practices. They are often severely limited in terms of both education and experience. Closed minds that lack a realization of a changing world of business cannot be alert to, or even aware of, possibilities for application of big business methods in the small firm.

The use of inept, second-generation owner-managers presents another facet of the problem of small business deficiencies in management. This does not mean that a father should not be succeeded by his son if the son has the requisite courage and skill to run the business. But nepotism that seats an untrained, unskilled son in his father's place at the head of a family business is unfortunate.

The small business entrepreneur also has a unique problem in arranging for the management succession. When a proprietor dies, for example, the heirs may reorganize the business and continue operations. Some heirs may be untrained and unequal to the management task. Selecting, training, and retaining a manager who is competent to assume leadership is most difficult. Such a manager is often ambitious to own, as well as to manage, the business. Even if the owner had sons and daughters, there would be difficulties. These heirs could create a partnership, but such partners would not necessarily be either able or compatible. A single son might be disinterested in the business, sell it in order to follow his own career interest, and so waste his father's efforts. Such a son might also be unequal to the job of running the business, with the result that he runs it into bankruptcy. Such situations are unlikely to occur in a big business firm.

Personal Lack and Misuse of Time

Deficiencies in management ability and a lack of management depth combine to create a closely related problem—personal shortage of time in which to manage the business. It is true that an executive in large business may also suffer from time pressures, but the manager of a small concern faces uniquely severe time pressures. Frequently, this individual bears the management burdens alone. The jobs are varied, and the limits on managerial responsibilities are few, if any. The manager is "jack of all trades and master of none." In a very small firm the manager may even help out at the worker level on occasion, packing a rush order in the small factory or delivering merchandise to a valued customer who insists on immediate service. This means that the manager does not have the opportunity to operate solely at the executive level.

This lack of time to manage is accentuated by participation in civic affairs and by time devoted to the family, hobbies, and recreational activities. Time budgeting and reasonable restraint exercised over participation in community affairs may overcome part of the total time pressure. But, characteristically, the manager has too much to do.

Financing

One problem of major significance to many small businesses is lack of capital and credit. Long-term capital is a particular need of many small concerns. This capital is obtained by personal investment or by long-term borrowing. Borrowing money to be paid back over a period of years is difficult for small firms. The banker ordinarily expects funds of this type to come from equity capital.[5] Borrowing from relatives or friends presents problems in that, in those cases in which it is a possibility, the relatives or friends often expect some voice in the management of the business. There may be instances where this type of credit would jeopardize the relationship of both parties.

The small firm has only limited access to capital markets that are open to larger concerns. Accepting partners or selling stock may involve the surrender of absolute control over the business, a situation the original owner may consider unacceptable. Expansion capital similarly must come from personally invested funds or from profits retained in the business.

These facts suggest that small business cannot have the entrepreneur's "rugged individualism" and independence of management except on terms of severely restricted equity capital and limited credit. In contrast, a medium-sized or large business that is well managed can procure needed capital and credit much more easily.

Taxes

Although there are a number of aspects of taxation that present problems to the independent entrepreneur, the federal personal and corporate income taxes are probably the outstanding source of trouble. The present two-step corporate income tax provides for a lower tax on earnings up to $25,000 and a higher tax on earnings in excess of $25,000. Even though such a tax structure appears to favor small business, it is actually more severe in its effects on the small firm than on the large one. The burdensome nature of the tax is caused by its reduction of potential expansion capital.

Small business does not have available to it the sources of capital that are open to larger and better-known concerns. As a result, it necessarily depends to a greater extent upon retained earnings to finance growth. This means that a heavy income tax sharply reduces the amount of capital that is available for expansion purposes.

This condition has led to numerous suggestions that the corporate income tax make some exception for the earnings of small corporations in order that

---

[5] Equity capital refers to the total funds invested in a business by the owner or owners in contrast to funds borrowed from a bank or other lenders. Equity capital is often referred to as "risk" or "venture" capital.

expansion capital might be available. This would help to equalize small and big business growth opportunities.

Research

Difficulty in undertaking product, process, and market research provides another serious problem for the small business entrepreneur. This difficulty arises principally from the demands for money and specialized talent necessary to conduct research. It costs many thousands of dollars annually to pay for a substantial research program. Small businesses do not have the available capital in most cases.

It also takes the time and the ability of someone in the management group to keep abreast of developments in methods, processes, and products. The advent and the usefulness of newly created materials may long remain unknown to the small industrialist. One does well to read several trade journals regularly and to ask questions of the salespeople who call at one's place of business.

Market research is seldom scientifically and seriously attempted. Small business entrepreneurs tend to rely on requests and complaints of customers and, sometimes, on trade surveys conducted by other organizations. Hence, they seldom are well informed as to the extent and the sales potential of their markets. Although they may develop a sort of sixth sense to divine the needs of customers, they are severely limited by lack of sufficient market information. The same is less true of big business; it has the necessary capital and trained experts to undertake product and market research on a large scale.

Manpower

Many entrepreneurs identify manpower or labor as one of their major problem areas. Union relationships are not usually specified as the primary difficulty in most such cases. Instead, managers often report difficulty in locating properly qualified personnel. Securing well-trained automobile mechanics, radio repairmen, or pharmacists may pose real problems. The manager of a diesel engine service concern, for example, searched six months to locate a well-qualified parts man who could also learn to supervise the office and record keeping activities. Recruitment of managerial and professional personnel may be even more difficult.

Of course, the need to recruit and train competent manpower is not unique with the small firm. The entrepreneur often has limited knowledge of selection techniques and is frequently unaware of sources of applicants used by larger firms. Training programs are customary in big business also, but the small business entrepreneur typically lacks a well-developed program and has little grasp of its significance.

There are numerous other ways in which small business personnel problems are different. In some industries, for example, the practice of "pattern" bargaining with labor unions tends to impose big-business labor requirements upon small firms. This practice often appears unreasonable to managers of small concerns. To illustrate, consider a contract provision limiting employees to a specified type of work. The small firm has greater difficulty in adhering closely to rigid job definitions of this type and needs considerable flexibility in shifting employees from one type of work to another. Some union contracts, it should be noted, have recognized such unique problems of manpower management in small firms.

Marketing

When the entrepreneur speaks of the problem of "competition," some aspect of selling is often stressed. In most small firms the rigors of competition make the manager painfully conscious of marketing weaknesses. Difficulties in managing the firm's advertising illustrate the nature of the marketing problem. How much should the firm spend on advertising? What media should be used? How can the effectiveness of advertising be measured? For small firms, many of these questions are particularly difficult to answer, and the entrepreneur must often guess at the right answer. Channels of distribution, product policy, salespersons' compensation plans, and other marketing issues likewise constitute significant problems for the small firm.

COMPETITIVE STRENGTHS OF SMALL FIRMS

In spite of their problems, small firms can compete vigorously in many industrial areas. Indeed, their smallness gives them a number of competitive strengths. When exploited skillfully, these strengths enable them to "carry the attack" to larger firms. Three of these strong points are discussed briefly below.

Knowledge of Customers and Markets

The bureaucratic structure of large corporations tends to isolate its management from customers and markets. Salespeople have regular contact with the marketplace, but their thinking is several steps removed from the influential decision-making levels of the corporation. Special effort is required to keep decision makers well informed. Market research, often in sophisticated forms, is a tool designed and used extensively by large concerns to probe the market and to reduce corporate ignorance of the market situation. It is also true that, even in small firms, there is often a need for good market research. But the small firm manager can know almost automatically some facts that can be gleaned by managers of larger corporations only with great effort. National chain stores have long recognized the problem of relating their merchandising practice to the varied, unique demands in the localities in which their stores are located.

The acquaintance of the small business entrepreneur with customers and markets is only a potential strength, however. It may not be realized in practice. The entrepreneur is close enough to his customers to understand the market situation in depth, but he may be blind. Both a sensitive awareness of customer needs and a careful discernment of market trends are necessary to make this potential strength an actuality.

Product and Market Specialization

Someone has suggested that graduate education teaches one more and more about less and less. The point is that one must specialize or concentrate upon a specific field of knowledge if one is to go beyond a superficial comprehension and acquire a depth of understanding. One cannot possibly know everything about everything.

In a similar way it is difficult to become a specialist in such broad areas as business generally; or in retailing, manufacturing, or construction; or even in particular types of retailing, manufacturing, or construction. As one narrows the range of business activity, an understanding of it and an expertise in providing such goods and services can increase accordingly. To some extent, geographic specialization provides a comparable situation. One can more easily develop a detailed knowledge of a specific locality than one can of an entire state, region, or country. As noted above, chain stores have recognized this handicap in trying to keep up with nimble, independent merchants. This also explains the strength of small business in specialty-shop areas of retailing.

To a greater or lesser degree, the independent entrepreneur specializes. The extent of specialization governs the potential limits of this strength or advantage. If a sufficiently narrow market segment is selected, the possibility of becoming a true specialist comes closer to reality. In fact, with sufficient effort the entrepreneur may come to know more about the firm's product, customers, and market than anyone else, including the giant industrial competitors.

Flexibility in Management

Rapid environmental change has become a way of life. Product life cycles become shorter, innovations appear with greater frequency, customers grow increasingly fickle, competitors move more quickly, and public expectations change more often. As a result, business firms are confronted with new demands and new situations. Change is a fact of life for business firms of all sizes. However, a difference exists in the small firm's adaptability or flexibility.

For example, heavy fixed outlays for manufacturing facilities, as in automobile production or steel making, lead to inflexibility. A small firm with a lower investment in fixed assets is in a much better position to change quickly.

In addition, decisions must be made quickly, and changed as conditions change. In spite of their practice of decentralization, the decision-making machinery of large corporations is more "creaky" than that of small firms. More people are involved in an important decision, and more levels of management must be consulted before making a change. In some cases the big company may allow red tape and tradition to grow to the extent that change is exceedingly difficult to make.

The small firm, in contrast, can "turn on a dime." Its reaction to changes in the marketplace can be prompt. Once again, the small firm's strength is only a potential strength. A prompt decision is not necessarily a good decision. If the necessary facts are considered, however, the decision may be both prompt and correct, giving the small firm an edge over its larger competitor.

THE FUTURE OF SMALL BUSINESS

Apprehension over the future of small business has been voiced by members of Congress, other politicians, labor leaders, friends, and even owners of small firms. Some, indeed, are quite pessimistic concerning the future prospects of small business establishments. Such a picture is discouraging to entrepreneurs.

But is it correct? Let us review the evidence. Much of the earlier discussion in this chapter is obviously relevant to a consideration of this issue.

Sources of Small Business Strength

Small business has in the past demonstrated an ability to control a substantial segment of American business. It seems clear that there is economic justification for this—the existence and the success of small units are based upon certain economic and technological advantages, a number of which have been noted already.

Big business itself needs small businesses as suppliers, providers of customer service, and retailers of big business products. Furthermore, it is impractical to conduct some lines of business, such as retail specialty shops, repair services, barbershops, florists, and laundries, except as small businesses.

The special strengths of small business noted in the previous section —detailed acquaintance with markets, specialization, and flexibility in management—contribute to its survival and growth. Of course, small business faces the various problems enumerated earlier in the chapter. In some industries these problems are particularly acute. Nevertheless, small business possesses the ability to cope with these problems and to match its market. Both small business and big business have their proper place. Small firms typically show greater profit and loss variations over the business cycle; the rate of decline in periods of business recession is greater than for big business. But most small businesses earn and pay their way while at the same time giving job satisfaction and independence to the entrepreneur.

Opportunities Inherent in Future Developments

The one thing we know about the future is that it will be different from the present. In the world of business, the future will entail different markets, different customer desires, different products and services, different channels of distribution, different production technology, different approaches to advertising and selling, different methods of financing, and different concepts of management. Small firms are born, function, and frequently die within this rapidly changing social and business environment.

Shift to a Service Economy. One major structural change that favors small business is the shift from a manufacturing to a service economy as described in Chapter 1. The manufacturing segment, in which big business predominates, is currently declining in relative importance. On the other hand, services, retailing, and wholesaling are growing in relative importance. These areas are fields in which small business has been traditionally strong.

Adaptability to Changing Conditions. Survival of small business will depend upon its ability to adapt to the changing environment within which it functions. Firms that continue to sell the same products and to follow the same practices that make them profitable today may be headed for trouble tomorrow because tomorrow will be different from today. The forces at work today will inevitably alter the business institutions and practices of the future. Today's innovations become tomorrow's products and methods. Electronic computers make today's accounting and research far different from that of one decade ago, for example, and their further application and development will continue to affect these fields over the next several decades.

There is no reason why change should automatically favor big business and handicap the small concern. Indeed, innovation may provide small firms with a powerful competitive weapon. Between 1939 and 1944, the inventor of the Xerox copying process was turned down by many large companies, among which were Remington Rand and International Business Machines Corporation. A small firm in Rochester, New York, however, contracted for the commercial rights and experienced a fabulous growth that came with the revolution in office copying. Some production and marketing developments will quite likely benefit by requiring investment and technology beyond the resources of small firms. Other developments, however, make small concerns even more competitive. Adaptation of electronic computers to small firm usage and development of automatic and numerically controlled machine tools with the flexibility required by small business provide new strength to small firms in their competitive struggle with the highly automated larger corporations.

Success in the future belongs to those firms whose managers are sensitive to the changing business scene and who are prepared to capitalize on its opportunities. Large size does not guarantee adaptability to changing conditions and may even mitigate against it. The very smallness of small business, on the other hand, may contribute to its flexibility. The quality of management is nearly crucial, then, in determining the future role of small business.

Government and the Future of Small Business

Preservation of a strong small business sector in the economy should require little in the way of governmental intervention. Superiority in the production and marketing of goods and services constitutes the greatest guarantee of continued life for a small business. The primary justification for using the strong arm of the government is to provide freedom of opportunity for the small firm.

In the belief, however, that small business needed assistance from government, Congress in 1953 established the Small Business Administration which has the four following principal responsibilities:

1. To assist small concerns in procurement of credit.
2. To help them get a fair share of government contracts.
3. To aid them in solution of management and production problems.
4. To provide financial assistance for owners of small businesses damaged or destroyed by acts of God (such as floods, fires, and tornadoes).

It seems obvious that the Small Business Administration is now a permanent agency of the federal government, and it is equally clear that it can be of assistance to small businessmen under appropriate circumstances. Creation of the Small Business Administration represents a positive attempt to strengthen small business—an approach that is infinitely preferable to the occasional legislative acts designed to help small firms by directly penalizing their larger competitors. Nevertheless, small business would do well not to constitute itself a "special interest" group dependent upon government assistance and preferential legislation.

Trends in Small Business Activity

As indicated in Chapter 1, the proportion of employment and sales accounted for by small firms has declined over the past few decades. The degree and extent of the decline varied considerably depending upon the industry. In most cases the drift is properly described as gradual. It is important to recall that the downward trend in the small firm's proportion of business activity has occurred in an expanding economy. The volume of small business activity has thus increased in absolute terms while dipping in relation to big business.

It is fair to assume some continuation of these long-run trends. Small firms will apparently grow in number and size while continuing to surrender a somewhat larger proportion of total volume to larger firms. It is also well to recall that the small business share of the total is still large and that the small firm is in no immediate danger of extinction.

 Summary

1. Values arising from the existence of small business include, among others, its contribution to freedom of opportunity, greater efficiency in certain areas, support of larger business concerns, encouragement of innovation, and stimulation of competition.

2. Two of the most pressing problems of small firms are the severe time pressures on the owner-manager and the lack of specialized skills and depth in the management group. Small firms also face such problems as financing, taxes, research, manpower, and marketing.

3. Long-term capital needs constitute a problem of primary importance for small concerns. Small business does not have available to it the sources of capital open to larger and better-known firms.

4. The problems of research, recruitment, and marketing are likewise complicated by the smallness of firms. The latter—marketing problems—are often described as problems of "competition."

5. Small business possesses the following potential strengths in its competitive struggle with big business: (a) an intimate acquaintance with customers and markets; (b) product and market specialization; and (c) flexibility in management.

6. Small business faces the future with those basic strengths that have permitted it to remain strong in the past, and owners of small firms may, by foresight and flexibility, exploit the opportunities provided by changes occurring in the economic environment. Although some governmental programs are designed to assure its future, small business should place greatest reliance upon efficient management in meeting the uncertainties of tomorrow.

Discussion Questions

1. Can there be freedom of opportunity without a large number of small business institutions?
2. If all small businesses could somehow be merged into large concerns, what would be the effect on industrial efficiency and on our standard of living? Why?
3. What is the relationship of technology to bigness in business?
4. (a) Explain what is meant by the interdependence of all kinds of business. (b) Give some examples.
5. In what way does small business stand as a barrier against monopoly?
6. In view of the fact that big business, as it is known today, has arisen since the day of Adam Smith, is his reasoning concerning competition still pertinent?
7. Would you favor legislation to establish minimum qualifications for entry into a given small business field? Why?
8. Why are the problems of small business different from those of big business?
9. How can time budgeting help the independent businessman in view of the varied demands upon his time?
10. What would be the diverse management skills ideally desirable in the following types of business: (a) retail hardware store; (b) photographic studio; (c) grocery wholesale firm; (d) sheet metal shop; (e) retail appliance store; (f) radio and television repair shop?
11. Why is it unlikely that one individual would have all the necessary specialized management skills?
12. Is attainment of high-quality management a greater problem for small firms than for big business? Why?
13. What is the relationship between financial problems and tax problems of the small concern?
14. (a) Why does research constitute a significant problem for small firms? (b) For what types of concerns would this problem be most acute?
15. To what extent does the lower tax rate on the first $25,000 of corporate income minimize the tax problem of small firms?
16. (a) What is your estimate as to the relative strength of small business 20 years from now? (b) What factors will be most significant in determining its role in the future?
17. Discuss briefly the role of the Small Business Administration in determining what the future of small business will be.

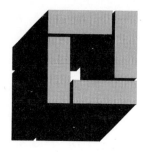

3

Strategy, Objectives, and Responsibilities of the Small Firm

Some of the most basic decisions for a small business are those pertaining to its nature and relationship to its environment. Management must answer the questions "What type of business are we?" and "What type of business should we try to be?" These questions direct attention to the firm's relationship to customers and competitors. In addition, management must consider in a broader sense the firm's relationship to environment—especially the orientation it will take with respect to the community, the general public, and the government.

DETERMINING BUSINESS STRATEGY

In planning for the future of a firm, the manager should begin at the most basic level—that of relating the firm's products and/or services to the needs of the marketplace and the offerings of competitors.

Importance of Strategic Planning

Strategy determination refers to the process by which managers "size up" the general situation pertaining to the business as a whole and decide upon necessary changes of a fundamental nature. Managers of small firms are frequently unaware of the possibilities for such strategic planning and unappreciative of the value of spending time and effort in this endeavor. Reflection of this type appears academic and unrelated to the practical, urgent problems of the moment. Time is always at a premium, and it is easy to dispense with speculation and philosophizing about the future. Any type of long-range planning seems to involve a large amount of guesswork. As a result of such thinking, many managers fail to see the study of strategy as a matter of any great consequence.

Unfortunately many of the changes that slip up on and surprise management are the type that can be detected only through an analytical approach to strategy. Obsolescence of product lines, aging of physical plant, shift of market demand, new moves by competitors, and deterioration of the organization are illustrative of fundamental changes that may occur without fanfare. Nevertheless, such changes are discernible, and the implications for the small firm can be analyzed. Strategy determination is concerned, however, not only with dangers to be avoided but also with opportunities to be exploited.

The economic environment within which the small firm functions is constantly changing. Some changes affect the products and/or services being provided by a particular firm. Only by watching these often-gradual changes closely can an entrepreneur assess the impact upon his firm in terms of both dangers and opportunities. On the basis of such observation and analysis, the manager can then decide upon proper action to cope with the situation.

The problem is not so much the fact that businessmen fail to think about the future. Everyone, including businessmen, thinks about the future. Rather, the planning deficiency arises from the lack of a systematic, analytical investigation of these questions and a failure to appreciate their significance.

Finding the Strategic Niche

In a pluralistic economy there is a place for both large and small firms. Head-on competition with large competitors is difficult and possibly fatal, however, unless the small firm has some natural advantages going for it. If possible, it is preferable for the small firm to capitalize on its potential strengths and to operate in the crack between larger businesses. Each firm has some area of greatest potential strength. Exploitation of this potential will provide the maximum competitive "muscle."

Small business strategy manifests itself in a number of ways depending upon the nature of the industry. Small firms better their larger rivals by such tactics as concentration upon a narrow product line, development of a highly specialized product or service, production to meet product requirements of a minority group, and provision of a product-service "package" containing an unusual amount of service. This possibility of providing a different product or filling a special niche deserves serious consideration in small business planning.

Particularly in manufacturing, the small firm should look for and emphasize the special niche it can best fill. If it can get a corner on the market for a particular specialized product, it will be in an unusually advantageous position. A few years ago, E. C. Highley started with the idea of finding a new use for the timber and employment for his neighbors around Salt Lick, Kentucky. He discovered that Delco Products Division of General Motors was in the market for pallets—small wooden platforms on which to stack and ship manufactured parts. So he got in touch with them and obtained an order for 250 pallets. Having both the lumber and sawyers available, he quickly filled this order. As a result, he obtained subsequent orders from Delco Products alone for 500 pallets a week. Soon, other General Motors divisions, and other companies as well, heard about the new business and submitted orders. Thus, Salt Lick had a profitable, new industry. It was the concentration on a single product which aided materially in the development of this company.[1]

Not all of the special niche cases, however, are confined to the field of manufacturing. Small retailers find similar possibilities in exclusive franchises and in merchandising of particular products. Indeed, the many small, specialized retail shops offer abundant evidence of the numerous special niches that characterize the retail field. Consider the example of certain drugstores of

---

[1] *Small Business and General Motors,* General Motor Corporation, undated pamphlet. (Now out of print.)

today which have turned to specialization in the filling of prescriptions. This is a special niche case which reverses the trend of drugstore diversification to lunch counters, cameras, gift wares, cosmetics, books, toys, and sporting goods.

The service goals of a business firm must be modified as consumer tastes change and as competitive products and services are developed. Peter Drucker has suggested that a business should classify its products, markets, and distribution channels in such categories as:[2]

1. Today's breadwinners.
2. Tomorrow's breadwinners.
3. Productive specialties.
4. Development products.
5. Failures.
6. Yesterday's breadwinners.

7. Repair jobs.
8. Unnecessary specialties.
9. Unjustified specialties.
10. Investments in managerial ego.
11. Cinderellas (or sleepers).

By looking at the business from this point of view, the manager can emphasize the firm's strengths—for example, "tomorrow's breadwinners"—and withdraw support from its weaknesses—for example, "investments in managerial ego."

The Process of Strategic Planning

Getting started with a study of strategy often seems difficult, and the owner-manager may find the experience frustrating! Unaccustomed as he is to systematic investigation of this type, he has difficulty finding an appropriate starting point. One approach he may take is to begin by asking a number of fundamental questions about his firm and then thoughtfully producing answers to these questions.

The questions on page 35 have been proposed by Frank F. Gilmore as a framework for small business strategic planning sessions.

Strategic decisions should be reduced to writing to insure completion of the strategy-determination process and to provide a basis for subsequent planning. The firm's strategy, moreover, should be incorporated into more specific plans of action. In this way the small firm can devise a system that assures the implementation of strategic thinking. Periodic review and evaluation sessions could be devoted to measurement of progress in following strategic guidelines and to dealing with problems that might emerge.

ENTERPRISE OBJECTIVES

The objectives of a small firm include strategic goals of the type discussed above. However, business goals are not limited to questions of strategy. In this section attention is directed to the firm's other objectives.

Service Objective

A privately owned firm is allowed to do business by society; therefore, it should be expected to serve the interests of society. Accordingly, a business

---

[2] Peter F. Drucker, *Managing for Results* (New York: Harper & Row, Publishers, 1964), Chapter 4.

QUESTIONS TO USE IN FORMULATING STRATEGY[3]

1. Record current strategy:
   a. What is the current strategy?
   b. What kind of business does management want to operate (considering such management values as desired return on investment, growth rate, share of market, stability, flexibility, character of the business, and climate)?
   c. What kind of business does management feel it ought to operate (considering management's concepts of social responsibility and obligations to stockholders, employees, community, competitors, customers, suppliers, government, and the like)?

2. Identify problems with the current strategy:
   a. Are trends discernible in the environment that may become threats and/or missed opportunities if the current strategy is continued?
   b. Is the company having difficulty implementing the current strategy?
   c. Is the attempt to carry out the current strategy disclosing significant weaknesses and/or unutilized strengths in the company?
   d. Are there other concerns with respect to the validity of the current strategy?
   e. Is the current strategy no longer valid?

3. Discover the core of the strategy problem:
   a. Does the current strategy require greater competence and/or resources than the company possesses?
   b. Does it fail to exploit adequately the company's distinctive competence?
   c. Does it lack sufficient competitive advantage?
   d. Will it fail to exploit opportunities and/or meet threats in the environment, now or in the future?
   e. Are the various elements of the strategy internally inconsistent?
   f. Are there other considerations with respect to the core of the strategy problem?
   g. What, then, is the real core of the strategy problem?

4. Formulate alternative new strategies:
   a. What possible alternatives exist for solving the strategy problem?
   b. To what extent do the company's competence and resources limit the number of alternatives that should be considered?
   c. To what extent do management's preferences limit the alternatives?
   d. To what extent does management's sense of social responsibility limit the alternatives?
   e. What strategic alternatives are acceptable?

5. Evaluate alternative new strategies:
   a. Which alternative *best* solves the strategy problem?
   b. Which alternatives offer the *best* match with the company's competence and resources?
   c. Which alternative offers the *greatest* competitive advantage?
   d. Which alternative *best* satisfies management's preferences?
   e. Which alternative *best* meets management's sense of social responsibility?
   f. Which alternative *minimizes* the creation of new problems?

6. Choose a new strategy:
   a. What is the *relative significance* of each of the preceding considerations?
   b. What should the new strategy be?

---

[3] Frank F. Gilmore, "Formulating Strategy in Smaller Companies," *Harvard Business Review*, Vol. 49, No. 3 (May-June, 1971), p. 80.

enterprise must provide a flow of goods and services to the public. This is a primary objective—the rendering of economic service to the community.

The privately owned firm has the obligation to do this for the society which permits its existence. But recognition of the objective may also be viewed as a mere reflection of intelligent selfishness. It is selfish because the business which fails to provide an economic service to the community will not survive. Because the business enterprise operates in a setting of competition and government regulation, some recognition of this objective is almost unavoidable. Mere recognition of service goals does not guarantee intelligent choice, however. Errors in judgment about the nature of products or services desired by customers may lead to mediocrity or failure.

Decisions about basic service objectives shape the very nature of a business. They are the strategic decisions discussed in the preceding section. Of course, these basic strategic objectives are subsequently broken down into more and more specific goals. The decision to diversify into Product Line A is a strategic and, therefore, a service objective. The later decision to carry Product Line A in 12 colors or quality levels establishes a narrower, nonstrategic service objective.

Profit Objective

Another goal of every privately owned business is profit. It is typically for this purpose that a business is founded. The necessity of profits lies in the need to reward the entrepreneur's acceptance of business risks and his performance of economic service to the community. Even more important is the need for profits to assure business continuity. Continuous losses inevitably result in failure unless the business is subsidized in some way. When working capital becomes depleted, the owner can hardly be expected to replace equipment if there is no prospect of a return on the investment.

It should be clear that profit making is not a short-range concern but rather a matter of long-range significance. Hence, the entrepreneur cannot be unduly concerned with the net profit reported on the income statement each month, each quarter, or each year unless this is part of a long-run trend or condition. Undue concern with short-range profit making is somewhat like clock watching on the part of the employee. Profit maximization over the long run should be the major goal with the periodic income statement regarded as a progress report.

Even though the desire for profits may be rooted in mankind's selfishness, profits are absolutely fundamental to business life. Without profit, a business firm can make no long-run contribution to employees, suppliers, customers, or the community.

It might also be noted that the profit-seeking goal of the businessman may be supplemented by certain nonfinancial objectives. He is more than an economic man. It is often true, for example, that he desires the prestige of being a successful businessman as much as he desires the dollars associated with that success. Similarly, he may be motivated by various altruistic considerations.

Growth Objective

A business philosophy concerned with economic service and profit making must also be concerned with enterprise growth. Some have gone so far as to suggest that a business must either grow or die. In an expanding economy, growth is normal for a healthy, successful business. Enterprise growth envisions the need for additional production facilities and so calls for retained earnings or new investment by the owners. Growth demands an awareness of technological advances. There must be a readiness to participate in the experimentation involved in attainment of progress. There must be a readiness to utilize new processes in the manufacture of new products. All of this requires effective long-range planning.

The importance attached to growth by different businessmen seems to vary considerably. Some managers are more inclined than others to accept the status quo and to feel little need for growth. The age of the businessman is an example of one variable that may affect his attitude toward growth. There are undoubtedly other factors, some of which are rooted in the personalities of the individuals. One research study of a small sample of business firms suggests the following three stereotypes as descriptive of three different viewpoints concerning growth:[4]

1. The conservative operator managing the relatively stable, often small firm. His major goal is survival, and he believes the best way to achieve this objective is to maintain the status quo. Growth in terms of production, revenue, or profit is not an objective.
2. The industry stalwart. He seeks an *acceptable* rather than an *optimum* rate of profit. Although he does not attempt to maximize growth, he strives to "keep up" with the industry.
3. The aggressive, innovating operator who manages a progressive, growing firm. He attempts to maximize firm profit, and he views production and revenue growth as means to this end.

Selection of a growth objective for a particular firm, then, involves a value judgment in terms of the alternatives outlined above.

SOCIAL RESPONSIBILITIES OF THE SMALL BUSINESS

In recent years public attention has been focused on the issue of social responsibilities of business organizations. Even businessmen and businesswomen have joined the chorus of those proclaiming the social obligations of the business community. These feelings of concern are seemingly rooted in a new awareness of the role of business in modern society. In a sense, managers now occupy a "trusteeship" position and must act accordingly to protect the interests of suppliers, employees, customers, and the general public, along with making a profit for the owners of the business.

Nature of Social Responsibilities

Managers of small businesses have recognized the same responsibility as clearly, if not always as eloquently, as the spokesmen for big business. In fact,

---

[4] F. Parker Fowler, Jr., and E. W. Sandberg, *The Relationship of Management Decision-Making to Small Business Growth*. Small Business Management Research Report. Prepared by Colorado State University Research Foundation under a grant from the Small Business Administration, Washington, D.C., 1964, Chapter 5.

many independent entrepreneurs speak of their satisfaction in serving the community as one of the major rewards from their businesses. Of course, this does not mean that all firms share this philosophy; some fail to sense or refuse to recognize any obligation beyond the minimum necessary to produce a profit.

Some sense of social responsibility may be perfectly consistent with the firm's long-run profit objective. A firm which consistently observes certain obligations makes itself a desirable member of the community and may attract patronage. Conversely, the firm which scorns social responsibilities may find itself the object of restrictive legislation and discover its employees to be lacking in loyalty. It seems likely, however, that the typical independent businessman contributes to the community and other groups simply because he feels it a duty and a privilege to do so, and not because he has cunningly calculated the profit potential in each such move.

Recognition of a social responsibility does not change a profit-seeking business into a charitable organization. Earning a profit is absolutely essential. Without profits, the firm is in no position to recognize social responsibilities toward anyone. The point is that profits, although essential, are not necessarily the only factor of importance in the thinking of the businessman.

Environmentalism and Small Business

In recent decades the deterioration of the environment has become a matter of widespread concern. One source of pollution has been business firms that discharge waste into streams, contaminants into the air, and noise into areas surrounding their operations. Efforts to preserve and redeem the environment thus directly affect business organizations, including small business firms.

Beneficial Effects on Small Firms. The interests of small business owners and environmentalists are not necessarily or uniformly in conflict. Some business leaders, including those in small business, have worked and acted for the cause of conservation. Many small firms, for example, have taken steps to remove eyesores and to landscape and otherwise improve plant facilities. Others have modernized equipment and changed procedures to reduce air and water pollution. In a few cases, small business has been in a position to benefit from the emphasis on ecology. Those whose products are harmless to the environment gain an edge over competitive products that pollute. Also, small firms are involved in servicing pollution-control equipment—the auto repair shop, for example, services pollution-control devices on automobile engines.

Adverse Effects on Small Firms. Some small firms, however, are adversely affected by efforts to protect the environment. Livestock feeding lots, cement plants, pet-food processors, and iron foundries are representative of industries that are especially vulnerable to extensive regulation. The cost impact in businesses of this type is often severe. Indeed, the required improvements can force closure of some businesses.

An excellent example is the instance of a small cheese-producing company in Wisconsin. Even though the owner-manager ran an efficient operation and had always operated on a minimum cost basis, the company's earnings were modest. Recently faced with the requirement to spend $200,000 on sewage treatment facilities, he closed his company and sold his product lines to a large company in another city. His company disappeared, as did the jobs of his former employees. A similar fate has befallen a small food-processing company in New York, a dairy in Michigan, two small construction companies in Pennsylvania, and numerous others around the country.[5]

The ability to pass higher costs on to customers is dependent upon the market situation and is ordinarily quite difficult for the small firm. Resulting economic hardships on small business must, therefore, be recognized as a cost of pollution control and evaluated accordingly as to its desirability. In some instances the controls are hardest on the small, marginal firm with obsolete equipment. Environmental regulation may merely hasten the inevitable demise of the firm. In cases of this type, the loss is unfortunate but unavoidable.

The level of government regulation poses another potential problem for small business. Legislation, whether state or local, may prove discriminatory by forcing higher costs on a local firm than on competitive firms outside the regulated territory. The immediate self-interest of a small firm, therefore, is served by regulations that operate at the highest or most general level. A federal regulation, for example, presumably applies to all U.S. firms and thereby precludes competitive advantages to low-cost polluters in other states.

Consumerism and Small Business Management

The concept of customer satisfaction has become increasingly important in the last few years. At one time the accepted philosophy was expressed as "Let the buyer beware." Today the new philosophy holds in contrast, "Let the seller beware." Today's sophisticated buyers feel they should be able to purchase products that are safe, reliable, durable, and honestly advertised. Government offices have been established to represent consumer interests, and national attention has been directed to consumer rights by Ralph Nader and other concerned citizens.

Advantages for Small Firms. Small firms are directly involved in the consumerism movement. To some extent they stand to gain from this type of attention. Attention to customer needs and flexibility in meeting these needs have traditionally been strong assets of the small firm. Their managers have been close to customers and thus able to know and respond easily to their needs. To the extent that these potential features have been realized in practice, the position of small business has been strengthened. And to the extent that small firms can continue to capitalize upon customer desires for excellent service, they can reap rewards from the consumerism movement.

Disadvantages for Small Firms. Consumerism also carries threats to small business. It is harder to build a completely safe product and to avoid all errors in service. Moreover, the growing complexity of products makes their service difficult. The mechanic or repairman must know a great deal more to render satisfactory service today than was needed two or three decades earlier. Rising

---

[5] Dale D. McConkey, "Ecological Problems Facing Small Business," *Journal of Small Business Management*, Vol. 10 (October, 1972), pp. 1-2.

consumer expectations, therefore, provide a measure of danger as well as opportunity for small firms. The quality of management will determine the extent to
which opportunities are realized and dangers avoided.

Business Ethics

The fact that America is a democracy which espouses the right of the individual to enter business at will does not endow that individual with the right to
do anything and everything without restraints. Although the competitive system and the action of government are both policing forces that tend to regulate
business conduct, they are not enough. The individual entrepreneur must also
have a code of business ethics—a moral sense—that polices his actions.

Consistency in Business Ethics. A manager cannot be honest in big things
and dishonest in little things. If one tries this, the cumulative effect of little
dishonesties will be such as to pervert one's perspective of life and management.
The manager is in a position of power; business success generates a sense of
power and infallibility in action. The manager is often tempted to engage in
small violations of ethical practice to enhance immediate business success. But
taking advantage of others in the small case leads eventually to complete moral
irresponsibility and improper exercise of administrative power.

It is indeed remarkable how those employed by a given firm can sense the
manager's moral code. Insincerity and a lack of integrity on the manager's part
cannot long be concealed from subordinates. The manager's moral code must
have a sound basis so that fair play and honesty in all relationships with workers, customers, and others become instinctive acts. One cannot turn on and off
good human relations practices and ethics as one can turn water on and off at a
faucet. The crux of the matter is that restraint cannot come entirely from law
but requires conscience in management of business. Self-imposed restraints
should characterize a free-enterprise economy in action. When these fail, people
turn to the government for a restraint which the collective conscience failed to
provide. As someone has said, free enterprise is not a hunting license to gouge
the other fellow for self-profit. Instead, it is the liberty granted by society to do
business, with freedom for others to compete, and with self-imposed moral
restraints by all so that undue advantage will not be taken by anyone.

Development of Business Morals. Only in recent years have businessmen
come to the point of viewing seriously the matter of ethical business practice.
Even now some dismiss it as being impractical for a firm seeking optimization
of profits. Others consider ethical practices and government regulation as virtually synonymous. Nevertheless, we have slowly attained a widespread acceptance of the view that business must act in the interest of its customers, employees, suppliers, and others affected by its operations, while also acting in its
own interest.

In part, this moral progress has been fostered by competition which forced
adoption of higher ethical practices in order to compete successfully with ethical competitors. Ethical business practices, in other words, have been found to
be good business. Enlightened self-interest has thus no doubt motivated much
ethical behavior. It is true also that the government, through pure food and drug

laws, Federal Trade Commission activities, and the like, has made a contribution to better business morals.

Nevertheless, much remains to be done. Our concern is not primarily with illegal practices. Legal conduct is assumed as the bare minimum for ethical behavior. In addition, management must be concerned with the borderline areas of ethical behavior. For example, the salesperson's expense account tends to become a "swindle sheet." Also, there is the tendency to be vulgar, misleading, and immorally suggestive in certain types of advertising. Purchasing agents may accept expensive gifts from order-seeking concerns. Unquestionably, this imposes some sense of obligation on their part and may create a conflict of loyalties. There is, indeed, a general recognition of inadequacy of ethical standards in American business.

Thus, the task of constructing one's own standards of business honesty falls on each manager. These standards should apply to small as well as large things and even to those areas where legal penalties are not involved. Accepted practice obviously provides no sure guide. Chances are that personal satisfaction and, in the long run, success in business will come to the manager who has developed a philosophy of ethical behavior.

Formal Code of Ethics. In some industrial and professional fields, group action has been taken to adopt formal codes of ethics. Doctors, lawyers, and public accountants are typical examples of professional groups that are closely regulated by self-imposed ethical codes. Doctors will not indiscriminately disclose to outsiders the physical condition of patients. Moreover, they accept the obligation to heal the sick under any circumstances—the country doctor, for example, drives to a farm in the middle of the night in order to attend a sick person. Public accountants carry their ethical practice so far as to preclude advertising other than by a simple announcement. Even the opening of a public accounting practice is typically announced only by a small newspaper notice giving the name and address of the firm.

A few years ago, owners of automobile repair shops in a small city met and formulated a code of ethics stressing the principle of fair play with employees and honest, good service for customers. This is significant as an attempt to do something constructive about ethics in the business field and thus to raise it to a professional level. Also, certain advertising agencies have led the way toward greater honesty in advertising.

A special reference should be made to work of trade associations and the Federal Trade Commission, often acting cooperatively, in formulating ethical codes for various industrial fields. The Federal Trade Commission sponsors trade-practice conferences in which representative business leaders attempt to develop codes to prevent unfair methods of competition. They are encouraged to discuss openly the practices and problems of their industries in arriving at codes of fair competition.

It would seem desirable for small firms to participate actively in any attempts to formulate such codes of ethics. Every such code instituted and adhered to elevates the moral tone of the business community and benefits the individual firm which adopts it.

Ethical Advertising. Unethical business behavior has perhaps been more apparent in advertising than in any other area. The public has the right to expect ethical advertising, however, because of its importance to the individual and its great persuasive power in the economy. It is a form of communication, and untruthfulness or other breaches of ethical behavior are as objectionable here as they are elsewhere. Because of its far-reaching influence, the advertiser must assume some social responsibility and must abide by ideals of honesty, reliability, and integrity.

First, advertising must be truthful without omitting material facts. Advertising which does not disclose all important facts is either dishonest or misleading. If only one or two items are being offered at a reduced price, this fact should be clearly stated. The advertisement for a soft drink cannot claim the drink is healthful if there are *any* ill effects. An ethical auto dealer cannot deceive a purchaser as to the nature of installment or interest payments. Merchandise represented as "formerly $10.98," should be merchandise sold by the advertiser at that price for a period of time. Terms of purchase should be clearly stated and should include definite statements as to conditions and time duration of any warranties or guarantees. Presentation of the facts may not be enough in some cases. A simple statement of facts should be supplemented or restated to avoid the confusion or misleading character of the advertisement.

There is also the question of good and bad taste in advertising. Advertisements bordering on the vulgar and immoral should certainly be avoided in all cases. Advertisements which reflect adversely on the home, religious beliefs, the nation, or minority groups should also be avoided. They are in bad taste and they tend to create resentment both toward the company and the product which it advertises.

Better Business Bureaus. Better Business Bureaus have been established by privately owned business firms in many cities to promote ethical conduct on the part of all business firms in the community. Specifically, a Better Business Bureau concerns itself with the business morals of the community, seeking out and preventing continuation of dishonest practices on the part of individuals or business firms attempting to sell goods or services in the community.

As a result, business swindles inevitably decline in a community served by a Better Business Bureau. Some shady operators are deterred from even entering the community by the presence of the Bureau, and its effective operation will persuade others that illicit practices are a losing proposition. In the interest of promoting ethical practices, small firms should share in the financial support of the activities of a Better Business Bureau and wholeheartedly endorse its activities in forestalling dishonest practices.

Application of Ethical Principles. The greatest statement of what is right in business, as in other relationships, is the Golden Rule. An increasing number of managers in both industry and government actually believe this to be a fundamentally sound principle for human relations. It means that all workers, as well as managers and supervisors, should be treated as human beings who have likes and dislikes, strengths and weaknesses, variations in talents, and emotional reactions to various stimuli. It means that management will treat individual employees and others with respect and fairness in all dealings.

All persons have individual differences, with the result that their attitudes and desires differ. Thus, management must attempt to project itself into the shoes of the affected individual and determine that individual's real outlook and desires. This process may reveal a condition contrary to management's original conception. If management is consistent in its attempt to play fair, to be objective, and to do what is right, it will come to enjoy increased understanding and better relations in all areas of the business.

The effect of business ethics on profits has been frequently debated. In some cases, ethical behavior seems to be profitable; in other instances, the ethical approach seems to be costly. Certainly, ethical business practices rest on a rather fragile foundation if their sole justification is the hope of greater profits. But even though ethics may not always increase profits of the business, it should at least decrease ulcers of the businessman. Peace of mind through right living may thus prove to be the major reward of ethical behavior.

Public Relations

Public relations consists of those activities which promote understanding between a business organization and those groups which constitute its public. In the case of a small business, the ultimate responsibility for good relations with all segments of its public rests directly and squarely on the entrepreneur.

Purpose of a Public Relations Program. The purpose of public relations activities is not to whitewash but to interpret the business organization to its public. It must be more than a veneer which conceals poor workmanship and a shoddy product. In the past, some managers have endorsed the need for good public relations and maintained a public relations staff while they enunciated policies and took actions which violated good public relations practice. This inconsistency, together with a lack of understanding of what public relations is and does, has tended to make the very phrase "public relations" unpopular.

One might say that public relations effort is designed to sell the company's objectives, policies, practices, and even products, to the various publics which the business serves. Public relations, if concerned solely with company publicity, falls far short of its mark. It uses various avenues of approach to the public to tell the company's story. Some of it may be publicity through the news columns of the paper and some may be paid advertising. But much of it also occurs in the daily contacts between members of the firm and the representatives of the public whom they contact.

Company Character and Reputation. The small firm has some type of reputation with those who are acquainted with it. Unfortunately, this reputation may not accurately portray the firm's true character. Its management may be ethical and its products excellent without public awareness of these qualities.

A public relations program lets a firm upgrade public understanding of its true character. A company must sell itself to its publics, so they will better appreciate the worth of the company, its program, and its products. Given efficient public relations efforts, character and reputation can be brought into a proper relation to each other, with the reputation of the firm measuring its true character rather than the former misconception of its true character.

It should be clear that, fundamentally, good character is the starting point for the public relations effort. Otherwise, public relations activities degenerate into a whitewash job intended to deceive the public. And it is a very difficult task to persuade the public that black is white.

Identification of the Various Publics. Public relations activities can be made more effective if different segments of the public are recognized. The firm has a different type of relationship to different groups and must appeal to them on different bases. Rather than one amorphous "general public," these groups may be treated as individual publics of the firm.

Employee Relations. The immediate objective in the case of employee relations is employee goodwill. Indirectly, the response of employees is transmitted to other segments of the community. Employees and their families express their likes and dislikes to friends and neighbors. Outsiders tend to view the employment relationship as the acid test of the firm's character and real intentions. A fuller discussion of employee relations in small business is given in Chapter 9.

Customer Relations. Achieving customer acceptance is of obvious importance if the business hopes to earn profits. Because customer contacts constitute an integral part of business operations, they are often viewed as something other than public relations. In reality, however, customers constitute the most critical public of most firms.

Stockholder Relations. Good relationships with stockholders in corporate enterprises, even in small industry, are essential in order to perpetuate management. In a very small corporation, of course, the stockholders may be active participants in the business, thus eliminating this as an area of concern. In other small corporations, however, a few outsiders may be owners, and their goodwill must be cultivated through provision of information on company affairs. Occasionally, a stockholder may be a major customer of the concern. In addition, stockholders provide a source of new capital; this, in itself, may be the most important reason for deliberately cultivating the goodwill of stockholders.

Supplier Relations. Good relations with suppliers of materials, equipment, and services are essential in modern business. A regular inflow of materials to a manufacturer or merchandise to a retailer are alike in their contribution to success. Supplier goodwill is particularly important when materials or merchandise is in short supply, when liberal terms of purchase are desired, and when quick delivery or other special treatment is necessary. Chapter 10 gives a more detailed treatment of purchasing and supplier relations of a small business.

Community Relations. As a business citizen of a community, a business concern enjoys a certain degree of local prestige or ill will. Community goodwill may result in more favorable local legislation, tax rates, and property valuation for tax purposes. It may also permit certain privileges such as parking permits or on-the-street parking in inset parking zones. Community goodwill also facilitates the recruitment of workers within the local community.

Government Relations. Governmental units whose goodwill must be cultivated by a small business include tax and regulatory agencies of government, whether federal, state, or local. Building contractors, for example, typically work closely with local building inspectors. Any lack of cooperation causes some interference with the construction efforts of uncooperative contractors. If there are unsatisfactory relationships, inspections may be delayed, or they may be made unreasonably severe.

Competitor Relations. Good relations with competitors help forestall uneconomic price wars and help to raise the level of competition. The philosophy of free enterprise does not require competitors to be constantly at each other's throats. It is also possible to get better cooperation from competing concerns through the organization and operation of a trade association. Competitors even work together in some industries in negotiating with organized labor.

The Public Relations Program in Action.
The regular contacts a firm has with its various publics constitute the heart of its public relations program. In a retail store, for example, customers form their impressions largely through their personal experiences with, and observations of, the store. The knowledge or ignorance of sales personnel is readily apparent to them. Even more evident are the friendliness, courtesy, speed, and accuracy with which customers are served. Physical features of the building—modern construction, cleanliness, lighting, and so on—and the displays of merchandise also contribute to their concept of the business. Telephone calls, monthly bills, and calls by service personnel provide still other check points for evaluation by the customers.

The attitudes of other groups are likewise vitally affected by the customary, regular, day-to-day or week-to-week contacts. Employees form their opinions of the employer on the basis of the employer's personnel policies and the quality of supervision they receive. Suppliers judge the firm on the basis of its promptness in meeting obligations and reasonableness of its requests. It is apparent that those employees having contacts with these and other groups are the ones most influential in creating the public image of the firm. Careful selection, training, and motivation of personnel are consequently of basic importance in a public relations program.

Viewed in this way, the public relations effort is not something to be turned on and off at the whim of the manager. Favorable public relations can be developed only by a skillfully designed, consistent program that continues over a period of time. In some cases, it is desirable to start public relations activities by seeking to discover the current attitudes of the firm's publics. Some managers have only the haziest notion of how their companies actually rate in customers' minds. Even though favorable attitudes must be built slowly, it is well to realize that a single incident can destroy existing goodwill in a very short time.

It is possible, of course, to add other features—those more commonly considered "public relations"—to this foundation of business contacts with the public. News items in the public press, institutional advertisements, public addresses by members of the firm, and letters to employees may all be desirable at times. Unless the foundation and substance of good relations actually exist, however, such formal communications are immediately perceived to be nothing but veneer.

Summary

1. By strategic planning, managers "size up" the business situation pertaining to the business as a whole and make necessary changes in the basic nature of business operations.

2. The small firm can maximize its competitive strength by finding a strategic niche, emphasizing its natural advantages, and avoiding head-on competition with big business.

3. The process of strategic planning may be structured around a series of suggested questions pertaining to current strategy, strategy problems, and improved strategies. Strategic plans should eventually be reduced to writing in such a way that they can be subjected to periodic review.

4. A set of objectives goes beyond a statement of business strategy. In addition to service (including strategy) objectives, the small firm may also adopt profit goals, growth goals, and social responsibility goals.

5. A sense of social responsibility characterizes many modern business leaders. Small businessmen, in particular, often speak of their service to the community as one of the major rewards from their business activity. The recent emphasis upon environmentalism and consumerism creates both opportunities and problems for small business.

6. A moral sense, stimulated by increasing public emphasis on ethical business practice, enables many businessmen to create and follow personal codes of ethics. Consistency and sincerity in the adherence to ethical codes are obligatory if ethical business practices are to be and remain effective. Ethical advertising is especially important, and local Better Business Bureaus have become common for dealing with unethical advertising, as well as with other objectionable business practices.

7. The purpose of a public relations effort is to interpret properly the business organization to its public. Fundamentally good character is thus its proper starting point. Among the various "publics" of the small firm are employees, customers, stockholders, suppliers, the community, government agencies, and competitors.

Discussion Questions

1. What is meant by "strategic planning," and how does it differ from other types of planning?

2. Give some examples of strategic moves that might be made by an independently-owned service station.

3. What is the concept of the "strategic niche," and what are its values for the small firm?

4. If the businessman thoroughly

believes in the free-enterprise system, should he be opposed to progressive income taxation? What should be his position regarding protective tariffs and fair-trade price laws?

5. Why must a business firm recognize and fulfill its service objective? Is this equally true in all types of businesses? Is the service objective equal to, or subordinate to, the firm's profit objective? Why?

6. What stake do the employees of a small firm have in its attainment of its profit objective?

7. Is maximization of profits a safe guide for business decisions? Would the nature of the market structure have any bearing on this question?

8. A men's clothing store has been opened by an extremely ambitious young man who seems determined to make a place for himself in the business world. He is strongly growth-oriented. How might this affect his operating methods and policies?

9. Is it necessary for the businessman to be a philanthropist to some degree to adhere to social objectives in his business? Why?

10. The environmentalism movement obviously affects automobile manufacturers, oil companies, and other types of big business. How does it affect small business? Illustrate.

11. Suppose that a used car dealer has just made an oral commitment to sell a car at a particular price. Before the deal is completed, another customer indicates a willingness to pay a substantially higher price. What is the ethical thing to do? Is it also practical and good business?

12. The owner of a damaged automobile was making arrangements for a repair job following a minor accident. He suggested to the garage owner that several dents and scratches that appeared older and not directly connected with the primary damage be corrected as part of the job. The garage owner was aware that the additional repairs would run the bill above the car owner's fifty-dollar "deductible" and thus cost the insurance company rather than the car owner. The automobile owner was a regular customer of the garage. How should the garage owner have met this issue?

13. Analyze the newspaper advertising of several small firms. Do any of these advertisements appear to be particularly objectionable or unethical in any way? Can you be sure whether it is ethical or not?

14. Consider a specific small business firm. What are the most important publics of this particular concern?

15. What types of activities appear to you to be most significant in the public relations program of a small business firm?

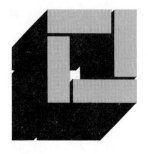

4

Salaried Employment

vs.

Entrepreneurship

An individual goes into business because he or she aspires to financial profits and certain nonmonetary rewards. One must pay a price, however, to realize these objectives. The benefits of salaried employment, i.e., the security and other rewards that come from working for someone else, must be given up, and the risks of ownership must be assumed. It is the purpose of this chapter to compare salaried employment with entrepreneurship and to evaluate the select group of individuals who choose to become entrepreneurs.

ADVANTAGES IN SALARIED EMPLOYMENT

There are several advantages to being an employee of a successful business. The most commonly proffered ones are discussed below.

Security of Employment

Many job seekers are impressed by job security. In recent years business and industry have emphasized both *current* security of job and income and *future* security through group insurance and retirement pensions. The result has been that competitive bidding for employees often turns upon fringe benefits quite as much as upon direct monetary remuneration. However, the regular paycheck now and the guaranteed pension upon retirement may build a false sense of security. One male office manager, for example, was 43 years old but lacked a college degree when his company was reorganized by bondholders. His position as office manager went to a "bright young man" from New York. He tried desperately to find other employment and finally undertook the selling of insurance, at which he made a scratchy living. His job security was wiped out overnight. The employee's security, therefore, is not perfect.

Pride in Employment

A second value commonly cited for employee status is that of association with a company whose prestige and business position are both secure and well known. Involved here is the matter of pride in the employer. The employee may take satisfaction in identifying with General Motors, Standard Oil, Prudential Insurance Company, Bank of America, or some other outstanding business institution. Another person, however, may prefer to take pride in personal achievements rather than to feel pride vicariously in the size and the accomplishments of an employer company. Many individuals, of course, are able to combine a pride in individual achievement in a key position with the pride of association with an outstanding concern.

Challenging Executive Careers

One must recognize the fact that large corporations employ thousands of professional managers. Many such managerial positions involve major responsibilities for decision making. Incumbents commit millions of dollars of resources and determine policies affecting thousands or tens of thousands of employees. In the corporate bureaucracy, therefore, many individuals may find satisfying, challenging careers. Any particular individual may rise above the more routine assignments at lower corporate levels and find duties corresponding to his own talents.

Less Demanding Work

Another possible advantage is the less demanding role of an employee—that is, supposedly, less managerial talent is required. There is no denying that a small business entrepreneur must be a generalist in management, a jack-of-all-trades. But it is dubious indeed that one who refrains from business ownership for this reason will ever climb very far up the management ladder in big business. To cite this as a reason for choosing employee status is to admit inferiority.

Shorter Hours, Less Worry, and Regular Paid Vacations

It is said that employees have no work and no worries after working hours are over. Moreover, they work fewer hours per day—and regular hours at that—drawing overtime pay if they are required to work beyond regular hours. This may be true of machine operators, typists, draftsmen, salespersons, and perhaps even some supervisors. But it is certainly untrue of executives in big business from the middle management level up. Numerous studies show that executives typically work 60 to 80 hours weekly. Many executives also admit that their only time for planning or for real creative thinking is "after hours." This feature is an "advantage," then, only in the lower positions in industry.

Regularity of paid vacations is another feature of salaried employment that appeals to many individuals. This is subject to qualification, however, because the timing of a vacation is still up to the employer. In many cases, employees must take their vacation in the hottest month of the year or before the children get out of school for the summer. The well-organized entrepreneur may experience no more difficulty in arranging a vacation than a key executive in a large concern.

No Risk to Personal Savings

Few salaried employees risk their personal assets in the business that employs them. The absence of investment risk might be cited as an advantage of salaried employment, particularly in comparison with business ownership returning comparable dollar amounts. A salary of $10,000 is preferable to a profit of $10,000 if the latter requires a substantial capital investment.

Although the lack of investment risk may thus be viewed as an advantage, the individual must at the same time forego the chance of realizing investment profits. In addition, one's capital may be otherwise invested elsewhere with some risk to oneself.

Pre-entrepreneurial Experience

A final advantage is that of procuring training and experience for subsequent small business ownership. In most cases such experience can best be gained on the payroll of another firm. The prospective owner of a men's wear shop, for example, should include employment in a clothing or department store as one part of his preparation.

There is the possibility, of course, that the prospective entrepreneur may be sidetracked by success achieved as an employee. While acquiring the years of experience preparatory to business ownership, any outstanding employee will probably climb one or two rungs on the management ladder. Thus, one may have the advantage of a good start up the ladder, together with a pension accumulation sufficient to make one reluctant to sacrifice security for the chance to own and operate one's own business. It is truly hard to quit a good job. If the employee is male, married, and has children, making a decision to strike out for himself may become virtually impossible. Even age may be a detriment.

DISADVANTAGES IN SALARIED EMPLOYMENT

Obviously there are also disadvantages in being an employee. While these may not outweigh the advantages for many individuals, they are significant to the few who desire to "be their own boss."

Subordination

Employees are subject to discharge for cause, or to transfer, even from one geographical location to another, at the discretion of their employer. If employees reach retirement age, they must then retire whether they feel like it or not.

Curbing of Initiative

During the years as an employee, one does not have unqualified right to exercise independent judgment; one's decisions and actions are circumscribed by company policy and the attitudes of superiors. In particular, an immediate superior can kill his employee's best ideas or steal the credit for them. Because the employee is always one in a group in line for advancement, promotions may come slowly, which tends to stifle initiative and permits only a partial use of latent managerial talents or special abilities.

Possibility of Mismatched Career

Many individuals fail to survey the field when offered jobs with big, successful concerns. As a result, they often become square pegs in round holes. One can never be happy, nor attain maximum success, when one is doing other than what he or she is fitted for and truly wants to do.

Limited Earnings

A final weakness in salaried employment is the salary limitation in many career fields. Earnings statistics show that lifetime earnings of employees are smaller in total than for entrepreneurs. This is a highly individualistic point, of course, because any specific individual may earn more as an employee than as an entrepreneur. The point to be made here is that there is no ceiling upon entrepreneurial earnings.

REWARDS OF ENTREPRENEURSHIP

Most individuals decide in favor of employment and against entrepreneurship. The minority deciding on entrepreneurship typically do so for a number of compelling reasons.

A Satisfying Way of Life

One important reason for many persons is the personal satisfaction realized from successful operation of one's own business. Running a business constitutes a way of living as well as a means of earning a living for the independent entrepreneurs and their dependents. Successful entrepreneurs enjoy the risks, the necessity for decision, and the many responsibilities. They like people, both individually and collectively, and they typically enjoy the active participation in civic affairs into which they are thrust by business ownership. They also often enjoy greater prestige within their community than the hired managers of big business. To some individuals, this standing in the community is of vital importance because they like the special status they have in the eyes of their fellow citizens.

Within the business, entrepreneurs are permitted to exercise all of their managerial talents; in fact, they are required to do so as entrepreneurs. There are no organizational restrictions that confine them to sales or advertising or production control. Opportunities for creativity and self-expression are enhanced. Self-respect and self-reliance are strengthened.

Desire for Independence

A second vital factor in the decision to become an entrepreneur is found in the human desire for independence. America has long been known the world over as a nation of rugged individualists. Many have a strong, even fierce, desire to make their own decisions, take risks, and reap the rewards for themselves. This desire is largely psychological in character, but it is very real and compelling because independence in itself provides a source of satisfaction to the entrepreneur.

For individuals who want to "be their own boss," the freedom of decision and action afforded by business ownership seems more a necessity than a luxury. Big businesses tend to be bureaucratic and often operate against an individual with creative imagination and aggressive drive. The result is that such an individual feels hemmed in, unable to venture and build, and so must decide on independent entrepreneurship.

Opportunity for Service

Another reason for undertaking business ownership is the fact that it affords a broad opportunity for service. Young persons who contemplate business careers like to feel that the careers they select provide a service to their fellow citizens and promote the general welfare of their home community.

As a salaried employee, one's contribution is less direct and perhaps less substantial than that possible as an independent entrepreneur. For individuals who are in business for themselves, there is little or no question about this contribution because they are providing jobs, supporting civic projects, and producing either a service or a product for their customers. Hence, when in business, individuals can expect to know that they are helping others while prospering themselves.

Profit Expectations and Security

Another factor of primary importance in most decisions to enter business is found in the prospect and definite expectation of financial gain. The rate of return to efficient, successful entrepreneurs is high. It covers interest on their invested capital, plus an additional return compensating them for risks carried and for the exercise of their managerial talents. Business profits of successful entrepreneurs may easily exceed the level of earnings they would realize in careers as salaried employees. The records of many individuals like John Wanamaker, Henry Ford, and R. G. LeTourneau, who started with nothing and became independently wealthy, demonstrate the rewards to be gained in business for oneself. The fact that many businesses fail, and thus fail to reward their owners, does not deter the confident young people who make the decision for entrepreneurship. They continue in the belief that their ventures will be successful.

Moreover, once a business is on a paying basis, its owner is both financially and occupationally secure. Both income and job are assured so long as the owner retains the goodwill of customers and the home community.

Desire for Power

Some go into business for another, less noble reason—to obtain the power that a position of business leadership will give them. In earlier times, some men chose military careers for the same reason. Caesar, Alexander, and Napoleon are examples of military leaders who acquired great power. In modern times, power is more likely to be gained in business or in politics. To some individuals, the desire for power over the lives of other people is insatiable, a craving that simply cannot be denied.

Protection of Business or Property

Still another, though perhaps less frequent, reason for deciding on business entrepreneurship is the desire to protect an inherited investment. Individuals who inherit a business must either sell it, employ a manager to operate it, or manage it themselves. Selling typically entails losses, and obtaining a manager with the requisite managerial ability is difficult at best. Even if available, such a manager may be reluctant to stay long in this position, for this person may become restless and desirous of also becoming an entrepreneur. The wrong manager can run the business into bankruptcy or cause other losses to the owner. Thus, on occasion, the only practical alternative open to heirs of a business is to manage the business themselves.

Somewhat akin is the matter of property protection. For example, the owners of a vacant business building may decide to open a business to protect their investment in the building. In one case the owner of a building originally used as a garage opened a glove factory after the building had remained vacant for a time. Another example is a former theater converted by its owner into a retail shop.

Miscellaneous Reasons for Business Ownership

Although many other reasons contribute to decisions for entrepreneurship, those discussed above are the ones most frequently stressed by actual entrepreneurs as the factors encouraging their entry into business. Some other possible reasons include the following:

1. Desire to prove one's ability to spouse, parents, or friends.
2. Desire to set one's working pace.
3. Inability to obtain salaried employment, due to age, physical handicaps, or business depression.
4. Desire to occupy time, try out one's ideas, or supplement income after retirement.
5. Desire to occupy time when financially independent, regardless of age.
6. Desire to utilize one's technical preparation for a profession or a trade.

NEGATIVE ASPECTS OF BUSINESS OWNERSHIP

In the preceding discussion certain distasteful or hazardous aspects of business ownership were mentioned or implied. Specifically, there are several serious risks that the prospective entrepreneur should understand.

Risking Loss of Capital

Perhaps the greatest risk is the danger of losing personal capital invested in the business. Opportunities offering large potential profits typically entail serious risks. If the investment were perfectly safe, someone else would have snapped up the possibility already. And, unfortunately, not all risks are subject to control by the entrepreneur. Price fluctuations, wars, fashion changes, and labor trouble on occasion may threaten and damage even well-managed concerns. When individuals fail in business, whether or not they are to blame, they also suffer a certain loss of reputation.

Irregular or Uncertain Income

Business income is typically less regular than the paychecks of a salaried employee. During the first six months or year of operation, many potentially prosperous firms return zero profits to the owner. Even after the business is firmly established, there may be profit fluctuations that require the entrepreneur to live upon personal accumulated savings.

Lack of Suitable Temperament

Furthermore, the responsibilities associated with entrepreneurship may be distasteful to any particular individual. Participating in civic affairs, negotiating with unions, satisfying customers, and dealing with suppliers and regulatory agencies of government may be one person's "meat" and most distasteful to another. To the person who is not temperamentally equipped for the entrepreneurial role, this burden of responsibility would be an undesirable aspect of such a career.

PERSONAL CHARACTERISTICS AND QUALIFICATIONS OF ENTREPRENEURS

According to the prevailing image, entrepreneurs are ambitious individuals whose desire for independence has led them to establish their own firms. Their thrift, skill, and persistence have presumably enabled them to overcome an unfriendly competitive environment and to create a successful business organization. Let us examine this conjecture by considering the types of individuals entering small business and the qualifications that enable them to be successful as entrepreneurs.

The Entrepreneurial Type

Is there an "entrepreneurial type"—a kind of person who is uniquely qualified to make good in private business? Does the independent businessman or businesswoman differ qualitatively from the salaried executive of a big business firm?

As an initial reflection, it seems likely that the entrepreneur possesses many of the same characteristics as do successful managers in big business. Aside from exceptional cases, success in either field requires intelligence, good judgment, honesty, dependability, aggressiveness, and emotional maturity. Leadership talent is required for effective management in any type of organization. Skill in communications is also essential.

Family Background. This does not mean, however, that entrepreneurs and salaried managers are identical in all respects. The entrepreneur, particularly the first-generation entrepreneur who launches the firm, seems to be different in a number of ways. A study of Michigan manufacturer-entrepreneurs by Collins and Moore showed, for example, that the entrepreneur's family background differs from that of the salaried executive.[1] Table 4-1 compares the occupations of the Michigan entrepreneurs with the occupations of fathers of big business leaders—the "American business elite." Of 80 Michigan manufacturer-entrepreneurs, 30 percent had fathers who were skilled or unskilled laborers. Only 3 percent were sons of executives or owners of large businesses. In contrast, only 15 percent of the big business leaders had fathers who were skilled or unskilled laborers, and 35 percent of these leaders had fathers who were business executives or owners of large businesses. A study of small businessmen in Poughkeepsie, New York, substantiates this general picture.[2] Almost 34 percent of the Poughkeepsie proprietors had fathers who were manual workers, whereas fewer than 4 percent had "business manager" fathers.[3]

Table 4-1
FATHER'S PRINCIPAL OCCUPATION: ENTREPRENEURS COMPARED WITH BUSINESS LEADERS

Father's Principal Occupation	Percentage of Entrepreneurs [1]	Percentage of Business Leaders [2]
Major executive or owners of large business	1	24
Minor executive (including foreman)	2	11
Professional man, clerk, or salesman	16	22
Farmer	19	9
Owner of small business	25	17
Laborer (skilled or unskilled)	30	15
Other	6	2

[1] Number of entrepreneurs reporting: 80.
[2] Percentages for business leaders are taken from W. Lloyd Warner and James G. Abegglen, *Occupational Mobility in American Business and Industry* (Minneapolis: University of Minnesota Press, 1955), p. 45.

Source: Orvis Collins and David G. Moore, *The Organization Makers* (New York: Appleton-Century-Crofts, 1970), p. 18.

It is also interesting to note that 44 percent of the Michigan entrepreneurs came from homes of farmers or small business owners. A smaller proportion of big business leaders (26 percent) came from fathers who were "independents"—that is, from families of farmers or small business owners. It seems, therefore, that families of the laboring and "independent" type are particularly important as a source of independent businessmen.

Individualist Attitudes. It appears, then, that the small business owner typically has a family background without roots in large organizations and institutions. In contrast to the corporate executive, the entrepreneur lacks some of the conditioning in the ways of large organizations. His attitudes also tend to

[1] Orvis Collins and David G. Moore, *The Organization Makers* (New York: Appleton-Century-Crofts, 1970).
[2] Mabel Newcomer, "The Little Businessman: A Study of Business Proprietors in Poughkeepsie, New York," *Business History Review* (Winter, 1961), pp. 476-531.
[3] *Ibid.*, p. 516.

be those of the individualist who chooses to go his own way rather than to identify himself with another organization. The personality structure of the Michigan entrepreneurs was probed by use of the Thematic Apperception Test, the results of which were analyzed by a clinical psychologist. A summary statement relating these findings to other phases of the research is given below:

> One point of congruence between our interview material and the TAT analysis is the place of adult figures in the world of the entrepreneur. It is the entrepreneur's relationship to these figures that, more than any other one factor, sets him off from the men who spend their lives in large organizations and who uncritically accept the mandates and directives handed down by "leaders." The entrepreneur, typically, cannot accept without reservation the leadership of others. He cannot live within a framework of occupational behavior set by others. He must, in the end, seek another way. It is this seeking of another way that, in the most fundamental sense, makes an independent entrepreneur of him.[4]

It is well to recall that the discussion above has been particularly concerned with businessmen who have personally developed their own business firms. It is possible that those who take over firms started by others may be more "administrators" and less "pioneers" than those launching new firms. On the basis of research to date, however, the typical independent businessman appears to be an individualist—the nonconforming, inner-directed antithesis of the organization man.

The Family Business. In a study of the entrepreneur, some attention should be devoted to ownership by inheritance. The founder or original entrepreneur frequently bequeaths the business to an heir who then becomes a second-generation entrepreneur. Family businesses, in fact, comprise an important part of the business landscape. Some major corporations—the Du Pont Company and Ford Motor Company, for example—still retain a close identification with the founding families. Among smaller companies, family-type concerns are much more prevalent. In many firms, management has passed from father to son through a number of generations.

The family relationship produces, potentially, both harmful and helpful effects upon the quality of leadership and the success of the firm. As one example, an inferior quality of management may result from the family relationship. A founder's business may disintegrate under the crude or uninspired leadership of his son or grandson. Capable personnel outside the family may avoid the enterprise or desert it if a lack of opportunity is evident.

The quality of management does not always suffer as a result of the family's control of a business firm, however. It may also benefit. The family relationship provides a powerful incentive for the young manager to stay with the firm rather than to succumb to more attractive offers from other companies. If the family manager is capable, the continuity in management is highly desirable.

Owners of small companies typically attempt to augment the management strengths inherent in the family business and to minimize the management weaknesses that are often so disastrous. Some firms go so far as to refuse

---

[4] Orvis Collins and David G. Moore, *op. cit.,* p. 48.

employment to relatives until they have first established themselves elsewhere. Another popular approach, workable in theory at least, is to permit employment of relatives on the basis of family connection but to base all advancement upon demonstrated performance.

The concern here has been with the impact of family considerations upon entrepreneurship. There are also other important strengths and weaknesses in the family business that go beyond the scope of the present discussion.[5]

Special Requirements of the Entrepreneur

It seems probable that certain characteristics are either peculiar to the entrepreneur or required in much greater degree than those required of the hired executive. Unfortunately most of these presently involve speculation and lack a firm basis of objective evidence.[6] Those that appear significant are discussed in the next five paragraphs.

Insatiable Drive for Accomplishment. The entrepreneur possesses an inner compulsion to do and to succeed that is never satisfied.[7] This is most imperative in the early months or years of business operation. These are the months and the years of greatest struggle when the entrepreneur must fight with real intensity of purpose to keep his business alive and growing. This requires single-mindedness and an obstinate refusal to give up even when the situation looks impossible. This necessitates energy; old-fashioned, aggressive initiative; ambition; and even an unashamed desire to make money and be a real success.

Readiness for New Challenges. The second characteristic is an eager readiness to discover new challenges. Enterprisers are intellectually curious about what is wrong with the world around them, and they can distinguish or visualize an opportunity in anything short of perfection. They perceive opportunities even in the complaints and the disagreeable tasks of others. Entrepreneurs are also intuitively and sensibly daring, undertaking risks and ventures that might stop those with less courage. In talking about this trait, however, the greatest stress must be on *eager* readiness. Entrepreneurs have an *active* incentive to seek new adventure; they are ready to accept challenges to accomplishment.

---

[5] See Robert G. Donnelley, "The Family Business," *Harvard Business Review* (July-August, 1964), pp. 93-105; Stanley M. Davis, "Entrepreneurial Succession," *Administrative Science Quarterly*, Vol. 13, No. 3 (December, 1968), pp. 402-416; and Harry Levinson, "Conflicts That Plague Family Businesses," *Harvard Business Review*, Vol. 49, No. 2 (March-April, 1971), pp. 90-98.

[6] Some early attempts to investigate entrepreneurial traits are reported in the following: John A. Hornaday and Charles E. Bunker, "The Nature of the Entrepreneur," *Personnel Psychology*, Vol. 23, No. 1 (Spring, 1970), pp. 47-54; John A. Hornaday and John Aboud, "Characteristics of Successful Entrepreneurs," *Personnel Psychology*, Vol. 24, No. 2 (Summer, 1971), pp. 141-153; and Michael Palmer, "The Application of Psychological Testing to Entrepreneurial Potential," *California Management Review*, Vol. 13, No. 3 (Spring, 1971), pp. 32-38.

[7] Extensive studies by David C. McClelland have demonstrated the existence of a high need for achievement on the part of entrepreneurs. The individual who strikes out on his own and establishes a business is a prime example, although McClelland also includes some types of corporate executives in the "entrepreneur" category. See, for example, David C. McClelland, "N Achievement and Entrepreneurship: A Longitudinal Study," *Journal of Personality and Social Psychology*, Vol. 1, No. 4 (1965), pp. 389-392.

Acceptance of and Dealing with the Unusual. The third characteristic is an ability to accept and deal successfully with the unusual. Someone once remarked that one learns carefully that all balls are round, but that the successful person will not be "thrown completely for a loss" when he or she first comes upon a ball with one square side. The latter type of person is required for leadership in a small business enterprise. Small entrepreneurs are continually confronted with new and unusual problems. Hence, they must be able to accept and deal successfully with this succession of new, troublesome situations.

Persistent Enthusiasm. Persistent enthusiasm is likewise exceptionally important to the independent entrepreneur. One cannot afford to bow to discouragement and give up; one must forge ahead. It is a fact, as John Adams once said, that one swims or sinks in the stream of life. Once having embarked on a given course of action, assuming it is right, the entrepreneur must fight through to the end. But this characteristic is not merely persistence. It is persistence with enthusiasm, which means ardent zeal or fervor.

Sensitivity to Civic Responsibilities. Finally, there is the trait of sensitivity to civic responsibility. This characteristic is required of the hired executive also; but the hired executive more often than not is conscious of civic responsibilities in a more humdrum fashion because he or she thinks, and the company's board of directors believes, that this is a proper executive task. To the independent enterpriser, however, civic responsibility is not a task or an assignment, but a built-in, pleasant preoccupation with the making of a contribution to the home community. That is where the entrepreneur lives and expects to continue to live; hence, the entrepreneur has a compelling interest in its well-being and an active sense of responsibility for helping it to grow and to be a good place to live.

Supporting Attitudes

Certain supporting attitudes are also required of the successful entrepreneur—and, in a varying degree, it must be admitted, of the successful hired executive also. Among these are the following:

1. A willingness to take responsibility and to make decisions.
2. A willingness to select assistants and then to depend upon them and to delegate to them.
3. A willingness to concede one's own limitations and to accept them in an adult manner.
4. A willingness to take advice.
5. A willingness to work hard.
6. A desire to render service, honestly and well.

Training and Experience

It is impossible to prescribe exacting educational and experiential requirements necessary to achieve success as an independent entrepreneur. There are fabulously successful exceptions to any minimum requirement one could specify. It is a matter of record, however, that many business failures result from avoidable inadequacies on the part of the entrepreneur. Analysis of business failures, therefore, provides a suggestion of what is normally a desirable background for success.

In a study of manufacturing failures, Hoad and Rosko discovered that experience and education deficiencies were associated with those failures.[8] Of 36 entrepreneurs who failed, 11 were deficient in education, 11 in experience, and 11 in both. Only three of the failing entrepreneurs, therefore, possessed the appropriate combination of training and experience.

Incompetence, a cause of many failures, may reflect inadequate educational preparation. Certainly a high school education is almost a necessity if one is to undertake business ownership. A college education, with graduate study in business, might be recommended as the ideal academic preparation.

The study of the Poughkeepsie business proprietor mentioned earlier showed him to be better educated than the average person in the total population.[9] There were wide differences, however, among the educational qualifications of proprietors in different types of industry. Barbers and shoe repair shop operators, for example, had less education than clothing store proprietors. This suggests that minimum educational requirements are dictated by the nature of the business. Although this study gave no definite answer as to the importance of college education for success in small business, it did show that the larger of the small business units had the "lion's share" of the college graduates.

Education is no substitute for experience, however. Lack of experience in the particular field of business, lack of managerial experience, and specialization of experience in only one aspect of business are all common causes of failure. Length of desirable experience naturally varies from one type of enterprise to another. Individuals contemplating a business of their own typically do well to consider several years of employment in a similar business. Preferably, this experience should be such as to bring them into contact with the full range of activities and problems associated with the given type of business.

Self-Analysis to Determine Personal Readiness for Entrepreneurship

Only the individual can determine whether he or she is ready or unready to undertake business ownership. It is a decision of vital and lasting significance. The individual who contemplates starting a business will do well to complete the checklist in Appendix A on pages 540-548, which is reprinted from *Small Marketers Aid No. 71*, published by the Small Business Administration.

---

[8] William M. Hoad and Peter Rosko, *Management Factors Contributing to the Success or Failure of New Small Manufacturers*, Michigan Business Report No. 44 (Ann Arbor: Bureau of Business Research, Graduate School of Business Administration, University of Michigan, 1964), Table 47. An entrepreneur was classified as "experienced" if he had more than five years' experience as owner-manager or manager of the same or a similar kind of business. He was classified as "educated" if he had formal education of one or more years beyond high school.

[9] Newcomer, *op. cit.*, pp. 485-487.

Summary

1. Advantages cited for many salaried positions include job security, pride in association with a well-known reputable business, challenging job opportunities, less demanding work, better hours, and regular vacations. The significance of each of these depends upon the particular position and company being considered.

2. Two other major advantages of salaried employment are the absence of investment risk and, for prospective business owners, the acquisition of pre-entrepreneurial experience.

3. Some of the disadvantages of salaried employment include the possibility of transfer or discharge at the desire of the employer, the limitation on the employee's right to exercise personal judgment and initiative, and salary limitations in particular fields.

4. Some of the rewards of entrepreneurship are a satisfying way of life, a feeling of independence, an opportunity for service to the community, and opportunities for profits and security. Other reasons why individuals operate their own businesses are desire for power or need to preserve an inherited investment.

5. The possibility of losing one's personal investment and the irregularity and uncertainty of business income are two of the greatest dangers in business ownership.

6. Successful entrepreneurs differ in background and attitude from salaried managers. In particular, entrepreneurs seem to be more individualistic in viewpoint and to enter entrepreneurship as an escape from the organizational constraints of large concerns.

7. For success as an independent businessman, the individual needs a drive for accomplishment, eagerness to discover new challenges, ability to accept and deal with the unusual, enthusiasm, and a sense of civic responsibility.

8. An adequate background of education and experience is also desirable for business owners. What is adequate depends upon the individual circumstances.

9. Only the individual himself can determine his readiness for business ownership by analyzing his own abilities, experience, education, attitudes, and financial resources.

Discussion Questions

1. What are the variables affecting job security in (a) salaried employment, and (b) business ownership?

2. Compare salaried employment and business ownership as to their demands for hard work and long hours.

3. How can you say whether the financial rewards are higher as an employee or as an independent businessman?
4. Is financial risk a weakness or an advantage of business ownership?
5. Suggest the desirable type and length of salaried employment to prepare one for operation of a (a) florist shop, (b) bowling alley, (c) cafeteria, (d) millwork manufacturing company, (e) drug wholesale company, and (f) shoe store.
6. What is the most significant, fundamental reason for choice of business ownership by the small business entrepreneur whom you know best?
7. The study of Michigan entrepreneurs shows that most of their fathers were not big business executives. What is there about the home or family life of a salaried business executive that might prevent the son's choice of an entrepreneurial career?
8. Does it seem likely that the greater independence of spirit on the part of the entrepreneur is a result of educational conditioning?

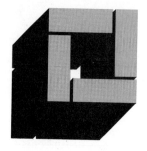

5

The Danger of
Small Business Failure

In the previous chapter attention was given to the personal characteristics, abilities, and backgrounds of entrepreneurs. Because of personal deficiencies, some entrepreneurs are doomed from the very beginning. Other entrepreneurs encounter business problems that exceed their ability or resources. For one reason or another, therefore, many small firms fail every year. This chapter is concerned with the patterns of failure, particularly in small business, and also with the prerequisites for successful operations.

FAILURE AND THE SMALL FIRM

In view of the obviously limited resources and lack of financial stability on the part of many small firms, it seems probable that small business mortality is greater than big business mortality. As a class, small business would seemingly be "hit harder" by failures than would be the case with larger firms. That this is apparently true is shown by the data in Table 5-1. Over 73 percent of the 1972 failures occurred in firms having less than $100,000 in liabilities. The problem of failure in business is thus an urgent problem of small business.[1]

Table 5-1
PERCENTAGE DISTRIBUTION OF BUSINESS FAILURES
BY SIZE OF LIABILITY, 1972

Size of Liability	Percentage of Failures
Under $5,000	4.1
$5,000 to $25,000	26.1
$25,000 to $100,000	43.4
$100,000 to $1,000,000	23.4
Over $1,000,000	3.0

Source: *The Business Failure Record: 1972* (New York: Dun & Bradstreet, Inc., 1973), p. 6.

---

[1] Additional research is necessary to establish conclusively the probable negative correlation between size of firm and rate of failure. For example, the percentage of failures in each size class in Table 5-1 should be compared with the percentage of firms in each size class. Unfortunately the latter data are not available. There is corroborating evidence, however, from other studies that show the greater failure-proneness of small firms. See O. D. Dickerson and Michael Dawaja, "The Failure Rates of Business," in Irving Pfeffer (ed.), *The Financing of Small Business: A Current Assessment* (New York: The Macmillan Company, 1967).

The special threat of failure to the small concern is further evident in the relative failure rate among various business areas. Retailing, an area in which small business predominates, shows a high rate of failure, particularly in small-scale lines of retailing. All of the lines of business shown in Table 5-2 have a failure rate which is higher than the overall 1972 failure rate of 38 per 10,000 firms.

Table 5-2
RETAIL FAILURE RATES, 1972

Line of Business	Failure Rate per 10,000 Operating Concerns
Cameras and photographic supplies	85
Books and stationery	54
Women's ready-to-wear	88
Appliances, radio, and television	42
Furniture and furnishings	63
Men's wear	97
Gifts	60

Source: *The Business Failure Record: 1972* (New York: Dun & Bradstreet, Inc., 1973), p. 5.

Rate of Business Failure

The rate of business failure fluctuates from year to year because of changes in general economic conditions and other factors. Figure 5-1 shows the rate of

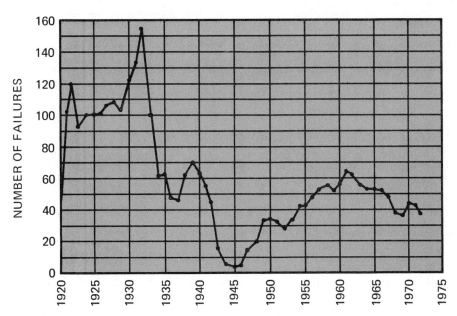

Figure 5-1
RATE OF BUSINESS FAILURE, 1920-1972
(Number of Failures per 10,000 Firms in Dun & Bradstreet Reference Book)
Source: *The Business Failure Record: 1972* (New York: Dun & Bradstreet, Inc., 1973).

failure each year from 1920 to 1972.[2] An examination of fluctuations in the rate of failure reveals that the rate in recent years is significantly lower than that of the 1920s. In view of this fact, one may take a more optimistic view of the chances for small business survival. Even though an alarming number of businesses die each year, the problem appears less serious when viewed in this historical perspective.

The rate of failure is closely associated with general business conditions. In the depression of the early 1930s, the failure rate reached its highest point. In the subsequent prosperous years of World War II, the rate dropped sharply. Since 1945, the consistently high level of economic activity has been accompanied by a lower rate of failure than existed some decades earlier.

Business Failure and Age of Firm

The relationship of the failure rate to the age of business firms is portrayed by Table 5-3. This table clearly shows the high rate of mortality among concerns in business five years or less. The concern that is going to fail typically does so during the initial five-year period. These years represent the "maiden voyage" for the new firm and provide real tests of capital, product, and business leadership.

Table 5-3
AGE OF BUSINESS FAILURE, 1972

Age in Years	Percentage of Total Failures
5 years or less	55.7
6 to 10 years	22.4
Over 10 years	21.9
Total	100.0

Source: *The Business Failure Record: 1972* (New York: Dun & Bradstreet, Inc., 1973), p. 9.

The Tragedy of Business Failure

There are a number of reasons why business failure constitutes a tragedy. Among these are the following:

1. Loss of capital on the part of the entrepreneur and creditors.
2. Psychological effect on the individual.
3. Elimination of a source of goods and services.
4. Reduction of employment.
5. Decreased tax payments.

The owner of a business that fails suffers a loss of invested capital, either in whole or in part. This is always a financial setback to the individual concerned; in

---

[2] The most comprehensive statistics pertaining to failure and changes in rate of failure are collected by Dun and Bradstreet, a business firm devoted to analysis and rating of the credit standing of other firms. Failures, as defined by Dun and Bradstreet, include only those discontinuances that involve loss to creditors; voluntarily liquidated firms with all debts paid are excluded.

some cases, he loses his life's savings. In the case of the retired individual who established a small business, this is a real tragedy inasmuch as his days as a productive employee of some other business are over. This individual is often thrown upon his family or the community for support.

Such a loss of capital is augmented by the losses of business creditors. Hence, the total capital loss is considerably greater than the sum of the entrepreneurial losses in any one year. To society as a whole, this loss of capital reduces the total sum of investment funds available to business. Thus, it is a factor contributory to business recession or a deterrent to expansion. It constitutes a social waste.

Moreover, the individual who fails suffers a real blow to his self-esteem. The business he started with enthusiasm and with high expectations of success has "gone under." The older entrepreneur, in many cases, lacks the vitality to recover from the blow. Even a younger man undergoes a gnawing doubt of his own ability unless and until he tries again and succeeds. Most unsuccessful entrepreneurs simply relapse into employee status for the balance of their lives. This, too, may constitute a serious social loss, as many of these "failures" possess managerial ability that is not utilized fully in an employee status.

The third reason why business failures are to be deplored is found in the elimination of firms supplying goods and services that the public needs and wants. This assumes, of course, that a real business opportunity existed, such as could successfully support a business concern. Customers find it inconvenient to travel farther than before to find the goods or services wanted. In some cases, replacement firms do not appear for months or years. In the meantime, it may be difficult to find as broad a choice of merchandise and services or as reasonable prices as before.

Again, the number of jobs available in the community is reduced by the failure of any enterprise. The entrepreneur himself becomes jobless; his employees, if any, join him at least temporarily in the ranks of the unemployed. The community thus suffers the loss of a business payroll.

Finally, the business that failed was a taxpayer, contributing to the tax support of schools, police and fire protection, and the services of government generally. The loss of tax income, whether from business failure or otherwise, can force a curtailment of local governmental services or deficit financing. Ordinarily, neither of these outcomes is socially desirable.

For these reasons, therefore, it is clear that business mortality is a personal tragedy to the entrepreneurs who fail and, at the same time, it is a source of social waste.

CAUSES OF BUSINESS FAILURE

Aside from the relatively few failures caused by fraud, neglect, and disaster, the root cause is found in managerial incapacity. The weaknesses of management manifest themselves in various ways, however. These manifestations might be thought of as the apparent or surface causes of failure.

Surface Causes of Failure

Even though we recognize that management is basically at fault, it is nevertheless profitable to note those areas in which management most frequently finds itself in trouble. Some of the more prominent difficulties are discussed in the next five paragraphs.

Competition. A frequently alleged cause of failure is intensity of competition. Independent grocery stores in small towns or city shopping centers may be run out of business by the advent of efficient chain or supermarket competition. Manufacturers serving a given clientele or area might also encounter new, efficient, well-financed competition for the first time. An efficiently managed, existent business, however, is a tough foe for any competitor. Perhaps too much stress has been placed on competition as a cause of failure, but it must be given proper consideration.

Lack of Capital. Starting business on the proverbial shoestring is generally unwise and often leads to failure. Even though initial capital may have been adequately provided, the entrepreneur may misuse that which is available. The result is the same—a lack of capital. The lack of capital may be only temporary but still cause failure. The results of overborrowing are often tragic. Lack of capital is typically an indication of poor financial management with the end result being business failure.

Location. In a certain city in Texas, within the space of one year, three eating establishments in succession were opened in a given shopping center. The failure of each was due, in part, to the choice of location. Choice of a successful location is partly a science and partly an art. It is obvious, however, that many locations are chosen without serious study, careful planning, or adequate investigation.

Premature Expansion. To expand any business unwisely may be fatal. Business expansion should be financed soundly, ordinarily from earnings or capital contributions of owners. In periods of business prosperity, with reasonable certainty of continued demand, a manufacturer might successfully expand physical facilities through bond sales or mortgage loans. Expansion, in any case, calls for careful advance planning. An expanding concern should never be top-heavy with debt.

The conditions that seemingly cause failure could be expanded at length. Some of the additional, more common surface troubles are: (1) inadequate sales; (2) heavy operating costs; (3) inventory difficulties; (4) excessive fixed costs; (5) bad debts; (6) payment of dividends whether earned or not; (7) ignorance concerning the market; and (8) difficulty in providing for management succession. These conditions are the results of inadequate management.

Management as a Cause of Failure

Among the many interrelated causes of business failures, the most important basic cause is a lack of skill in management. This indictment of the manager is amply supported by the extensive analysis of business failures conducted by Dun & Bradstreet. Consider, for example, their analysis of reasons for failures occurring in 1972, as depicted in Table 5-4.

Table 5-4
CAUSES OF FAILURES IN 1972

Neglect		2.0%
Fraud		1.5
Inexperience, incompetence		93.1
Inadequate sales	45.4%	
Heavy operating expenses	8.5	
Receivables difficulties	9.6	
Inventory difficulties	5.7	
Excessive fixed assets	3.8	
Poor location	4.3	
Competitive weakness	26.4	
Other	6.5	
Disaster		0.9
Reason unknown		2.5
		100.0%

Source: *The Business Failure Record: 1972* (New York: Dun & Bradstreet, Inc., 1973), pp. 11-12. Since some failures are attributed to a combination of causes, percentages for the items in the inset column do not add to 93.1%.

In small business especially, management seems to be the number one problem of the enterprise. The able manager utilizes his time wisely and gives proper attention to the various managerial functions. This includes careful attention to customer and public relations, financial planning, employee relations, production control, selling, and other key factors of a business. Often the ostensible causes of failure, such as inadequate sales, excessive fixed assets, and poor location, are merely reflections of the owner's inadequacy.

Case Histories of Failures

A number of case studies have served to confirm the Dun & Bradstreet analysis that places the blame for failure upon deficient management. To cite only one example, the University of Iowa, in conjunction with the Small Business Administration, compared the management policies and practices of 37 unsuccessful manufacturing firms with those of 53 successful companies in the same industries.[3] The purpose of the study was to determine points of contrast that might explain the failures.

The contrasts were indeed sharp. Product policies constituted one major point of difference. For example, some poultry processors went out of business when the broiler industry shifted to the South. In contrast, other processors changed their operations to processing dried and/or frozen eggs. As another example, one bakery failed while concentrating on a limited product line of bread and buns, whereas a successful bakery of similar size developed higher markup products in the more lucrative pastry line. In these various examples there is evidence of a gap in managerial planning.

---

[3] Clifford M. Baumback and Leonard J. Konapa, "Management Miscues of Small Manufacturers," *Journal of Small Business Management*, Vol. 7, No. 3 (July, 1969), pp. 4-7, 11.

Collection difficulties with many slow-paying customers was another problem of unsuccessful small manufacturers. These resulted from ill-advised credit policies and practices that created a shortage of working capital. In many cases, customer credit standing was not checked with credit bureaus or banks. Even in those firms receiving credit reports, management failed to take them seriously. These practices indicate a major weakness in the performance of the management control function.

Other differences likewise reflected contrasts in management, and the authors of the study drew the following conclusions:

It is evident from this study the successful small manufacturers adopted marketing guide lines early in their life whereas the unsuccessful firms either drifted hazardously or capriciously determined their product, credit, price, channel of distribution and sales promotion policies subsequently. It seems natural to conclude, therefore, that the formulation of even tentative policies is more likely to result in a successful business venture rather than simply allowing them to develop haphazardly during the early years of the enterprise.[4]

SYMPTOMS OF BUSINESS FAILURE

The types of change discussed below are symptoms of impending business failure. These are the red flags that alert the entrepreneur, and any one of them may point to trouble. As groups of symptoms converge, however, the danger grows more evident, and corrective action becomes necessary to avoid failure.

Deterioration of Working Capital Position

Deterioration of a firm's working capital position is evidenced by a progressive decline in working capital adequacy. Working capital, which includes receivables and inventory in addition to cash, will also typically become less liquid, that is, less rapidly convertible into cash. Factors contributing to declining adequacy and liquidity include:

1. Continuing operating losses.
2. Unusual, nonrecurring losses, such as those due to theft, flood, tornado, and adverse court judgments.
3. Payment of excessive managerial bonuses and unearned dividends.
4. Frozen loans to officers, subsidiaries, and affiliates.
5. Overinvestment in fixed assets from working capital funds.
6. Bond or long-term loan payments in excess of a proper share of annual profits.

Liquidity of working capital is essential to a satisfactory working capital position. The average number of days that accounts are outstanding and the inventory turnover ratios are measures of working capital liquidity. Regular taking of all purchase discounts is another indicator of both adequacy and

---

[4] *Ibid.*, p. 7.

liquidity. The current ratio and acid-test ratio are direct measures of working capital adequacy.[5]

If company ratios are unfavorable in comparison with industry standard ratios, working capital is relatively inadequate and illiquid. Management should then seek new equity capital, retain profits in the business, enforce a tighter credit policy, and reduce receivables and inventories. Excess fixed assets may be sold, officer loans collected, and dividends to stockholders passed until the situation is improved.

Declining Sales

Sales decline represents a serious situation for any business. This is because operating expenses—particularly fixed overhead expenses—do not decline in proportion to sales. Hence, sales declines result in reduced profits or actual losses when continued too long.

Some of the recommended steps to be taken in the face of declining sales include: (1) market research to measure sales potentials by sales areas or customer groups; (2) selective selling to profitable customers; (3) increased, properly planned advertising expenditures; (4) improved sales promotion; and (5) development of new products and services.

Declining Profits

Profits that go downward from month to month or year to year are also symptomatic of business failure. The cause may be declining sales, increasing merchandise cost, higher labor costs, higher taxes, or many other factors. Two key ratios to watch in this area are net profits on net sales and net profits on tangible net worth, that is, on proprietorship investment. The operating expense ratio, which is the ratio of expenses to sales, should also be watched carefully. These should be held at figures comparable to the industry standard ratios.

Higher Debt Ratios

Progressively higher debt ratios constitute still another symptom of possible business failure. If current liabilities get out of hand and bills or payrolls due for payment cannot be paid, the concern's situation might rapidly deteriorate into involuntary bankruptcy. Nor should a company's fixed, long-term liabilities be allowed to become excessive. Key ratios for use in determining trends and comparisons with industry standards include the following:

1. Current liabilities to tangible net worth.
2. Current liabilities to inventory.
3. Fixed assets to long-term liabilities.
4. Total liabilities to tangible net worth.
5. Number of times bond interest, if any, is earned.

---

[5] It is not necessary to be overly concerned with precise definitions at this point. The "current ratio" may be thought of as the ratio of all current assets—particularly cash, receivables, and inventory—to liabilities which must be paid within one year. "Acid-test ratio," on the other hand, is the ratio of only the very liquid current assets—cash and receivables, but not inventory—to liabilities which must be paid within one year.

It is recommended that small business expansion ordinarily come from retained profits. To increase its percentage of total industry sales, a firm should procure added equity capital. For the small business, ownership capital should constitute 60 percent of its total capital, or higher, for safety.

PREREQUISITES FOR SUCCESS IN BUSINESS

Having considered the causes of failure, it is now possible to formulate certain of the prerequisites for success. In contemplating any business venture, it is desirable to consider the factors that are essential for survival and growth.

Existence of Business Opportunity

The first prerequisite for business success is the existence of a real, not merely an apparent, business opportunity. This means that the firm must sell goods or services needed and desired by the public. It also requires enough customers who are willing to buy at a price and in sufficient volume to permit continuing profitable operation.

Obviously, a small entrepreneur must verify the public need for his goods and services. First, this involves the measurement of sales potentials at various prices to ascertain both the magnitude and the degree of elasticity of demand. Second, an evaluation should be made of how much sales can be expanded through advertising. The prospective businessman must also demonstrate that the number of existing firms is too small to serve the present demand efficiently. Favorable findings of this kind tend to guarantee the existence of a real business opportunity.

Management Ability and Background

The second prerequisite for success in both large and small business firms is real management ability on the part of the manager or management team. Concretely, this means skill in handling men, money, and inventories, along with the ability to formulate wise policies, select proper methods, merchandise aggressively, and create good relationships with employees, customers, and the general public. Ability of this type requires a background of training and experience. A minimum of three years' experience in the given line, or a closely related line, is recommended. Preferably some time should have been spent in a management capacity.

Experience should be supplemented by adequate formal training in business administration. Training and experience make it possible for the small entrepreneur, as well as for the big business executive, to know tax angles, insurance needs, relationships to regulatory agencies of government, and the labor laws currently in force that apply to his business. They acquaint him with operating and office methods and procedures, the need for adequate records and reporting systems, the meaning and the proper use of various controls afforded by accounting and statistics, and the importance of participation in civic affairs. By experience, the entrepreneur becomes conversant with trade practices and customs, including standard business papers used in business transactions. He learns also about equipment care and replacement, how to control expenses, and how to solve personnel problems.

Adequate Capital and Credit

Another requirement for success is adequacy of capital and credit, together with a knowledge of how to use both properly in financing operations. It has been recommended previously that equity capital be 60 percent of total capital, or more, in the average small business. Working capital, at the inception of operations, should be sufficient to assure continuing operations for six months and preferably for twelve months. It requires some time for most new businesses to begin to show a profit, and thus provision must be made for an early no-profit period. In a small enterprise, initial capital or savings must also be sufficient to provide for the family living expenses of the owner until the business does show a profit. This may require from 6 to 24 months.

Modern Methods

Another prerequisite for business success, closely related to that of management ability, is the use of modern methods, research, and a scientific approach to solution of the problems of the business. Many small businessmen feel that the use of such methods is precluded by their high cost. Actually, the reverse is true. It is the high cost of antiquated methods and of lack of research that makes modern methods and the scientific approach imperative in every business. Merchant pools may be set up to engage in market research collectively. The chamber of commerce initiates studies and then makes the results available to members. Private research organizations, such as Southwest Research Institute of San Antonio, Texas, are available. And the small entrepreneur can keep abreast of new developments by reading trade literature and by talking to sales representatives who call on him. New materials, new equipment, scientific construction of advertisements, market research, sales planning for selective selling, integrated data processing, budgets, and the like are all available.

Insurance for Measurable Risks

A final prerequisite for business success is the identification of all possible business risks and the carrying of adequate insurance covering all those that are insurable. One may insure against fire or flood loss; business interruption; injury to customers and members of the public; health and accidents of employees; auto theft, collision, and liability; loss of a key executive by death; property loss (equipment, inventory, etc.); marine and other transportation losses; and theft, embezzlement, and fraud.

In fact, one can insure against almost any business risk except those that are not measurable, such as depressions, wars, or declines in sales and profits. Business operation should not be a gamble; hence, there is a need for all pertinent forms of insurance.

A Sound Management Philosophy

There are those in business who would scorn the notion that the managerial philosophy of those operating a business can make a contribution to business success. But management must believe in business and in America. It must perceive America's new frontiers. Business opportunities are still as readily found as in former years. Management must believe this and then search for its own special opportunity. In so doing, management must:

1. Be readily adaptable to new methods and new products.
2. Adhere to the theory and practice of mass production for mass distribution, if practicable. For firms catering to special markets—such as specialty grocers who sell imported delicacies only—this is not practicable.
3. Play fair with labor, recognizing the worker as a partner in the enterprise.
4. Exercise a well-developed sense of civic responsibility.

By so doing, a business remains competitive, turns a low unit profit into maximum total profit, enjoys good employee relations, and serves as an enlightened citizen in its home community.

 Summary

1. The rate of business failure during the past decade has been substantially lower than the failure rate in the 1920s. The rate is closely related to general business conditions, increasing during periods of recession and dropping during periods of prosperity.
2. The mortality rate among small firms is particularly high. Many lines of retailing in which size of firms is typically small show disproportionately high rates of failure.
3. New firms, particularly those less than five years old, have a much higher failure rate than do older firms.
4. Business failures are costly not only to the businessman who fails but also to creditors and to the community.
5. The underlying cause of most business failures appears to be the incompetence and inexperience of the management. This factor is often obscured by such "surface" causes as severe competition, lack of capital, poor location, and premature expansion.
6. Some symptoms of impending business failure are: (a) deterioration of working capital position; (b) declining sales; (c) declining profits; and (d) increasing debt ratios.
7. Some of the essential factors in achieving business success are: (a) the existence of a real business opportunity; (b) management ability; (c) adequate capital; (d) modern methods of operation; (e) insurance for measurable risks; and (f) an adequate management philosophy.

Discussion Questions

1. What is the long-run trend in business failure?
2. (a) What are the effects of depressions and wars on the rate of business failures? (b) Why do these effects occur?
3. (a) In what areas of business are the rates of failure most severe? (b) What do you think accounts for this?
4. Explain the relationship between business failure and business age. Is this a causal relationship?
5. Enumerate and describe some of the costs of business failure.
6. Justify the statement that most business failures are caused by management weaknesses.
7. (a) Explain the symptoms of business failure described in the chapter. (b) Can you suggest others?
8. What is the basis of a real business opportunity?
9. Outline the minimum educational and experiential requirements you think necessary for the following types of business: (a) restaurant; (b) drugstore; (c) small supermarket; (d) public accounting firm; (e) TV repair shop; (f) independent house builder; and (g) small town bank.
10. Discuss the meaning of "adequate" capital. Can any amount of credit obviate the need of ownership capital? Why?
11. What is the most essential type of insurance for business success?
12. (a) What is your idea of the connection between management philosophy and business success? (b) Do you know of firms that are apparently succeeding with unethical methods?

Case A-1

TEXAS METER & DEVICE COMPANY *

Texas Meter & Device Company is a small family-owned business specializing in the service and rebuilding of electric meters. Most of its operations are located in a small shop in Waco, Texas. The president of the company, Ted Kramer, has recently become interested in a business opportunity related to a new product developed by Westinghouse Electric.

Company's Background

The company's services include testing and repairing of electric meters, building of customized metering equipment, and rebuilding of meters for sale in foreign countries. The company has earned an excellent reputation as a dependable company in its field of specialization.

The nature of the business has given Ted Kramer frequent contacts with all utilities in the region—large private utilities, municipal systems, and cooperatives. These same utilities are also the customers of Westinghouse Electric. Through contacts with electric utilities, Kramer became aware of Westinghouse's new product and the difficulties they were experiencing in marketing it.

New Product's Background

Westinghouse Electric, a large utility equipment manufacturer, had recently developed a new instrument to record energy usage by large industrial consumers. Electric utilities have historically utilized data on peak power loads as one factor in computing the cost of service. An improved recording device,

therefore, could be of value to them in measuring power usage and computing monthly charges. A utility could install a device of this type at the electrical service entrance of a large industrial consumer.

Traditionally, peak power loads were recorded, with less than complete accuracy, by a device having an inked pen that drew a line on a moving chart. Other types of demand meters were read in the field and then reset to zero. At the end of the month, the utility correlated peak load and energy usage data in billing the customer. These systems often contained interpretation errors, were slow to implement, and seldom could be counted on to reproduce accurately a customer's energy usage pattern.

Westinghouse's new and innovative recording device employed a magnetic tape recorder as a replacement for the traditional charting device. The system used electrical impulses to record power load usage. Some systems even contained a separate emergency power pack which could operate the system in case of a power failure. The new recorder provided readings of greater accuracy, showing peak power consumption by 15-minute periods or by any other interval specified by the utility. Its recorded information could also be used for other types of reports on power consumption. In spite of the new recorder's superiority, however, Westinghouse experienced difficulty in its marketing, installation, and use.

Need for Translating Equipment

Although the new recorder was superior in performance, it possessed one design feature that limited its adoption and use. The recorder had been designed to be competitive in price with existing equipment, and this fact restricted the sophistication of its design. It was not possible to incorporate a basic logic system and memory unit into the recorder without making the cost prohibitive. As a result, the new device

---

* This case was prepared by Professor Alan N. Cook and Professor Justin G. Longenecker of Baylor University.

recorded electrical impulses on a ¼" magnetic tape. However, these recorded impulses did not constitute computer language, and the tape could not be fed directly into a computer. To be processed by computer, it would be necessary to translate the data into computer language while transferring it to a ½" computer tape.

The problem, therefore, was how to transfer information from the ¼" magnetic tape to the ½" computer tape. Westinghouse designed a machine to perform this translation, but its cost of $45,000 tended to price it out of the market. By purchasing such a translator, a utility could use the new recording devices in the plants of major customers and bring the various tapes into a central location for analysis. However, the cost appeared quite high because most utilities lacked a sufficient number of industrial customers large enough to justify installation of a $45,000 translating machine. In addition, further cost would be involved in developing software—that is, in writing computer programs necessary to retrieve information from the magnetic tape.

As a result of these cost considerations in buying translators, utilities were understandably reluctant to purchase and utilize either the translator or the new recording devices. In view of these considerations, therefore, the market for the new recorders and translators failed to develop as desired.

Selling a Translating Service

It seemed clear that utilities that were unwilling to invest in costly translating equipment might be willing to purchase a translating service. In this way, they could use the new recording technology and obtain needed information of greater accuracy without heavy capital investment.

Sensing the attractiveness of this idea, Westinghouse instituted a translating service and sold some of the new recorders. However, the operation of a translating service by Westinghouse differed sharply from its basic function of manufacturing and its primary interest in production. Because of this or other reasons, the translating service seemed unsatisfactory to many users. Major complaints centered on lost tapes and slow service. Utilities wanted 24-hour service, if possible, but service was much slower than that. In spite of available translating service, sales of the recording device continued to lag.

Small Business Opportunity in Problems of Westinghouse

The difficulty of Westinghouse in providing satisfactory translating service provided a potential business opportunity. Ted Kramer thought that a small service business might succeed where Westinghouse had experienced difficulty. Small firms reputedly had greater flexibility and a possibility for speedier service than that offered by large corporations. If Texas Meter & Device Company could provide such service, the strengths of small business could be coupled with the manufacturing and research strengths of big business to the mutual advantage of both. If successful, Texas Meter & Device Company would profit from the sale of a translating service, and Westinghouse would profit from the sale of new recorders to the utilities.

Successful operation would require Texas Meter & Device Company to earn profits where Westinghouse had failed. As a small business, Texas Meter & Device Company was quite different from large corporations like Westinghouse. For example, it was a business that emphasized service rather than the manufacture and sale of heavy equipment. Texas Meter & Device Company, moreover, was experienced in providing testing and repair services to the utilities which might need the translating service.

Problems in Offering a Translating Service

Offering a translating service necessitated access to a computer, and

Texas Meter & Device Company had no computer. Computer time could be purchased, however, from another firm in the same city.

Texas Meter & Device Company also lacked experience in the use of a computer. Even with computer service available, the company would need a computer programmer to write the programs necessary to retrieve the data. In all likelihood this would not require a full-time employee. A qualified individual might be paid to perform the necessary programming on a consulting or part-time basis. Once a particular program was written, it could be used over and over. There was need for more than a single program, however. Additional programs would be required to retrieve various data in addition to the peak power load information available on the tapes and to meet the special requirements of each customer.

An investment of $45,000 would be necessary to obtain a translating machine from Westinghouse. This represented a substantial investment for Texas Meter & Device Company, and there was some danger in obsolescence. If the industry switched to recorders that produced a ½" computer tape, the translating machine would have little further use.

Reaching a Decision

To attempt establishment of a translation service, Kramer needed to submit an offer to Westinghouse to act as a translation center for the more accurate, new recording system. If a proposal appeared practical, Westinghouse should approve. Their own difficulties with the service had made continuation of the service more of a burden than an attractive opportunity to them. At the same time, provision of the service was essential for the sale of their new recording devices. Consequently, they should welcome an opportunity to cooperate with Texas Meter & Device Company in the establishment of an independent translating service facility. The question faced by Ted Kramer was whether his small firm could succeed where big business had failed.

QUESTIONS

1. What are the major strengths of Texas Meter & Device Company that are related to the proposed venture?
2. What can Texas Meter & Device Company do that Westinghouse is not already doing to make this a success?
3. What should be Ted Kramer's decision with respect to this opportunity?

Case A-2

ACME ELECTRO-VIDEO, INC. *

After three years in the electronics program at a leading southwestern university, Terry Baker enlisted in the Air Force, where he spent four years as a radar technician. When he was released from the military, he went to work testing prototype radar systems. During this period, Baker became familiar with television systems and recognized the great market potential television had in the security field. After two years in the radar-testing field, Baker had an opportunity to join a small company which was involved in selling and servicing video surveillance systems. He spent seven years with this organization in both a sales and service capacity, and then decided to start his own business.

With his own savings and some family financial support, Baker formed the Video Engineering Corporation to install and service television surveillance systems in

* This case was prepared by Brent D. Werley and Professor O. Hoyt Gibson of Texas Christian University.

banks. The Tulsa-based firm had three employees: Baker, doubling in sales and service; an installation/repair man; and Baker's wife acting as a secretary/accountant.

From the beginning, Baker was pleased with the progress he was making with his new venture. He found new markets opening up in unexpected areas, but the small size of the company precluded taking advantage of these opportunities. The company needed new capital very badly, but sources of capital were not available.

At this particular time Robert Simmons, a successful Oklahoma City electronics distributor, was searching for a sales-oriented but technically competent manager who could revitalize his Tulsa video sales and service company. Simmons' company sold and serviced surveillance systems that were designed for security systems in penal institutions, banks, and large corporations. The firm also solicited educational television studio/systems business from the colleges and universities in the area.

When Simmons heard that Baker's business was experiencing difficulties, he proposed a marriage that would allow a newly chartered company to continue exploiting the highly lucrative television surveillance market.

On September 15, 1967, the new company, Acme Electro-Video, Inc., was formed for the purpose of selling and servicing both video and audio equipment. The board of directors consisted of Baker and Simmons. Simmons was chairman of the board, and Baker was president of the corporation. The articles of incorporation authorized 50,000 shares of common stock at 15 cents per share. Simmons held 50 percent of the shares and Baker had the other half.

The organization consisted of Baker, who devoted most of his time to sales; two installation/service men; and one secretary (see Exhibit 1).

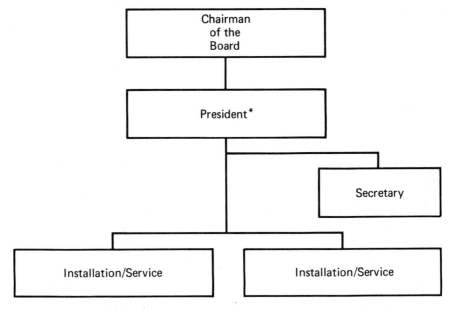

*In the beginning the president functioned primarily as the sole sales representative.

Exhibit 1
ACME ELECTRO-VIDEO, INC., ORGANIZATION CHART, SEPTEMBER 15, 1967

The market area to be covered by the new company extended approximately 125 miles in all directions from the Tulsa office. Within this area Acme had three competitors, who were approximately the same size as Acme and sold and serviced identical equipment and systems.

Cold prospecting generated most of the early sales, but some support came from suppliers' leads and referrals. The sales approach was to emphasize the system's capabilities and, if pressed, to discuss the company's service policies. When a sale was consummated, the company purchased the required hardware on credit, installed it, and paid suppliers when the job was paid for.

First Year

The first year's efforts resulted in sales of $234,301, and a net income after taxes of $17,048. There were no personnel additions, and no significant changes in operating procedures (see Exhibits 2 and 3 for financial information).

	1967-1968	1968-1969
Sales	$234,301	$441,518
Cost of Goods Sold		
Inventory-Beginning	0	31,264
Merchandise Purchased	183,026	611,598
Freight In	2,722	7,253
Available for Sale	$185,748	$650,115
Inventory-Ending	31,264	304,067
Total	$154,484	$346,048
Other Costs		
Selling and Administration Expense	$ 52,609	$113,110
Depreciation	3,138	1,417
Interest Charges	1,741	6,132
Total	$ 57,488	$120,659
Total Cost of Goods Sold	$211,972	$466,707
Taxable Income	$ 22,329	$ 0
Income Tax	5,281	0
Net Income After Taxes	$ 17,048	$(25,189)

Exhibit 2
ACME ELECTRO-VIDEO, INC., COMPARATIVE STATEMENT OF PROFIT AND LOSS (Fiscal Years 1967-1968 and 1968-1969)

Second Year

The company moved to a larger building to accommodate its increased sales volume. Two additional station wagons were leased to facilitate moving men and equipment to installation sites.

Ralph Weaver, previously a store manager with a leading audio distributor, was hired to be vice president of operations. Weaver had three years of college training in electronics, and 11 years' experience in sales and maintenance of many types of audio and video equipment. An additional installation man and a sales repre-sentative were also added. As a result of the additional installation man, the market area was increased by almost 30 percent.

Baker was still doing most of the sales work because the new sales repre-sentative was not yet completely familiar with Acme's operation. During the second year, sales increased to $441,518, but the company showed a loss of $25,189 (see Exhibits 2 and 3).

Current Situation

Four new employees were added during the first half of the current year. Weaver,

	1967-1968		1968-1969
Current Assets			
Cash	$ (616)		$ 56,336
Accounts Receivable	96,283		56,052
Inventories	31,264		304,067
Total Current Assets	$126,931		$416,455
Fixed Assets			
Building and Equipment	$ 6,816	$7,475	
Accumulated Depreciation	3,139	4,555	
Total Fixed Assets	3,677		2,920
Other Assets	462		1,043
TOTAL ASSETS	$131,070		$420,418
Current Liabilities			
Accounts Payable	$ 71,567		$202,306
Notes Payable	24,600		218,438
Payroll Taxes Payable	4,104		1,412
Total Current Liabilities	$100,271		$422,156
Long-Term Liabilities			
Notes Payable (exceed one year)	973		0
Total Liabilities	$101,244		$422,156
Stockholders' Equity			
Common Stock	$ 7,500	$7,500	
Retained Earnings	22,326	(9,238)	
Total Stockholders' Equity	$ 29,826		$ (1,738)
TOTAL LIABILITY AND STOCKHOLDERS' EQUITY	$131,070		$420,418

Exhibit 3
ACME ELECTRO-VIDEO, INC., COMPARATIVE BALANCE SHEET
(Fiscal Years 1967-1968 and 1968-1969)

charged with the personnel functions, indicated that no formal job descriptions existed, but spelled out the general responsibilities of the 11 employees (see Exhibits 4 and 5).

Direct mail advertising is now being used regularly to augment the three sales representatives' efforts to cover intensively an unchanged market area. Baker devotes only 60 percent of his time to sales since the new salesmen joined the firm. The rest of his time is spent in administrative work.

Currently Acme has 45 percent of the market in its market area. In part, this results from the fact that Acme is the sole distributor for one of the major suppliers of audio and visual surveillance equipment. Meanwhile, the number of Acme's competitors has risen from three to five over the past 18 months.

Acme's bidding strategy is to be first on the job so that it can write the specifications on the equipment it would like to supply. To avoid the disappointment of bidding a job with good equipment and losing the contract to a competitor who underbids by using inferior equipment, Acme has a policy of rendering three bid prices. A high bid is provided for those companies who may receive additional appropriations for the project and may wish to upgrade their system. The second is approximately midway between the high and low bids. It is the one the company tries to push. The low bid is provided to keep Acme competitive with the firms that bid inferior hardware.

When an order is received, the preliminary drawings and specifications are reconfirmed. The customer prepares

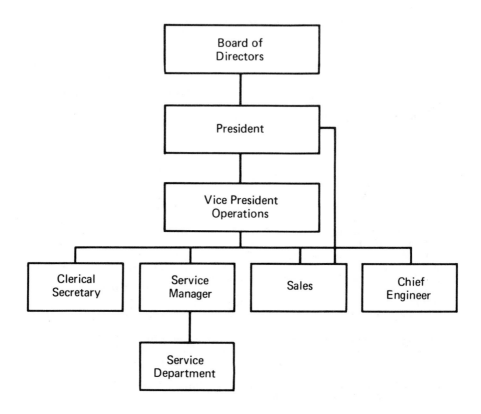

Exhibit 4
ACME ELECTRO-VIDEO, INC., ORGANIZATION CHART, SEPTEMBER 1, 1970

PRESIDENT—Devotes 60 percent of his time to sales; responsible for all legal and financial matters; approves all contracts.

VICE PRESIDENT OF OPERATIONS—Devotes 80 percent of his time to installation and service problems; spends an additional 10 percent of his time in sales work, and the remaining 10 percent is divided between personnel and purchasing functions.

SERVICE MANAGER—Directly supervises the installation and maintenance of all company projects; develops installation and service schedules and controls vehicle utilization.

CHIEF ENGINEER—Inspects customers' locations, develops specifications for the total system, and checks to see that the system is being installed according to specifications.

SERVICE/INSTALLATION MEN—Service and install equipment as directed.

SALES REPRESENTATIVES—Sell systems and maintenance packages; write contracts on all their sales.

CLERICAL PERSONNEL—Maintain accounting system, write purchase orders, maintain time cards, pay bills, and type correspondence.

Exhibit 5
ACME ELECTRO-VIDEO, INC., JOB RESPONSIBILITIES, SEPTEMBER 1, 1970

and forwards a purchase order, which is carefully examined for accuracy, assigned a job order number, and used to prepare Acme's purchase orders. It usually requires 60 to 100 days to secure current production models. Older models can be expected within 15 days. Acme usually bears the transportation costs between the supplier's factory and its service facility. Often equipment must be airmailed to meet contract completion dates.

All hardware is shipped to Acme's shop for a complete on-line evaluation because suppliers are frequently remiss about quality control and adequate packaging. Acme absorbs all the repair expenses associated with these deficiencies.

When a piece of equipment arrives, a shop order is issued. One copy goes to the shop, two copies go to the office, and the remaining copy goes to the customer. The packaging slip is attached to the piece of equipment it describes and goes with it until it is ready for installation.

After a piece of equipment is pronounced operational, it awaits transportation to the customer's site in one of Acme's station wagons. Frequently this takes considerable time because scheduling is complicated by a small work force trying to satisfy a workload that outweighs it. The scheduling difficulty is further compounded when a contract is negotiated for a building under construction or yet to be built. As the building is being erected, men must be available to install conduit and wire. When that step is completed, the job will languish for as many months as it takes to complete the building.

Installing a system takes from two weeks for a small three-camera bank job to four months for a large 35-camera job at a state prison. After the system is operational, the biggest maintenance problems are caused by poor operator technique. It is customary for the hardware suppliers to conduct a comprehensive training program for the customer's operators, but for some reason Acme's service personnel spend a significant amount of time retraining operators.

Equipment manufacturers rarely provide replacement parts. When equipment repairs require parts, Acme must usually purchase an entire unit from the manufacturer to get the part. This is especially true for equipment that is being currently produced. Parts are more readily available for equipment that was produced three or more years ago.

The office workers are charged with maintaining the ledgers on payables, receivables, man-hours, and supplies. The payables and receivables ledgers are maintained religiously, but the others are maintained as time permits. Also, an organized file system to support ledger entries does not exist.

Now, with the demand for surveillance systems slowed, Acme is beginning to reduce its backlog of maintenance and installation work, giving Baker and Weaver more time to think of the control techniques that both admit are badly needed.

QUESTIONS

1. How well is Acme Electro-Video doing? Present your evaluation or "size up" of its situation.
2. What are the most obvious causes of the decline of the firm's business?
3. Identify and discuss the management errors observable in this case.

Case A-3

NIKIPOULIS GROCERY STORE*

George Nikipoulis, owner of the Nikipoulis Grocery Store located in a small city in a large Midwestern state, has been approached by the local salesman for a large national dairy, Reliance Milk Company. If Nikipoulis promised to buy all his milk from Reliance, the salesman would give Mr. Nikipoulis a ten percent rebate off the wholesale price of the milk. Nikipoulis would continue to be billed at the wholesale price by Reliance. However, he would receive a personal check from the salesman for the rebate each month. The salesman explained that he was willing personally to take a lower commission in exchange for getting all the milk business from the Nikipoulis Grocery Store. He claimed that several other groceries had already accepted his proposal.

The state in which the Nikipoulis store is located, like many other dairy states, maintains fixed wholesale prices on milk to protect its dairy industry. In recent years, there has been considerable protest from consumers as well as from the large dairies against these fixed prices. The dairy farmers, however, have a strong influence in the state legislature and have prevented the ending of fixed prices. Nikipoulis has purchased all his milk from the Acme Dairy Company for the last three years. When told of the Reliance salesman's offer, the Acme salesman claimed it was illegal and said he would not be able to offer a similar rebate. The Acme salesman further claimed that the rebate was offered by Reliance itself and would not, in fact,

be deducted from the salesman's commission.

Nikipoulis is wondering whether he should accept the Reliance salesman's offer. Nikipoulis runs his grocery with the help of his wife. The store is currently faced with strong competition from large supermarket chains, as are other "Mama and Papa" stores. Mr. and Mrs. Nikipoulis are able to stay in business only through such services as staying open later than the chains on evenings and weekends, granting credit to customers, and the reputation for friendliness and personal attention which has been built up after 34 years in the grocery business at the same location. Nevertheless, the business is marginal at best and furnishes the owners with but a small income. Mr. and Mrs. Nikipoulis have no other source of income apart from the grocery.

If Nikipoulis accepts the rebate, he could reduce the retail price of his milk to the price charged by the supermarket chains or else pocket the rebate as an additional profit in the neighborhood of ten to twenty dollars a week.

QUESTIONS

1. Is the rebate ethical if it is paid by the Reliance Milk Company? If it is paid by the Reliance salesman?
2. Would there be an ethical issue if the price-fixing law did not exist? Is such a law ethical?
3. Would it be ethical for Mr. Nikipoulis to accept the rebate if he reduced prices accordingly, thus helping his customers?
4. Can Mr. Nikipoulis afford to look closely at the ethics involved in view of the marginal nature of his business?
5. Should Mr. Nikipoulis accept the Reliance salesman's offer?

---

* This case is the work of Professor Donald Grunewald of Rutgers, The State University. It appears in *Cases in Business Policy* published by Holt, Rinehart and Winston, Inc., 1964.

Case A-4

GIVING JERRY THE BUSINESS*

As he talked on the telephone, Professor Alan Stone watched his graduate assistant, Jerry Weston, shifting nervously in his chair. When Stone had completed his call, the following conversation with Jerry took place.

Stone: Sorry we were interrupted, Jerry! You said you have a problem. How can I help you?

Jerry: Dr. Stone, I'll be finishing my M.B.A. next month, and I still haven't been able to decide which job offer to accept. Two of the companies want answers next week, so I simply have to make some decisions.

Stone: Well, Jerry, you will have to make the final determination yourself, but we can certainly discuss the various alternatives. As a matter of curiosity, did any of the consulting work we did for General Electric ever result in a job offer?

Jerry: Yes, sir! GE has offered me a really intriguing project-planning job in their Appliance Division in Louisville at $14,800. I would have a lot of responsibility from the start, and I would be coordinating the efforts of personnel from several functional departments. If all went well, they have indicated I'd probably have a good chance to be the head of product development for the entire division. Of course, they would pay all moving expenses, and they really have a package of fringe benefits.

Stone: That sounds awfully good! What else do you have?

Jerry: Samsonite, Shell Development, and Boise Cascade. If my wife has her way, we'll go to San Francisco with Samsonite. My only question is, can two people live in San Francisco on $13,000 a year, particularly if one of them is my wife?

Stone: Say, what about the family business? Have you given up the idea of being the biggest construction equipment dealer in Billings, Montana?

Jerry: No, sir, not really! As a matter of fact, that is one of the complicating factors. I've been getting some pressure to go back to Billings.

Stone: How do you mean, Jerry?

Jerry: Well, I never really noticed how subtle Dad has been until I started thinking about it. As far as I can recall, he has never specifically said that he thought I should come into the business. But he always said that the opportunity was there if I wanted to take it. His classic statement is how good the business and Billings have been to the family, and I think it is fair to say he influenced me to go to Iowa State, his alma mater, and even to major in accounting. My uncle, who is the accountant in our company, is retiring this year, and I see now that I was probably being prepared all along for that position.

Stone: Does your mother voice an opinion?

Jerry: Yes, sir! She voices more than an opinion! To give you an idea, the last time I talked to her about some of the job offers, she burst into tears and said that it would break my father's heart if I didn't join the business. She said they built the business for me and that they hadn't worked all those years to turn it over to some stranger. Since my uncle has to retire because of his health, she accused me of turning my back on Dad just when he needs me the most. By the time she finished, she had me feeling confused, miserable, and mad!

Stone: Mad?

Jerry: Yeah! Mom made some statements about Carol, my wife. Mom thinks Carol is trying to persuade me not to go back to Billings because it's too small and I'd be

---

* This case was prepared by Professor John E. Schoen of Baylor University.

too close to the family. I suppose I wouldn't have been so angry if it hadn't been partially the truth!

Stone: You mean your wife doesn't want to go to Billings?

Jerry: Oh, I'm sure she'll go if that's what I decide to do, but I think she'd greatly prefer San Francisco. She is from Seattle and likes all the bright lights and activity in big cities. In addition, she has a degree in interior design and the opportunities for employment and learning would be greater in San Francisco than any of the other places, particularly Billings. She has worked to help put me through school the last two years, so I may owe this to her. She also believes it would be better for me to stand on my own two feet and asks why did I get an M.B.A. if all I was going to do was join the family business. She made me mad, too, last week when she said the worst thing she can imagine is being barefoot and pregnant and eating at my folks' house three times a week.

Stone: What about the Shell and the Boise Cascade offers?

Jerry: Oh, they're really just offers I've had. It is basically San Francisco, GE, or home!

Stone: Well, Jerry, you do seem to have a problem. Can you compare the nature of the work in each job?

Jerry: Yes, sir! The GE job looks very interesting, and the possibilities for advancement are good. Samsonite, on the other hand, has a typical cost accounting position. I suppose it would be all right for a couple of years while Carol does her thing and we see if we like San Francisco, but something else would have to come along eventually!

Stone: What about your work in the family business?

Jerry: That's the funny part of it! Everything about the GE offer—the salary, fringes, authority, prestige, promotion possibilities, and so forth—appeals to me, but I like the family business, too. I mean I've grown up in the business; I know and like the employees, customers, and suppliers; and I really like Billings. Of course, I'd be working as an accountant for awhile; but I would eventually succeed my father, and I've always thought I'd like to run the business someday.

Stone: What about salary in the family business?

Jerry: That's a part I've forgotten to tell you! Last week, my uncle was in town, and even he was dropping broad hints about the family looking forward to our return to Billings and how he will give me a short orientation and then "get the heck outa Dodge." His parting comment was that he was certain Dad would match anything the big companies could do on starting salary.

Stone: Even $14,800?

Jerry: Apparently! Well, there it is, Dr. Stone! What do you think? I've got to let General Electric know by the end of the month.

Stone: I don't know, Jerry. Could you go with GE or Samsonite for a couple of years and then go back to the family business?

Jerry: I thought of that possibility, but I think that if I'm going to go with the family business, this is the right time. Uncle Phil is retiring, so there is a position; and I know Dad was a little hesitant about the M.B.A. versus getting experience in the family business. Dad is approaching sixty, and the business is hitting all-time highs, so I believe he will try to sell it if I go somewhere else. No, I think it's now or never!

Stone: Well, you were right about one thing, Jerry. You do have a dilemma! This reminds me of the cases in management textbooks—no easy solution! Good luck, and let me know your decision.

Jerry: Thanks, Prof!

QUESTIONS

1. Does Jerry have an obligation to the family to provide leadership for the family business?
2. What obligation does Jerry have to his wife in view of her background, education, and career interests?

3. Should Jerry simply do what he wants to do? Does he know what he wants to do?

4. In view of the conflict between Jerry's own interests and those of his wife, what should his career choice be?

Case A-5

MIDWEST RESTAURANT *

Fred Wilson was a labor union leader in a Midwest steel town, with 16 years of seniority on his job. He was well liked by his fellow workers, and found his dealings with management at the bargaining table interesting and challenging. But Fred did feel that he could go no farther in his job, and he and his wife talked often about a business of their own.

A newspaper advertisement of a drive-in restaurant franchise attracted Mrs. Wilson and, at her urging, Fred inquired about it. A meeting was arranged with a company representative, at which time the Wilsons were exposed to the company's management, sales territories, advertising policies, cost and profit projections, and financing arrangements. At the conclusion of the meeting, the Wilsons were convinced this was their golden opportunity.

The Wilsons did not have very much capital because Fred's salary had been invested in paying off the mortgage on their home as rapidly as possible, and they enjoyed the luxury of a fine automobile each year. However, the Wilsons' credit was excellent, and they borrowed what they lacked from their local banks, setting up a rapid repayment schedule, just as they had done with their home. The projected income figures indicated to Fred that this was feasible.

Less than a month later, the former steel worker was listening to market experts, food technicians, and experienced accountants explain the franchise operation. The training period was brief, but quite thorough, and Fred decided that whatever he didn't quite understand at the moment he would learn as he went along. Filled with enthusiasm, Fred returned home, eager to enter into his new business.

In the initial few days of operation, a company representative helped him operate the business. Store traffic was excellent—Fred's enormous circle of friends began to patronize the establishment immediately, and the pleasure of being the "boss" masked the strain of the long hours in the new enterprise.

When the company's representative left, Fred and his wife both worked in the restaurant, and, although the traffic of the first few days slackened a bit, the Wilsons were still working a good 16-hour day. After the first 2 months, Fred and his wife felt that the strain on them was too great—Mrs. Wilson had not worked previously, and Fred was quite used to his comfortable 40-hour week. So the Wilsons made a decision to hire additional help to ease their burden.

Two new employees were hired and given a 2-day on-the-job training course by a franchisor company representative. By the end of the week, Fred was convinced that the new employees could handle the job, and he let them take over the evening shift.

After 2 weeks, it became apparent that this system wouldn't work—and the

* Case taken from *Franchising: Instructor's Manual, Management Development Program*, prepared by the Small Business Administration.

Wilsons split up the workday—Fred and one employee took one shift, and Mrs. Wilson and the other employee took the other shift. The system seemed practical—the customers were being served properly, and all looked well—until the Wilsons looked at their accounts.

The additional costs of the help, on top of the financial obligations the Wilsons faced to repay their initial investment, were not leaving them very much. They were working very hard and realizing less money than Fred had earned at his previous job. The only decision the Wilsons could make was to let the help go and continue to do all of the work themselves, on a 6-day week, 16 hours a day. By the time the sixth month had

rolled by, Fred was searching earnestly for a buyer for his restaurant.

QUESTIONS

1. How compatible was Fred Wilson's background with the type of business he entered?
2. What advantages did entrepreneurship seem to hold for Wilson?
3. What was the principal reason for Wilson's lack of success?
4. What financial arrangements could have been made to ease the Wilson's financial burden? Explain.
5. What would you suggest as a solution to the problem facing the Wilsons?

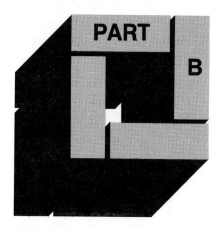

PART
B

Managerial Functions, Relations, and Practices in Small Business

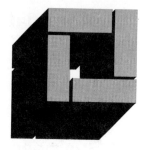

6

The Process
of Management

To function effectively, any organization, including a small business firm, requires leadership and decision making. Entrepreneurs must possess more than craftsmanship or salesmanship unless they limit themselves to tiny one-person businesses. In the typical small business that entails group effort, the manager provides direction by activities that are described as *management functions*. This chapter will examine in a general way the nature of these important functions, as well as other aspects of the *management process*. Later chapters will provide extensions and applications of these basic ideas.

NATURE AND IMPORTANCE OF MANAGEMENT

An understanding of the nature of management is necessary for effective direction of the small business firm. Too many people have misconceptions concerning the nature of management—deriving perhaps from news stories, statements of politicians, criticisms of union leaders, or even personal misinterpretations of what managers themselves say and do. Such misconceptions must be corrected.

Management consists of all activities undertaken to secure the accomplishment of work through the efforts of other people. Hence, it is an art, although it makes considerable use of the scientific method in the analysis of current problems and in planning for the future of the business.

Good Management and Attainment of Enterprise Objectives

If all managers perform their functions efficiently and obtain effective business teamwork, enterprise objectives, such as discussed on pages 34-37 in Chapter 3, will be attained. If management is inefficient in the performance of its functions, the enterprise objectives will not be fully attained. Good management is absolutely essential to successful operations—and so to survival—of a business.

This requirement of good management applies equally to small and large concerns. It is independent of a firm's scale of operations. Hence, the small entrepreneur must perform the same general functions as the executive in a large firm. Small business owners and prospective entrepreneurs must understand this fact, or they may neglect the development of requisite managerial skills.

Management and Decision Making

A manager constantly faces the necessity of making decisions. Proper guidance of the enterprise requires decisions on business objectives, scale of operation, marketing policies, products and product cost, product quality, work assignments, pay rates, and employee grievances, among many others. Virtually every managerial activity involves a choice among alternatives, thereby requiring a decision by the manager.

In making decisions, the business manager is often tempted to rely upon intuition. Indeed, one may be forced to do so because of the intangibles involved or the absence of necessary information. The intuitive decision may be criticized, however, if it disregards factual information that is already available or that is easy to obtain. Past experience is another basis for decisions which has both strength and weakness. There is an important element of practicality that comes from experience, but, at the same time, past experience is no sure guide to the future. In making decisions, therefore, the manager should have a healthy respect for factual data and utilize them as extensively as possible.

Management and Creative Thinking

Creative thinking assures a more successful performance of the managerial functions. As leader-manager of a business, the entrepreneur has the responsibility for idea production. Often, creative thinking is done under severe pressure for production of useful ideas.

The present age is one of progress, the rate of which is constantly accelerating. Tomorrow's world will be full of new and wonderful things. Consider the possibilities of space travel, atomic and solar power, automated processing in factories, high-speed electronic computers, two-way radio and closed-circuit television communication, and antibiotics. The future should be very different—and better than the present. But if this expectation is to be realized, the entrepreneur must think creatively as never before. The search for new or better products and services and improved methods can never stop.

The one best way, if it exists, has never been found—and probably never can be. This is true of every area of business activity, which makes idea production vital to business success and survival.

The small entrepreneur cannot financially support a highly paid research staff. Therefore, since a constant flow of new, workable ideas is required, the entrepreneur must think creatively—reaching new answers to old problems—in order to stay competitive. It is also desirable that others within the organization be led to think creatively.

It is not enough merely to produce ideas. People often resist change. Creative entrepreneurs, therefore, must convince their suppliers, employees, and customers of the worth of their ideas. Any explanation and persuasion must be convincing in order to overcome inertia, adherence to custom, fear of that which is new, and especially fear of personal loss of status as the result of the change. Only thus does idea production lead to effective innovation—and this process requires time.

MANAGEMENT FUNCTIONS AND THEIR BROAD APPLICABILITY

It is desirable that owners and managers of small firms understand the general functions of management. These are: planning, organizing and staffing, actuating work accomplishment, and controlling. Effective performance of these management functions, among other things, calls for ability to lead and inspire other people. It is the manager who must secure the integration of divisional, departmental, and personal goals with those of the enterprise as a whole. In the truly small enterprise, of course, there will be no divisions or departments, but only the entrepreneur and perhaps one or two managerial assistants. However, the assistants might have personal goals divergent from enterprise objectives. It is the entrepreneur who must reconcile such divergences, persuading the subordinates of a mutuality of interests.

Planning

Planning is concerned with such matters as the following:

1. Determination of company objectives.
2. Formulation of policies, programs, and procedures designed for attainment of company objectives.
3. Designation of performance and cost standards and their incorporation in a budget. This serves as a short-range plan of operations and as the basis for operating control during the budgetary period.
4. Long-range planning, which will govern the development of the company's line of products, services, and processes.

Even the daily decisions of supervisors on work plans fall in this functional area.

Planning is advance decision concerning, and systematizing of, a future course of action. It is primarily the responsibility of the manager. This does not mean that employees never make decisions relative to their own daily tasks, but rather it means that their need to make decisions is minimized by good managerial planning. This need for effective planning and decision making on the part of management is independent of company size and of type of enterprise. It is required equally of small and large company managers.

Certain procedural steps are involved in managerial planning. To some extent, of course, these steps are applicable to all problem solving and decision making, but they are particularly pertinent to the formulation of business plans. These steps are:

1. Determination of the issues involved and of company needs.
2. Collection and analysis of all pertinent facts, insofar as time, cost, and other pressures permit.
3. Consideration of the facts, including the tax impact of the possible alternative courses of action, by the manager.
4. Tentative decision among the possible alternatives.
5. Testing of the practicality of this tentative plan, by trial and error, with modification into a final plan fully satisfactory to management.
6. Announcement, as of a stated effective date, of the plan as finally determined.

Specific and concrete action to implement this plan must follow. All members of a management team must participate in the action taken if desired results are to be obtained.

Organizing and Staffing

The next function of management to be considered is organizing and staffing. *Organizing* involves the assignment of functions and tasks to organizational components and to individual employees. It includes the delegation of authority to subordinate managers and operating employees, so they can properly carry out their duties. Thus, organizing establishes the pattern of relationships observed by all members of the organization.

Organizing properly culminates in a formal statement of enterprise structure. Ordinarily, this takes the form of an organization chart showing all the managerial levels and positions. Some companies also prepare a supporting organizational manual to show the detailed functions assigned each executive and each supervisor on the management team.

For the typical small business, the management group may, and probably will, consist of a very few persons. It will grow as the small business itself grows. Two examples of organization structure are presented in Figures 6-1 and 6-2.

A study of the organization structure serves to clarify organizational arrangements that may otherwise be hazy in the minds of employees. Whether

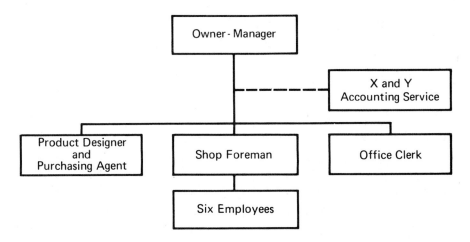

Figure 6-1
ORGANIZATION OF A SMALL MANUFACTURING PLANT

Explanatory Notes:

This chart portrays the organization of a plant manufacturing plastic novelties. It has contracted its entire output to a New York jobber, thus eliminating the need for a sales department in the company.

The dotted line connecting the X and Y Accounting Service indicates that it is an outside organization which acts as accountant for the firm.

The owner's wife performs the dual function of product designing and purchasing. The shop foreman directly supervises factory operations. The office clerk serves as receptionist, opens mail, types letters, answers the telephone, maintains files, and performs other routine clerical duties.

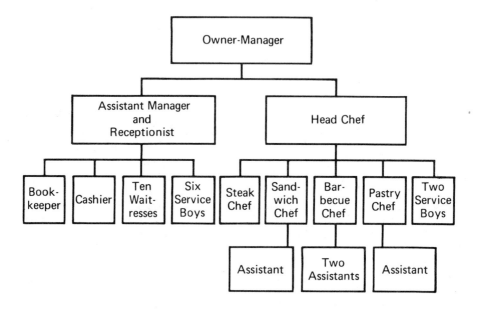

Figure 6-2
ORGANIZATION OF A RESTAURANT

Explanatory Notes:

The restaurant specializes in steaks and barbecue and is open from 11:00 a.m. to 11:00 p.m. It can be seen that the organization is divided into two departments, (1) kitchen or food preparation, and (2) dining room or food service. In the food service department, the bookkeeper serves as a second receptionist during rush hours.

the structure is reduced to writing or not, it is desirable that relationships among members of the organization be logically conceived and thoroughly understood by all. In the very small concern, of course, this may be satisfactorily accomplished without a written chart or manual.

The objective in organizing is to set up a work team that can function efficiently and profitably. To accomplish this, channels for the flow of authority and of up-and-down communications must be clearly stipulated, and balanced teamwork—in terms of actual personnel used—must be obtained. A business organization is a group of people who work together to attain common goals.

Accordingly, *staffing*, which includes the choice and development of personnel, is quite important. It is the people in it who make a business organization successful or unsuccessful. The best techniques of selection and development should be used in order to get a work team that functions effectively.

Development of personnel is often a neglected aspect of staffing in small firms. Many large concerns have formal executive development and personnel training programs; such programs would benefit the small business quite as much as the large business. For many small entrepreneurs, however, formal programs are prohibitively expensive and impractical—but achievement of their objectives still should be sought. Personnel training is intended to yield better job performance, fewer accidents, better understanding of company policies, practices, and products, and employees who are capable of promotion to supervisory positions. Executive development is intended to improve supervisory and leadership performance of each executive job-holder, to develop the potential that this executive possesses so that the person next higher up may be relieved of lesser responsibilities and thus let the superior spend time on more important duties, to transform the specialist in management into a well-rounded executive, and to provide for managerial succession through creation of a reserve of trained replacements against the day a higher-level manager changes jobs, retires, dies, or is promoted.

Of these executive development objectives, provision for management succession is the most difficult in a small firm because the owner-operator may personally provide most of the top management. This individual may limit the board of directors to routine meetings and lack a strong supporting managerial staff. Often there is no line of managerial succession set up as in the big firm, no understudy to take over; this is a situation which could lead to a real emergency. Prior provision for managerial succession can mean continued business life to a small firm. Since continuity of business life is rarely an issue in a big company, it follows that prior provision for managerial succession is even more vitally important in the small firm than in the large one.

Actuating Work Accomplishment

The third management function is actuation of work accomplishment on the part of associates and subordinates. *Actuating* involves the several activities discussed below.

Order Giving. Orders may be given in person or in writing. Written orders may take the form of notices on bulletin boards, standards, policies, shop rules, budgets, and standard operating procedures. They may be addressed to a specific person or to groups of persons. They may be given in an authoritarian manner or put in the form of suggestions or questions. The modern concept of order giving is one of democratic directing rather than of autocratic commanding.

Supervising. Supervision is the activity of management concerned with the training and discipline of the work force. It includes the checkups required to assure the prompt and proper execution of orders, and thus it is also a part of the control function which is discussed in the next section. Supervising is a required function for every member of a management team, from chief executive down to first-line supervisors. In the small business it is a required activity for the owner-manager and for each managerial assistant.

Leading. Leadership is the ability to inspire and influence others to give maximum effort and cooperation, willingly and voluntarily, for attainment of group objectives. Obviously this is essential to getting work done through and by others, which is the manager's task. The leader may find certain techniques helpful for getting people to do better work. Among these are:

1. Being a good listener and a ready, accurate communicator.
2. Being always considerate of other people.
3. Using suggestions or requests to make one's wishes known, and being sure to give the reason why.

4. Criticizing and reprimanding in private, but praising, when praise is due, promptly and in public.
5. Studying subordinates to find out the most effective type of motivation for each.
6. Taking subordinates into plans and programs before decisions and commitments are made—and soliciting their suggestions and assistance, giving them credit for ideas used.
7. Building up subordinates in ability and judgment through a development program for independent decision making.
8. Always letting subordinates know where they stand.
9. Expecting and tolerating some "griping."
10. Admitting one's own mistakes promptly.
11. Delegating functions effectively to subordinates.

The leader will also be careful to create a good work climate. The good work climate is productive of loyalty, efficient teamwork, and good interpersonal relationships among all work team members. Provision of good working conditions and adequate employee facilities constitutes the first step in creating the good work climate. Necessary also are adequate pay, fair treatment, prompt grievance handling, and good opportunities for advancement. A personal interest in each worker—sincerely felt and demonstrated on the part of the manager—will help greatly. Matching of employees to jobs and creation of congenial work teams also contribute to the work climate. When a good work climate has been attained, loyalty, a sense of security, and efficient teamwork will result.

Motivating. Creation of the good work climate is a natural by-product of good leadership. But it also contributes materially to motivation of better work performance. Actuation of work accomplishment is never a finished task; motivating followers to maximum achievement is a continuing managerial problem. It is well to keep in mind that most people respond to a clear challenge and that everyone takes pride in accomplishment. A number of motivating factors exist, several of which may be used to augment favorable employee response. Among these are loyalty, a spirit of competition, job and old-age security, job safety, fair pay, fair treatment, training and promotional opportunities, good machines on which to work, and only the necessary minimum of disciplinary action. Real loyalty also depends upon pride in one's job, in the firm's product or service, and upon a personal sense of belonging—of "being on the team." Such is the genesis of loyal efficient teamwork.

Communicating. Communicating with employees is the final aspect of the effort to actuate effective work performance. It depends upon formally established channels for communicating, up and down the chain of command; it depends also upon admitting the grapevine exists and, possibly, making use of it to disseminate facts. It depends, most of all, upon prompt transmission of all pertinent facts which can be revealed and upon being a good listener to the subordinate with a "gripe" or a suggestion (which includes the practice of consultative supervision). Managers communicate verbally, by written notice, by well-timed silences, and by extending or withholding status symbols from their subordinates.

Controlling

The fourth management function is that of controlling operations. *Controlling* involves the establishment of standards and the appraisal of operating results, followed by prompt remedial action on the part of management when results are significantly below par. Evaluation of operating results involves appraisal of managerial performance, policy and employee relations audits, review of cost and performance control reports, and analysis of financial transactions.

Control is required in the areas of sales, costs, profits, output, quality, labor turnover, accidents, employee morale, and labor relations, among others. The cornerstone of control is the budget, in which accurately set cost and performance standards are incorporated. Cost and performance reports should go to all executive and supervisory personnel.

In the very small business, cost and performance standards may not be formally determined, nor is it likely that the budget will be reduced to writing. Nevertheless, the efficient entrepreneur will have in mind what cost and performance should be, will keep track of actual results, and will investigate —looking toward prompt remedial action—whenever the actual results vary from what they should be.

Similarly, control follows from prompt issue of financial statements, ratio analysis of those statements, comparison of actual and standard ratios, investigation of significant variances from standard, and prompt action to implement findings and improve current results. Such is the control procedure whatever the area of control. Its proper execution is just as important in a small business as in a large business.

Applicability Independent of Business Size

The functions of management described above are the same for all firms, regardless of size. Small business planning is as necessary and, when well done, as effective as that done by the executives of a big business. Control is as essential and tools of control as available to small entrepreneurs as to billion-dollar corporations. Supervision of subordinates is required in every business, whatever its size. The importance of setting up and staffing the organization likewise is independent of business size, although the problems faced vary somewhat in nature and scope. Leadership and creative thinking are also vital in every business, as are congeniality and loyalty within the work force. No function of management, in fact, varies much in utility or importance with business size.

Applicability to All Levels of Management

The functions of management similarly are performed at all the levels of management: top, middle, and supervisory. Top management, for example, must plan overall company operations, while first-line supervisors plan the work of their subordinates. Of course, the scale and the complexity of planning, control, delegation, and the like decrease with descending levels of management.

Applicability to All Organizational Units

In the same manner the functions of management apply in all the business activities of an enterprise. Major business operations for industrial firms are:

1. Production.
2. Purchasing.
3. Employee procurement and relations.
4. Marketing.
5. Engineering and research.

6. Finance and corporation records.
7. Office services.
8. Public relations.
9. Legal service.

In a small manufacturing organization, various combinations are possible, such as the subordination of purchasing to production or the combination of financial records and office services. Such combinations should be tailored to fit the needs of the particular firm. In the small retailing organization, production and engineering are not found as organizational units, while sales and purchasing are almost always combined. In very small plants, stores, and service firms, organizational subdivisions are simply nonexistent. In such a case, management is one-individual or partnership in character, with one or two persons responsible for all areas of management.

Management functions must be performed regardless of the degree to which the small firm subdivides its organization. If sales or production units are used, their managers must perform the various management functions described earlier. In the case of a one-person management, the owner must personally perform all management functions.

OUTSIDE MANAGEMENT ASSISTANCE

In carrying out their managerial functions, entrepreneurs are often less effective than they should be. Frequently, they encounter problems that they themselves cannot solve. A progressive owner-manager then turns to a management consultant. This step of seeking outside counsel is not an admission of failure or incapacity, but rather a logical move to supplement and strengthen one's management abilities.

Management Consultation: A Valuable Service

The value of management consultation does not vary directly with business size. The management problems of small concerns may be fully as perplexing to their management staffs as are the problems of large corporations to their management teams. Many small firms clearly recognize this fact and regularly utilize outside management advisers. One trucking firm, for example, with fewer than 50 employees, regularly uses consultants. Even very small firms of the corner grocery type consult with their bankers or public accountants.

Consultants provide a service that has long been used by large firms for solving technical and managerial problems in order to improve operating results. In view of the management deficiencies prevalent in small firms, the need and the opportunity for successful use of consultants are even greater in the area of small business. By using consultants, small entrepreneurs overcome some of their own deficiencies in managerial capacity. Furthermore, an "insider" directly involved in a business problem often "cannot see the forest for the trees." To offset this limitation of managers, the consultant brings an objective point of view and new ideas, supported by a broad knowledge of proved, successful, cost-saving methods. The consultant can also help the manager improve decision making through better organization of fact-gathering and introduction of scientific techniques of analysis.

Ideally, the consultant should have an "on call" relationship to the small business, so that improved methods may be put into use as the need arises.

Sources of Management Assistance

The small entrepreneur needs to know where to go for outside help. The list below is not exhaustive but it suggests some of the varied potential sources of management counsel.

Sources of Outside Management Counsel

1. Management consultants.
2. Certified public accountants.
3. Bankers.
4. Attorneys.
5. Suppliers and equipment manufacturers.
6. University professors and research bureaus.
7. Trade associations.
8. Small Business Administration field offices.
9. Market research agencies.
10. Advertising agencies.
11. Local credit bureaus.
12. State, railroad, and public utility business-location agencies.
13. Chambers of commerce.
14. Private research organizations.

No doubt there are numerous, less obvious sources of management knowledge and approaches to seeking needed help. For example, entrepreneurs may increase their own skills by consulting public and university libraries, attending college classes at night, or considering suggestions of friends and customers. A group of noncompeting small firms might conceivably retain the services of a retired executive or a college professor who would give part-time service to each firm.

Service Corps of Retired Executives (SCORE)

Small business managers can now obtain free management advice from a group called the Service Corps of Retired Executives (SCORE) by appealing to any Small Business Administration field office. SCORE is just what it says—an organization of retired business executives who will consult on current problems with small entrepreneurs. They function under the sponsorship of the Small Business Administration. This group provides an opportunity for retired executives to be useful again to society, and it helps the small entrepreneurs solve their problems. Hence, the relationship is mutually beneficial. It may also encourage small entrepreneurs to utilize paid consultants as their firms grow by demonstrating the worth of consulting service.

One example of the quality of service provided is the reported case of the luncheonette which was on the way to business failure when it appealed for help to the SBA. A SCORE counselor was assigned, and within the year following, this enterprise was restored to a sound operating status.[1]

An Investment in Cost Reduction

The entrepreneur should regard the service of a competent management consultant as an investment in cost reduction. Many small concerns could save as much as 10 to 20 percent of annual operating costs. The advantage inherent in the use of able consultants is suggested by the existence of thousands of consulting firms. They range from large, long-established firms to small, one- or two-person operations. Qualified small consultants can provide useful services to the small firm.

Two broad areas of service exist:

1. To help a client get out of trouble.
2. To help prevent trouble by anticipating and eliminating its causes.

Formerly, businessmen typically used consultants only to help solve problems they could not handle alone. This is still done, but an even greater service is provided by daily observation and analysis that keeps problems from becoming "big." To forestall trouble is better than getting out of trouble after it arises. This view of the role of consultants greatly enlarges their service potential.

Cost of Consulting Service

Consultants may be hired on a fixed-fee basis (by the day or the engagement) or on an annual retainer basis. Retained consultants are "on call" to the small firms that have contracted for their services, thus assuring their clients of regular assistance. This makes it possible to deal with problems before they reach emergency status.

The direct cost of consulting service often appears high. An example is the local drug chain that paid $40,000 for a few weeks' consulting service. Individual consultants often charge from $100 to $500 per day for their services. Such fees may seem prohibitively high to many entrepreneurs. The cost savings made may not be immediately measurable, but they are probable and should be evident if competent counsel is obtained.

Moreover, the small entrepreneur may propose a fee contingent upon demonstrable results (in the form of lower costs and higher profits). Small consulting firms can reasonably accept such an arrangement, and the client firm reduces its cash outlay thus and makes sure that it is money well spent. Another

---

[1] "Riding to the Rescue of Small Businessmen," *Business Week*, No. 1902 (February 12, 1966), pp. 118 and 120. See also "A Big Plus SCORE for Small Business," *National Business Woman*, Vol. 49, (July, 1968), pp. 9-11.

possibility for the small corporation is to let the consultant take a part of the fee in company stock.

Choosing the Right Consultant

The selection of a consultant is a matter of vital importance. The small business may well be wary of firms using "high-pressure" approaches. An ethical consulting firm will not engage in offensive self-promotion any more than it will haggle over fees. For an estimate of a consultant's character and ability, one may refer to satisfied clients or to one's attorney, CPA, or banker. High ability and good character are both requisites. It is well also to learn some things about the consultant such as length of time engaged in business, training, and experience, and financial status. Fees to be paid and time stipulated for accomplishment of results should be contractually specified. And both consultant and client should require a clear definition of the consultant's task.

Cooperation of Client with Consultant

Cooperation between client and consultant is highly important. The small entrepreneur can contribute to improvement of the consultant's service by throwing open the establishment and its business records to the consultant. The entrepreneur must trust the consultant implicitly. Data requested should be promptly and accurately furnished—with no pertinent facts withheld. Problems noted by either client or consultant should be promptly called to the other's attention and full exploration made so that a solution may be found quickly. Promptness in taking remedial action reduces the scope and impact of many problems.

Some Common Criticisms of Management Consultants

A quick look at some frequent criticisms of consultants is in order. One such criticism is that there are charlatans among the reputable consultants, claiming a background of skill and experience they do not possess. Even though this is true, it does not warrant suspicion of able, ethical consulting firms. Instead, it calls for care in the selection of a consultant.

It is also pointed out that consultants, unlike doctors and public accountants, need not be licensed by the state to practice and are not subject to ejection from the profession by a professional association in the event of unethical practice. There is, however, the Association of Consulting Management Engineers to which the larger firms belong. Thus, a start toward self-policing has been achieved. Moreover, careful selection should assure the consultant's good character and ability.

A third charge against consultants is that they may insert themselves unduly into management and take over its responsibilities. Fulfillment of responsibilities is up to the managers themselves. They cannot be forced to turn them over to a consultant. Hence, if responsibilities shift from manager to consultant, it is the manager's own fault.

A fourth common criticism concerns lack of ability. Information on percentage of satisfied clients, like that on frequency of repeat engagements, is difficult to obtain. According to one report, "Most consultants claim that well over 90 percent of their work satisfies their clients, and by and large their clients will say that they got their money's worth."[2] This criticism should again alert small entrepreneurs to the need of selecting an able consultant.

TIME FOR MANAGING

Much of the manager's time during the working day may be spent on the firing line—meeting customers, solving production problems, listening to employee complaints, and so on. The manager spends a great deal of time seeing people, including outsiders interested in getting contributions for charity, selling insurance, seeking recruits to serve on some civic project, and the like. The manager of the small firm faces the problems of management with the assistance of only a small staff. All of this means that the manager spreads himself thinner than big business competitors.

The Problem of Time Pressure

The problem of time pressure is a real one, not fictitious. Many managers work from 60 to 80 hours per week. Even so, the pressure of nonmanagerial duties makes it difficult to find time to manage—that is, time in which to plan for future operations, to organize the firm for attainment of its objectives, to think creatively about new processes, products, and services, to plan the motivation of people, and to evaluate the results of their performance.

One frequent and unfortunate result of overwork is the inefficient performance of those tasks that some managers do attempt or for which they are responsible. They may be too busy to see traveling salespeople who can supply market information on new products and processes. They may be too busy to read the technical or trade literature in order to discover what others are doing and the improvements being created that might be adapted to their own use. Because managers are too busy, they fail to listen carefully to employee opinions and grievances or to reach an understanding with employees. Because they are too busy to give instructions in a proper manner, employees may not know what to do or how to do it properly.

Time-Savers for Busy Managers

One important answer to the problem of lack of time is a good organization of the work. This permits delegation of duties to subordinates who are then permitted to discharge those duties without close supervision. Of course, this requires the selection and training of individuals to assume responsibility for the delegated functions.

Sometimes a manager must see some visitors who may overstay the necessary time. Various devices have been tried by managers who have faced this problem, including the use of uncomfortable chairs, secretarial

---

[2] Perrin Stryker, "The Ambitious Consultant," *Fortune* (May, 1954), p. 85. Courtesy of *Fortune Magazine.*

interruptions with reminders of other appointments, and the like. A more direct approach is simply to tell the visitor in advance that the manager is busy and can allot at most ten minutes, and then stick to this time limit. Another means of conserving time is to provide some type of dictating equipment which permits dictation at convenient times and transcription by the secretary without frequent interruption. In addition, the secretary can sort out unimportant mail, screen incoming phone calls, and keep a schedule of appointments.

Another major time consumer is the business conference with subordinates. Often these meetings just happen and drag on without any serious attempt to control them. The manager should prepare an agenda for such meetings, set starting and ending times, hold the conferences to the subjects to be discussed, and assign the necessary follow-through to specific subordinates. In this way the contribution of business conferences may be maximized and the manager's own time conserved, along with that of subordinates.

Some other general hints on effective time utilization include the careful planning of work before doing it and arrangements that permit uninterrupted concentration during the period of actual work. This may necessitate use of a "hideout" occasionally. It may also require relaxation during off-duty hours, in the form of a hobby, athletics, reading, social contacts, or change of activity. If personal affairs can be kept in order, the manager's mind will be free to concentrate upon management functions during working hours.

Planning the Use of Time

Perhaps the greatest time-saver of all is the effective use of time. If an individual flits from one task to another and back again, it is likely that little will be accomplished. Effective, sustained effort requires some planning to prevent the haphazard use of time that occurs if there is no planning.

The first step in planning one's use of time should be a survey of time normally spent on various activities. Relying on general impressions is unscientific and likely to involve considerable error. For a period of several days, or preferably several weeks, the manager should record the time spent on various types of activities during the day. Analysis of these figures will reveal the pattern of activities, those projects and tasks involving greatest time expenditure, and factors responsible for waste of time.

On the basis of this analysis, it is possible to plan or budget the workday. In most cases, considerable flexibility is required, but some planning will typically save time in the same way that a monetary budget conserves money.

 Summary

1. Management consists of all activities of an entrepreneur (or executive) undertaken to accomplish useful work through and by other people. Thus, it is the key to

success in business and the activating force in enterprise activity. It is both an art and a science.

2. The manager must constantly reach decisions pertaining to all aspects of business activity. Although these may be based upon intuition, experience, facts, or a combination of these, a healthy respect for factual data is recommended.

3. Business progress in a competitive economy demands creative thinking by the manager and his associates.

4. The general functions of management include planning, organizing and staffing, actuating, and controlling.

5. The planning function is concerned with the formulation of company objectives, policies, programs, and procedures.

6. The organizing and staffing function includes the allocation of functions to organizational units and individuals, delegation of authority, and selection and development of personnel.

7. The function of actuating work accomplishment entails such overlapping activities as order-giving, supervising, leadership, motivating, and communicating.

8. The controlling function involves the appraisal of operating results, followed by prompt remedial action to correct any results which are significantly below par.

9. General management functions are the same for all kinds and sizes of businesses. They also apply to all levels of management.

10. Managers may have to utilize expert consultants to help them solve certain problems. Help of this kind is available from many sources. While some services are free, most consultants charge fees that initially look high. However, competent consulting service actually is an investment in cost reduction.

11. Outside help is available from many different sources. Often the same types of assistance may be obtained from a variety of agencies. Just the right consultant—competent and ethical—should be selected.

12. A special source of free help is available to the small entrepreneur with problems. This is SCORE (Service Corps of Retired Executives), which is contacted through the Small Business Administration.

13. Consultants bring broad experience and expertise to the solution or prevention of management problems. For effective service, the consultant's task should be carefully defined.

14. Time pressure constitutes a real problem for the entrepreneur, particularly by limiting his performance of managerial functions. By effective planning and scheduling of his available time and by use of various time-savers, this problem can be minimized.

Discussion Questions

1. Define "management" from the points of view of managers, labor leaders, and politicians.

2. What are the general functions of management? What are their interrelationships? Which

function, if any, is more closely related to scientific method?

3. What values accrue to the small business entrepreneur who prepares a written organization chart? How does the organization manual reinforce and supplement the organization chart?

4. Is the budget more closely related to planning or to controlling? Why?

5. What are the activities involved in actuating work accomplishment?

6. Why is idea production such an important responsibility of the small entrepreneur?

7. Is provision for management succession of greater importance in the small or the large firm? Why?

8. What differences are there in the general functions of management as performed in a large manufacturing organization and a small-town bank?

9. In what ways can management consultants help the small business firm? Why is it that "inside" management needs help? Explain.

10. Is it reasonable to believe that an outsider coming into a business could propose procedures or policies superior to those of the manager who is intimately acquainted with operations? Why?

11. What are the relative advantages of engaging a consultant on a retainer basis versus engaging him to deal with a special problem when it arises?

12. What practices can a small business manager utilize to conserve time?

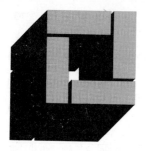

7

Planning and Tools for Decision Making

Whatever the type of activity involved, planning is a thinking process which deals with the reasoned determination of a future course of action. A business planner must formulate objectives, evaluate alternatives for reaching those objectives, and select a strategy to be followed by the firm. More specifically, he must decide what action should be taken, when it will be taken, and how it will be implemented.

THE PLANNING FUNCTION IN SMALL FIRMS

Planning covers production, sales, finance, personnel, and all other phases of business operation. Planning culminates in the formulation of business goals, programs to be undertaken, policies which establish guidelines for the firm's managers, and specific operating methods and procedures. It also embraces other specific decisions relating to the firm's operations, such as selling a piece of equipment or adding a sales territory.

Critical Importance of Planning

During its first years of operation, the success or failure of a new business hangs in the balance. Throughout this critical period, it is the quality of management that causes the firm to move toward success or failure. Planning is especially important during this period, and its neglect constitutes a major hazard to business success. When a prospective businessman approaches a banker, one of the banker's first inquiries concerns a proposed budget or estimated profit and loss statement. Such evidence of planning is regarded as absolutely essential if the proposed business is to succeed.

A launderette was opened in a suburban shopping center. Recognizing a need for careful planning, the owner had systematically studied the equipment and other financial requirements for such a business. In fact, he had attended a training course sponsored by his equipment supplier. In spite of such thorough preparation, he still overlooked certain hidden expenses. These were readily apparent to him later, but he failed to anticipate them in the pre-operating stage. Fortunately he was able to increase the size of his loan and to dip into some personal savings, thus avoiding failure. A more serious error might have occurred without intensive investigation. This experience reveals not only the difficulty but also the critical nature of small business planning.

Someone once said that a businessman should plant his feet firmly on the ground but let his head soar in the clouds. This does not imply that he is to be a daydreamer. Instead, it means that along with the day-to-day practical operation of his business he will be thinking and planning creatively for subsequent operations. In the modern business world some managers do not think at all, and others follow a standardized thinking pattern. This is dangerous. In planning, a businessman must anticipate future problems, keep overall objectives in view, and develop policies and programs that will contribute directly to profits and continued business life.

Tendency to Neglect Planning

The independent businessman sometimes neglects the planning function as the result of severe business pressures. If he becomes too entangled in day-to-day operations, he finds it easy to put off the policy making and planning that is so essential to continuing success. For example, when there is a choice to be made between waiting on a customer or getting out an order and planning operations for the next six months, the owner must attend to those matters that require immediate attention. As a result, the time left for reflecting upon the future course of the business may be small. In this case, a lack of appreciation of its value may be coupled with the limited time available to reduce the amount of planning. In any event, planning is "postponable" and may not appear to be an absolute necessity.

Postponement of planning is dangerous because failure to plan results in ineffective, undirected action. The action taken may contribute to failure rather than to business success.

Organizing for Planning

The entrepreneur himself is directly and personally responsible for business planning. Typically, he does not have, and cannot have, a full-time planning staff, such as many large firms have. He does not have either the money or the personnel for such a staff. Consequently, the owner must do his own planning, and a great proportion of his time will be spent in planning. Nevertheless, this responsibility may be delegated by him to some extent because some planning is required of all the members of the enterprise. If the organization is of any size at all, the manager cannot specify in detail the program for each department. Furthermore, there is a need for some factual information which can be supplied only by members of the organization.

The concept that the boss does the thinking and the employee does the work is rather misleading. Progressive management has discovered that employees can think and that their ideas are often helpful in developing solutions to company problems. The salesman, for example, is closer to the customer and usually best able to evaluate his reactions. Actually, the entrepreneur has staffed his organization with people who he thinks will be effective in helping him to find the solutions to his firm's business problems. It is not enough for them to call attention to problems—they must also turn up recommendations and solutions.

However, the primary responsibility for planning remains with the entrepreneur himself. And he must deliberately take time to plan for future operations, with specific times set aside in which planning will be done. Evenings and weekends often are so used. One businessman stays in a hotel occasionally to guarantee an uninterrupted period for planning. Others reflect and plan while traveling. The exact time used for planning is less important than the provision for future planning in the absence of daily pressures and without undue physical strain on the entrepreneur.

Importance of the Tax Factor

Much has been said in the literature of management, accounting, and taxes about the importance of the tax factor in business planning. Most of this, perhaps, is addressed to large business. Nevertheless, taxes can vitally affect profits in a small business also. Hence, the small enterpriser needs to be well informed regarding tax matters in order that planning can be most effectively carried out.

Tax avoidance is neither illegal nor morally wrong. Opportunities to avoid or postpone taxes have been specifically granted by Congress and the courts in many areas. Such tax avoidance or postponement is highly technical in most cases. Consequently, the small enterpriser must consult periodically with his tax adviser on the impact of tax regulations on particular plans.

As an example of tax considerations in financial planning, consider the small corporation's need for capital funds. It might procure these, without loss of control, by sale of preferred stock or by long-term borrowing. If money is borrowed, the interest paid for the funds is tax deductible and has the effect of reducing the corporate income taxes. On the other hand, the dividends paid on preferred stock constitute the cost of the money so obtained. In this case, however, there is no tax-deductible item for the use of the money. Moreover, the same small corporation could retain earnings to promote long-term business growth. Thus, stockholders would avoid, for the time being, payment of individual taxes on the dividends which would otherwise be paid. Eventually they can sell their stock and pay only the lower capital-gain tax on the increase in its value.

Tax considerations are not limited to financial planning, of course. Personnel planning, equipment planning, real estate transactions, and many other areas of business planning require attention to tax laws and regulations.

STEPS IN THE PLANNING PROCEDURE

There are a number of specific steps required in planning. Although the ensuing discussion emphasizes initial planning prior to the inception of a business, the same approach is useful in the planning of business operations on a year-to-year or day-to-day basis. Furthermore, the planning steps are described sequentially, although in actual practice there is a tendency for them to overlap.

Identification of the Problem

The first step in planning is identification of the problem to be solved. Until the issue is clear, it is impossible to develop a sound plan which will provide an adequate solution. Although this sounds easy, the true nature of a problem is not always evident on the surface. It is a well-known fact, for example, that a complaint about wages may be completely misleading and only a camouflage for another grievance. To assume that wages is a problem might lead to a plan that misses the mark completely because it solves the wrong problem.

Not all planning is problem-centered, however. For example, planning is involved in merely carrying out organizational objectives. In such planning, the first step might be better described as recognizing the need for action. The first step in opening a restaurant, for example, would involve recognition of a need for planning the location, physical facilities, personnel requirements, financial structure, operating procedures, and so on. After the restaurant is under way, the manager would recognize a need to plan menus and purchasing even though he might not describe them as problems. Of course, he would also experience difficulties or problems that require planning for their solution.

In summary, then, a planner must begin by understanding clearly the occasion or need for reflective thinking. The advantage of systematic planning is clearly evident in this first step.

Collection and Classification of Facts

The second step in the planning procedure is the collection and classification of pertinent facts. Prior to opening the business, a prospective entrepreneur cannot obtain precise information on what conditions will be like after inception of operations. He must resort to trade publications, government and trade association data, and knowledge gleaned from his own experience and that of his co-workers.

Not all facts are significant to particular issues and, therefore, to particular planning activity. In this preliminary analysis, the entrepreneur must distinguish the significant facts, classify them, and note causal relationships. Moreover, he must recognize any gaps in the available data and arrange to secure the needed facts. He must realize, however, that time and cost pressures, among other factors, may prevent his obtaining these additional pertinent facts.

In planning physical equipment of a restaurant, for example, the entrepreneur would investigate the types of equipment available and the various possibilities for its arrangement. Some of this information would no doubt be derived from his past experience and observation. He would quite likely supplement this by discussions with equipment suppliers, visits to other restaurants, contacts with a trade association, and perusal of trade publications. From these various sources, he would secure detailed information regarding initial cost, durability, operating cost, efficiency, appearance, and size of the different types of equipment. The effects and demands of various types of equipment upon personnel would be particularly noted, as would the types of financial arrangements available. For example, a particular unit might provide exceptional convenience of operation for personnel and require a down payment of one half its total cost.

Distinguishing Alternative Courses of Action

As factual information is collected and examined, various possible courses of action begin to suggest themselves. If planning is thorough, each of the major practical solutions or courses of action will be carefully identified. Here again, the process seems simple, but creative thinking is required to visualize possibilities not immediately apparent. Many times the obvious solution is not the best.

Returning to the case of the proposed restaurant, there would no doubt be many alternatives with regard to the physical equipment that might be installed. Possible hypothetical alternatives might be:

1. Purchase of new Type A equipment from Supplier A at a cost of $1,500.
2. Purchase of new Type A equipment from Supplier B at a cost of $1,450 but with slower delivery.
3. Purchase of new Type B equipment from either supplier for $2,200.
4. Purchase of used Type A equipment from Supplier C for $950.

It should be clear that the possible alternative actions existing in most situations would be numerous. Only the most likely appearing possibilities would be retained for further consideration.

Analysis of Facts

In preparing to choose among various alternatives, the planner must carefully weigh and evaluate the factual information he has collected. This involves a comparison of advantages and disadvantages, an assessment of the importance of particular factors, and a judgment concerning the significance of certain "unknowns."

Perhaps one's initial approach is the utilization of past experience as a guide for future action. To a certain extent, the belief that experience is man's best teacher may be correct. There is some danger, however, in relying solely upon past experience. This is because one does not always perceive the causes of his own failure or recognize his own mistakes. There is also the probability that the particular situation differs from those which have been experienced.

It is desirable, therefore, to engage in additional exploration and reasoning concerning the available information. Such analysis would include, but not be limited to, the lessons of experience. The matter might be evaluated by the entrepreneur alone or discussed with his subordinates. This simply means that there will be a discussion of the pros and cons of the situation to try to determine which of the alternatives is best. Then the problem should be broken down into its components so that each may be separately considered.

In choosing restaurant equipment, the prospective restaurateur would weigh the merits of each alternative. Type B equipment, for example, is more modern—but it costs more money. This involves a consideration of financial resources. Are funds available to purchase the higher-priced equipment? What are its virtues? How much saving, if any, will be realized in labor or other operating costs? Will the newer equipment produce greater customer satisfaction? If so, will the increased satisfaction be substantial or insignificant in amount? Many other questions would occur in any such analysis.

When planning, it is usually necessary to make certain assumptions concerning the future. For example, it may be assumed that a competitor will not establish a restaurant directly across the street during the next five years. Although assumptions are necessary to permit any type of planning, they should be completely logical.

Research and experimentation may sometimes be used to see what would happen under given circumstances. Insofar as experimentation can be utilized, it is well to do so because it will save hours of analysis and discussion, much of which might prove fruitless. The prospective restaurant owner may be able to visit another restaurant, observe Type B equipment in operation, and talk with its operator. Of course, one is thrown back upon the discussion of the pros and cons of the situation and upon analysis by mental trial and error if research and experimentation are too costly or if they are precluded by time pressure or by lack of technical skill.

The study of the situation will involve a consideration of both the tangible and intangible factors inherent in it. The tangible factors can be more easily measured in terms of their impact on profits. Estimating the effect of the intangible factors is more difficult. The businessman planning the restaurant knows that each item of modern equipment adds something to the atmosphere of a restaurant. This better atmosphere would appeal to both customers and employees, but the precise contribution of each item is difficult to determine.

Perhaps the first step in the measurement of intangibles is to identify them precisely. Then one must try to quantify them so that they can be measured in quantitative terms. If this is impossible, good judgment is required in weighing their importance.

Selection of a Course of Action

The final step involves a selection of one of the alternatives. This step is taken after reflection upon all the tangible and intangible factors in the case. The businessman is a man of action although he desirably takes a reasonable time to consider the issues. One cannot postpone decisions unduly merely because uncertainties and unknowns exist.

The final step should flow naturally from the preceding steps. If alternatives have been clearly stated and carefully examined, the most desirable choice is usually apparent. Applying this step to the case of planning restaurant equipment, it is at this point that the prospective entrepreneur decides, perhaps, to buy Type B equipment.

KINDS OF PLANS

Business plans may be classified in several ways. On the basis of business functions, they may be identified as financial, production, sales, procurement, and personnel plans. In terms of duration, they may be viewed as long-range plans or short-range plans. According to purpose, they may be considered as operative or corrective. With regard to frequency of use, they are single-use plans or standing plans.

Another grouping that provides a convenient framework for discussion is as follows: target plans, policies and standard operating procedures, long-range operating plans, and short-range operating plans (including budgets and detailed operating programs).

Target Plans

Planning the future operation of a business begins with the determination of definite objectives. Such objectives may also be considered target plans for the business. They constitute the goals which the firm plans to achieve. The businessman has the objective of making a profit, and, to accomplish this, the firm must provide some useful product or service to its customers. Specifying the type of product or service in some detail provides one overall objective. It is not enough to say merely that a new restaurant will serve food to its patrons. It is necessary to know whether it will be steak or fish, high-quality or low-quality, with waitress service or cafeteria serving line, and so on.

These major objectives, of course, will be implemented by more specific objectives applicable to particular areas of the business. If the business is departmentalized, each department would have its overall goal that would contribute to accomplishment of the firm's objectives.

Business Policies and Standard Operating Procedures

Business policies constitute another form of business plan. They may be defined as fundamental statements which serve as guides to management practice. Some policies are general in that they affect the whole business, while other policies affect particular departments or portions of the operation. In a small manufacturing firm there are product policies, sales policies, manufacturing policies, financial policies, expansion policies, personnel policies, and credit policies, among others. To cite a specific example, any small firm establishes a personnel policy when it determines the amount of vacation to which its employees are entitled. Similarly, the same firm establishes sales policies when it determines the geographical scope of its market and the type of customer to be sought.

Function of Policy. Policies enable an entrepreneur to make a prompt decision on a specific problem in the light of an already-decided policy. This does not mean that the policy dictates the decision because a policy allows a certain latitude for judgment in the individual case. Nevertheless, the policy prescribes guidelines that govern the potential action and so restrict the range of possible decisions. Actually, this means that a complete analysis is avoided each time that the specific problem arises. For example, an employer need not decide each year the amount of vacation each employee should receive. He simply and quickly applies the general statement of policy to individual cases.

Saving time is only one of the advantages in the use of definite policies in a small firm. Decisions are made on the basis of a careful consideration of all pertinent factors and are thus arrived at logically. Without policy in particular areas, the businessman is forced to make decisions under pressure and without the opportunity to think through the implications of his action.

Policies also serve to guide other members of the organization without detailed oversight by the manager. Furthermore, policies provide consistency of action from one time to another, a matter of value to both customers and employees of the firm.

Written Policies. Policies may exist and be understood without appearing in written form. This is often the case with very small firms. Numerous small firms, however, have discovered advantages in the reduction of policies to writing. Writing the policy forces careful consideration of the issue and encourages precise statement of the firm's position. In addition, employees affected by the policy can act with greater confidence and feel more secure in their relationship with the employer.

Two small manufacturing firms located in the same general area, and similar in many other respects as well, differed sharply in productivity and morale. One of the few striking differences between them was the use of well-defined, written personnel policies by the more efficient firm. Observation of other prosperous, well-managed small businesses strengthens the conclusion that written policy is vitally related to good management.

Standard Operating Procedures. A standard operating procedure is similar to a policy in that it is a standing or continuing plan. Once a method of work or a procedure is worked out, it may be standardized and referred to as a standard operating procedure. For example, the steps involved in taking a credit application, investigating the applicant, approving or disapproving the request, and subsequent authorizations of particular purchases by approved customers may be completely standardized.

Long-Range Operating Plans

To make current decisions intelligently, a manager must know what the firm will be doing several years in the future. If he fails to take the "long look," the business may find itself on a "dead-end" street at some point in the future. The manager must concern himself with long-run trends or developments in income levels, market size, product use, business district location, merchandising and manufacturing methods, and so on. If a firm's competitors are installing improved equipment, it is probable that the firm should be similarly modernized within a few years. Current equipment decisions should reflect long-range considerations of this type. The entrepreneur may also have established targets that demand long-range planning if they are to be realized. Of course, the target plans are themselves long-range plans, but the emphasis here is upon the activities that must be undertaken over a period of years in achieving the overall business objectives.

To be sure, there is considerable guesswork when long-range planning is attempted. Certain trends are discernible, however, to one who studies the position and problems of the business. Large business concerns make their planning departments responsible for peering far into the future. Five- and ten-year forecasts are not unusual. In the small firm, it is long-range planning which is most easily neglected.

Many progressive small businesses, however, are alert to long-range considerations and are operating consistently in the light of their future goals and of the long-run trends which affect them. One motel owner in New Jersey constructed a modern 20-unit motel on a highway that will probably be relocated within five or ten years. The location has excellent profit potential at present, and the motel may pay for itself before the highway is changed. The owner did not ignore the possibility of highway relocation, however. When the motel was constructed, he had it built in such a way that each two units can be uncoupled and moved with relative ease. In this way, he protected himself against possible total loss by keeping his eyes open to long-run developments.

Another small firm, a retail store with eight departments, has planned and carried out an expansion program over a period of several decades. Its management has kept in close touch with the development of the district in which it is located and the growth trend of its potential customers. By knowing the direction in which it should go and the appropriate rate at which it can expand, the business has operated wisely in day-to-day administration. Decisions concerning debt reduction, profit distribution, real estate purchases, modernization, and staffing have reflected management's expectations for the long-run future of the firm. Such long-range planning avoids the opportunism, the hit-or-miss decisions, and the many uncertainties associated with myopic management.

Short-Range Operating Plans

A classification of plans between long-range and short-range is necessarily arbitrary. That is to say, there could be intermediate-range plans as well.

One of the best-known and most-used short-range plans is the budget. A *budget* is a device for expressing future plans in quantitative, usually monetary, terms. A budget is usually prepared for one year in advance with a detailed breakdown by months. It is the principal short-range plan for any business. It constitutes a program of future action and, at the same time, provides a set of yardsticks by which operations can be controlled. Thus, a budget is more than a mere estimate of income and expenses. Its cornerstone is an accurate forecast of sales. Based upon this forecast are estimates of inventory, purchases, and various expense items. The budget as a management tool is discussed in Chapter 21.

Entrepreneurial planning is incomplete until detailed action programs are prepared on the basis of the business budget. Such programs must be worked out in detail for every aspect of the firm's operation and properly timed as to sequence of action so that maximum results will be obtained.

Consider a simple illustration. Suppose that the budget provides for the purchase of a truck. The detailed action program includes assembly of price quotations and essential information on performance characteristics. These data must then be analyzed to determine the most desirable purchase. In addition, the action program would include planning the operation and maintenance of the truck. Some of the planning might be left to the driver himself, such as the time for servicing the truck. The purchase of the truck also requires financial planning to provide cash when needed for payment.

QUANTITATIVE METHODS TO AID DECISION MAKING

In both large and small businesses, certain quantitative tools may be utilized to improve decision making. Most owners of independent businesses associate these quantitative tools with big business, considering them quite inapplicable to small firms. This belief is erroneous. In this section we will demonstrate the potential usefulness of quantitative tools to the small firm.

All the quantitative tools discussed in this section depend, in part, on the *theory of probability*, which deals with the rational calculation of chances of specific outcomes from a contemplated course of action. Much has been said about the taking of calculated risks in business. Nevertheless, relatively few businessmen typically calculate the risks involved in a specific course of action. All the quantitative tools available to planners, however, take account of determinable risks, thus leading to better decision making.

As a practical matter, few owners of small firms have sufficient knowledge of advanced mathematics and statistical theory to apply these tools personally. Their consideration is pertinent, however, for at least two reasons. First, these tools can be applied to certain problems by referring them to management consulting firms. Secondly, the growing use of these techniques points up the need for increased training in quantitative methods on the part of small business operators. Even though an individual lacks the necessary technical knowledge for using the tools, it is desirable that he appreciate their possibilities, advantages, and limitations.

Sampling Theory

Sampling theory is concerned with the selection of random samples of adequate size and truly representative of the underlying population or universe. In this way, the businessman avoids the necessity of obtaining one hundred percent of a given type of data. In fact, sampling is essential for the simple reason that the underlying universe of data can hardly ever be investigated in totality. Cost and time pressure, for example, often make this prohibitive.

The main advantage of sampling, thus, is the avoidance of time-consuming data collection and processing without impairment of accuracy of findings. It makes possible the prompt discernment of trends and prompt action in the light of those trends.

Specifically, one possible application of sampling theory in the small factory is its use in quality control. The final acceptance of entire lots or batches of product may be based upon inspection of a properly selected sample. Sampling plans can be designed to provide a fixed low risk of incorrect rejection of a good lot by chance, coupled with a fixed low risk of incorrect acceptance of a bad lot as being good. This means that good lots typically will be accepted quickly after inspection of a sample—with bad lots equally quickly rejected.

Another potentially useful small business application is the survey of customer opinion concerning a product, service, or organization.

Linear Programming

Linear programming involves the use of mathematical formulas for the solution of business problems. In particular, it assists the businessman in evaluating the results from several alternative courses of action, each of which involves a number of variables. The method is used to discover the solution that will minimize costs or maximize gains.

As an example of the type of problem that could be analyzed by linear programming, consider the manufacturer who is using two basic, but scarce, raw materials. Assume that only a limited quantity of each material is available for production. Both raw materials may be used to produce three different finished products. The total production can be sold, however allocated among them, but the amount of each raw material needed for each final product varies. Furthermore, the profit per unit is different for each final product. These variables might be illustrated as follows:

Material	Quantity Available	Amount Needed per Unit for		
		Product A	Product B	Product C
I	30,000 lbs.	3 lbs.	4 lbs.	5 lbs.
II	20,000 lbs.	6 lbs.	4 lbs.	2 lbs.
Profit per unit		$10	$15	$20

The manufacturer's problem is to determine which product or combination of products to produce in order to maximize his profits. Specifically, he needs to know how much of each product to produce. The number of variables obviously complicates the decision. The technique of linear programming will solve the problem by determining the most profitable mixture and level of production.

Linear programming can deal with variables only as they are expressed in quantitative terms. Even after variables have been so expressed and the solution found, there will still be some need for the administrator to exercise his judgment. Suppose that the answer in the case above turned out to be the concentration of all materials in the production of Product C. It is possible that the firm might wish to produce some quantity of Product B, even though at a lower profit, in order to "take care" of certain loyal customers. In other words, it is difficult to incorporate every variable in quantitative form in the linear programming equations.

Linear programming can also be applied to many other types of problems, such as determining the best product mixture using given equipment. It may even be used to determine which parts to make and which to buy, to evaluate for purchase alternative types of equipment, and to compute optimum monthly production rates for a seasonal product.

Queuing Theory

Queuing theory is waiting line theory. It consists of the use of calculated probabilities for determination of the number of persons who will stand in a line. Examples might include the number of depositors who will stand in line for service at a bank teller's window, or customers who will stand in line at checkout counters in a supermarket, or car owners who will wait in line at car wash establishments. Military examples would include servicemen standing in line for shots or waiting in line to get into the mess hall.

Governing Selection Procedure. A waiting line factor which must be known is the governing selection procedure, which may be based on *random selection*; *first-come, first-served*; or *prior appointment*. Let us consider the case of a doctor's office as an example. The doctor might accept patients on a first-come, first-served basis, or in the order of appointments made in advance, or in a random order. A knowledge of both arrivals of patients and servicing rate distributions is required for useful decisions. Given a knowledge of these factors, the doctor can determine the number of chairs that must be made available in the waiting room. The need for another doctor as a partner may also be measured in this manner. Such input-output information completely specifies a queuing situation.

Knowledge of the System State. One must also know whether the system state is *steady, transitional,* or *explosive* to evaluate correctly the waiting line properties that underlie decisions to add, drop, or combine service facilities. A certain restaurant in Waco, Texas, features a popular "dinner" at half price each Wednesday. The customer who goes at noon on that day finds a waiting line that is already long and steadily growing longer. Such a waiting line situation evidences the *explosive* state. Somewhat later, there is a brief period during which the *transitional* state prevails—in which a change from *explosive* to *steady* state occurs. Given a *steady* state, one can measure the waiting line properties—and so predict and (largely) control its behavior. It is only in the steady state that arrivals and services are well-matched so that waiting lines are short and customers are promptly served.

The importance of knowledge of the system state is shown in the case of a barber facing retirement at age 65 in order to draw his social security pension. He considered the alternatives of selling out, trading his two-chair shop for a one-chair shop (to be operated weekends only), or keeping his present shop open on Fridays and Saturdays. A college professor who was a steady customer worked out the waiting line simulation for him covering a one-chair shop open only on Fridays and Saturdays. This showed that the barber would work continuously, without rest breaks or meals, from 8 a.m. to 10 p.m. if all arriving customers waited until served—even though the shop door was locked for an hour at noon and locked again for the day at 5 p.m. Knowing this was untenable, the professor also made the simulation for a two-chair shop open only on Fridays and Saturdays. This proved to be workable, except that the barber would still make too much money to be legally entitled to his social security checks. Hence, the waiting line simulations suggested a different solution: the barber sold out and contracted to work for another barber on Fridays and Saturdays only, taking full pay for his services up to the limiting monthly amount and letting the shop owner take everything over that figure. This case exemplifies the application of waiting line theory for guidance of a small entrepreneur's decision to sell out.

Simulation

Another tool for the improvement of decision making is simulation. Simulation makes possible the inexpensive, rapid reproduction of large-scale events over a considerable period of time through the use of a "model" of the situation. Ordinarily the use of the simulation technique also requires the availability and utilization of a digital computer. The small entrepreneur might get around this costly factor, however, through use of a rented computer. That is, one might have either a management consulting firm's computer or a machine service center computer made available to him.

The simulation technique requires input to the computer of the actual business situation in terms of marketplace pricing, inventory data, production capacity, and all other pertinent factors which can be included in the business model. When these are fed into the computer, it makes possible the playing of a business game. The entrepreneur can set up such a game and participate with his co-workers in its execution. Each player would be faced with a limited range of possible decisions including such things as increasing or decreasing output, raising or lowering prices, buying or selling productive equipment to increase or decrease capacity, investment (or failure to invest) in research and development, purchase of information as to a competitor's action, and the like. Such a business game simulates the real business world effectively if all of the possible factors are included in the model, so that the possible decisions outline all the alternatives for action. A particular decision, when made, is fed into the computer, with the result that the effect of that decision is then calculated and stipulated by the machine to the participants in the game. Thus, all participants see the consequences of specific actions. This forecasts actual results of given decisions and so guides the making of decisions. This also tends to broaden the entrepreneur's experience in days, or even in hours, instead of through years of actual operations.

Game Theory

Game theory is concerned with the formulation of a strategy of action against the competition of an informed opponent. Inherent in its use is the assumption that business situations have a strong resemblance to games, both involving elements of competition, chance, and strategy.

Game strategy consists of a set of directions, or plan of action, for a given player for the playing of a complete game, including instructions on what to do in case of every contingency that may arise during the course of the game. Prior to the taking of action, one must assume that the competitor either knows or does not know one's own strategy. If he is assumed to have discovered one's strategy in advance, game theory may then be utilized to formulate a new strategy that will be effective in providing the maximum countering action.

One's choices are then governed by this strategy as long as he assumes that his competitor is unaware of his strategy. The outcome of the game for each competitor is discernible if the strategies of each are known and are pursued to the close of the game (under the assumption by the players that competitors are ignorant thereof).

Search Theory

This is concerned with the allocation and utilization of limited means in searching out unknown objectives. In the military case, this might be the finding of a target within a general area whose exact location is unknown. In the business case, it might be concerned with the location of mineral ore deposits.

Monte Carlo Method

Sometimes an economic model equation is not capable of computation by ordinary methods. In such an event, the Monte Carlo method may be used to provide the answer fairly rapidly and inexpensively. This involves the setting up of an experiment to duplicate the features of the problem under study. It also involves calculation, based upon feeding into a system a set of random numbers and obtaining the resulting answers from the system. Because of the use of random numbers, however produced, the name Monte Carlo has been attached to this method. The statistical procedure of confidence limits may be utilized to determine the range of error likely in the answer obtained.

Limitations of Quantitative Tools

The use of quantitative tools does not preclude the requirement of feedback control. This means that information concerning operating results is fed back to the planner so that he may modify plans, programs, and instructions accordingly. When a budget exists, for example, there will be reports which describe deviations from the budget. After these are received, the budget is modified or other corrective action is taken.

It must be emphasized that quantitative tools are just that—they are tools, and no more. When used properly, they tend to improve entrepreneurial decision making. These probabilistic decision-making tools do not eliminate business risk totally. Risk is inherent in the use of present resources and production facilities for the creation of new goods. It is inherent also in the purchase of merchandise for resale. Decision-making tools are designed merely to minimize risk by providing a rational approach to business problems.

Quantitative tools do not preclude the exercise of entrepreneurial judgment, which is definitely required because of the human factor and the other intangibles inherent in a problem situation. In this sense, there is inevitably a need for tools as a means to an end, but they are not the end itself. Thus, the entrepreneur needs to know about these tools, but his judgment remains the decisive factor in planning.

Summary

1. Planning may be defined as the reasoned determination of a future course of action.
2. Even though planning is of critical importance to a new firm, the pressure of other activities often leads to its neglect.

3. Effective organization of planning entails the solicitation of ideas from various members of the firm and the allocation of some time specifically for planning.

4. Tax considerations affect planning in financial as well as other areas of the business.

5. The steps in planning include the identification of a problem, collection and classification of facts, determination of possible courses of action, analysis of the facts, and selection of a course of action.

6. The planning of business operations begins with the determination of objectives or goals which might be thought of as "target plans."

7. Business policies are plans that serve as guides to management practice. Although policies may exist without being written, there are advantages in placing them in writing.

8. Long-range planning is necessary to avoid opportunism and hit-or-miss decisions in business operations. Too often, it is left undone.

9. The budget is an example of a well-known and widely-used short-range plan. Plans of this type are an essential supplement to long-range plans.

10. Quantitative tools useful for the improvement of decision making include sampling theory, game theory, search theory, linear programming, queuing theory, simulation, and the Monte Carlo method, among others.

11. The application of such tools for better decision making may require the use of outside consultants. At the least, however, their advantages and limitations should be known to the entrepreneur. As tools, they assist in reaching a decision but do not preclude the use of business judgment.

 Discussion Questions

1. Is planning too often a neglected managerial function in the small firm? If so, what accounts for its neglect?

2. Can employees be of assistance in business planning? If so, how can the manager motivate them to make a maximum contribution to planning?

3. Can a small entrepreneur improve his own ability to plan? If so, how should he go about doing so?

4. What are the steps in an effective planning procedure? Explain each.

5. Give examples of various "target plans" that might be used by (a) food wholesalers, (b) electrical contractors, (c) newspapers, (d) bakeries, (e) service stations, and (f) savings and loan associations.

6. What values are present in written, as contrasted to unwritten, policies? How large

should a firm be to justify putting its policies in written form? Why?

7. What major blunders might result from a lack of long-range planning by a small manufacturer?

8. It is said that a budget constitutes a guide to future operations. Specify just how this might be true of procurement and repayment of working capital loans made at the bank.

9. To what extent are the sophisticated, quantitative decision-making tools discussed in the chapter actually applicable in small business management? Explain concisely.

10. Stipulate the advantages and limitations inherent in the use of linear programming and queuing theory for improving entrepreneurial decision making.

11. How might the owner of a local theater chain use queuing theory?

12. Can you suggest uses of sampling theory in small firms, in addition to those mentioned in the chapter? Of search theory?

8

Organizing and Staffing

A sound organization is essential to business success. In this chapter we shall therefore examine the nature, principles, and values of organizing in the small firm. In view of the fact that organizing terminates in the selection of employees to fill the various positions, this chapter also considers the subject of staffing in the small business. Viewed in broad perspective, organizing includes the provision of physical facilities and capital. These topics, together with personnel, are discussed at length in other chapters. In this chapter, the major emphasis is on bringing business functions, facilities, and personnel into a proper relationship with one another.

NATURE AND IMPORTANCE OF ORGANIZING

A *business organization* is a group of people working together to operate a business at a profit, with each individual assigned specific functions and with each business function assigned to some member of the group. This definition applies equally to large and small businesses. Without a clear statement of the functions and responsibilities of each member of the organization, inevitably friction, frustration, and a lack of teamwork will develop. And the chances for organization friction increase many times faster than the number of jobholders. Everyone's responsibility becomes no one's responsibility, in most cases. Buck-passing then becomes commonplace. Decision making can easily become paralyzed when there is a lack of clearly defined authority and matching responsibility. This is why a prospective entrepreneur must set up the organization properly in order to minimize friction and maximize teamwork.

Organization Planning

Many small organizations just grow like Topsy. Certain employees begin performing particular functions when the firm is small and retain those same functions as the company grows in size. Other responsibilities remain diffused in a number of positions, over a period of time and growth. Herein lies grave danger. The natural organization structure which develops with growth is not necessarily a logical structure.

Serious weaknesses in organization structure may arise in this way which only conscious organization planning can overcome. In many cases, careful initial planning can forestall the development of such weaknesses. Initial planning is seldom complete, however, and subsequent growth invariably calls for organization change. In view of these facts, the entrepreneur should take a critical look at organizational relationships at regular intervals subsequent to starting the business. Even two partners may fail in business merely because of a lack of understanding or agreement concerning their relationship to the firm. For example, if one partner works only on sales while the other one concentrates on production, neither may think about money problems or overall administrative problems.

Human Considerations in Organizing

In the process of organizing, the businessman must constantly realize that he is organizing the work of people. Someone has remarked that "organization is people." Organizing cannot be accomplished satisfactorily by adopting a textbook formula for organization without regard to the particular individuals involved. In fact, it is the effective and coordinated performance of individual employees that constitutes the goal in creating an organization structure.

At times, conflicts develop between organizational ideals and human considerations. Suppose the limitations of certain otherwise desirable executives prevent assignment of all the responsibility they should theoretically bear. Must the manager dismiss such employees? There is, of course, no hard-and-fast answer. Although the businessman cannot flagrantly disregard the important principles of organization, he will find it necessary to bend these principles at times in the interest of enabling his particular firm to operate effectively. The important thing is that departures from an ideal structure be supported by logical thinking and that they be recognized for what they are—temporary deviations from the theoretically desirable arrangement.

As a starting point, an attempt should be made to create a sound organization, and deviations should be grudgingly conceded. This is another way of saying that, ideally, the organization should influence selection of personnel rather than having availability of given individuals determine the structure of the organization.

Types of Business Organization

Small firms may use any of several types of organization structure. Some of these types are described in the next four paragraphs.

Line Organization. A line organization is one in which each person working for the organization has one supervisor to whom he looks for instructions and orders and to whom he reports. Thus, a single, fixed chain of command exists. All employees are engaged directly in getting out the work—producing, selling, or arranging financial resources. There are no "staff" specialists to perform "helping" functions. Most very small firms—for example, up to ten employees—use this form of organization (see Figure 8-1).

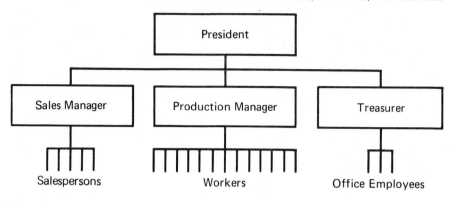

Figure 8-1
LINE TYPE OF ORGANIZATION STRUCTURE

Functional Organization. A functional organization is one utilizing a different supervisor for each principal function. Employees look for instructions and orders to several different supervisors, each of whom supervises one specific aspect of the work. This means there is a division of authority which tends to interfere with efficient operations. As a result, this type is almost never used in its pure form and is seldom desirable for a small firm.

Line-and-Staff Organization. This type of organization is similar to line organization in that each worker reports to a single supervisor. However, there are also staff specialists who act as management advisers in special areas. Examples include a personnel manager, a production control clerk, a quality control specialist, or an assistant to the president. This does not make for divided operating authority. The staff advisers can advise or help only. Orders must come through line channels. Small firms ordinarily grow quickly to a size requiring some staff specialists. Consequently, this is the most prevalent type of organization in small business (see Figure 8-2).

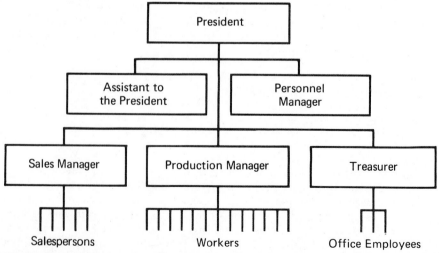

Figure 8-2
LINE-AND-STAFF TYPE OF ORGANIZATION STRUCTURE

Committee Organization. This type of organization is a variation of the previous form. There is superimposed on the line-and-staff organization a set of committees, such as executive and finance committees. One retail store with 60 employees, for example, utilizes an executive committee composed of the general manager, assistant manager, and controller. Committees are designed to help line officers reach necessary decisions by exploration of the pros and cons of a given situation. In a very small firm, only the entrepreneur and perhaps one or two assistants are empowered to make major decisions. As a result, the use of committees in small business is typically unnecessary and is often inefficient.

Choice of Type of Organization

In organizing, the problem of a choice of organization type is a relatively simple one. The only two practical alternatives for most small firms are the line organization and the line-and-staff organization. The decision as to which of these two types should be utilized can usually be made on the basis of the company's size. Of course, there is always an important question as to the point at which the addition of a particular staff specialist is justified.

Informal Organization

Even in the small organization, informal relationships arise among employees. Although such informal relationships do not constitute a part of the formal organization, they should be understood by the entrepreneur and evaluated as to their effect on the functioning of the total organization. Through friendships and associations developed on the job and elsewhere, the employees are affected to some extent by each other as well as by the formal management. Ordinarily there is no serious conflict between these informal groups and the company's formal management.

It is possible, of course, that a "natural-born" leader will arise and attempt to influence employee behavior contrary to the wishes of management. In most cases, formal management would be weak to permit this to happen. It might be necessary, in such a case, to discharge such an employee. Another possibility would be to use the informal leader in some way to supplement the activities of management. In any case involving troublesome cliques or other informal organizations, there is need to scrutinize carefully the formal organization to discover the cause of the negative attitudes.

BASIC FACTORS IN STRUCTURING A BUSINESS ORGANIZATION

Organizing is a dynamic process. The small business will incur changes in personnel, production technology, product lines, customer services, or other areas. The environment of the small firm also changes rapidly. Both factors have an almost inevitable impact upon the organization structure. Hence, this section considers a number of basic factors applicable not only to initial organizing decisions but also to subsequent changes that are required.

Grouping Activities by Function

In grouping activities into positions and departments, similarity of function provides a practical guiding principle. To use an obvious example, production activities would be placed under a shop foreman while sales activities would be directed by a sales manager. Such homogeneous assignments of functions and tasks contribute to effective operation.

Larger companies sometimes use a product pattern or a territorial pattern rather than the functional pattern of organization. There are major product divisions or geographical divisions of such companies. Small business firms are seldom in a position to utilize such organizational plans. Their very smallness typically dictates top-level organization according to the business function.

Delegation of Authority

Given a proper concept of delegation of authority, an executive will grant to subordinates, on the basis of their competence, the right to act or to decide. By delegating authority, the superior frees himself for more important tasks by turning over less important functions to subordinates.

This may well be the weakest point in small business organizations generally. Although the problem is found in all organizations, it seems to be peculiarly a problem of the independent businessman. The background of the small businessman usually contributes to this situation. Frequently he has organized the business, and he knows more about it than any other person in the firm. Thus, to protect his business and to use his own knowledge, he is inclined to keep a firm hold on the reins of leadership.

Inability or unwillingness to delegate authority is manifested in numerous ways. Employees find it necessary to "clear it with the boss" before making even a minor decision. A line of subordinates is constantly trying to get the attention of the owner to resolve some issue which the subordinates lack authority to settle. The owner himself is exceptionally busy, rushing from assisting a salesman to helping iron out a production bottleneck to setting up a new filing system. Frequently he laments the fact that the pressure of day-to-day work prevents him from giving proper attention to long-range planning.

Delegation is important for satisfactory operation of a small firm and an absolute prerequisite to growth. This factor alone is the reason why many firms can never grow beyond the small size that can be directly supervised in detail by the owner. One owner of a small restaurant operated it with excellent profits. As a result of this success, he acquired a lease on another restaurant in the same locality and proceeded to operate it for one year. During this year, he experienced constant "headaches" with the second restaurant. He worked long hours, tried to observe both operations, and finally gave it up as a bad job. He had never learned to delegate authority.

The independent businessman may find delegation as painful as pulling teeth, but it is fully as necessary. Admittedly, he will experience difficulties if his subordinates are incompetent or untrained. In such a situation, he should work in the direction of eliminating the basic weakness and proceed with the delegation of authority. If he succeeds in doing this, he will not only improve the morale and interest of most employees but also provide a means for development of his personnel.

Span of Control

Another related difficulty of small organizations is the tendency for the owner's span of control—that is, the number of subordinates who report to him—to exceed his "reach."

Although some authorities have stated that six to eight supervisors or departments are all that a top manager can supervise effectively, span of control actually is a variable depending upon a number of factors. Among these are the nature of the work and the entrepreneur's knowledge, energy, personality, and abilities. In addition, the abilities of subordinates should be considered. If these are greater than average, the manager's span of control may be enlarged accordingly because such employees are capable of more independent work.

There is a limit on the number of operative employees who can be effectively supervised. Of course, the span of control is greater in the case of personnel performing routine assignments than it is in the case of technical, professional, or administrative personnel.

The problem of span of control in a growing business is illustrated by the Liverpool Machine Tool Company which produced metal-forming machinery.[1] Its president had begun by working as a designer and sales expert for many years. He arranged for the machines to be built elsewhere to his specifications and supervised only a salesman and a few clerks in his own organization. The manufacturing function was added in 1930, and the company secured a major order from the Mexican Government that permitted expansion even during the depression years.

The president hired clerks to help on production and accounting and foremen to supervise production employees. Eventually, he was supervising six foremen, four sales supervisors, plus production scheduling clerks and accountants—a total of 13 subordinates reporting directly to the president. Of his average work week of 60 hours, he spent 20 hours on designing and 15 hours on personal selling. Financial problems and relations with outsiders took another 20 hours. The remaining five hours—roughly 20 minutes per subordinate per week—could be spent in supervision. The need for organizational change was clear.

The steps in creating a smaller span of control involved the appointment of a production manager, a purchasing manager, a treasurer, and a sales manager. Further changes were also made as the company continued to grow. The span of control that had developed naturally through the years was obviously inefficient for the stage of growth that the company had achieved.

Clear Lines of Authority and Responsibility

The lines of authority and responsibility in a small firm should be clear, nonoverlapping, and known to all members of the organization. In other words, the chain of command and channels of communication must be clearly defined and followed by both managerial and nonmanagerial personnel.

---

[1] This case is reported by Ernest Dale in *Planning and Developing the Company Organization Structure* (New York: American Management Association, 1952, Sixth printing, July, 1959), pp. 66-69.

Trying to serve many masters is as disagreeable in a small firm as in a large one. Unclear organization lines permit dual supervision as well as other questions and misunderstandings concerning supervision of particular positions. Only clear organization lines permit every employee in the organization to know his own status, to whom to look for orders and instructions, and to whom he is responsible for achievement.

In keeping with this concept of clear organization lines, orders should be transmitted through proper channels. There is a tendency for the manager to establish a formal channel and then ignore it in practice. Unfortunately, the leader's bad example is followed by others, making it difficult to maintain the organizational lines. His action in short-circuiting regular channels of supervision expresses an attitude of contempt for the organizational framework which the employees, in turn, are quick to adopt.

A frequent criticism of administrators which relates to authority and responsibility is that the superior does not always delegate sufficient authority to the subordinate. The boss expects the subordinate to get out production or achieve a given volume of sales, but limits him by unreasonable financial or personnel restrictions or imposes excessive demands upon his time. Equity demands that the subordinate be held responsible only for that which is within his range of authority.

Charting the Organization

Several types of organization charts are commonly used in American business. The one most often used begins with a box representing the entrepreneur or chief executive at the top (see Figure 8-3). Descending levels of authority and responsibility are represented by horizontal rows of boxes, one row beneath the other. The supervisors under the entrepreneur would occupy the second level, that is, the second horizontal row. In a small organization, the workers would probably be found on the third level, that is, in the third row of boxes. Vertical lines connecting the rows indicate the patterns of flow of authority and accountability. The same channels, of course, would be used for up-and-down communications. In appearance, such a chart is seen to fan out from the top down to both left and right.

No chart will actually show all existent relationships or the complete social organization of the business. Even with six or eight employees, there will be informal relationships which cannot appear on such a chart. If their portrayal were attempted, the chart would be so crisscrossed with lines that there would be no understanding and no visualization of channels of authority and of communication.

EFFECTIVE USE OF DIRECTORS IN SMALL CORPORATIONS

All too often, the majority stockholder in a small corporation appoints a board of directors merely to fulfill a legal requirement. Such owners make little or no use of directors in managing their companies. Some entrepreneurs, however, have found an active board to be both practical and beneficial. Not to

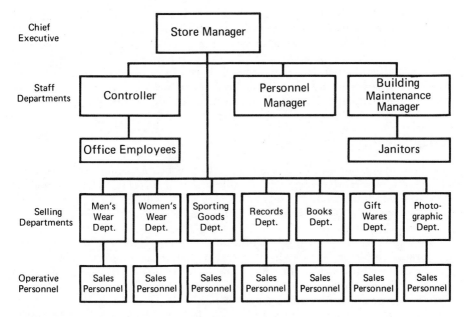

Figure 8-3
ORGANIZATION CHART FOR A DEPARTMENTALIZED RETAIL STORE

use the directors for business counsel is a waste. In fact, one authority has said that "the board of directors has been the most wasted asset" of a corporation.[2]

Contribution of Board of Directors

As noted earlier, the chief executive of the small firm makes the major decisions for his firm in all areas of operation, including finance, distribution, production, personnel, and general administration. He often lacks the requisite experience or skill in one or more of these areas, and frequently he has no expert on his payroll. In a board of directors, the wise executive in the small corporation can find one means for combating his own deficiency.

A properly assembled directorial team can bring supplementary knowledge and broad experience to corporate management. The board should meet regularly at least once a month to provide maximum assistance to the chief executive. This is in sharp contrast to the perfunctory annual meetings of many small corporation boards. Such monthly board meetings should be conferences in which ideas are debated, strategies determined, and the pros and cons of policies explored. In this way, the chief executive is assisted by the combined experience of all his board members. Their combined knowledge makes possible more intelligent decisions on major issues.

Such a practice of utilizing the combined experience of a board of directors does not signify that the chief executive of a small corporation is abdicating active control of its operations. Instead, it means merely that he is consulting

---

[2] Eugene E. Jennings, in a study prepared for Lamalies Associates, Inc., as quoted subsequently in the press.

with, and seeking the advice of, the board's members in order to draw upon a larger pool of business knowledge in decision making and formulation of policy.

The active board of directors serves him in several important ways. The first of these, of course, is the board's review of major policy decisions. But there is also the matter of advice on external business conditions and on proper reaction to the business cycle. Moreover, some directors are willing to provide individual advice informally, from time to time, on specific problems that arise.

Selecting Board Members

There are a number of sources open to the businessman attempting to assemble a cooperative, experienced, able group of directors. The selection is indeed highly important. The firm's attorney, its banker, its accountant, other businessmen, and local management consultants might all be considered as potential directors.

Business prominence in the community is not essential for the small corporation director. Rather, it is desirable that this individual be one who really understands small business and sympathizes with its problems. Moreover, he should be one who is interested in sharing his knowledge and who has the personality and ability to get across his knowledge to the chief executive. The director, in this sense, is a little like a football coach who must instruct his players by example and by precept so that they will play winning ball on the gridiron.

A prospective director of a small corporation should be a person whose background of experience and special skills in management properly complement the abilities of the entrepreneur. That is, each director's skills should cover up one or more of the weaknesses of the entrepreneur.

Compensation of Directors

The small corporation director usually does not accept a directorship because of the fee which he will earn. Rather, he is much more interested in the challenge to his management capacity presented by the small corporation's problems. However, it is possible that fees from $10 to $100 per meeting might be paid.

Also, to whet the interest of directors, the owner might offer to sell them small amounts of stock—perhaps up to 10 or 15 percent of the total. A partial ownership on the part of the director is more or less a guarantee of his continuing interest in the firm's operations. Of course, this step would be unacceptable to an owner who wishes to maintain 100 percent ownership.

STAFFING THE ORGANIZATION

The organization can be no better than the people in it. Thus, staffing is of critical importance to the small firm and is discussed in some detail in the next chapter. It is desirable at this point, however, to give some attention to the broad problem of assembling an initial staff, with major emphasis upon filling managerial and supervisory positions.

Importance of Staffing to the Small Firm

There is always a risk in hiring subordinates in the small business. In fact, this risk is greater in the small firm than it is in a larger business. The large firm can draw upon a wider market, can sometimes compete better in terms of salary and fringe benefits, and so can recruit able employees more readily. Because it also hires many persons, it develops more effective hiring techniques.

Each key employee of the small firm assists in executive decision making and thus influences the future of the enterprise. This means that the entrepreneur must plan wisely and utilize all available aids for the effective selection of subordinates.

Criteria for Selection

A major question concerns the kind of individual to select. Certainly, the enterpriser does not want to select an applicant to fit a rigid specification of education, experience, family background, age, race, religion, and the like. Rather, he must concentrate upon the ability of an individual to fill a key assignment in the business—much the same type of ability that is sought by the large firm.

If the small entrepreneur cannot directly outbid large concerns in hiring, he may need to consider those who are able but excluded from hiring by the larger concern. For example, this might be the older employee with seasoned experience, or it could be the individual whose personality does not make him compatible, in the eyes of the large firm, with an existent work team.

As a beginning step, the prospective entrepreneur should analyze the functions required and determine the number and kinds of jobs to be filled. In this way he will know the job requirements in terms of physical, emotional, mental, skill, and experience factors. Knowing the job requirements, he is then in a better position to survey job applicants and determine their respective capabilities. In such an analysis of an applicant, the entrepreneur may administer tests, conduct an interview, check references and business experience, and ferret out every possible fact about the applicant which can be determined. Knowing the job requirements as well as capacities and characteristics of the individual applicants, the entrepreneur can then make a more intelligent selection of persons to be hired and placed on specific jobs.

In particular, in the small enterprise, the entrepreneur must attempt in his initial staffing to obtain individuals whose capacities and skills complement his own abilities. This might cause him to choose individuals other than those whom he would have otherwise chosen but for the fact that he needed to supplement his own capacities and offset his own weaknesses.

Two quite similar manufacturing firms followed directly opposite policies in selecting their key personnel. One firm selected individuals experienced in the trade but with little regard for other qualifications. In the other company, the president deliberately sought applicants with the highest possible level of ability. In fact, he frankly stated that he hoped and expected some of them to be superior to him at least in certain areas. After several years of experience under these different approaches, the latter plant was far ahead of the other company both in terms of effectiveness and overall morale.

Summary

1. The efficiency of a small business depends in part upon the quality and type of organizational relationships that are used.
2. Organization structure should be developed carefully and thoughtfully with adequate consideration of the human problems involved.
3. The small firm must choose between the line type of organization—that most appropriate for very small concerns—and the line-and-staff type of organization, which uses staff specialists such as a personnel manager or a quality control manager.
4. Informal relationships among employees arise rather automatically and supplement the formally prescribed superior-subordinate relationships. Ordinarily, there is no serious conflict between the formal and informal organization.
5. Delegation of authority is particularly important and, at the same time, unusually difficult for the independent businessman.
6. The desirable size of the span of control is a variable depending upon such factors as the nature of the work and the ability of both manager and employees.
7. Other important factors deserving consideration in the design of organization structures are the principle of functional similarity in grouping positions and the need for clear lines of authority and responsibility.
8. Although an organization chart is only a picture of organization relationships, it can be used to clarify and communicate the nature of the structure to those involved in it.
9. A board of directors may be used to provide experience, knowledge, and counsel to supplement the ability of the firm's management. The selection of each director should be made on the basis of his understanding of small business problems and his interest in the particular concern.
10. Staffing managerial and supervisory positions is of critical importance for the small firm. The entrepreneur must know the type of individual he wants—and just what criteria to apply in his or her selection.

Discussion Questions

1. How large must a small firm be before it encounters problems of organization? As it grows, do its problems become more difficult to solve? Explain.

2. Define "organizing" and "organization structure."
3. What is entailed in properly constructing a good organization structure? Whose responsibility

is it? Can the organizer safely disregard human values and interpersonal relationships? Why?

4. What surface difficulties would you expect to find in a firm of 25 employees lacking good organization? Why?

5. What type of small firm might properly use the line type of organization? When should its type of structure require change? To what type? Why?

6. How does the concept of line-and-staff organization attempt to harmonize the ideas inherent in line and in functional organization structures?

7. When one employee becomes the recognized head of an informal organization overlapping the formal organization structure and having goals at variance with entrepreneurial goals, just what should the entrepreneur do to correct the situation?

8. What are the two more likely causes of failure to delegate properly? Is this important? Why?

9. Explain the relationships, if any, between "span of control" and "proper delegation."

10. Is the matching of authority and responsibility, positionally speaking, of importance in setting up an organization? What problems are caused if authority exceeds responsibility and if responsibility exceeds authority? To what level in the organization should any given amount of authority be delegated?

11. In small firms, should authority ever be granted to a committee? If so, specify the circumstances.

12. In what way is a top manager of a small business most likely to violate his own organizational structure?

13. Of what value is an organization chart? Is it as necessary in the small firm as in the large firm? Why? And why is it frequently not used by small concerns?

14. Just how might a board of directors be of real value to management in the small corporation? What are the qualifications essential to a person chosen as director in a small corporation? Is stock ownership in the firm a necessary prerequisite?

15. What staffing problems are of peculiar importance in the small firm? How can the entrepreneur get around such problems?

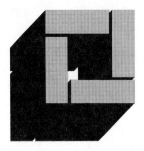

9

Employee Relations

As noted in Chapter 6, the process of management involves work achievement through the efforts of others. One might think that a small firm, employing only a few individuals, would avoid serious personnel problems; but this is true only of a one-person firm. Any one employee may ignore or misunderstand instructions, feel underpaid, take unauthorized rest breaks, or work inefficiently. Any one employee may also perceive a lack of opportunity for advancement and quit unexpectedly. The lesser dimensions of the personnel task in small business do not eliminate personnel problems.

Labor frequently accounts for more than 50 percent of total operating expense of a business. But cost is not wholly synonymous with the importance of personnel. Consider, for example, the significance of employee contacts with customers. What retail store customer will ignore the salesclerk who is inattentive or takes another customer out of turn?

HOW EMPLOYEE RELATIONS ARE DIFFERENT IN THE SMALL FIRM

Smallness creates a unique situation in personnel management. The small plant is not merely a miniature version of a large plant. The owner of a small retail store, for example, cannot use the personnel program of Sears Roebuck—which has more than 350,000 employees—by merely trimming it down to fit his store. This condition is both good and bad for the small business. Some of the features of the small store enable its owner to do a better job than Sears in managing its employees. At the same time, the small entrepreneur has some handicaps that do not bother Sears. In beginning a discussion of employee relations, then, it is important to understand these distinctive conditions that create both problems and opportunities for small firms.

Employees and Manager Are Personally Acquainted

Employees in the small firm will get to know the "boss" personally. If their relationships are good, they will know they are more than mere cogs in the business machine. The employees are not unappreciative of the advantages inherent in such a situation. Consider, for example, the case of Fred White who has worked as a machinist in a small machine shop for 12 years. Previously, he had been employed for several years by a manufacturing organization of national reputation with branch plants in several states. One feature of the smaller plant that appeals to Fred is the personal contact he enjoys with Ben Thacker, the head of the organization. As Fred expresses it, "Ben and I have come to know each other pretty well during the last 12 years. He knows what I can do, and I can count on him to treat me right when I have a personal problem. Every two or three days I see him in the shop, and he usually takes time to talk for a few minutes. If something important comes up, I can always catch him in the office or call him at home."

In such a situation, the employee develops a strong feeling of personal loyalty to the entrepreneur, coupled with a stronger sense of responsibility than is likely in a large concern. How could one feel deeply about the president of a large corporation whom he has never seen? Clearly, the small firm has an advantage here.

On the other hand, there is a danger in the reluctance of an entrepreneur to discipline or curb those employees who are also old friends. Employees may engage in acts that would not be tolerated in a larger, impersonal organization. To cite one example, the proprietor of a small supermarket employs an older widow as a cashier. He is acutely aware of her need for employment and realizes it would be difficult for her to find employment elsewhere. In performing her work, however, she is extremely "choosy" about what she will or will not do. She refuses to arrange stock on the shelves or perform other necessary work when there are no customers to be checked out. The long-suffering owner permits this situation to exist because of his sympathy for her as an individual.

Relationships with Employees Are Typically Informal

Written personnel policies and records are ordinarily used in large companies. The same is not true in most small firms. The danger inherent in informal solution of personnel problems on a case-to-case basis is that solutions may not be thought through. The quick answer may not be the right answer, and precedents may be established that will prove embarrassing later.

The advantage of the small firm's informality is found in the manager's ability to devise a solution to fit the particular case. Individual considerations may be taken into account, and problems that do not fit a rule book may be solved in the most appropriate manner.

The Small Entrepreneur Has a Different Attitude

The attitude of a typical small entrepreneur toward employee relations is often quite different from that of large business managers. It is natural for this person to feel or say, "This is *my* business." This may be literally true, of course, by virtue of both personal ownership and personal contribution in building the business. Undue emphasis upon this fact, however, may cause the entrepreneur to say, "If they don't like it, they can quit"—and to flare up emotionally when anyone questions personnel practices in *his* business. It can destroy a sense of partnership between employees and management.

Some Employers Concentrate Upon "Production" or "Sales"

Many small entrepreneurs enter business with a rather specialized background in production management or in sales management. A traveling salesman, for example, may decide to go into business for himself, or an engineer may decide to manufacture a product he has devised during spare time. In the day-to-day operations, there looms a diversity of pressing production problems, sales problems, and financial problems. Personnel problems, in contrast, appear less critical, at least in their early stages. As a result, the entrepreneur may become so enmeshed in problems of buying, selling, producing, or financing that the matter of personnel relations is ignored until the entrepreneur is forced to give it proper attention.

The Employer Lacks Specialized Personnel Know-How

Most small businesses have no personnel manager. Even those that can support a personnel specialist cannot specialize as intensively as do large companies. In a huge corporation, for example, one would find specialists in personnel testing, job analysis, union negotiations, performance evaluation, and so on. This means that the manager of a small firm must be jack-of-all-trades in personnel relations. It also means that the manager frequently lacks the personal background and skill that would be ideal for solving personnel problems. The alert manager attempts to minimize such limitations by personal development and by thoughtful consideration of personnel problems.

The Influence of the Boss Is Felt Throughout the Business

Introduction of a new personnel philosophy is a difficult problem in the large firm. Its penetration of lower echelons of management will be time-consuming indeed. It often requires years to educate lower-level supervisors who may misunderstand or even try to sabotage new personnel policies. In contrast, a weakness in personnel philosophy may be "seen" and corrected immediately by the small entrepreneur. Suppose, for example, that the decision has been made to change from fighting a union to cooperating with a union. If the entrepreneur is the only manager in the business, the educational program is complete. If there are additional managers, the new policy can be quickly explained to them.

Small Firms Use Less Elaborate Personnel Tools

Large firms can and do utilize personnel tools and procedures that are far more complex than those found in small firms. Examples of these more involved techniques include extensive recreational programs, elaborate testing methods, comprehensive personnel records, a variety of training programs, and complex job evaluation plans.

Some may think that the essence of personnel management lies in such tools and procedures. Nothing could be further from the truth. Rather, it is to be found in the relationship between manager and subordinates. A personnel program may be simple and yet facilitate the management of people. Although simplicity is not always a virtue in itself, neither does it brand the small firm's personnel relations as inferior. For example, a small business owner may by day-to-day contact and conversation with a handful of employees let them know how they stand and give them encouragement to do a good job. In contrast, an appraisal and counseling effort of a large corporation may fail dismally in achieving such results.

While some of the large company's personnel techniques could be adopted by small firms, other methods are simply not practical for smaller organizations. The test of effectiveness of a small business personnel program is not its complexity nor the degree to which it mimics that of large firms. It is found instead in the efficiency with which personnel are utilized and in the degree of harmony achieved.

RECRUITMENT AND SELECTION OF EMPLOYEES

The intial step in a sound personnel program is the recruitment of capable employees. No stream can rise higher than its source, and failure in recruitment and selection may doom the firm to the use of inefficient or mediocre employees who cause high costs.

When hiring, the entrepreneur should consider whether the current need is for an employee to be closely supervised or an employee to be an independent decision maker. The entrepreneur can expect "workers" to be closely supervised and "management personnel" to be somewhat unsupervised decision makers. Thus, the individual selected must have ability and must fit into both the organization and the community. Also, management assistants selected should have skills complementary to those of the entrepreneur so as to compensate for the latter's weaknesses.

Need for Aggressive Recruitment

In the labor market the entrepreneur is in competition with both large and small businesses. One cannot afford to let competitors take the cream of the crop while one picks up the remainder. Yet, this may be one's fate unless one recruits aggressively and selects carefully. Aggressive recruitment means that the small business operator should contact or use enough sources of employees to find a number of likely applicants for each job vacancy. In a sense, the entrepreneur goes out to look for employees. One who does not recruit aggressively simply selects from those applicants who offer their services or those who can be located without active effort. Then, all too often the poor quality of employees is lamented! Although one cannot lay down ironclad rules to be followed in recruiting, the point to be grasped is that the employer should take the initiative in locating applicants and should search until enough applicants are available to permit a good choice.

A Good Organization Helps Attract Good Employees

Selling products is an art mastered by successful salespeople. In much the same way a personnel recruiter must "sell" the organization to job applicants.[1]

---

[1] For a discussion of recruiting strategy, see Ronal G. Borgman, "Winning the Recruiting Battle in Small Business," *Journal of Small Business Management*, Vol. 11 (July, 1973), pp. 22-26.

The recruiter wants the best applicant, and the applicant wants the best possible employer. The better the applicant, the keener the competition for his or her services. An entrepreneur with a poor organization to offer is unlikely to obtain the best employees. To attract the best applicants, an organization must possess both good management and good personnel relations, along with competitive strength in all directions.

Sources of Employees

To recruit effectively the small entrepreneur must know where and how to secure good applicants. Possible sources are numerous, and one cannot generalize about the best source in view of the variations in labor requirements and quality of sources from one locality to another. Some of the major sources are discussed below.

Unsolicited Applicants. In a loose labor market, there may be a substantial number of qualified applicants in this group; but when workers are scarce, the majority of such job seekers are unsuitable for employment. In the interest of good public relations, such applicants should be treated courteously even though unsuited for employment.

Schools. Secondary schools, trade schools, colleges, and universities are desirable sources for certain classes of employees, particularly those who do not need specific work experience. Colleges and universities can supply candidates for positions in management and in various technical and scientific fields. In addition, many colleges are excellent sources of part-time employees for businesses located in the same city. Secondary and trade schools provide applicants with a limited but useful educational background.

Public Employment Agencies. State employment agencies, which are affiliated with the United States Employment Service, offer, without cost, a supply of applicants who are actively seeking employment. These agencies attempt to place applicants on the basis of work experience, education, and extensive psychological testing. Branch offices of state agencies are located throughout each state.

Private Employment Agencies. In all large cities and in some cities of smaller size, private agencies offer their services to a business as employment offices. In most cases, the employer receives their services without cost because the applicant pays the fee to the agency. However, some larger businesses will pay the fee if the applicant is highly qualified. Whether such a service can be profitably used depends upon those available and their areas of specialization.

Friends and Acquaintances of Present Employees. If present employees are good employees, their recommendations may provide excellent prospects. Ordinarily, they will hesitate to recommend applicants thought to be inferior in ability. Many small business owners admit that this source provides more of their employees than any other.

Advertising. The "Help Wanted" sign in the window of a business establishment is one form of advertising used by small firms. If the work is unskilled and labor is plentiful, such advertising may produce acceptable results. More aggressive advertising usually takes the form of advertisements in the classified pages of local newspapers. The effectiveness of advertising as a source of good employees has been questioned by some. The fact remains that many well-managed organizations recruit in this way, particularly for highly skilled tradesmen, scientists, and other professional employees when there is a shortage of such applicants from other sources.

Handicapped and Older Workers. The entrepreneur might well give careful consideration to the employment of handicapped and older workers. It has been discovered by many employers that the handicapped or older worker who is properly matched to a job is frequently superior in performance and attitude to the average worker.

Evaluating the Applicant

Occasionally a small employer knows the background and ability of an individual applicant. This is particularly true of employers located in small towns. Unfortunately there are many cases in which such knowledge of the applicant does not exist. How extensively a business can engage in investigating unknown applicants depends somewhat upon the size of the company. Many of the large-company evaluating techniques are available to the small business in one form or another. By following the series of steps described below, an uninformed, blind gamble on new employees may be avoided.

Step 1—Completion of Application Blank. Application blanks are almost universally used by large business organizations. There is a reason for such widespread use even though they may appear to be unnecessary "red tape" to the small entrepreneur. The value in using an application blank is in systematically getting background information that might otherwise be overlooked. Such background information is useful in sizing up an applicant and in making a more detailed investigation of his or her experience and character. If an application blank is not used, some vital information will invariably be overlooked. The employer may forget to ask or to record the applicant's answers.

Application blanks need not be elaborate or lengthy. They need not even be printed forms. The important questions to be answered by an applicant can be determined and several copies then typed for use as needed. Such a form is illustrated in Figure 9-1 on page 138. After the application has been used in evaluating and investigating the applicant, it may be destroyed but is better placed in the file for possible future reference.

Step 2—Interviewing the Applicant. A small business owner should conduct an employment interview. There is good reason for a conversation of this type. In this way the employer can get some idea of the applicant's appearance and personality, factors which may be important in the job to be filled. Although the interview is an important step, one should be cautious of making it the only step. Some individuals have the mistaken idea that they are infallible judges of human nature on the basis of interviews alone.

The interview can be more or less profitable depending upon the skill and methods of the interviewer. Any employer can improve the quality of

APPLICATION BLANK

1. PERSONAL DATA

Name _____

Address _____ Tel. No. _____

If married now
    Wife's (husband's) name _____
    Number of children _____

Number of other dependents _____

2. WORK EXPERIENCE

Present or last job:
    Name and address of employer _____
    Dates of employment _____
    Title of your job _____
    What kind of work did you perform? _____
    _____
    Why did you leave? _____

Next-to-last job:
    Name and address of employer _____
    Dates of employment _____
    Title of your job _____
    What kind of work did you perform? _____
    _____
    Why did you leave? _____

3. EDUCATION

High School
    Name and address of school _____
    Did you graduate?_____ When? _____

College or Specialized School
    Name and address of school _____
    Did you graduate?_____ When? _____
    Nature of course _____

4. REFERENCES (List three references not mentioned above)

      NAME   *ADDRESS*   *OCCUPATION*

_____

_____

_____

Figure 9-1
SIMPLIFIED APPLICATION BLANK

interviewing by following generally accepted principles of interviewing. Some of the basic techniques of good employment interviewing are:

1. Determine the questions you want to ask before beginning the interview.
2. Conduct the interview in a quiet atmosphere.
3. Give your entire attention to the applicant.

4. Put the applicant at ease.
5. Never argue.
6. Keep the conversation at a level suited to the applicant.
7. Listen attentively.
8. Observe closely the applicant's speech, mannerisms, and dress if these characteristics are related to the job.
9. Try to avoid being unduly influenced by trivial mannerisms or superficial resemblances to other people you know.

Step 3—Investigating the Applicant's Background. It has long been recognized that most references listed on application blanks give a rose-colored picture of the applicant's character and ability. However, careful checking of former employers, school authorities, bankers, and certain other references can be most constructive. The way in which references are checked has an important effect upon the quality of the results. Written letters of inquiry are probably the weakest form of investigation. Individuals who provide little useful information in response to a written request often speak more frankly when approached by telephone or in person. There is a hesitancy to put damaging statements in written form.

For only a few dollars, the small employer can supplement the investigation with an inquiry by firms specializing in investigational work. The Retail Credit Company, with headquarters in Atlanta, Georgia, and with branch offices in major cities of all states, is an example of a privately owned corporation providing this type of service. The value of such investigations is principally in uncovering information of a derogatory nature. If the applicant has a police record or certain defects of character, this evidence can be considered carefully before appointing this person to a position of trust.

Step 4—Testing the Applicant. The small employer is often unaware of the possibilities open in testing applicants for employment. Many types of work lend themselves to performance testing. The typist may be given some material to type, or the mechanic may be asked to complete a repair job. With a little ingenuity, employers may improvise practical tests pertinent to most of the positions in their businesses.

Psychological examinations may also be used by small business firms, but the results can easily be misleading because of difficulty in interpretation or in adapting the tests to the particular business. For small firms desiring to use such examinations, a number of agencies have developed tests which they sell at a nominal cost to business concerns. The principal benefit from both performance and psychological tests is the discovery of incompetence rather than the prediction of varying degrees of success.

Step 5—Physical Examination of Applicant. Physical examinations, though frequently neglected, are of practical value and are possible for the small business. Although few small firms have staff physicians, arrangements can be made with a local doctor who will administer the examinations. The employer, of course, would pay for the cost of the physical examination. In a few occupations, physical examinations are required by law, but it is always wise to discover physical limitations and possible contagious diseases of all new employees.

Inducements to Offer to Selected Applicants

A number of inducements may be offered to selected applicants in order to persuade them to accept positions. Among these are the following:

1. A challenging task with good pay.
2. Individual recognition for achievement.
3. Opportunity for advancement within the firm (including eventual part ownership) and outside it (through assistance in getting a more lucrative job with another firm, when ready for promotion).
4. Relative freedom of action.
5. Fringe benefits.
6. Offer of employment to one who is older or physically handicapped.
7. Better-than-average compensation.
8. Opportunities for self-development through experience, formal executive development training, college courses, and other types of development.

These inducements add up to the provision of "job satisfaction" on the part of the prospective employee, plus a challenge to his or her abilities and growth on the job.

TRAINING AND PROMOTING EMPLOYEES

There are very few positions in industry for which no training is required. Even in the small business, the new employee seldom arrives with a complete knowledge of what the duties and responsibilities on the job are. To develop skill and knowledge, the employee is trained by the manager or a senior employee. If the manager fails to provide training, the new employee must figure it out for himself, frequently with waste of time, materials, and money. Training to improve skills and knowledge is not necessarily limited to newcomers; the performance of veteran employees may often be improved through training.

Much time and money may be required in the training process to make it effective. One small business providing pest extermination service for hotels, restaurants, and other commercial establishments has service representatives in several different cities of the Southwest. The owner estimates that $2,000 is expended for the six months on-the-job training for each new representative, the outlay being required because of the specialized knowledge and skill required of employees. It would be a rare individual who had an adequate background at the time he made application for employment.

In addition to developing employees in their present positions, another type of training is designed to prepare an employee for promotion. In view of the fact that personal development and advancement are prime concerns of able employees, the small business can profit from careful attention to employee development. If employees can grow and move up in an organization, it not only improves the morale of present employees but also offers an inducement for outsiders to accept employment with that organization. The fullest benefit from a training program is realized, then, if it is coupled with a program of promotion from within.

Training for Management Positions

The small business faces a particularly serious problem in training managerial employees. This is true even though the owner is the only supervisor or manager in the firm. When the time arrives for the owner to withdraw from active direction of the business, it is imperative that a replacement be available.

In many types of business, the new manager should have months and perhaps years of preparation before assuming the position of leadership. Consider the small accounting firm whose accounts have been developed and serviced by the head of the business. What would happen to such a business if the owner were hospitalized for an extended period of time? The absence of a competent individual trained to step in when the original manager steps out might easily cause liquidation of such a firm. The process of liquidation, furthermore, is ordinarily a money-losing proposition, because the typical enterprise is worth far more as a going business.

If the business is sufficiently large that there are other managers in addition to the owner, the need to develop individuals in and for these positions also exists. Frequently, there is a family connection on the part of one or more potential managers, a situation which may tend to discourage other capable individuals in the organization. Whether or not there is an "heir apparent" in the business, it is easy for the owner to assume that management personnel will develop naturally and be available when needed. Some fathers are even reluctant to delegate enough responsibility to their sons to permit them to learn the business.

Once the manager of a small business senses the need for some management development, the question arises as to how the manager should go about it. In most business situations, all or at least most of the training must be of an on-the-job variety. In accomplishing this management training, the manager should give serious consideration to the following factors:

1. Determine need for training. What vacancies are expected? Who needs to be trained? What type of training and how much training does each need?
2. Develop the plan for training. How can the individuals be trained? Do they have enough responsibility to permit them to learn? Can they be assigned additional duties? Should they be given temporary assignments in other areas—for example, shifting them from production to sales? Would additional schooling be of benefit?
3. Establish a timetable. When should training be started? How much can be accomplished in the next six months or one year?
4. Counsel with employees. Do the individuals understand their need for training? Are they aware of the prospects for them in the firm? Has an understanding been reached as to the nature of training? Have the employees been consulted regularly about progress in their work and problems confronting them? Have they been given the benefit of the owner's experience and insights without having decisions made for them?

Training Nonsupervisory Employees

The problem of training nonsupervisory employees may be small or great depending upon the number of employees, the amount of labor turnover, and the complexity of the work. In a very small established business, the one or two veteran employees may know their work so thoroughly that there is no training problem at the moment. Even here, however, the need for training will arise as replacements are made or expansion occurs. In recent years, progressive managers have viewed the job of training as including attitude development in addition to building technical job skills. The subject of attitude development will be considered later in the chapter.

Whether it occurs regularly or infrequently, most training is accomplished on the job. Its weakness in small firms results from the use of haphazard learning in contrast to planned, controlled training. Any training can be accelerated and improved in quality as consideration is given to the objectives, methods, and limitations of the training. One plan designed to make on-the-job training more effective is known as Job Instruction Training (JIT). The steps of this program, listed below, are intended to help the manager who is not a professional educator in "getting through" to the employee. The steps are simple but they are often overlooked even by experienced supervisors. The process of instruction can be improved materially by any manager who will make a conscious effort to observe these steps.

1. Prepare the worker. Put the worker at ease. Find out what he or she already knows about the job. Get the worker interested in learning the job. Place the worker in an appropriate job.
2. Present the operations. Tell, show, illustrate, and question carefully and patiently. Stress key points. Instruct clearly and completely, taking up one point at a time—but no more than the worker can master.
3. Try out performance. Test the worker by having him or her perform the job. Have the worker tell, show, and explain key points. Ask questions and correct errors. Continue until the worker knows that he or she knows.
4. Follow up. Check frequently. Designate to whom the worker goes for help. Encourage questions. Get the worker to look for the key points as he or she progresses. Taper off extra coaching and close follow-up.

WAGE POLICIES

As leaders of unionized businesses would testify, an entrepreneur does not always have a free hand in establishing wage levels. Wages cannot be established on an individual basis when employees are represented by a union. When the small entrepreneur is dealing with a powerful union, wage policies may be determined by the legal representative of the employees.

Most small entrepreneurs do not operate under strict union control. A business is permitted to work out individual wage agreements with employees. Even here, however, the small business typically has less freedom of choice than appears on the surface. If wages are set at less than the going rate, the result is inferior employees. On the other hand, the small firm cannot afford to pay more than its competitors unless the higher wage stimulates greater productivity.

Another external influence on the wage policies of some small firms is legislation providing for minimum wages and overtime compensation, a subject which is discussed later in the chapter.

Internal Alignment of Wages

Many "beefs" from employees about wages are not concerned with the absolute wage as such. Rather, they are such complaints as "I work as hard as

Joe, but he gets more money," or, "I've been here longer than Mary, but she draws the same salary I do," or, "Bill and I do the same type of work, but he earns more." Remarks of this type point to three factors affecting an internal alignment of wages that will be considered as "fair":

1. The best producer should be rewarded financially.
2. The employee with long service is entitled to more than a newcomer.
3. More difficult or more responsible work deserves higher pay.

To some extent, these factors conflict, but it is possible to devise a wage program that will give some weight to all three factors.

The relative emphasis to be placed upon the first and second factors depends upon the relative importance attached to individual efficiency and length of service. To the extent that efficiency is used as a guide in setting wages, the employer must measure the performance of employees. When this is done formally, it is called performance rating or merit rating. If the number of employees is quite small, the relative efficiency of all employees may be known to the manager without special study.

Efficiency, and possibly length of service, should be permitted to influence wages within a certain wage bracket. But the wage bracket of a janitor should not be so high as that of a forklift truck driver. The janitor, for example, might draw from $2.00 to $2.35 per hour, depending upon his efficiency. The forklift truck driver, in contrast, might draw from $2.65 to $3.00 per hour. The idea that the type of work should also affect the wage level is expressed by the phrase, "Equal pay for equal work."

If the number of positions is very small, the manager probably has a correct mental picture of the various jobs and their comparative difficulty. As an organization grows, it is necessary to analyze the positions carefully in terms of difficulty of work, nature of working conditions, extent of responsibility, supervision given and received, and requirements for training and experience. In its simplest form, the analysis can be made by ranking the positions after careful review of these factors. In somewhat larger firms, more refined techniques of job evaluation are desirable, such as the job classification method or the point system.

Incentive Wages

Whether wages should fluctuate with output is another question basic in the determination of a firm's compensation policy. Most employees in American industry are paid day wages; that is, their income does not vary directly with their productivity. In many occupations, in contrast, incentive wages of some type are traditional. Many salespeople, for example, are paid partially or entirely on a commission basis. Incentive wages are also prevalent in many types of manufacturing.

Adoption of an incentive wage plan should be preceded by careful analysis of all aspects of the problem. In favor of incentive wages is the spur to production provided for employees. Under favorable conditions the improved performance is substantial. In adopting an incentive system, however, an employer often encounters opposition and antagonism of employees or unions. Quarrels over time or output standards exemplify this condition. In addition, the management must undertake more extensive record keeping and perhaps employ specialists in this area. Furthermore, the emphasis of most incentive systems is upon quantity, and this may interfere with the quality standards of the business.

Some types of work are not easily measurable and accordingly do not lend themselves readily to wages based upon output. It must also be recognized that output seldom fluctuates on the basis of money alone. An incentive plan can never take the place of good personnel practices. Mutual confidence between management and employees is an essential prerequisite for success with any wage program. One group incentive plan—the Scanlon Plan—which has achieved outstanding results in some plants, is based upon the principle of labor-management cooperation both in adoption and operation of the plan.

Profit Sharing

Profit-sharing plans have functioned successfully in many small companies. In fact, the large company probably has greater difficulty than the small firm in using profit sharing as a production incentive. This is because an individual employee's work seems to have such an insignificant effect upon profits of the large company as a whole. In a small organization, the connection between individual performance and company success can be more easily understood and appreciated by employees. These plans are similar to group incentive plans in their appeal to the group rather than to the individual employee directly. The incentive value of profit sharing is frequently weakened by the presence of nonlabor factors which affect profits. In other words, employees may work diligently and the company still experience a loss. In addition, the company must be prepared to disclose financial information to employees in adopting a plan of this type.

Although profit sharing distributes company profits to employees, it is possible to deduct such payments (up to a specified percentage of total profits) as wage expense in computing the income tax of the small corporation.

Fringe Benefits

Many large companies, as a matter of policy, grant several fringe benefits to their employees. These include such items as paid vacations, paid holidays, group insurance, pensions, and severance pay. Since World War II, unions have also bargained vigorously—often as hard as they bargain for wages—for benefits of this type. The effect is to add substantially to the direct wage costs, as much as 75 cents per hour in many cases.

Although large companies are usually the first to grant fringe benefits, union pressure is also applied to some small businesses. For the other small business establishments, there is the usual problem of meeting the competition. Most employees view their compensation as a combination of their paycheck and fringe benefits. If the small firm is to compete effectively for good employees, it cannot ignore fringe benefits.

Having spent money in this way, an employer should use it as a personnel tool, stressing to employees the cost and nature of benefits provided. Otherwise, there is a tendency for some employees to become accustomed to the extra benefits and to think only in terms of the paycheck.

HUMAN RELATIONS IN THE SMALL ORGANIZATION

On a typical day in a small shop, a veteran supervisor tried hard to get out a rush order but found it an uphill job. One employee was absent without explanation. Two others carefully observed every authorized minute of the coffee break. And to top it off, those on the job lacked inspiration and plodded along without a sense of urgency or concern for customer or employer. Such an absence of teamwork demonstrates the serious deficiency in that company's human relations.

To some extent, the personnel practices discussed earlier in the chapter contribute to the establishment of good relations between employees and management. A satisfactory wage policy and company picnics do not guarantee harmonious relations, however. Successful human relations involve more than a technique, a set of tools, or a personnel program. They are concerned with the team effort of individuals in accomplishing the group objectives.

Communication with Employees

One of the essential ingredients in achieving effective teamwork is given the label of "communication." The practical meaning of this concept is simply that there should be a constant interchange of information and ideas between management and employees. This sharing of information may be accomplished by the usual informal conversations of the small business. It does not require formal meetings, although these may be useful in larger organizations.

Communication is a two-way process. There is, to be sure, much communication in the form of orders and instructions that must go from management to workers in the ordinary course of business. Many of these are inadequate communications, however, because they fail to say "why." The manager may ask, "Am I required to explain and justify my every move to the employees or the union?" To be sure, the manager is not required to do so, but it is difficult for the employees to be either intelligent or enthusiastic teamworkers if they do not know the "why." Furthermore, management frequently *tells* the employees without bothering to *listen* to them. Most employees can tell a great deal to the manager who will take the time and has the patience to listen.

Some entrepreneurs do an excellent job of communication. The employees know where they stand, how the business is going, plans for the future, and other information pertinent to the business. On the other hand, there is another type of businessman who keeps all but the necessary information "under his hat." No doubt, there may be a little information that must remain a secret lest it fall into the hands of competitors. Most of the gaps in communication, however, are explained by the fact that the manager does not have (or does not take) the time to talk things out with the subordinates.

Other Methods of Building Good Human Relations

If communication is extended to the point of consulting either formally or informally with employees, an even longer step may be taken toward successful human relations in a business. The opportunity to contribute one's ideas and opinions before the manager decides an issue adds dignity to the job in the eyes of most employees.

In various other ways, a manager may appeal to the employees' desire for recognition and wish to belong, to be accepted, and to accomplish something worthwhile. There is no intended implication that negative disciplinary action is unnecessary, but positive motivation must be the primary tool in establishing good employee relations. Perhaps the most fundamental concept to keep in mind is that employees are people. They quickly detect insincerity, but they respond to honest efforts to treat them as mature, responsible individuals.

Use of a Personnel Manager

A firm with only a few employees cannot ordinarily afford to pay the salary of a full-time specialist on personnel problems. In such an organization the proprietor may easily combine functions of ownership, supervision, financial control, and personnel relations. Some of the more involved personnel tools and techniques which are required in larger businesses may be unnecessarily complicated for the four- or five-person business. As an organization grows in size, however, its personnel problems increase in both number and complexity.

As a small business adds employees, then, it reaches a point at which it becomes logical to appoint a personnel manager. This point cannot be specified precisely. Each entrepreneur must decide whether the type and size of the business could profitably pay for a personnel specialist. A part-time personnel manager might be a logical first step. The title is not particularly important; it may be "employment manager," "industrial relations manager," or any of a dozen other titles.

One survey of small manufacturing firms showed the following relationship of plant size to use of either full-time or part-time personnel managers:[2]

Number of Employees	Percent of Firms Using Personnel Managers
Less than 25	5.4
25 to 74	13.7
75 to 149	36.9
150 to 299	66.7

Conditions That Favor Appointment of a Personnel Manager. It is obvious from the above figures that some very small manufacturers have personnel managers, whereas others of substantial size operate without a specialized personnel staff. It is also true that the situation in manufacturing would not necessarily be identical to that in marketing or service industries. However, it is possible to identify some conditions that encourage the appointment of a personnel manager, and these are:

1. When there is a substantial number of employees. (What is "substantial" varies with the business, but 100 employees is suggested as a guide.)
2. When employees are represented by a union.
3. When the labor turnover rate is high.

---

[2] Alton W. Baker, *Personnel Management in Small Plants* (Columbus: Ohio State University, 1955), p. 29.

4. When the need for skilled or professional personnel creates problems in recruitment or selection.
5. When supervisors or operative employees require considerable training.
6. When morale is unsatisfactory.
7. When competition for personnel is keen.

Advantages in Early Appointment of a Personnel Manager. It is interesting to note that some companies of fewer than 25 employees have personnel managers. There are a number of advantages associated with early recognition of the personnel function to the extent of designating a personnel manager. Among these are the following:

1. Centralization of recruiting and other functions that are otherwise less efficiently performed by a number of supervisors.
2. Efficient performance of personnel functions by a specialist with superior background and training for these tasks.
3. Provision of a management staff member who carefully analyzes the human problems of the organization.
4. Availability of guidance and advice for managers who sense a weakness in human relations skills.

It should be stressed that hiring a personnel manager does not relieve line management of personnel responsibilities. The personnel manager is simply a staff expert who takes over some personnel duties and provides valuable advice in the case of other duties. It is the line manager, particularly the chief executive of the small business, who must bear ultimate responsibility for leadership in employee relations. A personnel program will not be accepted by employees or by other management personnel unless it is strongly supported by the top executive. Only as the entrepreneur grasps this simple truth will the personnel manager have the stature necessary to fill the job effectively.

LABOR PROBLEMS AND LEGISLATION

Although small business is generally less unionized than is large business, size is no guarantee against unionization. Small manufacturers, small printing establishments, small trucking firms, small construction companies, and barbershops are all very likely to become objects of union organization. Other types of small business, of course, are not immune to unionization. In some parts of the country, even small retailers have been unionized. Small firms located in heavily industrialized areas are more likely to become targets for union organization.

Union-Management Relations

The small entrepreneur who has developed a business and built strong personal relationships with employees may view their organizing efforts as a personal betrayal. In order to avoid such emotional reactions and to deal with the union on a businesslike basis, it is well to recognize that there are numerous reasons why employees become members of a union. Affiliation with a labor organization does not necessarily imply disloyalty to the employer. The factor of wages is often cited as the major reason for unionization. The factors of job security, fear of capricious action by the employer, and a desire for recognition are also among the motives causing employees to join unions. Some of the intangible factors are certainly as important in specific cases as the desire for higher wages.

Employers currently display a variety of attitudes concerning labor unions. Managers of some firms maintain that the problems of labor relations can be solved more adequately by working with a union than by dealing with employees individually. Other companies take a strong antiunion position. In between are those employers who simply accept unionization as a necessary way of life, attempting to make their relationships with the union as harmonious as possible. Unionization need not be regarded as a tragedy. Many employers have operated successfully for many years while dealing with responsible labor organizations. A responsible, mature viewpoint on the part of management will serve to stimulate the same type of approach by labor. A defensive union can hardly relax sufficiently to participate in a program that might be labeled as cooperative.

The absence of an adequate personnel program may encourage unionization. It seems highly questionable, however, whether an employee relations program should be installed for the purpose of avoiding a union. Furthermore, individuals do not change their human nature when they begin to carry union cards. An employer's control of employee relations may be circumscribed somewhat by the advent of a union, but the basic factors in good human relations remain the same.

Major Areas of Labor Legislation

A small manufacturer recently discontinued the coffee break (with free coffee) that he had previously permitted his employees to enjoy. As a result of taking this action unilaterally, the employer was found to have violated a federal law controlling labor relations! The circumstances behind the decision were most significant, of course. The discontinuance of the coffee break occurred immediately after the employees had voted to be represented by the International Association of Machinists. This act of management was held to be an illegal reprisal because of the timing and the company's refusal to bargain with the new union concerning it.

This incident serves to illustrate the fact that governmental control is not limited to minimum wage laws and safety regulations. On the contrary, labor legislation permeates the whole area of personnel relations. Labor laws provide the framework or the boundaries within which a personnel program operates. Good laws encourage constructive personnel relations, but scrupulous attention to the letter of the law does not guarantee success. Legal counsel may be required at times, but one should be wary of turning the personnel function over to an attorney. A good personnel program calls for more than the minimum required by law.

It is the purpose of this section to outline the major legal boundaries for personnel management by summarizing the basic labor laws, both federal and state. The extreme variation in state laws prevents a detailed consideration of these laws. In most states, the executive branch of the state government will provide a summary of state labor laws free of charge. By obtaining a booklet of this type, the small businessman can note any regulations that are peculiar to his state.

Unions and Collective Bargaining. Employers engaged in interstate commerce are required by the National Labor Relations Act to bargain collectively if a majority of employees desire unionization. In fact, discrimination of any type against an employee for union activity is strictly forbidden. The majority of states also recognize by statute the right of labor to organize. In a number of states, "right-to-work" laws limit the extent of unionization by outlawing the union shop.

Payroll Taxes. Employers, large and small, are both taxpayers and tax collectors. To finance old age and survivors' insurance, employers must pay a tax on the employee's earnings and deduct a comparable amount from the employee's salary. The Social Security Act also provides for an unemployment compensation tax, although most of this tax goes to the state government. Variations exist among the states regarding rates and coverage, and merit rating provisions permit lower rates for employers who stabilize employment.

Workmen's Compensation. Accidents and occupational disease have become the subjects of state legislation. Although the laws differ from one state to another, most of them require employers to pay insurance premiums either to a state fund or to private insurance companies. The funds provided in this way are used to compensate victims of industrial accidents or occupational illness. Premiums are based on rates that reflect the hazards involved and safety program effectiveness.

Wages and Hours. A minimum wage, which is adjusted by amendment from time to time, is specified by the Fair Labor Standards Act for employers engaged in interstate commerce. In addition, the Act establishes a standard workweek of forty hours, requiring payment of overtime compensation at the rate of time and one half for hours in excess of standard. Many states have also legislated in the field of wages and hours. For the most part, these laws specify maximum hours for women and children only. Minimum wage provisions of state laws are generally lower than those of the Fair Labor Standards Act.

Child Labor. The minimum age for employees is covered not only by the Fair Labor Standards Act but also by law in practically all states. For the most part, these laws establish a minimum of 14 to 16 years (the federal minimum is 16) with a slightly higher minimum often specified for hazardous occupations.

Discrimination Against Minorities. Recent legislation has narrowed, if not eliminated, the right of business owners to discriminate against minority groups. The most comprehensive legislation of this type is the Civil Rights Act of 1964, which was amended by the Equal Employment Opportunity Act of 1972. This Act forbids discrimination against applicants and employees on the basis of race, color, religion, sex, or national origin. An Equal Employment Opportunities Commission (EEOC), created by the Act, accepts complaints of discrimination and assists in implementing the Act's provisions. The law requires all employers who have 15 or more employees to avoid discrimination in advertising for applicants, the use of psychological tests, selection, compensation, promotion, and other ways. In addition to this federal law, a number of state laws also make it illegal to discriminate against minority groups.

Safety Legislation. The Occupational Safety and Health Act of 1970 (OSHA) established elaborate safety requirements for both large and small business firms. Safety devices and special equipment required for some businesses entailed the expenditure of thousands or even hundreds of thousands of dollars. In some cases, small firms were forced out of business because of their inability to meet the requirements and remain profitable. Others, however, adjusted to the new law without undue difficulty. There is no doubt that the Act created special problems, particularly in the early days of its enforcement, for many small firms.[3]

Summary

1. The smaller dimensions of the personnel task in a small firm change but do not eliminate the personnel problem. Relations between management and employees differ from those of large concerns because of such factors as the following: (a) the close personal acquaintance between management and employees; (b) the informality of relationships; (c) the proprietary attitude of the owner-manager; (d) the small employer's concentration upon "production;" (e) the lack of specialized personnel "know-how;" (f) the direct influence of the entrepreneur's attitude throughout the firm; and (g) less elaborate personnel tools.

2. To secure capable employees, the small firm must take the initiative in seeking applicants. A strong, healthy organization is one of the best "lures" for prospective employees.

3. Sources of employees include applicants who come seeking work, schools, public and private employment agencies, friends and acquaintances of present employees, and different forms of advertising.

4. Steps in evaluation of the applicant include the use of an application blank, employment interview, background investigation, testing, and physical examination.

5. Employees of small firms require training to develop skill and knowledge in their jobs and to prepare them for promotion. The need for developing personnel at the managerial level in these ways is particularly acute.

6. External influences upon wages include union pressure, competitive influence of other firms, and legislation. The internal alignment of wages is affected by work efficiency, longevity, and difficulty or responsibility of work.

7. Wage-incentive and profit-sharing plans may be used to motivate higher-level production in small concerns.

8. Many types of small business must bargain with unions representing their employees. Management personnel in small concerns display a variety of attitudes

---

[3] See "New Job-Safety Rules Perplex the Owners of Small Businesses; 'Needless' Costs Cited," *The Wall Street Journal*, February 20, 1973, p. 1.

with respect to unions; some have operated successfully for many years while enjoying good union-management relations.

9. The absence of teamwork in a business demonstrates a lack of effective human relations. Good human relations, which involve more than a technique or a personnel program, are particularly dependent upon the manager's communication efforts toward achieving mutual understanding and the use of positive motivation in dealing with employees.

10. The point of growth at which a personnel manager should be added cannot be specified precisely. Even after a personnel manager has been employed, the chief executive must continue to assume a strong responsibility for employee relations.

11. Labor legislation affects many areas of business management by regulating collective bargaining, imposing payroll taxes, requiring workmen's compensation, restricting wages and hours, prohibiting child labor, prohibiting discrimination against minority groups, and imposing safety regulations.

Discussion Questions

1. Are personnel relations more critical in a retail store or in a manufacturing plant? Why?

2. Do the personal acquaintance and informality in employee relations in small firms constitute more of an advantage or a handicap? Why?

3. What accounts for the fact that owners of small businesses frequently place undue emphasis upon technical factors in contrast with personnel factors?

4. Suggest some ways in which the manager of a small business might be aggressive in recruiting employees.

5. Are small companies that cannot afford elaborate employment procedures and fringe benefits at a competitive disadvantage in comparison with larger firms? Why?

6. Discuss with the owner or manager of some small business the sources he uses for new employees. What is his opinion concerning the comparative value of the different sources?

7. What factors should be considered in deciding the extent to which outside schools should be used for training employees?

8. Consider the small business with which you are best acquainted. Has adequate provision been made to replace key management personnel? What type of management development, if any, is being used?

9. What values are obtainable by use of a job evaluation plan in a small business? How could you overcome the difficulty inherent in the lack of a job classification analyst?

10. What problems are involved in using incentive wage systems? Are these more serious in the small than in the large firm? What effect would the nature of the work have upon your decision concerning the use or nonuse of incentive wages?

11. Is the use of a profit-sharing system desirable in a small firm? What major difficulties do you foresee for its use with the intent of motivating employees?

12. Why have labor unions succeeded better in organizing efforts in small manufacturing than in small merchandising firms?

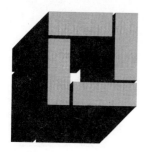

10

Purchasing and Supplier Relations

Purchasing is the activity involved in the acquisition of goods or merchandise. A manufacturer buys raw materials, parts, and factory and office supplies. A wholesaler or retailer purchases merchandise for resale to customers. Thus, for all businesses, purchasing makes possible the sales or production operations and the maintenance of plant and equipment.

Good relations should be maintained with all firms acting as suppliers, as good relations make more effective purchasing possible. A firm benefits from dealing fairly and honestly. Hence, this chapter considers not only purchasing functions, policies, and procedures, but also vendor relations.

IMPORTANCE OF EFFECTIVE PURCHASING

The quality of finished products cannot be better than the quality of the raw materials placed in process. If tight tolerances are imposed on the firm's product by design requirements, this in turn requires the acquisition of high-quality materials and component parts. Then, given an excellent process, excellent products will be produced. But even a superior process will not consistently turn out superior products if inferior materials or components are used. Therefore, factory purchasing is crucial in the manufacturing process. This is particularly true of plants spending 50 percent or more of the total cost dollar for materials and purchased parts. Similarly, in merchandising, the acquisition of quality merchandise makes sales to customers easier. Effective purchasing does more than this, however, since it also reduces the number and amounts of markdowns required for selling the purchased merchandise.

It is also vitally necessary that the delivery of goods be timed to meet the exact needs of the customer firm. In a small factory, failure to receive materials, parts, or equipment on schedule is likely to cause costly interruptions in production operations. Machines and men are idled until the items on order are finally received. And in the mercantile firm, a failure to receive merchandise on schedule may mean the loss of one or more sales, and, possibly, the permanent loss of the disappointed customer or customers.

PURCHASING FUNCTIONS

Since purchasing is such an important activity, the entrepreneur needs an understanding of its specific functions. A discussion of the various purchasing functions follows.

Issuance of Purchase Orders

Purchasing may be said to begin with the issuance of purchase orders for materials, component parts, supplies, and items of equipment or tooling. A standard form (see Figure 10-1) should be designed and used in all buying operations; this should have three sections. The first is the heading, which identifies the purchasing company, shows the date and purchase order number, and specifies the supplier's name and address. It may also specify shipping instructions, such as date of shipment and routing via stated common carriers. The second part is the main body of the form. It identifies the items to be purchased by name and/or number, states the quantity desired, and lists the latest price quoted by the seller. The third part is the signature section and carries the signature and title of the buying officer. When the order is accepted by a vendor, it becomes a binding contract. In the event of a serious violation, the written order serves as the basis for adjudication.

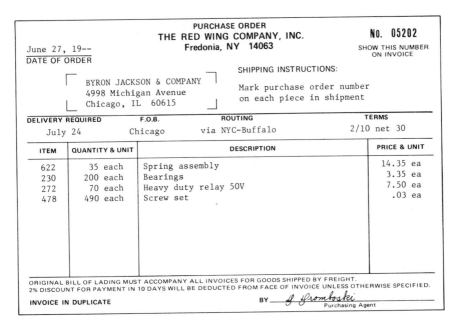

Figure 10-1
A PURCHASE ORDER

A purchasing agent should do all the firm's buying. Hence, this individual should have full authority to buy—which means full authority to sign and dispatch to suppliers purchase orders that legally bind the firm. Nevertheless, if other than the entrepreneur, the purchasing agent is responsible to the entrepreneur for proper, efficient procurement and is properly empowered to buy only what the firm needs within total authorized monthly spending amounts; that is, the budget permits buying only to a certain dollar amount each month. Purchase orders for goods or equipment whose dollar cost exceeds the monthly authorized expenditure should certainly require the counter-signature of the entrepreneur himself.

Record Keeping

Record keeping is a second important function of purchasing. Both buying and warehousing records are required. First of all, stores cards should be maintained, showing the supply on hand of each kind of raw material, each purchased part, and each separate supply item carried in the storeroom. These records may not be maintained by the purchasing agent; they are discussed in greater detail in Chapter 20.

Other records which the purchasing officer should maintain include all of the following:

1. Price quotations and credit terms—by suppliers and by kinds of materials or parts.
2. Purchase records showing outstanding orders and receipts from suppliers for each commodity. This provides a history of procurement of individual items.
3. Record of contract commitments.
4. Vendor quality and yield ratings.
5. Miscellaneous supplier data records, showing such things as willingness to inform the buying firm of new materials developed, cooperativeness in meeting delivery schedules and in improvement of quality control over purchased materials and parts, attempts at bribery to procure orders, and other such things.

Collaboration with Engineering and Production

The purchasing agent must also collaborate with engineering and production officers for an accurate determination of consumption standards applicable to the raw materials. Joint setting of the standard amount of raw materials required per unit of finished product will yield a better standard than will be obtainable if the product designer alone sets the standard. That is, the purchasing agent knows the quality of materials procured from given suppliers and the yield which can be expected from the goods. The purchasing agent is also in a position to discover new materials on the market and bring them to the attention of the engineering department. Hence, this individual has a real contribution to make in the setting of materials consumption standards. The product designer also has an intimate knowledge of materials and has the responsibility of designing a salable product which can be made at a competitive cost. And production people alone see the manufacturing operations at first hand every day, so that they are best acquainted with the current actual yield and the production troubles with given materials during processing. Hence, each has a vital contribution to make in determining workable materials consumption standards.

Related Functions

There are several functions closely related to purchasing. Some of these are assigned to the purchasing agent as administrative responsibilities, particularly in small firms. Such assignments should not be made blindly, however, because the separation of some functions permits cross-checking to eliminate errors and fraud.

One function frequently related to purchasing is the receiving room operation. The receiving clerks take physical custody of incoming materials and parts from the common carrier, check their general condition, and sign the carrier's release. Receiving inspection follows to assure an accurate count of

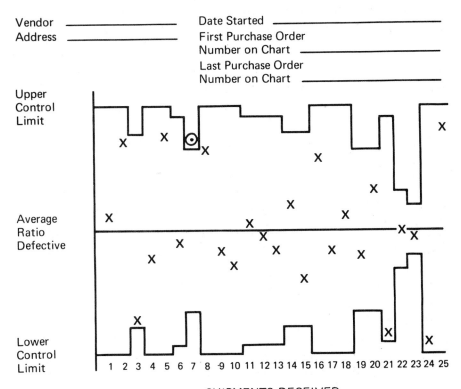

⊙ Out of Control

Shipments of all types of raw materials from the particular vendor are entered on such a p chart. Each shipment is treated as being one "random sample." Although some shipments may be for the same type of raw material, others may involve different types of raw materials.

Moreover, the size of shipment will vary—even for the same raw material, at times, and assuredly for different types of materials nearly every time. It is this variation in shipment size which produces the uneven upper and lower control limits.

The average ratio defective used on such a chart for 25 consecutive samples is the computed weighted average of the ratios defective for the preceding 25 shipments received.

In the present instance, the ratio defective exceeded the upper control limit only for shipment number 7. Therefore, this is the only "blemish" on the current quality record of this vendor.

Figure 10-2
OVERALL VENDOR QUALITY RATING p CHART

Materials Yield Summary
The Iowa Manufacturing Company

Stores Item _____ Week Ending _____

Stores Item Number _____ Quarter Ending _____

Supplier	Units of Product Put in Process	Allowance per Unit of Finished Product	Total Units Allowed	Actual Units Used	Usage as % of Units Allowed
1	2	3	4 = 3·2	5	6 = 5/4 (100) (Quotient) = %

    The materials yield summary provides an analysis of the quality of the given material (or part), as supplied by each vendor, for the given week (or quarter). Both weekly and quarterly summaries are made for each major stores item—using this same form. Since the standard usage percent of units allowed = 100, actual percentages for each supplier afford the purchasing agent concrete evidence of which suppliers are good and which are bad.

    Percentages under 100 (given high quality output) are favorable yield ratings; percentages over 100 are unfavorable.

Figure 10-3
MATERIALS YIELD SUMMARY

items received, together with assurance of proper quality and kind of items received. All items are counted, but the quality check may be performed on a sampling inspection basis by a representative of the quality control department.

    Inspection records are the basis of the buying officer's vendor quality ratings (see Figures 10-2 and 10-3). Even more important is their service to provide specific quality data on the supplier's products.

    Some purchasing agents are also charged with the storekeeping operation. This consists of the warehousing of raw materials, purchased parts, and supplies. The subject is discussed at some length in Chapter 20. Another related function is that of traffic planning, which includes the designation of the common carriers who will transport the inbound shipments. It includes the determination of optimum routing, considering the freight costs involved and the desired delivery dates. Since outbound shipments also involve traffic planning, purchasing is not the only logical department for the location of this function.

PURCHASING POLICIES

Buying policies can significantly affect the cost of buying, but they may be even more important for the preservation of good vendor relationships.

Confidential Dealings

One important policy that is essential to good relations with suppliers is the confidential treatment of all price quotations and bids received. The purchasing officer should never show bids and price quotations of one firm to sales representatives of other firms. This is an ethical practice of treating others as you would be treated.

Reciprocal Buying

Some firms try to sell to those from whom they purchase other materials. The concept involved is that one company can secure additonal orders by using its own purchasing requests as a bargaining weapon. Although the typical order of most small companies is not large enough to make this a potent weapon, there is a tendency for purchasers to grant some recognition to this factor.

This policy would be damaging if it were allowed to obscure quality and price variations. Otherwise, there is probably little to be lost (and perhaps little to be gained) from such a policy.

Ethical Policies

Ethical purchasing policies include the following:

1. Refusal of gifts from suppliers which might render the recipient indebted to the giver.
2. Marking purchase orders "rush" only on the basis of need.

The second of these ethical procurement policies could affect cost almost as much as it affects supplier relations. When the really rush order comes along and the supplier disregards it because he has heard the cry of "wolf" once too often, the resulting delay in production operations may completely shut down the buyer's plant, leading to higher costs, shipping delays, and the possible loss of some customers.

Making or Buying Component Parts

Another purchasing policy decision required of some manufacturers is whether to make or to buy component parts. In considering this problem, one must note several arguments on both sides. The arguments in favor of making the component parts are:

1. Uses otherwise idle capacity, thus permitting more economical production.
2. Makes one more independent of suppliers so that there are fewer delays and interruptions resulting from difficulties of suppliers.

3. Protects a secret design.
4. May be cheaper by avoiding payment of the supplier's selling expense and profit factors.
5. Permits closer coordination and control of total production operations, facilitating scheduling and quality control.
6. Permits better control over timing of design changes.

Some of the reasons for buying the component parts instead of making them are the following:

1. May be cheaper, as shown by cost studies, due to the supplier's concentration on production of the given part, which makes possible specialized facilities, added know-how, and greater efficiency.
2. A shortage of space, equipment, personnel skills, and working capital may exist, thus precluding "in-plant" manufacture of the part.
3. Requirement of less diversified managerial experience and skills.
4. Greater flexibility; for example, seasonal production of a given item makes its manufacture risky.
5. Frees "in-plant" operations for concentration on firm's specialty (finished products).
6. Partial purchase of components serves to check the efficiency of one's own parts-fabricating operations.
7. The increasing pace of technological change enhances the risk of equipment obsolescence, making diversion of this risk to outsiders a sound procedure.

The decision to make or to buy, once made and carried into effect, may be expensive to reverse. This lends importance to the initial decision, which should certainly be based on long-run cost and profit optimization. Making the parts, thus, should not be decided upon merely because it permits expansion. The underlying cost differences need to be analyzed very carefully since small savings in purchasing or making may greatly affect profit margins.

The entrepreneur in a small firm should approach this policy decision with an open mind and should be receptive to the arguments on both sides of the question. In particular, the entrepreneur should be perceptive of the outsider's added costs (and profit factor) as against his own firm's ability, capacity, and costs (overhead, administration, records and payroll, materials, design, tooling, equipment, and supervision). There is no definitive formula to guide one's decision. The decision must be independently made in the light of the currently governing factors and of company capacities and incapacities.

Substitute Materials or Products

Still another policy decision which must be made is one concerning the use of new or substitute materials. New types of materials are constantly being developed; some of these may be both cheaper and better. Quality considerations must be carefully evaluated. A new type of steel shank for ladies' shoes might eliminate the problem of breaking shanks; or, it could create such a problem. Similarly, in the same type of plant, certain upper leathers stretch just right for lasting of shoes, while others might be almost impossible to "last" without wrinkling of the vamps (foreparts of the shoes).

Nevertheless, the purchaser must consider not only the impact on the product and its cost but also the effect upon the process. A change in materials may alter the sequence of operations, or may even cause the deletion or addition of one or more operations. In turn, the new or altered operations would require new motion and time studies to reset accurately the hourly output rates demanded of the workers on those operations.

On occasion, a change of materials is forced upon the purchaser. Wartime scarcities constitute an obvious example. But the same is sometimes true in peacetime, as when a source of supply "dries up," so that the materials which were formerly used become impossible to obtain.

The small merchandising firm may be faced with a similar problem—the impossibility of continuance of a given product in its line. Consider the case of a small wholesaler of appliances, such as tape recorders, record players, and other items involving electronic elements. This wholesaler served as a service agency, supplying repair service for the units sold by the four or five retail outlets served. One day, this small wholesaler was notified by the New York office of a foreign manufacturer of a certain tape recorder that henceforth the minimum order it could accept and ship would be 20 units. Since this would involve an investment in the neighborhood of $2,500, the wholesaler had to discontinue his dealership for that kind of tape recorder. Located in a city of about 100,000 population, he did not sell that number of machines to his industrial and retail customers for several months. Hence, his own turnover was too low to justify the amount of investment required per order.

Purchasing policy should be sufficiently flexible to permit ready consideration of different materials or merchandise than those previously used or sold. Of course, a change must be based upon the possibility of producing or selling a better, cheaper product. However, as noted in the tape recorder case, circumstances may sometimes force a decision for a given change.

Taking Purchase Discounts

Any firm must decide whether or not to take available purchase discounts. One argument in favor of taking all purchase discounts available is that this evidences financial strength to one's suppliers and may tend to promote good relationships with suppliers. Even more important is the fact that discounts provide a source of actual savings. If the discount is taken on terms of 2/10, n/30, the savings are equivalent to interest at the rate of 36 percent per year (under the banker's rule for interest calculation). This is such a good rate that it pays to borrow at the bank in order to take the discount if one is short of cash on the discount date.

Concentration of Purchases

In the purchase of a particular item, there is a question whether it is desirable to use two or more suppliers. Division of orders among several suppliers can be a form of insurance against difficulties with a sole supplier. For example, a strike or fire might eliminate the supply for a time. The purchaser would then experience the delays involved in placing initial orders with a new source of supply. Moreover, if there is only one source, the purchaser is limited to just one quality of goods. This might eliminate the best available raw material to a small manufacturer or prevent a small merchandiser from meeting competition effectively. An even greater danger is the fact that failure to "shop" may result in a loss of the lower prices and superior service offered by other suppliers.

Nevertheless, the arguments on this problem are not all in favor of diversification of sources of supply. With centralized buying from one firm, the purchaser may acquire the right to special quantity discounts and other favorable terms of purchase. Special service, such as prompt treatment of rush orders, is readily granted to established customers. Moreover, the single source of supply may provide financial aid to the regular customer who encounters financial stress. It will also provide management advice and market information. It may even grant an exclusive franchise or dealership for the merchandising of certain branded goods.

Some firms follow a compromise policy by which they concentrate enough purchases to justify special treatment. At the same time they diversify purchases sufficiently to provide alternative sources of supply.

Purchase Quantities

At least three answers are available to the policy question of "how much to buy." These answers are discussed below.

Hand-to-Mouth Buying. This means the buying of small amounts as needed; for example, a firm might buy just what it requires for one week's operations. If storeroom space is at a premium, hand-to-mouth buying may be a necessity. Hand-to-mouth buying also presumes that the goods will be readily available from the supplier and that transit time for inbound shipments will be at a minimum. There are several advantages of this type of buying; among these are the following:

1. Simple determination of purchase requirements.
2. Avoidance of loss from price decline on quantities overstocked.
3. Reduction of dollar investment in inventory.
4. Shorter time cycle from purchase to use or sale, providing increased inventory turnover and reduced deterioration or obsolescence.

Correspondingly, hand-to-mouth buying presents certain disadvantages:

1. Higher cost of procurement, due to loss of quantity discounts, higher freight cost of LCL (less than carload) shipments, and repeated ordering costs.
2. Higher receiving and stores warehousing costs of handling small quantities per order.
3. Lower reserve stock with possible tie-up of production operations if deliveries are not made on schedule.

Speculative Buying. A second answer is speculative buying, which means buying substantially in excess of quantities needed to meet actual use requirements. This is done in the expectation that prices are going up. Price appreciation produces inventory profits. The great danger is that speculative buying entails gambling on the continued rise of prices. Broad price declines subsequent to heavy, speculative buying could bankrupt the speculator. Unless one is very stable financially and very wise, speculative buying should be avoided. It is typically used when the business cycle is on the way up; its use during a depression would be suicidal.

Scheduled Budget Buying. A third answer is scheduled budget buying to meet anticipated requirements. This is planned buying; it involves adjustment of purchase quantities to estimated production or sales needs. The quantity ordered may well be the *economic order quantity* for purchasing, which will minimize the total cost of the given item or raw material over a period of time.[1] Such an economic order quantity will be determined in the light of fixed costs of preparing and receiving an order, as against the stores or merchandise inventory carrying charges.

Budget buying in economic order quantities will assure the maintenance of planned inventories and the meeting of production schedule requirements without delays in production due to delayed deliveries. It can also encompass the planned expansion of dollar and unit holding of inventory, or the contraction thereof, depending on the scale of the firm's operations over the year and over the business cycle. It strikes the middle ground between hand-to-mouth buying, with its planned understocking of materials and its occasional delays due to late deliveries, and speculative buying, with its careful overstocking which entails risks as it seeks speculative profits. It gears procurement to planned production and planned sales requirements; it represents the best type of buying for the conservative small entrepreneur.

THE PURCHASING PROCEDURE

Buying standard stock items is closely related to inventory control, a topic discussed in detail in Chapter 23. Each regularly stocked kind of material or part normally has a stores card showing the reorder point. When the inventory balance is brought down to the reorder point, the stores clerk or shop foreman (whoever is responsible for issues of materials to the shop) notifies the purchasing agent of the need to reorder. Making and mailing the purchase order follows this notification.

Procedure in Factory Buying

If special orders which require materials not carried in stores are accepted, the manufacturer must prepare a bill of materials showing kinds and amounts of special materials required for the particular order. Purchase orders are then prepared and mailed.

If special materials or supply items become a necessity at any time, the buyer is notified by a requisition, following which a purchase order can be prepared. Likewise, in buying equipment for plant or office, the buyer is guided by the instructions or specifications prepared by the foreman, office manager, or plant engineer.

Written records—usually copies of the purchase orders—should be retained for all purchases made. Initially, these should be so filed as to facilitate traffic

---

[1] See Chapter 23 for an extended discussion of economic order quantities.

expediting of inbound shipments and to help assure the prompt arrival of the goods or equipment ordered. Follow-up of all purchases to assure delivery on schedule is necessary. Subsequently, there is the receipt and inspection of the goods, followed by their transfer to the storeroom or shop. Finally, there is the matter of payment. Payment should be made by check in order to facilitate both accounting and cash control.

The purchasing procedure is not complete until the buyer follows the materials and parts into the plant to determine production results. This is essential to provide information to guide future buying so that the best quality materials and parts will typically be purchased.

Total budgeted expenditures for materials, parts, and equipment should not be exceeded by the buying officer. Even an owner who does the buying should reconsider the need of given purchases which would surpass budgeted expenditure totals. Of course, if the need exists and a profit can be made, the owner will arrange the financing and go ahead with the purchase or authorize the purchasing agent to do so.

While price quotations received should always be retained in a "price quote" file, a buyer would be wise to obtain price confirmations before actually mailing any major purchase order. Some suppliers' prices are stated to be subject to change without notice. Price confirmation avoids embarrassment resulting from receipt of a shipment and invoice showing a considerably higher unit price than expected. Invoice prices should always be compared with quotations.

Procedure in Mercantile Buying

In small wholesale and retail establishments, purchase authorization is based on a combination of expected sales and inventory levels. Tools used for determination of balanced inventories include basic stock lists and model stock lists. Model stock lists are used, for example, in retailing of furniture.[2]

Retailers and wholesalers must check the quality and condition of goods received, present claims for damages or report shortages in shipments, verify prices billed, and the like.

It is very important also that merchants follow up merchandise purchases to see how well and how fast they sell to customers. This tends to improve future purchasing by elimination of slow-selling items. Among the sources of follow-up data will be rates of turnover, customer complaints, markdowns, and customer returns. Annually, perhaps, small retailers may even want to "age" their inventories so that nonselling items can be removed from stock. This should be done even though such items must be given away or thrown away.

Tests of Buying Efficiency

Poor buying may result from either incompetence of personnel or improper procedures in buying. Sound procedures and policies have been stressed earlier in the chapter. Departure from sound practice—whether by unwise reciprocal buying, failure to seek out the best suppliers, lack of follow-up, or a number of other factors—results in inefficient buying.

---

[2] See Chapter 26 for a discussion of purchasing techniques for a retail store.

There are two tests of buying efficiency. The first of these is the cost of buying. Estimates of the average cost of processing a manufacturer's purchase order range from $2 to $20. Larger concerns placing many orders per year tend to have a lower "per order" buying cost, whereas the average cost of a purchase order typically is higher in the small firm.

The other test of good buying is fulfillment of the purchasing objective: to buy the right kind and grade of goods at the right price, and to secure delivery of the right quantity at the right time and place. Buying at the right price means that one has the ability to compete on a cost basis. Securing proper deliveries means that the merchant does not lose sales due to lack of goods for timely display and that the industrialist does not suffer costly production delays.

SUPPLIERS—SELECTION AND RELATIONS

Selection of suppliers depends on a number of factors. Before making a choice of vendors, however, the purchaser must know the materials or merchandise to be purchased, including details of construction, quality and grade, intended use, maintenance or care required, as well as style factors and their importance. In addition, the buyer for the small factory must know how different grades and qualities of raw materials affect various manufacturing processes.

Supplier's Price Quotations

Knowing what materials and/or merchandise are needed, the purchaser is ready to consider and select a supplier. One of the most important considerations is the supplier's price quotations relative to prices of other suppliers. Quantity price discounts and shipping charges require attention in the comparison of price quotations. Price differences are significant if other factors are equal or do not offset price advantages.

Price considerations force attention to quality and its verification. The buyer should know the standards and specifications applying to the items purchased. These are dictated by actual use requirements. The supplier must meet the product specifications if he is to be retained as a supplier. The buyer, however, must still inspect and test incoming items to make sure that the goods meet specifications. Of course, some quality differences are difficult to detect and a number of items, varying in quality, may all be satisfactory. The issue is not always clear cut.

Vendor Quality Ratings

Corollary to this factor is the need for vendor quality ratings. On some types of material purchases, statistical controls may be used; for example, p charts (refer to Figure 10-2) may be prepared on the basis of receiving room inspection, with the ratio defective on all inbound shipments from a specific vendor computed and plotted on the chart. In this way, the buying firm obtains an overall or average quality rating for each vendor. This does two things for the buyer. First, it enables the buyer to protest—with concrete supporting evidence to back the protest—deficiencies in quality of incoming shipments and to claim allowances. Second, it enables the buyer to work with the vendor to upgrade quality or to cease buying if quality improvement cooperation is withheld by the supplier.

Supplier's Abilities and Services

Attention must also be directed to the supplier's ability to meet delivery schedules promptly. In the small factory, continuity of operations is necessary to minimize production costs. In the small retail store, failure of goods to arrive on schedule might result in a substantial loss of business.

The kinds and quality of services provided by the supplier must also be considered. Extension of credit by suppliers provides a major portion of working capital requirements of many small firms. Some suppliers are helpful in providing merchandising aids, planning sales promotions, and furnishing management advice. In times of depression, some small retailers have even received direct financial assistance from major suppliers of long standing. Another important service is the provision of repair services by the supplier.

Supplier's Reputation

One less tangible factor is the general reputation of the supplier. This may be implied by some of the factors mentioned above but deserves specific identification. Can one depend upon the supplier's word regarding quality and delivery dates? Does the supplier stand behind his goods, making prompt adjustments on legitimate claims? Any weaknesses of this sort constitute a major question mark in vendor selection.

Sources of Supply

The small firm will find a number of ways in which to learn of the existence of particular suppliers. On important purchases, the small business owner should actively search for new sources of supply. Perhaps the best lead to new suppliers is the supplier's traveling representative. Other possibilities include (1) trade association listings, (2) advertising for bids, (3) the company's own files, (4) trade literature advertising, and (5) directories of manufacturers.

Relations with Suppliers

Good relations with suppliers are essential for firms of any size, but they are particularly important to small businesses. The small buyer, because of his lack of financial strength, is sometimes at the mercy of the supplier. In periods of business recession and depression, many small firms are on "thin ice." They may go under if the supplier refuses deliveries because of questionable credit standing or lack of a good relationship. Even with a satisfactory credit position, the small firm may be discriminated against by the supplier if the materials ordered are distinctly scarce. The supplier might then allocate the total supply to certain choice customers, refusing deliveries to the given small firm.

Even in periods of prosperity, the small firm has much to gain by maintaining good relationships with major suppliers. Materials and equipment suppliers do not regard themselves as business consultants. Nevertheless, they make available to small manufacturing firms management advice and information on the development of new materials, equipment, and tooling. On occasion, they even extend financial assistance. If small buyers find themselves in straitened circumstances, they may be allowed exceptional credit terms. Wholesalers and manufacturers selling to industrial consumers and retailers provide similar services to them. For small retailers they will also provide merchandising aids and management counsel. All this is in addition to regularly extended services. Thus, sellers can be of material assistance at all times, regardless of what the prevailing business conditions may be.

The Suppliers Can Call the Tune. Perhaps the cornerstone of good supplier relationships is found in the small buyer's realization that the supplier is more important to the buyer than the buyer (as a customer) is to the supplier. The buyer is only one among dozens, hundreds, or perhaps thousands trading with that supplier. Moreover, the small buyer's volume of purchases over a year and the size of the individual orders are often so small that the business could be eliminated without great loss to the supplier. Small orders cost as much to process and fill as large orders, and they may be unprofitable to the supplier. Hence, in the interest of improving supplier relationships, the small firm should buy in as large a quantity as is consistent with its own sales volume and inventory turnover rate. Incidentally, this is a good argument for buying from one major supplier rather than scattering orders among several suppliers.

Fair Play Is the Best Policy. To implement the policy of fair play and cultivate good relations, the small customer firm should try to observe the following practices:

1. Pay all bills promptly.
2. See all traveling sales representatives promptly, according them a full, courteous hearing.
3. Accord confidential treatment to information obtained from the supplier or his representative (including price quotation, amounts of formal bids, and data as to newly developed materials).
4. Avoid "rush" orders, lest the supplier lose faith in all such requests.
5. Present complaints and damage claims promptly, with full supporting evidence.
6. Inform the supplier of receipt of inspection quality rating (established via p-charting) and seek to cooperate for its improvement.
7. Do not summarily cancel orders merely to gain a temporary advantage.
8. Do not argue over prices, attempting to browbeat the supplier into special concessions and unusual discounts. Even if these are finally given in the attempt to get the order, a bad impression is left with the supplier.
9. Cooperate with the supplier by making suggestions for product improvement and/or cost reduction whenever possible. Also, permit the supplier to make suggestions, such as the use of a standard part in replacement of a part made to your specifications (adopting any such suggestion which can be successfully used).
10. If gifts are returned or reciprocal purchase contracts refused, give a courteous explanation of the reasons underlying the decision.

If buying officers for small firms are tactful, courteous, friendly, and good listeners, they should be able to build better relationships with suppliers. Moreover, small buyers must remember that it takes a long time to build good relationships with a supplier, but that good relations can be destroyed by one ill-timed, tactless act.

Summary

1. The importance of purchasing is based upon the close connection between the buying and the resale of products by marketing institutions and upon the critical need for a specified quality of raw materials in most industrial processes.

2. The major purchasing functions are the issuance of purchase orders; maintenance of buying and warehousing records; and, through collaboration with production and engineering, the determination of materials consumption standards.

3. Purchasing policies should cover such objectives as confidential treatment of price quotations, reciprocal buying, ethical practices, making or buying of component parts, use of new or substitute materials, purchase discounts, concentration of purchases, and purchase quantities.

4. In deciding whether to make or buy a particular part or assembly, the manufacturer must balance such factors as existence of idle capacity and dependence upon outside suppliers against other such factors as cheaper manufacturing by a specialized producer and shortage of equipment or skilled personnel.

5. In determining purchase quantities, the purchaser must decide whether to buy merely to meet needs of the business or whether also to engage in speculative buying. In buying to meet business needs, there is the further question of the economic purchase quantity.

6. Choice of a supplier entails consideration of the supplier's price, quality, ability to meet delivery schedules, quality of service, and general reputation.

7. Factory buying involves control procedures on standard stock items, bills of materials covering special requirements, price quotations, purchase orders, written records, and budgetary controls.

8. In wholesale and retail establishments, purchase quantities are determined by a proper combination of expected sales and inventory levels.

9. Buying efficiency may be evaluated by measuring the cost of buying and the extent to which the purchasing objective has been fulfilled.

10. Good relations with suppliers are important and require consistent, fair purchasing policies and practices on the part of the small firm.

Discussion Questions

1. What conditions make the function of purchasing a particularly vital one for any given business?

2. When should authority to buy be retained by the owner? When should it be delegated to subordinates? Consider the specific example of a small department store in formulating your answer.

3. Of what value are purchasing records to a small firm?

4. What weaknesses or difficulties might be involved in assigning the purchasing officer such related functions as receiving room operation and storeskeeping? Explain.

5. How would the policy of reciprocal buying apply, if at all, to a (a) food wholesaler, (b) plumbing contractor, (c) taxi company, (d) shoe repair shop, (e) service station, and (f) jewelry store?

6. Is there anything unethical in the owner of a small firm accepting complimentary passes to baseball or football games from a prospective supplier? How about the acceptance of somewhat larger gifts?

7. Summarize the arguments in favor of outside purchasing instead of manufacturing parts within the particular firm.

8. What is the magnitude of the loss under the banker's rule if purchase discounts permitted by terms of 1/10, n/20 are not taken?

9. Compare the arguments for and against the concentration of purchases with one or two sources of supply.

10. What is "hand-to-mouth" buying? What costs are associated with it?

11. Under what conditions would it be least dangerous to engage in speculative buying? Is speculative buying more dangerous for a small retailer of furniture than for a large department store? More dangerous for a small grocery store than for a grocery chain?

12. Is price of greater importance than quality in the selection of a supplier? What bearing does the type of business have on this question?

13. Suggest several types of help that might be available to small firms from suppliers?

14. What is a "bill of materials," and how is it related to purchasing?

15. What specific practices are necessary for a small manufacturer of belts and leather novelties to maintain good relations with his suppliers?

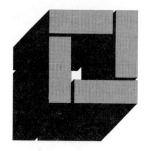

11

Customer Credit Practices

Nearly all business firms buy and sell on credit. This chapter focuses attention on the granting of credit by a business to its customers. Chapter 14 deals with the use of credit as a source of financing.

NATURE AND USEFULNESS OF CREDIT

Credit is the selling of goods or services subject to some form of deferred payment, with current delivery of goods if any are involved, and with transfer of title normally accompanying delivery. Transfer of title is sometimes delayed, as in conditional sales installment contracts.

Classes of Credit

There are two broad classes of credit—consumer credit and trade credit. *Consumer credit* is granted by retailers to final consumers purchasing for personal or family use. *Trade credit* is extended by nonfinancial firms, such as manufacturers or wholesalers, to customers which are other business firms.

These two categories of credit differ in a number of respects. Consumer credit information is obtained from local credit bureaus, and the sources which can be contacted for supplementary credit information are limited. Trade credit ratings, on the other hand, are available from national credit agencies, such as Dun & Bradstreet, and sources of supplementary data are more numerous. Consumer and trade credit differ also as to types of credit instruments used and sources for financing receivables. Still another important distinction is the availability of credit insurance for trade credit only. Finally, they differ markedly as to terms of sale.

Trade Credit Terms

Business firms usually purchase goods on open account; their purchases are subject to specified terms of sale, such as 2/10, n/30. This means that a two percent discount is given by the seller if the buyer pays within 10 days. Failure to take this discount makes the full amount of the invoice due in 30 days. Other discount arrangements in common use are listed below.

Sales Term	Explanation
3/10, 1/15, n/60	Three percent discount for first 10 days; one percent discount for 15 days; bill due net on 60th day.
M.O.M.	Billing will be on the 15th of the month, including all purchases made since the middle of the prior month.
E.O.M.	Billing at end of month, covering all credit purchases of that month.
C.O.D.	Amount of bill will be collected upon delivery of the goods.
2/10, n/30, R.O.G.	Two percent discount for 10 days; bill due net on 30th day—but both discount period and 30 days start from the date of receipt of the goods, not from the date of the sale.
2/10, n/30, M.O.M.	Two percent discount for 10 days; bill due net on 30th day—but both periods start from the 15th of the month following the sales date.
2/10, n/30, E.O.M.	Two percent discount for 10 days; bill due net on 30th day—but both periods start from the end of the month in which the sale was made.

Another sort of business buying on credit involves the use of "extended datings," which are common in seasonal industry selling. Extended datings have the effect of deferring the buyer's payments. For example, payments due on an invoice may be 10 percent after 30 days, 20 percent after 60 days, 30 percent after 90 days, and the remaining 40 percent after 120 days. This will give the small independent dealers, who buy seasonal goods from a manufacturer, time to obtain funds for payment by reselling the goods.

Sales terms are affected by the kind of product sold and by the buyer's and seller's circumstances. The credit period often varies directly with the length of the buyer's turnover period, which obviously depends on the type of product sold. The larger the order and the higher the credit rating of the buyer, the better the sales terms that can be granted if individual sales terms are fixed for each customer. The greater the financial strength and the more adequate and liquid the working capital of the seller, the more generous the seller's sales terms can be. Of course, no business can afford to allow competitors to outdo it in reasonable generosity of sales terms. In many lines of business, credit terms are so firmly set by tradition that a unique policy is difficult if not impossible.

Types of Consumer Credit Accounts

The four major kinds of consumer credit accounts are ordinary charge accounts, installment accounts, budget accounts, and revolving credit accounts. Many variations of these also are used. The most desirable type of account depends upon such factors as the kind of merchandise, the customer's financial position and income, and the customer's ability to budget expenditures and to stick to a budget.

Charge Accounts. The ordinary charge account results from charging merchandise when purchased, with payment due when the bill is sent to the customer. Stated terms typically call for payment at the end of the month, but customary practice allows a longer period for payment than that stated. The charge account is best used for recurring family expenditures. Small department store accounts provide a good example of such use. Use of the charge account for irregular purchases in large amounts should be avoided because of the difficulty of paying the entire bill at one time.

Installment Accounts. The installment account is the vehicle of long-term consumer credit. It is useful to the consumer for large purchases, such as automobiles, washing machines, and television sets. It is evident from Figure 11-1 that most consumer credit is of this type.

A down payment is normally required, carrying charges are added to the cost, and the most common payment periods are from 12 to 36 months. The down payment should typically be 20 percent or more. Only reasonable carrying charges should be made.

The merchant must also determine, in view of the state laws, whether the credit should be secured by a conditional sales contract or a chattel mortgage. Both of these permit repossession if the customer defaults a payment. Under a conditional sales contract, legal title to the product does not pass until the customer makes his last payment; immediate repossession is possible in case a payment is defaulted. When a chattel mortgage is used, legal title passes when the sale is made but is subject to the dealer's lien. When a payment is defaulted, the dealer can take court action to repossess and resell the goods.

Budget Accounts. The budget account, sometimes called an extended-payment account, might be defined as a short-term installment account. It results from charge purchases in amounts typically ranging from $100 to $200, and payment is ordinarily spread over a period of three months. Purchase of a power lawn mower or a set of tires, for example, might be financed in this way. This service is readily extended by many small merchants, but a service charge normally is added to the price when payments are deferred over 90 days. Monthly statements are usually not sent, which eliminates billing cost and places the responsibility for adhering to payment schedules on the customers.

Revolving Credit Accounts. The revolving credit account is another variation of the installment account. The merchant may grant a line of credit up to $200 or $300, for example, and the customer may then charge purchases at any time if purchases do not exceed this credit limit. A specified percentage of the outstanding balance must be paid monthly, which forces the customer to budget and limits the amount of debt that can be carried. Interest is computed on the unpaid balance at the end of the month.

Benefits to Businesses, Customers, and Society

If credit buying and selling did not pay both parties to the transaction, its use would cease. Businessmen give credit to customers because they can obtain increased sales volume by so doing. They also expect the increase in revenue to more than offset the cost of credit selling, so that profits will be larger.

Buyers benefit also from credit operations. The most obvious advantage is the deferred payment privilege. A merchant can sell the merchandise before remitting to the supplier, and an ultimate consumer can buy an automobile or television set without paying cash. The consumer is thus able to enjoy a higher standard of living than he otherwise could.

There is also a social impact of credit selling. When new sales on credit exceed total payments for the same period, the economic effect is inflationary. Until full employment is reached, however, the result is beneficial. When repayments exceed new credit sales, the effect is deflationary. A decline in business activity may consequently be aggravated by credit contraction.

By permitting more people to purchase more goods and services, credit has made possible the mass consumption of goods necessary for mass production. Furthermore, the judicious extension of credit by suppliers to small firms supplies working capital to them and also permits continuation of marginal businesses that would otherwise expire. Later on, such firms can make it "on their own."

It may be noted, however, that independent businessmen have little concern for the social impact of credit selling. Their one objective in extending credit is to enhance sales and profits.

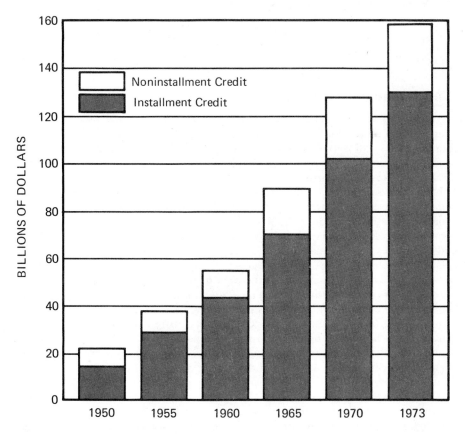

Figure 11-1
AMOUNT OF U.S. CONSUMER CREDIT FOR SELECTED YEARS
Source: *Statistical Abstract of the United States*, 1973, p. 455.

Extent of Use of Credit in the American Economy

Credit selling has expanded greatly during the past few decades. As indicated by Figure 11-1, outstanding consumer credit in the United States increased more than sevenfold between 1950 and 1973. The use of trade credit (that is, credit granted to other business concerns) has also grown in recent years. Thus, the function of credit management is increasing in importance in small firms. Nearly 80 percent of consumers now use some form of debt.

It seems clear that manufacturing and wholesaling concerns extend much more credit in proportion to sales than do retailers. Estimates suggest that 90 percent or more of industrial and wholesale sales are credit sales, whereas some 40 percent of retail sales are thought to be on a credit basis. Some of the reasons accounting for the greater use of credit by wholesale and industrial firms are:

1. Physical separation of buyer and seller.
2. Working capital needs of the buyer.
3. Buyer's desire to inspect goods prior to payment.
4. Reduction of risk in transfers of large amounts of cash.

Such a widespread and expanding use of credit selling would seem sufficient to attest its importance—both to sellers and customers.

Development of Credit Cards

The history of credit cards began around 1914, a year which saw major city department stores first issue credit cards to customers with proved credit standings. The objective was faster consummation of credit sales. Holders of cards could gain credit approval merely by submitting their cards. This also reduced customer waiting time and inconvenience.

The next significant development was the issuance of credit cards by large oil companies. Again, these sought to limit issuance of cards to individuals with good credit standings, duly checked after dealer recommendation. Eventually, potential cardholders with good credit standings became identifiable, and the oil companies began issuance of unsolicited cards. Again, credit selling became faster and safer.

The third development lay in the area of travel and expense credit cards. Diners' Club cards were first issued in 1950. Subsequently, Carte Blanche cards entered the competition, followed in 1958 by American Express Cards.

Applicants for credit cards complete application blanks showing employment and other personal data. The application blank also specifies the annual membership charge and asks for designation of the account as business or personal in nature. A thorough screening and card issuance or rejection then follows.[1]

Credit cards are honored by many hotels and motels, restaurants, service stations, and airlines, thus making almost cashless travel possible. Other services frequently available include low-cost group accident and life insurance,

---

[1] Today some clubs and oil companies screen potential card holders and, after they are approved, invite them by mail to accept a credit card.

hospital service and (in many major cities) medical treatment, and opportunities to purchase certain merchandise at bargain prices. In all cases, the holder enjoys both the convenience of credit almost anywhere and the tax benefit of proof of business travel expenses.

Bank Credit Cards. In 1951 the Franklin National Bank, Franklin Square, New York, issued the first bank credit cards. This is now the most important development in the credit card movement. By 1953, some 100 banks had emulated its example, but most of these found the cost too great and discontinued credit card operations. In 1958, a second group of larger banks began the issuance of credit cards, including Bank of America and Chase Manhattan. Chase sold its credit card business in 1962, and some others also discontinued their operations. Banks that continued operations in this field gradually brought their operating costs down, until finally profits emerged, largely through computerized procedures. A third wave of bank credit card issuance started in Pittsburgh in 1965. Then, in 1966, Bank of America set up a network of franchise-holding banks for issuance of its BankAmericard. Soon after, Interbank was created (as an association of banks) and issued Master Charge cards.

The banks have resorted to mass issuance of unsolicited cards to individuals with approved credit standings and to computerized handling of merchants' accounts in order to hold down costs and gain the volume required for profitable operations. Most individual banks discontinued their own cards and joined one or the other of the networks (BankAmericard and Master Charge), which became the two dominant bank credit card systems. At the start of 1970, there were some 24 million cardholders, as against two or three million a decade earlier. There were also 5,000 participating banks, as against some 500 in 1960.

Participating banks are franchised and recommend merchants for account holding and participation. Banks also authorize issuance of membership cards to persons of good credit standing. Consumers can then purchase on credit from a wide variety of retail establishments. Credit buyers buy several times as much as cash buyers, per sale and in total. They pay all accounts to one source, a distinct convenience. The banks have merchants report sales, sales returns and allowances, and other credits on special forms, charging and crediting their deposit accounts accordingly. The necessary speed in record keeping is provided by computerization of the transactions.

Nonparticipating banks may, at some future date, find themselves disadvantaged through loss of too many business depositors. Very small banks cannot afford computers and so cannot seek a franchise from a network.

Implications of Expanded Use of Credit Cards. The unsolicited bank credit card could cause the consumers to buy on credit beyond their means, particularly if the issuing bank establishes too high credit limits for them. Many banks have been accused of wholesale distribution of cards without adequate evaluation. The ease of buying on credit constitutes a real temptation—and perhaps, in some cases, a solvency threat as well. Of course, unsolicited credit cards merely irritate some recipients, so that the cards are never used—or are little used.

The participating retailer pays fees of four percent on sales made, together with a joining fee, in order to participate. There are also cash accommodation fees, merchant membership advertising fees, and rental charges for imprinting machines used for recording sales. The merchant gains from increased sales volume and from elimination of certain record keeping costs. Individual sales are more quickly accomplished also.

There are social implications in all this. If a cashless society is eventually achieved along this line of development, merchants' total costs might increase, thus causing overall higher prices to consumers. This could occur even though unit fixed costs are reduced by the larger sales volume. In addition, the growth of use of bank credit cards may cause inflationary pressures. Insofar as the public uses credit cards for buying that otherwise would not have occurred, this will be true.

THE DECISION TO RUN A CASH OR CREDIT BUSINESS

Nearly all small businesses can sell on credit if they wish, and so the entrepreneur must decide whether to sell for cash or on credit. In some cases this is reduced to the question, "Can granting of credit to customers be avoided?" Credit selling is standard trade practice in many lines of business, and in other businesses, credit-selling competitors will always outsell the cash-selling firm.

It should be obvious that most manufacturers and wholesalers—one exception being the small group of cash-and-carry wholesalers—must extend credit to customers. It seems equally obvious that many small retailers do have a choice of a cash or credit business, especially in the merchandising of non-durable, lower-priced goods. Even in retailing, however, the trend is toward more credit sales, so that pressure to extend credit to customers is increasing.

Limiting Factors Affecting Credit Decision

Numerous factors bear on the decision concerning credit extension. The seller always hopes to increase profits by credit sales, but each business must also consider its own particular circumstances and environment. Among the pertinent factors requiring consideration are the following:

Type of Business. Retailers of durable goods, for example, typically grant credit more freely than small grocers who sell perishables. Indeed, most consumers find it necessary to buy appliances and automobiles on an installment basis; the product's life makes installment selling possible.

Credit Policy of Competitors. Unless a firm offers some compensating advantage, it is expected to be as generous as its competitors in extending credit. Wholesale hardware companies and retail furniture stores are businesses that face stiff competition from credit sellers.

Occupation and Income Level of Customers. The occupation and income level of customers are significant factors in determining a retailer's credit policy. Consider, for example, a corner drugstore adjacent to a city high school; high school students are typically unsatisfactory credit customers because of their lack of maturity and income.

Availability of Adequate Working Capital. There is no denying the fact that credit sales increase the amount of working capital needed. Money that the business has tied up in open-credit and installment accounts cannot be used to pay business expenses.

Profitability of Credit Operations

It is axiomatic that income-creating benefits should exceed expense-increasing disadvantages to justify credit operations. For those firms that have an option, particularly in the retail field, it may be well to reflect on the pros and cons of credit extension.

The major objective in granting credit is an expansion of sales by attracting new customers and an increase in volume and regularity of purchases by existing customers. Some retail firms—tire dealers, for example—cater to newcomers in the city, newly married couples, and others by inviting the credit business of individuals with established credit ratings. In addition, credit records may be used for purposes of sales promotion by direct mail appeals to credit customers. Adjustments and exchanges of goods are also facilitated through credit operations.

Offsetting these advantages to some degree are the increased costs associated with credit sales. Additional bookkeeping expense in recording sales and billing customers illustrates this type of cost. These costs are discussed in greater detail later in the chapter.

Development of a Credit Policy

The independent entrepreneur must weigh the advantages and costs of credit extension. Normally a decision to extend or not to extend credit precedes the starting of business operations, but it is possible to transform a cash-and-carry business into a credit-granting enterprise, and vice versa. This decision is important for future business success no matter when it is made. If the decision is for credit operations, as so often occurs because of the advantages, competitive pressures, and the other factors discussed above, then additional problems present themselves. The progressive entrepreneur will face up to these problems.

There is often a dangerous tendency for the owner of the small firm to "do what comes naturally" with respect to credit. Decisions concerning credit extension and credit terms are made on the spur of the moment without consideration of fundamental principles that might serve to keep credit under control. To avoid this danger, it is desirable to plan carefully each facet of the firm's credit policy.

Place of the Credit Manager in an Organization

In the very small business, the volume of credit work may not justify the use of a separate credit manager; therefore, the entrepreneur must undertake credit management as an additional task. Other small business firms—furniture stores, for example—often find the volume of credit work such as to call for a full-time or part-time credit manager. This individual's position and functions in the organization both require precise definition.

If the credit manager is placed under the company treasurer, who is typically pessimistic about borderline credit risks, sales and profits may be unnecessarily reduced by the treasurer's insistence upon rejection of all borderline risks. Conversely, some companies place the credit manager under the authority of the sales manager. This is often unfortunate also because the sales manager is desirous of increasing sales as much as possible. Hence, the sales manager is characteristically too optimistic about borderline credit risks.

Preferably, the credit manager should be independent in position in order to be objective and impartial in decisions about credit risks. Borderline risks that are probably safe should be approved, to enhance sales and profits; those probably unsafe should be rejected, to reduce bad debt losses and conserve working capital.

TO WHOM AND HOW MUCH CREDIT TO EXTEND

Most firms can expand sales simply by extending more credit. However, if a firm is careless in approving credit applications, bad debt losses may exceed the profit on the additional volume. To avoid unnecessary losses, therefore, the seller must evaluate the credit standing of each prospective customer. Although credit evaluation does not eliminate all risk, it permits the rejection of applications that involve the greatest risk.

The Four Credit Questions

In evaluating the credit standing of applicants, the entrepreneur must answer the following questions:

1. Can the buyer pay as promised?
2. Will the buyer pay?
3. If so, when will the buyer pay?
4. If not, can the buyer be forced to pay?

The answers to questions 1, 2, and 4 must be "yes" and to question 3, "on schedule," before credit is approved. The answers depend in part on the amount of credit requested and in part on the seller's estimate of the buyer's ability and willingness to pay. Such an estimate constitutes a judgment of the buyer's inherent credit worth, a subject discussed in the following section.

Basis of Credit

Every credit applicant possesses credit worth in some degree so that extended credit is not necessarily a gift to the applicant. Instead, a decision to grant credit merely recognizes the buyer's earned credit standing. That is, the seller decides that the buyer can pay and probably will pay when the account is due. But the seller faces a possible inability or unwillingness to pay on the buyer's part. In making credit decisions, therefore, the seller decides the degree of risk of nonpayment that must be assumed.

At the time a seller makes a credit sale, the buyer's willingness and ability to pay must be evaluated. Willingness to pay is evaluated in terms of the applicant's *character*. Ability to pay depends upon the applicant's *capital* and *capacity*—and upon the prevailing economic *conditions*. These "four C's of credit" constitute the basis of credit[2] and are discussed below as a background for judging ability and willingness to pay. Together these "four C's" reside in the credit applicant, to be perceived and evaluated by the credit grantor.

Character. Character refers to the fundamental integrity and honesty which should underlie all human and business relationships. In the case of business customers, it takes shape in the business policies and ethical practices of the firm in its operations as a business citizen of the community. Applicants for credit must also be known to be morally responsible persons.

Capital. Capital consists of the cash and other assets owned by the business or individual customer. In the case of a business customer, this means capital sufficient to underwrite planned operations. There should be adequate owner-invested capital.

Capacity. Possession of this trait indicates that the customer is capable of conserving assets and faithfully and efficiently following financial plans. The business customer with capacity utilizes the invested capital of the business firm wisely and capitalizes to the fullest extend on business opportunities.

Conditions. As a result of business cycles and changes in price levels, economic conditions result which may be either favorable or unfavorable to payment of debts. Other adverse factors might include fires and other natural disasters, advent or termination of war, new legislation, strong new competition, or labor trouble. Certainly, prevailing conditions may augment or limit the customer's ability to pay.

Credit Investigation of Applicants

In most retail stores, the first step in credit investigation is the completion of an application form, an example of which appears in Figure 11-2 on page 178. The information obtained on this form is used as the basis for examining the applicant's financial responsibility. Local credit bureaus and credit investigating agencies are often consulted in connection with such investigations. Because these outside agencies are used to evaluate credit standing and to establish credit limits, they are discussed in more detail on pages 180 and 181.

The small manufacturer should similarly investigate credit applicants. One small clothing manufacturer has every sales order reviewed by a Dun & Bradstreet trained credit man, who maintains a complete file of D&B credit reports on all of the several hundred customers. Recent financial statements of dealer-customers are filed also. These, together with the dealer's account receivable card, are the basis for decisions on credit sales. The major emphasis

---

[2] Around the turn of the century, a noted financier and venture capitalist said that he would provide anyone with CHARACTER and CAPACITY with the necessary capital for launching a business, thus suggesting that only two factors are really needed. However, the borrower's capital position and the prevailing economic conditions would either facilitate payment or make it difficult.

THE MODEL STORE

CREDIT APPLICATION BLANK

Date _____

Credit Limit Requested _____ Set _____

IDENTIFICATION

Name of applicant _____ Age _____
Present address _____
Last prior address _____

EMPLOYMENT

Employer _____
Employer's address _____
Position held _____
How long employed _____

FINANCIAL STATUS

Monthly salary _____
Securities owned _____
Amount of life insurance carried _____
Home owned ( ) Rented ( )
        Value _____ Mortgage _____
        Monthly payment _____ Monthly rent _____
Other income _____
             _____
Bank account with _____ Average balance _____

FAMILY DATA

Ages of children, if any _____
Ages of other dependents _____

CREDIT BUREAU REPORT FINDINGS _____
_____
_____

4 Trade references_____
                   _____
                   _____
                   _____
Sales terms _____

NOTICE: Interest will be charged at 1½% per month on amounts past due 60 days.

_____
                            Signature of Applicant

Figure 11-2
CREDIT APPLICATION BLANK

is on the D&B credit reports. Credit limits are set at the time of the initial sale in ratio to the dealer's latest year's sales. They are reviewed with each new sale.

Factors to Consider in Fixing Credit Limits

Having selected a credit customer, the next problem ordinarily is "how much?" (As a practical matter, of course, these questions are often answered simultaneously.) The proper credit limit for a given customer depends upon a number of factors. Perhaps the most important is the customer's ability to pay the obligation when it becomes due. This in turn requires an evaluation of the customer's financial resources, debt position, and income level.

The type of credit required by the customer is the second factor that requires consideration. Customers of a drugstore need only small amounts of credit. On the other hand, business customers of wholesalers and manufacturers typically expect larger amounts of credit because it is needed and because competing vendors will grant their credit requests.

In the special case of installment selling, the amount of credit should not exceed the repossession value of the goods sold. Automobile dealers follow this rule as a general practice.

Sources of Credit Information

One of the most important and frequently neglected sources of credit data is found in the accounts receivable records of the seller. Properly analyzed, these present the past payment experience of the vendor company with its credit customers. They show whether the customer regularly takes cash discounts and, if not, whether the account is typically slow.

Pertinent data may also be obtained from outsiders. Arrangements may be made with other suppliers to exchange credit data. Although these arrangements may be informal, there are organizations of credit managers established to facilitate the exchange of ledger information. Such credit interchange reports are quite useful in learning about the sales and payment experiences of others with one's own credit customers or applicants.

A third source of credit data, on commercial accounts particularly, is the customer's banker. Some bankers are glad to supply credit information about their depositors, considering this a service in helping them to obtain credit in amounts they can successfully handle. Other bankers feel that credit information is confidential and should not be disclosed in this way.

The use of financial statements, local credit bureaus, and large credit agencies as sources of credit information is sufficiently important to justify separate discussion below.

Financial Statements. Manufacturers and wholesalers frequently can use financial statements submitted by firms applying for credit as an additional source of information. Obtaining maximum value from this source requires a careful ratio analysis of the statements which will reveal working capital position, profit-making potential, and general financial health of the firm. (Ratio analysis is discussed in Chapter 20).

Working capital position must be determined to be satisfactory or unsatisfactory in the light of industry standards. It is also very important to know whether the working capital position is improving or deteriorating.

Profit-making potential is evaluated by a comparison of actual with average profits for the type of business. Comparisons make it possible for the seller to determine whether profits are satisfactory in amount and whether they are on the uptrend or downtrend.

Determination of the general financial health of the firm in question is obviously important. Of particular interest is the ratio of owner investment to creditors' equity in the assets. Overinvestment in fixed assets or in inventories would also be dangerous.

Supplementary information, too, is of value to a credit manager in analyzing a credit risk. It may come from the applicant or from other sources. For example, the fact that a customer firm's officers "play" the stock market with company funds, or that they gamble on horse races, would be damaging information so far as a favorable verdict on a credit application is concerned. Or, the information that the applicant's inventory consists of shopworn or obsolete items would be helpful in correctly evaluating the applicant's working capital position.

Local Credit Bureaus. A credit bureau serves its members—who are retailers and other firms in a given community selling to final consumers—by summarizing the credit experience of bureau members with particular individuals. A local bureau can also broaden its service by affiliation with either the National Retail Credit Association or the Associated Credit Bureaus of America. This makes possible the exchange of credit information on persons who move from one city to another.

Some valuable services provided by local credit bureaus are:

1. Issuance of written and telephone credit reports on credit applicants.
2. Investigation of newcomers in the city in anticipation of requests for credit data.
3. Notification service to member firms, warning them that given customers have become poor credit risks.
4. Skip-tracing to locate debtors who move to other cities without leaving a forwarding address.
5. Collection of past-due accounts.

Of these services, the most important is the reporting of customers' credit standings. The usual credit report covers such items as the following:

1. Credit accounts maintained by the credit applicant, how long they have been maintained, dates of last purchases, balances due, and promptness of payment.
2. Ownership or rental of home. If the latter, promptness of payments is stipulated.
3. Evaluation of income and income sources.
4. Employment data, including position held and length of service.
5. Character evaluation and police record, if any.

A merchant need not be a member of some bureaus in order to get a credit report. The fee charged to nonmembers, however, is considerably higher than that charged to members.

Credit Agencies. Trade credit agencies are privately owned and operated organizations which collect credit information on business firms. These data are analyzed and evaluated, after which credit ratings are made available to client companies for a fee. They are concerned with trade credit ratings only, having nothing to do with consumer credit.

Dun & Bradstreet, Inc., is a general trade credit agency serving the nation. Manufacturers and wholesalers are especially interested in its reference book and credit reports. The reference book covers all U.S. businesses; it shows credit rating, financial strength, and other key credit information. It is available to subscribers only.

Periodic Review of Credit Limits

Factors underlying credit decisions can obviously change rapidly. For example, a customer firm may sign a large sales contract, discover a secret process, or hire a new president and thus gain in terms of economic advantage or managerial capacity. Credit data must be kept up to date. Periodic review of credit limits of customers is required, accordingly, with revision if and as necessary. Limits should also be reconsidered each time a new order threatens to carry a customer above the set limit, upon receipt of a new financial statement, or upon arrival of a new credit agency report.

Informing Customers of Credit Limits

There are arguments for and against informing customers of their credit limits. If the limits are inflexible, these should be indicated to the customers—particularly for any marginal account. Informing customers of their credit limits makes it easier to enforce the credit terms without stirring up resentment on their part. But, if new customers' credit limits are set too high, a potentially bad situation is created by informing them of their limits, for they might be tempted to overbuy. The final result could be lost customers as well as losses on bad debts. Informing customers of tight credit limits is unfortunate also if they reduce their purchases to stay within those limits despite business growth which warrants additional purchases.

RECORD KEEPING FOR CREDIT OPERATIONS

Record keeping for credit operations must be complete and accurate because the necessary paper work and organizational relationships can greatly affect the control of credit.

Credit Forms and Records

Depending upon the nature and extent of credit business, credit forms will be more or less elaborate. In the smallest organization—one in which there is personal acquaintance between seller and customer and only a few credit sales—the records may be extremely simple.

One of the key records is the file on each credit customer. In the case of trade credit, this may be a folder containing credit reports, financial statements, or other data on the customer. In the case of consumer credit, a card consisting of the applicant's original application with added entries to show his subsequent credit history may suffice. In either case, the record should indicate the credit standing and credit limit of the customer. Some firms, particularly in trade credit, find it desirable to supplement the folder with a card file that provides a quick reference to the customer's credit status.

Procedural Steps in Maintaining Credit Records

The essential steps in a sound procedure are few in number, but modifications and additions may be required as the business grows in size. Only the basic steps are described below.

Opening the Credit Account. Following investigation and approval of a new customer, credit records are established for this individual. These consist of the credit customer file folder or card and accounting ledger card or account.

Customer Identification and Sale Approval. Customer identification and sale approval should be a matter of routine. Written orders received by manufacturers, wholesalers, and other nonretailing firms may easily be checked to see that the sale does not exceed the customer's approved credit limit. Retail and service establishments sufficiently small to permit personal acquaintance between buyer and seller likewise have no difficulty with customer identification. Some small firms have enough customers, however, to require a formal procedure to identify the customer and approve the sale. Procedures for identification of customers include the following:

1. Word of customer. The clerks in one small drug chain, for example, simply ask, "Cash or charge?" If the customer says "Charge," the salesperson writes the customer's name on the completed sales slip and turns over the merchandise.
2. Informal identification. The procedure above may be improved by checking the customer's driver's license or other identifying papers.
3. Credit cards. Some firms, such as department stores, issue credit cards to each approved customer. Cards may also be prepared which can be used to imprint the customer's name and address on the sales slip, thus serving a double purpose.

These steps of identification may be supplemented by further checking to ascertain the customer's credit limit. In some organizations the salesclerks telephone the credit office, and, of course, contacts with credit managers in other stores are frequently made. If the customer has a credit card, however, small purchases are usually approved without further checking.

Recording Transactions. All credit sales, payments, returns, and other transactions are recorded on the customer's account. This is essentially a bookkeeping function and is generally performed outside the credit department if the business is departmentalized.

Billing Customers. In trade credit transactions, the invoice is typically forwarded at the time of shipment of the goods. Retail customers with open charge accounts, on the other hand, are typically billed monthly. In recent years, cycle billing has gained acceptance in contrast to the billing of all customers on the same date. With cycle billing, the accounts are arranged into groups of similar size, with different groups assigned to the different days of the month. This avoids a peak work load at the end of the month.

Review of Accounts. Some periodic review is desirable to detect delinquent accounts. In a simple system this may take the form of a periodic perusal of the ledger accounts. In other cases, it may require a tickler file to draw attention to those that become delinquent on each day.

CONTROLLING THE COST OF CREDIT

If a business firm extends credit to customers, increased expenses are almost inevitable. The following direct costs are related to credit sales:

1. Bookkeeping and billing costs.   4. Collection costs.
2. Financing costs.   5. Bad debts.
3. Credit investigations.

Increased bookkeeping expenses are usually the greatest of these, but each adds something to the total expenses of any firm with a substantial credit business. The final credit problem of the entrepreneur is the control of these expenses.

Use of Principles of Credit Control

Control of credit expense is made less difficult if the principles of credit discussed earlier are strictly observed. For example, a complete investigation of all credit applicants should produce credit customers who are less likely to become delinquent, and the business should thus experience lower collection costs and bad debt expense. Of course, such expenses could be reduced to nearly zero by sacrifice of considerable sales volume. A practical solution, however, seeks only to hold expenses within reasonable limits.

Expense Control Ratios

In controlling expenses associated with credit sales, it is possible to use various expense ratios. Ratios of this type are useful primarily in the analysis of trends and in comparisons with industry averages.

The best known and most widely-used ratio is the bad debt ratio, computed as follows:

$$\frac{\text{Bad Debts}}{\text{Total Credit Sales}} = \text{Bad Debt Ratio}$$

Typical ratios for selected small retail businesses are shown in Table 11-1 on page 184.

The bad debt ratio reflects the efficiency of credit policies and procedures. A small firm may thus compare the effectiveness of its credit management with

Table 11-1
BAD DEBT LOSS RATIOS OF SELECTED TYPES OF BUSINESS, 1969-1970

Type of Business	Bad Debt Loss Ratio
Apparel stores	.02%
New car dealers	.02%
Bookstores	.10%
Building materials dealers	.03%
Feed stores	.02%
Convenience food stores	.02%
Furniture stores	.83%
Gift shops	.02%
Dry cleaning shops	.03%
Liquor stores	.02%
Music stores	.02%
Pharmacies	.14%
Repair services	.04%
Service stations	.02%
Variety stores	.02%

Source: "Expenses in Retail Business," NCR Corporation, Dayton, Ohio, 1971, pp. 4, 6, 8, 14, 15, 17, 19, 27, 28, 32, 35, 36, and 40.

that of other firms. There is a relationship between the bad debt loss ratio on the one hand and the type of business, profitability, and size of firm on the other. Small profitable retail firms have a much higher loss ratio than large profitable retail concerns. Even though some small firms control credit adequately, the unfavorable experience of other small firms indicates a general deficiency and a need for improved credit management.

COLLECTION OF PAST-DUE ACCOUNTS

Slow accounts are a problem because:

1. They lead to losses from bad debts.
2. They tie up the seller's working capital.
3. They prevent further sales to the slow-paying customer.

Even if the customer is not lost, relations with this customer are strained for a time at least.

A Serious Problem in Small Firms

Bad debt losses of small business firms range from a fraction of one percent of net sales to percentages large enough to put the creditor firm out of business. Excessive bad debt losses are particularly troublesome in small firms because of the customary shortage of working capital. Furthermore, inadequate records and collection procedures often fail to alert the small firm in time to permit prompt collections. Also, the entrepreneur should not hesitate to apply pressure for payment even though he may know the customers personally, for it has been aptly said that "he who hesitates is lost."

Conceding the seriousness of the problem, the small firm must know what steps to take and how far to go in collecting past-due accounts. The small concern must decide whether to undertake the job directly or to turn it over to an attorney or a collection agency.

Collection Procedure

Perhaps the most effective weapon in collecting past-due accounts is the debtors' knowledge of possible impairment of their credit standing. This impairment is certain if an account is turned over to a collection agency. Delinquent customers who foresee continued solvency will typically attempt to avoid damage to their credit standing, particularly an impairment that would be known to the business community generally. It is this knowledge that lies behind and strengthens the various collection efforts of the business.

Promptness in detecting past-due accounts and initiating collection action is essential. If accounts are permitted to remain delinquent without action, they become that much more difficult to collect. Furthermore, some customers may be unimpressed with the urgency for payment of their accounts if the seller is lax in initiating and continuing collection efforts.

Most business firms have found the most effective collection procedure to consist of a series of steps each of which is somewhat more forceful than the preceding one. Although these typically begin with a gentle written reminder, they may include additional letters, telephone calls, registered letters, personal contacts, and referrals to collection agencies or attorneys. Timing of these steps may be carefully standardized so that step two automatically follows step one in a specified number of days, with subsequent steps similarly spaced.

Collection Letters

Because of their wide use in business, some discussion of collection letters is desirable. As a small business collection tool, it must be admitted that a personal contact may well prove superior at various stages. This is particularly true if the entrepreneur knows the customers personally; a friendly call may determine the cause of nonpayment and make possible a satisfactory arrangement for payment.

Nevertheless, collection letters are widely and often successfully used. The objective of a collection letter is to obtain payment while keeping the customer's goodwill. The tone of such a letter must accordingly be one of courtesy; the first communication often appears to be a strictly routine reminder. An interest-provoking, intriguing approach gets the best results, particularly when an initial reminder is unsuccessful. Probably a straightforward statement of the debt overdue will not succeed with most delinquents; something out of the ordinary in form and approach is required. As later letters in the collection series are found necessary and composed, the element of goodwill receives less emphasis while forceful expression is given to need for payment. Unfortunately some customers are aware of the series nature of collection letters and simply wait until postponement is no longer possible.

Use of Attorneys and Collection Agencies

Once the account appears uncollectible by ordinary methods, it should be turned over to an attorney or collection agency. Of course, the seller must be willing to accept the loss of a customer's future business when such a drastic step is taken. If an attorney is used, this person first investigates to determine the possibilities of collection out of court. If this is impossible, a lawsuit is logical, provided that the seller feels reasonably sure of winning and can collect the judgment.

Use of a collection agency is an equally serious and final step. Some credit managers prefer a collection agency to an attorney because an agency has more specialized experience and a buyer knows that refusal to pay will be broadcast widely by an agency. It is important to select a reputable agency if the business decides to use this approach.

At times, the mere threat of referring a delinquent account to an attorney or collection agency is sufficient to stimulate payment. If the customer has any desire to protect a credit reputation, the pressure for payment becomes greatest at this point.

THE USE OF CREDIT INSURANCE

Some small firms have the opportunity of insuring against certain credit losses. An intelligent decision concerning the use of credit insurance demands answers to such questions as the following:

1. What is credit insurance?
2. To whom is it available?
3. What particular advantages does it offer the small firm?
4. What are the customary provisions of such policies?

Nature of Credit Insurance

Credit insurance protects businesses from *abnormal* bad debt losses. It does not cover *normal* losses predictable on the basis of past business experience. The insurance company computes the *normal* rate on the basis of industry experience and the loss record of the particular firm being insured. Unusually high losses might result from a customer firm's insolvency due to tornado or flood losses, depressed industry conditions, business recession, or other factors.

Availability of Credit Insurance

Credit insurance is now available only to nonfinancial firms, such as manufacturers and wholesalers, who sell to other business firms. Thus, only trade credit may be insured. There are two reasons for this. The more important reason is found in the relative difficulty of analyzing business and ultimate consumer risks. The other reason is that retailers have a much greater number of accounts receivable, which are smaller and provide greater risk diversification, so that credit insurance is less acutely required. It may be noted also that retailers often know their customers personally, while manufacturers and wholesalers usually do not. Hence, there is a greater demand for trade credit insurance.

Credit Insurance and the Small Firm

In addition to general advantages of credit insurance, there are some specific reasons why it is particularly useful to the small firm. First, such firms often lack the financial stability necessary to withstand large unexpected losses. By its nature credit insurance is applicable to losses that exceed predictable amounts.

Secondly, the collection service of the insurance company makes available legal talent and experience that may otherwise be unavailable to a small firm. Furthermore, collection efforts of insurance companies are generally conceded to be superior to those of regular collection agencies.

A third factor, applicable in some cases, concerns the credit standing of many small firms that might use credit insurance. The credit rating of a firm that protects itself through credit insurance is enhanced. The seller can show his banker the steps that have been taken to avoid unnecessary risks and thus obtain more favorable consideration in securing bank credit.

Provisions of Credit Insurance Policies

It has already been noted that credit insurance is insurance against abnormal, rather than normal, bad debt losses, and that policies typically provide for a collection service on bad accounts. Although collection provisions vary, a common provision requires the insured to notify the insurance company within 90 days of the past due status of the account and to turn it in for collection after 90 days.

Although the vast majority of policies provide general coverage, policies may be secured to cover individual accounts. A ten percent, or higher, coinsurance requirement is included to limit the coverage to approximately the replacement value of the merchandise. Higher percentages of coinsurance are required for inferior accounts in order to discourage reckless credit extension by insured firms. Accounts are classified according to ratings by Dun & Bradstreet or ratings by other recognized agencies; premiums vary with account ratings.

 Summary

1. Credit selling is selling of goods and services subject to deferred payment, with title transfer normally accompanying delivery of goods. A majority of business firms buy and sell on credit.
2. There are two broad classes of credit—consumer credit and trade credit.
3. Trade credit terms are illustrated by the expression "2/10, n/30," which indicates the buyer is granted a two percent discount for payment within 10 days.
4. Four major kinds of consumer credit arrangements are ordinary charge accounts, installment accounts, budget accounts, and revolving credit accounts.

5. Extension of credit is of value to firms granting the credit, to customers, and to society as a whole.

6. Credit is used even more extensively in transactions among business firms than in sales to ultimate consumers.

7. Credit cards have become a significant force in retail credit selling. First issuers were large city department stores, followed by the major oil companies. Next, travel and expense cards came to the fore in the 1950s. Finally, bank credit cards were developed.

8. Two networks today dominate the bank credit card field: BankAmericard and Master Charge. Bank of America and Interbank, the original issuers, have franchised member banks to issue the actual cards to individuals with satisfactory credit standings, with participating mercantile firms having deposit accounts in the franchised bank. The bank keeps the records covering member firms' credit sales, billing consumers from a single source.

9. Some dangers are to be foreseen in bank credit cards. Franchised banks must computerize if operations are to be profitable, which tends to freeze out small banks. Small banks may eventually lose too many deposit accounts. Consumers may also be tempted by the credit card to overbuy on credit. Merchants may find costs of participation too great and quit. If overall costs are enlarged, higher retail prices would result. And the growth of use of bank credit cards could be inflationary during a period of inflation, as well as causing possible dislocations in access to credit for borrowers other than credit card holders.

10. The decision as to whether a firm should operate on a cash or credit basis is conditioned by such factors as the type of business, credit policy of competitors, income status of customers, and adequacy of working capital.

11. Development of a credit policy requires a balancing of the additional sales that result from credit extension against the increased costs of a credit business.

12. Choosing profitable credit customers requires an evaluation of the credit applicant's "four C's"—character, capital, capacity, and economic conditions.

13. Determining credit limits necessitates investigation of credit data of various types. In addition to reviewing previous experience with the applicant, the firm may analyze the applicant's financial statements and utilize the services of local credit bureaus and other credit agencies.

14. In controlling the cost of granting credit, attention must be given to bookkeeping costs, billing costs, financing costs, credit investigation costs, collection costs, and bad debt losses.

15. Among the organizational and procedural problems in the extension of credit are the establishment of credit records, stipulation of procedural steps, and definition of the credit manager's responsibilities and place in the organization.

16. Slow accounts are a serious business problem, threatening loss to the seller. They also tie up the seller's working capital and prevent further sales to the slow-paying customer.

17. Perhaps the most effective weapon in collecting a past-due account is the debtor's fear of possible impairment of his credit standing. In collecting such accounts, it may be necessary, as a last resort, to use an attorney or a collection agency.

18. Trade credit insurance is available to protect a business against abnormal bad debt losses.

Discussion Questions

1. What differences as a customer service are there in installment credit versus open-account credit? Do all customers view credit as a service?

2. What benefits can you suggest that come to the retailer who extends credit to his customers?

3. What values are inherent in the use of gasoline credit cards? Are the credit cards of the major oil companies of equal value to holders? Why?

4. Trace briefly the history of the development of bank credit cards. Also, explain their values to the franchised banks, retail firms participating, and consumers, respectively.

5. As a department store manager, suggest some sales promotion ideas you might use if you had access to credit records.

6. Why does wholesale trade show a larger proportion of credit business than does retail trade?

7. What would be the effect of incorporation on the credit standing of a small retail store? Defend your conclusion with at least one valid reason.

8. What values can you see in placing credit policies in written form in a small business?

9. What is the difference between consumer credit and trade credit?

10. Which of the costs involved in selling on credit appears most substantial? Why?

11. What is meant by the terms 2/10, n/30? Does it pay to take discounts?

12. What type of credit account would be most appropriate in the sale of (a) pianos, (b) groceries, (c) men's suits, (d) golf clubs, (e) motorboats?

13. What information is typically secured from the applicant on the credit application blank? Can you think of other data which should be collected in this way?

14. Which of the "four C's" seems most important in considering extension of credit to an ultimate consumer? Is the same true in extending credit to a manufacturer or wholesaler?

15. Describe the services provided by a local credit bureau.

16. What types of business might logically utilize the services of Dun & Bradstreet? How can a traveling salesman use state credit manuals to enhance his selling efficiency?

17. Why should credit insurance be limited to trade credit?

18. Should the small department store use cycle billing, or should it close its books on the 25th and mail statements in time to reach customers on the first of the next month?

19. What is wrong with placing the credit man under the sales manager of the business? Would this always be a bad practice?

20. Does the fact that a business is small make personal contact superior to letters in collecting past-due accounts?

21. If the small businessman has adequate investment to cover all of his working capital needs, does it cost him as much to sell on credit as it costs a company that must borrow? Why?

Case B-1

THE SCOUTMASTER *

Tom Daniels was one of several foremen working for Robert McGraw, the equipment manager of an independent telephone company. As shown in Exhibit 1 below, he had a number of two-men work crews under his supervision.

Yesterday morning, Daniels called in Jack Worley, a workcrew leader whose helper was off for the day, and gave him his assignment. He was to complete the hookup of a new automobile agency's switchboard. The cut-over time was 5 p.m., but Daniels emphasized that the job was to be completed today even if it took longer. The point didn't seem very important at that time since both men agreed that the job was one that should be completed well before five.

At 5 p.m. Worley called in to the office and asked for Daniels. He did this although he knew—as did all workcrew members—that at 5 p.m. Daniels customarily was at another company location where he could be reached by telephone. When informed that Daniels was out of the office, Worley asked to speak to McGraw.

As soon as he had the equipment manager on the line, Worley explained that he

was on a job that was going to take longer than expected because of some complications that had arisen. He then asked for permission to complete the job the next day so that he could get home in time to meet the boy scout troop of which he was the scoutmaster. McGraw—not knowing, of course, anything about the details of the assignment—OK'd his request to leave and finish the next day.

At 5:30 Daniels returned to the office and tried to contact Worley's location. Getting no answer, he went out to the site. He found that the job had not been completed and that Worley had left. He was unable to get the job finished that night because of the press of work and the lack of available crews.

The next morning, seething because of the customer complaint he had just answered, Daniels went in to McGraw's office to explain the situation. He was then told by McGraw that it was he who had given Worley permission to leave.

QUESTIONS

1. What is the *organizational* problem in this case?
2. Justify or criticize Worley's decision not to work.
3. Justify or criticize Worley's method of implementing his decision.
4. Evaluate McGraw's handling of the situation.
5. What should Daniels do about his problem?

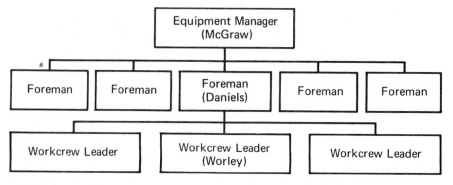

Exhibit 1
ORGANIZATION CHART

* This case was prepared by Professor A. Ranger Curran of Youngstown State University.

Case B-2

TEXAS STEEL FABRICATORS *

Texas Steel Fabricators is a manufacturer of metal products in Abilene, Texas. Its principal products are structural steel for buildings, nonbuilding industrial steel fabrications, home and playground steel products, metal bleachers, and industrial equipment.

Texas Steel Fabricators was founded in 1902 by Watson Gerrel I. In 1919, at the end of World War I, Watson Gerrel II returned from the war and became active in the business. Two years ago, a group of nationally recognized management consultants suggested to Watson Gerrel II that he and the four vice presidents under him should all consider retiring and turning the business over to younger men. At this time each of the vice presidents, along with Watson Gerrel II, retired, putting in a young president and four young vice presidents who are all in their mid 30's. The present organization is shown below.

After two years of operations, the young team was experiencing no difficulty in profitably operating the business.

Product Areas

Contract Work. Structural steel for buildings was fabricated for contractors constructing warehouses, service stations, churches, and industrial developments. In addition to these building applications, Texas Steel Fabricators also fabricates large nonbuilding structures such as oil refineries and chemical plants constructed by industrial design companies.

Small Fabrications. Individuals and local entrepreneurs frequently contract with Texas Steel Fabricators for special projects such as backyard bar-b-ques, outdoor tables and chairs, swing sets, and other items desired for individual use or limited local sales opportunities.

Warehousing. In addition to products that are manufactured by Texas Steel Fabricators, the company is frequently requested to supply standard steel stock such as dimension steel and prefabricated

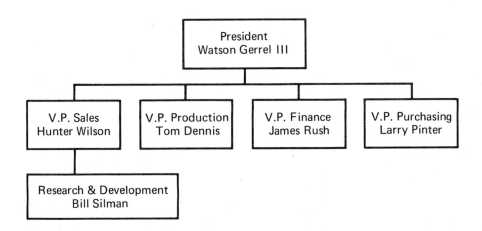

Exhibit 1
TEXAS STEEL FABRICATORS' ORGANIZATION STRUCTURE

* This case was prepared by Professor Richard C. Scott of Baylor University.

beams. Texas Steel Fabricators acts as a warehouse or sales activity only for these standard items, but performs no alteration or change of form to this stock.

Metal Bleachers. The metal bleachers fabricated by Texas Steel Fabricators consist of the steel standards that comprise the major structural portion of this type stand. This product area also includes thin aluminum covering for the bleacher seats and standards for mounting all types of outdoor recreational lighting equipment.

Manufactured Products. The manufactured products area is a recently inaugurated section designed to develop and market proprietary products designed by Texas Steel Fabricator's R & D or by outsiders who contract with Texas Steel Fabricators for production. These products range from relatively simple products, such as commercial playground equipment, to relatively complex equipment such as motorized, self-propelled industrial sweepers and vacuums.

Sales

All product sales are the responsibility of Hunter Wilson, Vice President of Sales. The approximate sales volume for each of the above areas is as follows:

Contract work ....$	7.4 million per year
Small fabrications	.7 million per year
Warehousing	1.1 million per year
Metal bleachers ...	.8 million per year
Manufactured	
products	.5 million per year
Total Sales ...	$10.5 million per year

New Division Proposal

About one year ago, Bill Silman, whose mother is on the board of directors, was brought to Texas Steel Fabricators from Texas Electronics to manage and develop the R & D group. As Silman sees his new job, the future of R & D lies in the expansion of the manufactured products group, since this group controls the destiny of all R & D output. Silman is not satisfied with

the way that the manufactured products group has been operating. He feels that it has taken second place to contract work, only being used to fill in slack production time when it is available.

Silman contends that, with the proper amount of effort, with an equal chance at the production facilities, and with an increased sales force devoted solely to the new division, a combined manufactured products and metal bleachers division can be developed into a $10 million annual sales division. Silman believes that manufactured products are 1.3 to 1.7 times as profitable as the contract work now being done by Texas Steel Fabricators. He also contends that the small fabrications group should be in this new division since it would be a source of R & D ideas for new manufactured products. On repeated occasions, Silman has come to Watson Gerrel and suggested that this new division be created under his supervision at a vice-presidential level.

The Problem

As Gerrel sees the problem, it is an organizational one. Gerrel believes that Hunter Wilson, Vice President of Sales, would feel that his division was being encroached upon if a new sales effort were launched out from under his functional control. Bill Silman feels that Wilson can never give manufactured products and steel standards a fair shake since Wilson was trained in the contract work part of the business. Watson Gerrel says that Silman is probably right in this but doesn't know how to introduce the subject to the V.P.'s. Gerrel hesitates to introduce change since Texas Steel Fabricators is now a successful small organization providing very adequate returns to its officers and stockholders. As Watson Gerrel sees it, the alternatives are as follows: (1) Retain manufactured products and steel standards, along with Bill Silman's ideas, as a secondary product area to be utilized only when the contract work division cannot use all of the facilities available; (2) Aggressively endorse and expand Silman's ideas.

QUESTIONS

1. What would Silman's reaction likely be if the decision is negative?
2. What would be the cost of this new endeavor if it were undertaken?
3. What is the possible gain?
4. What possible loss could result from undertaking this new venture?
5. What would you do if you were Watson Gerrel III?

Case B-3

THE BARTON COMPANY *

It was 7 p.m., and George Clark was finally on his way home. The traffic on the expressway was light now. He found himself relaxing a bit and thinking about the events of the day, particularly the events of the past two hours. Apparently his recommendation had resulted in the firing of a top vice president of the Barton Company, a small manufacturing firm in which he was serving as a management consultant. He wondered if the best course of action had been taken. He also had a question about his own role in advising William Barton, the company president.

The Barton Company was a manufacturer of plastics products with about 150 production employees. With the exception of three continuing contracts for pleasure boat windshields, all the company's business came from small, custom jobs, ranging from $1,000 to around $50,000. Some of these were completed within a week. Others lasted for several months. Some were handled by a

single craftsman; for others, the process resembled an assembly line. Prior to the last year, no jobs had been time studied, and no employees had been paid on piece rates.

Until recently, moreover, the organization structure of the production department had been more like that of a family than a business. All relationships were informal, and the processes were inefficient. There was no cost accounting, and nobody knew which jobs were profitable and which were not. However, the company became too large to survive with such poor controls, and at times bankruptcy seemed inevitable. It was obvious that professional management was necessary. Thus, a position of Production Vice President was created.

Through personal contacts, William Barton located a man he believed could handle the job. After a thorough investigation, Clark agreed, and Ralph Holden was employed. Holden had been a brilliant student. He held three degrees: a bachelor of mechanical engineering, a BBA, and an MBA. He had also taken correspondence courses and passed his CPA exams.

Holden's work history consisted of the following: 2 1/2 years for a ball bearing company (engineering), 1 1/2 years in a small business partnership (executive search firm), 3 years in a large electronics firm (production), and 2 years with a toy

---

* This case was prepared by Professor J. Clifton Williams of Baylor University.

manufacturer (industrial engineering and trouble-shooting). He explained his reasons for leaving these jobs in terms of "a better opportunity," "disagreement with top management over policy," and "boredom." His private business venture was not successful. After leaving one job, according to his résumé, he and his wife traveled in Europe for five months.

The pre-employment investigation led to several findings that seemed relevant to Clark and Barton. Some of these are described in this paragraph. On his jobs Holden worked long hours and at a fast and efficient pace. He was an aggressive problem solver and in the process often made enemies. His family life appeared stable, and he had little debt. On the other hand, his net worth was minimal for a person of his age and experience. Two previous employers remarked about his unique ability to organize, systematize, and increase the efficiency of an operation. Clark's assessment led him to conclude: "Holden will be a good 'hatchet man' to clean up the operation, but I see him as a two-year man at the most."

His performance at the Barton Company was true to form. In less than a year the windshield operation was paid on a piece-rate basis and required about half the previous number of employees. The cost and profit of every contract was routinely determined. Written personnel policies and procedures were established for all aspects of interpersonal relations in the production department. Two new foremen were selected and trained. Generally speaking, morale was acceptable, and most employees were motivated to be highly productive.

Clark had worked closely with Holden during his 14 months with the company. Specifically, Clark had attempted to help him be more effective in interpersonal relations, and, considering the tough job Holden had faced, he seemed to have been reasonably successful. In recent weeks the production department had been running smoothly, but a conflict intensified between Holden and Earl Smith, the Sales Vice President. Holden felt that the sales department was hurting the company by cutting prices to the point that no profit could be made regardless of how

efficiently the production department operated.

As Clark saw the situation, Smith "operated too much by the seat of his pants," using intuition where hard cost data were available for the asking. But, Smith and his salesmen had all been with the company for several years and had met with considerable success. Over a period of about three months, Barton had sensed a battle brewing and had, on occasion, made decisions as a kind of arbitrator. Clark felt that Barton should exercise stronger leadership in the company, but Barton viewed himself as a superior delegator and preferred to let the conflicts work themselves out.

Finally an impasse developed between Holden and Smith. When Holden realized he could not significantly influence sales policy, he went to Barton with an ultimatum. Either Smith should be fired, or Holden would leave the company. After a lengthy conference with Clark about the issues involved, Barton asked Clark what he would do if he were president. At first Clark hedged, but he finally indicated that he would be forced to let Holden go if he had to choose between the two.

At six o'clock Barton called Holden in and told him that he had discussed the matter with Clark and that Clark had recommended his dismissal. Barton watched Holden as he packed his personal possessions, turned in his keys, and left. Barton said, concerning Holden, "He seemed dejected and couldn't understand why Clark would 'knife him' after all the time they had worked together."

QUESTIONS

1. What do you think of Barton's actions? Of Clark's?
2. Assuming Holden would have carried out his threat to resign, could you in any way justify firing Smith?
3. Are any ethical issues involved in this case?
4. How would you have handled this situation differently from the way it was handled by Barton and Clark?
5. What do you see as the ideal role for a consultant to play in problems of this kind?

Case B-4

THE GOLDEN ACCOUNT *

Bob McFarland was the president and principal stockholder of Iowa Tractor Supply Company, a farm and construction equipment distributor located in Marshalltown, Iowa. The firm employed 27 persons, and in 1971 sales and net profit after taxes reached all-time highs of $1.4 million and $34,500, respectively. Ending net worth for 1971 was slightly in excess of $228,000.

Bob was highly gratified by these figures as 1971 was the first full year since he had appointed Stan Stockton as general manager. Although the company had been in operation since 1947, it had prospered only from the time Bob had purchased it in 1959. Having been a territorial sales manager for the John Deere Company, Bob was able to obtain that account for Iowa Tractor, and it typically contributed two thirds or more of the annual sales volume. After struggling successfully for 10 years to build Iowa Tractor into a profitable firm, Bob decided that it was time to take things a little easier. Accordingly, he promoted Stan and delegated many of his day-to-day duties to him. Fortunately Stan seemed to do an outstanding job, and during the summer of 1972, Bob felt secure enough to spend six weeks in Europe with his wife.

One day shortly after he had returned to work, Bob looked up from his desk and saw his accountant, Marvin Richter, approaching with several ledger cards in his hand. Marvin entered the office, carefully closed the door, and began to speak earnestly.

"Mr. McFarland, I think you should look at these accounts receivable, particularly Jordan Construction. I've been telling Stan to watch out for Jordan for two

months, but he just says they're good for it eventually. I got the latest Dun & Bradstreet monthly report today which didn't look very good, so I've called Standifer Equipment in Ames and the Caterpillar branch at Cedar Rapids. Jordan seems to have run up some pretty good bills with both of them, and Carter at Standifer said some of the contractors in Des Moines think that the two jobs Jordan got on Interstate 80 are just too big for them to handle. If Jordan can't finish those jobs, we are going to be in trouble! Carter says they're probably going to put them on C.O.D. and call in the rental equipment."

Bob examined the data for a few minutes, asked Marvin several questions before dismissing him, and then summoned Stan to his office.

"Stan, I've just been looking over the sheets on Jordan and the amount really scares me. Apparently, they are over 90 days on nearly $11,000; between 30 and 90 days on another $9,000; and the total due is more than $25,000. Payments on their account have been dropping off since April, and last month they barely covered the interest on the amount outstanding."

"I know, Bob. I've been over to talk to old man Jordan twice in the last three weeks. He admits they are having some trouble with those jobs on the Interstate, but he claims it is only temporary. I hate to push him too hard because he has bought a lot of equipment from us over the years."

"That's right, Stan, but we're talking about $25,000! At this rate, we'll soon have more money in Jordan's business than he does! I'm not so sure we shouldn't put Jordan on C.O.D until he makes some substantial payments on their account."

"I don't think so, Bob! Old man Jordan has a real mean streak, and the first time I went over there he really cussed me out for even questioning his account. He reminded me that he had been a good customer for more than 10 years, and he threatened to cut us off if we put any pressure on him."

"Yes, but you've heard that before,

* This case was prepared by Professor John E. Schoen of Baylor University.

Stan. Here we are contributing capital to his business involuntarily; we never get a share of his profits if he succeeds, but we sure get a share of the losses if he goes 'belly-up.' Stan, I don't want any $25,000 losses!"

"Well, I won't say that Jordan doesn't have some problems, but Harry thinks they'll be all right. It's just that if we put them on C.O.D. or pick up the rental equipment and they make it, I'm sure they'll never spend another dollar in here."

"Harry thinks they'll be O.K.?"

"Yes, sir."

"Get Harry in here!"

In a few minutes, Stan returns with Harry Reiser who is the sales manager for Iowa Tractor.

"Stan says you wanted to talk to me?"

"That's right, Harry. We've just been discussing Jordan Construction, and I'd like to get any information you have on them."

"Well, they're pretty good customers, of course. I rented them two tractor-backhoes last month. There are some rumors about their Interstate jobs, but I don't think there is much to it because Jordan was talking about buying a couple of crawler tractors last Friday. I think we have a good chance to get those crawlers if that joker over at Ames doesn't sell his below cost."

"Just a minute. You rented them some backhoes last month?"

"Yes, sir, two model 533's."

"How much are we getting for those units?"

"$1,100 a month each and I think we have a good chance to convert them to a sale if Jordan gets six months' rent into them."

"Did you check with anybody before you put those units out with Jordan?"

"Well, I think I asked Stan. No, I think he was busy that day. I'm really not certain, but Jordan Construction is one of our best accounts. Isn't it?"

"That's what we are trying to determine, Harry. Did you know that their accounts receivable is over $25,000?"

"No! That's great! I knew we'd really been selling them. I'm sure those rumors. . . ."

"And did you know that $20,000 of the $25,000 is past due and $11,000 is over 90 days?"

"Oh!"

"Stan, I think we've established what Harry knows about Jordan. Why don't we get Marvin in here and see what information he has. Then I think the four of us need to decide the best approach to getting as much of our money back as soon as possible."

QUESTIONS

1. Evaluate the quality of the information provided Bob by each of his subordinates.
2. Evaluate the various alternatives in solving the Jordan situation.
3. What action should Bob take regarding the Jordan account?
4. How could Bob improve the credit and collections procedure of Iowa Tractor to minimize problems of this nature?
5. Evaluate the performance of Marvin, Stan, and Harry in handling the Jordan account. Do the circumstances warrant any type of disciplinary action?

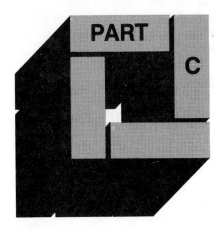

PART C

Initial Problems in Starting a Small Business

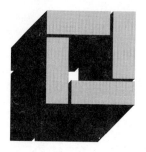

12

Roads to
Business Ownership

An individual may enter into the ownership and operation of a small business in one of three ways: buying an existing business, inheriting an existing business, or launching a new business. This chapter will consider each of these roads to business ownership, and the subject of investigating business opportunities will also be discussed.

Care should be exercised in entering business in any one of the three ways mentioned above. Even the continued operation of an inherited business would be unwise if it were heavily in debt or had recently lost much of its customer clientele. Similarly, the purchase of an existing firm could be dangerous. For example, a small factory for sale might have largely obsolete equipment and a top-heavy inventory of outmoded products. And starting a new business would be suicidal unless there were a real business opportunity, adequate financing, and genuine management capacity. If failure resulted from a venture into business, the entrepreneur would not only lose his capital but also impair his reputation as a manager.

BUYING AN EXISTING BUSINESS

Here we shall discuss the advantages inherent in buying an existing business and the various steps that a prospective entrepreneur should take in evaluating the business before "closing the deal."

Advantages in Buying an Existing Business

There are several reasons why a prospective entrepreneur might choose to take this road to business ownership. First, the fact that a business is already a going concern reduces the uncertainty of successful operation in the future. Second, the effort, time, and cost of the many steps required to launch a new concern may be avoided or minimized. Finally, the existing business may be available for purchase at a bargain price. Each of these reasons is discussed in more detail below.

Reducing Uncertainties of Successful Future Operation. Speculation concerning the profit potential of a contemplated enterprise yields results far less trustworthy than those obtained from a study of the operating history of an existing business. A successful, going concern has demonstrated an ability to attract customers, to control costs, and to make a profit. Of course, future operations might yield a different rate of return. The new owner, if lax and incompetent, might obtain a smaller profit—or even sustain a loss. Or, if efficient and capable, the new owner might increase sales or reduce costs, with the result that profits would be greater. It is a fact, however, that the firm's past record reduces uncertainty as to what the firm could do under given conditions. Naturally, the existence and extent of profitability must be verified by careful evaluation—a step discussed in the following section.

A major uncertainty involved in starting a new business is avoided by the proved location of the going concern. Correct location is of vital importance to a small business. Restaurants and mortuaries, for example, should not be placed next to each other. Nor is it likely that two record shops located side by side would both be successful. And sometimes small retailers could increase profits materially by moving across the street, a few doors down the street from the present location, or around the corner. Traffic counts and cost estimates are useful, but the acid test comes when a business opens its doors at a given location. And this test has already been met in the case of an existing firm, with the results available in the form of sales and profit data.

Another major uncertainty is eliminated by the existence of an established, growing customer clientele. This not only reduces uncertainty as to customer attitudes but also minimizes the time required to work up a trade in the given community, whether the entrepreneur is a professional, merchant, or service operator. Even a small manufacturer must build a solid group of customers. If an established customer clientele can be taken over "as is," a long and confident step toward business success has been taken by the new entrepreneur.

Reducing Effort, Time, and Costs Associated with Launching a New Business. The seller of a going concern has already assembled the personnel, inventories, and physical facilities for carrying on the business. This could be a major advantage because of the time and effort otherwise required for contacting suppliers and acquiring inventory items and equipment. Of course, this assumes that inventories on hand are neither shopworn nor obsolete—and that equipment is not worn out. Again, the skilled, experienced employees of the former firm constitute a valuable asset if they will stay on under the new management. But they must be truly capable and enjoy good relations with customers. Externally, the business may have established banking connections and valuable relationships with trade suppliers. But such worthwhile relationships must be demonstrated; they cannot be merely assumed to exist.

Buying at a Bargain Price. The final advantage cited for buying an established firm is availability at a bargain price. Whether the business offered for sale is a bargain is open to question. The price may appear low, but the business may be losing money, or the quality of the location may be deteriorating (or even vanishing overnight, as when a highway is to be relocated), or the seller may even intend to reopen as a competitor. The business may also have alienated many customers, may have been notified of discontinuance of its franchises, or may have earned a low credit standing with its bank and its suppliers. Such factors could make the "bargain price" anything but a bargain.

However, if the three major advantages cited truly exist, then the purchase of the existing business may well be a wise investment. Their existence (and the worth of the business) can never be assumed, however. The value of the business must be verified by careful appraisal of all pertinent factors if the investor is to avoid the purchase of a "white elephant."

Steps in Evaluating an Existing Business

Before an existing business can change hands, buyer and seller must reach agreement on the sale price. From sentiment, not always unmixed with greed, the seller tends to overvalue his business; hence, the buyer needs to start an investigation with his own appraisal of its worth. There are numerous outside experts who can help him make a realistic appraisal. Among these are public accountants, lawyers, bankers, realtors, representatives of trade suppliers and public utility companies, local industrial district officers, and chamber of commerce experts.

Conducting an Independent Audit. The first step is to arrange for an audit of the seller's records and financial statements by a competent public accounting firm. Of course, if the seller has been audited recently by such an independent certified public accountant, reference may be made to that audit report if it can be obtained directly from the auditor. There should be a detailed current audit, and in addition the auditor should obtain sales and profit figures (from tax returns, for example) for as many earlier years as possible. If audit reports are available for five or ten years, or even longer, it is so much the better because some idea of business trends can be obtained in this way.

The major purpose of the audit is to reveal the accuracy and the completeness of the financial data. It also determines whether the seller has used acceptable accounting methods, such as proper procedures in depreciating equipment and in valuing inventory. The buyer may be reasonably confident of the accuracy and completeness of financial statements prepared by a competent, independent auditor. But it would be dangerous to accept statements prepared by the seller's bookkeeper without an independent audit.

Capitalizing the Profit. A knowledge of the amount of net profit and the current worth of the net assets does not in itself provide an equitable purchase price. Translating profit into business value requires use of a process known as capitalization of profit. All this means is that the buyer determines what amount of investment would logically earn the annual profit obtainable from the business in question.

Assume that the annual net profit is $10,000. What should a buyer be willing to pay to secure such a return? This calls for a consideration of several factors and estimates, including the following:

1. Estimating probable future profit on the basis of past data. For example, the buyer should adjust past profit figures to eliminate nonrecurring gains or losses.
2. Allowing for personal time invested in the business. Since his salary must come from profit, the buyer should deduct a reasonable amount for his own labor before capitalizing the profit.
3. Estimating the degree of risk involved in the business. One might expect a 20 to 25

percent return in enterprises that entail considerable risk, whereas 10 percent or 12 percent might be quite satisfactory in a less hazardous venture.

4. Determining the existence and the amount of goodwill, if any. Goodwill tends to be less durable than other assets and thus is worth proportionately less to the buyer.

Computing the Business Value and Goodwill. Let us illustrate the computation of business value, assuming an annual net profit of $10,000. If the prospective owner places a value of $5,000 on his own time and effort, this leaves $5,000 to be capitalized. Suppose that the buyer evaluates the investment as moderately safe and feels that a 10 percent profit would be a good return on investment in comparison with alternative investment opportunities. It would seem that a simple calculation could be made as follows:

$5,000 = 10% profit
$5,000 ÷ .10 = $50,000 = business value

The $50,000 figure would provide a bench mark for use in negotiating the purchase of the business.

A reservation must be made, however, relative to goodwill. Goodwill derives from exceptional loyalty of customers or other advantages that cause earnings to be exceptionally high in view of the physical resources involved. The intangible and somewhat fragile nature of goodwill makes it unwise to treat it in the same way as other physical assets. Income attributed to goodwill should, therefore, be capitalized at a higher rate than that applied to other profits.

To illustrate, using the original example, suppose that the market or replacement value of net assets, exclusive of goodwill, amounted to $40,000. Using the 10 percent figure, the investor would expect a $4,000 profit from these assets. In view of the fact that the other $1,000 annual profit is based upon goodwill, it should be capitalized at a higher rate, say 20 percent (a common figure for capitalizing such earnings). On that basis, the asset value associated with this $1,000 profit would be $5,000 rather than $10,000, and total enterprise value would be $45,000.

Computing the Book Value of Net Assets and Goodwill. Another approach would consider the book value of the net assets (or the amount of the proprietor's investment in the business). If this is only $30,000, the 10 percent normal profit would be only $3,000. With actual profit at $5,000, the excess profit over normal would be $2,000. Capitalized at 20 percent, this excess profit would yield a value for goodwill of $10,000. The total net purchase price should then be only $40,000. To pay $45,000 would recognize an appreciation of the seller's actual investment, in addition to the goodwill computed on the basis of book value.

Nevertheless, in this case, perhaps the fairest price to both seller and buyer is $45,000 price. If the seller is aware, or believes, that his net business assets have a greater value than shown on the books, he would be reluctant to sell for $40,000, a figure which understates the true value.

If, however, the book value of the proprietor's net assets is $60,000, a 10 percent profit would amount to $6,000. Hence, actual profits of $5,000 would show an absence of goodwill and an apparent managerial inefficiency resulting in failure to earn the proper normal profit. But, if replacement value of net assets is only $40,000, normal profit would be $4,000; actual profit, $5,000; and goodwill, $5,000. The fair purchase price, once more, would be $45,000. In this case the recorded book value of the seller at $60,000 is an inflated or watered value, which the buyer should not pay.

Analyzing Financial Records Intensively. Using the audited financial statements, the buyer might next proceed to analyze in detail the following various aspects of profitability and financial condition. This investigation may confirm or modify the estimate of net worth determined above. The auditor may be able to help the buyer in portions of this study, but the buyer can also undertake certain of these analyses on his own. The buyer will be limited, obviously, by the quality and the number of financial statements available. A study based upon statements for the past 10 years would be superior to one based upon statements concerning only the most recent accounting period.

Enterprise Earning Power. Net profit is a definitive measure of earning power, but a more detailed examination is required to discover whether the full earning potential is being exploited. The following areas, in particular, should be studied as carefully as possible:

1. *Expense ratios and trends.* Operating expense ratios, for example, should be compared with any available ratios published by Dun & Bradstreet, trade associations, or other sources.
2. *Profitability of products and territories.* In the case of a manufacturing firm, the profitability of each product and territory should be estimated as carefully as possible. In other businesses, the service or selling departments may be evaluated.
3. *Sales potential and selling methods.* An analysis of the market may reveal either a saturated or an unexploited market. By plotting company and industry sales on a single ratio chart, the buyer can compare this firm's growth with that of the industry.
4. *Gross profit analysis.* Any unfavorable gross profit trend should be scrutinized. In addition, variations in gross profit should be analyzed to determine the reasons for these variations.

Adequacy and Liquidity of Working Capital. The seller's working capital position should also be carefully studied in the audit and subsequent investigation. The amount of working capital should be adequate. Adequacy may be tested in part by comparing the firm's current ratio with that which is standard for the given industry or line of business. The working capital should also be sufficiently liquid. This means that all current assets should not be tied up in inventory and receivables and that inventories and receivables should be regularly converted into cash within the normal number of days. When a firm needs ready cash—for example, for taking advantage of purchase discounts—the need is urgent. The need for cash would be even more pressing for meeting payrolls and paying bills. The fact that the business is small does not make the pressure any less. The working capital turnover ratio is an overall check. If it is too low, it is a danger signal, indicating inefficient use of resources. If it is too high, it may merely reflect strain on insufficient working capital (although it could represent efficient use of resources).

Overall Financial Health. The buyer is also interested in the general financial condition of the seller's business. Here, with the auditor, he will look at ownership and creditor equities in the assets, at the percent of noncurrent liabilities, at the adequacy of insurance carried both as to amounts and kinds, at the size of cash reserves for contingencies, and the like. In particular, the buyer is interested in seeing if there has been overexpansion of either fixed assets or inventories, considering the firm's relatively small scale of operations.

Verifying Listed Assets. In auditing records of the seller, the public accountant verifies the existence and the worth of certain assets by checking inventory age, quality of accounts receivable, and so on. There are further steps, however, that can be taken by the buyer to establish more fully the existence and the value of all listed assets.

An appraisal may be required, for example, to make sure the seller's fixed asset values, which are usually shown on the books at cost less depreciation, are realistic and representative of current values. This means that equipment, whether for factory, warehouse, office, or store, should be currently operational and not functionally obsolete. All these items of equipment must be capable of making a contribution to profits.

The buyer's attorney should check all leases, franchises, and long-term contracts that will be taken over from the seller. Their continuation for the buyer as new owner of the business should be formally verified. Trick clauses, if any, should be exposed. Property titles, if any, should be examined by a title agency and brought up to date. By so doing, existence of tax liens, if any, will be discovered, and the buyer will be assured that the seller is the titleholder of record, capable of transferring a good title.

Checking Tax Angles. The purchase of an existing business also presents tax problems. Questions of this type are quite technical, so the prospective buyer should check tax considerations and possibilities with a tax expert.

For example, the buyer is especially interested in what tax cost basis will prevail after the purchase. If the buyer pays cash for the business assets, the purchase price becomes his tax basis in computing such expenses as depreciation. On the other hand, if he buys the capital stock of an existing corporation and keeps it alive, his tax basis is that of the corporation.

Numerous other possibilities require checking by a tax expert. These might be illustrated by the following:

1. In buying capital stock and taking over a corporation intact, the buyer subjects himself to future taxes on dividends paid from the accumulated surplus existing and acquired at time of purchase.
2. Interest expenses connected with installment purchase of business assets may be tax deductible.
3. Property taxes are the obligation of the titleholder of record at the time the tax is imposed; the purchase agreement should require prorating of tax between buyer and seller.
4. The buyer may be able to deduct, for tax purposes, payments made to the seller in return for the seller's agreement not to engage in direct competition.

Considering Other Factors. A number of other factors remain to be explored. Among these are the following:

1. The extent and intensity of competition and the location of competing enterprises. In particular, the buyer should check to see whether the business he plans to buy is gaining or losing in the race with competitors.

2. Sufficiency of customers in the area served to maintain all competing business units, including the one to be purchased. This determination entails market research, study of census data, and personal, on-the-spot observation at each competitor's place of business.
3. Future developments in the community. Examples include the following:
   (a) Changes in zoning ordinances already enacted but not yet in effect.
   (b) Prospective land condemnation suits for construction of a public building, a municipally operated parking lot, or a public park.
   (c) Change of highway location, or change from two-way traffic flow to one-way traffic.
   (d) Discontinuance of streetcar or bus routes that will eliminate transportation for customers and employees.
4. Status of any contingent liabilities or unsettled lawsuits.
5. Union contracts in force and the quality of the firm's employee relations.
6. Restrictions on access to buildings—that is, whether there is access to the building without crossing the property of another. If necessary, a right-of-way should be negotiated before the purchase contract is closed.
7. Quality of the buildings housing the business, particularly the fire hazard involved.
8. The impact of possible future national emergencies. Of particular interest would be price and wage controls, energy shortages, manpower shortages, raw material priorities, and the like. Conversely, of course, a war situation might open the way to profitable subcontracting on war goods contracts.
9. Mortgages of record against any of the real property acquired.
10. Comparison of a merchant's product prices with manufacturer's or wholesaler's catalogs or by shopping competing stores in the locality. This is to assure full and fair pricing of goods whose sales are reported by the seller on his statements.

Investigating Seller's Reasons for Selling. Another question of vital interest to the buyer is: Why is the business being sold? The following are typical of the many reasons offered by sellers for disposing of a business:

1. Old age.
2. Illness.
3. Desire to transfer to a larger city.
4. Desire to move to a better climate.
5. Desire to try another line of business.
6. Offer of such a good position with a large firm that the opportunity cannot be turned down.
7. Discouragement caused by labor trouble, high taxes, or increasing governmental regulation.

There is always the danger that the reason offered is fictitious. It may be intended to conceal some undesirable feature or to camouflage the seller's plan to reenter business in competition with the buyer. Hence, the prospective buyer must probe deeply to make sure he has found the real reason or reasons.

If the seller's reentry into business would be injurious to the buyer, as might be true in the case of a men's clothing store, for example, the buyer may insist that the seller sign a contract not to reenter business in local competition for a specified period of time. Such a contract may require annual payments to the seller for the stated number of years. Another related question concerns the future name of the business. If there is goodwill, the buyer should contract for the right to continuance of the business under the same name in order to avoid loss of this goodwill.

It might develop that the undisclosed reason for sale is the unprofitability of the business, discontinuance of an exclusive sales franchise, expiration of a vital patent, impending condemnation of the business building for public use of the land, or rerouting of a highway or bus route, among other factors. Knowing such concealed reasons enables the buyer to evaluate the business opportunity more intelligently.

Closing the Deal

Once more, it should be emphasized that any contract to buy an existing business should not be consummated before the buyer has talked in person with an independent accountant, banker, chamber of commerce representative, attorney, and, if the business is unionized, representatives of the labor union.

Before final consummation of the purchase of an existing business, the prospective buyer's attorney should assist him in a final checking of all vital points. The attorney should also check the purchase contract itself.

INHERITING AN EXISTING ENTERPRISE

Potentially the same advantages exist for operating an inherited firm as for a purchased firm. It is a going concern, is already located, possesses an established customer clientele, and has the requisite equipment and inventory on hand.

However, the inherited firm might actually be without such values. Hence, the heir should establish its worth by an independent audit, appraisal of the building and equipment, checking the worth of the present location, and studying the firm's financial records. The latter study should show that the firm has an adequate, liquid working capital; an undiminished earning power; and a strong overall financial condition. Existence of tax problems and unfortunately negotiated long-term contracts of purchase or sale should be carefully analyzed. Other problems—such as labor troubles recently settled or still pending and community growth or recession—should also be investigated.

Inheritance is the least frequently followed route into business ownership, and an heir might want to sell unless his investigation of the inherited firm seemed wholly favorable. Even if all is favorable, an heir who has other professional or occupational commitments may wish to sell out or liquidate. Some who inherit businesses have no desire to manage them. Thus, only a portion of those persons who inherit businesses will continue to own and operate them.

STARTING A NEW BUSINESS

For a number of reasons, some individuals prefer to start completely new businesses rather than to buy out existing firms. Some of the considerations prompting a choice of this kind are the following:

1. Starting from scratch enables the owner to select his own:
   (a) Location.
   (b) Products and services.

(c) Merchandise.
(d) Equipment.
(e) Workers.
(f) Suppliers.
(g) Banker.

2. A new concern avoids the unfortunate and undesirable binding precedents, business policies and practices, and legal commitments of an existing firm.
3. A loyal customer clientele can be developed without assuming any ill will of an existing business.
4. There may be no existing firms of the type contemplated by the prospective entrepreneur.

The first three factors are significant advantages only if businesses available for purchase are unfavorably located, poorly staffed, or otherwise inefficiently managed. It is a mistake to assume that well-managed, profitable enterprises are never offered for sale. If there is an idea for a completely new type of business or one that is substantially different from others in a competing area, however, the individual is forced to pioneer. Opening the first sporting goods store or the first telephone answering service in a particular town would illustrate this situation.

Justification for a New Business of an Existing Kind

Two valid reasons justify the formation of a new business similar to other existing concerns. These are as follows:

1. A real, permanent expansion of the market, such that the market is not adequately served by existing business units.
2. Inefficient management of existing firms, with the result that the market is not adequately served by existing firms.

With respect to the first of these situations, it must be emphasized that the market expansion should be real and permanent. An influx of population to a community during the construction of a nuclear power plant, for example, could be sizable and yet inadequate because the population will quickly decrease when construction is completed. A temporary increase in population is not a dependable base on which to build a new business. Of course, one could, in such a situation, go into business with plans for temporary operation, large profits, and closure when the "boom" is over.

The second valid reason for justifying entry into a new business of an existing kind is best illustrated by the following examples. Some years ago, a young couple from Chicago settled in a small, downstate city and opened a junkyard. This operation was continued only a year or so, during which time they sized up their local business firms. In their opinion a furniture store was the least efficiently managed, and they offered to buy it, threatening to enter into competition if its owner did not sell. Surprisingly enough, he sold out at once. Another case is that of a Texas bottled water company. It was just about breaking even on operations when two young men offered to buy, with the same proviso—if the owner did not sell, they would enter into competition and attempt to drive him out of business. He did not sell. The two men opened a competing enterprise, and after eight years of operation they had a firm hold on half the market.

Justification for a New Business of a New Kind

When contemplating a completely different type of business, the prospective entrepreneur faces a different type of problem. It is a situation that typically entails the maximum of uncertainty and risk. The only reasons for opening such a completely new business are:

1. A new product has been created, which is useful and needed by the public.
2. A new service has been originated, which the public will use and pay for.

Obviously, combinations of these two cases and combinations of either of them with existing business also are possible. The latter combinations would result in partially new—not wholly new—types of businesses.

Two other observations are pertinent. First, the completely new enterprise, selling either a single new product or single new type of service, is a rarity. When a new product or service is developed, it is usually combined with existing products and/or services. Second, market analysis is necessary to prove that the new product or new service will gain consumer acceptance at a price and volume that will be profitable to the business. Formal market research, thus, is required to verify that the business opportunity is genuine. This is considered in the final section of this chapter.

Before concluding the present section, however, one might recall the products invented or developed in this century that have led to whole new industries. Among these are the automobile, the airplane, nylon, plastics, atomic energy, radio, and television. It should be clear that new ideas, new products and processes, and new customer services, if they gain public acceptance, can be highly profitable.

INVESTIGATION OF BUSINESS OPPORTUNITIES

An error of judgment in unwisely launching a new enterprise can quickly take the personal savings and the business reputation of the entrepreneur. To some extent, such risk haunts the entrepreneur in the establishment of any business. As noted earlier in the chapter, this risk is greater if the entrepreneur considers opening a new business unit in contrast to taking over a functioning enterprise. The uncertainties become greatest, however, when the contemplated venture is completely unique—a situation that not only prevents the study of the business enterprise itself but also eliminates the possibility of studying similar units already in operation.

Need for Statistical Data

To minimize this inherent risk, the prospective owner of a new business must resort to investigation and analysis. Each situation is unique; and the analysis must be tailored to fit the proposed business and the data that are available or that can be economically obtained. Appraising the market and the profit prospects for a new manufacturer would differ materially from a corresponding study for a contemplated restaurant or retail store. In each case, all possible statistical evidence should be carefully weighed as a supplement to personal observation.

To illustrate the type of facts that might be examined, consider the data in Table 12-1 pertaining to the metropolitan areas of New Orleans, Louisiana, and Portland, Oregon.[1]

Table 12-1
CENSUS DATA FOR NEW ORLEANS AND PORTLAND

Kind of Business	New Orleans		Portland	
	Number of Establishments	Population per Establishment	Number of Establishments	Population per Establishment
Jewelry stores	106	9,866	112	9,010
Department stores	20	52,290	21	48,053
Shoe stores (with payrolls)	104	10,055	73	13,824
Eating places	1,114	939	1,011	998
Drug and proprietary stores	240	4,358	203	4,971
Women's apparel stores	146	7,163	135	7,475
Furniture and home furnishings stores	228	4,587	257	3,927
Tire, battery, and accessory dealers	120	8,715	143	7,057
Florists	84	12,450	103	9,797

Source: *Census of Business, 1967.*

The interpretation of such data must depend on collateral evidence. For example, one might conclude that New Orleans would be a better city in which to locate a florist shop because of the larger population for each florist shop. On the other hand, one might find that more people in New Orleans grow their own flowers and that florist shops are generally as busy in Portland as in New Orleans. It is possible that the average income levels of the population in the two cities are substantially different and that this might affect buying habits. The extent to which each city attracts patronage from outside its metropolitan area would also influence the amount of business available for each establishment. To tell which verdict is correct, or whether some other explanation is pertinent, more intensive study of factual data and supporting personal observation over a period of time would be required. If florists in New Orleans appear to have a flourishing business, this would tend to confirm the picture presented by the above data. Preferably, one should have national and regional averages, as well as local data supported by personal observation. (The problem of choosing a business location is treated more fully in Chapter 15.)

---

[1] According to the 1970 Census of Population, the New Orleans metropolitan area population was 1,045,809 while that for Portland was 1,009,129.

Recognition of Symptomatic Conditions

If the opportunity for a new business rests upon inefficient operation of other firms, there are basic symptoms that may be evaluated. Using the retail field to illustrate, some of these symptoms might be: (1) prevalent out-of-town buying; (2) high prices; (3) slow or inferior service in stores; and (4) dirty, down-at-the-heel appearance of stores. These symptoms may be detected by personal observation or by consumer surveys conducted by newspapers, chambers of commerce, or other organizations. The study would be designed to discover whether the observed conditions were truly symptomatic of an inefficient business.

Direct Contact with Prospective Customers

In the case of an entirely new type of business, direct contact with a sample of prospective customers is perhaps the most critical phase of the investigation. If one contemplates producing a tool for use in industrial plants, for example, there is no substitute for seeking the reaction of industrial buyers prior to creating a factory to produce it. Many illuminating contacts with prospective customers can be made by the individual who is contemplating the formation of a new firm. A market research agency may properly be employed if a more elaborate study appears necessary.

Causes and Dangers of Inadequate Investigation

Prospective entrepreneurs have been told many times by many different authorities of the need for adequate investigation before launching a new business. For a number of reasons, however, the investigations made are all too often inadequate. Some of the most common reasons are:

1. An impatience to get started.
2. Insufficient funds to carry on expensive market studies or even much personal observation.
3. Lack of training and skill to undertake an adequate business opportunity investigation.

The preliminary consequences of inadequate investigation and planning are:

1. Poor business location.
2. Inadequate sales potential.
3. Unplanned or ill-planned distribution procedures.
4. Working capital shortage.
5. Crushingly strong competition.

The ultimate consequence to be expected is business failure. Hence, it must be said again and again: a prospective entrepreneur must investigate adequately and carefully before inaugurating a new small business.

Summary

1. There are three ways for a prospective entrepreneur to get into business for himself: by purchasing an existing business, by inheriting ownership of a going concern, and by starting a new enterprise.

2. Among the advantages in buying an existing business are the existence of an historical operating record that reduces uncertainty, the avoidance of some of the time and effort necessary in launching a new concern, and the possibility of purchase at a "bargain price."

3. In negotiating for the purchase of a going concern, the prospective purchaser can arrange for a certified public accountant to make an audit of the firm's business records and thus discover the accuracy and completeness of financial data.

4. The transformation of a net profit figure into a business value figure requires a process known as "capitalizing the profit."

5. A buyer should also analyze the financial statements to determine the earning power of the firm, the adequacy and liquidity of working capital, and the overall financial health of the enterprise.

6. It is desirable that consideration be given by a purchaser to the appraisal of fixed assets, checking of leases and other legal documents, and analysis of all tax angles involved in the purchase.

7. The seller's reason for selling, if it can be discovered, is helpful in evaluating the prospects of a going concern.

8. A new business of an existing kind may be justified by an expansion of the market or by inefficient management of existing concerns.

9. An entirely new type of business requires the development of a new product or service that will be purchased by the public.

10. It is imperative that a thorough investigation be undertaken prior to entering the business world as an entrepreneur. The actual existence of a business opportunity must be verified. All too often, the investigation conducted is inadequate, so that operating the proposed business is fraught with danger of failure. In fact, an adequate investigation of business opportunity is most difficult in those cases in which it is most needed, namely those involving great uncertainty.

Discussion Questions

1. What reasons for buying an existing business, in contrast to starting from scratch, appear most important?
2. Is uncertainty eliminated or merely minimized when an existing business is purchased? Explain.
3. What value is there in a current independent audit of a business that is being purchased?
4. How should a buyer determine the profit rate or rates to use in capitalizing business profits?
5. How should previous nonrecurring losses—for example, loss from a flood or a major fire—be treated in capitalizing profits?
6. Explain the steps necessary in calculating the value of goodwill.
7. What can be learned by intensive analysis of financial records concerning the value of a firm that is not evident from capitalizing the profits?
8. What is the significance of the seller's real future plans? How might you discover them?
9. What contractual arrangements can be made to prevent future competition by a seller of a business? Are these legally enforceable?
10. Describe the conditions that create a favorable opportunity for a new business of an existing kind.
11. Can you suggest a product or a service not currently available that might lead to a new small business? How safe would it be to launch a new small business depending solely on that one new product or service? Why?
12. What sources might be most appropriately consulted in investigating possibilities for a new (a) restaurant, (b) drugstore, (c) shoe repair shop, (d) service station, and (e) coin-operated, self-service laundry?
13. Can the investigation of a potential opportunity for a new business ever be too thorough? Explain.

13

Selecting the
Legal Form
of Organization

Should the new small firm be set up as a sole proprietorship, a partnership, or a corporation? Whether an owner buys, inherits, or starts the business, he faces this question at once. Moreover, the problem reappears as a business grows; firms begun as sole proprietorships later may find it desirable to become partnerships or even to incorporate.

These three forms of legal organization—sole proprietorship, partnership, and corporation—are most common. In fact, 99 percent of all firms fall in these categories. Other rarely used forms may be best for given ventures, however. Such minor forms include (1) limited partnership, (2) mining partnership, (3) partnership association, (4) joint-stock company, and (5) trust. Because they are rarely used, these forms are not described in this text.[1]

Before we discuss the most common forms of legal organization, it would be appropriate first to point out the merits of selecting an attorney who can give the prospective entrepreneur competent legal counsel, not only in selecting the form of business organization but also in many other legal matters involved in the operation of a small business.

ROLE OF THE ATTORNEY

An attorney's major function in serving a small firm is preventive in nature. That is, the objective is to insure observance of all legal requirements in the establishment and operation of the client firm. Other functions of the attorney include representing the businessman in court, before various regulatory bodies, and before other governmental agencies; serving in the negotiation of labor contracts with a union; and drawing up real estate or other contracts.

Subject Areas That Necessitate Legal Advice

A number of significant areas in which the small business entrepreneur may be given legal assistance by an attorney are briefly summarized on page 213.

---

[1] The interested small businessman should consult his attorney as to their nature and their possible usefulness to him. For other readers, these forms have no real significance; hence, they warrant no further exposition.

Choice of Form of Business Organization. The legal differences between the proprietorship, the partnership, and the corporation are important. These will be analyzed in later sections of this chapter.

Compliance with Labor Laws. In both unionized and nonunionized firms, the various laws pertaining to such matters as minimum wages, working hours, unemployment compensation, and industrial safety must be understood and followed carefully.

Acquisition of Real Property. In the purchase of real estate or in leasing property, the use of an attorney is highly desirable. In leases, for example, an attorney will check provisions regarding options to renew, ownership of improvements, subletting rights, and other details.

Purchase of Stock of Merchandise. Purchasing the stock of merchandise from another business—as in the purchase of a retail store—requires compliance with the *bulk sales law* or other relevant laws of the state. These laws are designed to protect creditors of the seller, and a clear title to the goods requires compliance with the laws.

Securing the Necessary Licenses. A *license* is a formal permission granted by a governmental body to carry on a stated business or to engage in a stated occupation which, without a license, would be illegal. Professionals such as certified public accountants, lawyers, dentists, and physicians require licenses. Businesses that require licenses include banks, insurance companies, bail bond companies, liquor stores, drugstores, collection agencies, and public warehouses. Personal service businesses or practitioners, such as barbers, beauticians, chauffeurs, electricians, morticians, optometrists, plumbers, and pilots, also require licenses.

Avoidance of Liens and Judgments Against the Seller. If the entrepreneur is purchasing an existing enterprise, the attorney should check the public records for possible existence of tax liens, mortgages, or judgments of record. There could also be undisclosed liabilities for taxes, outstanding product warranties made by the seller, tort claims against the seller not yet voided by the statute of limitations, consigned inventory items, payments due and unmade under lease or purchase contracts, and the like.

Observance of Local Ordinances. Prospective business owners should be interested in local ordinances such as building codes, sanitary requirements, and zoning. For example, to a small manufacturer who is renting his first building, the building code is important if the building requires alterations to make it useful for the intended business. Sanitary ordinances include those pertaining to all forms of pollution control and cleanliness practices. Zoning ordinances are also highly important because a business building must be in a properly zoned area, and no adverse zoning changes should be in prospect.

Choice of an Attorney

Of paramount importance in selecting an attorney is the quality of legal service that he or she can provide. Speed and cost are of secondary importance. An attorney must know the law, be an accurate interpreter of legal trends and judicial opinions, and be able to forecast outcomes of lawsuits. An attorney serves best when courtroom battles on the part of the client can be avoided.

Because of the range of legal issues involved in conducting a business and their frequency in arising, the relationship of the small business to its attorney should be a continuing one. Once a lawyer-client relationship is set up, the client should utilize the attorney's services promptly whenever the need arises.

RELATIVE IMPORTANCE OF FORMS OF BUSINESS ORGANIZATION

The relative importance of the different legal forms of organization varies from one industrial area to another. In retailing, for example, a sole proprietorship is most often used. However, Table 13-1 shows that corporations outsell all other organizational forms combined, while proprietorships outsell partnerships. Thus, a tendency for large firms to use the corporate form is discernible from these data.

Table 13-1
RELATIVE IMPORTANCE OF DIFFERENT FORMS OF LEGAL ORGANIZATION IN U.S. RETAIL TRADE

Form of Organization	Percent of Establishments	Percent of Sales
Sole proprietorships	68.8	25.1
Partnerships	8.1	6.7
Corporations	22.5	66.9
Other legal forms	0.6	1.3

Source: U.S. Bureau of the Census, *Enterprise Statistics: 1967, Part 1*—General Report on Industrial Organization (Washington: U.S. Government Printing Office, 1972).

Table 13-2
PERCENT OF RECEIPTS OF SELECTED U.S. SERVICE TRADES BY FORM OF LEGAL ORGANIZATION

	Sole Proprietorships	Partnerships	Corporations	Other Forms
Total Selected Services	**29.0**	**11.7**	**58.4**	**0.9**
Beauty shops	66.8	7.8	25.0	0.4
Auto repair shops	57.2	11.0	31.3	0.5
Hotels, motels, tourist courts, and camps	19.6	9.6	69.3	1.4
Laundries and dry cleaning plants	29.9	9.4	60.1	0.6
Miscellaneous repair services	54.1	7.7	37.6	0.5

Source: U.S. Bureau of the Census, *Enterprise Statistics: 1967, Part 1*—General Report on Industrial Organization (Washington: U.S. Government Printing Office, 1972).

Within the field of retailing, the relative importance of legal form varies from one line to another. Although retailing corporations outsell proprietorships overall, the reverse is true for gasoline service stations, florists, gift shops, and sporting goods stores.

In the service trades, as shown in Table 13-2, incorporated businesses account for 58.4 percent of total industry receipts. In auto repair and beauty shops, however, noncorporate forms are more numerous and account for the bulk of the receipts. Beauty shops exemplify the highly personal service typically provided by proprietorships; sole proprietorships account for 66.8 percent of all beauty shop receipts.

Table 13-3
PERCENT OF RECEIPTS IN U.S. WHOLESALE TRADE
BY FORM OF LEGAL ORGANIZATION

Form of Organization	Percent of Establishments	Percent of Sales
Sole proprietorships	31.5	10.6
Partnerships	8.0	6.5
Corporations	57.4	77.0
Cooperatives and other forms	3.1	5.9

Source: U.S. Bureau of the Census, *Enterprise Statistics: 1967, Part 1*—General Report on Industrial Organization (Washington: U.S. Government Printing Office, 1972).

Table 13-4
PERCENT OF ESTABLISHMENTS AND SALES IN U.S. MANUFACTURING PLANTS
BY FORM OF LEGAL ORGANIZATION

Form of Organization	Percent of Establishments	Percent of Sales
Sole proprietorships	21.2	1.2
Partnerships	4.3	0.8
Corporations	73.8	96.6
Other forms	0.7	1.3

Source: U.S. Bureau of the Census, *Enterprise Statistics: 1967, Part 1*—General Report on Industrial Organization (Washington: U.S. Government Printing Office, 1972).

It is evident from Table 13-3 that the corporation is much more important in wholesaling than in either retailing or the service trades. This is undoubtedly due to the larger size of establishment needed in wholesaling.

In manufacturing, the tendency towards corporate form is even more pronounced. Table 13-4 shows that more than 96 percent of manufacturing sales are accounted for by corporations. It seems clear that the larger the amount of capital required by a business, the more likely it is to choose the corporate form of organization.

THE SOLE PROPRIETORSHIP

Sole proprietorship is the name given to a business owned and operated by one individual. It is the oldest form of business organization known to man (with an origin lost in antiquity).

A sole proprietor has title to all enterprise assets, subject to the claims of creditors. He owns all the profits—but must also assume all losses, bear all risks, and pay all debts of the business. In most cases, he supplies the capital needed, assembles physical facilities and merchandise, and manages the business. By its very nature, it is obvious that the sole proprietorship is well-suited to small-scale enterprise.

Preliminary legal steps in establishing a proprietorship should include provision against the contingency of death of the sole proprietor. Death terminates the business, and the executor or heirs often must liquidate it because no heir is in a position to run it. A sole proprietor should make a will giving an executor testamentary powers to run the business for the benefit of the heirs until they can take over or until the business can be sold.

Incapacity of the proprietor is also possible. If he were badly hurt in an automobile wreck, and unconscious for weeks, his business could be ruined. But the proprietor can provide against such a contingency by giving a power of attorney to a legally competent person enabling the latter to carry on for him in such a situation.

THE PARTNERSHIP

A *partnership* is a voluntary "association of two or more persons to carry on as co-owners a business for profit." [2] Because of its voluntary nature, a partnership is quickly set up—without the legal formalities incident to corporate organization. It pools the managerial talents and capital of those joining together as business partners.

Qualifications of Partners

Under the law any person capable of contracting may become a partner in a business firm. Individuals may become partners without contributing to capital or sharing in the assets at the time of dissolution; they are then partners only as to management and profits.

Aside from legal aspects, however, partnership formation deserves serious study. A strong partnership requires partners who are honest, healthy, capable, and compatible. Also, ordinarily each should make both capital and management contributions to the firm.

Rights and Duties of Partners

Partners' rights and duties should be stated explicitly in the *articles of partnership*. In the absence of specific agreements to the contrary, however, a partner is generally recognized as having certain explicit rights. For example,

---

[2] This is the definition given in the Uniform Partnership Act—now adopted by most states.

partners share profits or losses equally if there is no pre-agreed profit-and-loss-sharing ratio. A partner is also entitled to a return of his invested capital upon dissolution of the firm—plus a share of accumulated earnings. In addition, a partner has the right to take part in management, receive pay for his services, obtain full business information, and inspect the books of account. Good faith, together with reasonable care in the exercise of management duties, is required of all partners in a business. Their relationship is fiduciary in character; hence, a partner cannot compete in business and remain a partner. Nor can he use business information solely for personal gain.

Articles of Partnership

The contract of partnership should, with the help of the attorney, be put in writing during the preoperating period. Articles of partnership should cover the following items as a minimum:

1. Date of formation of the partnership.
2. Names and addresses of all partners.
3. Statement of fact of partnership.
4. Statement of business purpose(s).
5. Duration of the business.
6. Name and location of the business.
7. Amount invested by each partner.
8. Sharing ratio for profits and losses.
9. Partners' rights, if any, for withdrawals of funds for personal use.
10. Provision for accounting records and their accessibility to partners.
11. Specific duties of each partner.
12. Provision for dissolution and for sharing the net assets.
13. Restraint on partners' assumption of special obligations, such as endorsing the note of another.
14. Provision for protection of surviving partners, decedent's estate, etc.

Termination of Partnership

Death, incapacity, or withdrawal of a partner terminates a partnership and necessitates liquidation or reorganization of the business. Liquidation often results in substantial losses to all partners. It may be legally necessary, however, because a partnership is a close personal relationship of the parties that cannot be maintained against the will of any one of them.

This disadvantage may be partially overcome at the time a partnership is formed by stipulating in the articles of partnership that surviving partners can continue the business after buying the decedent's interest from his estate. Or, the executor might act as a partner until the heirs become of age. In the latter case, the agreement should also provide for liquidation in event of unprofitability or in event of major disagreements with the executor as partner.

THE CORPORATION

In the Dartmouth College Case of 1819, Chief Justice John Marshall of the United States Supreme Court defined a *corporation* as "an artificial being, invisible, intangible, and existing only in contemplation of the law." By these words the court recognized the corporation as a legal person and a business entity. This means that it can sue and be sued, hold and sell property, and engage in business operations stipulated in the corporate charter.

Nature of the Corporation

The corporation is the creature of a state, being chartered under its laws. Its length of life is independent of owners' lives. It is the corporation, and not its owners, that is liable for debts contracted by it. Its directors and officers serve as agents to bind the corporation.

Status of the Stockholders

Ownership in a corporation is evidenced by stock certificates, each of which stipulates the number of shares held by the given stockholder. An ownership interest does not confer a legal right to act for the firm or to share in its management. It does evidence the right to receive dividends in proportion to stockholdings—but only when they are properly declared by the board of directors. And it typically carries the right to buy new shares, in proportion to stock already owned, before the new stock is offered for public sale.

In addition, a stockholder casts one vote per share in stockholders' meetings. Thus, indirectly, he participates in management by helping elect the directors. The board of directors is the governing body for corporate activity. It elects the firm's officers, who manage the enterprise with the help of hired subordinates, all of whom should be management specialists in their areas of activity. The directors also set or approve management policies, receive and consider reports on operating results from the officers, and declare dividends (if any).

The legal status of stockholders and managers is fundamental, of course, but it may be overemphasized in the case of many small corporations. The owners may also be directors and managing officers. If one man owns most of the stock, he can control the firm as effectively as if it were a sole proprietorship. In such a case, he names his attorney and wife as fellow directors, perhaps, and the directors meet only when legally required to do so. They can elect him president and general manager of the firm. This is not to imply that it is good business practice to ignore a board of directors but simply to point out that direction and control may be exercised as forcefully by a majority owner in a small corporation as by a sole proprietor. The corporate form is thus applicable to individual and family-owned businesses.

Corporate Charter

In most states, obtaining a corporate charter requires application by three or more persons to the secretary of state for permission to incorporate. After preliminary steps, including required publicity and payment of the incorporation fee and initial franchise tax, the written application is approved by the secretary of state and becomes the corporation's charter. Such a corporation charter typically provides for the following:

1. Name of the company.
2. Formal statement of its formation.
3. Purposes and powers—that is, type of business.
4. Location of principal office in the state of incorporation.
5. Duration (perpetual existence, 50-year life and renewable charter, etc.).
6. Classes and preferences of classes of stock.
7. Number and par or stated value of shares of each class of stock authorized.
8. Voting privileges of each class of stock.
9. Names and addresses of incorporators and first year's directors.
10. Names and addresses of, and amounts subscribed by, each subscriber to capital stock.
11. Statement of limited liability of stockholders (required specifically by state law in many states).
12. Statement of alterations of directors' powers, if any, from the general corporation law of the state.

A corporation's charter should be brief, in accord with the law, and broad in the statement of the firm's powers. Details should be left to the bylaws. The charter application should be prepared by an attorney. When the charter is received from the secretary of state, it should be recorded immediately with the county clerk, after which the incorporators should hold the formal organization meeting, adopt bylaws, and elect officers.

Limited Liability of Stockholders

One of the advantages of the corporate form of organization is the limited liability of owners for debts of the firm. However, new small business corporations often are in somewhat shaky financial circumstances during the early years of operation. As a result, the stockholders, few in number and active in management, frequently assume personal liability for the firm's debts by endorsement of its notes.

Death or Withdrawal of Stockholders

Unlike the partnership, ownership in a corporation is readily transferable. Exchange of shares of stock, evidenced by stock certificates, is all that is required to convey an ownership interest to a different individual.

In a large corporation, stock is being exchanged constantly without noticeable effect upon the operations of the business. In the small firm, however, the change of owners, though legally just as simple, may produce numerous complications. To illustrate, suppose that two of the three equal shareholders in a business, because of a disagreement or for other reasons, sold their stock to an outsider. The remaining stockholder would then be at the mercy of the outsider, who might decide to remove him from any managerial post he happened to hold. In fact, he may be legally ousted from the board of directors and have no voice in the management whatsoever.

The death of the majority stockholder could be equally unfortunate. An heir, executor, or purchaser of the stock might well insist upon direct control, with possible adverse effects for the other stockholders.

To prevent problems of this nature from arising, legal arrangements should be made at the time of incorporation to provide for management continuity by surviving stockholders as well as for fair treatment of heirs of a decedent stockholder. As in the case of the partnership, mutual insurance may be carried to assure ability to buy out the decedent. This would also require an option to permit purchase by the corporation or surviving stockholders ahead of outsiders and specification of a method for determining the price per share to be paid for the stock. A similar purchase option and pricing arrangement might well be included to protect remaining stockholders if a given stockholder wished to retire from the business at any time.

FACTORS AFFECTING SELECTION OF FORM OF ORGANIZATION

The advantages and disadvantages inherent in the three major forms of organization cannot fail to be of interest to a prospective entrepreneur. They should be ascertained—and duly weighed—prior to selection of the form of business organization to be used.

Management Control

In the sole proprietorship there is no question as to who is "boss." The individual proprietor has total, undivided authority in running his business. In contrast, a partnership requires consultation with partners, and a corporation requires consideration of other stockholders and officers.

Control of a business is shared in varying degrees, depending on the form of organization used. In a partnership, each partner has *agency power* and so can bind all members of the firm. In a corporation, stockholders elect directors, who then select officers to run the business. In the smaller corporation, thus, a major stockholder has the legal right to control so long as he respects the rights of minority shareholders. Questions of authority are not always settled, however, by referring to the legal status of other owners; in practice, an owner controlling a small business may often consult with co-owners even though they own only a small part of the business.

Given one-man control, an entrepreneur avoids the possible conflicts and delays that afflict companies run by a management team. If an owner-manager makes decisions wisely, subsequent to thorough investigations of the facts, he can act freely in any emergency, without wasting time and effort in explanation of his decisions to associates. Otherwise, a colleague might block a desirable course of action.

However, for those who work well with others, a partnership provides potential advantages. Partners share the burdens of management and the decision-making responsibility. They provide counsel of a sort unavailable to the sole proprietor. When properly selected, each partner brings to the firm both capital and some sort of specialized management skills. In the corporation a number of co-owners (1) similarly may pool diverse managerial talents, and (2) may also hire other management specialists to work for them. Thus, neither of these forms lacks management depth as a sole proprietorship typically does. There is a potentially serious drawback to collective management, however, because of possible conflicts of personalities.

Accordingly, in choosing a form of organization, the prospective entrepreneur must decide how important it is to have complete authority and control. His decision involves a consideration of how well he can work with others and of how much he trusts their honesty and business judgment. Only he can make this decision—after weighing all pertinent factors.

Sharing of Profits

A prospective entrepreneur must also consider ownership of profits before deciding to be a sole or a part owner. If willing to share profits, he or she may decide on a partnership or corporation. If unwilling to share profits, a sole proprietorship or a one-person corporation is the better choice.

In a partnership, profits and losses are shared according to a ratio stated in the contract of partnership. In the corporation, however, the owners actually receive profits only when their elected representatives (the directors) declare a dividend. If a majority owner is interested primarily in business growth, the board of directors might pass all dividends for years—until the minority stockholders are forced to go to court to secure an accounting for profits. Hence, the right to share in profits, in the case of a small corporation, is a qualified right that is sometimes of little value.

Transfer of Ownership

Sole proprietors transfer an ownership interest at will simply by selling their businesses to others. No one can prevent such a sale unless the bulk sales law is violated. In a corporation, also, it is easy to transfer an ownership interest. One merely sells his stock and delivers the covering stock certificate to the broker or the buyer. The consent of co-owners is not legally required.

In the case of a partnership, transferring an ownership interest is much harder. A partnership is an intimate, personal relationship in the eyes of the law, and one partner cannot sell out to an outsider without his partners' consent. This is true even when a partner wishes to retire for cause (such as disability, old age, or other incapacity) or wishes to transfer his interest to a son. Hence, partnership life depends on a retiring partner's ability to find a satisfactory, able, compatible person to take his place. This is a serious drawback to this form of organization, as it can lead to forced liquidation of a profitable firm. Losses for all partners are then likely. Of course, if they can pay his price, the remaining partners could buy out the one who is retiring. Moreover, the same type of problem arises whenever a partner dies.

Operating and Expansion Capital and Credit

The owner should supply most of the initial capital of a sole proprietorship, and expansion funds must come either from retained earnings, new owner investment, or borrowing. Credit is available but limited in amount. This poses a real problem since most would-be entrepreneurs are not rich. Even the sum of $5,000 is beyond the resources of many who wish to start a business. Capital limitation, initially, as well as for expansion, is a major weakness of the sole proprietorship.

A partnership is in a better position to acquire capital funds. Initial capital comes from two or more persons, and so it is typically greater than that of a sole proprietorship. Moreover, expansion funds are easier to obtain due to the partnership's larger line of credit.

A corporation, however, can draw its initial capital from savings of the general public. If it does offer stock to the public, initial capital is limited only by the amount of capital stock authorized and the investors' willingness to buy. Even when there are but few investors, the corporate form often is superior to a partnership for combining their resources. In the case of *close corporations*, of course, there is no attempt to pool the capital of many persons. The major shareholder's investment is essentially the total, and total equity capital is thus determined by his financial capacity.

Liability for Enterprise Debts

If a business fails, its creditors have claims against its assets. These must be sold, if necessary, to pay such claims. If the proceeds do not satisfy such claims in full, the creditors may then attach the nonbusiness assets of a sole proprietor. The latter has unlimited personal liability for his firm's debts. This is a potent legal disadvantage of the sole proprietorship unless the proprietor invests substantially all his assets in the firm.

Similarly, each partner in a partnership has unlimited personal liability for enterprise debts, up to the full extent of his personal resources. This is true even when the articles of partnership specify a profit-and-loss-sharing ratio as between the partners. Such an internal agreement does not bind outsiders. This form of organization often is unattractive, because a wealthy partner might see his personal assets taken for partnership debts in the event of business bankruptcy. In return, he would get only a claim against his insolvent partners. Such a claim is often worthless. This liability-for-debt disadvantage may be even more significant for a partnership than for a proprietorship.

In the case of a corporation, however, the individual owners—called stockholders—have limited liability for debts contracted by the firm. Their personal assets cannot be attached by the firm's creditors in the event of bankruptcy. This is a major advantage of the corporate form. Nevertheless, a would-be enterpreneur should weigh for himself the extent of risk involved in personal liability for debts of the firm before rejecting the proprietorship and partnership forms of organization. If he has few nonbusiness assets, limited liability may be of negligible value to him.

Taxes and Government Regulation

Sole proprietors and business partners enjoy several tax advantages. They pay only a personal tax, at the current individual tax rate, on net taxable income including business profits. And because their remuneration comes solely from profits, they escape income taxes entirely in years of business losses. A corporation, however, pays an income tax on profits, if any, and stockholders receiving cash dividends from the same profits pay a second, personal income tax. Moreover, even in years of business loss, salaries of owner-managers of small corporations are personally taxable. In addition, shareholders are subject to stock transfer taxes, while the corporation pays an annual franchise tax. These differences tend to make the corporate tax position inferior to that of the other forms.

However, it is impossible to state categorically that any particular form of organization is superior from a tax standpoint. Much depends upon the particular business—its level of income, other income of owners, number of owners, and so on. The various tax characteristics of the different forms have been noted earlier, but almost every feature of business taxation has a reservation or a modification that makes it pertinent or meaningless for the making of a particular decision. For example:

1. The corporate form causes double taxation of income; but small, closely held corporations can qualify in some cases for taxation as partnerships.
2. Double taxation of corporate income may be unimportant if the business pays such salaries (consistent with tax regulations) to its owners that the business shows no profit. The same thing is true if the business operates at a loss for any reason.
3. Only the corporate income tax must be paid on earnings retained in the business—which avoids, at least temporarily, the "double tax" feature. This corporation tax may be less than the individual tax applicable to incomes of persons in high tax brackets.

The sole proprietorship and partnership also escape a considerable amount of government regulation. For example, both forms are legally free to operate in any state due to their common-law origin. Nevertheless, small partnerships and proprietorships engaging in interstate commerce are subject to some regulation. Examples include the Social Security laws and the regulations covering collection of employees' income taxes. Both also are subject to the price-fixing controls of the Federal Trade Commission.

Corporations, however, undergo greater regulation than the other organizational forms. They must report annually to stockholders. They cannot issue bonds without formal approval from the Securities and Exchange Commission. They must make regular income tax withholding and Social Security reports. They are supervised by the Federal Trade Commission and other federal agencies. Nor can the corporation do anything not explicitly authorized by its charter. In fact, it cannot do any business in states other than the one that issued its charter without first qualifying in other states as a foreign corporation.

 Summary

1. The legal problems involved in starting and operating a business make it desirable to establish quickly a working relationship with a competent attorney.
2. An attorney is needed to approve or draw up contracts, deeds, or other legal documents; represent the firm in lawsuits; assure that the enterprise is legally started; and furnish advice on specific questions and pertinent legal trends.

3. Practically all small businesses are organized as sole proprietorships, partnerships, or corporations. The minor forms of organization are only rarely used.

4. In retailing, most (68.8 percent) of the firms are organized as proprietorships. However, corporations account for almost 67 percent of the sales. In some specific lines of retailing, such as gifts and sporting goods, the proprietorship is relatively much stronger. In the service trades, wholesaling, and manufacturing, corporations account for well over one half of total sales. The corporate form is thus the dominant form in each area when measured in terms of sales volume.

5. In sole proprietorships, one individual is sole owner. He risks the loss of his investment, but he owns all the profits. In establishing a proprietorship, provision should be made to protect against the death or incapacity of the owner.

6. A partnership is a voluntary association of two or more persons as co-owners, each of whom can act unrestrictedly for the firm in dealing with outsiders. A unique legal aspect of the partnership is the general agency status of each partner that permits him to bind the firm and the partners. The partnership agreement should be in written form and should include all significant elements in the relationship. Death, incapacity, or withdrawal of a partner terminates a partnership and necessitates liquidation or reorganization of the business.

7. A corporation, while owned by its stockholders, is a legal entity in its own right. Some small corporations, family dominated, are known as *close corporations*. In beginning as a corporation, the firm must procure a corporate charter from the state. One major advantage of the corporate form of organization is the limited liability of stockholders, since the corporation itself is liable for its debts. Another is that ownership shares are readily transferable by exchange of stock certificates.

8. Some of the major factors affecting the choice of legal form of organization are the following: (a) the extent to which management control is shared with others; (b) extent to which profits are shared with others; (c) ease with which ownership of a business can be transferred to others; (d) amount of capital available through the various forms of organization; (e) personal liability for business debts in some forms of organization; and (f) impact of taxes and government regulation.

Discussion Questions

1. Of what significance is the small entrepreneur's choice of an attorney? Upon what types of problems should the attorney be consulted?

2. For which form of legal organization is the attorney's assistance most essential in starting a new business? Explain.

3. Suppose you are entering the field of building contracting (with emphasis upon home building). Should you have an attorney under retainer? Why? Upon what basis would he be selected?

4. Discuss the relative importance of the major forms of organization in (a) retailing, (b) wholesaling, (c) manufacturing, and (d) service trades? How do you account for these differences?

5. Evaluate the three major forms of organization from the standpoints of management control by the owner; of sharing the firm's profits; and of ease of transferring ownership interests.

6. It is said that the corporate form permits a larger aggregation of capital. Would a prospective entrepreneur always be able to procure a greater total capital by use of the corporate form? Explain.

7. Is degree of liability for debt ordinarily a significant factor in choosing the legal form of organization? Why? Is it ever possibly a factor of negligible concern in selecting the form of organization? Why?

8. What seems to be the most important factor in choosing the legal form of organization? Why?

9. What legal requirements are there that apply equally, or similarly, to proprietorships, partnerships, and corporations?

10. In what types of businesses, if any, are local ordinances (zoning, licensing, and the like) of negligible importance? Why?

11. Should a small businessman have a will? If he does need a will, should it have a section dealing with his business and its disposition? Why?

12. Why is the general agency status of business partners of great importance?

13. Suppose a partnership is set up and operated without formal articles of partnership being drawn up and signed. What problems might arise? Explain.

14. If a general partner in a business retires or dies, what happens to the partnership?

15. The life of a corporation is independent of the life of any one or all of its stockholders. This being true, how might a stockholder's death create business and legal problems? Explain.

16. Explain the relative impacts of government regulation on each of the three major forms of legal organization. What effect might this have upon an entrepreneur's choice of form of organization?

17. Given normal business growth, would the initially chosen form of legal organization be changed eventually? Why? If so, at what point?

14

Obtaining Capital and Credit

The most important problem in starting a small business is to make a thorough study of the amount of capital needed to promote and organize the new venture. A companion problem is that of determining which sources to utilize in raising the funds required.

Beginning capital consists of *owner capital* and *creditor capital*. Traditionally it is said that the ownership equity in a new firm should be at least two thirds of the total capital. If the venture involves a total initial capital of $12,000, for example, the owner should invest $8,000 from his personal funds. The balance of $4,000 would then be supplied by creditor capital in the form of bank loans, loans from individuals, trade credit, or credit from equipment suppliers. This "two thirds" dictum is quite conservative, and many small businesses are started with ownership equities that are smaller. However, many small firms fail every year due to inadequate ownership equity. The conservative approach thus provides the prospective entrepreneur with a margin of safety that the shoestring operator lacks.

NATURE OF CAPITAL NEEDS OF A NEW BUSINESS

The specific nature of a proposed business venture governs the nature of its financial requirements. If the firm is a food store, financial planning must make provision for the store building, cash registers, shopping carts, inventory, office equipment, and other items required in this type of operation. An analysis of capital requirements for this or any other type of business must consider several types of needs. These needs include working capital, fixed asset capital, promotional expense capital, and funds to cover personal expenses for an initial period of operation.

Working Capital

The businessman often refers to the sum total of current assets as the working capital of the firm. It is more precisely defined as the excess of current assets over current liabilities. According to the former, less technical definition, working capital consists of the cash, accounts and notes receivable, immediately marketable investments, and trade inventories of the business. *Circulating capital,* a term which is sometimes applied to working capital, emphasizes its constant change from cash to inventory to receivables to cash, and so on.

Cash. Every firm must first provide for the cash essential for current business operations. This reservoir of cash is needed because of the uneven flow of funds into the business (as income) and out of the business (as expense). The size of this reservoir is determined not only by the volume of sales but also by the regularity of cash receipts and cash payments. Uncertainties also exist because of unpredictable decisions by customers as to when they will pay their bills and because of emergencies calling for substantial cash outlays. If an adequate cash balance is maintained, the firm can take such unexpected developments and irregularities in stride.

Accounts and Notes Receivable. The firm's accounts receivable, that is, the payments due from its customers, comprise another important item of working capital. If the firm expects to sell on a credit basis—and in many lines of business this is virtually imperative—provision must be made for financing receivables. The firm cannot wait until its customers pay to restock its shelves. Of course, the proportion of cash and credit sales significantly affects the size of receivables, as do the terms of sale offered to credit customers. The size of the necessary investment in receivables is likewise affected by seasonality of sales and by changes in business conditions which influence promptness of payment by many of the customers.

Inventories. Although the relative importance of inventories differs considerably from one type of business to another, they often constitute a major part of working capital. Factors affecting the size of the minimum inventory include the seasonality of sales and production. In the case of manufacturing firms, the length of the production cycle likewise influences the minimum work-in-process inventory.

It is apparent that some of the working capital remains in the business continuously. Whether it be January, July, or any other month, this minimum is required in the form of cash, inventory, and receivables. In addition, most businesses find need for temporary increases because of seasonal or other fluctuations in the level of their business activity. Retail stores, for example, may find it desirable to carry a larger-than-normal inventory during the Christmas season.

Fixed Asset Capital

Fixed assets are the relatively permanent assets that are intended for use in the business rather than for sale. They are not converted into cash quickly as is true of the current assets. To illustrate, a delivery truck used by a grocer to deliver merchandise to customers is a fixed asset. In the case of an automobile dealer, however, the delivery truck he intends to sell would be a part of his inventory and thus a current asset of his business.

Capital is needed in the new business to provide for the following types of fixed assets:

1. Tangible fixed assets.
   (a) Building, machinery, and equipment.
   (b) Land, including mineral rights, timber, and the like.
2. Intangible fixed assets—including patents, copyrights, goodwill. Many new firms have no intangible fixed assets.
3. Fixed security investments. These include stocks of subsidiaries, pension funds, and contingency funds. In most cases, a new business has no fixed security investments.

The nature and size of the fixed asset investment are determined by the type of business operation. A modern beauty shop, for example, may be equipped for around $30,000, whereas a motel sometimes requires fifty or more times that amount. In any given kind of business, moreover, there is a minimum quantity or assortment of facilities needed for efficient operation. It would seldom be profitable, for example, to operate a motel with only one or two units. It is this principle, of course, that excludes small business from automobile manufacturing and other types of heavy industry.

A firm's flexibility is inversely related to its investment in fixed assets. Investments in land, buildings, and equipment involve long-term commitments. Equipment is typically specialized, and substantial losses and delays often occur in liquidation. The inflexibility inherent in fixed asset investment underscores the importance of careful investigation and correct evaluation of fixed asset needs.

Promotional Expense Capital

The third kind of capital needed to initiate a new enterprise is promotional expense capital. Those who expend time and money organizing a business expect repayment of their personal funds and payment for their services as promoters. Payment of the promoter may take the form of a cash fee or of an ownership interest in the business. Of course, many new enterprises come into being as sole proprietorships, with the entrepreneur acting as his own promoter. In this case the proprietor must have sufficient funds to pay all necessary out-of-pocket promotional costs even though he may contribute his time.

Promoters often spend both time and effort on financial and legal planning. Then there are expenditures for utility company deposits, options for purchase or lease of land and buildings, attorney's fees, state organization tax and first year's franchise tax (if a corporation), clerical help, searching out and committing sources of equity capital, finding a suitable business location, and the like. All these are legitimate outlays.

Funds for Personal Expenses

In the truly small business, financial provision must also be made for the personal living expenses of the owner and his dependents during an initial period of operation. Technically this is not a part of the business capitalization, but it must be considered in connection with the business financial plan of the hopeful entrepreneur. The reason for such advance preparation to meet personal expenses is found in the typical failure of small concerns to produce profits at the very beginning even though long-run profit prospects are good.

Inadequate provision for personal expenses will inevitably lead to diversion of business assets and departure from the financial plan.

ESTIMATING CAPITAL REQUIREMENTS

In determining financial requirements, the prospective entrepreneur faces a necessary but difficult task. Part of the difficulty results from the problem of trying to peer into the future. If the business is to be an entirely new venture, the entrepreneur quickly feels the need for a "crystal ball" to use in making forecasts. If an established business is being taken over, the uncertainties are reduced, but they are by no means eliminated.

The previous background of the entrepreneur often is such as to make financial planning appear exceedingly complex and distasteful. For example, one whose experience is in production or sales may be unfamiliar with even simple accounting technology. Worse yet, a prospective entrepreneur might regard financial planning as a task that involves only "paper work."

Although the prospective entrepreneur should personally dig as deeply as possible into future financial needs, he or she should also seek factual information and counsel from various outside sources. It is often quite feasible to visit other businesses, similar to, but not directly competitive with, the proposed business. The prospective entrepreneur can sound them out as to capital requirements and inspect their physical facilities for doing business. In addition, guidance and specific data on certain points can often be obtained by consulting suppliers, wholesalers, CPA's, bankers, trade associations, and chambers of commerce.

Determining Probable Sales Volume

As a first step in estimating capital requirements, it is necessary to determine the volume of sales that may be expected. This step is required because the minimum amount of so many assets fluctuates directly with business volume. It obviously requires more inventory and accounts receivable, for example, to operate with sales of $500,000 than it does with sales of $250,000. Similarly, more cash is needed to pay expenses if the larger volume of sales is anticipated.

One approach to sales prediction is to select a desired profit figure and to work backward from that to sales. Suppose that the proposed business is a job printing shop and that the prospective entrepreneur hopes to earn annual profits of $15,000. If the industry standard ratio shows that job printers typically earn 5 percent on sales, the prospective entrepreneur must then achieve sales of 20 times the proposed profit, or $300,000.

The $300,000 sales figure now constitutes the minimum sales one must secure to make the venture sufficiently attractive. It does not prove, however, that the proposed business will guarantee this amount of sales. In fact, this figure should be cross-checked in as many ways as possible. If it is an existing business, there are past sales records for comparison. In a new business, the sales records of other, somewhat similar firms may provide a bench mark for checking. Those with close contact and experience in the line of business—suppliers, possibly—may have a more informed opinion as to whether one might reasonably hope for $300,000 worth of business.

Translating Sales Data into Asset Requirements by Use of Industry Standard Ratios

Having arrived at a sales figure as objectively as possible, the next step is to compute the amount of assets necessary for that particular sales volume. Once again, the prospective entrepreneur may use the double-barreled approach of applying standard ratios and cross-checking by empirical investigation.

Industry standard ratios are compiled for numerous types of business concerns. They are available from Dun & Bradstreet, bankers, trade associations, and many other organizations. If no standard data can be located, the estimating inevitably involves even more guesswork.

Some suggested approaches in the use of standard ratios to compute figures on various types of assets are described below.

Inventory. The ratio of net sales to inventory can be used to determine the inventory requirements. If the net sales of a drug wholesaler are typically six times inventory, a $100,000 inventory to accommodate sales of $600,000 would be required. After all estimates for working capital have been completed, inventory might be further checked by noting its industry standard relationships to current liabilities and to net working capital. The drug wholesaler, for example, might find that inventory is typically 60 percent of current debt and 90 percent of net working capital.

Accounts Receivable. If the average collection period and amount of credit sales are known, the average amount tied up in accounts receivable can be calculated. Machine shops, for example, may have an average collection period of 37 days, which means that 37 days' sales are "on the books" at any given time. If annual sales are $400,000, the owner must have 37/365 of this amount, or $40,548, in accounts receivable (to conform to the industry standard firm).

Cash. The inflow and outflow of cash are by no means synchronized. The amount of cash needed to provide for heavier outflow might be estimated initially by first computing current assets and then subtracting the amounts for inventory and receivables, as determined above. Also, the out-of-pocket expenses can be determined by noting their usual relationship to sales. By estimating the number of days these expenses must be paid before cash is received to cover them, the required amount of cash is evident. For a new business, however, it is customary and desirable to provide cash reserves to meet unexpected contingencies, so considerable subjective judgment is needed in estimating the desired cash balance.

It should again be emphasized that the standard ratios may specify an amount of cash that is too small for a new business. For one thing, the prospective entrepreneur is typically overly optimistic. Unexpected emergencies may also occur, and mistakes may be made in estimating normal capital requirements. Conservative financial planning would call for the establishment of cash reserves to cover unanticipated demands of this type and to counterbalance the rose-colored view of future prospects.

Fixed Assets. Total investment in fixed assets may be estimated by comparing fixed assets to tangible net worth, which, itself, may be derived from sales.

Suppose a shoe retailer with expected sales of $400,000 discovered that net sales typically are four times tangible net worth. This would indicate that tangible net worth should be $100,000. If fixed assets are usually 13 percent of tangible net worth, the shoe retailer would have to plan in terms of a $13,000 fixed asset investment.

As a final check, it may be possible to obtain a break-even point percentage for the proposed type of business. This is the percentage of capacity or normal level that must be reached to avoid loss. The fixed costs, for example, may be such that operating at less than 75 percent of normal would cause losses for the business. If the proposed investment would result in a break-even point that is lower than normal for the industry, the estimates are probably safe. If the break-even point exceeds that for the industry, there is cause for concern and need for rechecking and modification.

Determining Capital Requirements by Empirical Investigation

Although ratio analysis is illuminating, it is hazardous to rely exclusively on this approach in determining capital requirements. Either prior to, simultaneously with, or subsequent to ratio analysis of capital requirements, the entrepreneur should make an independent, empirical investigation of capital needs. If there are substantial discrepancies in estimates provided by the two different approaches, rechecking would be necessary to discover which appears more likely to be accurate.

Working Capital Requirements. In estimating working capital requirements, the entrepreneur must first compute the amount of cash necessary to cover anticipated expenditures before revenue begins coming in. This involves a study of anticipated payments for labor, utilities, rent, supplies, and other expenses following initiation of the firm. In many types of business, a cash balance adequate to pay one or two months' expenses is desirable. The estimated cash figure should be checked with an experienced person to assure realism. As noted earlier, the time required to achieve a satisfactory volume and the possibility of unexpected expenses call for a generous estimate of cash requirements. The same type of investigation should be used to ascertain the probable investment in accounts receivable.

Inventory Requirements. In analyzing inventory requirements, the specific type and quantities of items to be kept in inventory must be considered. In the case of a clothing retailer, for example, the entrepreneur must make a distribution by sizes and styles of items to be sold to customers. The costs in stocking this merchandise can then be computed by reference to prices quoted by suppliers. A prospective manufacturer identifies the types and quantities of raw materials to be kept on hand, considering the rate of usage, location of suppliers, and the time required to replenish supplies. Schedules may also be prepared showing the labor and material costs going into the production process so that adequate provision is made for both finished goods inventory and work-in-process inventory.

If possible, all such inventory projections should be checked with those who have experience in the particular line of business. Suppliers—wholesalers, for example, if the proposed firm is a retail establishment—are among the best sources of advice concerning inventory, among other requirements. From a furniture wholesaler, for instance, the prospective furniture dealer might obtain a model stock list.

Fixed Assets Requirements. In calculating capital needed for procurement of fixed assets, price quotations are often available. Land and building cost estimates may be based on prices asked by sellers. Equipment suppliers can quote prices for machinery, equipment, tools, furniture, and fixtures. Actual price quotations should be obtained; and, as with working capital items, the adequacy of proposed fixed assets should be checked with those acquainted with the particular line of business.

Common Weaknesses in Capital Estimation

The need for adequate working capital deserves special emphasis. A common weakness in small business financing is the disproportionately small investment in current assets relative to fixed assets. In such weakly financed firms, too much of the capital is tied up in assets that are difficult to convert to cash. Danger arises from the fact that the business depends upon daily receipts to meet obligations coming due from day to day. If there is a slump in sales or unexpected expenses, creditors may force the firm into bankruptcy.

The lack of flexibility associated with the purchase of fixed assets suggests the desirability of minimizing this type of investment. Often, for example, there is a choice between renting or buying property. For perhaps the majority of new small firms, renting provides the better alternative. A rental arrangement not only reduces the capital requirement but also provides a flexibility that is helpful if the business is more successful or less successful than anticipated. It also provides a tax deductible operating expense.

SOURCES OF FUNDS FOR A NEW BUSINESS

The relative importance of different sources of funds to small firms is indicated in Table 14-1. According to these data, it appears that a bit less than half (44.1 percent) of the capital of small corporations must be supplied by the owner or owners. It is also apparent that small firms rely more heavily upon short-term financing—accounts payable and notes payable—than do larger firms.

It is possible that firms beginning operation may differ somewhat from existing small firms in the sources of capital which they use. Unfortunately completely adequate data are not available. It is probable that personal savings are more important for the beginning business than for the existing firm.

The sources of funds discussed in this chapter are particularly important in establishing the original financial structure of the new firm. Of course, these and other sources of funds are used both in initial financing and in the subsequent day-to-day financing of business operations. Those sources which are more closely related to "going concern" financing are treated in Chapter 19.

Table 14-1
LIABILITIES AND NET WORTH,
ALL AND SMALL NONFINANCIAL CORPORATIONS, 1969 *

Item	All Sizes Amount (In Billions)	Percent	Assets Under $250,000 Amount (In Billions)	Percent
Accounts and notes payable	$ 221.9	20.5	$18.8	33.1
Bonds and mortgages	247.2	22.8	8.5	14.9
Other current liabilities **	79.6	7.4	4.5	7.9
Net worth	533.2	49.2	25.0	44.1
Total liabilities and net worth	$1,081.9	99.9***	56.8	100.0

* Excludes banks, insurance carriers, and real estate firms.
** Other liabilities include reserves for estimated expense, prepaid income, and accrued expenses.
*** Does not total 100% because of rounding.

Source: Internal Revenue Service, *Statistics of Income 1969, Corporation Income Tax Returns*, pp. 26 and 50.

Personal Savings

In the business world there is an ever-present danger of loss. The private business venture combines risk of ownership with a possibility of profit. One who takes the risks of losing personal capital will require a prospect of profits and a right to a proportionate share of them. This means that a substantial part of the capital for new businesses, whose futures are uncertain, must of necessity be risk or venture capital. It is unrealistic to expect bankers to supply venture capital at their ordinary loan rate of interest, which merely repays the lender for the use of his money without substantial risk.

Although stock may occasionally be sold to outsiders, a possibility discussed in Chapter 19, the ownership equity must typically come from the founder or founders of the business. It is not only difficult but also quite hazardous to borrow venture capital. The requirement of fixed interest charges and definite dates of repayment means sure failure if prospects fail to materialize exactly as expected. It was for this reason that a two thirds ownership equity was recommended earlier in this chapter.

Commercial Bank Loans

Although commercial bankers tend to limit their lending to working capital needs of going concerns, some initial capital does come from this source. If the small firm is adequately financed in terms of equity capital and if the entrepreneur is of good character, the commercial bank may loan on the basis of signature only. Of course, this is less likely for the beginning firm than for the established one. In any event, collateral is often required.

Collateral Arrangements. On some notes the name of a cosigner provides adequate security to satisfy the bank. If the borrowing firm is a corporation, such an arrangement is often used to hold the principals personally liable. Collateral arrangements include a wide range of assets and security provisions. Inventory, for example, is often pledged as collateral for short-term loans. In *floor planning*—one type of inventory financing—the bank loans money on items specifically identified by serial number (such as automobiles, boats, or major appliances). When a particular item is sold to a customer, the dealer must either pay his obligation to the bank or arrange for the bank to substitute an installment contract with the purchaser. In another variety of inventory financing known as *field warehousing*, a warehouse company takes over a portion of the borrower's facilities—a section of a grocery wholesale storage area, for example—and controls the inventory supporting the loan.

In addition to inventory, other assets serving as collateral include accounts receivable, life insurance policies, equipment, and real estate. Chattel mortgages and real estate mortgages are particularly useful in supporting longer term loan requests.

Long-Term vs. Short-Term Borrowing. Short-term borrowing should be limited to working capital loans, the repayment of which is not only scheduled by the lender but budgeted for and reasonably within expectation of the borrower. The purpose of such borrowing is to acquire funds to meet temporary needs for cash, such as to pay for merchandise, cover payrolls, or take care of other maturing obligations. Permanent working capital and fixed assets should be supplied by owner investment or long-term loans. It is often disastrous to finance a substantial portion of the fixed investment by short-term borrowing because the debt matures before the fixed investment can be amortized from the income it yields.

Long-term borrowing actually is divided into intermediate-term and long-term borrowing. Intermediate-term borrowing consists of loans maturing from two to five years after the loan is negotiated. Long-term loans are those maturing after five years from the date of the loan; they are likely to be 10- to 25-year loans. The funds from such loans go to obtain physical facilities for production of goods, for store fixtures, and the like.

Unused Debt Capacity. Initial financing should be carried out with an eye to the future. This means that initial commitments should not preclude further financial moves that will become desirable or necessary later. If emergencies arise, the new firm may need additional capital to weather the storm. As the business is successful, it will also need additional capital to finance expansion. For these reasons, the firm should not totally exhaust its borrowing capacity at first. The unused debt capacity can then be used for either emergency or expansion purchases.

Choosing One's Banker Wisely. The varied services rendered by a bank to a small firm make the choice of a bank highly significant. The provision of checking account facilities and extension of short-term (and possibly long-term) loans are the two most important services to the typical firm. Normally loans are negotiated with the same bank in which the firm maintains its checking account. In addition, a small firm may desire to use the bank's safety deposit vault or its services in collecting notes or securing credit information. An experienced banker can also provide management counsel, particularly in financial matters, to the beginning entrepreneur.

The factor of location exerts a practical limitation over the range of choices possible for the small firm. For reasons of convenience in making deposits and in conferring with the banker concerning loans and other matters, it is essential that the bank be located in the same vicinity. Any bank is also interested in its home community and, therefore, tends to be sympathetic to the needs of the business firms in the area. Except in very small communities, however, two or more local banks are available, thus permitting some freedom of choice.

Lending Policies of Banks. Lending policies of banks are not uniform, and this fact deserves consideration in choosing the firm's bank. Some banks are extremely conservative, while others are more venturesome in the risks they will accept. If a small firm's loan application is neither obviously strong nor obviously weak, its prospects for approval depend as much upon the bank involved as upon the borrowing firm. Such differences in willingness to lend have been clearly established by research studies as well as by the practical experience of many businessmen. In addition to variations in their conservative or venturesome orientation, banks also differ in length of loans, interest rates, types of security required, and other such features.

Bank's Flexibility. The bank's reputation for sticking with a firm in times of adversity is also pertinent. Some banks are more flexible than others in assisting a firm that is experiencing temporary difficulty. The beginning small business certainly needs a banker who is willing to make reasonable concessions in times of stress.

Line of Credit. The entrepreneur should arrange for a line of credit in advance of actual need. The lender is interested in extending credit only in situations in which he is well-informed. Procuring a loan in an emergency, on a spur-of-the-moment type of application, therefore, is usually impossible. If this is attempted and fails, the business usually becomes a bankruptcy failure. Moreover, the line of credit, arranged prior to inception of operations, should be for the maximum amount likely to be needed, as shown by projected business plans. When the loan is subsequently requested, the recipient should be ready to demonstrate that the firm's current financial condition still provides an adequate basis for borrowing.

Trade Credit

Credit extended by suppliers is of unusual importance to the beginning entrepreneur. In fact, trade (or mercantile) credit is the small firm's most widely used source of short-term funds. By its very nature, such credit is of short duration—30 days being the customary credit period. Most commonly, this type of credit involves an unsecured, open-book account. Inventory is sent to the purchasing firm, and a corresponding *account receivable* is created in the seller's records. The source of funds is shown by the buyer as an *account payable*.

In considering the use of trade credit, attention should be given to the pertinent costs. There may be a cost of *not* using trade credit if payment is made before the permissible date for lowest cash payment. By paying early, the firm commits funds that might have been used for other purposes. The more critical cost, however, is the cost involved in failure to take an offered cash discount. The real cost of financing in this way, stated in terms of equivalent annual interest, is much higher than the nominal discount rate.

Normally both bank loans and trade credit should be used only for working capital. Other use of such credit is risky to both parties. If short-term funds were tied up in fixed assets, the entrepreneur would have taken a first big step toward bankruptcy.

Line of Credit with Suppliers. The amount of trade credit available to a new firm depends upon the type of business and the suppliers' confidence in the given firm. For example, shoe manufacturers extend business capital to retailers by granting extended datings on sales made at the start of a production season. The retailers, in turn, sell to their customers during the season and make the bulk of their payments to the manufacturers at or near the end of the season. If the merchant's rate of stock turnover is greater than the scheduled payment for the goods, the merchant obtains cash from sales before he is required to pay for the shoes.

Suppliers are inclined to place greater confidence in the new firm and to extend credit more freely than bankers do because of the suppliers' interest in developing new customers. A bank might require financial statements and possibly a cash-flow budget. A supplier, on the other hand, usually checks the general credit standing of the purchaser and extends credit without requiring detailed financial statements. The supplier also tends to be less exacting than a banker or other lender in requiring rigid adherence to credit terms.

Selection of Trade Creditors. Important suppliers of merchandise or raw materials on credit should be selected carefully. This is true whether the small purchasing firm is a retailer, wholesaler, manufacturer, or service firm. A supplier should have a reputation for maintaining scheduled deliveries of materials or merchandise so that the purchaser will neither lose sales nor experience operating delays by reason of late deliveries. The trade supplier who is willing to participate in advertising is a boon to the small entrepreneur. Moreover, in times of unavoidable emergency, it is desirable for a firm to have a supplier who is willing to wait for payment and, in some cases, to extend direct financial assistance.

Equipment Supplier Loans

Some small business establishments—restaurants, to take only one example—utilize equipment that may be purchased on an installment basis. A down payment of 25 to 35 percent is ordinarily required, and the contract period normally runs from three to five years. The manufacturer or supplier typically extends credit on the basis of a *conditional sales contract* or mortgage on the equipment. During the loan period, this equipment cannot serve as collateral for a bank loan.

There is a danger in contracting for so much equipment that it will be impossible to meet installment payments. The entrepreneur is tempted to take on too many installment payments, just as the ultimate consumer tends to commit an excessive proportion of his income in this way. It is a mark of real management ability to recognize the desirable limits in borrowing of this type.

Equipment leasing, a practice that has grown rapidly in recent years, provides an occasionally attractive alternative to equipment purchase. Cars, trucks, business equipment, and machinery used in manufacturing are examples of assets that may be obtained in this way. Possible advantages of leasing equipment include the greater flexibility of investment and the smaller capital requirement made possible by leasing. Offsetting these advantages is the typically higher total cost of leasing rather than purchasing. Leasing may also be desirable when continuing specialized maintenance and protection against obsolescence are necessary—as with electronic computers, for example.

Funds from Friends, Relatives, and Local Investors

Another source of new small business financing is loans from friends or relatives. At times, such individuals may be the only available source. As a source of funds in initial financing, however, friends and relatives are frequently less satisfactory than outsiders. This is because they tend to feel that their close personal relationship with the entrepreneur, backed up by their capital loans, confers on them the right to give management advice or even actively to interfere in management. In consequence, it is desirable that the initial financial plan provide for repayment within the first six months of operations.

Local capitalists—for example, lawyers, physicians, or others who wish to invest funds—also are possible sources of equity funds. The small firm must compete with numerous other investment opportunities for the resources of such financial "backers." As a result, local capitalists are not inclined to invest money in risky small business ventures unless there is the prospect of a significantly better rate of return than is available elsewhere. The entrepreneur must also surrender some degree of control when he engages in this type of financing. For these reasons, such equity sources are used less frequently than other sources and are typically arranged as a last resort by the promoter.

Even though friends, relatives, or capitalists constitute primary sources of funds for particular firms, these sources probably supply only an insignificant part of the total capital used by small businesses.

 Summary

1. Capital is supplied by both owners and creditors for use in the business. One rule of thumb suggests that two thirds of the capital should be owner-supplied.
2. In starting business operations, funds are needed for use as working capital, purchase of fixed assets, payment of promotional expenses, and payment of the owner's personal expenses during an initial period of operation.

3. Estimating capital requirements is difficult because of the uncertainties involved in forecasting; it is also a distasteful task for some businessmen who are strongly oriented toward sales or production.

4. Capital requirements may be determined by estimating sales volume and translating sales data into asset requirements.

5. It is also possible to estimate capital requirements by means of empirical investigation. In fact, this method may be used to check results obtained through the sales-volume approach.

6. The largest source of capital for small firms appears to be that of personal savings. Capital obtained through bank loans and supplier credit is also of substantial importance. Other sources of beginning capital include equipment supplier loans, loans from friends and relatives, and loans from local capitalists.

7. Commercial bank loans are typically used to supply short-term funds, but longer-term loans are also extended by some banks. Some loans are unsecured; others are supported by various forms of collateral—including inventory, equipment, and real estate.

8. Short-term borrowing is properly used to provide working capital, whereas long-term borrowing can be used to finance fixed assets.

9. A banker should be chosen wisely because he can provide management counsel as well as the essential financial services.

10. Trade credit, the most widely used source of short-term funds, typically takes the form of open-book accounts. It is usually obtained with somewhat greater ease than are bank loans.

11. In view of the substantial importance of supplier credit, it is desirable to choose vendors—from among those able to maintain delivery promises consistently—who can best provide the management assistance and financial help needed.

12. Equipment leasing provides a flexible, though usually more costly, alternative to purchasing of equipment on an installment basis.

Discussion Questions

1. If you were a prospective small business entrepreneur, would you adopt the conservative rule that owners supply two thirds of the proposed firm's capital? Why? Might a safe proportion of equity capital vary with the type of business? Explain. Under what circumstances, if any, might a small entrepreneur start on a shoestring (for example, with an ownership equity of 20 percent of total capital)?

2. Define working capital. From what sources should it normally be obtained?

3. What is promotional expense capital? What justification is there for payment by a prospective entrepreneur to a promoter?

4. What estimate of personal expenses should be included in the initial financial planning?

5. How does probable sales volume affect estimates of capital requirements?

6. Does the use of industry standard ratios or empirical investigation appear the more practical method of estimating capital requirements? Why?

7. Which sources of funds account for the largest proportion of capital for small businesses?

8. Compare commercial bank loans and trade credit as capital sources for new firms.

9. List the major criteria for use in selecting a banker.

10. Suggest and evaluate the criteria to be applied in the selection of trade suppliers of materials and/or merchandise items.

11. What are the major problems involved in obtaining loans from friends and relatives? How soon ought they be repaid? Why?

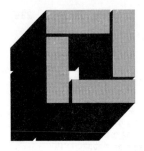

15

Locating the Enterprise

According to one motel proprietor, the three most essential factors in achieving success with a motel are "location, location, and location!" To him, other factors affecting business success are relatively minor compared to proper location. And the many half-busy or abandoned motels in virtually any city tend to verify the great importance of good location. A good location, however, is important not only for motels but also for most lines of business. When well located, a business has a better chance to earn a profit and survive.

In the last several years, the problem of achieving a good location has become much more complex. This is due to the increased attention being given to ecology and protection of the environment. According to one report:

> How land is used has become a pivotal issue in the new environmental activism. . . . All sorts of businesses that depend on the availability of land are finding themselves suddenly caught up in political turmoil. . . .
> . . . Where the federal and state agencies fail to crack down, such environmentalists as the Sierra Club, the National Audubon Society, the Friends of the Earth, and countless *ad hoc* local groups are carrying issues to court—and often winning.
> All evidence indicates that even tougher fighting over land use lies ahead.[1]

Since this movement is countrywide and affects many businesses and land developers, small businesses are also limited by these new constraints.

IMPORTANCE OF A WELL-CHOSEN LOCATION

For most small businesses, a location decision is made only when the business is first established or purchased. Occasionally, however, a business considers relocation to reduce operating costs, get closer to its customers, or gain other advantages. Also, as a business expands, it sometimes becomes desirable to begin additional operations at other locations. The owner of a drive-in hamburger and malt shop, for example, may decide to open a second unit in another section of the same city or even in another city.

---

[2] "The Land Use Battle That Business Faces," *Business Week*, August 26, 1972, p. 40.

Continuing Effect of Location Decisions

It is not the frequency but the lasting effects of location decisions that make them so important. Once the business is established, it is costly and often impractical, if not impossible, to "pull up stakes" and move. If the business depends upon a heavy flow of customer traffic, a shrewdly selected site that produces maximum sales will increase profits throughout the months and years of its existence at that location. In contrast, a site with light traffic will reduce the sales figure on every income statement throughout the life of the business. If the choice is particularly poor, the business may never be able to "get off the ground," even with adequate financing and superior ability in purchase and sale of merchandise. This enduring effect is so clearly recognized by national chain-store organizations that they spend thousands of dollars investigating sites before establishing new stores.

Importance Varies with Nature of Business

Very few businesses can safely ignore the factor of location, but it is much more vital in some lines of endeavor than in others. To illustrate, the site chosen for a millinery shop can make or break it. In contrast, the exact location of a painting contractor is of relatively minor importance. Even painting contractors, however, may suffer from certain locational disadvantages. All cities have buildings that need painting, but property is kept in better repair and painted more frequently in some communities than in others.

It also seems clear that there is more than one satisfactory location for most businesses. Even though the quest should be for the one best location, there are unquestionably several possible locations that meet the minimum requirements for success. Sometimes there is little to choose between two good locations. An automobile garage may do an equal amount of business at either of two corner buildings. On the other hand, many undesirable locations appear satisfactory on the surface. Only careful investigation will reveal the good and bad features of any particular location.

FACTORS AFFECTING CHOICE OF LOCATION

There are a number of facets to the problem of location. Among these are personal preferences, geographical considerations, and comparative analyses of costs and other factors. Large business firms have professionally qualified personnel whose analysis and advice are invaluable in evaluating prospective locations. In contrast, the small business entrepreneur must do the major part of his own investigational work. The prospective entrepreneur may lack the time, money, or knowledge of investigational techniques necessary, but he must surmount such difficulties and investigate fully each possible location. Several sources of outside help are open to him, and these are discussed in a later section of this chapter.

Owner's Personal Preferences

All too often, a prospective entrepreneur considers only the home community for locating the business. Frequently the possibility of locating elsewhere never enters one's mind. Home community preference, of course, is not the only personal factor influencing location. The owner may, for example, wish to locate in an area of the country that offers cool weather, fishing opportunities, or a desired religious or social atmosphere. Whatever the origin of or the reason for one's personal preference, it is an important factor in locating one's business. If one strongly dislikes a given area, it must be regarded as an unacceptable location.

Virtues in the Hometown Location. Choosing one's hometown for personal reasons is not necessarily an illogical decision. In fact, there are certain advantages. For one thing, the individual generally accepts and appreciates the atmosphere of his home community, whether it is a small town or a large city. From a practical business standpoint, the beginner can more easily establish credit in his home community. The hometown banker can deal more confidently with him, and other businessmen may be of greater service in helping the beginner evaluate a given opportunity. If customers come from the same locality, the prospective entrepreneur would probably have a better idea of their tastes and peculiarities than an outsider would have. Relatives and friends may also be one's first customers and help to advertise one's services. The establishment of a beauty shop in the home community would illustrate a number of these advantages.

Dangers Present in a Hometown Location. Locating a small factory on a rural site near the owner's home, for example, may force employees to commute from other places, taking them an hour or more to drive to work while the owner reaches the plant in 10 minutes.[2] They may resent this. Such a factory might also find materials inaccessible except at a high transportation cost. Personal preferences should not be allowed to cancel out location weaknesses even though it may logically be a primary factor in locating a small business. Just because an individual has lived in a given town all his life does not automatically make it a satisfactory business location.

Geographical Considerations

For some businesses—a barbershop or a drugstore, for example—the choice of a particular geographical area is a question of little significance. They can operate successfully in all areas of the country. Other types of small businesses, however, need to analyze this problem with extreme care.

Choice of Region. Some markets for goods and services produced by small business are restricted geographically. The following examples will make this point clear:

1. A ski lodge is practical only in an area with slopes and snow.
2. A boat repair service must locate near the water.
3. Stores selling home air conditioners have a larger market potential in the Southern states than in the Northern states.

---

[2] See "When Business Moves Where the Boss Lives," *Business Week*, September 30, 1972, p. 69. Although this article deals primarily with business relocation difficulties, it does point up the illogic of inconveniencing employees by forcing them to commute to work so that the boss can live close to his business.

4. Subcontractors to aircraft manufacturers produce parts for use in nearby production plants.

Regional choice factors are particularly important to manufacturers and, to a lesser extent, to other types of businesses that do not serve a regionally restricted market. The relative importance of these factors varies according to the nature of the business. Several basic considerations that enter into evaluations concerning a regional choice are discussed below.

Nearness to Market. Location near the center of the market is clearly desirable if other factors are approximately equal. In particular, this is true of industries in which the cost of shipping the finished product is high relative to its value. In the case of bricks and soft drinks, for example, this results in production close to the consuming markets. Other manufacturing plants—for example, toy manufacturers—are able to serve national or even international markets; but they must think, nevertheless, in terms of their heaviest concentration of customer orders.

Availability of Raw Materials. If raw materials are not abundantly available in all areas, the best raw material sources offer locational advantages to manufacturing plants. Bulky or heavy raw materials that lose much of their bulk or weight in the manufacturing process are powerful forces affecting location. The sawmill is an example of a plant which must stay close to its raw materials in order to operate economically. When it is impossible to achieve an optimum location with respect to both raw materials and markets, a compromise is required.

Adequacy of Labor Supply. A manufacturer's labor requirements depend upon the nature of the production process. In some cases the need is for semiskilled or unskilled labor, and the problem is to locate in a surplus labor area. Other firms find it desirable to seek a pool of highly skilled labor—the highly skilled machine trades of New England is a well-known example of such a labor supply. Wage rates are particularly important for firms that have a high percentage of labor cost, and a history of peaceful industrial relations is another attractive feature to a manufacturer. Not only the wage rate but also the productivity of labor is important. There is some evidence indicating that rural workers are superior to urban workers—and that workers differ in productivity from one region to another. One executive of a company with branch plants in Texarkana, Texas; St. Louis, Missouri; and Bloomington, Illinois, feels that the Texarkana employees are more productive than those in the other two locations. In explanation, he speaks of their intense desire to do a good job, their willingness and ability to absorb training more rapidly, and their pride in putting out a day's work for a day's pay. The variability of nonlabor factors, however, makes it impossible to establish objectively the existence, as well as the magnitude, of such differences.

Other Factors. Land costs, waste disposal, and water supply must also be given consideration. For a given business, any one of these may be a critical factor, though for industry generally they are less significant than markets, sources of raw materials, and labor. Still other factors of ever-increasing importance are:[3]

---

[3] Maurice Fulton, "New Factors in Plant Location," *Harvard Business Review*, Vol. 49, (May-June, 1971), pp. 4-6.

1. Environmental protection.
2. Need to employ minority groups.
3. Greater reliance on employee job commuting.
4. Greater technical demands on the labor force.
5. Increased foreign competition.
6. Rising tax and insurance costs.
7. Rail service curtailment or abandonment in many areas.
8. More costly municipal services.

Choice of City. For several decades many cities have tried to attract new industry. Much of this effort has been directed toward obtaining new manufacturing plants, but other types of business are welcomed also. In the last few years the drive for environmental protection has led some cities to reduce or abandon the attempts to entice new industries. This seems even more true where suburban, rather than central-city, locations are contemplated.

Growing or Declining City. Some cities are on the upgrade. They are growing in both population and business activity. Income levels of their citizens are advancing, and an atmosphere of prosperity is evident. In contrast, other cities are expanding slowly or even declining in population. Certain economic factors—shifts in markets, technological changes, and transportation advantages—apparently favor some cities at the expense of others. As an example of different growth rates, note below the varying percentages of expansion in nonagricultural employment between 1960 and 1970.[4]

Standard Metropolitan Area	Percent of Growth
Anaheim-Santa Ana-Garden Grove, California	152.7
San Jose, California	97.0
Phoenix, Arizona	80.1
Houston, Texas	64.8
Dayton, Ohio	33.7
Erie, Pennsylvania	27.9
Springfield, Vermont	9.3
South Bend, Indiana	7.8

In practically all cases, a new business properly wishes to locate in an up-and-coming city. The problem, of course, is how to detect economic trends in the various cities under consideration. Frequently the trend is obvious, and anyone acquainted with business conditions in the area can accurately describe the direction of business activity and income level. Less extreme forms of growth or decline are more difficult to detect and assess accurately.

The subjective judgments of bankers and businessmen are desirable supplements to one's personal observations in analyzing this characteristic. The Department of Commerce also publishes data that are useful for this purpose. Census reports, particularly the Census of Business, enable one to note differences in business conditions occurring between census dates. In addition, the Department of Commerce publishes biennial reports entitled "County

---

[4] Calculated from employment data given in the Bureau of Labor Statistics Bulletin 1370-9, *Employment and Earnings: States and Areas, 1939-1971.*

Business Patterns" that permit analysis of changes in the level of business activity by counties. These serve to illustrate, but do not exhaust, the sources of data that may be used in making such a study.

Below is a sample questionnaire presented to illustrate the general nature of questions that should be answered in comparing cities with respect to this trait.

Points to Check When Deciding on Jewelry Store Location [5]

Economic Factors. Don't be misled by the outward appearance or climate of a city. Both should be considered, but much more important is a hard look at where the community is heading. If the main industry, for instance, is a buggy-whip factory, the outlook for prosperity for the residents is not favorable, to say the least. The best community for you is one that has a number of different industries, that is not dependent on seasonal peaks and valleys, and that shows growth both in industry and in population.

Industry: Farming, Manufacturing, Trade

Trend: Is the industry growing, stationary, or declining?

Permanence: Is the industry old and well established, new and promising, or recent and uncertain?

Diversification: Are the sources of income varied, or is the town dependent on one major industry?

Stability: Is the industry very stable, average, or subject to wide fluctuations?

Seasonality: Is there little or no seasonal change in industry, mild seasonal change, or extreme seasonal fluctuation?

Outlook: Is the future of industry in the community promising, uncertain, or poor?

Population

Trend: Is the population growing, stationary, or declining?

Income: Is the community wealthy, well-to-do, moderately well off, or poor?

Character: Is the population native born, mixed, or chiefly foreign born?

Competition. Competition can be a blessing or a curse. Lively stores selling up-to-date merchandise in an attractive setting give an overall tone to the business area that draws customers. On the other hand, your chances for success would be slim in a community that already has more than its share of jewelry outlets.

Number of stores: Are there few, many, or too many jewelry stores?

Management: Is the management unprogressive, average, or alert and aggressive?

Chains: Are there no chain jewelry stores in the community, a few chains, or many well-established chains?

Appearance: Are the jewelry stores very attractive, average, unattractive?

Department stores: How many department stores sell jewelry—none, a few, many?

Facilities of the Town. You will want to be in a community that has good public transportation, ample parking space, good banks, active organizations, and other facilities for living as well as doing business. You should also be reasonably near your suppliers. Check these points:

---

[5] Small Business Administration, *Starting and Managing a Small Retail Jewelry Store, 1971,* pp. 29-31.

Transportation facilities   Churches
Wholesale suppliers   Medical and dental services
Banking facilities   Amusements
Civic associations   Climate
Schools

The People. You wouldn't try to open a store in Zenobia unless you spoke and understood Zenobian. Be choosy about where you decide to go into business. Pick a community that is "you." You might succeed elsewhere, but why do things the hard way?

Extent of Local Competition. Most small businesses are concerned with the nature and the amount of local competition. Manufacturers who serve a national market are an exception to this rule, and there are perhaps others. But overcrowding can occur in the majority of small business fields, and one would wish to avoid an overcrowded community. The quality of competition also affects the desirability of a location. If existing businesses are not aggressive and do not offer the type of service reasonably expected by the customer, there is likely to be room for a newcomer.

Published data can sometimes be used to shed light upon this particular problem. The average population required to support a given type of business establishment can frequently be determined on a national or a regional basis. By comparing the situation in the given city to these averages, it is possible to get a better picture of the intensity of local competition.

Unfortunately objective data of this type seldom produce unequivocal answers. The income level of the population and nearness to other shopping centers might account for certain discrepancies. There is no substitute for personal observation. In addition, the businessman will do well to seek the opinion of those well acquainted with local business conditions. Wholesalers frequently have an excellent notion of the potential for additional retail establishments in a given line of business.

Other Considerations. There are also other considerations in choosing a given city for business location. One of these concerns the availability of suitable personnel and the status of labor relations in the community. The supply of skilled labor, for example, may be a significant factor in the choice of city as well as the choice of region. The city of Portsmouth, Ohio, has an adequate supply of skilled shoe workers, while Detroit and Flint, Michigan, have a large pool of auto workers. The prevailing wage scale is particularly important for manufacturers competing with other firms who have lower wage costs. If the community has a record of constructive and peaceful labor relations, this is obviously preferable to a situation in which labor disputes typically lead to open strife.

The amount and the character of industry in a given city is likewise significant. A one-industry town is often subject to severe seasonal and cyclical business fluctuations in contrast to a city of diversified industries. In addition, the city should preferably contain necessary customers and suppliers of essential services.

Some cities are so eager to attract new industry that they offer free plots of land, financial aid in building, and tax concessions for several years. Of course, these lures must not be allowed to obscure less desirable features of the city.

Local government can similarly be such as to help or hinder a new business. In choosing a city, the prospective entrepreneur should be assured of satisfactory police and fire protection, streets, water and other utilities, street drainage, and public transportation. Unreasonably high local taxes or severely restrictive local ordinances are to be avoided.

Aside from local government, the city should also qualify with respect to civic, cultural, religious, and recreational affairs. This involves such features as schools, churches, theaters, golf courses, swimming pools, newspapers, radio and TV stations, civic clubs, restaurants, hotels, and concern for social and charitable organizations. These make the city a better place in which to live and do business.

Choice of Business Site. Having chosen a region and a city in which to locate, the businessman must next select a specific site. It is dangerous to undertake site selection before the best city has been found. It might be that the attractiveness of a particular site and building, located in a given city, would overshadow important economic advantages enjoyed by other cities. If the city is properly chosen, suitable sites usually can be found.[6]

Cost as a Critical Factor. Business may be divided into two general categories depending upon the more compelling factor in choosing a site. In the first group are those firms that stress the costs associated with the site—purchase costs and operating costs at that particular location. In the second group are businesses whose location must be customer-oriented.

If the customer does not come to the business establishment, the entrepreneur may disregard the problem of customer accessibility. Most manufacturing firms and wholesale establishments fall into this category. Other businesses of this type are bookkeeping services, commercial laundries using pickup stations, plumbing contractors specializing in repair work, radio and TV repair shops, and painting contractors. It would be foolish for such firms to pay high rent for locations in central business districts. Instead, their concern is with production efficiency and relative costs associated with the site. Questions to be answered by these businessmen are summarized below.

1. How does the purchase price or rent on this property compare with that of other available sites?
2. Will the foundation soil stand the weight, vibration, and other physical features of business operations?
3. Is the site properly zoned for intended use?
4. Are buildings adequate and in good repair?
5. Do existing highways and public transit systems make the site reasonably accessible to employees, and does it have enough parking space for employees and to meet city regulations?
6. Does the site have railroad siding and truck dock, and is it favorably situated with respect to transportation facilities?
7. Is there ample space for future expansions?
8. Are water, electrical, sewer, and other connections already installed, and are they adequate?

---

[6] In cities that have urban renewal programs, the prospective small entrepreneur should check on urban renewal areas for possible sites, along with other areas. In particular, the small manufacturer should do so if the renewal program includes the setting up of an industrial park.

9. Is it likely that there will be additional assessments for street paving, sidewalks, or other improvements?
10. Are property taxes in line with those of other sites?

Customer Accessibility as a Critical Factor. Some business sites must be chosen to attract the customer. This does not mean that the cost factors discussed above can be disregarded, but it does mean that the first and foremost consideration is customer accessibility. Businesses of this type are best exemplified by retail stores, and even among these the factor is of varying importance. A shoe store or a drugstore may fail simply because it is on the wrong side of the street. Customer traffic is the key to successful location in such businesses. A store that sells a specialty good—say pianos—has greater freedom in selecting a site. Some restaurants have achieved such distinction that customers drive for miles to patronize them in spite of relatively inaccessible locations.

Unless one has a product or a service sufficiently powerful to attract the customer, however, one must locate where the customer wants to buy. In the case of motels and service stations, this means a location convenient to many motorists. For clothing stores and variety stores, it means a downtown or suburban shopping center location. For some drug and food stores, it means a location in or close to the residential areas. The first step, then, in choosing the site is to analyze the type of product or service, the nature of the market, customer buying habits, and the effect of those factors upon prospective sites.

Of course, other factors in addition to amount of traffic must be taken into consideration. The general location must be in keeping with the prestige of the product or service. Business neighbors may likewise contribute to making a given site either desirable or undesirable. To illustrate, a high-class restaurant generally could not successfully locate in a low-income neighborhood. Neither would it locate adjacent to a laundry. If one is selling a shopping good, such as ladies' clothing, it is desirable to locate near competitors. On the other hand, both candy and record shops (convenience goods stores) would suffer from nearby competition. Consequently, two adjacent, similar shops would simply divide the available customers between them.

Measuring Customer Traffic. Customer traffic is recognized and discussed more frequently than it is measured. This is a mistake, because measurement of traffic is one of the easiest precautionary steps that can be taken in evaluating prospective business sites.

To make a count of pedestrian traffic, the investigator stations himself in front of the potential site and records the number of passers-by. This may be done at alternate half-hour intervals during the day for enough different days to get a representative sample of the traffic. These results should be compared with the amount of traffic at other available sites and sites known to be successful. Of course, the traffic must also be evaluated carefully to tell whether it provides prospective customers for the particular business. A ladies' shoe store, for example, will profit little from a high flow of pedestrian traffic that is primarily male. Pedestrians walking to or from a bus station may likewise be unlikely customers for a clothing store.

Growing or Declining Sites. In an earlier section it was pointed out that certain cities are on the decline while others are growing more or less rapidly. What is true of cities is also true of sections within cities. City growth occurs in a given direction, and that section thrives as a result of the development. Older sections of the city are blighted and display the picture of a past more prosperous than their present. Small retail firms and, to some extent, small service businesses must consider this factor in the selection of a business site.[7]

Suburban Trend. The trend toward suburban shopping centers has been an impressive development of the last two decades. Increasing suburban population, greater use of the family car, traffic congestion and lack of parking space downtown, and other factors have contributed to the relative decline of central business district activity in many cities. Suburbanites who find it difficult or unpleasant to shop downtown turn to shopping centers located nearer the residential areas.

The extent of this trend between 1963 and 1967 for a growing city is indicated in Figure 15-1. Although the city of Miami has gained more than 10 percent in population since 1950, the Miami suburban population has increased

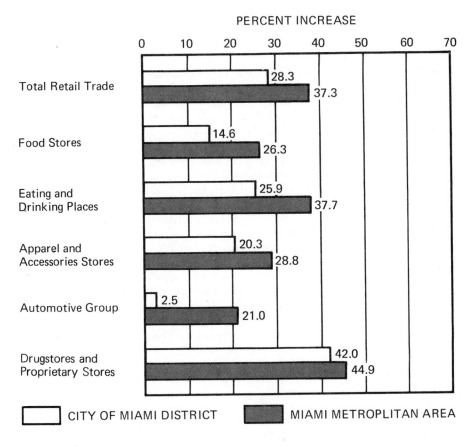

PERCENT INCREASE

Figure 15-1
CHANGES IN RETAIL SALES IN CITY AND METROPOLITAN AREA OF MIAMI, FLORIDA, 1963-1967

---

[7] The small retailer should also consider the impact of urban renewal programs on site values in or close to renewal areas. Blight can be eliminated.

far more. In Figure 15-1 the moderate increase in "City of Miami" sales contrasts sharply with the larger increase in "Miami Metropolitan Area" sales, the latter including both city sales and suburban sales. It is apparent that the suburban business establishments accounted for the "lion's share" of the area's business growth during the four-year period.

This shift of business has created problems in the downtown area as well as offered opportunities in the suburbs. For the small retail business, an opportunity is often presented by the shopping center or other suburban location that has a greater future and that can be handled with limited capital more easily than a downtown spot. Of course, the store site needs to be checked out carefully, whether it is a downtown or a suburban location.

Comparative Analyses of Costs and Other Factors

The complex of factors involved in the location decision of a cost-oriented business is resolved by determining the comparative costs of the various available locations. Cost comparisons are important even for the customer-oriented business, but they are the very crux of the problem for the cost-oriented entrepreneur. A location is most favorable, normally, when it enables delivery of the product or the service to the customer at the lowest cost. This means minimum operating (especially labor) costs, cost of shipping materials (or merchandise) and fuel inward, and cost of shipping finished products (or delivering purchases) to customers.

Figure 15-2 on page 251 shows the major cost factors that the manufacturer must analyze on a comparative basis. For any one business, there may be other significant costs that require serious study.[8]

The process of cost comparison and analysis can become extremely involved and difficult. Some location problems are sufficiently complex as to justify the use of professional help. After extensive preliminary investigation, the entrepreneur may conclude that the services of a consultant acquainted with problems of this nature are required.

Use of Work Sheets. Besides cost analyses, an entrepreneur who must make a business location decision can set up work sheets covering all significant region, community, and site selection factors. Evaluative ratings—ranging from unfavorable to favorable in perhaps five degrees—are then entered on these sheets, with supporting and explanatory remarks. The completed work sheets will facilitate the making of final decisions.

Use of Maps. Regional and city maps will also prove useful in making both the regional and site comparisons necessary. The regional maps should show territory embraced, population, cities, lakes and rivers, railways, and highways. The city map should show the downtown district, shopping centers, parking lots and parking meter areas, bus routes, streets (including designations of one-way thoroughfares), highways, railways (including sidings at projected sites),

---

[8] See Gerald J. Karaska and David F. Bramhall, *Locational Analysis for Manufacturing* (Cambridge, Mass.: The M.I.T. Press, 1969); and Leonard C. Yaseen, *Plant Location* (Roslyn, New York: Business Reports, Inc., 1952). The latter manual provides useful data on the making of cost comparisons and other evaluative studies of different available business locations.

MANUFACTURER'S COMPARATIVE COST ANALYSIS FORM			
Cost Element	Location A	Location B	Location C

MATERIALS
    Raw Materials
    Fuels			

OPERATING COSTS
    Labor
    Rent (or Depreciation)
    Power and Heat
    Other Utilities
    Insurance			

TAXES
    Property
    Income
    Payroll
    Other			

TRANSPORTATION
    Raw Materials
    Finished Goods			

Figure 15-2
MANUFACTURER'S COMPARATIVE COST ANALYSIS FORM

prospective competitors' locations, workers' residential areas, other major residential areas, airports, and the like. It is obvious that separate maps will be required for each region considered and for each city in which specific sites are under consideration. Such maps will be helpful in making and supporting the rankings on the location survey and work sheets.

SOURCES OF OUTSIDE HELP

Large firms often engage consulting specialists to solve their location problems. Small businesses may likewise find it desirable to make use of such help in important location decisions. Frequently, however, the small business entrepreneur will find a practical solution by consulting and using the free help that is available from sources noted below.

Bankers

A knowledge of local business conditions and the history of given sites makes bankers especially valuable in the choice of section of city and specific site. Their contribution would be rather limited in the case of a business whose choice must be based on differences in costs and who have technical operating requirements governing the selection. However, some banks now have real estate departments that provide advice helpful in achieving proper location.

Chambers of Commerce

Although chambers of commerce may tend to oversell locations in the hope of attracting business, they can be of substantial aid in locating and recommending desirable sites. The effort they expend enhances community prestige. Therefore, the service they render benefits all parties concerned.

Wholesalers and Manufacturers

As noted earlier, wholesalers and some manufacturers have experience and knowledge of the way products are currently marketed in a given location. They often know whether there is room for another aggressive business in a given line.

Trade Associations

By their close contact and study of problems in a given line of business, trade associations often can furnish valuable advice on conditions in a specific area.

Government Agencies

The field offices of the Department of Commerce and the Small Business Administration will assist a prospective entrepreneur in choosing an optimum location for the business or suggest other leads that one may follow up.

Organized Industrial Districts

While a different type of source than those listed above, industrial districts—often called industrial parks—can frequently help manufacturing-type businesses in finding a suitable location.[9] The industrial park has some rather appealing features for small businesses. It is somewhat similar to an apartment building, with facilities and equipment already installed. The small firm is able to occupy a unit of the district without excessive costs for street paving, sewage systems, building design and construction, railroad sidings, and the like. Everything is provided.

Other Sources

Still other outside sources of business location information include railroads, power companies, and state industrial development agencies. The railroad seeks to attract industry to sites adjacent to its tracks. The power company attempts to promote location in the area it serves. The state agency desires to attract new industries to locations within the borders of the state. Valuable information is obtainable from such sources, which frequently is unavailable elsewhere. Typical data obtainable are:

---

[9] See C. Everett Steichen, "Should Your Company Locate in an Industrial Park," *Business Management*, Vol. 40 (August, 1971), pp. 24 and 26, for a more extended discussion of industrial parks and business location.

1. Cost and availability of raw materials.
2. Available transportation and communications facilities in the area.
3. Type, condition, and cost of buildings located on given sites.
4. Land costs.
5. Adequacy of water, power, and fuel supplies.
6. Size and skill level of the labor force.
7. Existing tax rates, labor laws, and laws and ordinances regulating business activity.
8. Market possibilities.

LOCATION GUIDELINES FOR CERTAIN TYPES OF BUSINESS

The final section of this chapter is devoted to a discussion of special locational problems for three major areas of small business: wholesaling, service, and retailing.

The Small Wholesaler

The small wholesaler and the industrial distributor face the same sequence of locational choices—region, city, and site. Perhaps the most significant of these is the selection of a city in which to establish the business. The wholesaler of consumer goods is particularly interested in the volume of retail sales, both for the lines of goods that will be handled and in total. Certain cities serve as wholesaling centers, and the wholesaler's market includes not only the central city but also the surrounding towns. It is important for the prospective small wholesaler to discover which city is the wholesaling center; such centers exist because of basic economic factors. Any measure of intensity of local competition is also significant in considering any given city.

Certain specialized types of wholesalers perform functions that dictate particular locations. A resident buyer of clothing, for example, must locate in a major market city, whereas an assembler of farm products must locate in a rural area.

Small wholesalers considering specific sites for their warehouses must often choose between locations within and outside the central wholesale district. They should be near the center of the trading area to be served, while remaining accessible to highways and railways. Central wholesale districts have grown up because of their proximity to transportation facilties. If one chooses a wholesale district location, one should expect higher rent—or less space for a given amount of rent. Locations outside the wholesale district, but still accessible to railways and highways and having suitable loading and unloading facilities, will often mean lower rent, more space, lower operating expenses, and faster deliveries—both in and out—and possibly newer and more attractive quarters.

The location problem may also be affected by the method of sale. If customers do not come to the wholesaler—as is true with most wholesale establishments—there is less need for attractive quarters and parking facilities.

The Small Service Firm

Regional and city choices for the small service firm are typically made on the basis of the owner's home location. The choice of community and specific site are highly important; the desirability of a given location varies with the kind of service business.

Some service firms are visited by their customers and must be located conveniently for them. This is true, for example, of barbershops, beauty shops, and photographic studios. Their location problem is much like that of a retail establishment. The convenient location is imperative except in the case of those firms that can build reputations for such high quality or unique service that customers will seek them out. Furthermore, the location must be one that avoids noise, dirt, and a generally shabby appearance.

Other service firms are more closely related to the manufacturer in their locational problems. The plumber or the TV repairman, for example, may work from his home or other low-rent location if he specializes in repair work. The calls for service are typically received by telephone, and customers seldom visit the business establishment. Such service firms would thus be governed by the factors that affect the manufacturer's choice—location of customers, access to raw materials, rental costs, zoning regulations, and the like.

The locational problems of professional men providing medical, legal, and accounting service, of banks in towns or small cities, and of agencies such as a retail credit bureau differ from those of the service firms already considered. Banks require a downtown or shopping district location, while doctors typically prefer a downtown office, a neighborhood clinic location, or a location close to a hospital. Lawyers tend, for the most part, to locate in the downtown area on upper floors of office buildings.

The Small Retailer

The prospective small retailer should choose an area suitable to the nature of the particular business. The suburban trend described earlier in the chapter provides excellent opportunities for many small retailers. In contrast, the older areas of a city are generally less preferable than the new, expanding areas.

The store location must be chosen to attract the customers who patronize it. Parking facilities must be adequate. The store and its arrangement should create just the right atmosphere, considering the type of customers and type of goods to be sold. Moreover, the window display areas should be suitable for showing the type of merchandise the store will carry.

Restaurants and other eating establishments are typically classified as retail businesses. Below is a summary of the special locational problems of these organizations. Much of the discussion in this summary is pertinent to retail business location in general.

Picking a Location [10]

It has been said that being at the right place at the right time is essential to success. That certainly applies to selection of a restaurant site.

However, finding the right place requires considerable study. Much time should be devoted to the search since, in the final analysis, the restaurant isn't likely to prove any better than its location.

---

[10] *Success in the Restaurant Business*, Merchants Service Department, The National Cash Register Company, undated pamphlet, pp. 16-17.

A wise man doesn't open a restaurant in the first vacant building discovered. All the factors affecting restaurant location must be weighed and analyzed.

First, the prospect usually decides the kind of eating establishment he prefers to operate. Attention should be turned to the neighborhood desired. What is its character? Is it a business locality? Industrial? Residential? Is it on the way up?

Study the Neighborhood

Many conditions that might appear comparatively unimportant have just as great an influence on successful restaurant operation. For instance, neighborhoods should be avoided if they harbor loafers, have an unpleasant odor, or are noisy. Restaurants seldom are popular when located in or near undertaking homes, hospitals, or cemeteries.

Churches and schools do not make good restaurant neighbors. They may alter conditions on liquor licenses, and quite often cause congestion on the sidewalks such as noise and other disturbing factors.

Parking facilities are a factor, too. A water hydrant at the front of a restaurant prevents parking, slows down food deliveries, and is very often responsible for puddles of water and congestion near the entrance. On the other hand, value may be increased immeasurably by such a simple thing as an abutting alley. The alley will provide delivery facilities not always available on the thoroughfare.

Competition must be studied. Is there ample opportunity for the business in the area, or is it already overcrowded with eating places? Are the other restaurants making a profit? What is their history?

To determine whether the area can use another eating place, it is necessary to ascertain the success of existing places, the types of patronage they are receiving. And it is wise to know whether or not the community is growing.

It will be important to know the population in surrounding businesses, hotels, apartments, and the like. Changing conditions in the area will have a bearing on value of the location. Just as construction work in the neighborhood causes traffic congestion that often temporarily drives away business, so new buildings on the opposite side of the street may deprive a restaurant of customers. It is a fact that the general public favors the side of the street having new buildings.

Being on a busy thoroughfare often enhances value of a restaurant, but value of the traffic cannot always be determined by counting the people as they pass. It is necessary to know where the traffic is going, and the type of persons riding. Many people may pass the restaurant, but the type of eating place planned may not necessarily appeal to sufficient numbers of them.

The new restaurant must be planned to suit the pocketbooks and the likes and dislikes of its potential customers, for the people who live and work around it are the ones who will eventually decide whether it is to succeed.

The new restaurant man will want to know where the customers come from, the kind of transportation they will use, what they will want to eat, how much they will be willing to spend, group potential, whether they will want quality, quantity—and the types of service.

If the location is in a residential section, the prospective restaurant man must realize that luncheon trade will be light, and should consider evening trade.

The very nature of the neighborhood will determine whether customers will come in singly, in couples, or in family groups.

Such information may be obtained through talks with other persons operating small business houses in the area, or with some of the older and representative residents of the neighborhood.

A restaurant located in an industrial area presents a special problem. Since much of its business will stem from the surrounding plants, it will be necessary to know whether the plants operate their own lunchrooms, how many persons they employ, the hours they work, and the percentage of persons who bring their own lunch.

The type of work the employees do and the wages they receive will have much to do with the kind of food they want and the amount of money they will be willing to spend on their meals. Here, of course, a convenient location is vital as workers will not travel far for the noon meal. Also, in an industrial neighborhood, the problem is to serve large portions at a reasonable figure. The best source of information will be the workers themselves. Why not ask them?

Regardless of the type of eating place, good transportation facilities are of prime importance. A corner location at intersecting streetcar or bus lines may attract many persons leaving streetcars or buses or waiting to board them.

A roadside restaurant or cafe has still other problems. It should be on a main highway, preferably just on the outskirts of a city. Plenty of parking space should be provided, and the place will require an attractive exterior if it is to catch the eye.

It is important to keep in mind that the restaurant should be in a neighborhood adequately supplied with gas, electricity, water, and fuel.

These are some of the factors governing wise selection of location. If followed, they will ease the problem of locating a profitable restaurant, but they must be approached with common sense and judgment, as conditions vary.

It is all very well to say that good food and service will cause people to "beat a path" to your door. But, save in such cases as outstanding "special occasion" dinner spots, people today want accessibility too. The ideal is a reasonably good location, yet not in the high rent district. Authorities set the average rent percentage at from 2½ percent to 5 percent of income.

Summary

1. The location decision of a small firm is generally affected significantly by the factor of personal taste. There are certain values in selecting a hometown location, but *every* business opportunity should be evaluated to make sure hometown preference or other personal desires do not lead to an unwise decision.

2. Important factors in choosing a region are market location, raw materials location, and availability of labor. Of course, various other conditions also deserve consideration and may even govern the location decision of particular firms.

3. Choice of a city is critical for some types of business. Preferably, a firm should be located in a growing, progressive, prosperous city. The extent and effectiveness of local competition is also a vital consideration for many firms.

4. In choosing a specific site, the most important factor may be either the factor of cost or the degree of customer accessibility. The nature of the business determines which of these considerations has priority.

5. The suburban trend has created numerous opportunities and problems for small firms, particularly retailers. The drive for environmental protection, currently popular, constitutes a major problem in this area for land developers and small manufacturers.

6. Comparative cost analysis is the crux of a location evaluation by a cost-oriented business (and is important for all businesses).

7. Various tools—such as regional and city maps or factor rating work sheets—can be used to help in evaluating different locations.

8. Sources of outside help in choosing a location include bankers, chambers of commerce, wholesalers, manufacturers, trade associations, government agencies, industrial districts, and consulting specialists.

9. The choice of city is probably the key locational decision for wholesalers and industrial distributors.

10. Regional and city choices for the small service business are typically made on the basis of the owner's home location. The choice of community and specific site are highly important.

 Discussion Questions

1. Why are the effects of a location decision so permanent?

2. Can you suggest a type of business in which the factor of location is of no significance whatever?

3. Is the hometown of the businessman likely to be a good location? Why?

4. Is it logical for an owner to allow personal preference to influence the decision on business location in one region or another? Why?

5. For the five small businesses which you know best, would you say that their location was based upon evaluation of location factors, chance, or what?

6. Suggest some illustrations of geographically-restricted markets that determine location in addition to those mentioned in the chapter.

7. In selecting a region, what types of businesses should place greatest emphasis (a) upon markets, (b) upon raw materials, and (c) upon labor? Explain.

8. Why is the question of regional selection more important to most manufacturers than to most retailers?

9. Why would a new business prefer to locate in a growing city in preference to a declining city? What else does a city need to attract new industry to itself? Why?

10. How may one measure the extent of existing competition in a given city? The quality of pedestrian traffic?

11. For what types of business does the suburban trend seem to be most important? Is this effect the same in cities of different size?

12. In choosing specific sites, what types of business must show the greatest concern with customer accessibility? Why?

13. Describe the site factor requirements for a suburban bank in a city of 100,000 population. How would they differ for a downtown bank in a large city? Why?

14. What types of business would profit most from utilization of an outside consultant in location?

15. How would the location advice received from a banker, chamber of commerce representative, power company, and an industrial park promoter differ? Why?

16. How do site factors differ for a manufacturer and a retailer?

17. Where would you recommend that a new wholesaler locate in relation to his market if he plans to serve only the New England states? Why? Only Texas and the Southwest? Why?

18. In locating a new business, or in relocating an existing firm, just what balance would you recommend between economic and environmental factors? Explain.

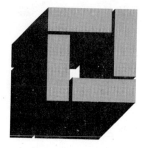

16

Providing
Physical Facilities

The physical facilities normally required in operating a beginning small business include at least one building and some equipment and tooling. This chapter will consider not only the various factors that a prospective entrepreneur must consider in acquiring the appropriate physical facilities, but also the problem of layout to make most effective use of these facilities.

THE BUILDING

A small business entrepreneur usually starts out by purchasing or leasing an existing building. The alternative to acceptance of an existing building is design and construction of a new building. Unfortunately this involves a greater investment which increases the risk of capital funds—a most significant factor for a small business. Furthermore, the process of building may delay the commencement of business operations.

The Problem of Leasing or Buying

Leasing and buying a business building both present certain advantages. The advantages of one are typically the disadvantages of the other. Among the advantages of leasing are:

1. Avoidance of a large cash outlay for purchase of a building. This means either that the entrepreneur will have a much smaller initial capital investment to make or that his working capital will be much larger and more liquid than would be the case if a building were purchased. Thus, by leasing, the small entrepreneur can avoid many financing problems.
2. Avoidance of danger of loss due to fire, tornado, hurricane, flood, and explosion.
3. Reduction of risk due to decline in property values (incident upon a neighborhood's becoming shabby, the moving of a highway, etc.).
4. Deductibility for income tax purposes of lease rentals paid (typically a larger expense item than allowable building depreciation).

In some cases the only available housing for a business at the chosen site is leased quarters. The owner of a desirable building may refuse to sell but agree to lease. Furthermore, the owner may also agree to pay for any building alterations initially required and to assume the cost of all subsequent repairs. An arrangement of this type provides major advantages to a small business entrepreneur. In view of the high mortality rate of new firms within the first five years of operation, such leasing advantages are very important. Moreover, upon expiration of a short-term lease, a young, growing, small business can move without risking loss on the sale of a building.

There are also advantages to buying the building. For example, ownership permits the adaptation of a building that will fit the special requirements of a business. In addition, a company cannot be forced—other than by government for public use—to move from quarters which it owns. Building depreciation is also deductible for income tax purposes. Offsetting these ownership advantages are such factors as the cost of repairs and maintenance, the necessity of selling a building when one moves a growing business, and the assessment costs for putting in sewers, waterlines, and streets. The small entrepreneur should give careful attention to this problem of leasing or buying; this is particularly important if his capital investment is modest.

Space Requirements

The building should be large enough to house the projected business operation and, typically, should include some space for future expansion. Too many small businesses have started operations in a building too small, with the result that the first ten years of successful growth have encompassed three or four moves to new locations.

The amount of space required varies with both the type and size of business. The number of workers employed is one index of business size. Obviously a business employing 50 workers will need more space than one employing five or ten people. As to type of business, a drugstore requires less space than a furniture store, because the latter must display living room furniture, bedroom suites, and other heavy, bulky items. Similarly, a jewelry store requires less space than a supermarket. A hot dog and hamburger stand does not need nearly so much space as a restaurant having many booths and tables.

Functional Requirements

The general suitability of a building for a given type of business operation is always an important consideration. The floor space of a restaurant, for example, should be on one level rather than divided among the floors of a four-story building. Similarly, the shape, age, condition, fire hazard, heating and air conditioning, entrances, and exits all are important factors to be considered relative to the particular requirements of a given business. Obviously these factors carry different weights for a factory operation as against a wholesale or retail merchandising type of business.

Accessibility is likewise important to employees, customers, and others coming to the place of business. Accessibility depends primarily on location, a problem discussed in the preceding chapter. In part, however, it depends on adequacy of access streets and on availability of highways and railroads in the community and area.

A desirable building should also have efficient internal transportation. This requires adequate aisles, traffic lanes, elevators and stairs (or escalators), together with equipment for the handling of merchandise in the store or raw materials and goods in process in the factory. The handling of materials or merchandise requires platforms and ramps for loading and unloading of trucks. There may also be chutes or conveyors required to transport materials to the receiving room. Other transportation facilities include handtrucks, dollies, pipelines, conveyors, hoists, cranes, and forklift trucks. The adequacy of transportation facilities must be evaluated in light of the firm's requirements.

Finally, there are a number of human problems relative to the functional character of a building. The comfort and convenience of workers and customers must be borne in mind. Heating, air conditioning, lighting, and service facilities all are important in this area.

Construction Requirements

The type of construction and physical condition of the building should provide for the safety of customers and working personnel as well as safe housing for the firm's merchandise and equipment.

Modernization. A structurally sound building may look out of date. Its architecture may identify it with a bygone era—a matter that is more or less serious depending upon the type of business. A traditional appearance could usefully imply stability and conservatism. There is the danger, however, that customers and others may identify old-fashioned architecture with outmoded, inefficient management. Most retailers desire a thoroughly contemporary atmosphere. Even factory workers are affected by the appearance of their factories. Other things being equal, most businesses find that modernization is highly desirable.

A modern appearance depends on good design and effective use of color. Use of glass as a structural material, skylights, and effective lighting contribute to a modern look.

Building Interior. A good color combination in the plant might include white ceilings, light green upper walls, darker green lower walls and machine bases, and bright orange moving machine parts. Traffic lanes could be indicated by black and/or white stripes, and floor storage areas could be enclosed with white stripes. The floor itself might be a neutral shade of gray. First-aid equipment might be the traditional green—and fire-fighting equipment, red. Such a color scheme enhances the safety and morale of workers.

Windows with sun exposure might also be provided with glareproof panes. This makes for eye comfort and a cooler building interior. This is particularly appropriate for a bank, office building, or restaurant.

Floors should be capable of supporting heavy equipment, be acid resistant, and have nonskid surfaces. Concrete floors are often used, but they are hard on shopworkers' feet. Store floors may require appropriate special finishes, such as hardwood blocks or rubber tile, while many professional offices frequently are carpeted.

Interior load-bearing walls and supporting columns must be adequate to carry the necessary load. Attention to this feature is particularly important for factories and other firms using heavy machinery in the production process. However, freestanding walls are extensively used today—and their use facilitates changes in plant layout.

The ceiling in both store and factory should be light in color to give proper light reflection. A modern trend in ceilings makes greater use of soundproofing materials; these absorb up to three fourths of the sound created in an average building. Soundproofed ceilings are especially useful, and regularly used, in exclusive shops, restaurants, noisy factories, banks, and supermarkets.

Building Exterior. The outside appearance of a building is important because of the impression it makes on customers and passersby. This is obviously much more important to a store or restaurant than to a manufacturer, wholesaler, or plumbing repair shop.

Among recent departures in exterior finish of buildings is the use of marble, bronze plate, aluminum siding, glass blocks, and translucent, two-pane insulating glass walls. In fact, an entire store front may consist of plate glass. If a store is clean and orderly, the ability to see in adds to the invitation to enter and purchase. The use of self-opening doors reinforces this invitation.

The foundation and exterior walls of an industrial or commercial building must be structurally sound and also strong enough to carry the load imposed upon them. And, of course, the building must meet minimum standards imposed by the local building and fire codes, considering the use to which it will be put, so as to assure the safety of employees, customers, and others.

Entrances and Exits. Entrances and exits should be such as to facilitate the quick and easy flow of people into and out of the building. Anything interfering with easy access should be avoided. For example, two doors should be provided (one on each side) if the building frontage extends over 35 feet. Or, if heavy customer traffic at a corner location suggests the need of two entrances, one can be placed at the front and the other at the side of the building.

At each entrance there should be a revolving door—or two swinging doors, one being for inbound customers and one for outbound customers. These swinging doors may be automatic in action, but this will cost more. Supermarkets, in particular, use automatically operated doors. They are also utilized by restaurants for the convenience of waitresses and busboys in going to and from the kitchen.

Differences in level between store floor and sidewalk constitute barriers to easy access. Older customers tend to resent the physical effort required to walk up and down steps; the psychological impact is generally bad. Rental prices reflect and attest the reality of this impediment.

Another major factor in evaluating entrances and exits has to do with inflow and outflow of merchandise and materials. Railway sidings and access ramps for trucks should lead to properly placed loading and unloading platforms. And, in stores, it is important that delivery entrances are separated from customer entrances.

Building Installations and Service Facilities. The owner of a small business cannot allow it to be outclassed in provisions for customer and employee comfort if he wishes to be directly competitive. One should certainly never go "second class" merely because one's business is small.

Air Conditioning. Air conditioning in factories is more rarely used. Some production processes generate so much heat as to make it impractical. In setting up a new plant, however, the owner of the small firm might well consider the possibility of air conditioning. Such a system is cheaper to install when the building is being built. Air conditioning often improves worker morale, and the owner may find his own efficiency increased with proper temperature control. It may be conducive to a better quality product and make equipment maintenance easier—especially where delicately adjusted equipment is being used. Air conditioning is especially useful in a factory where materials require controlled humidity to avoid deterioration.

Lighting. Good lighting must also be provided in both factory and store. In a factory the objective is adequate illumination for workers. In a retail store an added objective is the creation of a pleasing atmosphere for customers.

In both factory and store, the electric wiring must be adequate. It is worthy to note that the voltage required to operate a fluorescent lighting system is different from that required to operate a conveyor or heavy-duty machine tool. It is different also from the voltage required for electric calculators or other business machines in an office. These variations must be borne in mind in assessing electric wiring requirements for a place of business.

Sanitary Facilities. Sanitary facilities required in a factory or store include lounges, rest rooms, washrooms, and drinking fountains. These must be conveniently located for the use of workers and customers. Sterilization devices may also be required in cafeterias, dairies, hospitals, laundries, dry cleaning shops, and food processing plants.

Another common problem is that of proper plumbing and a good waste-disposal system. In addition to the ordinary plumbing required in any installation, a factory may require a vacuum-suction pipeline system for the removal of sawdust or metal chips which result from the process. Removal and decontamination of waste created in chemicals processing also create problems for plants which use such processes.

EQUIPMENT AND TOOLING

The procurement of a building is the initial step in providing physical facilities for a business. The next step is to procure the necessary equipment and tooling items for the intended business.

Factory Equipment

Machines in the factory may be either *general-purpose* or *special-purpose* in character. General-purpose machines for metalworking include lathes, drill presses, and milling machines. In a woodworking plant, general-purpose machines include ripsaws, planing mills, and lathes. In each case, jigs, fixtures, and other tooling items set up on the basic machine tools can be changed to permit accomplishment of two or more shop operations. This makes the general-purpose machine flexible in use.

Advantages of General-Purpose Equipment. General-purpose equipment requires a minimum investment and is well adapted to a varied type of operation. Small machine shops and cabinet shops, for example, utilize general-purpose equipment. General-purpose equipment also contributes the necessary flexibility in industries where the product is so new that the technology has not yet been well-determined or where there are frequent design changes in the product.

Advantages of Special-Purpose Equipment. Special-purpose equipment permits cost reduction where the technology is fully established and where a capacity operation is more or less assured by high sales volume. The large-volume production of automobiles, for example, justifies special-purpose equipment costing hundreds of thousands of dollars. Not all special-purpose equipment is that expensive, however. Even though it is used most in large-scale industry, application of the same principle on a more modest scale is possible in many small manufacturing plants. A bottling machine in a soft drink bottling plant and a milking machine in a dairy both illustrate specialized equipment used by small firms. Nevertheless, a small firm cannot ordinarily and economically use special-purpose equipment unless it makes a highly standardized product on a fairly large scale.

The use of a specialized machine using permanently set up special-purpose tooling results in greater output per machine-hour operated. Hence, the labor cost per unit of product is lower. The initial cost of such equipment and tooling is much higher, and its scrap value is little or nothing due to its highly specialized function. The cost of maintenance also is less, due in part to the use of built-in lubrication systems.

The small entrepreneur, thus, must consider initial cost, cost to maintain the equipment, allowable depreciation, and length of life, together with the conversion cost per unit of product resulting from the use of special- or general-purpose equipment. The risk that invention will make a machine functionally obsolete before its normal replacement date must also be evaluated. Moreover, achieving economy of repair service and reducing the variety of supplies required for machine servicing depend on having standardized equipment.

Retail Store Equipment

Small retailers must have such equipment as merchandise display counters, storage racks, shelving, mirrors, seats for customers, customer push carts, cash registers, and various items necessary to facilitate selling. Such equipment may be costly, but is usually less expensive than equipment for a factory operation.

Restaurant Equipment

The prospective restaurateur must consider at least five points when buying items of dining room equipment. These are:

1. Functional utility and size of the item
2. Durability and ability to withstand abuse
3. Impact on comfort of customers
4. Appearance
5. Cost

Essential items for the dining room include not only tables and chairs but also such items as coffee urns, silverware, china, table linen, and the like.

Kitchen equipment needed for food preparation includes kitchen utensils, ranges, refrigerators, and ovens, together with such accessories as potato peelers, electric mixers, meat choppers, meat slicers, bread slicers, vegetable slicers, and the like. There is also a need for worktables, sinks, and dishwashers.

Office Equipment

Both stores and factories require office equipment for typing, billing, bookkeeping, and other clerical tasks. The increased use of mechanized record keeping systems, even among smaller firms, adds to the investment required for the most efficient office equipment.

Some of this equipment may be rented, which reduces the capital outlay but still entails substantial operating costs. One dairy with fewer than 150 employees, for example, leases an International Business Machines punch card system at a cost of $20,000 per year. The purchase cost of the same equipment is about $100,000. Another firm with fewer than 25 employees produces and sells phonograph records with the aid of a punch card system which is leased for about $15,000 annually.

Automated Equipment for Small Business

Automation has come into use to a limited extent in small business wholesaling and merchandising operations. It is quite well-developed in some general office operations. However, some persons say that it is too expensive for the small business entrepreneur. Others disagree, saying that automation can be used on a small scale as well as on a large scale.

In a small plant the major barrier to automation is found in short production runs which do not require the automated process to be in action most of the time. But if a small plant produces a given product in large volume, with infrequent changes in design, the owner should seriously consider the many benefits derived from automation. Among these are:

1. Automation tends to eliminate operator errors with the result that it improves quality.
2. Automation increases speed of operation and machine efficiency, thereby lowering processing cost.
3. Automation tends to conserve manpower, while upgrading personnel skill requirements at the same time.
4. Automation promotes safety of manufacturing and handling operations.
5. Automation tends to reduce inventory requirements because of faster processing.
6. Automation improves both maintenance and inspection by incorporating lubrication systems and inspection devices in the automatic transfer machines.

LAYOUT OF THE BUSINESS

Layout involves the logical arrangement of all the physical facilities of a business in order to provide efficiency of operations. What is efficient and logical, however, depends to a considerable extent upon the type of business. In order to avoid makeshift arrangements, the inexperienced prospective entrepreneur would be well-advised to obtain the services of an architect, an engineer, or one who is sufficiently skilled to make an effective arrangement of the available facilities.

Factory Layout

Factory layout is a three-dimensional space problem. Overhead space may be utilized for power conduits, pipelines for exhaust systems, and the like. A proper design of storage areas and handling systems makes use of space near the ceiling. Space must be allowed also for the unobstructed movement of machine parts from one location to another.

The ideal manufacturing process would have a straight-line, forward movement of materials from receiving room to shipping room. If this ideal cannot be realized for a given process, backtracking, sidetracking, and long hauls of materials can at least be minimized. This will reduce production delays. The factory layout should also place service facilities at appropriate locations. There must be adequate space for storerooms, tool cribs, aisles, conveyors, pipelines, and power conduits.

Process and Product Layouts. Two contrasting types of layout are used in industrial firms. One of these is called *process layout* and has like machines grouped together. Drill presses, for example, are separated from lathes in a machine shop layout. The alternative to such a process layout is called a *product layout*. This is used for continuous-flow, mass production—usually conveyorized, with all machines needed for balanced production located beside the conveyor. Thus, similar machines are used at the same points on the different conveyor lines set up to process a given product. In the smaller plant, which operates on a job-lot basis, such a product layout cannot be used because it demands too high a degree of standardization of both product and process. Thus, small machine shops are generally arranged on a process layout basis. Small firms with highly standardized products, such as dairies, bakeries, and car wash firms, can use a product layout.

Tools for Planning Layout. Three tools available for planning layouts deserve special attention. These are scale-model layouts, scale-template layouts, and flow charts.

The *scale-model layout* uses miniature replicas of the machines, conveyors, pipelines, and other items to be installed in the plant. Service facilities are also constructed in miniature to scale. Then, each of these is juggled into just the right position. The finalized layout should have no waste or misuse of space.

The *scale-template layout* is somewhat less effective because it considers the problem of layout in two dimensions only. Thus, a machine that has a moving part might be so located and installed as to shear through an overhead pipeline, for example. Consequently, a scale-model layout is better than a template layout. Either one, when used, should be accompanied by a *flow chart* of the process, showing all processing machines and operations, together with storage and inspection points, distances traveled, direction of movement of materials in process, and the like. Standard symbols are used on a flow chart to portray graphically the various steps in processing, movement, inspection, and storage. Along with a scale-model layout, such a chart helps in visualizing the layout.

Layout of Work Stations. The work space allocated to any given machine and operator must itself be properly laid out, with standard positions for all tools, parts, supply items, packaging items, and the like. This is necessary so that the operator need not make more strenuous or wasteful motions than are actually required. An operator's work cycle will be speeded if he does not need to search for any part or tool. In some cases a standard arrangement makes possible repetitive movements without looking or conscious thought.

Layout of the Office. The layout of the general office is also a problem in the new small factory. Its location relative to the rest of the factory is perhaps even more important than the internal arrangement of its physical facilities. Hence, the total office space should be scaled and considered in the juggling of items for the total factory layout. Within the offices, the desks and chairs, safes, files, typewriters and tables, and other necessary items require adequate space and proper arrangement for efficient office operations. Thus, a set of office equipment miniatures will be needed for preparing the internal layout.

Store Layout

The objectives in retail store layout differ from those of factory layout. Among the goals of the small retailer is the proper display of merchandise in the various departments of the store, so as to make possible the maximization of sales. A second objective is customer convenience and service. Normally efficient, prompt service, together with convenience and attractiveness of surroundings, is required to justify a customer's continued patronage. Good layout also contributes to operating economy. A final objective is protection of the store's equipment and the goods on display. In achieving these objectives, the flow of customer traffic must be anticipated and planned as a part of the store layout problem so that it will be effectively facilitated when the store is opened for business.

Making the Store Layout. The store layout problem begins with a tentative floor plan, considering the respective values of different areas of the store building itself. Space for the different departments and, within departments, the different counters, shelves, and displays must be allocated in terms of the sales and profit potentials of the respective lines of merchandise. That is, the total space available must be divided properly among the various selling departments, stock rooms, and service facilities. Essential store service facilities include receiving room, general office, cashiering, credit checking, packing and delivery rooms, and the like. Space is required also for customer services such as gift wrapping, public telephones, and rest rooms.

Once the tentative floor plan is set up, a flow chart should be prepared, properly scaled as to distances. It should show the flow of customer traffic, the flow of goods within the store, and the movements of store personnel in the performance of their duties.

Self-Service Layout. The most revolutionary change in store layout in recent years has been the change to a self-service arrangement. The old-fashioned counters are gone, and customers have direct access to merchandise. Not only does this reduce the selling expense of waiting on customers, but it also permits shoppers to examine the merchandise before buying. In grocery merchandising this principle is now almost universally followed. It is also rapidly gaining acceptance in many other lines.

During a period of transition to a different type of selling and layout, it is the merchant with imagination and foresight who can capitalize on such trends. The successful small merchant dares not blindly follow the traditional practices that bankrupt so many firms. A progressive attitude leads to an analysis of his merchandise in order to determine the possibilities inherent in self-service layout. It leads also to a continuing study of the methods used by competitors.

Sales Strategy and Store Layout. For the proper display of goods, it must be remembered that some types of merchandise—for example, ladies' hosiery, cigarettes, magazines, and candy—are often purchased on an impulse basis. Impulse merchandise should be placed at the front of a store and at other points where customers can see it easily. Products which the customers will buy anyway and for which they come in specifically may be placed in less conspicuous spots.

The different areas of a retail store differ markedly in sales value. Customers typically turn to the right upon entering a store, and so the right front space is the most valuable. The next most valuable are the center front and right middle spaces. One department store places high-margin gift wares, cosmetics, and jewelry in these areas. The next most valuable are the left front and center middle spaces. And the left middle is fourth in importance. The back areas are the least important so far as space value is concerned. In consequence, most service facilities and the general office typically are found in the rear of a store. Certainly the best space should be given to departments or merchandise producing the greatest sales and profits.

The first floor has greater space value than a second or higher floor in a multistory building. Generally, the higher the floor, the lower its selling value to the merchant.

Cafeteria Layout

In view of the myriad types of small business, layout problems are unique to a considerable extent. The consideration of cafeteria layout in this section will illustrate one of the many fields presenting individual layout problems and an approach to their solution.

Dining Room Layout. In selecting tables and chairs for a cafeteria, at least half of the tables should seat four persons. Tables seating just two persons are often arranged along the wall. Booths provide another possibility for the seating of cafeteria patrons along the walls. In fact, according to some restaurateurs, most customers prefer booths. Of course, booths may also be placed on either side of a dividing wall in the central dining area.

In laying out a dining room, proper aisle space must be provided so that customers, tray in hand, can easily reach a vacant table or booth. Customers are understandably annoyed if they must creep by others while carrying trays of food—or if busboys carrying containers full of dirty dishes bump into them.

Perhaps the ideal layout is achieved by having customers enter through the front door into a small reception space which, in turn, funnels them into a corridor leading to the serving line. Modern cafeteria managers have discovered that a layout which shields the waiting and serving lines contributes appreciably to the atmosphere of the dining area.

The serving line constitutes a layout problem in itself. There is a question as to the order in which meats, vegetables, salads, desserts, drinks, and the other food items should be placed. Customers probably want to choose their meat near the beginning of the line, although some cafeterias reserve the first area for salads or rolls. Of course, the very first items on the service counter are trays, napkins, and silverware.

Before patrons leave the service line, their purchases are totaled by a cashier; they may pay for their food then or later when leaving. The advantage of deferring payment until later is the elimination of delays in the serving line that are inevitably involved in making change. Postponing payment until after dining will require an additional cashier at the exit, which may be too costly in small cafeterias.

Kitchen Layout. There are several principles to observe in preparing an efficient kitchen layout. The first principle of kitchen layout is the provision of adequate worktable space. At least four linear feet of worktable space should be allowed for each employee active in preparing food on the worktable. There must also be worktable space for laying out foods before and after cooking. Such items as individual casseroles require abnormal amounts of space for such post-cooking layout.

The second principle is that worktables connected with cooking must be reasonably close to the cooking equipment. This will reduce the accident hazard as well as the effort and time required for moving food from stove to table and vice versa. Storage space for accessories must also be provided at worktables.

The third principle requires that aisles of adequate size be provided. Some of these will be "working aisles" for the use of individual employees while others serve as "arterials" for moving from one part of the kitchen to another.

Main traffic aisles should be clearly defined and clearly separated from work aisles. This means that workers in one kitchen area should traverse their own aisles, without competition in their use from other kitchen or dining room workers. Thus, work aisles should be perpendicular to, or parallel to and separated from, the main traffic aisles. Observance of this principle will promote kitchen efficiency and reduce accident hazards in the kitchen.

According to the fourth principle, there should be a physical separation of the different types of cooking and preparation functions. For example, preparation of salads, meats, and pastries may properly be separated and different tables used for each. Here, too, the purpose is increased kitchen efficiency and reduced accident hazards.

The fifth principle is that equipment and materials should be located as near the point of use as possible. It may be impossible in a cafeteria kitchen to have a straight-line flow of materials. Workers in hot food preparation must be doing several things concurrently. Every effort must be made, however, to place mixers, utensils, flour, and sugar at points convenient to those who use them. Similarly, water pitchers and other supplies should be located conveniently for waitresses serving the dining area.

The last principle is that major equipment units should be so located as to maximize convenience and minimize interference among kitchen workers. In hot food preparation, there are four typical arrangements for equipment such as ranges, ovens, griddles, broilers, deep-fat fryers, and steam cooking equipment. The four typical methods of arranging this equipment are straight-line, L-shaped, parallel-back-to-back, and parallel-facing.

 Summary

1. The small business must usually begin by using or adapting an existing building. Erection of a new building is possible for the new firm, of course, and it often becomes desirable as a firm grows. In either case, the space should be adequate in amount and suitable in nature for the particular type of business.
2. There are various advantages and disadvantages associated with the question of leasing or buying physical facilities. The significance of these must be weighed in the light of each business situation.
3. The type of construction and physical condition of the building should provide for the safety and comfort of customers and working personnel and the safe housing and effective display of merchandise and equipment. Building service installations must also be adequate and properly located.
4. A decision between general-purpose equipment and special-purpose equipment must hinge upon the nature of production operations, the volume of production, and the costs of different types of equipment.
5. Each type of business and each division of a business has its individual equipment needs.
6. Automation is becoming a practical possibility for many small plants. The extent to which it can be effectively used depends primarily upon the size of production runs.
7. Efficiency of operation is the objective of plant layout. What is efficient depends, to a considerable extent, upon the nature of the business. Outside expert assistance often proves helpful in achieving the best layout.
8. Factory layout may be either a process-type layout or a product-type layout, depending upon the type of operation involved. Factory layout attempts to minimize materials handling.
9. Store layout attempts to maximize sales through effective display of merchandise and contribution to customer convenience. A self-service type of layout has become widely accepted in certain types of retailing. Store space varies considerably in its sales-producing value on the basis of its location.

Discussion Questions

1. Contrast the kind and extent of facilities as well as amounts of investment required by a neighborhood theater in a city suburb and by an 80-employee plant manufacturing house slippers. What types of small business require little or no physical facilities? Also, what types of small firms find substantial amounts of investment in facilities necessary?

2. In what way is the decision regarding physical facilities related to (a) type of business, and (b) location decision?

3. Should a small-city, downtown bank buy or lease its first building? Explain.

4. Would provision for possible expansion space be more important for a small retailer than for a manufacturer? Why?

5. What problems might be associated with the use of a multistory building by (a) a small manufacturer, (b) a small retailer, (c) a steam laundry?

6. How important is the appearance of modern construction, inside and outside, for (a) a small retailer, and (b) a local theater? Why?

7. Discuss the conditions under which a new small manufacturer should buy general-purpose and special-purpose equipment respectively.

8. Should a small manufacturer seriously consider machine and conveyor leasing? Why?

9. Is customer convenience and safety more important for the small retailer than for the small manufacturer? Why?

10. Stipulate a small retailer's possible uses for automated equipment, if any.

11. Should a new small factory avail itself of the services of a management consultant in designing the initial factory layout? Might the entrepreneur understand the layout problem better than the management consultant?

12. When should the small manufacturer utilize process layout, and when product layout? Explain.

13. What is a "flow" chart, and just how is it related to layout?

14. Define "backtracking" and "sidetracking" as they apply to factory layout and materials movement. Do they affect operating costs? If so, how?

15. Describe the unique problems concerning store layout and merchandise display that confront a new small jeweler.

Case C-1
INTERNATIONAL FLIGHT ACADEMY *

Proposed Flying School

A flying school was available for purchase, and Walter Hunter could see the opportunity of getting into business for himself. For the past year, he had managed the flying school which was associated with Lynn Aircraft, Inc., a fixed base aircraft operation. Lynn Aircraft wished to dispose of the flying school, which was operating at the break-even point, effective November 1. It appeared to Hunter that the business could be expanded and made into a highly profitable venture if he could raise the necessary financing and make the purchase on reasonable terms.

The flying school owned and operated five planes which were used in pilot instruction. Through this instruction, pilots could earn the following ratings:

1. Private
2. Commercial
3. Instrument
4. Multi-engine
5. Instructor
6. Instrument instructor
7. Airline transport

The school was situated in Lubbock, Texas, a location that made possible operation on a year-round basis. Student personnel were primarily local residents who took part-time pilot training. Hunter also visualized the possibility of having full-time resident students.

Another incidental source of revenue for the proposed business might come from taxi or charter service. Hunter realized this would not be a primary source of income but felt that it might supplement income received through the flying school.

Personnel

Hunter would be the manager and primary instructor in the proposed business. He was 34 years of age and a thoroughly experienced pilot. He had more than 12,000 flying hours to his credit and held the airline transport rating plus the necessary instructor ratings. He had served as a commercial airline pilot for eight years and had managed two flying schools at other locations for a total of three years prior to entering his present position.

Two other instructors were on the staff and would be available for service in Hunter's flying school. Both were experienced and capable instructors—one with 11 years' and the other with five years' experience in this field.

Hunter thought it would be necessary to employ one secretary, perhaps on a part-time basis initially. Maintenance and overhaul work would be contracted so that there would be no need for employing service or maintenance personnel.

Aircraft Investment

The major financial commitment would result from the purchase of five aircraft. Lynn Aircraft was willing to sell the five planes without down payment. In other words, Hunter could take over the aircraft and merely continue the payments on them. The outstanding loan balances on the five planes totalled $53,000. The original cost of the aircraft was more than double this amount.

The planes available for purchase are listed in Table 1.

Income Projections

Hunter realized that income from the flying school would vary from month to month because of weather conditions. This would cause the months of November through February to be the low-income period of the year. In contrast, the summer months of June

---

* This case was prepared by Professor Richard C. Scott and Professor Justin G. Longenecker of Baylor University.

Table 1

Estimated Current Value	Age	Type	Hours Since Last Overhauled	Use
$ 5,300	2 years	Cessna 150	1,243	Two-passenger, primary trainer.
$ 5,400	2 years	Cessna 150	180	Two-passenger, primary trainer.
$ 8,000	1 year	Cessna 172	960	Four-passenger, primary trainer and cross-country airplane.
$12,500	1 year	Piper 180	900	Instrument trainer, cross-country, and possible charter service.
$21,800 $53,000	9 years	Piper PA-23-250	900	Twin-engine Aztec, multi-engine trainer and possible charter service.

Table 2

	Hourly Rental Rent	Estimated Monthly Rental Hours (June-Sept.)	Estimated Monthly Rental Hours (Nov.-Feb.)
Cessna 150	$14	125	85
Cessna 150	14	125	85
Cessna 172	20	176	120
Piper 180	20	131	90
Piper PA-23-250	50	43	30

The rental hours noted above include the estimate of rental service during instructional flights.

Table 3

	Hourly Rate	Estimated Monthly Instruction Hours (June-Sept.)	Estimated Monthly Instruction Hours (Nov.-Feb.)
Flight instruction	$6	260	200

through September would be the high-income period. All flight instruction produced two types of income to the school—aircraft rental income and flight instruction income. His estimates of aircraft rental hours and of flight instruction income are shown in Table 2 and Table 3.

Estimated Operating Expenses

Hunter attempted to project the expenses that would be encountered in the business. Table 4 shows the general monthly expenses that he anticipated. In addition, Hunter estimated the expenses

Table 4

		Monthly Expense
Payment on airplanes [1]		$1,450
Aircraft insurance		575
Salaries		
Walter Hunter	$1,200	
Instructor #1	650	
Instructor #2	600	
Secretary	400	
Miscellaneous	200	3,050
Employee benefits		280
Advertising		300
Office and administrative expense		225
Payment on equipment and fixtures [1]		125
Lease of premises (including utilities)		300
Total		$6,305

[1] The monthly payment for aircraft and equipment would approximate a conservative monthly charge for depreciation. It is possible that depreciation may occur somewhat more slowly than this would indicate.

Table 5

	Cessna 150	Cessna 172	Piper 180	Piper PA-23-250 [1]
Gas expense	$2.48	$4.02	$5.08	$11.47
Oil expense	.25	.25	.28	.60
Maintenance expense	1.25	1.32	1.40	3.20
Overhaul expense [2]	.75	.69	.83	3.85
Total hourly expense	$4.73	$6.28	$7.59	$19.12
Operating hours	1600	2000	2000	1500

[1] It should be noted that the Piper PA-23-250 is a twin-engine plane. Hourly expenses shown are sufficient to cover both engines. It is assumed that both engines will require overhaul at the same time.

[2] The overhaul figure is the hourly rate necessary to establish a reserve for complete engine overhaul when the engines reach the number of hours indicated on the "operating-hours-before-overhaul" line.

related to aircraft by referring to the aircraft manufacturer's cost project publications. Hourly operating costs and maximum engine hours between overhauls are shown in Table 5.

QUESTIONS

1. What is the minimum amount of capital needed by Hunter to begin operations? What would be the optimum amount of capital to have available?

2. Project the operating revenues for the first year.

3. Assuming Hunter's projection of operations is reasonable, should he initiate this business?

4. Assuming Hunter has no personal savings and that he wishes to maintain control, how can he raise the necessary capital?

5. What future avenues of expansion are available for Hunter?

Case C-2
DIESEL
POWER SUPPLY
COMPANY

Clair D. Weller, owner of Diesel Power Supply Company, was considering the retention of an attorney to provide legal advice and assistance for the firm.

During the 10-year history of the business, an attorney had been used only infrequently. On one occasion, an attorney was used to obtain a judgment against a delinquent debtor. An attorney's services were also required in the purchase of real estate and in drawing up a will. Weller had also consulted with an attorney in analyzing the advisability of incorporation. The firm had grown to more than $300,000 annual sales, and it was clear that an attorney should be retained at some point in its growth.

Weller could see the potential usefulness of an attorney, but there was a question as to whether his contribution at this point would be sufficient to justify the $200 to $400 annual retainer fee. He had little serious intention of using an attorney for collection purposes. (The fee would undoubtedly be greater if such use were contemplated.) His experience had led him to believe that in his operation legal action against debtors simply did not pay for the cost involved. For occasional property transactions, he could always find an attorney on a one-time fee basis.

Even though Weller had decided against immediate incorporation, he intended to continue his consideration of the corporate form. Conditions could easily arise which would make it logical to incorporate. Further, with rapidly changing laws affecting business, he felt a need for guidance by someone who was keeping abreast of the law. Such an attorney who was also abreast of his business could alert him to laws affecting his business or to changes needed in the business to maintain conformity to the law. Although not absolutely necessary, he felt it would be helpful to have an attorney with some background knowledge of the firm and its operations. Also, he felt he would like to have an attorney look after family interests in the event something happened to him personally. The firm was worth more than the book value of its net worth, and this needed to be recognized in selling the business, paying off bank loans, or making other decisions in settling the estate. It was quite essential that the business be maintained as a going concern to avoid loss of established goodwill value.

The firm's banker recommended its own legal firm to Weller for his consideration. Weller hesitated to accept this recommendation, however, questioning whether such an attorney would be completely independent in representing his interests with the bank. Could such an attorney protect the family interest in the event of his death, or would his primary concern be with repayment of bank loans? At least one other leading law firm might be contacted, and there were, of course, other smaller law firms and independent attorneys available.

Weller felt that any attorney would need his complete confidence in order to provide adequate legal service. This meant the attorney must understand and be sympathetic with the basic operating philosophy and character of the firm. So, the question facing him was not only whether to retain an attorney but, if so, what type of attorney to select.

QUESTIONS

1. What seem to be the most pressing legal problems that face this firm?
2. Does this firm have sufficient need of legal services to justify retention of an attorney?
3. If retention of an attorney is justified at this point, should Weller select the bank's attorney? If not, what alternative should he follow?
4. What type of problems can a business encounter by failing to keep abreast of changes in the law?
5. In a small business, what is the relative importance of having legal counsel versus trained insurance counsel?

Case C-3 LOUISVILLE MARINA *

Sgt. Oliver of the U.S. Army was assigned to the ROTC Detachment at the local university. He has put in 22 years in the Army and is scheduled to retire in six months (about April 1, 1966) with a medical discharge. Oliver is 44 years of age. He has savings of about $8,000 and would receive $185 per month in retirement.

During the past two summers, Sgt. Oliver spent most of his leisure working at a cove marina west of the city along the Ohio River. This was possible since Oliver's duties were relatively light at the Detachment during the summer. His primary duties at the marina involved running the restaurant, but he did spend some time running the marina operation. He was assisted in the restaurant by his wife who worked as a waitress. The restaurant was open from 12 noon until 9:00 p.m. every day except Tuesday during the boating season. It served snacks and light hot meals. It did not cater to outside trade.

The marina is for sale and Sgt. Oliver would like to buy it and operate it himself.

Facts About the Marina

The marina is located about 20 miles west of Louisville. It is the last cove type marina down the river from the city, and one of only two such marinas in the area. A cove type marina differs from a dock on the river in that a cove marina is usually a dug-out basin with a channel leading to the river. Boats are protected from debris and the constant pounding into docks caused by waves (factors not present in docks on the river). The cove and land surrounding it comprise an area of 44.95 acres. The dug-out harbor is connected to the Ohio River by a channel of about 300 feet in length. Water covers most of

the land when the river floods. For example, water enters the restaurant when the river level reaches 58 feet. Consequently, all equipment in the restaurant is portable and is removed when there is danger of a flood. There is one section of land, about 5 acres, which is higher and is safe from flooding up to a river stage of 73 feet. The river has not reached this level since the great flood of 1937.

At the present time there are 84 boat slips (docking spaces) in the cove. These are all rented, and there is a waiting list for spaces. This is due to the desirable features of the cove. On-river docking is not this crowded. The slip docks are on floats so they do not have to be removed for minor flooding. They are normally pulled from the water in the winter, however, to prevent damage from freezing and to prevent their breaking away in very high water. When removed, they are stored in the open on the high ground. In addition to the slip docks and restaurant, the marina also has a gas float and dry dock. The gas float is maintained and serviced by Ashland Oil Company, whose products are sold at the float. The dry dock can be rented by boat owners and used for boat repair and maintenance. There is also a ramp which can be used to launch small boats, but this traffic is limited, if not discouraged, by the lack of personnel to aid in launching.

The marina is owned by Bob Baker and Jim Higgins. The former is in the building business and the latter is in the contracting business. Baker had owned the land for several years and conceived the idea of the marina. Higgins contributed the equipment and men to do the excavation work. Both contributed to build the slip docks and restaurant. As a result, the men are equal partners. According to Baker, Higgins has not shown much of a working interest in the marina in the past two or three years due to growth of his contracting business. This has put an additional burden on Baker who manages the operation. Baker is anxious to sell the marina for two reasons. First, he is not happy with the partnership arrangement and,

* This case was prepared by Professor John E. McDavid of East Tennessee State University.

second, he wants the cash to build a golf course.

In addition to himself and the Olivers, Baker hires a part-time worker during the boating season to help with the chores and a watchman to care for the boats during the off hours. Baker runs the marina and draws a salary for his services.

During the past year, the marina earned a profit, before Baker's salary and taxes, of approximately $20,000. The income and expense items are shown in Exhibit 1. According to the partners, the land, buildings, slip docks, restaurant, etc., have a value of $150,000, as shown in Exhibit 2. The marina has no long-term debt. The asking price for the land and facilities is $200,000, but Oliver feels it can be bought for $175,000 cash.

Oliver's Proposed Changes

If Sgt. Oliver purchases the marina, there are several changes he would like to make. First, he would like to build 30 new slip docks which would increase the moorage income by $10,000 per year. Moorage charge is based on the length of the boat. Construction of these slip docks would cost approximately $14,000. There are enough people on the waiting list to rent these new slip docks and still leave some waiting. The new slip docks would be on floats similar to the present ones and would be removed in the winter.

The second thing he would like to do would be to create more interest in launching small boats on the weekends. This would require an outlay for help

Income		
Moorage	$20,000	
Restaurant (net)	2,000	
Dry dock	1,500	
Gas and oil sales (net)	3,000	$26,500
Expenses		
Water	$ 50	
Electricity	1,000	
Telephone	200	
Insurance	1,200	
Salaries	4,160	6,610
Net Income		$19,890 [1]

[1] Before Baker's salary and before federal income taxes.

Exhibit 1
OPERATING STATEMENT, 1965

Assets		
Cash		$ 4,000
Fixed assets	$168,000	
Less depreciation	18,000	150,000
Total assets		$154,000
Liabilities and net worth		
Accrued taxes		$ 3,000
Accounts payable		1,000
Total current liabilities		$ 4,000
Owner's equity		150,000
Total liabilities and equity		$154,000

Exhibit 2
BALANCE SHEET, DECEMBER 31, 1965

only, since the launching ramp is available. If enough of this business were forthcoming, it might be necessary in the future to enlarge the parking area to accommodate the cars and trailers. Sgt. Oliver anticipates that $3,000 can be earned from the ramp during the season.

The third thing he would like to do is to build a pole barn on the high ground to accommodate boats in winter storage. Most boats in this section of the country are either removed from the water and require storage or taken south for the winter. This building could be built in two sections, with half being built the first summer and the remainder the second. Total cost of the building would be $6,000, and the completed structure would earn about $14,000 per year in storage charges. Storage charge is based on $7.00 per foot of boat stored. In addition to storage, some income can be generated from the labor required to remove the boats from the water and winterizing them, and then by dewinterizing them and returning them to the water in the spring. Also, some income can be earned by providing a trickle charge to the boat batteries over the winter.

If Oliver acquires the marina, he would like to improve the restaurant after a year or two. At such time he would like to establish the restaurant as a club and obtain a club license in order to sell liquor to members. Dues could be set at $10, and he feels that most persons with boats at the marina would join. He does not anticipate that he could obtain a regular liquor license that would permit him to cater to outside trade. He estimates that the improvements necessary on the restaurant would cost $10,000; and he has made no estimate of income from the added food and liquor sales.

Another idea he had is to sell boat and engine parts to bring in extra income. This would make his the only marina for about 50 miles, 30 east and 20 west, that would be selling parts.

The cost of first-year improvements would be $17,000: $14,000 for slip docks and $3,000 for the pole barn. This amount would be financed. Second-year improvements would be $3,000 for the second half of the pole barn and $10,000 for the improvements to the restaurant. Funds for the second-year improvements would be generated from profits.

Net income before taxes would be about $32,000 for the first year after the improvements. Exhibit 3 shows the estimated income statement for 1966.

Income		
Moorage	$30,000	
Restaurant	4,000[1]	
Dry dock	2,000	
Boat launching	3,000	
Winter storage	7,000	
Gas and oil sales (net)	4,000	$50,000
Expenses		
Water	$ 50	
Electricity	1,200	
Telephone	250	
Insurance	1,700	
Salaries	15,050[2]	18,250
Net income before taxes		$31,750

[1] Income after deducting expenses for food, but not for labor.
[2] Includes wages for restaurant and marina management.

Exhibit 3
ESTIMATED OPERATING STATEMENT, 1966

Alternative Financing Plans

Sgt. Oliver is considering financing the purchase of the marina (land, equipment, and buildings) by either the formation of a corporation, or borrowing the money, or a combination thereof. He figures a down payment of about $40,000 would be required to purchase the marina and the remainder to be provided by mortgage funds. If a corporation is formed, he anticipates authorizing 40 shares of stock to be sold at a book value of $1,000 per share. He could buy some of this stock with his savings and sell the remainder. At the present time, he knows of three or four individuals who are parking boats at the marina and are interested in buying stock. The corporation would then finance the remainder of the purchase price by borrowing funds from a savings and loan association or bank and mortgaging the assets. These funds would cost about 6.5 percent.

A second method Oliver has in mind is to use his savings and personally borrow from a bank or other financial institutiion the remaining $32,000 for the down payment. The property could then be mortgaged to obtain the remaining funds. These funds would also cost about 6.5%, and Oliver would be personally liable for the loan. This plan would give Sgt. Oliver sole ownership and control of the operation, something the first plan lacks.

The third alternative is for Sgt. Oliver to raise the $40,000 cash for a down payment and allow Baker to finance the purchase. Baker is willing to accept a cash down payment and give the buyer a 5% mortgage on the remaining $160,000 for 10 years.

QUESTIONS

1. Calculate the worth of the Louisville Marina as a basis for negotiating its possible purchase from the present owner.
2. If the marina is purchased, how should it be financed?

Case C-4
BEN FRANKLIN VARIETY STORE *

Parnell McNamara and his brother Mike are the owners of a prosperous 4,400 square foot variety store in Waco, Texas, a city of 100,000 people. This is the only variety store that Parnell and Mike own, and it is a franchise unit of the Ben Franklin voluntary chain. They estimate that 90 percent of their customers are women.

The store is situated in a community shopping center in a growing area and currently serves a neighborhood of approximately 15,000 people. A bridge is near completion which will bring more traffic into their area. A new junior college with great potential is in the vicinity. The college presently has 2,000 students.

The Park Lake Shopping Center in which the variety store is located is on both sides of Park Lake Drive, a moderately travelled street; and North 19th Street, a busy street which runs along one side of the Center (see Exhibit 1). They are

* This case was prepared by Professor Curtis C. Reierson and Professor Justin G. Longenecker of Baylor University.

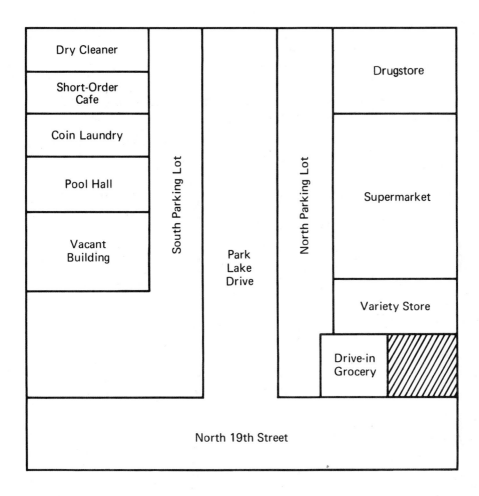

Exhibit 1
PARK LAKE SHOPPING CENTER

located on the north side of the street between a large supermarket and drive-in grocery. There is also a modern drug store in the center. The supermarket customers take up much of the available parking space, and the location of the drive-in grocery also limits the number of parking spaces in the area of the variety store.

Across the street is a vacant building formerly occupied by an auto parts store. The vacant building contains 6,600

square feet and is located at one end of the community center. The business adjoining it is a large pool hall. A coin operated laundry, short order cafe, and a dry cleaner make up the remainder of the south side of the Park Lake Shopping Center.

Parnell and Mike and the Ben Franklin representative agree that the variety store needs more space. According to the franchisor, the trend in variety stores is toward stores of much larger size that provide certain economies of scale. The vacant building is the only nearby location available. However, a location expert has advised against the proposed new site for the variety store.

The new south side location would have the advantages of a 50 percent increase in selling space and doubling the present parking space.

Parnell and Mike realize that their rent at the new location will increase proportionately to the increase in square footage, and that the neighboring business firms will not bring in as much "drop in"

trade for their store. However, they must consider the need for more selling and parking space.

QUESTIONS

1. Evaluate the advantages of the current location.
2. What are the advantages or weaknesses of the adjacent business firms in each of the two locations in relation to the variety store?
3. Should Parnell and Mike move to the larger available location across the street?

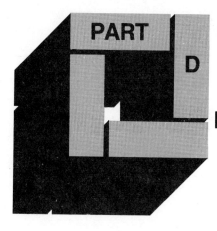

PART D

Selling and Marketing Research in Small Business

17

Selling the Products or Services

Effective marketing programs and policies are as important as production activities for the typical small firm. In designing an effective marketing program, the small business must consider such factors as the product line, pricing, advertising and sales promotion, personal selling, and sales planning and control. The importance of each of these factors varies according to the nature of the business, but the total marketing effort is a highly critical element in the stability and growth of most businesses.

PRODUCT LINE DECISIONS

The product or assortment of products produced by a small manufacturing firm constitutes its *product line*. Decisions are often required as to whether this product line should be altered, contracted, expanded, or held constant. For example, a company bottling and distributing milk may decide to expand by manufacturing and distributing ice cream. Product line decisions for retailing and wholesaling firms are concerned with the types of merchandise to be sold. Service firms also must determine the scope of services offered to customers.

Product and merchandise lines have a tendency to grow rather haphazardly. Lines may be added with a hope of greater profit but without a careful analysis of profit potential and without the subsequent serious attempt to evaluate the profit contributed by the added products. In the well-managed business, however, product line decisions are based upon a study of all pertinent data.

The Life Cycle of Products

Successful products go through a recognizable life cycle. They begin with an *introductory stage* of low customer acceptance and proceed through a *growth stage*, in which sales gains are rapid, to *maturity*. Eventually, a period of *decline* is encountered, and sales fall off. The length of each stage depends upon the nature of the product. Because of the rapid rate of technological development and the increasing pace of business change, the average life of products continues to decrease.

If a small firm is to survive, therefore, it must constantly examine and reexamine its product line. The rate of growth in the firm's new products, for example, may be declining; or sales for all products may be leveling off. New or modified products are required to replace products that reach the final stage of their life cycle.

Introduction of New and Improved Products

In adding different or improved products to its line, a business firm is faced with a fundamental business policy decision. These products may have been developed by the firm itself; they may be inventions that have been purchased; or they may be products acquired by purchase of, or merger with, another firm. In any event, launching a new product is typically a hazardous step. Avoidance of costly errors requires careful attention to the several factors noted below. Although the discussion of these is directed primarily at manufacturers, much of the reasoning is also applicable to marketing and service firms.

Relationship to Existing Product Line. A going manufacturing concern has a given variety of products and established distribution channels. Any products to be added should be consistent with, or properly related to, this existing product line. For example, a new product may be designed to fill a gap in the company's product line or in the price range of the products it currently manufactures. If the product is completely new, it should normally have at least a family relationship to existing products. Otherwise, the new products may call for drastic and costly changes in manufacturing methods, distribution channels, type of advertising, or manner of personal selling.

Cost of Development and Introduction. One problem in adding new products or introducing improved products is that of underwriting the cost of development and introduction thereof. The capital outlays may be considerable. These include expenditures for design and development, market research to establish sales potential and company volume potential, advertising and sales promotion, patents, and the equipment and tooling that must be added. It may be from one to three years before profits may be realized on the sale of the contemplated new or altered product. This calls for the ability to finance operations until the inception of profits.

Personnel and Facilities. Personnel and facilities should be available for production and marketing of the proposed product. Obviously having skilled personnel, including management executives of the right kind, and production equipment to do the job is better than having to add skilled personnel and buy new equipment. Hence, introducing new or improved products is typically more logical if the personnel and the required equipment are already at hand.

Competition and Market Acceptance. Still another factor requiring consideration is the character of the market and the existing or potential competition facing the proposed product. Competition must not be too severe. Some businessmen, for example, think that new products can be introduced successfully only if a 5 percent share of the total market can be secured. The ideal solution, of course, is to offer a sufficiently different product or one in a cost and price bracket that avoids direct competition.

Production-centered decisions regarding the product line are dangerous. Customers must accept the new product, and their choices often differ from the seller's choices based on his personal tastes or availability of equipment and personnel. If the product is radically new, market research will be necessary to determine market acceptance.

Small Business Limitations and Strengths. All the factors stated above apply to both small and large firms in all lines of business. The factors of available capital, facilities, and personnel are particularly significant to the small firm. As to capital, the large corporation has a distinct advantage in its financial strength. Likewise, the facilities of a large manufacturer are frequently more nearly adequate for the required task. The small manufacturer, on the other hand, often has to expand production facilities considerably to introduce the same new product. The limited management, production, and sales ability and experience in many small firms constitute even more severe limitations.

Nevertheless, the small firm possesses strength as well as weakness in its choice of a product line. Chapter 3 introduced the concept of strategy in selecting products and/or services that provide a competitive edge. By using its flexibility, which larger competitors do not have, the small business may attack at the point of greatest weakness in the large firm. Selling to a mass market often leads large corporations to choose products and services that appeal to the mass taste. Products desired by only a segment of the market are much less attractive to them. By finding a nonstandard product area which large firms are not exploiting, a small firm may compete effectively in the marketplace. This might mean either a higher-priced product or an economy model. On the other hand, it might involve fast deliveries or short production runs of special items. Or, the high quality of the product or the service that is offered with the product may make it superior to comparable products offered by others. Properly selected, the small firm's product may occupy a special niche in the market.

Product Line Expansion

Product line expansion is called *diversification*. Its objective should be to increase profits and to contribute to the long-range growth of the company. Diversification can be so planned as to result in stabilization of production, employment, and payrolls. It can also fill out a product line as a service to customers. In addition, diversification can spread the overhead costs of administration over more units so that overhead cost per unit is reduced.

Small retailing institutions provide numerous examples of diversification in practice. The addition of general merchandise lines to drug prescriptions constitutes a type of diversification that has been followed by almost all drugstores. Service stations have also experimented with various types of additional services and products. Some of these, such as car wash installations, auto repair shops, and trailer rental services, are closely related to the service station business. Others, however, are quite different in nature. Some stations, for example, have added self-service laundries, grocery departments, dry cleaning stations, restaurants, auto rental facilties, and tool rental services.

Whether any particular step toward diversification is logical and desirable depends upon the particular circumstances. The factors discussed in the preceding section—for example, availability of necessary facilities and skills—should affect the decision. Moreover, the firm must be able to deal creatively with all of the problems which diversification will entail, or it can hardly be expected to succeed. Then it is possible that the cost of diversification may exceed the increased sales.

Product Line Discontinuance

In contrast to diversification, management should also consider contraction of product lines. Dropping of products is wise if the market has disappeared for the product or if the firm is losing money on the production of a certain product or group of products. Many manufacturers, small and large, have discovered that weeding out excess products and concentrating upon a narrower line can produce substantial operating economies. Product discontinuance certainly is to be recommended if income lost by discontinuance is less than the costs that will be eliminated thereby.

Measuring the benefits from product discontinuance requires another pertinent consideration. Can the company, after product discontinuance, still use its employees and equipment so that no unemployment will be created and no idleness of expensive equipment results? Money invested in facilities is a "sunk" cost which is difficult to recover. Moreover, a company typically must still use its sales force, service personnel, and executives after a product discontinuance. If the executive, sales, service, and factory personnel time and the facilities cannot be utilized on the remaining products, product discontinuance may be unwise.

Product Profitability Analysis

The amount of profit that might be realized from a new product may be estimated by comparing the incremental costs with the incremental sales revenue. Incremental sales revenue is normally the sales dollars expected from the new product. It is possible, however, that the new product may cause a reduction in sales of an existing product. In such a case, the net incremental sales revenue is more pertinent to the analysis. Such an analysis must consider both production and distribution costs of both a variable and fixed nature. The ideal new product provides a substantial spread between its selling price and variable costs while requiring no increase in total fixed costs for the company. Fixed costs may remain the same, for example, if the new product can be manufactured with existing equipment and sold by the present sales force.

Many firms do not know the cost of the products they make and/or sell. Their cost accounting systems should be revised to provide the pertinent cost information. Such a revision should make it possible to determine the income contribution of each major class of products or services in the present line.

In summary, it should be reiterated that the small business should carefully estimate the profit on each of its present products as well as the potential profit on new products. If pertinent cost information is not available, an accurate evaluation of profit effects of product line changes is difficult or impossible.

Product Packaging

The primary function of any package or container is to protect its contents. This job of product protection begins the instant the product is packaged and does not end until the last of the product is consumed. It may be weeks or months after the product leaves the filling machine, or even after a consumer has purchased the product.

At one time, the package was merely a container which facilitated handling and protected its contents. Today's package should also help to sell the product, particularly products purchased by ultimate consumers. It is no longer enough for the package merely to show the manufacturer's name and the product trademark. The immediate product container must also serve as an advertising medium, enhancing the value of the product to the customer's eye.

PRICING DECISIONS

What appear to be pricing problems in small firms are often different types of problems in disguise. Frequently small businesses hesitate to match prices directly with larger competitors. One reason for this reluctance is the small firm's difficulty in covering costs and providing some margin of profit at the lower price. The size and resources of the larger business make possible more efficient operations. Thus, the problem is stated in terms of price, but in reality it is a matter of relative operating efficiency.

An uneconomic location of a small firm might make it impossible to engage in direct price competition with better located businesses. In this case a location problem masquerades as a pricing difficulty. All problems in pricing, however, cannot be shrugged off as the result of other organizational weaknesses. Some pricing uncertainties and decisions cannot be avoided even by the well-managed small business.

Product or Service Differentiation

Only in rare cases are identical "packages" of products and services offered by competing firms. In many cases the products are dissimilar in some way. Even when products are the same, the accompanying services typically differ. Speed of service, credit terms, delivery arrangements, personal attention by a top executive, and willingness to stand behind the product or service are but a few of the areas that serve to distinguish one business from another.

The pricing implications depend on whether the small firm is inferior or superior in these respects to its competitors. There is no inherent reason why the small business may not excel in a number of ways. In fact, it may well have "natural" advantages which its management may carefully exploit. Certainly, there is no absolute imperative for the small business to conform slavishly to the prices of others. Its unique combination of goods and services may well justify a premium price.

This suggests the possibility that a particular firm's contribution might be valued more highly by certain potential customers than by others. An opportunity thus exists for the small business to cater to a certain segment of the market rather than attempting to appeal to all customers. For example, a small grocery store with credit and delivery services may develop a successful business by appealing to customers who desire this combination of services. It might in this way continue successfully to price above supermarket prices.

Business Costs and Pricing

In a successful business, price must be adequate to cover total cost plus some margin of profit. *Total cost* includes three elements. The first is the *cost of goods* (or services) offered for sale. An appliance dealer, for example, must include in the price the cost of the appliance and freight charges. The second element is the *selling cost.* This includes the direct cost of the salesperson's time as well as the cost of advertising and sales promotion. The third element is the general *overhead cost* applicable to the given product. Included in this cost are such items as office supplies, utilities, taxes, office salaries, and management salaries. Most of these are fixed charges in that they do not change in total amount with the amount of sales.

The final component of price is profit. This is the necessary return to the entrepreneur for his services and risk of doing business.

Flexible Pricing Practices. Although many firms do make a determination of their costs and use total cost as a point of resistance, most of them take into consideration demand for the product and practices of competitors in arriving at their prices. The following cases[1] illustrate this point:

Contractor A estimates the full cost of producing a house, but he modifies the price to meet market conditions. Even his concept of cost reflects variable estimates of the opportunity costs of his time. His time is less valuable in the winter, when business is slack, than at other seasons; he adjusts his estimates of cost accordingly. He also shades price on a cash sale of a house, recognizing the avoidance of a risk as compared with sales involving complicated financing. Thus the stress on full cost does not mean inattention to demand.

Printing Company A also pays considerable attention to full-cost estimates. While the management insists that prices *should* be kept on a full-cost basis, actual practice is more flexible. The managers are critical of "rate cutters," who, they claim, are responsible for the low industry profits, but they themselves show some willingness to adjust to market conditions when the necessity arises.

Furniture Company D starts with a cost estimate, including an allocation of indirect labor and factory overhead. But the management modifies the target return to meet market conditions.[2]

Pricing at Less Than Total Cost. On certain occasions it may be logical to price at less than total cost. For example, if a business has idle facilities, their cost may be continuing regardless of whether they are used or are idle. In any case, the price should cover all marginal or incremental costs—that is, those costs specifically incurred to get the added business. In the long run, however, all overhead costs must be covered as well.

Price Cutting

Other factors being equal, a firm should reduce price whenever the added volume resulting from so doing will produce more than enough sales revenue to

[1] W. Warren Haynes, *Pricing Decisions in Small Business.* Small Business Management Research Report. Prepared by the University of Kentucky under a grant by the Small Business Administration, Washington, D.C. (Lexington: University of Kentucky Press, 1962), p. 27. Used by permission of the publisher.

[2] *Ibid.*, pp. 28-29.

offset the added costs. The logic of price cutting, thus, is to increase product acceptance by one's customers.

Elasticity of Demand. The elasticity of demand for a product is one factor affecting the wisdom of price cuts.[3] If demand is highly elastic, customers will respond with substantially higher orders when offered a price reduction. Price cutting, therefore, must be considered as a sales promotion technique. It should be used only when it is superior to other techniques.

Inelasticity of Demand. Given inelastic demand, however, price cutting becomes intolerable because there will be a loss in sales revenue without a corresponding decrease in cost. For example, a retailer selling an $80 item for $100 makes a gross profit of $20. If the price is cut 10 percent (to $90), gross profit per item would drop to $10. This means that two items must be sold to realize the same gross profit as before. Because of the inelastic demand, however, no more than a negligible increase in sales volume would result. This illustrates the folly of price cutting when demand for a product is inelastic.

Probable Reaction of Competitors. The probable reaction of competitors is a critical factor also in determining whether to cut prices below a prevailing level. A small business in competition with larger firms seldom is in a position to consider itself the price leader. If competitors view his pricing as relatively unimportant, they may permit him to introduce and maintain a price differential. This may well be the reaction if the price-cutting firm is sufficiently small. On the other hand, established firms may view a smaller price cutter as a direct threat and move to counter his cut with reductions of their own. In such a case, the original price cutter accomplishes very little.

Whether price reductions are appropriate, therefore, depends upon the nature of demand and the probable reaction of one's competitors. Unfortunately price cutting is used unwisely in many cases because the entrepreneur is unaware of other promotional schemes or refuses to deal with the basic problems of inefficiency.

Price Concessions to Individual Customers. In some lines of business, the selling firm makes price concessions to individual customers even though it advertises and presumably uses a uniform price. One study of the sale of high-unit-value home appliances discovered that 86 percent of the establishments customarily practiced variable pricing.[4] Such concessions were made for various reasons, one of the principal considerations being the customer's knowledge and bargaining strength. In some fields of business, therefore, pricing decisions involve two parts: the level of the stipulated "list" price and the extent of price concessions to particular buyers.

Markup Computations

In calculating the selling price for a particular item, retailers, wholesalers, and even manufacturers must add a markup percentage to cover the following:

---

[3] Methods of estimating price elasticity for products of small firms are suggested in William J. Kehoe, "Demand Curve Estimation and the Small Business Manager," *Journal of Small Business Management*, Vol. 10 (July, 1972), pp. 29-31.

[4] Walter J. Primeaux, Jr., "The Effect of Consumer Knowledge and Bargaining Strength on Final Selling Price: A Case Study," *The Journal of Business*, Vol. 43, No. 4 (October, 1970), pp. 419-426.

1. Operating, particularly selling, expenses.
2. Operating profit.
3. Subsequent price reductions—for example, markdowns and employee discounts.

Markups may be expressed as a percentage of either the *selling price* or the *product cost.* For example, if an item costs $6 and is selling at $10, the markup of $4 would be 40 percent of the selling price or 66 2/3 percent of the product cost. Although either method is correct, consistency demands that the same method be used in considering the components entering into the markup. If operating expenses amount to 35 percent of sales and a profit of 5 percent of sales is desired, the markup (assuming no markdown) must be 40 percent of sales price. This is clearly different from 40 percent of cost. In fact, an incorrect application of the 40 percent figure to cost would produce a markup amounting to less than 29 percent of sales, less than enough to cover operating expenses. Of course, it is easy enough to convert a sales percentage to a cost basis, or vice versa. Table 17-1 shows markup percentages based on cost. Table 17-2 on page 290 presents simple formulas for markup calculations.

Table 17-1
SELLING PRICE MARKUP TABLE

How to use this table. Find the desired markup percentage based on selling price in the column at the left. Multiply the cost of the article by the corresponding percentage in the column at the right. Add this amount to the cost in order to determine the selling price.

Desired Markup Percentage (Based on Selling Price)	Equivalent Percentage of Cost
5.0	5.3
6.0	6.4
7.0	7.5
8.0	8.7
9.0	10.0
10.0	11.1
12.5	14.3
15.0	17.7
16.7	20.0
20.0	25.0
25.0	33.3
30.0	42.9
33.3	50.0
35.0	53.9
37.5	60.0
40.0	66.7
42.8	75.0
50.0	100.0

A common business practice uses an "average" or "normal" markup for the entire business or for particular departments. One possible weakness in this practice is its failure to recognize cost differences in selling different products. Cost studies often reveal differences in the variable expenses of distribution, among which are receiving, checking, advertising, personal selling, delivery,

Table 17-2
FORMULAS FOR MARKUP CALCULATIONS

Cost + markup = Selling price
Cost   = Selling price − markup
Markup   = Selling price − cost

$$\frac{\text{Markup}}{\text{Selling price}} = \text{Markup expressed as a percent of retail}$$

$$\frac{\text{Markup}}{\text{Cost}} = \text{Markup expressed as a percent of cost}$$

If a seller wishes to translate markup as a percent of selling price into a percent of cost, or vice versa, the two formulas below are useful:

$$\frac{\text{Markup as a percent of selling price}}{100\% - \text{markup as a percent of selling price}} = \text{Markup as a percent of cost}$$

$$\frac{\text{Markup as a percent of cost}}{100\% + \text{markup as a percent of cost}} = \text{Markup as a percent of selling price}$$

---

service, and credit extension. If there are substantial cost differences in selling product A and product B, a "normal" markup percentage may produce a loss on one product and a greater-than-average profit on the other. To the extent that cost analysis can determine the selling cost of particular products, therefore, an attempt should be made to price the product accordingly. Departmental markup percentages, when based on such reasoning, may be superior to a single percentage for the entire business.

It might be observed that the markup percentage, even when it is realistically computed, is only the starting point. It may need to be modified because of any of a number of factors. Competitors' prices, traditional prices, and loss-leader or promotional pricing illustrate these other influential factors.

Price Lines and Price Strategy

A *price line* is a range of several distinct prices at which merchandise is offered for sale. Men's suits, for example, might be sold at $75, $100, and $125. The general level of the different lines would depend upon the income level and buying desires of a store's customers. The policy has the advantage of simplifying choice for the customer and reducing the necessary minimum inventory. *Price strategy*, on the other hand, is the offering of goods for sale only for price and quality lines in which the merchant meets little or no competition. That is to say, he sandwiches his offerings of merchandise in the price and quality levels at which his competitors are not offering goods for sale. Obviously, for unstandardized shopping goods, price strategy may work, whereas it is not used in the case of standardized staple goods.

The limitations of price lines and price strategy may force the merchant to alter the initial sales price as determined by ordinary markup procedures. More likely, however, it would simply close the door to handling of merchandise of qualities that would fall in between regular price lines. The selling price would be set first and would serve as a guide for buying.

ADVERTISING AND SALES PROMOTION

Advertising is the impersonal presentation of a sales-creating message to large groups of people. It utilizes mass media, including, among other forms, newspaper advertising, radio and television advertising, direct mail advertising, billboard advertising, and handbills. Doing business without advertising is like winking in the dark—the businessman knows what he is doing, but potential customers do not.

Objectives of Advertising

It is the function of advertising to draw attention to the existence or superiority of a firm's product or service. To be successful, it must rest upon a foundation of quality workmanship and efficient service. Advertising can bring no more than temporary success to an inferior product. A restaurant, for example, may entice customers to give it a trial, through advertising; but only good food, fair prices, and service can build repeat business. Advertising may also accentuate a trend in the sale of an item or product line, but it seldom has the power to reverse such a trend. It must, consequently, be closely related to changes in customer needs and preferences.

Used superficially, advertising may appear to be a waste of money. It seems expensive, while adding little utility to the product. Nevertheless, the major alternative is personal solicitation of potential customers, which is often more expensive and time-consuming.

Types of Advertising

From the foregoing objectives, one may discern that there are two types of advertising—product advertising and institutional advertising. *Product advertising* is direct-action advertising, designed to make potential customers aware of a particular product or service and of their need for it. *Institutional advertising*, on the other hand, is concerned with the selling of an idea regarding the business establishment. It is intended to keep the public conscious of the company and of its good reputation.

No doubt the majority of small business advertising is of the product type. Retailers' advertisements, for example, stress products almost exclusively, whether those of a supermarket featuring weekend specials or a men's shop focusing upon suits or sport coats. At times the same advertisement carries both product and institutional themes. Furthermore, the same firm may stress product advertising in newspapers and, at the same time, use institutional appeals in the yellow pages of the telephone book. Decisions regarding the type of advertising used should be based upon the nature of the business, industry practice, media used, and objectives of the firm.

When to Advertise

When to advertise is always an important question for the small business. Institutional advertising, if justified at all, should be done periodically if not continuously. Attempts to stimulate interest in a company's products or services should be part of a continuous advertising program. One-shot advertisements which are not part of a well-planned advertising effort lose much of their effectiveness as a result.

Some noncontinuous advertising, of course, may be entirely justified. This is true, for example, of advertising to prepare consumers for acceptance of a new product. Similarly, special advertising may be employed to suggest to customers new uses for established products. This is true also in the case of advertising special sales.

Where to Advertise

The question of where to advertise is particularly significant for the small business. Most small firms are necessarily restricted either geographically or by class of customer. Advertising media should reach but not overreach the present or desired market. From among the many media available, the small entrepreneur must choose those that will provide the greatest return for his advertising dollar.

Selection of the right combination of advertising media depends upon the type of business and its governing circumstances. A real estate sales firm, for example, may rely almost exclusively upon classified advertisements in a local newspaper, supplementing these with listings in the yellow pages of the telephone book. A transfer and storage firm may use a combination of radio, direct mail, and telephone directory advertising to reach individuals planning to move household furniture. A small toy manufacturer may place greatest emphasis on trade paper advertisements and participation in trade fairs. A local retail store may concentrate upon display advertisements in a local newspaper. The selection should be made not only on the basis of tradition but also upon an evaluation of the various ways to cover the particular market.

How Much to Spend for Advertising

No small business has unlimited funds to spend for advertising. Consequently, the outlay of funds for advertising must be wisely planned. Insofar as the small firm has money to spend on advertising, it should be guided by the standard ratios for the line of business or type of industry. In addition, there is the fact that spending must vary with the type of product; the location, age, and prestige of the firm; the extent of its market; the media used; the current business cycle position; and the amount of advertising by competitors.

A firm's advertising policy may also regulate the amount spent for advertising given products or given classes of merchandise. One small business followed the practice of spending two thirds to three fourths of the total outlay on one product or merchandise class. Other products or classes of merchandise were given incidental advertising. This was accomplished by giving them small amounts of space at the bottom of each advertisement in which the main product or merchandise class was headlined. It may also be done by sporadic advertisement of minor products, with the regular advertisements playing up the main product or merchandise class.

In passing, it should be noted also that timeliness and impact of advertising vary seasonally, as do the sales of most business firms. Hence, advertising expenditures should be varied seasonally and be proportional to normal, expected sales.

The Advertising Program

It is important that the various aspects of advertising and sales promotion be woven into a carefully planned program. This involves first a statement of objectives and a determination of amounts to be spent for advertising and supplementary sales promotion. It also requires consideration of timing of advertisements, choice of media, liaison with outside experts or advertising agencies, and the relationship of advertising to marketing research results. Haphazard, uncoordinated advertising efforts may constitute a waste of business resources.

In addition, there are underlying principles or precepts upon which the successful advertiser regularly depends. Some of them are the following:

1. A quality product or service should be properly priced and made readily available to purchasers.
2. Advertising should be truthful, honest, and in good taste.
3. Advertising must be regularly and consistently used for maximum impact.
4. The advertising message should reach the right people—the potential customer clientele.
5. The business should have factual knowledge of its market, so that the advertising will be properly designed with appropriate appeals.
6. Each type of advertising should fit into a total advertising program designed for maximum sales impact.

One often hears the statement that it pays to advertise. A little reflection upon these principles of successful advertising reveals this to be only a partial truth. Only *effective* advertising actually pays.

Use of Outside Help

An advertising agency stands ready to design a firm's advertising program, to evaluate and recommend the advertising media with greatest "pulling power," and to attempt an evaluation of the effectiveness of different advertising appeals. It will also perform design and artwork in the preparation of specific advertisements. Again, it will advise on sales promotion and merchandise display problems. Moreover, it can furnish mailing lists and make market sampling studies to evaluate product acceptance or area sales potentials. Of course, the quality of particular agencies varies greatly, and only the competent agency can be of real aid to the advertiser. Since an advertising agency may charge a fee for its services to supplement what it is paid by the media, the advertiser must make sure that his return from those services will be greater than the fees paid by him.

Other outside sources may also provide assistance in formulating and carrying out an advertising program. Suppliers often furnish display aids and even complete advertising programs to their dealers. Trade associations also are active in this area as in other areas.

Analysis of Advertising Results

Although extremely difficult, it is important that the sales impact of each advertising effort be checked as closely as possible. Only in this way can the advertiser know whether his advertising money is being well spent. Of course, he can never answer this question precisely. He knows that only a portion of his advertising is effective, but he has difficulty knowing exactly which part.

Evaluating the effectiveness of advertising is complicated by a number of factors. Consider the time element, for example. Some sales may be generated immediately, but other sales may result a month or a year after the advertisement. In addition, customers are subject to numerous forces affecting their behavior in addition to the advertising. These other forces do not remain constant. Business conditions change, and competitors change their advertising as well. The continuing change in these numerous variables makes it impossible to isolate the effects of any one variable in advertising.

The difficulty in measuring advertising effectiveness varies, of course, with the type of advertising. Institutional advertising is the most difficult to evaluate, whereas direct mail product advertising might be evaluated quite effectively. In order to judge advertising effectiveness, records must be maintained to show the timing of the release, the media used, weather, appeals used, and sales results. At best, however, most evaluations of this type require a considerable measure of subjective judgment.

Nature and Objectives of Sales Promotion

Sales promotion includes not only advertising but also a wide range of activities and techniques designed to build sales of products and services. One of these activities—personal selling—is discussed in a later section of this chapter. Other promotional devices or activities include contests for salesmen, aids furnished to dealers, counter and window displays, publicity, visits by Santa Claus, autograph parties with the author of a book, special sales, and use of trading stamps.

In retail stores, window displays and counter displays should be frequently changed to help bring the merchandise to customer attention. Some aid in this type of advertising is available from manufacturers. Eastman Kodak, for example, supplies retailers with counter displays and leaflets describing Christmas cards that can be made from a customer's picture. Manufacturers, in addition to furnishing display materials, advise on store layouts and personnel training programs and provide free advertising mats. The manufacturer or wholesaler might also provide a two- or three-day factory training course for sales personnel of key distributors. Or, they could maintain a staff of sales engineers to act as troubleshooters for customers' problems. All of these might be considered promotional techniques.

Quality of product and service in itself constitutes a type of indirect sales promotion. One service station looks much the same as another. It is principally the quality of service which serves to distinguish one from its competitors. The satisfied customer not only returns but also speaks favorably of it to others.

Many a small automobile repair shop has built a rush business largely on this particular basis.

Philosophy of Advertising and Sales Promotion

Any businessman should assume that his competitor has a product or service as good as his own, a sales organization as effective as his own, and competitively equal prices. Hence, he must predicate his sales program on the theory that creative merchandising will be required to accomplish better sales results than those of his competitors. Creative merchandising depends upon the ingenuity and quality of ideas invested in the planning and promotion of sales. Moreover, it depends upon the joint cooperative effort of all members of the firm. It also depends upon the philosophy that customers buy ideas rather than products. Hence, sales promotion must sell people ideas which sell products and services.

The quality of products, organization, advertising and selling effort, customer service rendered, and the like are all without much point unless the product or service is brought face to face with the largest possible number of customers under circumstances which influence those customers to buy from the given firm instead of from a competitor. One's philosophy and practice of sales promotion, accordingly, must be designed to bring the maximum number of potential customers into direct contact with the product at a possible point of sale. One might summarize by saying that sales promotion properly consists of every activity which is both legal and moral and which will promote sales.

PERSONAL SELLING

Few products or services are sold without personal salesmanship. Sales procured via catalogs, direct mail, and other impersonal techniques are merely exceptions to the general rule. Personal selling includes the activities of both the inside salespersons of retail, wholesale, and service establishments and the outside sales representatives who call on business establishments and ultimate consumers.

Product Knowledge

Effective salesmanship must be built upon a foundation of product knowledge. If salespersons know the product advantages, uses, and limitations, they can educate the customer and successfully meet objections. Most customers frankly look to the salesperson for such information, whether the product is a camera, suit of clothes, automobile, paint, machine tool, or office machine. Customers seldom are specialists in the products they buy. They immediately sense the knowledge or the ignorance of the salesperson, however. The significance of product knowledge is revealed by the fact that personal selling degenerates into mere order-taking where such knowledge is not required of the salesperson.

A salesperson may be able to suggest new uses of the product that the prospective customer had not contemplated. Sales case histories, kept on tap for use when needed, may help to convince a doubtful customer about the benefits deriving from the use of the product by showing specifically how it has benefited others.

Making the Sales Presentation

The heart of personal selling is the sales presentation to the prospective customer. At this crucial point the order is either secured or lost.

Salespersons must adapt their sales approach to the customer's needs. A "canned" sales talk will not succeed with most buyers. The salesperson of bookkeeping machines must demonstrate the capacity of the equipment to handle a customer's particular bookkeeping problems. Similarly, a boat salesperson must understand the special interests of particular individuals in boating. In this connection, the salesperson must talk the customer's language. Every sales objection must be answered explicitly and adequately.

There is considerable psychology in successful selling. The salesperson, as a psychologist, must know that some degree of enthusiasm, friendliness, and persistence is required of him or her. The enthusiastic, persistent salesperson is the one who gets the sales orders. Perhaps 10 percent of all salespersons secure as much as 80 percent of all sales made. This is because they are the 10 percent who persist and who bring enthusiasm and friendliness to the task of selling.

Some salespersons have special sales "gimmicks" which they use with success. One salesclerk, selling boys' clothing, kept a supply of dimes in his pocket. When a boy came in with his parents for a new suit, the clerk asked the usual questions about price, color, and style, and then allowed the boy to try on a couple of coats for size. After this, he selected a suit he thought would best satisfy the boy and please the parents as well. He would then slip a dime into the righthand coat pocket, knowing that boys typically put their hands into coat pockets of new suits when trying them on. It was his boast that hardly any boy who felt the dime in the pocket was able to turn down the suit.

Cost Control and Profit Creation in Personal Selling

There are economic and wasteful methods of achieving the same volume of sales. For example, efficient routing of traveling salespersons and the making of appointments prior to arrival can conserve time and transportation expense. The cost of an outside sales call on a customer may be considerable—perhaps twenty dollars or more—which emphasizes the need for efficient, intelligent scheduling. Moreover, the salesperson for a manufacturing firm can contribute to cost economy by stressing products which most need selling in order to give the factory a balanced run of production.

Profitability of sales is increased to the extent that sales are on the basis of quality and service rather than price cutting. All products do not have the same margin of profit, however, and the salesperson can maximize profits by emphasizing high-margin lines. The salesperson's compensation plan may be devised to encourage such sales.

Building Customer Goodwill

The salesperson must look beyond the immediate sale to build customer goodwill and to help create satisfied customers who will patronize the company in the future. One way to accomplish this is to preserve a good appearance, display a pleasant personality, and demonstrate good habits in all contacts with the customer. One can also help build goodwill by understanding the customer's point of view. Courtesy, attention to details, and manifested friendliness will help to gain acceptance with the customer.

High ethical standards are, of course, of primary importance in creating customer goodwill. This rules out misrepresentation and calls for confidential treatment of a customer's plans. Certainly, the salesperson who receives secret information from a buying firm should preserve the confidence of that firm. He or she should not disclose its secret plans to competitor firms.

High-pressure selling is no longer so popular as it once was because it is less productive than it was several decades ago. More than a slick personality and high-pressure tactics is required for successful selling today. Low-pressure salesmanship, on the other hand, which allows the salesperson to sell through having a good product and a complete knowledge of it, is more effective in obtaining sales and in getting repeat orders from permanently satisfied customers.

SALES PLANNING AND CONTROL

There should be a proper balance between sales tactics and sales strategy. *Sales tactics* refer to sales techniques used, which may vary from day to day. *Sales strategy*, on the other hand, includes preparation of the product for the market, preparation of the market for the product, and creation of customer confidence in the firm. All these objectives of a sales strategy can later be translated into actual sales by means of sales techniques.

Sound Sales Strategy

A good sales strategy must rest on the base of thorough market knowledge. A study of sales records, talking to customers themselves, and market sampling studies will enrich the entrepreneur's market knowledge and permit him to plan a good product line, together with an effective sales promotion and selling program. Even the production line cannot be ignored in planning market strategy because it is there that quality is built into a product or omitted from it.

Entry into New Territories and Dropping of Old Territories

Earlier in the chapter, it was noted that products should be added or dropped when it becomes profitable to do so. Similar planning is required before a company enters a new market or drops an old one which is unprofitable. Profitability of operation is the proper basis for continuance or introduction of operations in a given territory. Entering a territory should generate more dollars of sales income than it adds to cost. Hence, entering a territory should be based upon a comparison of incremental costs and incremental income. The same is true when dropping a territory—it should be dropped when its cost contribution exceeds its income contribution.

Sales Forecasting and Sales Quotas

Sales quotas provide targets for the firm as well as for individual salespersons, departments, or sales territories. The establishment of sales quotas involves one type of marketing research—a topic discussed in the following chapter. As such, it must be based upon facts as far as it is possible to do this. For example, it might include market sampling studies and study of census data to determine sales potentials. Of course, such a study should also make due allowance for the extent and intensity of competition in the respective territories served. Furthermore, the knowledge of salespersons achieved through customer contacts should be utilized. Statistical analysis and projection based on past sales may also be used. Because market information is continually changing, sales quotas quickly get out of date, requiring annual and/or seasonal review.

The final sales forecast is the cornerstone of the whole budget of the firm. It also provides specific sales quotas for specific salespersons and territories. Hence, sales forecasting cannot be taken lightly and must be done accurately at the proper time. It cannot be avoided. The small entrepreneur who thinks he has avoided sales forecasting is kidding himself, for he will be forecasting by "off-the-cuff" estimates if he has not made a formal forecast.

Sales Analysis and Control Reports

Sales management by intuition simply will not work well. Sales managers need information on actual and projected sales in order to control the marketing program. Control data should be in proper form and available at the earliest possible time. Out-of-date information is relatively worthless.

In sales reports, the stress should be placed on major facts and trends rather than on details. Sales records provide data on actual sales. The budget, as revised in the light of current sales conditions and operating facts, provides the yardstick with which actual sales must be compared. All variances between budgeted and actual sales should be clearly noted in the control reports. All significant variances require immediate investigation to find their causes so that appropriate remedial action may be promptly taken.

 Summary

1. Products typically follow a life cycle beginning with an introductory stage and ending with a period of decline. Because of this fact, a small firm must give continuing attention to changes in its product line.

2. Decisions regarding a firm's product line require consideration of such factors as the relationship of the various products to each other, cost of development and introduction, availability of personnel and facilities, intensity of competition, market acceptance, and profitability of the product. Increasing the size of the product line results in diversification which may be desirable or undesirable depending upon the availability of necessary facilities and skills.

3. One of the difficulties in pricing comparisons is the dissimilarity of the "package" of products and services offered by different firms. Differentiation of this "package" may make it possible for the small firm to differentiate its price as well.

4. In the long run, price must be adequate to cover total cost plus some margin of profit. Decisions concerning price cutting must consider elasticity of demand and the probable reaction of competitors.

5. Price lining is the offering of merchandise at several distinct price levels; price strategy is the offering of merchandise at price levels which meet little competition.

6. Advertising is the impersonal presentation of a sales-creating message. It draws attention to the existence or superiority of a firm's product or service and may be classed as either product advertising or institutional advertising.

7. Important direct methods of sales promotion include advertising, personal selling, window displays, counter displays, contests for salesmen, dealer aids, publicity, and use of trading stamps. Quality of product and service indirectly promote sales.

8. Effective personal selling demands adequate product knowledge and a courteous, clear sales presentation. The salesperson must look beyond the immediate sale in order to build customer goodwill.

Discussion Questions

1. A manufacturer of power lawn mowers is considering the addition of a line of home barbecue equipment. What factors would be important in a decision of this type?

2. Would either diversification or restriction of product lines appear to be inherently better for a small firm? Why?

3. What advantages would a small manufacturer find in a policy of reduction of the product line?

4. In addition to profits from increased sales, what reasons might a firm have for product diversification?

5. Under what conditions would it be desirable to keep a product in the line even though it did not show a profit?

6. For what types of business is the packaging of products most important? For what businesses is it unimportant?

7. Examine and report on packages observed in a retail store which show imagination, help sell the product, and are used to package the product of a small manu-

facturer.

8. How may pricing problems indicate inefficiency in a small firm?

9. Under what conditions can a small firm take the role of a price cutter?

10. Should small firms always try to match the prices of larger competitors?

11. Should price always cover total costs of producing and/or marketing the product or service by the selling firm? Why?

12. What difference does it make, if any, whether markup is computed on the basis of cost price or selling price?

13. What difficulties may arise from using "normal" markup percentages?

14. What business firms might concentrate on institutional advertising?

15. What nonadvertising activities are included in sales promotion programs? What are "indirect" methods of sales promotion?

16. What kinds of selling help might small firms obtain from large suppliers?

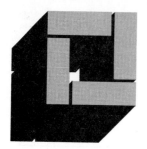

18

Marketing Research

Many managers of small firms are skeptical about the value of marketing research. Some of them do not see how it can contribute to their success. Others suggest that it is too expensive to be practical. These doubters do not understand that the foundation of marketing research is an attitude of inquiry toward marketing problems—an attitude that seeks to discover the facts of a situation and to improve the marketing program.

NATURE AND SCOPE OF MARKETING RESEARCH

Marketing research is distinguished from other areas of industrial research by its concentration upon marketing problems. In dealing with a marketing problem, a research study reveals the essential facts and frequently makes possible a better solution than would have been the case without research.

Study of Consumer Behavior

Marketing research experts have devoted much attention to the study of consumer behavior, or *motivation research*. At one time, it was thought that, for the most part, consumers reacted rationally to products and advertising. Even when the importance of emotional and psychological factors was realized, business generally lacked an understanding of the nature of these reactions with respect to particular products and companies. Worst of all, consumers, if asked why, often cannot, or will not, explain the reasons for their buying behavior. For example, some years ago a man told his wife that he was uninterested in acquiring a television set, believing it could do nothing for him. She agreed, and they owned no TV set until his brother gave them one. Today this family of three owns four TV sets: two in color and two in black and white.

A qualitative approach to market research seeks enlightenment on consumer motivation, and so it is potentially useful for a wide range of decisions in marketing. Unless researchers understand the underlying reason behind certain attitudes, they cannot take adequate corrective action. It should be noted that motivation research is not limited to its use in depth interviewing by a trained psychologist. A business manager may quite informally develop an awareness of, and a method of discovering, the attitudes of his customers. To illustrate, if the operator of a television and radio service firm called on a sample of his customers two weeks or a month after completing service calls, he would discover that most customers are willing to express opinions regarding technical proficiency, speed, and cost of service.

Identification of Customers and Trading Area

One important area of marketing research concerns identification of the firm's customers and trading area. Strangely, perhaps, many businesses do not really know who their customers are. The "reach" of a business may also be greater, or less, than management realizes. The location, race, income bracket, occupation, and educational level of customers obviously constitute valuable information for many types of business decisions. A firm can use such information in planning for advertising intended to expand its market and enhance its sales.

Investigation of Customers' Wants and Reactions

Even more neglected in the study of customers is the careful investigation of their desires. One cannot safely assume that he knows what customers want. What the businessman thinks customers want and what they actually desire may be vastly different. Of course, customers may not always know just what they want. Sometimes, however, they are fully aware of their needs. Where this is true, market studies will produce valuable information. This is true even though a company's sales already are high. Good sales might be translated into excellent sales by a greater knowledge of customer wants.

A particularly fruitful sort of marketing research is that directed toward determining the reaction of consumers to new products, restyled products, new or altered services, and changes in product packaging. Of course, an investigation of customer attitudes and needs involves quite different approaches depending upon the nature of the business. Whether the business is that of manufacturing ice cream or retailing drugs, however, the manager ideally should know his customers and be aware of their evaluation of his product or service.

Evaluation of Sales Potential

Another type of marketing research activity is that directed toward an evaluation of sales potential for the industry and the firm. With such an objective in mind, research studies are directed toward the measurement of population, income level, purchasing power, and other indexes of sales potential in the trading area. A local retailer investigates these factors with respect to the community in which he is located. In contrast, a manufacturer or wholesaler selling on a regional or national basis includes a correspondingly larger area in the study. After establishing market potential for the area and industry, a specific firm can apply its estimated percentage[1] of total industry sales to obtain

---

[1] This percentage or market share can be closely estimated by a typical going concern on the basis of past sales experience of the industry and company. It is not a "guessed" figure.

its own sales potential. A determination of the firm's sales potential is essential for the establishment of accurate sales quotas and for the measurement of effectiveness in selling. Another advantage is found in the greater accuracy with which expenditures for advertising and sales promotion can be specified.

Evaluation of Sales Promotion Program

Marketing research may also be directed to the effectiveness of a sales promotion program. The "pulling power" of individual advertisements can be studied, and the ability of customers to identify an advertiser with his products can be investigated. Certainly, the need for obtaining maximum impact from advertisements and other sales promotion devices is sufficient to warrant such evaluation studies.

Determination of Profitable Channels of Distribution

A careful study of the most profitable channels of distribution constitutes still another practical objective for marketing research. The product of a particular manufacturer may be sold through wholesalers, various types of retail outlets, door-to-door salesmen, catalogs, and in other ways. The firm should know which distribution channels will maximize its sales and profit.

STEPS IN MARKETING RESEARCH

Marketing research activities vary greatly as to the degree of formality involved. Managers of small firms, to the extent that they engage in marketing research at all, rely primarily on the more informal methods.

Recognition of the Problem

Whether the research is formal or informal, it begins with the recognition of a problem which creates the need for information. This problem might be a need to know the size of a firm's potential market or to determine the effectiveness of its advertising.

Problems are frequently somewhat vague or confusing as the businessman faces them. One must start, therefore, by determining the real nature of the difficulties facing the firm. This focuses management attention on its real troubles. Unfortunately, small business managers sometimes work diligently but are solving the wrong problems simply because they have not carefully analyzed the situation confronting them.

Preliminary Investigation and Planning

Having identified the marketing problem, the next step is a review of the facts already known. In some cases the answer may be quickly determinable in this way. In others, added data will be required.

This second step may involve discussion with other people inside or outside the firm, reading of trade publications, or tapping of still other sources of information in order to discover exactly what facts are required to deal with one's problem. At this stage, the manager knows what facts are needed to deal with the identified problem and what facts he already has available. Comparison of these two sets of facts shows clearly what facts are needed but not on hand. The manager can then make plans for procuring the data needed.

Gathering Factual Information

The heart of marketing research is found in this stage of ferreting out the objective information pertaining to a given business problem. The sources of information are indeed numerous and vary with the nature of the problem under consideration. Techniques appropriate to the gathering of needed facts often are dependent upon the available sources of information.

Primary Sources of Published Data. A primary source of data is one compiling and first publishing the given data. Examples include U.S. census reports and the broad analysis of the market and methods of building materials dealers published some years ago by U.S. Gypsum Company, along with local market surveys made by chambers of commerce. Data from primary sources may not be generally available; they may be either comprehensively or narrowly applicable. Sometimes they may be usefully intermixed with data that is collected from secondary sources.

Secondary Sources of Published Data. A secondary source of published data is one containing data originally compiled and published elsewhere. Usually such data are of general-purpose character. Frequently they were published originally as a public service. The secondary source then republishes the data to make them more generally available. Perhaps the most widely used secondary sources are government publications, such as *Survey of Current Business* and *Statistical Abstract of the United States*. Others include *World Almanac*, trade association reports, chamber of commerce studies, university research monographs, trade journals, and newspapers.

Secondary sources sometimes take the form of a comprehensive study, which provides all facts needed to solve a given problem. Often, however, they appear in isolated tables and must be pieced together with still other facts in the process of solving a problem. Obviously, if such data exist and will help solve a business problem, money and time are saved by finding and using them.

Primary Sources of Unpublished Data. Published data may not suffice to solve a business problem. In this event, original data must be collected. One may use internal data from the firm's own records. Or, one may use external data acquired from dealers, competitors, and ultimate consumers. In either case, time and cost pressures may preclude getting all the data needed. One must then resort to sampling, a technique discussed on pages 304-305.

Classifying and Interpreting Information

A solution is not always clearly evident from the basic factual information applicable to a particular problem. When the answer is not obvious, it is necessary to classify and fit together the various data available. This demands careful thought in determining the significance of certain facts, their interrelationships, and their implications for the business. This is true whether the data be in the form of dollar figures, verbal opinions, trade association estimates, or any other form.

In this step, the manager is searching for the meaning of the facts, and a high degree of skill and insight is required in achieving a reasonable interpretation. Common sense, also, is certainly in demand in this stage of the market study. In many situations the best information available is still inadequate, and numerous intangibles may also complicate the analysis.

Reaching a Conclusion

If the research is successful, it will lead to some conclusion. In some cases this may be essentially negative in nature, but the manager will still know more than he did at the beginning of his investigation. The conclusion should follow logically from the interpretation and reasoning involved in the preceding step. Even though the impact of intangibles is unclear and gaps in information exist, the conclusion will be based on objective data.

RESEARCH TECHNIQUES FOR SPECIFIC MARKETING PROBLEMS

The use of quantitative methods is the time-honored approach to a study of industry market potential, investigation of consumer reaction to changes in products or product packaging, and determinations as to the effectiveness of advertising. Given a good sample design, efficient coding and tabulation, accurate analysis, and common sense in drawing conclusions, one can get good results from such methods. Corroborative collateral evidence is helpful also, when available.

Sampling Surveys

The design of sampling surveys involves the use of statistical techniques, and a small firm may need help from a specialist. If sample survey designs are not efficient, the analysis of data and the accuracy of the findings will both be impaired. A *random sample* is required so that the laws of probability will govern the interpretation of results. Two other basic requirements, only slightly less important, are that the sample used must be representative and adequate. The *representative sample* is one which is like the universe of which it is a part with respect to variables, such as race, religion, occupation, sex, or income level, which might affect the accuracy of the sample-provided answers. An *adequate sample* is one large enough to yield a truly dependable answer.

Two types of survey research techniques are available—the *questionnaire* and the *personal interview*. If the survey subject matter is complicated—for example, if technological factors require explanation—personal interviews are virtually required if the needed information is to be obtained accurately. Moreover, the interviewer must have high skill to assure dependable results. Questionnaires sent by mail have the advantage of economy in comparison with most interviewing plans.

Manufacturing managers often admit the value of sampling techniques in consumer market research but consider it inapplicable to industrial sales research. They feel that their product is unique and that it takes the whole universe of market data to enlighten them about their market. This belief is often false. An adequate, random, representative sample for industrial sales research can be obtained by determining who buys the particular product and devising a sample to include enough of the various types of buyers, randomly selected and in proper proportions. Such a sample can acquaint them with the important characteristics of their market.

Sequential Sampling of Consumers' Packaging Preferences

An accurate determination of the packaging preferences of consumers is frequently important to such firms as dairies, bakeries, cosmetic manufacturers—indeed, to producers of almost any product sold in packaged form. *Sequential sampling* is a statistical technique that can be utilized in making such determinations. It involves the use of a number of successive, randomly chosen members from a large group. An analysis of properly drawn sequential samples can quickly reveal the characteristics of the entire group. This technique typically permits the use of smaller samples than are required for other types of sampling, without any increase in the risk of error in the judgments reached. In fact, a statistician can determine the probability of accuracy of a judgment reached at any stage of a sequential sampling investigation. When a sufficiently accurate judgment is attained, the investigator ends the sampling.

Let us assume that a dairy has 1,000 home customers. It has made experimental use of paper cartons for two weeks and is considering their permanent substitution for glass bottles. If the change is made, the dairy's increased cost would require a price increase of one cent per quart. Hence, the dairy operator has decided to take a random sample from the whole group of home customers, explaining the price differential and inquiring as to their preference. He will reject the use of paper cartons if no more than one third of the customers like them and will adopt them if two thirds or more approve.

The investigator must first decide upon an acceptable maximum probability of error—say one chance in twenty of getting a wrong answer.[2] Then, using standard statistical formulas, he can proceed with investigation of successive sample members—individual randomly selected customers in this case. If they should give unfavorable answers on the first, second, third, sixth, seventh, eighth, and ninth interviews, the seventh unfavorable answer out of the first nine would lead to a judgment that the total group of home customers disliked the paper cartons. Thus, with only one chance in twenty of a wrong decision, such random sampling of the thousand customers has provided a definitive answer in only nine interviews.[3]

---

[2] This is because any sampling procedure involves some degree of uncertainty as to accuracy of the survey results.

[3] All statistical sampling procedures properly provide for precise determination of margins of error in indicated results.

Testing Market Acceptance

Small business firms that are contemplating the introduction of new products can reduce risks by first investigating the market reaction to those products. This can be done by *test marketing*. The manufacturer should produce a model of the new product and let prospective users examine it and provide critical evaluations. Or, if a wholesaler is considering the addition of a line of frozen foods, he can sample the sentiment of retail customers. The important thing is to discover the probable reaction of customers as early as possible. If their response is completely negative, the firm can move slowly—or even abandon the project.

Choosing the Test Market. If the firm sells to a regional or national market and can conduct formal research, it may wish to select a test city in which to investigate market opinion. The test market must be carefully chosen. For researching acceptance of a consumer product, the test market should be one which is independent of the trading areas of nearby cities in order to avoid distortion of results. If the chosen city has diversified industry, its citizens should have stable income and buying power, which is desirable. The market should be typical of the national or regional economy and be neither depressed nor booming as the result of purely local conditions. This means that the city used should provide typical consumers with average incomes, all the normal advertising media, and a full quota of retail outlets. Though carefully picked, such a test city may still distort the picture due to some inherent bias.

Market Testing. Of course, the pilot run testing can be extended to include the advertising and marketing program itself. One goes further than mere "test marketing" (or acceptance of the new product) to what is called *market testing*, involving both acceptance testing of product and the marketing program. Any unforeseen "bugs" in the marketing program may be detected and eliminated in this way.

Only when all possible facts about a proposed new product and consumer reaction to it are known and are favorable can a company afford to invest heavily in a full-scale production and sales program to launch that new product. To stay competitive, most businesses must develop and launch a new or improved product fairly regularly. This makes the testing of market acceptance a matter of vital importance.

Measuring a Firm's Share of the Market

The market trend and potential of an industry often can be determined from past sales, sales trends, and other projections. To establish a particular company's share of the market, the manager typically compares company sales with industry sales in past years. If adequate industry data are available, this technique ordinarily produces accurate results. Frequently, however, the firm wishes to establish its share of the future market, rather than that of the past market. The *trend of the company-to-industry sales ratio* may itself be studied if enough years of data are at hand for both company and industry. This would show whether the firm is gaining on, or losing ground to, its competitors. In predicting the future market share, a manager must allow for changes in product quality and in promotional programs. An element of judgment is thus required to supplement the statistical projections.

The small firm cannot allow itself to become complacent over its present market share, as such complacency might lead to a fatal do-nothing complex. In addition, overall success, reflected by a satisfactory market share, may cover up a failure in one or more territories or product lines. A study of one's share of the market often calls for remedial action. If a men's clothing store, for example, discovers that its hat sales are disproportionately small compared to other such stores, an opportunity for improvement is immediately apparent.

Measuring the Effectiveness of Sales Efforts

The typical entrepreneur understands the need to increase sales volume and to control, or reduce, the cost of marketing. Suppose, for example, that a small manufacturer examines the overall position of his business and finds that total cost is rising faster than sales. Suppose also that production costs are not to blame. The manufacturer must then turn to the marketing area to locate the trouble, whether it be a lack of sales efficiency or a rise in the cost of distribution, or both. Assume that he has five sales territories, each served by one salesperson.

Determining Sales Potential. The proper starting point is an accurate determination of the sales potential for each of the five territories. The percentage of total company sales which should be achieved by each territory is computed first by using some *market index*. In the illustrative work sheet shown in Table 18-1, this step reveals that Territory 1 should account for 36 percent of total company sales. By applying this percentage to actual company sales for last year, it is discovered that Territory 1 should have produced $360,000 sales. The amounts so obtained (in column 3) represent the dollar volume for each territory that would have been secured if the sales efficiency of each territory exactly equaled the company's average sales efficiency.

Table 18-1
ILLUSTRATIVE WORK SHEET FOR DETERMINING SALES EFFICIENCY BY TERRITORIES

Territory	Percent of Total Sales*	Computed Standard Sales**	Actual Sales Last Year	Index of Sales Efficiency***
1	36.0	$ 360,000	$ 300,000	83.3
2	17.5	175,000	200,000	114.3
3	15.2	152,000	180,000	118.4
4	20.1	201,000	160,000	79.6
5	11.2	112,000	160,000	142.9
	100.0	$1,000,000	$1,000,000	

* Computed by use of a market index reflecting area potentials.
** Actual total sales for last year multiplied (for each territory separately) by the territory's ratio to total sales.
*** Actual territory sales divided by 1/100 of the territory's computed standard sales.

Comparing Actual Sales Volume with Potential. Next, the actual sales volume for each territory is stated and compared with its potential. The illustration, for example, shows that Territory 1 secured only $300,000 in sales instead of $360,000. Expressed as a percentage, Territory 1 thus had a sales efficiency of only 83 percent. Such percentages of standard performance for each of the territories clearly identify those in which actual performance does not measure up to what it should be.

It is desirable at this point to back up and look at the market index used in computing the sales potential of each territory. There are various possibilities for establishing such an index. It could be based upon arbitrarily weighted factors such as population, personal income, and retail sales. Such a market index would have some value, but a more specific index may be easily obtained and might be more useful. For example, if the hypothetical manufacturer produced electric appliances, he might acquire data on the number of wired homes in each territory. Then, the number of wired homes in each territory could be related to the total number of wired homes in the firm's entire marketing area to determine territory potential.

Allowing for Errors in Market Indexes. The manufacturer need not expect or strive for perfection in establishing territory sales potentials. Suppose the market index was 10 percent in error for Territory 4. Such an error would make the Territory 4 market index percentage either 18.09 percent or 22.11 percent instead of 20.1 percent. The territory indexes of sales efficiency corresponding to these market index figures would be 88.4 and 72.4, respectively. A 10 percent error in the market index would not remove the spotlight from Territory 4 as being the "weak sister" territory.

Three other observations are pertinent here. First, the range between the highest and lowest indexes of territory sales efficiency is likely to be much greater than that shown in the table. This is especially true for a firm serving a large sales area.

The second observation is that the salesperson in Territory 4 should not be arbitrarily dismissed because of bad performance. Of course, dismissal could be the right answer. But the analysis merely shows a failure to achieve a desired and presumably possible level of sales; it does not reveal the cause. The salesperson is only one of many variables involved. The manufacturer should at least consider the length of service of this individual, as well as his total record with the company. He might also train this individual to use the techniques used by the firm's leading salespersons.

The third observation is that the territory with the lowest sales efficiency index offers the firm its greatest challenge and sales opportunity. By concentrating its best efforts in the low-sales territories, the firm might maximize the improvements from a given amount of sales effort.

Adjusting to a Changing Market

Many small businesses serve unwieldy or uneconomic sales territories. This may be due to the fact that the markets themselves are constantly changing. In the case of the consumer market, population shifts create substantial changes in market geography. Buying habits are subject to change also. Customers may shift from hometown to out-of-town buying—or from shopping downtown to buying at outlying shopping centers. The reasons for such shifts are of obvious interest to the entrepreneur. Some of the significant factors are population shifts, availability of free parking, easier accessibility, better assortment and quality of goods, more efficient salespersons, and differences in customer services. Market studies are required to determine the significant factors, so that appropriate action may be taken. In the case of a downtown retailer, for example, such a study might suggest moving to a shopping center or opening a suburban branch store.

Analyzing Internal Records

Up to this point, little attention has been paid to the contribution that analysis of the firm's records can make in the area of marketing research. For example, a firm may make an accounting analysis of the profitability of selling to particular customers or of selling particular product lines. Such an approach often identifies certain low-quantity, high-cost customers to whom sales are unprofitable. Once such customers have been identified, their orders may be refused or upgraded in quantity until they become profitable customers.

Many wholesale firms have used this type of study with outstanding success. To cite one illustration, a Michigan wholesaler with 35 employees investigated the cost of serving a number of its accounts. Allocated to each account were the direct costs associated with it, such as salesmen's commissions, truck operation, invoicing, billing, order picking, drivers' loading expense, and delivery expense. It was discovered that accounts of less than $50 per month in gross credit sales were unprofitable and that sales in the $50 to $100 group merely broke even. Consequently, this firm decided to review carefully all accounts providing less than $75 credit sales per month and to retain only those customers giving promise of becoming potentially profitable. Accounts not meeting the $75 minimum were to be handled on a strictly cash basis.

Sales records, particularly those on profitable credit customers, may also be analyzed to discover what and when these customers buy. Knowledge gained in this way is pertinent to merchandising decisions—such as what products should be sold—and to developing effective sales promotion programs. The retailer, for example, can discover the residential areas from which his customers come and the relative importance of each area. Given an accompanying analysis of purchasing power of the various residential areas, he can determine whether sales, including sales in specific lines, such as women's shoes, are in proper proportion for each area. In addition, a study of the records will reveal the normal interval between shoe purchases by customers, the price brackets in which shoes sell best, and the percentage of credit customers who buy shoes. Moreover, the retailer can find out whether shoe buyers also purchase gloves, bags, and similar accessories in his store. Information of this type would be useful to store managers.

USE OF MARKET RESEARCH CONSULTANTS

Perhaps the greatest drawback to research work by the staff of a small business is the lack of "know-how" and training in research techniques. It must be admitted that this is a formidable barrier which severely limits the nature of the projects that can be safely attempted. Fortunately many research efforts may be relatively simple in their purpose and scope. In such situations the manager is required simply to direct his general knowledge and managerial ability toward solution of the marketing problem.

On research projects which appear too complex for the talents or time of an inside staff, the services of outside experts may be secured. The most obvious example of this type is the marketing research consulting firm. Such a consultant makes available, for a fee, the necessary experience and ability to undertake an extensive investigation of various marketing activities and marketing problems.

A marketing research agency is qualified to make market sampling studies designed to determine area sales potentials, to evaluate probable dealer and/or consumer acceptance of new or redesigned products, or to determine population shifts and changes in area standards of living. Other marketing analyses will determine the level of purchasing power in the company's sales regions served, evaluate probable consumer reaction to altered product packaging, or analyze traffic flow and parking problems in downtown and suburban shopping centers. The marketing research firm may also ascertain elasticity of demand for a company's products. It will undertake a study of causes of declining sales and profits. Finally, among still other services, it will determine a company's potential position within its industry or the proper pricing of new products.

Outside help other than that from marketing research agencies is sometimes available, as we have noted earlier. The trade association, for example, may be equipped to provide extensive service in this area. The same is frequently true of local or regional chambers of commerce. Bankers may also furnish assistance. The field offices of the Department of Commerce and Small Business Administration also stand ready to be of service in this area.

The managers of small firms often are unaware of the possibilities for profit inherent in the use of marketing research consultants. They lack knowledge concerning consultants' services and frequently feel that the firm cannot afford such services.[4] In some cases, too, managers simply do not recognize the existence of problems justifying the use of a consultant. Information regarding reputable marketing consultants can be secured from such sources as trade associations, the Small Business Administration, the American Management Association, or local bankers and lawyers.

---

[4] Competent consulting service typically results in overall cost savings even though consultants' fees appear to be high.

Summary

1. Marketing research is the objective analysis of various aspects of the firm's marketing program and policies. It may be used to identify a firm's customers, investigate their desires, determine reactions to new products, study market potential, evaluate advertising effectiveness, and analyze marketing channels.

2. The steps in marketing research are as follows: (a) recognition of the problem; (b) preliminary investigation and planning; (c) gathering factual information; (d) classifying, analyzing, and interpreting information; and (e) reaching a conclusion.

3. Secondary sources of data are those reprinted from an earlier published version. Primary sources of published data are compiling, first publishing sources. Both may contribute importantly to effective marketing research decisions and, if available, should be used to save time and money.

4. Original unpublished data can also contribute to effective marketing research, when required.

5. Various research techniques and approaches are available for investigating particular marketing problems. These techniques include sampling studies, opinion surveys, indexes of sales efficiency, test marketing, and analyses of internal records. Some are quantitative; others, qualitative.

6. One major limitation to marketing research in small firms is the lack of "know-how" and training in research techniques. It is possible to supplement the abilities of a firm's own staff, however, by use of outside specialists such as marketing research organizations.

Discussion Questions

1. Suggest some types of marketing research that might be appropriate for (a) a florist shop, (b) a small bakery, (c) a laundry, (d) a service station, (e) a corner drugstore, and (f) a lumberyard.

2. Identify as many types of information as possible which might be sought through some type of marketing research.

3. Explain the various marketing research steps which would be involved in measuring customer satisfaction with a combined automobile dealership and service department located in a medium-size city.

4. How can salesmen be used as marketing research assistants?

5. What is the difference between primary and secondary sources of data? Which would be more applicable to the problems of the small firm?

6. What is the fundamental idea involved in sequential sampling? Could it be used without a knowledge of statistics?

7. In what way could a small firm obtain information which would

permit measurement of the firm's share of the market? Answer the question in terms of plumbing contractors, furniture retailers, and large city employment agencies.

8. What qualitative research might be utilized by retail food stores? By TV service firms?

9. Is it possible that a small firm might be engaging in marketing research without knowing it? Explain.

10. What types of cooperative research projects might be possible and profitable for small firms?

11. A small manufacturer has had reasonably good success in selling a certain type of inspection gage. Other, larger firms sell a similar product. If the small firm is contemplating expansion, what are some desirable types of marketing research that might first be attempted? Explain.

12. An auto supply store locates in a suburban shopping center, but its sales volume during the first year does not come up to expectations. What kind of marketing research might indicate the reason for the unsatisfactory sales situation?

13. What types of useful research information might be gathered from the internal records of a small department store?

14. Should a small business attempt marketing research if its personnel are completely lacking in training in research methodology? Why?

15. What types of outside specialists are available to assist small business firms in marketing research efforts?

Case D-1
QUALITY MOBILE HOMES, INC. *

Charles Johnson is owner and operator of a mobile home business which currently has local franchise rights for four brands of coaches. Johnson's business is the retail link in a channel of distribution in which the coach manufacturer ships directly to him, and he in turn sells directly to the individual customer.

Johnson's business is located in a large metropolitan area of about 150,000 population; the major central city has a little under 100,000 population. Sales were exceedingly good during the later 1960s as were most other mobile home dealerships, while the industry enjoyed tremendous growth. However, during the early 1970s Johnson's sales were beginning to level off, reflecting a more competitive and possibly saturated market situation.

Johnson is a very progressive businessman who is always eager to make appropriate changes in his marketing mix if he feels they would increase sales. He is, however, quite critical of many of the promotional gimmicks which are common in the industry. For example, some competitors advertise their coaches with a special deal like, "This week only you can get an air conditioned coach at no extra cost," when, in fact, any week one can easily negotiate an equivalent price with air conditioning. Therefore, in effect, the customer does pay directly for the air conditioner. Johnson feels that many competitors have given a bad image to the industry by the use of such "come on" promotional techniques. He believes in providing a quality mobile home and in keeping his customers happy. Word-of-mouth advertising is always important to him. He feels that, if he can get the customer to his business, he can sell that customer his product. His coach lines are constructed well and are not like many of the "box" mobile homes that many dealers sell. The public as a whole, unfortunately, is not able to recognize easily these quality differences.

Johnson rents about 50 percent of his 30' × 60' sales office space to a mobile home service business. This makes it quite convenient to get coaches delivered to customers and set up on their lots—a seemingly important selling point with most customers. Johnson has an arrangement with the mobile home service manager to deliver homes to customers and to charge Johnson—not the customer—with a fixed fee. This mobile home service company provides repair service for the public on all kinds of mobile home problems. The service company also is the local, exclusive authorized dealer of a major, add-on air conditioning unit. Since most mobile homes do not have central air conditioning, this is usually a heavily demanded option by customers. However, the presence of the service business does limit the amount of space which Johnson can use for display of the many coach options which are available in paneling, carpeting, and furniture styles. Since mobile homes require a great degree of structural standardization in order to lend themselves to mass production techniques, the coach options which are available give the inside of the coach some degree of distinctiveness and provide quite an important selling point to potential customers. The coach manufacturers are quite willing to provide samples of all the available options to retailers like Johnson. With four coach lines each having approximately four options within each optional area (rug types, colors, furniture styles, etc.), Johnson has been unable to display properly all samples. Customers have difficulty, therefore, visualizing how their own "personalized" coaches might look. Since delivery time on coach orders is two or three weeks, many customers prefer to order their homes. They can, of course, choose among the standard model coaches on Johnson's lot.

* This case was prepared by Professor Carlos W. Moore of Baylor University.

Johnson's lot space will park only about 15 coaches but, fortunately, the producer of his major selling brand is located only five blocks away. This location allows Johnson to take customers to the manufacturing lot to show additional coaches which he cannot afford to stock in his limited inventory.

Like the majority of other mobile home dealers, Johnson participates in radio spots on local stations and classified advertisements in the local newspaper. Currently manufacturers do very little promotion which is directed toward the final consumer. Johnson also gives out specialty items, such as calendars and pens, but these are only given to customers on special holidays. Johnson is concerned as to whether or not he is making proper use of his promotional budget. He feels a significant amount of his promotion may be missing its target. But since he has not analyzed his own customer data files, he himself is not certain of his exact customer profile. The producer of his best-selling coach has made available a great deal of such information. Johnson feels this information might be helpful in planning his promotional strategy. Among these materials is a summary of demographic information of mobile home purchasers which has been obtained by follow-up questionnaires sent by the manufacturer to all purchasers of that brand coach throughout the nation. Preliminary analysis suggests that there may be a unique customer profile for mobile home purchasers. Youthfulness and status as renters seem to be characteristics of people in the mobile home buying market. In other words, young families who have been renting homes are seemingly heavy mobile home purchasers.

Since Johnson's business is located alongside a major traffic artery, he is considering using some billboard space. Also, he feels that a direct mail campaign might stimulate market interest.

QUESTIONS

1. What additional information do you think Johnson should have before he plans his promotional strategy?
2. What are some of the major considerations which Johnson should evaluate as he plans his promotional strategy?
3. What promotional changes, if any, would you recommend to him?
4. What would you see as the potential of better promotion by Johnson at his present sales office location?

Case D-2
MAPLE BROTHERS, INC.

Greg Smith is Texas Manager for Maple Brothers, Inc., a small California corporation. He has been struggling recently with the problem of declining sales volume in his sales area.

Company History and Products

Maple Brothers, Inc., has for 25 years wholesaled raw, or unfinished, wood moulding to the lumberyards and building supply houses of Southern California. Some eight years ago, the company also started manufacturing prefinished mouldings. (Prefinished mouldings differ from raw, or unfinished, mouldings in that they are painted and imprinted with a simulated wood grain.) These prefinished mouldings were sold originally to a mobile home manufacturer, and this type of sales expanded with the growth of the mobile home industry. Eventually, Maple Brothers accounted for 60 percent of the Southern California mobile home market for prefinished mouldings. In summary, then, the firm sold raw wood mouldings primarily through lumberyards and prefinished mouldings, both wood and plastic, primarily to the mobile home industry.

Two years ago, Maple Brothers extended itself beyond its Southern California home territory and entered the highly competitive Texas market, selling prefinished mouldings to the mobile home manufacturers. Greg Smith was appointed manager of this Texas sales territory; in two years he made Maple Brothers the area's leading supplier of prefinished mouldings. The firm maintains a warehouse in Central Texas to which mouldings are shipped from the California manufacturing facility. The business employs a total of three employees and has one delivery truck. Smith does most of the selling himself.

Maple Brothers' sales to lumberyards and building supply houses in California have been limited almost entirely to raw, unfinished wood mouldings. Many of these lumberyards and building supply houses also sell prefinished mouldings. However, Maple Brothers has been unsuccessful in attempts to sell prefinished mouldings to the same lumberyards and building supply houses. Their failure to market prefinished mouldings through this channel might be partly explained by relatively low dollar volume in lumberyard sales of prefinished mouldings versus mobile home sales of the same mouldings and by the firm's traditional strong emphasis on raw, unfinished mouldings for the lumberyard market.

Current Market Conditions

Beginning in the summer of 1973, the mobile home building industry experienced a severe slump. The slump was attributed to a number of causes—to high interest rates and tight money in particular, but also to market saturation, tightening code requirements inspired by consumerism, uncertainty over the Watergate affair, rising fuel costs, and so on. Whatever the cause, mobile home manufacturing nose-dived and with it the primary market for Maple Brothers' products.

As he watched the drop in moulding sales, Smith realized that he faced the possibility of falling below his break-even point. At the existing overhead and selling expense level, Smith estimated the break-even point for the Texas sales territory at $10,000 sales per week. (A small portion of this amount represents prorated overhead of the California plant.) Even though Maple Brothers had established itself as the leading supplier, its sales volume from the volatile mobile home industry could vary from more than $20,000 per week to less than $10,000 per week. If sales fell below $10,000 per week, which was a distinct possibility, the firm would be losing money in its Texas territory.

In seeking to offset the effects of the mobile homes drop in sales, Smith looked for other markets with potential. One market that interested him was the sale of prefinished moulding to lumberyards and building supply houses in the Central Texas area. Transportation and sale of raw wood mouldings to this market did not appear feasible from a competitive standpoint. It seemed impossible, therefore, to duplicate the California lumberyard sales of raw mouldings in the Texas market. However, there was a possibility that prefinished mouldings might be sold to these same Texas lumber dealers.

Market Research Project

To decide upon the wisdom of entering the new market, Smith decided to launch a modest market research project. The major part of this research involved interviews with officials of lumberyards and building supply houses—those who would be potential customers. At first, Smith talked informally with dealers but soon discovered he had overlooked certain important questions. He then developed the interview guide shown in Exhibit 1 on page 316. In some cases Smith was able to go beyond the questions shown on the guide. If he established good rapport, for example, he asked about the dollar volume of the firm's moulding sales.

1. What types of prefinished mouldings do you sell?

   Wood _____ CPVC _____ Both _____? Preference _____

2. List below the shapes, lengths, and prices of the prefinished mouldings:

Shape	Volume	Price
_____	_____	_____
_____	_____	_____
_____	_____	_____
_____	_____	_____
_____	_____	_____
_____	_____	_____
_____	_____	_____

3. List below the colors in which the prefinished mouldings come:

_____	_____	_____
_____	_____	_____
_____	_____	_____
_____	_____	_____

4. What is your estimate of your share of market for the city? _____Percent

5. List below the names and address of your suppliers:

Name	Address
_____	_____
_____	_____
_____	_____
_____	_____

6. What is the lead time? _____ Order frequency? _____

7. What is your minimum order quantity? _____

8. What is your initial stock requirement? _____

9. Is freight prepaid? _____

10. What is your quantity discount? _____ Prompt pay discount? _____

11. What are your supplier's strengths or weaknesses:

    Quality _____ Service _____

    Sales aids _____ Price _____

12. What are the types of sales aids?

    Catalogs _____ Sample chains _____ Pricing sheets (illustrated) _____

    Other _____

13. What are your payment terms? _____

Exhibit 1
INTERVIEW GUIDE

Market Potential

On the basis of his interviews, Smith estimated that the Central Texas market—principally the Waco and Fort Worth areas—had a sales potential for prefinished mouldings of approximately $60,000 per month. Smith suspected that the Austin-San Antonio areas represented another $40,000 potential per month. Large retail chains were thought to represent $30,000, or 30 percent, of this $100,000 total. Major retail chains in the area included the following:

Buddy's Handy Man Centers ...5 stores
Payless Cashaways ....7 stores
Homer's Handy Man Centers ...7 stores
Kier Building Materials ....5 stores
Handy Dan Stores ....5 stores

Smith estimated that, in addition to the retail chains, there were 100 lumberyards and building supply houses in the Waco-Fort Worth area and another 100 in the Austin-San Antonio area. There were also some firms that served as distributors to retail lumberyards and building supply houses. The mobile home industry to which Smith sold consisted of approximately 40 manufacturers, and the total prefinished moulding sales (of all suppliers) to this market was estimated at $250,000 to $300,000 per month.

Interview Results

After interviewing a number of dealers, Smith summarized his conclusions as follows:

1. The profiles (the configuration of the moulding) sold through Central Texas lumberyards were, with the exception of one very popular ceiling cove, all standard Maple Brothers' profiles.

2. No one source supplied all popular colors. Consequently, many dealers were carrying two or more brands to obtain the colors they wanted. Maple Brothers felt they could offer standard products in the five most popular colors, giving the dealer the opportunity of buying all of his mouldings from one source.

3. Prevailing prices were equal or higher than those obtained by Maple Brothers in the mobile home market.

4. Manufacturers supplied free storage racks to the dealers with a specified minimum order. They also supplied sample chains (containing samples of different colors and shapes of moulding), point-of-sale displays, and small pamphlets illustrating use of the moulding. Maple Brothers currently had none of these sales aids.

5. The standard minimum order quantity was approximately 50 cartons, but the cartons used in this area were much smaller than those used by Maple Brothers in shipping to mobile home manufacturers.

6. Standard credit terms were 2/10, n/30.

7. The quality of competitive mouldings did not appear to be superior to those of Maple Brothers. In fact, Smith knew that his mouldings were better than some of those he had seen stocked in lumberyards and building supply houses.

8. Nine competitors were currently splitting up the $100,000 monthly business volume.

Inventory Requirements

As noted above, an inventory was maintained in a Central Texas warehouse for the mobile home industry. This ran from $20,000 to $40,000 depending on sales level.

If Maple Brothers sold to lumberyards and building supply houses, an additional inventory would also be needed for this purpose. If he sold directly to individual lumberyards, Smith believed he would need an additional investment in inventory equal to the monthly sales dollar volume. In other words, he would need a $10,000 inventory to support a monthly sales volume of $10,000. On the other hand, he might reduce the inventory to a one- to two-weeks' volume level if he sold through a distributor.

Decision

Smith attempted to assess his prospects on the basis of the evidence he had compiled. Although he hoped for improved conditions in the mobile home market, he could not count on this occurring immediately. Therefore, he needed to decide whether the other market held sufficient potential to justify his entry.

QUESTIONS

1. Evaluate Smith's method of obtaining data. Would there have been an advantage in using a questionnaire rather than interviews?

2. Should Smith have considered using a less formal discussion with prospective dealers rather than using a patterned interview?

3. What should be Smith's decision regarding entering the new market?

4. If Smith decides to enter the market, should he sell directly to individual lumberyards and building supply houses, through a distributor, or both?

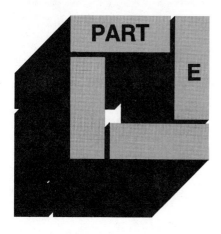

PART

E

Financial and Administrative Controls in Small Business

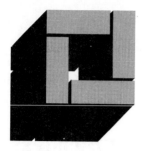

19

Financing the
"Going Concern"

The financial considerations in establishing a new business were discussed in Chapter 14. We now turn our attention to those financing problems that are involved in "going concern" operations.

THE SMALL FIRM'S FINANCING PROBLEMS

A going concern must constantly replenish or maintain its capital. Otherwise, its initial capital would soon be gone, and operations would have to cease. Hence, as spending occurs, there must be a replacement of cash resulting from sales to customers. If the firm makes a profit, the return flow of cash will sustain operations at the starting level. If the firm is to grow, however, it requires additional capital.

Need for Additional Funds

Many manufacturing firms are under constant pressure for capital equipment investment. In a recent study, 84 percent of responding small manufacturers said that they found it necessary to invest in added equipment regardless of profitability in the short run.[1] Investments were required, for example, to meet competition or to maintain output. Presumably the investments would be profitable in the long run.

The adequacy of capital for financing small business operations is not really known. However, there is a widespread feeling that inadequacy of capital constitutes a significant problem for small firms. This need is most acute in the area of long-term financing and is reflected in various governmental programs designed to give financial aid to small firms. Some inability in acquiring funds is not unnatural, for not all businesses can qualify as sound credit risks. The fundamental question concerns the degree to which reasonably well-managed companies are hampered by a lack of funds.

---

[1] David F. Scott, Jr., Otha L. Gray, and Monroe M. Bird, "Investing and Financing Behavior of Small Manufacturing Firms," *MSU Business Topics* (Summer, 1972), pp. 32-34.

The degree of need for additional funds varies with the age and stage of development of a given firm. A new business typically has strained finances, and its production resources are fully used. Its working capital is often too little. But, as the business matures under sound management, available assets become more clearly compatible with the firm's operating needs. Under these conditions capital resources also become more plentiful due to the firm's history of successful operations. It is the new, rapidly expanding firms, therefore, that are regarded as having the most serious shortages of funds.[2]

Higher Cost of Capital

The interest cost of loans to small firms is typically greater than that of large businesses. Moreover, among small businesses, the newer the firm, the higher its interest costs. This is normal since it is precisely these new firms that face maximum hazards and are least likely to make satisfactory profits. Once a small business passes the early critical years, it may enjoy a lower interest cost, although this will not be as low as that of large firms.

According to a Federal Reserve System study of small business financing undertaken some years ago, the short-term interest rate for all firms was 5.0 percent, the intermediate-term interest rate was 5.7 percent, and the long-term interest rate was 4.7 percent. For small firms with assets of $50,000 to $250,000, the short-term rate was 5.6 percent, the intermediate-term rate was 7.1 percent, and the long-term rate was 5.6 percent. In both cases these were the average rates on loans made between July 1 and the survey date in October. This is clear-cut evidence of the interest rate disparity between loans to small and to large firms.

The higher capital costs can be explained, in part at least, by lenders' cost differences in extending and servicing small loans. A more critical underlying factor, however, is the greater risk involved in the small firm. There is little diversification in the typical small business, and this implies a greater concentration of risk. The lack of knowledge or experience in financial matters and the deficiency in general management ability tend to accentuate this risk.

Small firms attempt to reduce their cost of capital by using a combination of invested and borrowed capital. The study of small manufacturing firms cited earlier described this practice in the following way:

Few firms choose to finance entirely with common equity funds because (1) the tax deductibility of interest payments provides a strong incentive in favor of debt as a means of raising external corporate capital, and (2) a favorable financial leverage effect achieved through the prudent use of debt and preferred stock instruments can magnify the rate of return on the common equity investment.[3]

---

[2] For an extensive treatment of the relationship of growth to financial management, see James F. Mahar and Dean C. Coddington, *The Financial Gap—Real or Imaginary?* Small Business Management Research Report. Prepared by the University of Denver under a grant by the Small Business Administration, Washington, D.C., 1962.

[3] David F. Scott, Jr., Otha L. Gray, and Monroe M. Bird, *op. cit.*, p. 35, *MSU Business Topics*, Summer, 1972.

Deficiencies in Financial Management

Financial practices of the small firm are adversely affected by the orientation and deficiencies of its management. The manager or management group in a new firm often lacks experience in financial management. Their background experience is frequently specialized in sales or production, and they are often strongly oriented accordingly. As a result, there is a noticeable inability to understand certain fundamental financial relationships as well as a lack of competence to deal with financial problems as they develop.

Although experience has some educational value, the deficiency in financial ability tends to be a persistent one. In the view of most observers, most well-established small firms are weak in this area when compared with big business. The larger businesses may have a chief executive who is financially oriented. If not, the management staff ordinarily includes a financial manager who is thoroughly experienced in the field of finance and whose counsel is typically given serious weight in management decisions.

Danger in One-Man Management. One danger to those supplying funds to small business lies in the critical importance of one man—or of a few key individuals. Many firms would be forced to close if they lost their chief executives. No other persons are prepared to step in and take over. The key individuals might die, quit voluntarily, take voluntary bankruptcy, or leave the business in some other way.

This contrasts sharply with larger businesses which have anticipated the problem of executive replacement and which have developed sizable management staffs. To the creditor or investor supplying funds, a reliance on one individual increases the risk involved in placing the funds at the disposal of a small firm. Even if the small business manager is personally competent, this risk must be taken into consideration in financial decisions. Incorporation of the firm confers unlimited life upon the business in a legal sense, but it fails to eliminate the fundamental problem. It merely changes the firm from a risky one-man proprietorship to a risky one-man corporation.

Furthermore, the entrepreneur typically holds a strongly favorable attitude toward risk taking. He is eager to exploit his ideas quickly and to make a profit. As a result, he is inclined toward more venturesome, less cautious decisions. His daring attitude, though commendable, conflicts with the conservatism of most financial institutions.

Weaknesses in Financial Planning. Informality is the keynote of much small business planning. The entrepreneur is busy at building a business and earning a profit. Directing operations and satisfying customers are obviously related to his primary goals. The time spent in financial planning, on the other hand, often appears to be time wasted on that which is not urgent. As a result, financial analysis is neglected.

Any relatively new firm also lacks important data even when it attempts financial projections. Older firms can begin with an established record of sales which have been achieved. This is far different from estimating sales revenue without the benefit of some hindsight. The manager is also likely to encounter difficulties in forecasting production levels, inventory levels, credit sales volume, personnel needs, and equipment requirements. In particular, it is difficult to measure the probable effect of these and other variables upon working capital needs. These uncertainties, coupled with the typical optimism of the entrepreneur, combine to produce estimates of cash needs that too often are unrealistically low. And it is the thinly financed operation that is least able to weather adverse economic conditions. Of course, it is also possible to err in the opposite direction. In that event, the effect of the errors is to produce a wasteful excess of cash.

Several years may be required before financial forecasting becomes reasonably accurate. In many firms, five years or more of data will be required to provide a sound basis for forecasting. Anything less yields forecasts which are little better than guesswork.

CAPITAL BUDGETING IN SMALL BUSINESS

Financial decisions by the manager of a going concern should provide funds from the best possible sources for use in the most profitable manner. The manager's activities in achieving these objectives are described as *capital budgeting*. Determining the most profitable use of funds requires an appraisal of the alternative investment opportunities open to the small firm. This process is the very heart of capital budgeting. In this section we shall examine the concepts of investment analysis and their relevance to small business firms.

Analysis of Alternative Investment Opportunities

Capital budgeting assumes that the firm's supply of capital is limited and that it should be rationed in such a way as to provide funds for the best opportunities. Because capital is insufficient to finance all possible projects, this means that the least promising opportunities must be postponed or rejected. Suppose, for example, that a small manufacturer is contemplating the following possible courses of action—each of which entails an outlay of funds:

1. Development and introduction of a new product that shows promise but requires additional study and improvement.
2. Initiation of direct mail advertising of the firm's products.
3. Installation of new data processing equipment.
4. Replacement of the company's delivery trucks with current models.
5. Expansion of sales activity into a new territory.
6. Construction of a new building.
7. Employment of several additional salespersons for more intensive selling in the existing market.

This list of possible outlays of funds could be extended. The cost of funds and the absolute limit on the volume of funds available to a particular firm require rejection not only of those that would be unprofitable but also of those that would be least profitable.

A thorough analysis of investment opportunities requires the following steps to be taken:

1. Search for investment opportunities.
2. Analysis of the supply and cost of funds.
3. Estimation of future cash flows—that is, the costs and income associated with each investment.
4. Ranking and choosing the most attractive project or projects.

In its broadest sense, capital budgeting includes investments of both a long-range and short-range nature. Our greatest concern, however, is with long-range financial commitments, and the discussion that follows deals exclusively with long-range movements of funds.

Traditional Methods of Investment Valuation

In evaluating business opportunities, entrepreneurs have traditionally utilized either the simple *return on investment* or the *payback period* method.

Return on Investment Method. The simple return on investment method was used in Chapter 12 to provide guidance in negotiating the purchase of a going concern. It may be calculated by the following formula:

$$\text{Return on Investment} = \frac{\text{Average Annual Profit}}{\text{Investment}}$$

In using this method, an entrepreneur who expects to earn 20 percent on an investment of $20,000 should expect to create an annual profit of $4,000. Such an investment is justified if more lucrative investments are not available and if a return of 20 percent is reasonable in view of the risk involved.

Payback Period Method. The payback period is determined as follows:

$$\text{Payback Period} = \frac{\text{Investment}}{\text{Average Cash Flow}}$$

If an investor expects an annual cash flow of $50,000 to result from an investment of $100,000, the payback period would be two years. Only two years would be required to return the original investment, assuming an accurate estimation of expected cost and profit.

In using either of these two methods, it is important to recognize that only net additions to costs or profits are significant. If a partially depreciated machine is to be replaced by a new, more efficient piece of equipment, the book value of the old machine is not included in calculating the cost of the change. Of course, any salvage or trade-in value of the old machine would be considered in computing investment cost. Similarly, only additional profits (over and above those that would be otherwise realized) are significant.

Perhaps the greatest value of these rule-of-thumb methods is their simplicity. They do provide a rough check for evaluating an investment. Although they have definite limitations when compared with the more sophisticated tools described later in this chapter, they are widely used and often provide satisfactory answers.

Weaknesses of Traditional Methods. These rule-of-thumb methods are subject to two major weaknesses. First, they fail to recognize the time value of money. A dollar today is worth more than a dollar a year from today because the dollar can earn interest during the year. Similarly, a dollar received two years from today is worth less than a dollar received one year from today. An outlay of a dollar at the end of a year is also less costly than today's expenditure of the dollar because interest may be earned during the year preceding payment. A theoretically correct method must take into account the timing of cash flows and apply the concept of the time value of money to determine the attractiveness of investment proposals. For example, an investment that promises favorable returns only after several years is much less appealing than one providing similar returns next year.

The second weakness of the traditional methods is their neglect of the economic life of a project. A payback period of three years may apply to an investment providing increased profits for three years or 30 years. Knowing that the investment will be recovered in a specified time does not distinguish between those with prospects of a long life and those with a short life expectancy. In a similar manner, a simple rate of return gives no indication of the length of time during which that rate of return may be expected to continue. A technique of valuation that reflects the economic life of investments would be obviously superior.

Theoretically Correct Methods of Investment Valuation

Two methods designed to correct the defects of traditional measures are the *discounted cash flow* method and the *present value* method.[4]

Discounted Cash Flow Method. The discounted cash flow, or discounted rate of return, method may be calculated by the following formula:

$$C = \frac{Q_1}{(1 + r)} + \frac{Q_2}{(1 + r)^2} + \ldots + \frac{Q_n + S}{(1 + r)^n}$$

where Q = post-tax cash flow in year t (where t is 1, 2, 3, . . . n)
C = cost of asset
n = useful life of asset
r = unknown rate of return
S = terminal salvage value

In using the discounted cash flow method, the investor discovers the rate of return which the projected cash flow will provide on the amount invested. A given investment may be shown to offer a return of 35 percent per year. This is a "true" return rate rather than a simple rate of return; it reflects the lower present value of future income.

---

[4] The formulas presented in this text, used with permission of the publisher, are from Martin B. Solomon, Jr., *Investment Decisions in Small Business*, Small Business Management Research Report. Prepared by the University of Kentucky under a grant by the Small Business Administration, Washington, D.C. (Lexington: University of Kentucky Press, 1963), pp. 13-17.

Present Value Method. The following formula permits calculation by the present value method:

$$V = \frac{Q_1}{(1 + r)} + \frac{Q_2}{(1 + r)^2} + \ldots + \frac{Q_n}{(1 + r)^n} + \frac{S}{(1 + r)^n} - C$$

where V = excess present value over cost
  Q_t = post-tax cash flow in year t (where t is 1, 2, 3, . . . n)
   S = terminal salvage value
   r = selected rate of interest
   C = cost of asset
   n = useful life of asset

The present value method calculates the present value by discounting future cash flows at some selected rate of interest. The interest rate utilized is usually the rate that could be earned on the money otherwise (the *opportunity cost* of the money). The present value figure represents the value of an investment opportunity over and above the stipulated rate of return. Using a rate of 15 percent, for example, the investor may find that a particular proposal has a present value of $4,000 over and above a 15 percent return on his investment. One advantage of this method over the discounted cash flow method is its ability to distinguish between long-run and short-run prospects. The discounted cash flow method may show the same return for a five-year project as for a ten-year project.

Limited Use of Theoretically Correct Valuation Methods. Even though these methods are theoretically superior to the traditional ones, they are not widely used in either small business or big business. The typical small businessman is unaware of the existence of such measurements and would not readily understand the underlying reasoning and analysis involved. The lack of knowledge of the entrepreneur, therefore, is a major factor limiting the use of such sophisticated techniques. In addition, the solution of such problems is often time-consuming and may require the use of an electronic computer.

Perhaps the greatest deterrent to the use of theoretically correct methods is the extreme uncertainty that surrounds many investment decisions. If great uncertainty about future demands or costs exists, the use of sophisticated measurements may provide little practical guidance. Instead, the entrepreneur may prefer to base decisions on short-run prospects—for example, approving an investment that seems likely to return his money in one or two years.

Solomon's excellent study of investment decisions in small business offers the following conclusion on the measuring devices discussed in this section:

> *Theoretical* methods of investment evaluation (present value and discounted rate of return) assume decision making under conditions of certainty. Usual business investments are not made under these conditions. Because some alternative methods are fairly accurate estimates of the discounted rate of return and because some of them can

rank proposals quite well, there is reason for substituting these alternative methods for those that are theoretically more accurate. Also, if uncertainty is so great that satisfactory predictions are not possible, no logical or mathematical significance may emerge in the results of theoretical methods.

Few businessmen, especially small businessmen, would be willing to predict the future outcome of an investment for more than a few years. Consequently, they are generally unwilling to invest when the profitability depends upon years beyond the prediction period. A break-even point of profitability is determined, the payback period. If it is strongly felt that the proposal will continue its returns for at least this time, the proposal may be accepted. The results are similar to a "go-no-go" gauge. Perhaps this is altogether satisfactory for the small businessman in our present state of knowledge.[5]

Search Activity in Small Business Investment Decisions

Investment decisions are presumed to involve a choice among several competing opportunities that originate from the investor's search. In evaluating competing opportunities, furthermore, the investor may seek information that permits an intelligent choice to be made. Solomon's study confirmed the suspicion that small business managers often reach investment decisions without extensive search.[6] In larger firms various investment opportunities seem to appear almost spontaneously. In small businesses, however, investment opportunities are often considered on a one-at-a-time basis. The businessman is seemingly less concerned with ranking a number of investment possibilities than he is with trying to determine the merit of one particular proposal. In the analysis of a single proposal, moreover, the investor often jumps to a conclusion on the basis of sketchy information. The following case illustrates an investment behavior pattern of this type:

Mr. E, a dry cleaner, had an opportunity to open a branch dry cleaning store in a new shopping center. After looking at the center, talking to associates, and computing a break-even point, he decided to invest. His demand estimate was based on information given to him by the promoter of the shopping center.

The search for information was both spontaneous and nonprogrammed. Mr. E had no predetermined approach to the collection of data. He devoted little time to finding sources of information for demand estimates, such as city planning and zoning maps of population. He had no time for such things because of involvement in the day-to-day details of his business. He did not delegate many routine tasks in maintenance, collections, and deliveries.

Similarly, the search for alternatives was neither planned nor programmed. Mr. E did consider the possible purchase of common stock as an alternative to opening the branch store, but the search went no further. Instead of seeking out still other alternatives, he considered only proposals brought to his attention; this was true of the branch store proposal itself. The issue in this case is whether the delegation of routine tasks would have profited Mr. E by providing him with time for more concentrated attention to investment alternatives.[7]

---

[5] Martin B. Solomon, Jr., *Investment Decisions in Small Business*. Small Business Management Research Report. Prepared by the University of Kentucky under a grant by the Small Business Administration, Washington, D.C. (Lexington: University of Kentucky Press, 1963), pp. 90-91. Used with permission of the publisher.

[6] *Ibid.*, Chapter 7.

[7] *Ibid.*, p. 96.

The apparent deficiencies in small business search activity provide an opportunity for improvement in the quality of small business investment decisions. By breaking out of the pattern of routine activity or by delegating such work to others, the entrepreneur can free himself for the search that leads to more profitable investments.

Instead of stressing refinement in ranking methods, many small businessmen can more profitably improve their capital budgeting procedures by setting aside a portion of the manager's or owner's time: time to view the firm as a whole and evaluate its progress; time to correct weak policies and practices and to emphasize those that are strong; time to search for and stockpile alternative prospective investments and information concerning them; time to assess the availability of funds; and time to compare and choose among alternatives.[8]

SOURCES OF CAPITAL FOR THE EXPANDING BUSINESS

The acquisition of funds prior to the inception of business operations was considered in Chapter 14. The major sources of funds that were discussed in that chapter were personal savings, commercial bank loans, trade credit, equipment supplier loans, and funds from friends, relatives, and local investors. Even after a firm is launched, these sources continue to provide funds for its operations. Of course, some sources may be eliminated—for example, loans from relatives may be liquidated—but the other sources are as vital for the going concern as for the new firm.

Many of the limitations of these sources apply similarly to their usefulness in supplying funds for expansion. Personal savings, for example, are usually used to the limit in launching the enterprise. Loans from relatives and friends are as objectionable in financing expansion as they are in original financing. The three remaining sources discussed in Chapter 14—commercial bank loans, trade credit, and equipment supplier credit—can be utilized to provide funds for business expansion.

Retained Earnings

Retained earnings constitute a major source of funds for financing expansion of small business operations. As profits are realized, they are plowed back into the business by foregoing dividends. Such internally-generated funds may be invested in physical facilities or used to expand the firm's working capital. Retained earnings provide a natural type of expansion for most small firms. It is likely that the majority of small firms experience an annual growth in net worth as a result of retention of earnings.

In using retained earnings, it is apparent that the rate of expansion is limited by the amount of profits generated by the business. In the case of a rapidly expanding small firm, these funds are often insufficient to meet the heavy capital needs.

---

[8] *Ibid.*, p. 122.

Financing through retained earnings provides a conservative approach to expansion. The dangers of overexpansion or too rapid expansion are largely avoided. Because the additional funds are equity, the firm has no creditors threatening foreclosure and no due dates by which repayment must be made.

The lack of an interest charge on funds secured in this way may create the impression that there is no cost involved in their use. Even though there is no out-of-pocket cost, there is a definite economic cost for these funds as well as for borrowed funds. If not retained in the business, such funds might be invested otherwise, and the income that could be so earned constitutes the opportunity cost of utilizing the funds within the firm.

Sale of Capital Stock

A second source of expansion capital is available through the sale of capital stock to outsiders. This involves, of necessity, a dilution of ownership, and many businessmen are reluctant to take this step for that reason. Whether the owner is wise in declining to use outside equity financing depends upon the long-range prospects. If there is an opportunity for substantial expansion on a continuing basis and if other sources are inadequate, the owner may decide logically to bring in other owners. He may be better off by owning part of a larger business than by owning all of a smaller business.

Private Sale of Stock. Sale of stock is difficult for the small firm because it is not widely known and has no ready market for its securities. When sold to selected individuals, the most likely investors include employees, acquaintances of the owner, local residents, customers, and suppliers. Sale of stock to employees can provide additional capital only to the extent that they have surplus funds available for investment. Because of the greater resources and personal interest of managerial personnel, this group is a more likely source than are nonmanagerial employees.

Public Sale of Stock. Even though there are real difficulties involved, some small firms "go public" by making their stock available to the general public. The reasons for this step are typically cited as the need for additional working capital or, less frequently, for other capital needs. The personal financial objectives of owners may also enter into the reasoning involved in the public sale of stock. For example, a conflict among owners may lead to an arrangement whereby the ownership or interest of one owner is sold to the general public. Some owners may also wish to diversify their investments or to minimize estate taxes.

In undertaking the public sale of stock, the small firm subjects itself to public regulation. There are state regulations pertaining to the public sale of securities, and the Securities and Exchange Commission also exercises surveillance over such offerings. The SEC is quite tolerant of small offerings, however, permitting "Regulation A" offerings (those under $300,000) to be sold with minimum requirements for financial data and information.

Common stock may also be sold to underwriters who guarantee the sale of the securities. The compensation and fees paid to underwriters typically make the sale of securities in this manner rather expensive. The fees themselves may range from 10 percent to 30 percent, with 18 percent to 25 percent being typical. In addition, there are options and fees that may run the actual costs considerably higher. The reason for the high expense is, of course, the uncertainty and risk element associated with public offerings of stock of small, relatively unknown firms.

Studies of public sale of stock by small firms reveal the fact that small companies frequently make financial arrangements that are not sound. Indeed, the lack of knowledge on the part of small firm owners often leads to arrangements with brokers or securities dealers that are not in the best interest of the small firm.

Small Business Administration Loans

Another source of long-term funds for small business is found in Small Business Administration (SBA) loans. These are available not only to small manufacturers but also to wholesalers, retailers, service establishments, and other small businesses for the purpose of business construction, expansion, facilities, machinery, working capital, and other needs. Loans to firms in certain lines of business—for example, amusement and recreational firms and firms which derive a principal portion of their income from sale of alcoholic beverages or gambling—are precluded by law. Loans are also unattainable if the firm seeking the loan is in financial trouble or if the loan is intended to finance the purchase of a business by an applicant who is not a member of the ownership group at the time of the loan application.

Qualification Requirements for SBA Loans. To qualify for an SBA loan, the prospective borrower must be unable to obtain financing from private sources on reasonable terms. At the same time, the loan must be of such sound value or so secured that repayment is reasonably assured. These loans are normally secured by real estate mortgages or chattel mortgages, or by assignment of accounts receivable, life insurance policies, franchises, securities, and so forth. In 1964, the Small Business Administration began to make character loans up to $15,000 without collateral.

SBA Direct Loans. Small Business Administration direct loans are made for a maximum amount of $100,000 and carry an interest rate of 5½ percent. They generally provide for monthly payments, with maturities up to 10 years. Many banks hesitate to make loans of more than two or three years. The longer terms of the Small Business Administration loans are thus helpful to the business which is unable to secure loans of this type from commercial banks. As mentioned earlier, the loan request must have been rejected by a private source before it will be considered by the SBA.

Other Types of SBA Loans. The Small Business Administration also guarantees bank loans (up to $350,000) or makes *participation loans,* which are loans made in cooperation with private banks in which the degree of participation by the Small Business Administration ranges up to 90 percent. *Disaster relief loans* constitute one important phase of the Small Business Administration lending program, examples of which are found in the loans extended to small businesses after the devastating tornadoes which occurred in

1974. In addition to granting regular business loans and disaster loans, the Small Business Administration provides *economic opportunity loans* to minority and other disadvantaged groups. Management assistance is given as a part of the economic opportunity loan program, and an effort is made to seek out deserving applicants in ghetto and other depressed areas.

Small Business Investment Companies (SBIC's)

In 1958, Congress passed the Small Business Investment Company Act, providing for the establishment of privately owned capital banks. These banks or companies were established for the purpose of providing long-term loans and equity capital to small business. Small business investment companies are licensed and regulated by the Small Business Administration. They may obtain a substantial part of their capital from the Small Business Administration at attractive rates of interest. For example, an SBIC beginning with $700,000 in equity funds can add $1,400,000 from federal loans for a total of $2,100,000. Small business investment companies that are larger can obtain proportionately less in federal funds, a factor that tends to limit their size.

Tax Advantages of SBIC's. The formation of small business investment companies is encouraged by the provision of certain tax advantages. Losses sustained on convertible debentures or stock of small businesses, for example, may be treated as ordinary loss deductions rather than as capital losses. The motivation for the formation of such companies, of course, is the earning of a profit on the financing of small business firms.

Emphasis of SBIC's on Equity Financing. Although small business investment companies may either lend funds or supply equity funds, the act was intended to place a strong emphasis upon equity financing. This may involve either direct purchase of stock or, quite commonly, purchase of convertible debentures—that is, bonds which may be converted into stock at the option of the small business investment company.[9] The investment company is strongly desirous of investing in companies with rapid growth prospects. In addition, the cost of investigating investment opportunities usually makes it more profitable for the lender to concentrate his attention upon the bigger investments required by the larger small businesses. These considerations and the reluctance of many small business owners to accept a dilution of equity have limited the use of small business development companies by small business firms that need long-term capital.

Types of SBIC's. As small business investment companies have grown, they have developed in different directions. The following summary describes the major types of small business investment companies:[10]

---

[9] Many SBIC contracts provide a measure of protection to the borrower by permitting him to reacquire his full equity at some stipulated price. The tendency of SBIC's to concentrate their funds in debt securities of small firms, rather than investing in their equity capital, was reported in a paper by Carolyn N. Hooper and J. Van Fenstermaker, "An Appraisal of the SBIC Industry," Southwest Social Science Association Meeting, April 1, 1972.

[10] Samuel L. Hayes and Donald H. Woods, "Are SBIC's Doing Their Job?" *Harvard Business Review* (March-April, 1963), pp. 180, 182.

1. *A specialist*— This type of SBIC, which is often affiliated with a parent company operating in the same industry, usually has a great deal of savvy in a specialized field. As a result, specialists will often be willing to make investments which other venture capitalists, not so familiar with your industry, would be reluctant to undertake.

2. *A term lender*—This type of lender is often *both* a specialist *and* an affiliate of a parent company. The advantage to you as a borrower is that there may be no dilution of equity, although the interest rate can run anywhere from 8% to over 16%. Responses to the survey indicate that few term lenders insist on board representation; instead they prefer to secure their loans with real estate or other collateral.

3. *A bank-related SBIC*—The survey indicates that 28% of all affiliated SBIC's are bank-connected. If your present bank has an SBIC connection, you may find the associated SBIC more willing to accommodate your needs than other venture capital sources, inasmuch as it will have access to the bank's records.

4. *A small, independent SBIC*—If your financial needs are modest and your need for management assistance negligible, a local "minimum capital" SBIC may prove to be a satisfactory source of financing. Although these SBIC's seldom have full-time managers and are therefore limited in their ability to extend management assistance, they often adopt a hands-off policy toward their investments and, because they are usually financed by local businessmen, their connections may be useful in attracting new business.

5. *A syndicate*—If you approach an SBIC manager who decides that your needs are too large for his firm alone to handle, he may suggest that a syndicate of SBIC's be organized to accommodate you. This has the advantage of giving you a much larger potential source of capital, not only for your immediate needs but also for subsequent needs to finance further growth. SBIC managers report that syndicates are often ineffective in exercising proper control over portfolio companies once the investment is made. From the standpoint of the borrower, this fragmentation of authority reduces the threat of effective interference in the company's affairs. However, SBIC managers also report that syndicates tend to be slow and cumbersome in making investment decisions; and, depending on the urgency of your financial needs, this may prove to be a disadvantage.

6. *A publicly owned SBIC*—If one can be found that is willing to help you, a public SBIC offers many of the advantages that you cannot always get from a single, small SBIC. The survey indicates that this type of SBIC has staffs of professional analysts of from two to more than ten men who can extend management help if needed. Its funds resources are usually large enough to handle your foreseeable capital needs, and if it is one of the better known firms, its sponsorship may facilitate a public offering of your stock at a later date.

On the other hand, with a wider assortment of investment opportunities than the small SBIC's, in terms of both industrial groups and geographical location, competition for the attention and funds of a public SBIC may be harder to get. Moreover, the public SBIC's are primarily interested in large deals of $400,000 or more, because of the expense of investigation and follow-up once the investment is made.

Many small business investment companies have provided not only funds but also counsel and advice to the small business firms whom they have served. It is not uncommon for an investment company to have a representative on the board of directors of the borrowing firm. The investment company does not normally wish to assume operating control of a business, but it is often able to provide constructive advice, particularly of a financial nature. Some small business investment companies provide management counsel and advice on a fee basis in addition to supplying the unofficial counsel that accompanies the original investment or loan.

Minority Enterprise Small Business Investment Companies (MESBIC)

A development since 1968, the minority enterprise small business investment company (MESBIC) is a small business investment company devoted solely to the making of loans or equity investments in companies owned and operated by members of minority groups.[11] A MESBIC is privately owned and is regulated solely by the Small Business Administration. Thus, it can and does cut the time and red tape involved in procuring a direct SBA loan. MESBIC's may not break even, although when fully mature they could become profitable. The government hopes that sponsors will consider their net outlays of funds as social investments, an objective considered to be significant in recent times.

Business Development Corporations

During the last 25 years, several states have formed business development corporations for the purpose of promoting the business and economic welfare of the state. In particular, they encourage the location, rehabilitation, and expansion of all types of business activity. Their capital is supplied by private sources interested in promoting industrial growth, such as banks, public utilities, and transportation firms. An example of financing through the business development corporation is provided by the following account of the Industrial Development Corporation of Florida:[12]

When Germfree Products, Inc., recently decided to build a $150,000 plant here, the newly formed breeder of birds and animals for research applied for financing at three local banks. The applications were quickly rejected.

Though Germfree's prospects seemed sound, the banks voiced concern about its lack of operating history in a new industry, the fact that collateral would consist largely of specially designed equipment which might prove difficult to sell in the event of liquidation, and Germfree's desire that the money be repaid over a lengthy 10-year period.

But Germfree got its money anyway—and on the terms it wanted. Supplying the cash was Industrial Development Corp. of Florida, a private lending institution which regards monetary risk as secondary to state pride. Supported by 97 Florida banks, 31 savings and loan associations and 10 insurance companies, among others, Industrial Development's principal aim is to develop increased job opportunities in the Sunshine State by supplying capital to firms that can't obtain it from more conventional lenders.

In addition to the state business development corporations, there are many local community development corporations. These corporations also operate on the basis of privately supplied funds which may be supplemented with

---

[11] See Richard H. Klein, "A Perspective on the MESBIC Program," pp. 45-51, *MSU Business Topics*, (Autumn, 1972). See also, "MESBIC Highlights," *The DAME News*, Vol. 4 (July, 1973), p. 2, for data on MESBIC Financial Corporation of Dallas, now sponsored by 50 Dallas banks and corporations. A further discussion appears in, "He Cuts the Risk for Minority Entrepreneurs," *Business Week*, October 20, 1973, pp. 72-73, 76.

[12] Burt Schorr, "State Boosters: Many Companies Join Lending Pools to Help Spur an Area's Growth," *The Wall Street Journal* (May 18, 1964), p. 1.

borrowed funds. The local development corporations typically function by building and leasing plants or by buying and leasing or selling sites for new plants. The community industrial foundation is often composed of various civic-minded persons who are interested in solving the economic and industrial problems of their community. Community development corporations may also supply funds to industries by lending or purchasing stock in them.

Miscellaneous Sources of Funds

Commercial finance companies lend money to small business firms on a secured basis. Their loans may be backed by inventories, accounts receivable, equipment, or other items. They participate in floor planning arrangements and also purchase installment paper from small firms. The interest rates charged by commercial finance companies tend to be larger than those charged by commercial banks.

Insurance companies have also made term loans available to small business. Although their major financing efforts have been directed toward big business, some companies have established small business loan departments. Insurance companies place considerable emphasis upon the submission of financial statements and projections by the borrowing company, and small companies are often reluctant to subject themselves to such effort and evaluation.

In addition to the sources discussed above, there are still other financial institutions and groups that make financing available to small business firms from time to time. Included among these other sources are savings and loan associations, mutual savings banks, factors, and personal finance companies.

Summary

1. The general adequacy of capital for financing small business firms is not known. However, there is a widespread opinion to the effect that a capital shortage exists—particularly in long-term funds. The capital needs of new and rapidly expanding firms are particularly acute.

2. The cost of both equity funds and loans to small firms typically is greater than the cost to larger business firms. To some extent, this disparity is explained by differences in risk and cost of service.

3. The financial strength and practices of small firms are adversely affected by deficiencies in financial management. In addition, there is a lack of depth in management (often one-man management), and there are weaknesses in financial planning.

4. In capital budgeting, the manager is principally concerned with allocating available capital to the most promising investment opportunities. Traditional methods for determining the relative desirability of alternative investment opportunities are the simple return on investment and the payback period. Although there are conceptual weaknesses in these tools, they have the value of simplicity and provide a rough and usually satisfactory check for evaluating investments.

5. Two superior methods of measuring investment proposals are the discounted cash flow method and the present value method. These methods take into account the time value of money and the economic life of the investment. They are more difficult to use, however, and they have very little application in small business at the present time.

6. A study of investment behavior of small business owners indicates that insufficient attention is given to search activities in connection with investment proposals. Investment opportunities are often considered on a one-at-a-time basis, and the typical investigation of a particular opportunity is superficial in nature.

7. Some capital for expansion is available from the same sources used in initiating the business, particularly commercial bank loans, trade credit, and equipment supplier loans.

8. Retained earnings constitute a major source of funds for financing the expansion of small business operations. Reliance upon this source of funds limits the rate of expansion, but it does provide a conservative approach to financing expansion.

9. The small firm faces a serious problem in the sale of capital stock because it is not widely known and thus has no ready market for its securities. As the firm grows, however, it may sell common stock to selected individuals or even "go public," although the latter course of action often entails payment of large fees to underwriting firms.

10. The Small Business Administration makes long-term loans available to small firms which are financially sound but which are unable to secure funds from private sources. These loans are either direct loans from the Small Business Administration or participation loans in which the Small Business Administration cooperates with private banks in making the loan. They also extend disaster relief loans and economic opportunity loans.

11. Small business investment companies, which make long-term capital available to small business, are licensed by the Small Business Administration and typically obtain a substantial portion of their capital from the Small Business Administration. These investment companies are particularly interested in investing in growth companies through the purchase of stock or, more frequently, convertible debentures.

12. As of 1968, the supplementary MESBIC program was instituted for the purpose of making loans and/or business investments in small firms run by minority group members who might otherwise not be able to procure funds.

13. Other sources of capital for the expanding firm include state business development corporations, community development corporations, commercial finance companies, insurance companies, and savings and loan associations.

 Discussion Questions

1. A small independently-owned data processing center began operations two months ago. How would its financial needs and problems differ significantly from those of IBM and NCR?

2. How are the financial needs and available resources of a firm related to the stage of its development?

3. A wholesale firm with a critical need for additional working capital has an inventory turnover rate slightly more than half of the average rate for its line of business. Is there any logical connection between these conditions? If so, what?

4. Why should interest rates be higher for small firms than for large firms?

5. Is the greater danger in lending money to a one-man firm imaginary or real? Justify your answer.

6. Why is it that those with greater ability in sales or production rather than finance seem to be the ones who launch new businesses?

7. What appear to be the principal weaknesses in capital budgeting by small business firms?

8. What are the principal advantages of the discounted cash flow method and the present value method as compared with the traditional methods of evaluating investment opportunities?

9. What is meant by "search" activity, and how is it related to investment by small business firms?

10. What would appear to be the most likely source of expansion capital for a going concern? What are the limitations of using additional equity capital supplied by outside investors?

11. What is your prediction as to the future usefulness of small business investment companies in financing small business firms? Justify your answer.

12. What seems to be the most plausible explanation for the failure of SBA loans to have become a major source of capital for small businesses?

13. The owner of a bowling alley has $13,000 of his own funds invested in the business. Is there a cost associated with the use of this money? Should it appear on the income statement of the firm? Why?

14. Suppose the owner of the bowling alley in Question 13 is a member of a minority group and is seeking a business loan of $10,000. To what sources might he turn? Which is most likely to advance funds more quickly? Why?

15. Some years ago the president of a major stock exchange proposed that the federal government should invest $250 million in the stock of small businesses and get a proportionate share of the dividends. Control would remain in the hands of the original owners, however. How would this differ from the small business investment company program? What would be its advantages and difficulties?

16. Would it be any easier for a firm to borrow from a bank three months after beginning operations than it was six months earlier? Why?

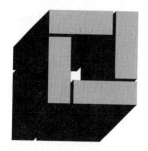

20

Record Keeping and
Financial Statements

In a small firm, as in the large one, effective decisions require a foundation of objective information concerning business operations. Data must be collected, tabulated, analyzed, and interpreted for the manager's use. Unless the firm is very small, with uncomplicated operations, the entrepreneur cannot rely solely on his memory. Hence, we shall consider a small firm's record-keeping needs and the relationship of business records to successful operations.

RECORD KEEPING IN THE SMALL FIRM

In spite of the obvious importance of record keeping in a business, many small firms do not maintain adequate records. A file of canceled checks and invoices alone is woefully inadequate. It has been discovered, for example, that small firms which have gone bankrupt typically had inadequate records. On the other hand, small firms which maintain adequate records reflect high-quality management because such records provide management a basis for more effective decision making and better control over operating results. Furthermore, adequate records make it easier to detect employee frauds, waste, spoilage, and other losses.

Objectives of a Record-Keeping System

The reasons for keeping adequate records might be translated into the following objectives of a record-keeping system for small business:

1. The record-keeping system should yield an accurate, thorough picture of operating results.
2. The records should permit a quick comparison of current data with prior years' operating results and with budgetary goals.
3. The record-keeping system should provide suitable financial statements for use by management and submission to prospective creditors.
4. The record-keeping system should permit prompt filing of reports and tax returns to regulatory and tax collecting agencies of the government.
5. The record-keeping system should reveal all possible employee frauds, thefts, waste, and record-keeping errors.

Automatic Data Processing for the Small Firm

Small business operators are characteristically slow to appreciate and adopt modern automatic data processing methods. Here is a sampling of comments reported after a recent study:[1]

"Computer systems cost too much."
"Computer systems take too much time to implement."
"As a small businessman, I don't understand the computer."
"I'm too small to afford, let alone use, computers in my business."
"My employees will be afraid that their jobs are going to be replaced by the computer."
"I don't have 'start up' funds for a computer system."
"A lot of computer systems don't work very well."

These comments either reflect caution concerning the introduction of a computerized management information system or indicate an outright negative attitude. In some cases, caution is well-founded. But progress in the use of computers is rapid, and small business entrepreneurs should certainly consider their use.

Practicality of Automatic Data Processing for Small Firms. Some minimum business size is clearly essential to make automatic data processing truly practical, but this level of operation is hard to pinpoint. Committed advocates of automatic data processing believe that it will pay its way even in very small firms. Improvement of programming methods and decrease in size of computers have reduced the necessary minimum business size for efficient use of computers. However, to justify the use of a computer, it is the number of transactions and record-keeping entries that is significant, not the mere size of the firm.

The following are estimates suggested by experienced analysts concerning automatic data processing in small firms:[2]

	General Electric Co. Estimate	Tabulating Consultants, Inc. Estimate	Lincoln Tabulating Center Estimate
Payroll	200 employees	50 employees	100 employees
Accounts receivable	500 transactions per month	500 source documents	300 to 400 statements
Inventory control	1,000 transactions per month	1,000 items in inventory	Fairly good sized firm

Use of a Data Processing Center. A few small firms purchase or rent electronic computers. This is costly, however, and requires a large volume of record keeping to make it economically feasible. Another, more widely used

---

[1] Robert E. Markland, "Can Computers Help the Small Businessman?" *Journal of Systems Management*, April, 1972, p. 29.

[2] These estimates were submitted to the Select Committee on Small Business. See U.S. Congress, Senate, A Report to the Select Committee on Small Business, *Automatic Data Processing and the Small Businessman*, 90th Congress, 2d Session, 1968, pp. 67-68.

approach to automating small business record keeping entails use of a data processing center. Data processing centers are service organizations that own computer facilities and provide processing services for a fee. Some of them are owned by computer manufacturers, such as NCR, Inc., and others are operated as independent businesses or as sideline operations of banks or other corporations.[3] There are 1,000 or more such centers in the United States, and the number is growing.

The advantage to the small firm is obvious. Recording equipment can be installed in the user firm with a relatively small investment and with minimal operating costs. For example, a punched paper tape may be prepared while the cash register is being used. This tape is taken or mailed to a data processing center. The center then utilizes its computer in preparing desired management reports which are returned to the small business user. The small businessman has access to the electronic computer without buying a computer or employing skilled programmers.

Impact on Small Business. To some individuals, developments such as the introduction of electronic data processing appear to constitute a threat to small business. As noted above, some small firms are discovering ways to utilize these modern methods of data processing. The financial limitation is not prohibitive, particularly when the data processing center is used. The primary threat, if one exists, is to small business management that is not alert to changes of this type and cannot adapt to modern technology in its office procedures.

Automatic data processing constitutes an opportunity as much as it constitutes a threat. By use of these methods, the manager of the small firm may be able to control inventory and receivables more effectively than was ever possible prior to development of the computer. Some have suggested that an automatic data processing center may be more effectively applied to the relatively simple operation of a small firm than to the more complex operation of a large corporation. The following is an observation by an executive of a firm manufacturing electronic computers:

> The weaknesses of a small business are first, limited financial muscle, if you want to describe it as such, limit in product line developments, and more important, limited staffs. Now, in every one of those instances, the availability of this computer system is going to enable these small businesses to overcome these weaknesses in a way relatively more significant to them than is the case in a situation involving a large business. These systems can be used to reduce inventory, improve receivables—obviously, they cannot borrow money for a small business, but they can make the operation of a business more efficient within the confines of the sums available.
>
> They can do analyses on product lines. They can substitute for large staff and give better results.
>
> One thing is clear, I think, and that is the ability to perform detailed analyses of products, lines, operations and so forth that will permit the small company to operate with the flexibility, speed, and product-marketing differentiation which it theoretically always had—we used to like to think that—but which in fact it probably did not.
>
> I believe there is no evidence to support the theory that the small businesses will not profit as much from the advance of this new technology and new industry as will the large

---

[3] Consider, as an example, Transaction Data Corporation (which has five employees), mentioned in "How a Tiny Store Keeps the Books," *Business Week*, January 9, 1971, pp. 80-81.

businesses. The computer can no more put a company out of business than it can keep one in business. It is a tool, a wonderful tool, and a powerful one, but its value lies in the skill of the user, and in that regard, the large computer user is not necessarily better than the small.[4]

If the foregoing analysis is correct, the advent of the electronic computer places a great premium upon the effectiveness of small business management. A professional approach to management has always been desirable, but it is becoming increasingly important because of developments of this type.

Accounting Records

Accounting records are designed to summarize the financial results of business transactions and to portray the firm's financial condition. As a minimum, the accounting records should provide information on the following:

1. Assets, including real estate, equipment, inventory, receivables, and cash.
2. Liabilities to banks, suppliers, employees, and others (including income taxes due).
3. Owner's equity in the firm.
4. Sales, expenses, and profit for the accounting period.

Accounting Systems Design. Accounting systems design is seldom well done by the amateur. The services of a public accountant ordinarily are required. The use of such an expert makes possible a system that will function better at lower cost. Alternatively, the sales engineers of office equipment manufacturers will design systems for small firms purchasing their equipment. Such manufacturers maintain many local sales and service centers which sell or lease punched-card tabulating equipment, sell the cards required, or even perform a client's data processing operations. Systems analysis is provided free in order to secure the sale or lease of the equipment, and it can be a major service to the small business whose office costs and records are major problems.

In setting up a system, careful attention must be given to the achievement of the objectives stipulated at the beginning of the chapter. In addition, the factors of economy, simplicity, and flexibility in operation are important for the small firm. Any accounting system, of course, must be consistent with accepted principles of accounting theory and practice—that is, a company must be consistent in its treatment of given data and given transactions. For example, inventory must be valued in the same way for each accounting period.

Design of efficient, economical forms is very important. They should be so prepared that completion time is minimized, while complete information is promptly provided. Undue duplication of forms must also be avoided. Each form should clearly state its purpose in its heading, and the form size should be suitable both for filing and for feeding into posting and bookkeeping machines. Forms should be kept simple and capable of completion by hand or on a typewriter. All frequently recurring information should be printed on the form. Finally, each proposed new form should be checked with the bookkeeper, clerk, foreman, or other prospective user, to avoid overlooking features which might keep it from being useful.

---

[4] Statement of Walter W. Finke, President, Electronic Data Processing Division, Honeywell, Inc., *Ibid.*, p. 1576.

Accrual vs. Cash Basis System. Most modern accounting systems are on an accrual, as distinguished from a cash, basis. In a cash accounting system, the accounts are debited and credited as cash is received and paid out. In the accrual method, income earned and expenses incurred are recorded at the time the sale is made or the expense is incurred. The use of the accrual method thus provides a more nearly accurate and up-to-date statement of profits.

Provisions for Internal Check. To safeguard business assets and prevent errors, the accounting system should provide for effective internal check. This means that the records should be accurately maintained, transaction by transaction, by the bookkeepers. No one employee should completely control any given business transaction. For example, cashiering and account collections should be divorced from bookkeeping, and the bookkeeper should never be allowed to authorize purchases.

In addition, data analyses and reports should ordinarily depend upon the efforts of at least two persons. Alternatively, of course, in a small business using cash registers, the cash register tape provides a double check on cash received by the cashier. Such procedures tend to prevent fraud and errors. If internal check is to operate with maximum efficiency, however, all employees must be properly selected and well trained. All this does not eliminate a need for supervisory responsibility for accurate preparation of records and reports.

As an alternative to account keeping by an employee or member of the owner's family, the firm may have its books kept by a public accountant or by a bookkeeping or computer service agency catering to small businesses. Very small firms often find it convenient to have the books kept and the statements and tax returns prepared by the same firm that makes the periodic audits. Numerous small accounting firms offer a complete accounting service to small businesses. Their services have been supplemented in recent years by the development of national firms which provide bookkeeping service on a mass-production basis to thousands of small businesses. Data are submitted by mail, and reports prepared by the agency are mailed back to the client firm.

Specific Types of Accounting Records.

In other chapters, reference is made to the records used in the various management areas—inventory control, purchasing, selling, production control, and so on. It may be helpful at this point, however, to indicate the major types of accounting records and the business decisions to which they are related.

Accounts Receivable. Records of receivables are vital not only to decisions on credit extension but also to accurate billing and to maintenance of good customer relations. Analysis of these records reveals the degree of effectiveness of the firm's credit and collection policies.

Inventory Records. Adequate records are essential to the control and security of inventory items. In addition, they supply information for use in purchasing, maintenance of adequate stock levels, and computing of turnover ratios.

Accounts Payable. Records of liabilities show what the firm owes, facilitate the taking of available cash discounts, and allow payments to be made when due.

Sales Records. Analysis of sales records is essential to studies of advertising effectiveness, market coverage, and customer profitability. In addition, sales records often provide a basis for compensation of salesmen.

Production Records. The production process is regulated by use of production control records. They provide a basis for product costing and permit detection of costs resulting from idle machines or idle manpower.

Payroll Records. The payroll records not only show the total payments to employees but also provide the base for computing and paying the various payroll taxes.

Cash Records. Carefully maintained records showing all receipts and disbursements are necessary to safeguard this asset. They yield a knowledge of cash flow and balances on hand; such information is essential for proper timing of loans and for assurance of cash to pay maturing obligations.

Various other accounting records are also vital to efficient operation of the business. Among these are the insurance register, which shows all policies in force; records of leaseholds; and records covering the firm's investments.

Statistical Records

There are numerous nonaccounting records used in a typical small firm, some of which are quite as important as those of a financial nature. For example, sales tabulations by class of merchandise, by department, or by sales territory may be highly informative in planning future sales effort. These are statistical tabulations, frequently machine made, but definitely not a part of the formal accounting records as such.

Another example is found in the personnel records of a firm. They include the application form, the individual job history form, a report of physical examinations, performance rating forms, and the like. Certainly, the employer can better deal with employee relations problems, including relations with unions, if he has adequate, accurate personnel records.

Records used in quality control, maintenance planning, and other areas of manufacturing management are still other types of nonaccounting records. It seems clear that many types of statistical data can contribute to effective managerial control in the small firm.

Records Management

Records management for the small business involves the following two major aspects to be considered here: retention and protection.

Retention of Records. The life of a record is not necessarily long. Nevertheless, some firms habitually keep all records without considering the future need for them. If a business is quite small and the records can be housed in just a few filing cabinets, the problem is not serious. For most firms, however, there are two weaknesses in such a policy. First, the excess storage equipment and unnecessary handling of records are wasteful. Secondly, loading the files with unnecessary material makes it difficult and time-consuming to locate important information when it is needed.

For tax purposes, steps should be taken to safeguard fixed asset and depreciation records, tax withholding records for each employee, detailed records of unusual business expenses (which might be suspect if an income tax auditor should appear), and records proving prior-period business losses which could be carried forward in future income tax returns. Other very important records include government contracts, partners' wills, partnership agreements, stockholder lists, and important sales and purchase contracts. Accounts receivable and payable records, inventory records, blueprints, and product specifications are also basic in business operation.

Essential records, including those legally required for possible government audit, must be maintained as long as the actual need exists. This may be three, five, or ten years—or even longer. Nevertheless, every firm should study its true needs and retain essential records only for the requisite time periods.

Once retention needs have been determined, there is the additional problem of reducing the cost of maintaining records. For example, microfilming is now widely used by firms that have a large volume of records; this greatly reduces the space required for records retention. A manufacturer with 100 employees, for example, might record a complete weekly payroll, including all supporting documents, on less than one spool of film.

Physical Protection of Records. Maintenance of records assumes another aspect—the protection of records during their essential life span. Fires, floods, tornadoes, and other disasters can occur at any time. Loss of all business records in one such disaster could bankrupt a firm. The blueprints of a manufacturer and a retailer's financial records illustrate the highly critical records whose loss might be fatal. Even a firm's claim against an insurance company for the amount of insured loss might be difficult to sustain in the absence of proper accounting records.

Some precautions are clearly desirable to minimize such dangers. How extensive these should be necessarily depends upon the importance of the records. Financial records may be stored in fireproof safes or cabinets on the premises; microfilmed copies of the originals, along with other very important business documents, might be stored in the firm's safety deposit box. Duplicate sets of blueprints might also be maintained at a separate location. A firm could also build a subsurface storeroom on company premises, separated from the main office and plant, for storage of basic or duplicate records. This will involve some expense, but the precautionary measures afford a protection that may be viewed as a type of business insurance.

ANALYSIS AND INTERPRETATION OF FINANCIAL STATEMENTS

Operating efficiency of a firm, ability to secure bank loans and trade credit, and attraction of new equity capital all depend upon the quality of a firm's management. This is reflected in its financial statements, properly analyzed and interpreted. Hence, we shall now consider the typical financial statements, together with some of the analytical approaches that are useful for their proper interpretation.

The Typical Financial Statements

The preparation of financial statements is made possible by the existence of accurate and thorough accounting records. Figure 20-1 illustrates an income statement of a manufacturing firm. For the same firm, Figure 20-2 on page 346 illustrates a schedule of cost of goods manufactured, and Figure 20-3 on page 347 presents a balance sheet.

THE PARKER MANUFACTURING COMPANY
Income Statement
For Year Ended June 30, 1975

Sales			$415,100
Cost of goods sold:			
Finished goods inventory, July 1, 1974		$ 38,500	
Cost of goods manufactured		294,675	
Total cost of finished goods available for sale		$333,175	
Less finished goods inventory, June 30, 1975		51,000	
Cost of goods sold			282,175
Gross profit on sales			$132,925
Operating expenses:			
Selling expenses:			
Sales salaries and commissions	$28,575		
Advertising expense	19,300		
Miscellaneous selling expense	2,500		
Total selling expenses		$ 50,375	
General expenses:			
Officers' salaries	$23,060		
Office salaries	8,300		
Depreciation—office equipment	1,800		
Bad debts expense	2,050		
Miscellaneous office expense	2,790		
Total general expenses		38,000	
Total operating expenses			88,375
Net income from operations			$ 44,550
Other expense:			
Interest expense			5,000
Net income before income tax			$ 39,550
Income tax			15,100
Net income after income tax			$ 24,450

Figure 20-1
INCOME STATEMENT

THE PARKER MANUFACTURING COMPANY
Statement of Cost of Goods Manufactured
For Year Ended June 30, 1975

Work in process inventory, July 1, 1974		$ 20,000
Raw materials:		
Inventory, July 1, 1974	$ 32,000	
Purchases	120,800	
Cost of materials available for use	$152,800	
Less inventory, June 30, 1975	28,725	
Cost of materials placed in production	$124,075	
Direct labor	98,750	
Factory overhead:		
Indirect labor $19,300		
Factory maintenance 8,000		
Heat, light, and power 11,800		
Property taxes 5,000		
Depreciation of factory equipment 17,600		
Depreciation of buildings 3,000		
Amortization of patents 2,500		
Factory supplies expense 6,000		
Insurance expense 2,600		
Miscellaneous factory expense 2,050		
Total factory overhead	77,850	
Total manufacturing costs		300,675
Total work in process during period		$320,675
Less work in process inventory, June 30, 1975		26,000
Cost of goods manufactured		$294,675

Figure 20-2
STATEMENT OF COST OF GOODS MANUFACTURED

Minor variations would be involved in preparing the same statements for a trading firm instead of a manufacturing business. Specifically, the cost of goods sold section in the income statement would make reference to purchases rather than manufacturing cost, and no separate schedule comparable to Figure 20-2 would be required. In the capital section of the balance sheet, the capital stock item shows this to be an incorporated business. If it were a proprietorship or partnership, the individual ownership investments would be shown.

Another useful statement (see Figure 20-4 on page 348) shows the sources and uses of funds in the business for the preceding year. It is important to distinguish this from the income statement. Profit for a period is only one source of funds. The various uses of additional funds are detailed by this statement.

THE PARKER MANUFACTURING COMPANY
Balance Sheet
June 30, 1975

Assets

Current assets:			
Cash			$ 22,240
Accounts receivable		$ 41,500	
Less allowance for			
uncollectible accounts		2,500	39,000
Inventories (at lower of cost or market)			
Finished goods		$ 51,000	
Work in process		26,000	
Raw materials		28,725	105,725
Factory supplies			4,000
Prepaid insurance			2,900
Total current assets			$173,865

		Accumulated	Book
Plant assets:	Cost	Depreciation	Value
Office equipment	$ 18,000	$ 8,100	$ 9,900
Factory equipment	276,000	163,500	112,500
Buildings	125,000	20,000	105,000
Land	35,000	—	35,000
Total plant assets	$454,000	$191,600	262,400

Intangible assets:	
Patents	27,500
TOTAL ASSETS	$463,765

Liabilities

Current liabilities:		
Accounts payable	$ 38,600	
Estimated income tax payable	15,100	
Salaries and wages payable	1,965	
Interest payable	1,250	
Total current liabilities		$ 56,915
Long-term liabilities:		
First mortgage 5% notes payable		
(due 1984)		100,000
Total liabilities		$156,915

Stockholders' Equity

Common stock, no-par (30,000		
shares authorized and issued)	$150,000	
Retained earnings	156,850	
Total stockholders' equity		306,850
TOTAL LIABILITIES AND		
STOCKHOLDERS' EQUITY		$463,765

Figure 20-3
BALANCE SHEET

THE PARKER MANUFACTURING COMPANY
Statement of Sources and Uses of Funds
For Year Ended June 30, 1975

Funds were provided by:		
Operations:		
Net profit (per Income Statement)	$24,450	
Add: Depreciation expense charged to operations	22,400	
Amortization of patents	2,500	$49,350
Funds were applied to:		
Dividends	$ 9,000	
Purchase of equipment	23,100	
Retirement of long-term notes payable	20,000	52,100
Decrease in working capital		$ 2,750

The decrease in working capital is accounted for as follows:

	June 30 1974	June 30 1975	Working Capital Increase	Decrease
Cash	$19,000	$ 22,240	$ 3,240	
Accounts receivable (net)	46,000	39,000		$ 7,000
Inventories	90,500	105,725	15,225	
Prepaid expenses and supplies	8,900	6,900		2,000
Accounts payable	28,200	38,600		10,400
Income taxes payable	14,500	15,100		600
Other payables	2,000	3,215		1,215
			$18,465	$21,215
Decrease in working capital			2,750	
			$21,215	$21,215

Figure 20-4
STATEMENT OF SOURCES AND USES OF FUNDS

Ratio Analysis of Financial Statements

A single item from a financial statement has only limited meaning until it is related to some other item. For example, current assets of $10,000 mean one thing when current liabilities are $5,000 and another when they are $50,000. For this reason, the practice of ratio analysis—relating different financial figures to each other—has gained wide acceptance. Ratios have been developed to relate different income statement items to each other, balance sheet items to each other, and income statement items to balance sheet items.

Most Widely Used Financial Ratios. Although numerous financial statement ratios can be computed, certain ones are widely used. Richard Sanzo, a respected financial analyst of small business, has suggested the following ratios as those that have the greatest usefulness for managers of small firms:[5]

1. Current assets to current liabilities.
2. Current liabilities to tangible net worth.
3. Turnover of tangible net worth.
4. Turnover of working capital.
5. Net profits to tangible net worth.
6. Average collection period of receivables.
7. Net sales to inventory.
8. Net fixed assets to tangible net worth.
9. Total debt to tangible net worth.
10. Net profits to net sales.

A careful interpretation of ratios is required to make them useful to a particular firm. A ratio may indicate potential trouble, but it cannot explain either the causes or the seriousness of the situation. A ratio may also be misleading. For example, higher inventory turnovers are usually considered favorable. But the rate of turnover could go too high and merely reflect an inadequate inventory (such as would cost the firm sales). To be sure, the greater danger is that the rate of turnover is too low, and a careful comparison with industry standards may show this to be true. Only careful interpretation can determine the significance of any given ratio.[6]

Most small firms find it profitable to compare their ratios with their own past experience and with industry standard ratios. Such comparisons reveal performance trends and measure managerial efficiency. Various sources periodically publish standard ratios for different types of business. Among others, Dun and Bradstreet, Inc., publishes annually a series of ratios for 72 lines of business in manufacturing, wholesaling, and retailing. Trade associations frequently collect and publish financial data concerning their members. And public accounting firms can locate appropriate standard ratios and advise on the interpretation of a firm's financial statements.

Testing Management Efficiency via Ratio Analysis of Statements. Three basic criteria for evaluating managerial efficiency through ratio analysis of financial statements are discussed below.

Satisfactory Profit Position. The first requisite for realization of satisfactory profits is the existence of a profit-making opportunity. To have a profit potential, a business must offer a product or service that customers are willing to purchase at a price and in a quantity that will permit profitable operation. The profit potential of a retail store, for example, is determined partially by the number of

---

[5] Richard Sanzo, *Ratio Analysis for Small Business* (Washington, D.C.: Small Business Administration, 1970), p. 6. This booklet contains an excellent survey and explanation of the process of ratio analysis.

[6] See also Constantine Konstans and Randall P. Martin, "Financial Analysis for Small Business," *Atlantic Economic Review* (March-April, 1973), pp. 26-31.

customers and partially by the number of competing stores in the city. Excessively intense competition may preclude profits for all of the firms of a given kind.

If a profit opportunity exists, the concern must be so operated as to earn a profit compatible with the profit potential. Whether an earned profit is satisfactory must be evaluated in terms of such ratios as net profit to net sales and net profit to tangible net worth. The actual ratios of a given business may be evaluated in the light of industry standard ratios and the firm's own historical ratios. Comparisons of the firm's profit ratios with industry standards require interpretation in the light of the firm's location, scale of operations, intensity of competition, and other pertinent factors.

Satisfactory Working Capital Position. To have a satisfactory working capital position, a concern's working capital must be both adequate in amount and liquid in nature. Working capital adequacy means that sufficient money must always be on hand to pay all maturing obligations. Payroll disbursement cannot be delayed. Discounts on purchases cannot be obtained unless bills are paid within the cash discount period—which usually is ten days. Taxes unpaid on the due date assigned by law will force a penalty payment in addition to the actual amount of the tax. Cash must also be available to meet the various contingencies which arise from time to time in every business. Then, there will be diversions of cash to pay for new fixed assets and to launch advertising and sales promotion campaigns.

Adequacy of working capital is tested by comparing certain company ratios with corresponding industry standard ratios. One of these is the *current ratio*, which is computed by dividing current assets by current liabilities. The "banker's rule" for this ratio is "at least two to one" for working capital to be judged adequate. Actually, the proper size of this ratio depends upon the type of industry, the season of the year, and other such factors. The acid-test ratio provides a second, more severe test of adequacy and is obtained by dividing the liquid current assets (total current assets less inventories) by the total current liabilities. This is a more rigorous test due to exclusion of the inventories. Their exclusion is justified since they are in part a fixed capital investment (since to operate at all requires a certain minimum inventory).

Working capital liquidity refers to the proportion of working capital made up of cash and all other assets quickly convertible into cash. In a store, for example, merchandise is carried in inventory until sold; a sale creates an account receivable. Presently, the account is paid, and the cash account is increased accordingly. The length of this cash conversion cycle affects the liquidity of the firm's working capital. The acid-test ratio tests liquidity as well as adequacy of working capital. Industry standard ratios show the proper average inventory turnover rate and the proper average collection period for accounts receivable. This permits an intelligent evaluation of the firm's own turnover rate and collection period. Also, the cash flow cycle of a firm reflects the overall efficiency of its management. Given an accurate knowledge of his firm's cash flow cycle, a small entrepreneur will perceive the impact of scale of operations upon cash requirements, the need to arrange additional financing before cash is exhausted, and the danger of overbuying and overexpansion.

Sound Financial Structure. Efficiently conducted small business operations maintain the soundness of a firm's financial structure. This is essential for continuance of the enterprise. It includes not only a large enough total capital and a satisfactory relationship between debt and equity capital, but also a proper balance among the various classes of assets owned. Of course, profit-making and a strong working capital position contribute to a sound financial structure.

For any given type of business, there is an appropriate amount of total required assets. For example, a restaurant serving 250 customers daily could not efficiently use the same amount of assets as a restaurant of similar quality serving 500 customers daily. If total assets are excessive for the volume of sales, they are not being used effectively and should be reduced in amount. In contrast, insufficiency of assets inevitably imposes financial strains on a firm. Hence, its working capital position may be weak, and it may have trouble meeting all obligations promptly.

To measure the sufficiency of total assets, one can use such ratios as *plant turnover* (which relates fixed assets to sales) and *operating asset turnover* (which compares total operating assets with sales).

The relative proportion of current to fixed assets is also highly important. Some firms have been launched only to discover that nearly all the equity funds were spent for necessary fixed assets, thus leaving an inadequate amount for working capital. The proper amount of investment in fixed assets depends upon the line of business. A soft drink bottler, for example, may have fixed assets equal to 60 percent of tangible net worth, and a grocery wholesaler may have fixed assets amounting to less than 15 percent of tangible net worth. In making comparisons, it is imperative to refer to the standard ratios of firms similar to the one whose financial structure is being analyzed.

It is also possible to evaluate the amounts invested in particular types of assets. Inventory turnover comparisons, as explained in Chapter 23, illustrate the nature of such analyses.

One of the most critical aspects of financial structure is the relationship between borrowed funds and invested capital. If debt is unreasonably large when compared with equity funds, the firm is skating on thin ice. According to the conservative rule of thumb first stated in Chapter 14, two thirds of the total capital in a business should be owner-supplied. In most lines of business, however, the industry standard ratio is somewhat lower. If a comparative analysis indicates that a given firm has an excessive debt, another type of check can be made by comparing interest expense with net profits before taxes. The number of times interest payments are earned provides evidence of the firm's margin of safety in meeting fixed interest charges.

Analysis of Gross Profit Variations

In the analysis of gross profit variations, causes are sought for the difference between actual and expected gross profit. There are four causes which act singly or together to produce this variation in gross profit. These are:

1. Sales price variation.
2. Cost price variation.

3. Sales volume variation.
4. Sales mixture variation.

The first three of these are self-explanatory. The sales mixture variation refers to the difference in gross profit occasioned by a change in the percentage distribution of sales of the various items in the firm's product line. Not all products carry the same percentage of gross profit, and this causes the variation. If product A is expected to provide 50 percent of total volume but actually accounts for only 25 percent of total volume, a significant difference between actual and budgeted gross profits may appear.

The formal techniques for ascertaining the specific amounts of variation are discussed in standard accounting texts. From a practical standpoint, a little thought or informal checking may point clearly to a particular contributing factor without resorting to the more sophisticated techniques.

Standard Cost Variations

Another type of appraisal of current operating results, useful in the small factory, is the analysis of standard cost variations. This type of analysis is limited to plants using a standard cost system.

Since there are three elements to manufacturing cost—namely, material cost, labor cost, and overhead cost—the analysis of standard cost variations requires the evaluation of variations in each of the three areas. The materials variation, in turn, is broken down into materials price and materials quantity variations to help identify the underlying difficulty. Similarly, the total labor cost variation can be broken down into labor rate and labor hours variations. Finally, the overhead cost variations can be subjected to detailed analysis. Standard cost accounting books explain the specific techniques for obtaining such variations.

As in the case of gross profit variation analysis, the manager should investigate sufficiently to discover the underlying cause of significant variations and take the necessary remedial action.

Break-Even Analysis

Another type of study—break-even point analysis—is performed in advance of an accounting year, although it utilizes information presented in earlier financial statements. It is more concerned with the future, however, than with evaluation of past performance.

The objective of break-even analysis is to determine the point at which a firm of given size and cost structure can begin to earn a profit. Figure 20-5 presents a simple break-even chart. The fixed expenses are portrayed as a horizontal section in view of the fact that they do not change with volume of production. The variable expense section slants upward, however, because of the direct fluctuation of variable expenses with output. The distance between the total expense line and the horizontal base line thus represents the combination of

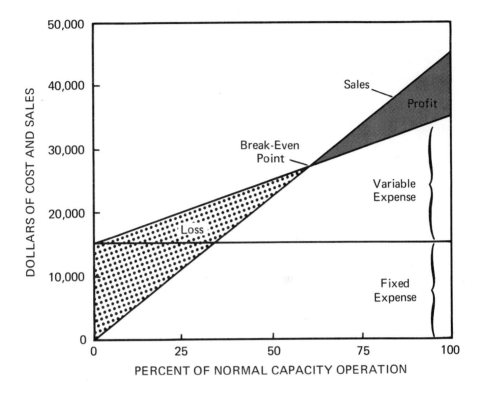

Figure 20-5
BREAK-EVEN CHART

fixed and variable expenses. The distance between the sales and total expense lines reveals the profit or loss position of the company at any level of production. The intersection of the two lines is called the break-even point because sales revenue covers total expenses at this point.

If a firm's break-even point is at too high a percentage of total capacity, it must seek means of reducing this point. Otherwise, a slight drop in output caused by business recession or other factors might be immediately disastrous.

This type of analysis reveals the probable effect on profits of expansion or contraction of volume, starting from any given point. It also shows the level of output required to cover both variable expenses and the fixed expenses of being in business, such as rent, property taxes, interest, and basic utilities. The analysis can be extended to show the percentage of capacity at which earnings will equal interest expense—or the level at which interest and preferred stock dividends can be earned. Still other critical operating points may be established in terms of both dollars and percentages of capacity at which to operate. Standard books on accounting and budgeting, which describe these procedures in detail, should be available.

Accounting Principles and Conventions

In seeking to analyze and interpret statements, a manager must realize that certain principles and accounting conventions govern the preparation of financial statements. For example, conservatism is a principle that guides accountants, and the most conservative method available is the one an accountant will typically choose. Another principle governing the preparation of statements is consistency. This means that a given item on a statement will be handled in the same way every month and every year, so that comparability of the data will be assured. Also, the principle of full disclosure compels the accountant to insist that all liabilities be shown and all material facts presented. This is intended to prevent misleading any investor who might read the firm's statements.

Certain accounting conventions also regulate, in part, the preparation of financial statements. One of these holds that incomes are realized when earned, whether or not received in cash, and that expenses are to be recorded when incurred, whether or not paid out in cash. Again, there is a valuation convention governing the balance sheet valuation of inventory, so as to state it fairly. Similarly, receivables are valued at their cash value less an allowance for possible bad debts, while fixed assets other than land are valued at their depreciated value based on original cost.

THE USE OF REPORTS IN MANAGEMENT CONTROL

In view of their informational purpose, control reports deserve a careful, immediate review by the manager and his assistants. They must appraise the operating results of the past period, search for causes of bad performance, and consider plans for the current and succeeding periods. To be truly effective, reports should be simple and economical of the user's time and effort. If reports show too many details, the user may easily get lost in the forest of figures and be unable to see the significant trees. In addition, reports should be tailored to serve the user's specific purposes and should reach him before the data become obsolete.

Content of Reports

The subject matter of reports varies with the user and the point of view appropriate to his position. Reports for the top manager of a small firm are concerned with such factors as profits, sales, gross margins, costs of marketing, income taxes, and return on investment. At the level of the shop supervisor, the control reports touch upon such subjects as output of individual operators and work groups, earnings of shop personnel, and total production. Still other reports of interest to a shop supervisor deal with number of defectives produced, amount and cost of rework, materials usage and waste, and number of labor hours used.

Nature of Reports

Reports may include graphic presentations which spotlight important data—such as significant cost and performance variances. It is said that a picture is worth ten thousand words. So far as general impressions and emphasis on significant figures are concerned, this is correct. Supporting tables are necessary, of course, in order to give the details of operating results needed for a full explanation of the data charted.

It is possible to view managerial reports as the end result or output of the management information system. And this point of view throws some additional light on the general nature of reports. If the information system is computerized, the reports can reach the manager in time to be of maximum usefulness.

 Summary

1. Good record keeping is characteristic of most successful businesses, while inadequate records are typical of firms that fail. This is true, at least in part, because good records are essential for effective control of operating results.

2. Automatic data processing may be used to improve record keeping in small business. Data processing centers provide computer services to small firms on a fee basis, thus making unnecessary the purchase or rental of a computer.

3. The use of an experienced accountant or systems analyst is desirable in devising a system that will function effectively at minimum cost.

4. Accounting records are designed to provide information on assets, liabilities, net worth, sales, expenses, and profits. To safeguard assets and prevent errors, the accounting system should provide for effective internal check. The accounting records make possible the construction of various types of financial statements covering the firm's operations and operating results.

5. There are numerous statistical nonaccounting records used in a typical small firm that are as important as those of a financial nature.

6. How long records should be retained depends upon the appraised future need for them, together with legal requirements affecting their disposal. Those retained require proper physical protection, the nature of which depends upon the value of the given records.

7. Ratio analysis of financial statements involves the determination of relationships among different financial figures. Present ratios may be compared with those of earlier periods and with the appropriate industry standard ratios. Such comparisons reveal trends in performance and measure managerial efficiency.

8. Ratio analysis also makes possible the evaluation of a firm's earning power, working capital position, and current financial structure.

9. Some of the approaches in interpretation of financial statements include analysis of gross profit variation, analysis of standard cost variations, and break-even analysis. In statement analysis, it is important to realize that certain accounting principles and conventions govern their preparation.

10. It is the function of reports to provide management with essential information for guidance of decisions on current and future action. To achieve their objective, they must be kept simple, be tailored to the user's needs, and conserve his time. They should also reach the decision maker promptly. Graphic presentation in reports has the advantage of spotlighting such important figures as significant cost or performance variances.

Discussion Questions

1. Many small firms that have failed have kept poor records. Did such failures occur because of the poor records and the consequent inadequate reports to management, or did the poor records result from inefficiency preexisting in management? Explain.

2. What records are essential for the successful operation of a small retail store? As the firm grows, will the volume of record keeping increase also? Why?

3. Even miniature electronic computers are costly to buy or lease. Since this is a fact, how can a small firm use automatic data processing? If it does set up a computerized system, what is the principal advantage obtained? Explain.

4. What is the relationship between systems design and the physical equipment used by a business?

5. How long should a small firm retain payroll and credit records? What about patent records or completed government contracts or the owner's will? And how should retained records be cared for and stored?

6. What is internal check? Is it necessary in very small firms? Just how might it be used in office operations? In factory operations?

7. What advantages accrue to the small entrepreneur from using a public accounting firm or computer service center for maintaining all the firm's accounting records. Which of these outside services would you favor? Why?

8. Define operating profit, gross profit, and net profit. To which of these does the income tax apply (assuming the small firm is incorporated)?

9. Explain the nature and purpose of each of the following financial statements of a business: (a) balance sheet, (b) income statement, (c) funds statement, and (d) cost of goods manufactured statement. What is the relationship between the income statement and the funds statement? Between the income statement and the balance sheet?

10. Discuss concisely the objectives of ratio analysis of a firm's financial statements, with respect to profit, working capital position, and general financial soundness of the concern. What standard of reference, if any, would be utilized in each case? How would the outcomes of the analysis be interpreted? Under what conditions would the manager need to take corrective action?

11. If a jewelry store finds sales volume up 10 percent, cost of merchandise up by 13 percent, and sales prices up 6 percent, what would be the overall effect on gross profit? Would your answer change if you also knew that both sales price and volume

increases applied totally to the 50 percent of the items having the largest markup, while item cost increases were uniform for all goods purchased and sold? Assume that group markups average 60 and 40 percent respectively.

12. Show graphically the difference between the break-even points of firms that have 80 percent vari-able costs and firms that have 20 percent variable costs. Explain why this difference appears.

13. Would it ever be desirable to operate a business at a sales volume below the break-even point volume? Explain.

14. Explain the nature, content, proper timing, and management use of management reports. Are they "means" or "ends?"

21

Business Forecasting and Budgeting

All too often, small business management tends to neglect financial planning and control; instead, it devotes its full time and attention to operating functions such as production and sales. Experience has shown, however, that a successful business depends upon more than producing at capacity and employing a persuasive sales force. It also needs to have effective control over sales revenue, business expenses, and inventories. Thus, forecasting and budgeting, which are the primary tools for management planning and control, will be considered in this chapter.

BUSINESS FORECASTING

Business forecasting refers to prediction of the course of business activity in the future from the facts currently known. Hence, forecasting permits the development of a management strategy based on the probabilities involved in the various courses of action open to management. Action based upon some understanding of the future is clearly preferable to a course of action selected blindly without regard for future prospects.

Need for Business Forecasting

Forecasting attempts to peer into the future and ascertain the future course of general business activity and of company sales. A knowledge of the trend of company sales in the future is essential to effective budgeting of next year's operations. As will be noted later in the chapter, the forecast of sales is the cornerstone of effective budgeting, which helps to integrate plans for overall, divisional, and departmental operations during the next period. Business plans must all hang together and be aimed at a common objective.

It is not only next year's business plans that require effective forecasting, however, because many business executives realize how much a knowledge of business trends contributes to more effective long-range planning. Some companies formulate plans extending 5, 10, or even 20 years into the future. And they view this as a serious matter, not merely as an academic exercise, because considerable time and money are invested in the development of long-range forecasts.

Long-range planning is concerned with prospects for company growth. The business outlook clearly affects decisions concerning expansion or replacement of fixed assets. A major investment can be justified and proved profitable only if the future volume of sales permits full use and amortization of that investment. Thus, effective forecasting enables a firm to commit its resources with maximum assurance of long-range profitable operations.

Nature of Forecasting Methods

Business forecasting requires a blend of scientific analysis and business judgment. Statistical techniques[1] are primary tools for economic forecasters, but few are willing to accept their verdict without qualification or interpretation. The limitations of quantitative analysis are too great and the uncertainties too numerous to permit complete confidence in even the most refined approaches. A consumer's buying intentions may be surveyed, for example, but no one can be sure of his future behavior until it occurs. As a result, it is unreasonable to expect 100 percent accuracy in such predictions about the future. The predictions are statements of probabilities and are based upon factual information which is seldom complete or beyond question. The forecast is no substitute for judgment, but it is an important tool or aid to judgment in managerial decisions involving future periods.

The type of information used and procedures for forecasting differ somewhat depending upon the nature of the prediction. Forecasting economic conditions for the coming year presents a different problem from predicting market growth for a particular product or service during the next 20 years. Population growth is a factor which would have little import for a short-run economic forecast, but it is very useful in long-range projections of market size.

In forecasting the trend of general business conditions, the forecaster typically watches quite closely a number of business indicators as business barometers. Some examples of these important business indicators are:

1. Index of industrial production.
2. Index of retail sales.
3. Cost of living index.
4. Index of wholesale prices.
5. Index of corporation profits.
6. Number of business failures.
7. Indexes of imports and exports into and from the United States.
8. Index of freight car loadings.
9. Index of bank debits outside New York City.
10. Index of cash farm income.
11. Estimated gross national product.
12. Index of common stock prices.
13. Index of leading business indicators.

Charts showing monthly or quarterly changes in these important indexes can be maintained to provide a current picture of business conditions and

---

[1] The specific statistical techniques involved in business forecasting cannot be explored in detail in a volume of this type. The reader is referred to standard textbooks on business statistics for such details.

trends. Such published indexes are reliable and valid in that they are consistent in performance and measure accurately that which they purport to measure. Their validity in accurately predicting business conditions for a particular firm is a different matter, of course; only a study of the firm's operating results can determine an index's validity for this purpose. Some of these indexes are sensitive to slight changes in business activity level; others are relatively stable, reflecting only major changes in business conditions. Still others possess a time lead of several months over the turning points in general business activity.

Short-Range vs. Long-Range Forecasting

Because forecasting is expensive and time consuming, a firm must determine which forecasts are most essential. Basically, there is need to forecast future operations at short range and over the long term for perhaps the next 10 or 15 years.

The short-range forecast is principally concerned with accurately forecasting sales to facilitate the construction and revision of the firm's budget. Such sales forecasting involves the determination of industry sales potential and of company share of the market in the light of past sales experience. One caution must be expressed. Sales forecasting is difficult indeed unless preceded by effective general business level forecasting and price forecasting. Moreover, sales forecasting should be preceded by long-range anticipation of the needs of the market.

Long-range forecasting is required for prediction of company growth and determination of fixed asset needs both for expansion and replacement purposes. A single year's results, reflected in financial statements, is actually but a page from business history. This is why the small business needs long-range business forecasting. In undertaking such forecasting, it is necessary to allow for population change over the years projected and for variations (typically upward in the United States) in the standard of living.

Limitation on Forecasting in Small Firms

Uncertainties concerning the future provide risks for small firms as well as for large ones. Business forecasting, therefore, is theoretically as essential and valuable for small business as for large business. For a number of practical reasons, however, it is not and cannot be used as much or as successfully by the small firm as by the large company.

One limitation is found in the inability of the typical independent businessman to use or to appreciate the methods of quantitative analysis. Unfortunately it is very unlikely that he has a forecaster on his payroll. To overcome this deficiency, some firms attempt to keep in close touch with industry trends through contacts with their trade association. The trade association is frequently better qualified from the standpoint of professional staff members to engage in business forecasting. Trade publications provide another source of information about business trends. Other publications and economic newsletters are also used by private business firms to provide current information of this kind. Examples of these include the *Kiplinger Washington Letter, Business Week,* and *The Wall Street Journal*. Government publications such as *Survey of Current Business, Federal Reserve Bulletin,* and *Monthly Labor*

Review are also of interest in a general way. Then there is the possibility of subscribing to professional forecasting services which provide forecasts of general business conditions or specific forecasts for given industries.

In the final analysis, an independent businessman must make his own forecast. He must accept or reject the information provided by professional forecasters, published indexes, or models, and decide what he will do in his own business. The business future of any firm is uncertain, but the businessman can avail himself of all possible information both in budgeting for the following year and in long-range planning. The more complete and reliable his information, the better his judgments and forecasts.

BUDGETING

A *budget* for a business enterprise is an overall financial plan which embodies its anticipated income and expense over a definite period of time. The typical budget period is one year, and this annual budget is in turn broken down by months or by quarters. When a business is departmentalized, it usually has a master budget which covers the whole enterprise, as well as departmental budgets which constitute the component parts of the master budget. The departmental budgets include those for sales, production, purchases, and so on. The master budget yields financial statements covering the expected operating results and shows the impact of operations upon the firm's asset values and equity interests. These financial statements typically include the budgeted balance sheet, the budgeted income statement, and the budgeted funds statement.

Basic Factors in Budgetary Control

An entrepreneur must predetermine expected normal performance in order to establish performance standards. These are required for the firm and for its various divisions and departments. Performance standards make possible the evaluation of operating results. To be functional for such evaluations, the standards must be reasonable and attainable in the light of expected business conditions. The only alternative is the creation of ideal standards, envisioning optimum operating conditions. But ideal standards would be difficult to attain because actual business conditions are seldom ideal. Hence, ideal standards must be rejected in favor of expected attainable performance.

Setting Cost and Performance Standards. In view of the central role of standards in budgeting, attention is directed at this point to the process of constructing cost and performance standards. These should be developed for the several areas of production, distribution, and general management.

Manufacturing Standards. In manufacturing, physical standards pertain to specifications covering products and raw materials, to manufacturing methods, and to equipment utilized. Product designs are translated into product tolerances on specific quality variables. Materials consumption standards specify the amount and kind of materials required per unit of finished product. Since they regulate both the quality and quantity of material used, such standards affect budgeted cost. Of course, the dollar value of materials budgeted also depends upon the budgeted unit cost prices for each kind of material. These are the expected future prices—which reflect current prices paid and anticipated economic changes in the business cycle and the price level.

Physical standards for processing are possible also. Underlying their establishment are methods, motion, and time studies, which objectively determine the best method of processing. The extent to which a given firm should use these refined techniques in setting processing standards depends upon the degree of product standardization, the repetitive nature of production, and other such factors. Processing standards cover machines and tooling to be used, the handling system, workplace layout and work methods, and the operator's motion sequence. All such standards affect the budgeted cost of labor by specifying the nature of its application. That is, they make possible the determination of the total standard hours of labor necessary to achieve the budgeted production on each shop operation. But the dollar cost budgeted for labor also depends upon the standard hourly rates paid to the machine operators on the various processing operations. These pay rates should be set in accordance with the principles of job evaluation to assure fairness, compatibility, and accuracy of standard labor costs.

Manufacturing overhead expenses—for example, depreciation, property taxes, and utility costs—are less susceptible to the setting of objective standards. But the proper amounts for many such items can be determined in the light of past experience and of the percentage of capacity operation expected. The amount of indirect labor, for example, may be specified as a percentage of the budgeted direct labor hours.

Standards in Selling and Administration. In the area of distribution and administration, standards of cost and performance are similarly required. For various lines of business, Dun and Bradstreet, Inc., the firm's trade association, and other agencies compile data on various expense items; these show average industry expenses as a percentage of net sales. Industry standard ratios and the firm's own past experience can be used to predetermine selling and administrative expense standards which are reasonably accurate and capable of attainment.

Most lines of business have well-established expense classification systems. It is true, of course, that too many of these systems record expenses by kinds rather than by functions. Rent is a kind of expense; so is warehousing labor in the finished goods stock room; whereas, warehousing, credit and collections, and order-filling in the stock room are examples of functions. Expenses can be controlled better by function than by kind, which argues in favor of functional expense classification.[2]

Certain rules for expense classification in the setting of selling and administrative expense standardards might be noted. First of all, the units of measurement used must be objective and clear-cut. For example, the unit of measure for order-procurement by a salesman might be the dollars spent per sales call made. Secondly, a separate classification should be made for each item of expense, with accumulation of expenses in terms of functional categories. Finally, expense classification should not be carried too far—that is, to the point where each minute kind of expense is identified and the amount separately accumulated regardless of its importance. A miscellaneous classification could be established for these minor expenses.

---

[2] See pages 373-374 for a discussion of functional expense classification.

Variables in Setting Standards. In the area of production, the volume of production is obviously a major factor affecting cost. Frequently, however, the budget is constructed as though volume were the sole determinant of cost variation. It is not. For example, the introduction of new products would be a major source of cost variation for the accounting period in which those new products were introduced. Another example is found in variation in the size of production orders.

Still other cost variation causing variables in a production situation are (1) materials quality variation, (2) rate of labor turnover, (3) varying labor efficiency, and (4) changes in handling or processing equipment. Similarly, in the area of distribution, such factors as changes in the product mixture of sales, changes in sales prices, changes in intensity of competition, entry into new territories, and deletion of old territories, among others, all are important. Moreover, in establishing administrative expense standards, many so-called fixed expenses are fixed only for a given period of time. With a sufficient change in sales and production volume and/or mixture, they must be varied upward or downward to a new fixed level.

Thus, in the final analysis, cost and performance standards must be set as objectively as possible in the light of expected conditions and in the light of existing cost variables.

Modern Statistical Techniques. Finally, attention should be called to the possibilities inherent in statistical analysis, linear and dynamic programming, and operations research. These tools are useful in both manufacturing and distribution areas. In marketing, they provide a means of utilizing past experience and expectation data to arrive at the ideal sales volume, price, and mixture combination. In the factory, they may be utilized to set up an ideal production program, with optimum inventories. Obviously, their utilization will improve the cost and performance standards incorporated in the budget. The fact that small business management lacks sufficient training in mathematics to understand these methods is a deterrent to their use, but alert managers can resort to consulting firms for assistance in the use of such techniques.

Prompt Reporting of Actual Versus Standard. Cost and performance standards are useless in themselves. Their effective use requires the prompt reporting of actual results together with variations between these results and those anticipated. Such reports must be issued as soon as possible after the close of a budget period.

While it is of interest to observe differences between actual and standard on all types of expenses, the real benefit derives from knowing the significant variations between actual and standard performance on controllable cost items. Concentration upon insignificant or uncontrollable cost variations is a waste of time. Moreover, such discrepancies may well reflect inaccuracy of the standard itself rather than management inefficiency. Prompt, accurate reporting to management on actual versus standard results should stress controllable costs.

Investigating Cost and Performance Variances. The third element in budgetary control is the immediate investigation of all significant favorable and unfavorable cost and performance variances that are reported. One objective in so doing is to locate and eliminate, if possible, the causes of unfavorable performance. Occasionally it is management itself which is at fault for failing to meet budgeted standards. And, sometimes, investigation reveals that standards were unrealistic or that the cause of bad performance is beyond management's control.

Significant favorable performance and cost variances noted should also be investigated. Such analyses may reveal loose standards, changed external conditions, or superior performance. If unusually good performance is noted, it may be possible to apply the effective methods in other sectors of the organization. Certainly, action should be taken to continue their use wherever possible.

Taking Management Action. Management action, when necessary, should be taken promptly to achieve correction of significant adverse variations between the budget and actual operating results. Delay is intolerable. Putting off action for several weeks or months allows the unfavorable conditions to continue, and this causes losses or reduced profits for such additional time periods.

An unfavorable variance is similar to a flashing red light. Something more than observation of the warning is required. Hence, prompt, decisive, effective, remedial action should be added to the other elements of budgetary control for optimization of business results. Concentration upon the significant variations from anticipated results is one form of "management by exception."

Revising the Budget During the Budget Year. Business operation is always full of uncertainties with the result that actual operations seldom correspond exactly, and sometimes not even closely, to the budgeted operating level. A need for budget revision during the budget year consequently arises. For example, the manufacturer budgets a given product mixture and volume for sales. If actual sales do not conform thereto in total amount and in product mixture, he must revise the budgeted sales and the corresponding expense budgets. Even if sales volume is accurately predicted in total, a different mixture may require budget revision. Moreover, to obtain sales in a competitive market, anticipated prices may have to be changed. This, too, may occasion a need for budget revision.

In the retail or wholesale establishment, changes in advertising and sales promotion emphasis, changes in style trends, changes in customer clientele, and other such factors lead to a similar need for budget revision. Of course, the use of a flexible budget would eliminate the need for change due solely to changes in total sales volume. But it might not allow for sales mixture change or various other types of change.

Unless needed budget changes are made, the periodic performance reports comparing results with budget standards will be misleading and make it difficult to attain operating control. This is why budget revision to fit current sales and other conditions is always a pressing problem. Operating control requires accuracy in budget standards so that only truly significant discrepancies are selected for exploration and action. Only when accurate budgets are compared with actual results and significant discrepancies are noted and investigated can management take remedial action to prevent recurrence of unprofitable conditions or to perpetuate favorable results.

Budgetary Control Deficiencies Common in Small Businesses

Even though budgets are designed to facilitate effective management, they sometimes fail to reach this objective for several reasons. One reason for unsatisfactory budgetary performance is the inaccurate determination of budget standards. Comparisons of actual results with budgeted amounts can then mislead management into the belief that all is well when, as a matter of fact, costs are uncontrolled and performance is inefficient.

A second common defect in the operation of a budgetary control system is failure to revise the budget as required. For example, the budget may be initially established for operation at 80 percent of capacity, but sales may permit only a 70 percent operating level. Expenses should vary accordingly. Similarly, changes in sales mixture for the whole line of products, in manufacturing methods, or in external business conditions may introduce distortions into the original budget. Failure to revise the budget when necessary makes it inaccurate as a yardstick for evaluating operating performance.

Another weakness of budgetary administration is the failure to include all key business activities in the budget. For example, one might budget the various expenses and the cash position but fail to budget sales and production. Control of expenses and cash position alone is not enough. All business activities must be incorporated in the budget if desired overall results are to be attained.

The tardy submission of control reports to designated recipients constitutes still another difficulty in budgetary control. Promptly provided information on operating performance makes possible management action to remedy the situation during the ensuing period. But if the budget reports are delayed more than a month in preparation, they are typically useless as guides to remedial action. In small firms, budgetary control reports are often late in arriving in the hands of the responsible officers or supervisors. Hence, for them, this difficulty is particularly acute.

Again, the manager and his subordinates sometimes find control reports difficult to interpret. Thus, they may fail to detect and act on controllable cost items with significant variances between actual and budget.

The top manager fails sometimes, also, to convince subordinates of the value of the budgetary control system. The budget must have the full support of top management. Two-way lines of communication must be maintained, factors indicating a need for revision of the budget must be promptly reported, and budget changes must be communicated promptly to subordinates. Also, management subordinates should be consulted when preparing the budget so that they will feel it is theirs rather than something imposed upon them by "the boss." It is likely that the budget's quality will be improved with their assistance.

Preparation of Budgets

Even in a small firm, the preparation of an annual budget is not a one-man job, nor is it one which is accomplished quickly. Some weeks or months of effort will be required. The small manufacturer, for example, would need to meet with his heads of departments frequently before the amounts and standards to be incorporated in the budget can be determined. Then the budget must be broken down by months. Finally, it must be typed, with copies for distribution to the department heads, each of whom will also have reviewed and agreed in advance to the annual and monthly figures.

Sales Budget. In view of the fact that most business activities must be geared to the level of expected sales, it is customary to begin with the establishment of the sales budget which serves as the cornerstone of the overall budget. The sales budget must be as nearly accurate as care and good judgment can make it because all of the other segmental budgets depend on the sales budget. Hence, careful attention is given to current economic factors and to important business barometers, such as the gross national product, the level of industrial production, wholesale price level, level of employment, level of total inventories, and level of consumer spending. Moreover, consideration should be given to the relative degree of price stability, the company's productive capacity and present percentage of capacity utilized, together with the current level of and probable changes in government spending.

Several methods of forecasting sales may be used in arriving at the final sales budget. One method is based upon market analysis of the various sales territories to discover the industry sales potential for the company's products. Coupled with a knowledge, based on experience, of the company's share of the market, this yields one estimate of possible sales. Still another approach is to ask each salesman to estimate possible sales for his territory. Since salesmen are often overly optimistic in anticipation of future sales, it is sometimes necessary to scale down such estimates. A third procedure is to compute the sales trend of the company and of the industry, respectively, and then extrapolate each forward one year. The industry trend, multiplied by the company's known percentage of total industry sales, yields one trend estimate of the company's anticipated sales for the next following year. The company's own sales trend, as projected for the following year, constitutes a second trend estimate of the company's expected sales. These two estimates should be fairly close in amounts projected, and together they comprise a trend estimate or forecast of next year's sales.

A fourth procedure is to make a detailed study of the preceding year's sales and a less detailed study of the last five years' sales of the company, by products and in total. Still another possibility is to correlate industry sales by months for past years with some business factor such as disposable personal income. Properly time lagged, one or more months, such a procedure yields a regression equation which will estimate industry sales that number of months in advance. Again, knowing the firm's share of the market makes possible an estimate of future company sales. Finally, as noted earlier, linear programming may be utilized to determine the optimum sales mixture.

Careful consideration of these various forecasts leads to a final sales forecast which is officially adopted for the total product line and for each product. Sales data for the year are typically broken down to monthly sales figures by application of the firm's seasonal sales indexes and then to territory quotas. When both units and dollars of sales per month are known, thus, the sales budget is finally complete.

Production Budget. The second budget is to be prepared is the production budget. This is tied closely to sales budgeted on the one hand and to finished goods inventory level planned on the other.[3] Given nonseasonal production, the monthly production will be exactly one twelfth of the annual budgeted production. If the sales pattern has seasonal fluctuations and if the starting actual inventory is large enough, planned inventory levels may be such as to permit absorption of all of the seasonal variations, thus allowing monthly production budgeted still to be exactly one twelfth of the budgeted annual production. If this is impractical or undesirable, the budgeted production for each of the respective months in the year may be obtained by multiplying one twelfth of the annual budgeted production by the respective monthly seasonal index ratios. Monthly ending inventories will still have to be planned, much as before. In any event, production must provide sufficient finished units to meet sales requirements, taking into consideration any planned inventory changes by months and for the year.

Production must be budgeted thus for each product in the line, separately. When the total monthly production in units has been determined for all products, the production budget is complete.

Materials Budget. The materials budget specifies by months the amounts of each kind of material required to meet production schedules. It must be noted, however, that the budgeted monthly production for each kind of product is not equal to the units to be placed in process for those months because of the planned work-in-process inventory variation. Hence, units to be produced must first of all be translated into units to be placed in process.[4] Once the units of each product to be placed in process monthly have been determined, it is possible to estimate the units of each kind of raw materials required. In determining materials requirements, it is necessary to predetermine the standard quantities of each kind of raw material necessary to process one unit of final product. Each such materials consumption standard is then multiplied by the number of units to be placed in process to obtain the number of units of the given kind of raw materials required. This computation is necessary for each kind of raw material and for each kind of final product. When the units of raw materials of each kind required for each month's production have thus been ascertained, the materials budget is complete.

Purchases Budget. Differences between monthly materials requirements and materials available in the storeroom will necessitate a purchases budget. The formula for determining the units of each kind of raw materials to be purchased is: units of material required for production plus planned ending raw materials inventory minus expected starting materials inventory. Obviously this computation must be made for each kind of raw material, separately, for each month. Annual purchases in units for each kind of material are then obtained by summation of the monthly figures. In turn, the budgeted purchases, in units, for

---

[3] The formula for units budgeted to be produced during the year is:

$$\text{Budgeted production} = \text{Budget sales} - \text{Starting finished goods inventory}$$
$$\text{expected} + \text{Ending finished goods inventory planned}$$

[4] The following formula must be utilized for monthly budgeted production for each of the products in the line to translate same into units to be placed in process:

$$\text{Units to be placed in process} = \text{Units to be produced, as budgeted} - \text{Units in expected starting inventory in process} + \text{Units in planned ending inventory in process}$$

any one kind of material may be multiplied by the standard price per unit of that kind of material to arrive at the dollar investment in purchases for that kind of material. This computation is required for each kind of material for each month. Each month's purchases budget, measured in dollars, may be obtained by summation of the dollar products so obtained for each kind of material for each given month. Summation of the monthly purchases in dollars will give the annual purchases budget.

Direct Labor Budget. In the direct labor budget, estimates are presented of direct labor to be used in production during the coming 12 months. If time and motion studies for each labor operations have been utilized, they will have prescribed a standard motion sequence and a standard rate of output per hour. Budgeted production divided by standard output rate per hour yields standard hours of direct labor. If time study has not been used, the labor estimate must be made on the basis of past experience. This computation of direct labor hours is required separately for each product in the line and for each labor operation. When all these computations are completed, summation yields the budgeted direct labor hours, by departments and for the plant, by months and for the year. Total hours for each operation times the standard hourly rate yields the standard labor cost.[5] Summed for all operations, one arrives at the total labor cost in dollars. This is done for each month and for the whole year, with department and plant totals for each.

Manufacturing Expense Budget. Manufacturing expense is also known as "burden" or "factory overhead." One of the most important items in the manufacturing expense budget is indirect labor. Computation of indirect labor expense requires a determination of the desired number of such personnel as stores clerks, stock and shipping clerks, model makers, shop supervisors, timekeepers, inspectors, mechanics, boiler room operators, night watchmen, and office clerks, most of whom typically are on straight salary. If so, their monthly salaries can be entered at once on the burden budget schedule.

For the other nonsalaried indirect labor operators, it is necessary to estimate the hours which the storeroom, stock room, shipping room, inspectors, and others will work. Or, approved ratios to direct labor hours, based on past experience, may be multiplied by budgeted direct labor hours to obtain budgeted indirect labor hours. Both job hour estimates may be multiplied separately by the standard hourly rates of pay to yield two cost estimates. The two must then be resolved into a final budget cost figure. With direct and indirect labor costs both known, thus, the employer's social security tax, unemployment compensation tax, and workmen's compensation premium payments may be computed next and entered on the burden budget schedule.

Property taxes are budgeted at the latest year's actual taxes, modified by any expected changes in property valuations or tax rates. Fire and insurance premiums are a matter of record or may be obtained by consulting one's insurance agent. Other indirect expenses typically included are building depreciation, machine depreciation, repairs, tools and fixtures, factory supplies, power and light, freight and express, models and patterns, rework, blueprints, and fuel and water, among many others. Each factory expense must be carefully and separately budgeted, by months and for the year.

---

[5] This agrees with the procedure discussed in the earlier section on setting of manufacturing standards, but here yields the labor budget in dollars, whereas the earlier discussion was concerned with the setting of fair standards.

Cost of Goods Manufactured and Sold Budget. In the materials budget schedule, the required units of material for the product to be started in process each month were specified. The dollar value, however, was not previously obtained. Hence, the number of units of material required for production each month must be multiplied by the standard price per unit for the particular kind of material. When this calculation is completed for the various products and materials, they may be added to give the monthly dollar cost of materials expected to be requisitioned for production. (This is not the same as the dollar value of materials to be purchased each month.) The dollar value of materials requisitioned each month may be added to get the total for the year. From the earlier budget schedules, the dollar value of direct labor hours and manufacturing expenses are known. The cost of materials, added to that for direct labor and manufacturing expense, yields the monthly and yearly cost of goods manufactured—after proper adjustment for the variation in expected starting inventory in process and planned ending inventory.

For balance sheet purposes, the budget-maker should now cost the respective month-ending inventories of each kind of raw material, totaling them to get the total dollar value of the month-ending inventories of raw material. The month-ending work-in-process and finished goods inventories should be similarly costed, in turn.

The value of the starting finished goods inventory is added to the monthly cost of goods manufactured. This yields a subtotal from which the month-ending finished goods inventory is deducted to find the budgeted cost of goods sold for the month. This will be done for each month and for the year. The ending inventories for the final month of the year will be the year-ending inventories as well.

This phase of budgeting culminates in monthly and yearly statements of the cost of goods manufactured and the cost of goods sold. These figures are required for preparation of the budgeted income statements.

Selling and Administrative Expense Budgets. After the manufacturing budgets have been completed, bugets for the selling and general administrative expenses of the firm should be separately prepared. Both of these normally require monthly breakdowns as well as an annual total. Salaries of administrative and clerical personnel and pertinent payroll taxes are entered on the administrative expense schedule. Other expense items, such as office supplies, contributions, telephone and telegraph, depreciation of office equipment, and other office administrative expenses, are included also to get the total budgeted amount for administrative expense.

The selling expense budget covers sales salaries and commissions, travel expense, sales promotion and advertising, and the like. The amounts budgeted tend to vary, however, with business volume to a greater extent than those for administrative expenses. For example, with constant prices, greater expenditures for both advertising and personal selling are normally required to achieve a higher level of sales.

Capital Expenditures Budget. Any type of business which utilizes physical assets must plan expenditures for such facilities. Such planning was considered in detail in Chapter 19. Hence, a few brief reminders will suffice at this point.

1. The most direct approach to budgeting of capital expenditures is to analyze plant and equipment needs. It is also possible to utilize the tools of statistical analysis to explore the relationships between fixed assets and sales.

2. If expansion is contemplated or if worn equipment must be replaced, purchase contracts should be initiated only as consistent with the firm's ability to meet maturing obligations. Acquisitions must not deplete working capital. A firm with adequate total assets could easily become financially embarrassed by committing too much of its total capital to long-term investment in facilities.
3. Fixed assets acquired by increasing the long-term debt also bear watching, to make sure a proper balance is preserved between creditor-supplied and owner-supplied capital.
4. Each year's cash and other budgets must allow for settlement or refunding of long-term debt maturities, as well as for interest payments.

Capital expenditures, therefore, require careful financial planning for at least ten years in advance, with only the first year's planned outlays included in the coming year's budget. The segmental budget chiefly affected is the cash budget, although the overall budget and the budgeted financial statements are also affected.

Accounts Receivable and Cash Budgets. The expected[6] starting balance of accounts receivable is entered as the beginning item on the January accounts receivable budget. Credit sales of the month (the normal fraction of total budgeted sales) are then recorded. Collections from receivables must also be forecast and entered,[7] and the ending balance is then determined. This process is repeated to get each of the other eleven monthly budgets.

Collections from accounts receivable are also entered on the cash receipts and disbursements budget schedule. Its starting point is the expected January 1 cash balance, to which collections on accounts and other budgeted cash receipts (duly forecast and itemized separately) are added to get the total additions to cash for the period. Then disbursements are budgeted and listed by kinds (with separate, detailed supporting schedules for the month prepared for accounts payable, payrolls, taxes, dividends, machines, tools and fixtures, supplies, insurance, fuel, contributions, traveling expense, repairs, and the like)[8] yielding a total disbursement figure. In this way, the ending cash balance is easily forecast.[9] This process is repeated for each month of the year.

Budgeted Financial Statements. The information for the budgeted income statement comes from the earlier budget schedules. It is constructed like any income statement except that both income and expense items are estimates derived from the schedules discussed above. An estimated balance sheet is also prepared and reflects the net results of operations expected. A final statement, the funds statement, shows the expected sources and applications of working capital during the budget year. Each is prepared monthly and yearly.

---

[6] The word "expected" is required here, as in several earlier cases, because at the time of budget preparation the starting balance is itself still unknown. Budgets typically are prepared in October, November, and early December for the following calendar year.

[7] Losses on bad debts must also be budgeted as expenses, monthly, via aging of accounts receivable and past experience, with offsetting credits to the Reserve for Bad Debts (deducted from Accounts Receivable on the budget balance sheet to evaluate its current worth).

[8] Some of these will have appeared in offset form on manufacturing or other expenses schedules, the labor budget, or elsewhere.

[9] Working capital loans required from one's bank will be identified as required during the month if there is a negative ending cash balance. They and their scheduled repayments (as disbursements) must then be incorporated in a revised cash budget for this month and in the budgets for the months involving the repayments.

Construction of the budgeted financial statements is facilitated by preparation of two work sheets. The first of these supports the preparation of the budgeted income statement and balance sheet. Its first two columns will be the starting trial balance for the budget year, as forecast at the budget-building date for the various accounts. The various budget schedule estimates will be entered in the second pair of columns, in lieu of operating data. The income statement items will appear in the third pair of columns, and the balance sheet account balances will appear in the fourth pair of columns, with the third and fourth pairs of columns balanced by the net profit budgeted. The second work sheet is that supporting the funds statement. Its preparation is so technical that the reader is referred to standard accounting textbooks covering this subject. The work of budget preparation is now complete on the part of the budget builder.

Flexible Budgets

As an alternative to the "static" budget procedure described above, it is possible to utilize a "flexible" budget plan. The latter entails a series of monthly budgets for each of several volume levels —for example, 50 percent, 60 percent, 70 percent, 80 percent, 90 percent, 100 percent, 110 percent, and 120 percent of normal capacity. Monthly normal capacity equals one twelfth of the average annual sales, in units, attained over a complete business cycle. Physical capacity of a plant typically is about 120 percent of normal capacity, which is why we stop at 120 percent. For each such level, a master budget and supporting budget schedules are prepared as in the case of the static budget. Data in units must be translated into dollar data. For any level, the annual budget is 12 times the monthly budget at that level. Seasonality of sales and production, if any, is ignored, except in selecting the appropriate budget level for each month.

One weakness in flexible budgeting lies in the fact that it presumes that volume change is the only cost-differentiating factor acting on a budget. This is untrue, as has already been noted.

Evaluation and Initial Acceptance of the Budget

Following preparation of the budget, it should be evaluated by the use of key statement ratios. These were enumerated in Chapter 20 and are discussed in detail in accounting and statement analysis textbooks. Such ratios evaluate estimated working capital position, profit expectancy, and ownership position, among other aspects of the overall financial condition of the firm.

If the ratio analysis indicates that the budgeted operations will produce unsatisfactory results, revision of the budget must be undertaken at once. But this revision must still be predicated upon reasonable expectation for next year's operations. If undertaken, it will proceed as the original budget preparation did, leading once more to budgeted financial statements (with supporting schedules) and to ratio analysis of these statements.

When the ratio analysis indicates that the budgeted operations will produce satisfactory results, whether on first, second, or still later trials, the budget may be considered completed.[10] Copies can then be prepared and issued to all persons concerned.

---

[10] Successive revisions may still indicate unsatisfactory profits, or even losses—and the entrepreneur, in the end, may be forced to accept unsatisfactory results as the best possible under the governing economic conditions.

CONTROL AND REDUCTION OF EXPENSES

The budget, when properly used, is perhaps the most effective tool in controlling expense. By providing a set of standards, or yardsticks, for expenses of each kind, the budget points up overspending or underspending. It can be seen, thus, that the budget and expense control are interrelated—that is, the budget is the cornerstone for expense control. In understanding the possibilities for controlling expenses, either by budget or otherwise, it is essential to examine several concepts pertaining to expense, its classification, and its control.

Classifications of Business Expenses

It is customary to divide business expenses into such categories as factory overhead expense, selling expense, and general administrative expense. Within each of these expense categories, there are several other classifications of expenses possible.

Actual vs. Imputed Expense. One additional expense classification is that of actual expense versus imputed expense. *Actual expenses* are those that actually accrue and require cash outlays. *Imputed expenses*, on the other hand, do not exist in the sense that they can be entered on the books of account and appear on the income statement. Consider, as an example, the interest on the owner's investment in a business. If he had invested the money in the stocks or bonds of other corporations or in government bonds, he would have received an income in the form of dividends or interest. The theory of imputing the expense of interest on the owner's investment lies in the fact that an income which could have been received from another source is lost if the money is tied up in one's own assets. This lost income is the imputed interest expense. An imputed salary expense for a proprietor or partner provides another example of imputed expense. The economist refers to these as *opportunity costs*. Certainly such imputed expenses cannot properly be included in the income statement. Consideration must be given to them, however, in many business decisions.

Fixed vs. Variable Expense. Another of these two-way expense classifications is fixed versus variable expense. *Fixed expenses* are those that do not vary in total amount for the accounting period—for example, a rental charge of $300 per month or a property tax of $800 per year. *Variable expenses*, on the other hand, are fixed on a per-unit basis but vary in total amount for month and year with the volume of goods manufactured or sold. As an example of a variable expense, consider machine operators in a factory who work on piece rates and receive a specified amount in dollars and cents per unit of product processed by them. If they process 100,000 units at five cents per unit, they receive $5,000. If they process 10,000 units at five cents per unit, they receive $500. Thus, the amount of the variable expense—in this case, direct labor—depends upon the number of units made. This distinction is also important in business decisions. For example, an order might be accepted under some circumstances at a price which would cover variable costs but fail to cover all fixed costs. As a practical matter, many expenses are neither completely fixed nor completely variable in nature.

Controllable vs. Noncontrollable Expense. A third classification of business expenses is controllable versus noncontrollable. Property taxes, for example, are noncontrollable, as is also true of rental payments during the life of a lease. Conversely, the manager determines the amount of advertising expenditures, so that advertising is fully controllable.

It should be observed that for actual (as distinguished from imputed) expenses, the categories of fixed versus variable and controllable versus noncontrollable are overlapping. That is, an expense may be fixed and noncontrollable, or fixed and controllable, and so on.

Functional Expense Classification. The traditional accounting breakdown of business expenses has been by kind. Examples include taxes, interest, office supplies, rent, payroll, advertising, travel expense, repairs, insurance, depreciation, and professional services. Such a breakdown of business expenses by kind is imperfect, because it does not provide a basis for functional expense control. Logically, a retailer requires a functional expense breakdown somewhat as follows:

1. Merchandising
   a. Buying
   b. Selling
2. Sales Promotion
   a. Advertising
   b. Window-display
   c. Point-of-purchase display
   d. Premiums and trading stamps
3. Store operation
   a. Store protection
   b. Employee training
   c. Switchboard operation
   d. Cashiering
   e. Delivery
   f. Receiving, checking, and marking
   g. Warehousing
   h. Elevator operation
   i. Utilities
4. Control
   a. Accounting
   b. Statistical tabulations
   c. Payroll preparation and distribution
   d. Auditing
   e. Credit investigation
   f. Collections
5. Management (only those portions of the expenses which cannot be allocated to other categories)
   a. Executive salaries
   b. Rent
   c. Taxes
   d. Insurance
   e. Depreciation

If the amounts recorded by kinds of expense in the books of account can be equitably distributed to these functional expense categories, then and only then can expense control be achieved. Consider the expense of payroll preparation, charged functionally to control. Involved is the cost of preparation of the payroll, distribution of the checks, and audit of the accuracy of the payroll expenditure. A unit of measurement is required for control; this is afforded best, perhaps, by the number of payroll checks written. If the average payroll preparation expense over the past year is taken as standard for budgeting purposes and expense control, the actual expense for a given pay period can be compared and discrepancies evaluated. It should be stressed that the payroll expense attributed to control functionally is not the amount of payroll itself, but the cost of its preparation, distribution, and audit. The payroll cost itself would be distributed to the various pertinent categories. Perhaps this example will indicate the nature of functional expense control. Certainly, payroll expense in total is not controllable as such, in the degree that it is controllable if allocated equitably to various functional expense categories. Only as the salary cost of payroll preparation, distribution, and audit is properly segregated can it be controlled.

Concentration on Controllable Expenses

It is important that management in a small firm should stress controllable expense almost to the exclusion of noncontrollable expense. Consider a lease with a flat rental. Once a lease has been signed, rental expense is not controllable during the life of the lease. Hence, attention should then be directed to other items of expense which are controllable.

In the small factory, for example, if a further mechanization of materials handling is possible and the capital expenditure is not prohibitive, the necessary equipment can be installed to reduce expenses. For a given system, however, expense control means that the system must be used more efficiently. For example, employees on hourly rates may be sent home when work is light.

Similarly, delivery expense is controllable to some extent. The truck driver's salary, truck depreciation, and operating cost can be more effectively used and better controlled if the truck is provided with two-way radio. In contrast, a retailer subscribing to a delivery service at a fixed amount per month is committed to a noncontrollable expense. Accordingly, there is little need for attention to it until time to renegotiate the delivery service contract. It pays to spend the available time on managing the controllable expenses.

Important Areas for Expense Control

Greater attention should also be given to major rather than to minor items of expense. Perhaps the most important expenses to the retailer, for example, are those of labor, advertising and sales promotion, rent, buying and receiving of merchandise, and inventory carrying charges. His biggest investment is typically in merchandise inventory. The productivity of labor can be so variable as to make labor a most important expense category.

The small manufacturer does not face the same important areas for expense control as does the retailer. For the manufacturer, the typically important areas for expense control are materials and supplies, direct labor cost, cost of equipment and its operation, cost of advertising and sales promotion, together with the costs of financing receivables and of freight. If the manufacturer uses traveling salespersons, their salaries and travel expense allowances may also be important categories of expense control.

Example of Expense Control

Expense control is frequently more important than expense reduction. Expense control may include expense reduction, but it may also involve the increase of expenditures for a given type of expense rather than either constant outlay or reduced outlay.

Let us now consider one specific example of expense control in a small factory which employs traveling salespersons who carry models and samples of the product to dealer customers. For car transportation expense, expense standards may be developed in terms of mileage allowances. Actual expenses then can be compared with, and controlled in terms of, these standards.

The so-called traveling expenses other than the cost of car operation are not so easily determinable and controllable, however. For example, the salesman may report weekly on hotel costs, meal costs, tips, entertainment of customers, and other expenses. It would be possible for him to pad the expense account. Other techniques are possible, however, to combat this danger. If he is supplied with credit cards honored by certain cafeteria or cafe chains, the exact cost of meals (including meals of customers) will be determinable. Hotel and motel bills, gifts, theater tickets, dry cleaning, garage services, and many other expenses can be incurred under credit card charges. For a small amount per year, thus, the business gets a part-time bookkeeper and prevents the salesman from juggling his expense accounts in such a way as to obtain additional income for himself.

Control of expenses, therefore, involves the predetermination of expense standards, the design and maintenance of adequate records, the possibility of audit of expense records, and the prompt reporting and comparison of actual expenses with expense standards. Lacking the tools or the ability to control expenses, management might as well face the fact that the business may not long survive.

Expense Reduction Program

A program of expense reduction, superimposed upon one of expense control, is invaluable if it can be achieved without reduction in sales volume, deletion of customer services, or loss of operating efficiency. Most business executives and management consultants will admit that a five percent or greater reduction in expenses could be achieved by almost any business. Thus, the small firm has the opportunity to reduce expenses as well as to control them. Expense reduction, if accomplished without loss of efficiency, makes possible price reductions or profit expansion, or both.

The entrepreneur must have creative imagination and persistence to inaugurate successfully an expense reduction program. Moreover, he must sell employees on it to the point of full cooperation with his efforts. Nor can he overlook the possible usefulness of management consultants whose broad experience could be harnessed in the effort toward expense reduction. Of course, their fees will represent a cost of achieving expense reduction in this case.

The tools of expense reduction are those of methods engineering and are discussed in Chapter 29. Primarily, these include job analysis, methods and motion studies, and work simplification. Analysis of work to eliminate inefficiencies and to find more productive methods is as applicable to sales and administrative functions as it is to manufacturing operations.

Expense reduction may be achieved by recruitment and retention of superior personnel perhaps more effectively than by any other means. Even at a higher salary cost, superior employees more than make up the difference by their greater contribution to the firm's production and distribution effort. Because of their greater efficiency, expense per unit of product or service or per item sold is reduced.

 Summary

1. Business forecasting attempts to look into the future and to determine the probable course of general business activity and of industry and company sales. Such a knowledge of future sales is an essential starting point for budgeting future operations. Long-range forecasting is essential for many types of decisions.

2. Business forecasting requires a blend of scientific analysis and business judgment. It may make use of various statistical techniques. The typical businessman's limited ability and experience in the use of quantitative techniques tend to make this a particularly difficult area for the small firm.

3. A budget is a statement of business objectives expressed primarily in monetary terms. It serves as the plan for future operations and provides yardsticks for appraising and controlling performance.

4. Use of a budget involves a determination of standards, a prompt comparison and investigation of actual versus standard results, and necessary corrective action.

5. Cost and performance standards may be developed to apply to manufacturing, distribution, and administrative activities. Variables in setting standards are the volume of production, size of production orders, materials quality, and labor efficiency.

6. Revision of the budget typically is required during the budget year because of the uncertainties involved in budget preparation. These revisions must be made if the periodic performance reports are not to be misleading.

7. Deficiences common in small business budgetary control include inaccurate determination of budget standards; failure to include all key business activities in the budget; failure to revise budget figures; use of a poor report form, making it difficult to spot significant variations from standards; and lack of a real understanding and acceptance of the budget by both management and employees.

8. Preparation of an overall budget is a task requiring considerable time and effort on the part of those in management and supervisory positions. Specific steps and subsidiary budgets required in the formulation of a master budget include sales forecasts, production budget, materials and purchases budget, direct labor budget, manufacturing expense budget, cost of goods manufactured and sold budget, selling and administrative expense budgets, capital expenditures budget, and accounts receivable and cash budgets, culminating in budgeted financial statements.

9. Flexible budgets may be substituted for static budgets.

10. Expenses may be classified in different ways, such as actual and imputed, fixed and variable, and controllable and noncontrollable. Also, the traditional

accounting breakdown of expenses has been by kind—for example, taxes, interest, and rent. A different classification provides for a functional expense breakdown, such as buying, advertising, cashiering, and warehousing. The latter arrangement may simplify the manager's control and make it more effective.

11. In controlling expense, it is important for management to stress controllable expense much more than noncontrollable expense. Major items of expense should also receive careful study in contrast to relatively minor expense items.

12. A program of expense reduction is a desirable supplement to the program of expense control. If accomplished without loss of efficiency, expense reduction makes possible a direct increase in profits.

Discussion Questions

1. If a small manufacturer is contemplating a plant expansion, what types of forecasts would be helpful in arriving at a sound decision?

2. If the manager of a small business is untrained in statistical techniques, how can he utilize business forecasting?

3. In view of the fact that sales volume is typically an unknown, how can a budget be both a plan of action and a tool for control? Explain.

4. If a business firm could predict its sales volume quite accurately, would there be any point in budgeting? Explain.

5. What differences or variations, if any, would occur in adapting the principles of budgeting to an automobile sales and service agency?

6. What would be the "predetermined standards" in budgeting by a retail hardware owner? Would they be the same for a dairy?

7. How would the concept of "prompt reporting of actual versus standard" apply to a hamburger stand with just five employees?

8. How large should a cost or performance variance be to justify management attention? Might such a variance ever be favorable? Would it call for management action any the less if favorable than if unfavorable? Why?

9. What factors might lead to a requirement for budget changes during the budget period? Explain.

10. Of the various budgetary control deficiencies identified in the chapter, which would seem to be the most critical for most small firms? Why?

11. What are the relationships between a firm's production budget and its sales, materials, and purchases budgets?

12. Can "fixed" expenses be controlled? Are they really always "fixed"? Cite some examples (for both answers).

13. What is the nature of an expense classification by function? Of what value is it to the manager?

14. Assuming that rent and purchases each accounts for the same proportion of the sales dollar, which should receive primary or initial attention of the manager? Why?

22

Business Risks
and Insurance

Risk is inherent in the operation of any business, but running a business is more than a "gamble." Most types of business risk can be dealt with if the practice of *risk management* is followed.

The risk manager . . . is perhaps the wettest blanket in his company, whether large or small. It is his job to say *no* to all kinds of ideas and arrangements which look good at first glance but which would unduly deprive the company of protection against loss. The risk manager . . . knows that the company cannot escape some losses. But through a vigorous program he can search out and eliminate many of the potential small losses and find ways . . . for his employer to absorb with the least pain the large losses that could be damaging.[1]

The entrepreneur of a small business must often be his own risk manager, and his profit on operations will reflect his skill and effort in combatting risk. The dangers involved in launching a new enterprise were considered in earlier chapters. This chapter focuses on the risks faced by a going concern.

COMMON BUSINESS RISKS

Several specific risks commonly confront entrepreneurs. Most of them are insurable, but some are not. Managers of firms, both large and small, should make and regularly update a risk survey of their companies. A knowledge of the existing risks must precede any action to eliminate or reduce those risks. The small firm does not face precisely the same risks as the large business since the nature of risks varies with the type of business, its location, its personnel, its customers, and its physical properties.

Uninsurable Risks and Noninsurance Forms of Protection

Entrepreneurs may use various methods of offsetting or avoiding uninsurable risks. These methods will be discussed in relation to the kinds of risk to which they are applicable.

---

[1] F. X. McCahill, Jr., "Avoid Losses Through Risk Management," *Harvard Business Review*, Vol. 49 (May-June, 1971), pp. 57-65.

Risks in Economic Conditions. In times of depression or recession, small business firms are particularly vulnerable to loss. Perhaps the major weakness lies in the failure of the small business to build reserves and increase ownership equity during a preceding period of business prosperity. As a result, they are frozen out due to losses incurred during depression. As a practical protective consideration, then, the small firm should utilize profits in a period of prosperity to increase the ownership equity and to build a strong working capital position.

Price fluctuations constitute another economic factor contributing to losses, as well as possible profits, for some firms. If the business carries a substantial inventory, price declines almost automatically result in inventory losses. This danger can be minimized by a policy of *hand-to-mouth buying* although such a policy requires a decision to resist the lure of speculative profits from possible price increases. A few large firms are able to gain price protection through *hedging* in the commodities market; however, this protection is unavailable to most small firms.

Obsolescence of Products or Processes. Industrial research expenditures today are vast, and technological progress is rapid. As a consequence, small manufacturers often find their processes and products becoming obsolete. About the only solution for the small firm is a progressive management which keeps up with industrial progress. Admittedly, the small firm has its limitations, but it need not fall asleep. Research possibilities for the small company were discussed in Chapter 18.

Sabotage and Other Wartime Risks. During time of war, sabotage and other military risks confront many small plants. For a plant engaged in war goods production, the threat of sabotage demands an effective system of plant protection. Although bombing by enemy planes or missiles has not happened to American industry in previous wars, it has occured in other countries such as Japan, Germany, Italy, England, France, and Russia. Ours is a shrinking world, and the increasing power of military weapons makes this a threat for both defense and nondefense establishments. Although a plant may be located in an area that is safer than others, the destructive power of nuclear weapons makes the outcome of this risk dependent upon the course of international relations.

A related risk for manufacturers producing under defense contracts is the uncertainty of contract duration. When a war ends, contract termination is customary. The changes involved in shifting to peacetime production are difficult and often costly.

Losses from Bad Debts. Any firm selling on credit runs the risk of losses on bad debts. The nature of this risk and the recommended procedures for dealing with it were discussed in Chapter 11.

Shoplifting. Shoplifting has been on the increase in recent years, amounting to 5 to 6 percent of sales revenue or about equal the profit a department store can make, for example. Unfortunately, an insurance policy covering the theft of merchandise during store hours is not available. Attempts to control shoplifting include careful surveillance and, occasionally, such measures as closed-circuit television cameras, sensitized tags on merchandise that trigger an alarm when the shoplifter starts to leave the store, and one-way mirrors. The entrepreneur, however, should take precautions that such protective measures against shoplifting do not offend legitimate customers.[2]

Insurable Risks

As mentioned earlier, most of the common business risks are insurable. The subject of insurance will be considered in the latter part of this chapter. Here the nature of some common insurable business risks and how they can be avoided or minimized by ways other than insurance will be discussed.

Fire Hazards. The possibility of fire is ever present. Buildings, equipment, and inventory items can be totally or partially destroyed by fire. Of course, the degree of risk and the loss potential differ with the type of business. Industrial processes that are complex and hazardous or that involve explosives, combustibles, or other flammable materials enlarge the risk.

Obviously the small firm needs to take every possible precaution for preventing fires and for dealing with the losses incident to the occurrence of a fire. Among the possible precautions are the following:

1. *Use of safe construction.* The building should be made of fire-resistant materials, and electrical wiring should be adequate to carry the maximum load of electrical energy which will be imposed. Fire doors and insulation should be used where necessary.
2. *Provision of a completely automatic sprinkler system.* With an automatic sprinkler system available, fire insurance rates will be lower—and the fire hazard itself is definitely reduced.
3. *Provision of an adequate water supply.* Ordinarily this involves location in a city with water sources and water mains, together with a pumping system that will assure the delivery of any amount of water needed to fight fires. Of course, a company may hedge a bit by providing company-owned water storage tanks or private wells.
4. *Institution and operation of a fire prevention program involving all employees.* Such a program must have top management support, and the emphasis must always be to keep employees fire-safety conscious. Regular fire drills for all employees, including both building evacuation and actual fire fighting efforts, may be undertaken. This program should also include an emphasis upon good plant housekeeping—a practice often neglected in small firms.

Other Disaster Losses. Floods, hurricanes, tornadoes, and hail constitute other sources of disaster losses. If flood waters sweep into a manufacturing plant, damage may well occur to materials in process, finished goods, physical equipment, and business records.

Such disasters are often described as "acts of God" because of human limitations in foreseeing and controlling them. Although the business firm may take certain preventive steps—for example, locating in areas not subject to flood damage—major reliance is placed upon insurance in dealing with such risks.

Business Interruption Losses. Fire, tornadoes, floods, and the like not only cause a direct property loss but also may interrupt business operations with consequent loss of profit to the firm. Still another cause of business interruption is found in such prolonged strikes as in the steel and automobile industries.

---

[2] This paragraph derives in part from "Shoplifting: The Pinch That Hurts," *Business Week*, June 27, 1970, pp. 72-73, 76.

During the period when business operations are interrupted, fixed charges, such as bond interest, rent, supervisory salaries, and insurance charges, continue. Management action to deal with such a risk is similar to that designed to combat the disasters causing the interruptions. In the case of a strike threat among suppliers, *stockpiling* is a widely used precautionary step also.

Liability Risks. Liability risks are those involving losses to third parties who make claims against a business. For example, a customer may sustain a personal injury on one's business premises by slipping on icy steps while entering the place of business, by walking into an open elevator shaft, or by falling down stairs. Or a customer might become ill or sustain property damage in using a product made or sold by a company. Still another example is that of a company-owned car or truck which is involved in an accident with a pedestrian or with another motor vehicle. Many other such possibilities exist, any of which could lead to damage suits.

The legal liability of the business would depend upon the extent to which the negligence of company personnel contributed to the accident or loss. In the case of the slippery steps, a court might construe as negligence the firm's failure to remove the ice. Hence, the businessman is at the mercy of juries' and judges' legal interpretations as to whether reasonable care was exercised in particular situations. Consider the following cases:

An Illinois jury awarded $930,000 to a woman who was blinded when a can of plumbing drain cleaner exploded in her face. . . .

Thalidomide damage awards against companies that manufactured the drug also have run into millions of dollars. . . .

In this age of consumerism, the law has shifted the burden of proof from plaintiff to defendant. *Caveat emptor* has become *caveat vendor* . . . And juries, with inflamed memories of a doctor who refused to make a house call, or of a toy that maims, are more and more inclined to soak the defendant. . . .

In 1968, Aetna Life & Casualty paid out $10 million more than it took in on medical malpractice policies alone.[3]

The liability loss threat is indeed severe, insurance is getting harder to obtain, and rates are considerably higher than formerly. With damage suits and injury awards both on the increase, it should be clear that the potential loss from claims of this kind may far exceed that due to fires and other disasters.

A small businessman should carry insurance, but he can also reduce such losses by the practice of good business housekeeping and sound management. In the winter, ice should be removed from sidewalks. Iron railings can be set up beside entrance steps, if any. The safety consciousness of truck drivers and other employees may be upgraded by a program of safety education. To prevent the manufacture of items which could be injurious to customers, safety in product design should be emphasized and quality standards in production should be maintained.

Business Frauds and Theft. Business swindles can amount to hundreds of millions of dollars a year. Small firms in particular are susceptible to swindles.

---

[3] "He's Insured—Sock It to Him!" *Forbes*, Vol. 105 (April 15, 1970), pp. 63-64.

Examples of these are bogus office machine repairmen, phony charity appeals, billing for listing in nonexistent directories, sale of advertising space in publications whose nature is misrepresented, and advance fee deals. Risks of this kind are avoidable only through the alertness of the business manager.

Thefts by employees may include not only cash but also inventory items, tools, metal scrap, stamps, and the like. Then there is always the possibility of forgery, raising of checks, or other fraudulent practices. The trusted bookkeeper may enter into collusion with an outsider to have bogus invoices or invoices double or triple the correct amount presented for payment. The bookkeeper may approve such invoices for payment, write the check, and secure the manager's signature. In addition to bonding employees, the firm's major protection against employee frauds is the system of internal check or control previously described in Chapter 20.

Another form of theft is *burglary*, which is the forcible breaking and entering of premises closed for business with the subsequent removal of cash or merchandise. Although insurance should be carried against such losses, it may prove helpful for a business to install burglar alarm systems and private patrol services.

Death or Loss of a Key Executive. Every successful small business has one or more key executives. The manager often has key assistants, some of whom may even be stockholders in the firm. These employees could be lost to the firm by death or through attraction to other employment. If the owner serves as manager, the uncertainty of his life and health constitutes a part of this risk. If key personnel cannot be successfully replaced, the small firm suffers appreciably and loses profits as the result of the loss of their services.

In addition to valuable experience and skill, there is also the possibility that the executive may have certain specialized knowledge which is not a matter of record but which is vital to the successful operation of the firm. For example, a certain manufacturer was killed in an auto accident at the age of 53. His processing operations involved the use of a secret chemical formula which he had devised originally and divulged to no one because of fear of loss of the formula to competitors. He did not reduce it to writing and place it in his safety deposit box. Not even his sons were told the formula. As a result of his sudden death, the firm went out of business within six months. The expensive special-purpose equipment had to be sold as junk. All that his widow salvaged was about $60,000 worth of bonds and the Florida residence which had been the winter home of the couple.

Two answers, at least, are possible to the small firm faced with this contingency. First of these is key-man insurance, which is discussed in the following section on insurance. The second solution involves the development of replacement personnel. A potential replacement may be groomed for every key position including the position of the owner-manager. In fact, development of potential replacements may also protect the company and facilitate operations during temporary absences for vacations and other purposes.

BUSINESS APPLICATIONS OF INSURANCE

Insurance provides one of the most important means of protection against business risks. Too often in the past, the businessman has paid insufficient attention to insurance matters and has failed to acquire skill in analyzing risk problems. Today, such a situation is untenable. A sound insurance program is imperative for the proper protection of a business.

Principles of Protection

The first principle is to determine the need for protection by identifying the most common business risks. Although these risks have already been pointed out, there are other checklists that can be used in identifying the most common risks. Other less obvious risks may be revealed only by a careful investigation. The insurance buyer must first obtain coverages required by law or contract, such as workmen's compensation insurance (in most states) and automobile liability insurance. Moreover, partial coverage often proves to be an expensive economy while over-insurance represents a waste of premiums. If *coinsurance clauses* are involved, the insured must bear a share of any loss if he has not met the coinsurance requirements stipulated in his policy. As part of this risk-identification process, the plant and equipment should be periodically reappraised by competent appraisers in order to maintain an adequate insurance coverage.

Another principle to observe is that insurance coverage should be acquired only for major potential losses. Thus, the firm must determine the magnitude of loss which it could bear without serious financial difficulty. If the firm is sufficiently strong, it may cover only those losses exceeding a specified minimum amount. The purpose of this principle is the avoidance of unnecessary insurance coverage. It is important, of course, to guard against the tendency to underestimate the severity of potential losses.

Finally, another insurance principle is concerned with the cost of insurance and its relationship to the probability of loss. Because the insurance company must collect enough premiums to pay the actual losses of insured parties, the cost of insurance must be proportional to the probability of occurrence of the insured event. As the chance of loss becomes more and more certain, a firm finds that the premium cost becomes so high that insurance is simply not worth the cost. Thus, insurance is most applicable and practical for improbable losses.

In buying insurance to cover appropriate risks, the small firm should use every possible means to reduce the cost of insurance. For example, policies may contain deductible or coinsurance clauses, and various policies may be placed on a three- or five-year basis and staggered as to dates of premium payment. Moreover, the small firm can seek out the insurance companies which charge the lowest premiums while still providing acceptable coverage.

Self-Insurance or No Insurance

Under some conditions, a large company can safely self-insure against even major risks. A chain store with retail outlets in many different cities and states, for example, might act as its own fire insurance company. This would require the store management to determine the probability of loss through fire and then set aside a sum determined by use of an actuarial method to meet those losses which are realized. It is clear that the risk would need to be spread so that any one fire would not destroy a substantial portion of the company's property. Self-insurance is seldom applicable to a small business.

There is the alternative, of course, of carrying no insurance. This is akin to self-insurance only insofar as it means that no outside company acts as insurer.

Self-insurance differs in that it is actuarially maintained, with cash reserves built up for use in case of loss.

The absence of insurance might reflect an ostrich-like attempt to ignore the risk. Or, it might indicate management's desire to rely on loss reduction or prevention rather than on insurance. Similarly, it may be based upon the premise that the loss would be small if it occurred, so that it could be safely borne by the firm. It should be clear, however, that not all losses are small and a lack of insurance could lead to serious losses.

Kinds of Insurance Required

There are several classifications of insurance and a variety of coverages available from different insurance companies. In this section the types of insurance that are normally required for a business are discussed.

Fire Insurance. Fire insurance, and the related lines of insurance against other disaster losses such as windstorm, tornado, explosion, riot, and so on, provides protection for the physical property of the firm. The coinsurance clause which is typical in such insurance contracts regulates the minimum coverage which can be secured without the insured's assuming a portion of the risk.

A special word is required about the insurance for losses that occur as the result of business interruption following property damage. In the event of fire, tornado, hurricane, or windstorm—if named as sources of business interruption losses in the policy—a firm is reimbursed for both the loss of profits during the period of interruption and the fixed expenses of "shutdown operations." Wages even for employees who are not required for "shutdown operations" can also be covered by special endorsement, but ordinarily this would be unnecessary. Typically, business interruption insurance coverage is for 90 days' interruption. Typically, also, business interruption policies are written with coinsurance clauses requiring one who underinsures to share the loss in part.

Marine Insurance. Marine insurance protects goods during shipment. It includes not only *ocean* marine insurance of shipments by water but also *inland* marine insurance covering transportation by rail or motor freight. One variety of inland marine insurance is the *commercial floater* which insures business property against various hazards no matter where it is located. Contractors' equipment, for example, may be insured in this way. This latter variety is not really transportation insurance even though marine insurance was originally designed to cover only the risks involved in transportation.

Casualty Insurance. Casualty insurance includes a variety of insurance differing from the categories enumerated above. Automobile insurance—both collision and public liability—is a major field of casualty insurance. Burglary, theft, robbery, plate glass, and health and accident insurance are other examples of casualty insurance. As pointed out earlier, liability policies are particularly important to small firms because of the very large losses which might be entailed in third party claims.

Fidelity and Surety Bonds. Fidelity and surety companies guarantee to the business firm that individuals in its employment and others with whom the firm has business dealings are honest or will otherwise fulfill their contractual obligations. Employees occupying positions of trust in handling company funds are customarily bonded as a protection against their dishonesty. The informality and highly personal basis of employment in small firms make it difficult to realize the value of such insurance. It might be noted in this connection that an untrusted employee is seldom given access to company funds and rarely absconds with the employer's money. Surety bonds protect one firm against the failure of another firm or individual to fulfill a contractual obligation.

Credit and Title Insurance. Credit insurance and title insurance are sometimes considered as subdivisions of the above category, or they may be classed as miscellaneous forms. The use of credit insurance was discussed in Chapter 11. Title insurance is of importance in the purchase of real estate; by such coverage, the buyer insures the acquisition of a clear title.

Life Insurance. By life insurance, protection for the business can be provided against the death of the entrepreneur or key executives of the firm. As noted earlier, a business may lose heavily when the services or capital of a key individual is lost. If the firm pays the premium as a regular business expense, it has at least a measure of protection against losses resulting from the untimely death of a firm member.[4]

Requirements for Obtaining Insurance

To obtain insurance, first of all, there must be a tangible risk to the insured which is measurable in monetary terms. That which is insured must possess a commercial, not merely a sentimental, value to the businessman.

As a second requirement, the insured must have little or no control over the risk. For the insured to have a valid claim under his coverage, the loss must arise from natural causes beyond control. It would be very difficult for an insurance company to attempt to protect against risks within the control of the insured.

A third condition for an insurable risk is that it must exist in large numbers. Furthermore, the insurance risk of a particular firm must be relatively small in comparison to the total risks which the insurance company assumes. Moreover, the insurance company must distribute the risk hazard geographically. Only in this way can the insurance company get an adequate, safe distribution of risk.

A fourth requirement is that the amount of risk be calculable. That is, it must be possible to develop actuarial tables showing the probability of loss. The idea here is that there is a fixed probability of loss due to the given type of causation but that those who suffer losses are not determinable in advance, even though the total number is predictable from the probability table. Only if the risks can be calculated will it be possible for the insurance company to determine fair insurance premiums to be charged.

The final condition for obtaining insurance is that the insured must have an insurable interest in the property or person insured. The purpose of insurance is reimbursement of actual loss and not creation of profit for the insured firm. Thus, the small firm cannot procure business interruption insurance against loss of $100,000 in profit in 90 days if the normal annual profit is $20,000.

---

[4] Further information on this subject will be found in Thomas L. Wenck, "Business Continuation Problems and Solutions," pp. 7-14, *MSU Business Topics*, Winter 1967. Reprinted by permission of the publisher, Division of research, Graduate School of Business Administration, Michigan State University.

Likewise, it could not insure a building for $500,000 if its true worth is actually $70,000. Again, the business concern cannot procure key-man life insurance on a banker, lawyer, or other nonemployees. The firm has an insurable interest, however, in the lives of key employees.

How Much Insurance is Enough?

The extent of coverage should be determined after consultation with an insurance counselor. Definitely there should be sufficient coverage against catastrophic and other major losses. Beyond this, the decision on insurance coverage requires a balance of such factors as the magnitude of possible loss, ability to minimize the loss, cost of insurance protection, and financial strength of the firm.

It is often apparent that small firms fail to carry sufficient insurance protection. Liability policies are obtained for specific liabilities when comprehensive policies should be purchased. Liability policies on company trucks and cars specify $5,000 or $10,000, when a safer figure would be $50,000 or more. Similarly, fidelity bonds on cash-handling employees should be larger than are typically carried; such policies frequently cover only a fraction of the amount embezzled. Having too little coverage for any type of insurance risk is dangerous, even though the premium cost is reduced by reduction of the coverage.

Provision of adequate coverage for operating assets may be facilitated by periodic appraisals of the fixed assets. Moreover, the company's accounting records should be able to support the replacement cost of properties in case an insurance claim must be presented.

It should be apparent that careful management dictates a study of adequate insurance policies in advance of a loss rather than after the occurrence of the event. By so doing, a manager may discover gaps in coverage and make appropriate corrections in time to forestall serious losses.

 Summary

1. Among the common business risks which are uninsurable are risks in economic conditions, obsolescence of products or processes, sabotage and other wartime risks, losses from bad debts, and shoplifting. The common insurable risks are fire hazards, other disaster losses, business interruption losses, liability risks, business frauds and theft, and death of key executives. Of these, liability losses are on the increase.

2. In developing an effective insurance program, a firm should first determine the extent of its need for protection by identifying its business risks. Excessive or unnecessary insurance should be avoided by limiting protection to major potential losses. The probability of occurrence of loss must be considered in connection with insurance cost in deciding whether to insure against specific risks. Every possible means of reducing the risk and the cost of insurance should also be used.

3. Some large firms use self-insurance or no insurance to cover their business risks.

Because of limited financial resources and single location, however, such a practice is ordinarily impractical for small firms.

4. Types of insurance typically used by small business firms include fire insurance, marine insurance, casualty insurance, life insurance, and fidelity and surety bonds.

5. To make insurance possible, there must be a tangible risk to the insured capable of monetary measurement. The object insured must possess commercial and not merely sentimental value to the owner. Furthermore, the insured must have little or no control over the risk. The risk must also exist in large numbers and be calculable in probabilistic terms.

6. The firm should carry enough insurance to protect against major losses. Beyond this, the decision on coverage requires judgment that balances such factors as magnitude of possible loss, ability to minimize such losses, cost of the insurance, and financial strength of the firm.

 Discussion Questions

1. Can a small firm safely assume that business risks will never turn into losses sufficient to bankrupt it and therefore avoid insurance and protective measures? Why?

2. How can a small business deal with the risk entailed in fluctuating economic conditions?

3. Can a small contractor deal with the problem of price fluctuations by use of an insurance policy?

4. Could a small firm safely deal with such hazards as property loss from fire by precautionary measures in lieu of insurance? Explain.

5. Is the increase in liability claims and court awards of special concern to small manufacturers? Why?

6. Are any kinds of business risks basically human risks? Are the people involved always employees?

7. Enumerate a number of approaches for combatting the danger of theft or fraud by employees and also by outsiders.

8. Under what conditions would life insurance on a business executive constitute little protection to the business? And when is it helpful?

9. What is the risk assumed by a business firm under a coinsurance clause? Is the use of coinsurance basically a conservative type of management?

10. When is it logical for a small business to utilize self-insurance? How does this differ from no insurance?

11. What types of insurance are required by law for most business firms?

12. Explain the requirements necessary for obtaining insurance to cover business risks.

13. A certain small manufacturer in a growth industry spends 7 percent of sales revenue on research and development. Is this policy justified? Is the amount too large—or too little? Why?

14. What do you think of the practice of yard storage of lumber by sawmills and lumber yards? Of yard storage of scrap metals by a small manufacturer? Why?

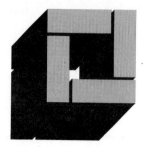

23

Inventory Control

Inventory management or control is another aspect of administrative control which can make a positive contribution to business success. For manufacturing and marketing (wholesaling and retailing) institutions, in particular, inventory control can make the difference between success and failure. The larger the inventory investment of a business, the more vital is its proper use and control.

This is not to say that other types of small business—for example, coin-operated laundries or dry cleaners, barbershops, plumbing outfits, automobile repair shops, and accounting firms—are not concerned with inventory control. Such service firms generally have relatively minor inventory problems, and some of these problems may deal only with what might be termed "office supplies." Lack of space precludes a complete treatment of inventory control in each of these separate types of establishments. Suffice it to say that many of the same principles and techniques of inventory control which will be discussed in this chapter in relation to manufacturing and marketing institutions apply to all other types of small business establishments.

OBJECTIVES OF INVENTORY CONTROL

Both purchasing and inventory control have the same general objective: *to have the right goods in the right quantities at the right time and place.* This is true of all types of enterprises—manufacturing, merchandising, service, financial, and so on. To achieve this general objective, other more specific subgoals have to be attained.

Assuring Continuous Operations

Factory processing operations require that work in process be moved on schedule. If a delay occurs due to lack of materials or parts needed in processing, it can cause a shutdown of a production line, a department, or even the whole plant. Such interruption of scheduled operations is both serious and costly. All conversion costs are adversely affected. Labor costs jump when skilled workers are idle or perform unnecessary work while waiting for materials. (The authors recall a case in which skilled production workers, rather than standing idle, were used to move stacked boxes of goods some 10 feet laterally to new locations. This action accomplished nothing.) When workers are idled, their machines stand idle also, and the overhead cost mounts rapidly. Given a long delay, fulfillment of delivery promises to customers may become impossible. Customers expect deliveries on schedule, and the irritation engendered by late deliveries may cause them to transfer present or future orders to other suppliers.

Securing Maximum Sales

When demand is sufficiently large, sales will be greater if goods are always available for display and/or delivery to the customer. Most customers desire to choose from an assortment of goods. A small store, for example, might concentrate so diligently on maximizing stock turnover, by reducing stock just prior to the taking of annual physical inventory, that customers are forced by narrow range of choice and/or stockouts to look elsewhere. Such a lack of merchandise may lose not only the given sale but future sales also. If the customer is lost permanently, the resulting reduction in future sales and profits will continue to reflect this error in inventory management.

Of course, the business might unwisely go to the other extreme and attempt to avoid the problem of stockouts or insufficient offerings by the unduly expensive practice of carrying too large an inventory. This both inflates the cost of carrying inventory and causes losses on unsalable or shopworn items, while an unexpected price decline could bankrupt the firm. Management must walk the chalk line, so to speak, between overstocking and understocking in order to retain customers and maximize sales. The cost of carrying inventory and maintenance of adequate merchandise stocks must be carefully balanced.

Protecting Assets

Inventory, like cash or equipment, is a valuable business asset. Hence, one of the essential functions of inventory control is to protect this asset against theft, shrinkage, or deterioration. Protective steps lead in a number of different directions.

For example, the efficiency or wastefulness of storeskeeping, manufacturing, and handling processes will affect the quantity and quality of usable inventory. Similarly, intelligent buying and merchandising minimize losses from obsolescence and physical deterioration of products or merchandise carried in stock. These are even more closely related to production and marketing than to inventory control.

The entrepreneur may also conserve his assets by minimizing the physical handling of goods and by improving handling methods. The more often an article is picked up and physically handled, the more chance there is for physical damage. Inventory items that need special treatment can also spoil or deteriorate if improperly stored. For example, humidity control may be required in a factory storeroom to prevent damage to certain kinds of materials. Others may need to be protected against heat, breakage, evaporation, or sunlight. Special storage in supermarkets is illustrated by refrigeration of meats, frozen juices, and dairy products.

Minimizing Inventory Investment

A major benefit deriving from control of inventory is that smaller inventories may be carried without disservice to customer or to processing. This means that the inventory investment is less. Moreover, it means lower costs for storage space, taxes, and insurance. And inventory deterioration or obsolescence is less extensive, as well.

In the factory, savings through minimizing inventory investment must be balanced against the economies of large production runs and large purchase orders. There is an economic lot size in manufacturing (discussed in a later section of this chapter) which leads to joint minimization of finished goods inventory carrying charges and manufacturing setup costs for any month (or other time period). Similarly, the fixed costs of preparing purchase orders and potential quantity discounts can be compared with the cost of carrying the larger stores inventory in arriving at an economic order quantity for purchases of raw materials and supplies.

A danger exists in reducing inventory to the point that a significant loss of sales or costly production inefficiency is experienced. The standard inventory turnover rate for the particular line of business constitutes one guide which may be used in determining the proper inventory level. If a firm's turnover rate is lower than average, there is an indication of unnecessarily large inventory, low sales volume, or too low a rate of materials consumption. Occurrence of frequent production delays or of lost sales, on the other hand, are warning signals that the inventory level may be too low.

Providing Records for Administrative Control

The inventory records provide data useful for various administrative uses. For example, inventory records provide basic information needed for determining proper purchase quantities and ordering dates.

Inventory levels must be measured in dollars for entry in the financial statements. Inventory is an important working capital asset for the manufacturer, but it is the major asset for most small retailers. If it is not correctly evaluated, accurate financial statements cannot be prepared. This could preclude getting a needed bank loan—or a supplier's approval of projected large credit purchases. It could also delude the entrepreneur into making excessive cash withdrawals from the business if it led to a serious overstatement of profits.

Moreover, inventory control records provide information which may help to evaluate management performance. For example, if the business has an inventory turnover ratio lower than is normal, the manager may be considered a less efficient manager of inventory than most of his competitors.

Factory inventory records will also yield data pertinent to improvement of buying and manufacturing performance. For example, accurate data on inventory issues of a particular part are essential for computing the "yield" from a given supplier's orders. This is highly pertinent to product quality control and to future buying or nonbuying from that vendor. Again, inventory information may provide data on the time actually required by suppliers to fill orders, thus making possible a reduction of the differential between reorder point and minimum number of units on stores cards. Thus, the average amount carried on inventory could be reduced by this amount, due to the obtaining of delivery at a faster rate.

Finally, the inventory records may be made the basis of audits which evaluate the degree of clerical accuracy. If this reveals too many clerical errors, it should lead to remedial action or to mechanization of inventory record keeping.

INVENTORY CONTROL IN MANUFACTURING

In the area of manufacturing, one would be concerned with three broad categories of inventory: *raw materials and supplies, work in process,* and *finished goods.* Raw materials and supplies include all items purchased for conversion into finished products, and this category often calls for maximum inventory control efforts. The amount of work in process, on the other hand, is determined by production requirements and is regulated in its flow via production control activities. The control of finished goods inventory involves accounting for products completed and awaiting shipment to customers. If the product line is small, this operation may be comparatively simple. Some firms, however, produce hundreds of products, many of which are made in numerous sizes and grades. As the shipping room requisitions stock for shipments to customers, the number of units shipped and their dollar value are ascertained and deducted from the finished stock inventory balance on stock cards.

Storage of Inventory

All storage rooms or areas must be suitably located and large enough to hold the maximum inventories planned. The raw materials storeroom should be placed between the receiving room and the first processing department. Work in process is stored on or adjacent to processing machines or assembly lines. Finished goods are best located between the final processing operations and the shipping room. Both the receiving room and the shipping room should be adjacent to loading or unloading docks and/or railroad sidings since they provide temporary storage of inbound and outbound inventory items.

Minimum Reserve Stock

Maximum inventory is related both to amounts ordered or manufactured at one time and to minimum inventory carried. The minimum carried could be zero, but a better practice of carrying several days' use requirements is generally followed. Such a minimum reserve stock allows for inaccuracies in planning and for unpredictably large customer orders which might otherwise exhaust the old supply before the new shipment arrives.

Several factors influence the desirable level of the minimum reserve stock. Some of these factors are the following:

1. *Time required to get production or delivery of additional supplies.* The longer the time so required, the larger the reserve stock which must be carried.
2. *Amount and frequency of withdrawals from stock.* If there are irregular withdrawals of large amounts, the minimum stock must be adequate for such occasions.

3. *Certainty of obtaining delivery of critical items within specified time limits.* The greater the risk of strikes or other disturbances which would interfere with deliveries, the higher the minimum stock needed. And since close control over arrival times for marine shipments is impossible, there should be a larger minimum for any material imported from abroad.

Techniques of Inventory Control

Although the keeping of certain records is unavoidable, a major emphasis in small firms should be upon simplicity of control techniques. Limitations of personnel and finance make it difficult to use elaborate systems. Furthermore, a relatively simple assortment of inventory items may be properly controlled by relatively simple techniques. Too much control is as wasteful as it is unnecessary. For some items, for example, mere visual inspection may provide adequate control.

Perpetual Inventory Method. In a perpetual inventory system covering raw materials and supplies, the *stores card* is the basic control tool. Its heading shows the maximum number of units to be carried in inventory, the reorder point number of units, and the planned minimum number of units. In the body of the card, there are sections for the date, for receipts and issues of materials each day, and for the new balance of stores. After each receipt or issue of any stores item, the new balance is computed in the latter section. With a separate perpetual inventory card for each raw material or supply item carried in stores, the firm will always know the number of units on hand and, if each receipt and issue is costed, their dollar value. Figure 23-1 is an example of a stores card.

STORES CARD

SHAFER SHOE COMPANY

Item: Metal Eyelets

Maximum No. of Pairs   60,000
Reorder Point No. of Pairs   24,000
Minimum No. of Pairs   12,000

	Receipts			Issues			Balance on Hand		
Date	Pairs	Price per Pair	Cost	Pairs	Price per Pair	Cost	Pairs	Price per Pair	Cost*
Jan. 1							14,000	$.00400	$ 56.00
2				2,500	$.00400	$10.00	11,500	.00400	46.00
3	48,000	$.00420	$201.60				59,500	.00416	247.60
3				2,000	.00416	8.32	57,500	.00416	239.28
4				2,100	.00416	8.74	55,400	.00416	230.54
7				2,000	.00416	8.32	53,400	.00416	222.22

*Minor discrepancies in this column are due to 5-place rounding in the preceding column.
The stores card is used by routing and planning clerks to assure an adequate supply of materials and parts to complete any given factory order.

Figure 23-1

Use of a perpetual inventory system may be justified in the small factory or wholesale warehouse. In particular, this might be desirable for expensive and critical items—for example, those which could cause significant losses through theft or serious production delays. Frequently, however, all items are controlled thus even in small plants—some of which may not actually require this type of control.

Perpetual inventory control for finished goods is similarly available, but the cards used in this case are known as *stock cards* rather than as stores cards. Techniques for the use of stock cards are the same as for stores cards.

Physical Inventory Method. The traditional method of taking physical inventory is for two people to go from item to item, with one calling off the kind of item and the number of units on hand while the other records this information.[1]

Even when perpetual inventory cards are maintained, periodic physical counts are required to check the accuracy of unit balances shown on the individual record cards. When the count is finished, each item is priced, and dollar values of the units on hand are computed, card by card. Finally, the total dollar value of the inventory is found by summation of the separate card balances. If perpetual inventory records are not maintained, physical inventory is the only method available for use in manufacturing and wholesaling firms.

The McKesson-Robbins inventory fraud of the late 1930's, involving several principal officers of the company, led the American Institute of Certified Public Accountants to prescribe tighter audit standards for the inventory assets of client firms. One standard requirement is that a representative of the public accounting firm making an audit shall plan and personally supervise the taking of the client's physical inventory. This is a good standard, and if physical inventories are taken only once each production season (or year), it may be possible to implement in practice. However, if the small business has the physical inventory taken day by day in the spare time of the stores and stock clerks, at the rate of one or two items a day, detailed supervision by the CPA will be impractical. Even then, he should plan the taking of inventory and make periodic, random spot checks.

One possible improvement in technique is to have a single stores clerk or stock clerk take the respective inventories by enumerating kinds of items and units counted, item by item, into a microphone attached to a dictating machine or tape recorder.[2] The inventory data sheets could then be typed directly from this recording.

Making a single employee responsible for inventory may enhance the efficiency of inventory control.[3] If inventory control does not constitute a full-time job, such an employee may also be made responsible for receiving. The important thing is to establish control responsibility clearly and to make it possible to achieve control by physical segregation of inventory storage from work areas. Release of items from inventory is normally authorized by written

---

[1] The use of two persons, thus, supposedly guarantees the honesty, accuracy, and completeness of the physical inventory, *as recorded.*

[2] The accountant would point out the absence of internal check in this type of system. And, if the taped sound is at all garbled, the transcription may show incorrect amounts.

[3] This system obviously lacks an internal check.

requisitions or shipping orders. Some items that are specialized, inexpensive, and not subject to damage—glue, for example—may be released to the work area without requisition and without detailed records being maintained. The objective of control should never degenerate into control solely for the sake of control.

Computer-Aided Inventory Control. Although manual control systems are customarily adequate, the use of computer-aided systems is becoming increasingly popular. To date, this type of automation has occurred primarily in larger firms. However, smallness does not preclude efficient use of such systems. The desirability of computer-aided control in many small firms is suggested by the following statement from a University of Michigan study:

> Inventory control is a widely accepted computer application in many industrial concerns. The relatively simplistic nature of basic inventory control theory has proved to be especially applicable to the concept of automated information systems, even for those firms with computer installations of somewhat limited size and capability. Yet a survey conducted by the Industrial Development Division of The University of Michigan has revealed that an astonishing number of small to medium sized manufacturing firms support grossly inefficient inventory and materials control policies. It was apparent that although there was a tremendous need for improvement of the existing manual systems, many of the inadequate controls could quite feasibly be tightened by a computer-aided system.[4]

Economic Order Quantity Method. This method of inventory control involves the production of an ideal quantity, known as the *economic lot size*, which is the number of units per lot that minimizes the cost of a month's supply of a given product. Ordinarily a month's supply will consist of several such economic lots.

In the area of manufacturing, there are two basic methods of producing goods for shipment to customers. One method is *production to customer's order*, in which case only sales orders determine the size of the lots processed. When the orders are completed and have passed inspection, they are shipped at once.[5] The second basic method of manufacture, to which the economic order quantity method applies, is called *production to stock*. This simply means that the manufacturer determines how many units to manufacture in any one lot and that completed lots are placed in the stock room to await shipment when a customer places an order. This method is used by job-lot firms that produce standardized products or component parts. Lots are moved through the process in single containers or in groups of containers moved simultaneously. When producing to stock, all output that passes final inspection is used to replenish the stock of goods carried in the finished goods stock room. Shipments are made from stock, pursuant to written shipping requisitions. When stock room

---

[4] Wilbert Steffy, William J. Buer, and Lawrence H. Schultz, *Inventory Controls for the Small and Medium Sized Firm* (Ann Arbor: Industrial Development Division, Institute of Science and Technology, The University of Michigan, 1970), p. 51.

[5] It follows that there is no finished goods inventory and no stock room in the case of production to customer's order. This means that there are no inventory carrying charges to oppose to the machine setup and other preparation costs, and so the total cost minimization possible for production to stock is here nonexistent. Hence, an economic lot size could not be calculated and used, given customer's order production, even if the sales order did not fix the lot size.

inventory declines to a predetermined number of units, called the *reorder point*, a new lot is put in process. When completed, it is inspected and placed in the stock room, in its turn.[6]

Nature and Significance of Economic Lot Size. Before standardized items can be produced to stock when stock room inventory needs replenishment, the manufacturer must determine the quantity to produce at one time. The small manufacturer, especially, is subject to two conflicting forces in determining economic order quantities. On the one hand, he realizes that a larger number of units per lot will lower the unit cost of production. This is because the fixed preparation costs—such as machine setup labor and ticket writing—are spread over a larger number of units per lot. On the other hand, he knows that expenses involved in carrying finished goods inventory would be decreased by having a smaller lot. There is a point of balance, however, where a determinable number of units per lot will minimize the total of these two types of costs over a period of time. It is obvious that such an operating cost situation is desirable in any manufacturing plant, whether small or large.

Computing and using an economic lot size, accordingly, requires production to stock—with resultant inventory carrying charges—of two or more standardized products, processed alternately so that there will be machine setup and other preparation costs.

Although it is not similarly an ironclad requirement, it is highly desirable to set and use cost and performance standards. In the absence of standard costs, use of an economic lot size becomes impractical since it would have to be recalculated for each new factory order in the light of the preceding order's actual costs. Moreover, it is also desirable to have a constant lot size for the whole plant. This is especially true in the small factory.

Inventory Cycling. The economic order quantity is related to the type of inventory cycle used. The economic lot size is the amount to be produced at one time, which, added to the minimum, determines the maximum number of units to be carried in stock. After the maximum is reached, succeeding days' shipments lower the inventory balance gradually until it reaches or closely approaches the reorder point. When this happens, a new factory order is written up. The difference between reorder point quantity and minimum quantity is the supply required until completion of a new production run. At the minimum, the new lot typically is finished, whereupon the balance on hand jumps again to maximum. The inventory cycle then starts again.

Standard Symbols and Formulas. The small entrepreneur need not construct his own formulas for calculating the economic order quantity if he uses the type of inventory cycling described above. If he manufactures two or more products intermittently, certain inventory formulas which are available for each of these products are given on page 396, following an explanation of the standard symbols used for such formulas.

---

[6] If a manufacturer made a single standardized product (or part), it would process the one product continuously, which would eliminate the periodic setups. There would also be no real need of a stock room, as the plant's output rate could be geared to its normal rate of shipments. Then, if a small daily excess were produced, it could be stored overnight at final inspection, or in the shipping room, while under-production could be caught up by one or two days' overtime. Hence, an economic lot size would not then be needed or calculated.

X = the economic lot size, stated in units
Y = the total dollar cost of a month's supply of the product
S = the budgeted monthly sales, stated in units
A = the lot preparation cost, stated in dollars
C = unit cost of manufacture (exclusive of all preparation costs)
T = the cost of handling and storing an item of finished goods for one month
K = taxes, insurance, and interest on inventory investment, stated as a monthly decimal fraction part of unit manufacturing cost
m = minimum number of units in stock
R = reorder point number of units in stock
M = maximum number of units in stock

1. Formula for maximum finished goods inventory: $M = m + X$

2. Formula for average finished goods inventory: $\dfrac{R + m + X}{2}$

In the case of lot-by-lot manufacture, using the standard symbols and the above-stated inventory formulas, the equation for monthly cost of the supply of a given kind of product is as follows:

$$Y = S\left(\frac{A}{X}\right) + T\,(m + X) + K\left(C + \frac{A}{X}\right)\left(\frac{R + m + X}{2}\right)$$

To minimize such a monthly cost equation, which is an upbending function, one must resort to the differential calculus. The first derivative of the Y cost equation is taken with respect to the variable X, is equated to zero, and solved algebraically for X. The result is the following economic lot size formula.

$$X = \sqrt{\frac{2\,SA + KA\,(m + R)}{2\,T + KC}}$$

The reader should note that any square root is either positive or negative. As a practical consideration, the negative square root does not apply since one cannot manufacture *less than no units per lot.*

This formula[7] can be checked by substituting the calculated X value in the Y cost equation, along with the values of the requisite constants. The Y cost in dollars corresponding to the calculated X quantity will be found to be smaller than the Y cost for any smaller or larger X value substituted in the given equation. This empirical procedure verifies the accuracy of both the X formula and the Y cost equation.

Significant Cost Factors. The two most significant preparation costs are those already mentioned—machine setups and ticket writing. Offsetting these, there are five inventory expenses which are normally significant in amount. These are taxes, insurance, imputed interest cost on investment in inventory in process

---

[7] Such an X is the economic number of units to process per lot in a job lot factory. A similar economic production run formula can be derived for use in continuous processing plants manufacturing two or more products alternately to stock. Consideration of such is omitted here, however, since *small* continuous processing plants of this sort are relatively few in number.

and in stock, cost of warehouse space, and warehousing labor charges. It is possible, of course, that there will be other significant cost elements which will require inclusion both on the side of preparation cost and on the side of inventory carrying charges.

It is noteworthy also that departures up to 25 percent, either above or below the economic lot size, are tolerable. Experience has shown that such departures do not occasion a significant cost increase for a month's supply of the product. This could mean that an experienced small manufacturer could "guess" satisfactory lot sizes inasmuch as he would hardly be wrong by more than 25 percent. But, despite long experience, he could never be *sure* of guessing a satisfactory lot size. Hence, in general, computation of the economic lot size seems desirable.

The small manufacturer may experience difficulties in the use of economic order quantities. Among these are the following:

1. It is easy to overlook a significant cost factor in setting up the cost equation, or to make arithmetic errors in computation, either of which makes the resultant economic order quantity erroneous and valueless.
2. It is necessary frequently to recalculate the economic order quantity, unless a standard cost system is used, because of variations in actual cost per lot. And setting up a standard cost system can be quite expensive and time-consuming.

INVENTORY CONTROL IN MARKETING INSTITUTIONS

The importance of inventory control in a small retail or wholesale establishment is attested by the simple fact that inventory typically represents the major dollar investment in such a concern. Thus, it is clear that the profit prospects of the firm depend greatly upon maintenance of balanced stocks of the various classes of merchandise. Balanced stocks imply both unit control—that is, numbers of items of each kind in proper balance for profit maximization—and dollar control—that is, dollar investment in each class of merchandise neither excessive nor too small.

Having a proper assortment of goods means having enough of each of the right kinds of goods, in the right grades, sizes, and colors. If the items are branded, a proper assortment must also include a suitable brand distribution. Moreover, the existence of price lines requires having the proper assortment of goods by price lines. Generally speaking, having the right assortment of goods on hand necessitates good planning. Inventory planning of staple goods is facilitated by use of basic stock lists. These may be formulated by the merchant for himself or may be obtained from a trade association or from major suppliers. For fashion goods, the merchant is assisted in inventory planning by model stock lists provided by major suppliers. Basic and model stock lists are described in Chapter 26.

Methods of Inventory Control

Most of the techniques of inventory control used by manufacturing firms may also be used by retail or wholesale institutions. In this section we shall discuss other control methods for merchandise inventory.

Personal Observation. First of all, the small retailer may rely upon personal observation as a basis of inventory control. Given experience in his line of trade, the retailer can inspect the store periodically and detect potential shortages of some items. An example of observational control of inventory, used as a supplement to other control techniques, is found in the textbook division of a college bookstore during a September or February buying rush. The manager inspects book stocks regularly to discover those books that are likely to be sold out during the registration period.

Inventory Turnover Ratio. Another frequently used tool for merchandise inventory control is the inventory turnover ratio. This ratio measures the efficiency of the merchant in maintaining a good working inventory and may be calculated weekly, monthly, quarterly, and annually. The merchandise inventory turnover ratio is properly computed by dividing the cost of merchandise sold by the average investment in inventory measured in cost dollars.[8] Goods are purchased, placed in stock, and sold to customers. If the cost of the average stock is equal to the cost of the goods sold in one year, the turnover rate would be one. Ordinarily, however, standard inventory turnover ratios are much higher than this. It is important to know the normal inventory turnover ratio for a particular line of business in order to have a standard for measurement.[9] This may be obtained from Dun and Bradstreet, a trade association, or other appropriate source. Too high a turnover, as well as too low a turnover, can be bad. The best turnover position is above, but not too far above, the industry standard turnover.

Retail Inventory Method. The retail method of inventory requires that starting inventory and purchases be recorded at both cost and retail, with sales, net markdowns, and net added markups [10] entered at retail only. The entries are so made that starting inventories, purchases, and net added markups can be totaled to provide cost and retail values of goods available for sale during the accounting period. Sales and net markdowns are separately recorded at retail and their total deducted from the total retail value of starting inventories, purchases, and net added markups, to arrive at the retail value of ending inventory. Then, with X defined as the ending inventory valued at cost, one can set up the proportion: X is to the ending inventory at retail as the combined cost of starting inventory and purchases is to the retail value thereof. Solved for X, this yields the cost value of ending inventory, measured in dollars. This is the value of the inventory for balance sheet purposes.

Example of Retail Inventory Method. A small department store, using the retail method of inventory, has the following April data:

---

[8] Most experts still insist on dividing oranges by apples, with respect to this ratio, by using net sales as its numerator. This is illogical because it divides sales price dollars by cost price dollars. Admittedly, it *does* provide a basis for measuring change even though it is technically inaccurate.

[9] The industry standard ratio numerator may also be stated in sales price dollars and so require adjustment to cost dollars; this can be accomplished from a knowledge of industry standard gross margin and cost of sales.

[10] Initial markup is the excess of initial sales price over the purchase cost of the goods and the pertinent transportation cost. Added markups are increases in selling price above initially marked prices. These may later be cancelled, in part, in which case the difference is the net added markup. Markdowns are reductions below original sales prices. These may be subsequently cancelled, in part, in which case the difference is the net markdown.

Sales	$75,000	
Added markups	6,000	
Markdowns	2,500	
Markdown cancellations	1,800	
Purchases	45,000 @ cost	$81,000 @ retail
Freight in	500	
Starting inventory	1,000 @ cost	$1,800 @ retail

Its ending inventory in cost dollars, showing all calculations, is found as follows:

	Cost	Retail	
Starting inventory	$ 1,000	$ 1,800	
Purchases	45,000	81,000	
Freight in	500		
Added markups (net)		6,000	$88,800
Goods available for sale	$46,500		
Sales		$75,000	
Markdowns (net)		700	75,700
Ending inventory			$13,100

The governing proportion in this case is: "Cost of ending inventory" is to "Retail value of ending inventory" as "Cost of goods available for sale during month" is to "Retail value of goods available for sale during month." Accordingly,

$$X:13,100 : : 46,500:88,800$$
$$88,800X = 13,100 \times 46,500$$
$$88,800X = 609,150,000$$
$$X = 609,150,000 \div 88,800 = 6,859.80$$

Because this derives from a method of averaging and because, obviously, all prior dollar values were rounded to even dollars, the balance sheet of this enterprise would show the merchandise inventory at $6,860 (rounded to the closest dollar), which is its value stated in cost dollars.

Primary Use of Retail Inventory Method. The retail inventory method was developed primarily for department stores as a basis for *dollar control* of merchandise stocks involving a multiplicity of items in a number of departments. Such inventory conditions, together with a high volume of sales, preclude the use of perpetual inventory cards for each item and also make the use of physical inventory methods arduous and unsatisfactory for control. But the retail method does not contribute to *unit control*.

Advantages of the Retail Inventory Method. The retail method of inventory is approved for income tax reporting, and it facilitates preparation of monthly financial statements, which would be prohibitively expensive if physical inventories were required as their basis. Moreover, the retail method gives a more conservative balance sheet evaluation than historical cost data would provide because it relates the inventory values to current sales prices—that is, it relates them to original sales prices plus and minus added markups and markdowns. The latter adjust for obsolescence and overstocking. Hence, the retail method of inventory gives valuations equivalent to the lower of cost or market value. These are potent advantages of using this method.

Weaknesses of the Retail Inventory Method. The retail inventory method has certain weaknesses:

1. Being based on averages and applied on a department-wide or class-of-merchandise basis, the retail method of inventory tends to overvalue certain merchandise items and undervalue others. That is, the inventory value on a balance sheet, computed under the retail method of inventory, shows a cost value for total inventory which assumes that all inventory items have the same relation between cost and sales price; this is frequently untrue.

    The retailer ordinarily finds it desirable or necessary to sell merchandise with different gross margins. To the extent that sales are not proportional among the merchandise groups carrying different gross margins, the inventory value computed by the retail inventory method may be distorted. That is, separate inventories, using this method, are required for each "gross margin" class, for complete accuracy.

2. Given very frequent markups and markdowns, the record keeping for the retail method becomes arduous and somewhat costly. This is particularly true if separate "gross margin class" inventories are individually maintained under this method.

3. The system also ignores stock shortages and employee discounts, and suffers disadvantages in the proper handling of trade-ins and customer discounts. Of course, physical inventory, used along with the retail method, helps reveal the "ignored" stock shortages. But this adds to cost and merely proves the method's inefficiency.

The retail method of inventory may be an effective system, and it is certainly a unified, integrated system of inventory control in a retail store. Nevertheless, its disadvantages may sometimes outweigh its advantages. Hence, the small retailer should consider carefully both its strengths and limitations before reaching a decision on its use.

Business Fluctuations and Profitable Inventory Levels

As noted earlier in the chapter, the major problem of inventory control in any business is maintenance of the proper amount of goods in inventory at all times. Small firms that do not maintain proper inventory levels at all times invariably get into difficulties. For example, suppose a small business finds itself with a large inventory when the crest of the business cycle arrives. Inevitably, a period of liquidation at falling prices ensues as management anticipates recession and attempts to reduce inventories. Such price decline losses are hard for a small business to undergo and survive.

Most businessmen insist that their policy is to gear inventory levels to sales levels. That is, they attempt always to maintain a relatively fixed ratio, properly applicable to their line of business or industry, between inventory and sales. Even with such a policy, there are many exceptions required because of business cycle, price level, and other business factor changes. Moreover, standard inventory data for an industry reflect both highs and lows in inventory levels. The industry obviously does not maintain the exact average inventory from month to month or day to day. By rigidly following a fixed ratio of stock to sales, the firm finds itself with high inventories at the crest of the cycle, to be liquidated at a loss in the ensuing price decline period; and, in the trough of the cycle, with too small an inventory, the firm finds that sales and profits are lost in the ensuing upsurge of business.

Perhaps the best answer for the small business is to compute the normal inventory-sales ratio for the particular line of business or industry. In so doing, account must be taken of any uptrend in sales present for the particular line of business or industry, together with cyclical and seasonal fluctuations. It is also desirable to remember that in practically every industry or line of business the inventory-sales ratio varies inversely with sales. It does not remain fixed over time, as sales vary in amount cyclically and seasonally.

Proper identification of the normal variation in the inventory-sales ratio as sales go up and down cyclically and seasonally makes possible more accurate budgeting for inventory. Since seasonal movements and unexpected economic factor changes may cause differences between budgeted sales and actual sales, the small firm should also gear the inventory level to actual sales, month by month, during a budget year. This means that it will not blindly follow the budgeted inventory-to-sales ratio, month by month, over the year, but instead will revise the budget in line with actual sales trends as the year develops.

 Summary

1. All businesses face the problem of inventory control, though the problem varies in importance with the type of business conducted.

2. The objectives of inventory management are the following: (a) assuring uninterrupted business operation; (b) maximization of sales; (c) protection of assets; (d) minimization of inventory investment; and (e) provision of records to facilitate administrative action and control.

3. The three categories of inventory in industrial concerns are raw materials and supplies, work in process, and finished goods.

4. Minimum inventory size is usually not zero but an amount that represents a "minimum reserve stock." Examples of factors affecting the size of this minimum amount are the time necessary to acquire additional inventory, amount and frequency of withdrawals, and certainty of obtaining deliveries of critical items within specified time limits.

5. Inventory control in manufacturing firms may be accomplished by using the perpetual inventory method or the physical inventory method. In some cases, computer-aided inventory systems are used. Calculation of the economic order quantity specifies the proper amount to purchase at one time and thus determines the maximum inventory size.

6. In producing two or more standardized items for stock, the ideal quantity of product to manufacture is the "economic lot size." This is the amount that minimizes the cost of a supply of the product over a month (or other period of time).

7. Inventory control in marketing institutions may be accomplished by other methods such as personal observation, the use of the inventory turnover ratio, and retail inventory method.

8. The retail inventory method is particularly useful in stores where physical and perpetual inventory systems are not practical because of the sales volume and the great number of items to be controlled.

9. Cyclical and seasonal fluctuations in sales also affect the determination of proper inventory levels.

Discussion Questions

1. One objective of inventory control is to assure continuous operations. Would this be more important for a retail store or a clothing manufacturer? Would this objective have any relevance to a bowling alley or barbershop?
2. Does maximization of inventory turnover also result in maximization of sales? Explain.
3. What types of costs would be magnified by maintenance of an excessively large inventory?
4. In what ways can assets be protected by inventory control? Explain the pertinence of your answers to various kinds of inventory items—for example, gasoline, dresses, jewelry, books, greeting cards, new and used automobiles, tractors, TV sets, cameras, fresh vegetables, etc.
5. Explain the nature of the following three types of factory inventories: (a) raw materials and supplies; (b) work in process; and (c) finished goods.
6. Is the "minimum reserve stock" fundamentally a current asset or a fixed asset? Explain.
7. Explain the conditions that would make it possible to hold the "minimum reserve stock" close to zero.
8. What are the advantages and disadvantages of a perpetual inventory system in contrast to a physical inventory system? For what kinds of inventory would a perpetual inventory system be impractical? Explain why.
9. On what types of inventory items would requisitions be justified in releasing them from stock? On what types of items would requisitions be unnecessary?
10. What would be the nature of inventory control in a "job shop" in which production is to fill specific sales orders?
11. Under what conditions can economic size lots be processed in a factory? Does this rule out their use in small plants? Why, or why not? What benefits and disadvantages are derived from use of economic lot sizes?
12. How does the use of economic order quantities affect inventory levels? Explain.
13. Can visual inspection ever provide effective inventory control? Explain.
14. What is the difference between the retail method of inventory and the traditional physical inventory method as used by a manufacturer?
15. Evaluate the policy followed by many firms that attempt to profit by speculative increases in inventory during periods of rising prices.
16. Does degree of effectiveness of inventory control distinguish good managers from poor managers? Explain.
17. Are quarterly inventory audits by the firm's CPA needed in small factories producing standardized parts for sale to industrial users? In a small town florist's shop? In a motel located in a large city? Why?

Case E-1

HOUSTON WIRE ROPE COMPANY

Late in 1967, Paul H. Rogers, major stockholder and president of Houston Wire Rope Company, faced the perennial capital-shortage problem of small business firms.

Background of the Company

In 1951, Rogers, then a sales representative for a major producer of wire rope, conceived the idea of a business which would specialize in the purchase and resale of used wire rope. Acting upon the idea, he established his business in Houston, Texas, purchasing used wire rope from the oil fields and selling it to mining, logging, and marine companies. In addition to purchasing and selling, some processing of the used rope was required. This involved rewinding onto new reels, inspection and grading of the rope, cutting out seriously defective pieces, and lubrication. The company quickly gained market acceptance and increased its sales volume each year.

In 1967, the Houston Wire Rope Company had attained an annual sales volume of approximately $1,193,000. It had added new wire rope imported from Holland, Belgium, Germany, Italy, and Japan to supplement its lines of used rope. In fact, new rope had grown to account for almost 58 percent of total dollar sales volume. Approximately 40 percent of used rope sales were made to the marine industry (including substantial sales to large dredging companies), 25 percent to the logging industry, and 35 percent to the mining industry. Of the imported new rope sales, about 60 percent went to industrial customers, 25 percent to marine customers, and 15 percent to oil producers.

Sales were made to a nationwide market and even to a few accounts in Canada. Branch warehouses were also maintained in Jeanerette, Louisiana, and Oklahoma City, Oklahoma. A warehouse at Eugene,

Oregon, had recently been closed. Although the major purpose of the branches was to purchase used rope from the oil industry in their respective areas, they also made sales in the same areas.

Need for Additional Funds

Throughout the history of the business, Rogers had felt the limitations imposed by inadequate capital. In starting each new branch, for example, a sum of $1,000 had been deposited in a local bank for use by the branch manager. This amount was increased as need developed for additional funds in the area. Competition had frequently been great, however, for all available funds.

The nature of the financing problem had changed somewhat over the years. In 1967, the company was being pressured by its bank to reduce short-term borrowing. In fact, the bank desired that outstanding loans be substantially reduced by a series of payments over the next few months. This pressure for reduction of short-term loans occurred at a time when the company was experiencing a need for all the working capital it could obtain. Working funds were required for normal operating requirements, and cash was also needed to pay income taxes and employees' bonuses at the end of the year.

Relationships with Local Bank

The bulk of Houston Wire Rope Company's banking business was transacted with a relatively small local bank. Rogers was a stockholder and also served as a director of this bank. Although the company was free to deal with any bank, there was a normal expectation that the company would concentrate the major part of its business with this bank. Although Rogers owned stock, it might be noted that he was not a major stockholder of the bank.

The size of this bank was such that its maximum loan limit to any one business firm was $40,000. A limit of this type was not particularly burdensome to the firm when it was small, but it did present problems as the company grew in size and in its loan requirements. The local bank did arrange for additional loans from a larger Houston bank as the need for funds exceeded its own capacity. Such loans were negotiated through the local bank, although occasionally Houston Wire Rope Company personnel had direct contact with the larger Houston Bank.

All notes payable to the local bank were secured by an officer's letter of guaranty. In effect, this meant that Rogers, the president, personally guaranteed every obligation of the corporation to the bank. This applied not only to unsecured loans, but also to notes supported by warehouse receipts (covering new wire rope) and installment notes secured by equipment. In effect, the loans were supported by the capital of the Houston Wire Rope Company, which amounted to a little more than $286,000, by collateral in the form of wire rope and equipment, and also by the personal signature of the president.

Unsecured Loans

The unsecured loans of the Houston Wire Rope Company amounted to $44,000 as of September 30, 1967. (This borrowing was supported by an insurance policy on the life of the president.) It is evident from the financial statement in Exhibit 1 that this type of borrowing had increased rather than decreased during recent years. Indeed, it had not been reduced to zero at any time.

The bank had expressed the opinion that this borrowing should be reduced to zero within the next few months. The bank took the position that it did not wish to provide intermediate or long-term capital for the company. The constant renewal of short-term notes, however, was equivalent to long-term financing.

As a result of pressure by the bank, Houston Wire Rope Company was attempting to reduce this loan by approximately $8,000 each month. It appeared that this would become increasingly difficult in view of the continuing demand for operating funds and the need for cash for income tax and profit sharing payments. This borrowing carried a 7 percent interest rate.

Borrowing Secured by Warehouse Receipts

Another type of bank borrowing used to finance inventory was secured by bonded warehouse receipts. New wire rope was placed in a bonded warehouse, and the bank proceeded to loan 80 percent of the cost value of this rope. As of September 30, 1967, this amounted to $60,092.80.

Only a part of the company's rope was housed in a bonded warehouse. All used rope and some new rope were kept in the company's warehouse and yard. The arrangement of keeping the wire rope in the bonded warehouse provided no great difficulty in meeting customer requests. In other words, the new rope could be obtained quickly from the warehouse as it was needed to fill customer orders. From a marketing standpoint, therefore, there was little problem involved in this method of financing.

The interest charge for this borrowing, to be computed realistically, would need to reflect not only the direct interest charge but also warehouse costs. When analyzed in this way, it appeared that the actual interest cost on this type of borrowing was between 9 and 10 percent per annum.

The larger Houston bank carrying the warehouse loan had expressed reluctance to continue the loan beyond the calendar year of 1967. From the standpoint of the bank, the element of danger in such a loan is determined by the stability or lack of stability in the value of the item being warehoused. According to the feelings of Houston Wire Rope Company personnel, new wire rope is not subject to extensive physical depreciation or obsolescence and thus should support a loan without undue concern to lending officials. However, the lending bank was pressuring for reduction of this type of borrowing.

Notes Secured by Equipment

Another type of borrowing was secured by equipment—primarily automobiles and trucks. As of September 30, 1967, such loans amounted to $18,153.93. These loans involved monthly installment payments. The rate of interest was 9 percent.

Houston Wire Rope Company
Comparative Balance Sheet
September 30, 1967, 1966, and 1965

	Sept. 30 1967	Sept. 30 1966	Sept. 30 1965
ASSETS			
Current Assets			
Cash on hand and in banks	$ 33,451.48	$ 17,745.45	$ 23,527.69
Accounts receivable:			
Trade	157,873.42	150,713.94	156,002.09
Employees and miscellaneous	642.64	950.15	1,580.73
Inventory:			
New wire rope (partially pledged as collateral on notes payable)	206,226.53	171,483.47	238,706.85
Used wire rope	46,107.48	50,876.61	43,250.73
Total Current Assets	$444,301.55	$391,769.62	$463,068.09
Other Assets			
Prepaid insurance	$ 8,289.19	$ 9,668.60	$ 10,661.72
Cash surrender value of life insurance	7,412.00	6,342.50	5,280.50
Club memberships	1,020.00	1,020.00	1,236.00
Airline and utility deposits	525.00	435.00	435.00
Prepaid interest	780.26	410.88	2,246.41
Prepaid rent	325.00	1,240.00	175.00
Total Other Assets	$ 18,351.45	$ 19,116.98	$ 20,034.63
Property			
Automobiles and trucks	$ 72,484.18	$ 93,052.91	$115,976.16
Machinery and equipment	25,673.56	23,200.41	18,630.03
Office equipment	17,171.79	14,297.05	11,658.02
Leasehold improvements	15,616.01	15,616.01	1,062.60
	$130,945.54	$146,166.38	$147,326.81
Less depreciation	57,488.05	67,246.56	58,329.57
Total Property	$ 73,457.49	$ 78,919.82	$ 88,997.24
TOTAL ASSETS	$536,110.49	$489,806.42	$572,099.96
LIABILITIES AND CAPITAL			
Current Liabilities			
Notes payable—bank (secured by officer's letter of guaranty):			
Secured by insurance policy on life of officer	$ 44,000.00	$ 24,000.00	$ 23,000.00
Secured by warehouse receipts covering new wire rope	60,092.80	34,465.20	81,160.52
Monthly installment notes payable due within one year, secured by equipment	18,153.93	6,861.47	27,984.68
	$122,246.73	$ 65,326.67	$132,145.20
Accounts payable—trade	96,217.77	108,032.89	123,788.51
Due to employees' profit-sharing trust	7,268.43	8,842.71	16,684.59
Bonus payable to employees	0	10,604.55	15,141.00
Estimated income tax payable	4,934.58	6,535.60	16,500.00
Payroll, property and sales tax payable	9,166.06	11,537.13	11,230.99
Accrued payroll	3,773.20	3,785.35	2,989.56
Total Current Liabilities	$243,606.77	$214,664.90	$318,479.85
Noncurrent Liabilities			
Installment notes payable due after one year	0.00	0.00	4,564.60
Note payable—loan on life insurance policy	6,342.50	6,342.50	0.00
Total Liabilities	$249,949.27	$221,007.40	$323,044.45
Capital			
Capital stock	$234,270.00	$234,270.00	$234,270.00
Earned surplus	52,518.82	35,113.52	14,785.51
	$286,788.82	$269,383.52	$249,055.51
Less stock held in treasury at cost	627.60	584.50	0.00
Total Capital	$286,161.22	$268,799.02	$249,055.51
TOTAL LIABILITIES AND CAPITAL	$536,110.49	$489,806.42	$572,099.96

Exhibit 1

In view of the installment basis of payment, however, the actual rate of interest was higher than the nominal rate.

Accounts Receivable

Trade accounts receivable constituted a substantial portion of the company's current assets, amounting to $157,873.42 as of September 30, 1967. Aging of these accounts for the last three years produced the following distribution:

used rope that at an earlier period were readily available. Management felt compelled to take advantage of every opportunity to purchase used rope whenever it was available at a reasonable price.

Net Worth Financing

As is evident from the balance sheet presented in Exhibit 1, the net worth of the company accounted for more than 50 percent of total liabilities and net worth.

Age	9-30-67	9-30-66	9-30-65
Current to 30 days	$ 90,411.52	$ 73,753.98	$ 84,303.97
30-60 days	24,614.62	30,184.44	35,760.14
60-90 days	14,149.65	15,577.69	15,768.63
Over 90 days	28,697.63	31,197.83	20,169.35
TOTAL	$157,873.42	$150,713.94	$156,002.09

Rogers felt that the growing age in accounts receivable was explained, in part at least, by the practice of selling to marginal customers, such as small oil drillers, who were frequently slow in their payments. There was no way to determine quantitatively, however, the extent to which this may have been responsible for the change.

Houston Wire Rope Company offered terms of sale of 2/10, n/30. In spite of the attractive discount for cash payment, however, the company was forced to carry the large accounts receivable balance.

Inventory Financing

The largest working capital item of Houston Wire Rope Company was that of inventory. As of September 30, 1967, the inventory account, both new and used rope, amounted to $252,334.01. Of this amount, $74,383.50 was pledged as collateral on notes payable. In other words, this represented new rope that was stored in the bonded warehouse.

The company was finding it increasingly difficult to control the inventory level of used wire rope. The supply of used rope had declined in recent years, making it more difficult to obtain quantities of

As of September 30, 1967, total net worth amounted to $286,161.22. This amount has been built up over the years by retaining a portion of net income in the firm. A comparison of sales and net income retained in the business is presented at the bottom of page 407. The profits that were plowed back into the business provided the funds for expansion. In fact, Rogers had reinvested substantially all earnings over and above expenses. His personal assets were thus largely tied up in the business.

Income taxes had obviously reduced the funds available for expansion. In the last three fiscal years, a total of almost $27,000 had been required for income tax payments (see Exhibit 2).

In addition, a cash bonus plan paid employees 25 percent of profits before income taxes, until 1967 when it was decided the reduction in profit would not justify any cash bonus. A profit-sharing (retirement) plan paid 25 percent of profits after bonus and before income taxes. Rogers felt that employees of the firm (28 in all) were in a large measure responsible for the success of the business and that these compensation plans were important in recognizing employee contributions. They obviously imposed a requirement for cash, however, that might

Houston Wire Rope Company
Comparative Income Statement
For Years Ended September 30, 1967, 1966, and 1965

	Year Ended		
	September 30 1967	September 30 1966	September 30 1965
INCOME			
Sales	$1,193,364.55	$1,240,073.05	$1,080,803.33
Less: Material cost	626,230.77	624,008.55	515,626.76
Gross profit	$ 567,133.78	$ 616,064.50	$ 565,176.57
Other income	6,442.25	4,803.11	4,322.79
	$ 573,576.03	$ 620,867.61	$ 569,499.36
EXPENSE			
Advertising	$ 6,600.70	$ 8,201.07	$ 5,072.98
Auto, truck and equipment leasing ...	36,119.72	17,089.48	356.36
Bad debts	6,537.74	7,827.51	8,516.76
Contract work	1,648.05	1,946.02	1,174.24
Contributions	305.00	178.90	492.50
Depreciation	26,268.88	33,681.62	32,852.56
Dues & subscriptions	1,568.30	1,397.00	1,398.65
Entertainment	2,099.45	3,481.10	1,901.26
Freight	35,370.37	38,814.53	32,698.42
Insurance	17,279.78	20,266.95	17,479.90
Interest expense	10,006.01	12,771.86	8,016.58
Legal & professional	10,385.53	9,397.61	8,281.10
Office expense	7,236.99	6,320.51	6,075.93
Pension expense	600.00	1,200.00	600.00
Reels & splicing	7,832.62	5,618.64	6,048.44
Rent expense	16,842.50	14,955.00	14,300.00
Repairs	4,359.37	3,240.91	3,220.01
Sales discount	14,045.60	15,423.15	11,831.28
Sales promotion	—0—	1,266.40	3,882.90
Supplies	10,234.59	9,905.80	10,375.40
Taxes	20,823.22	20,539.40	18,562.43
Travel expense—moving employees ..	77,757.11	94,692.69	76,644.88
Utilities	15,530.03	16,228.45	13,623.35
Wages, salaries & bonus	213,359.29	238,565.70	217,811.94
Bonded warehouse expense	1,691.45	2,486.49	1,543.13
	$ 544,502.30	$ 585,496.79	$ 502,761.00
NET INCOME BEFORE OTHER DEDUCTIONS	$ 29,073.73	$ 35,370.82	$ 66,738.36
OTHER DEDUCTIONS			
Profit-sharing plan	$ 7,268.43	$ 8,842.71	$ 16,684.59
Estimated income taxes	4,400.00	6,200.00	16,360.63
	$ 11,668.43	$ 15,042.71	$ 33,045.22
NET INCOME	$ 17,405.30	$ 20,328.11	$ 33,693.14

Exhibit 2

Sales and Net Income Retained in the Business

Year Ended	Sales	Net Income Retained in Business
9-30-67	$1,193,364.55	$17,405.30
9-30-66	1,240,073.05	20,328.11
9-30-65	1,080,803.33	33,693.14

otherwise have been available for other uses. They had received some criticism from the lending banks for paying out such a large percentage of profits to employees when it was needed as additional working capital in the business.

Key employees have the privilege of buying company stock at book value, and to some extent the cash bonuses had been used for this purpose. As of September 30, 1967, seven employees held approximately 11 percent of the outstanding stock and Rogers owned 89 percent. No stock was held by outsiders, and Rogers wished to avoid sale of the stock to individuals who were not directly associated with the business.

Term Financing

It is evident from the financial statement in Exhibit 1 that the Houston Wire Rope Company had no intermediate- or long-term debt financing. From time to time, it appeared logical that some long- or intermediate-term loans should be substituted for the short-term financing. This would not only facilitate expansion, but it would also reduce the pressure from short-term financing sources.

The possibility of obtaining longer-term funds had been explored only tentatively in the past. At one time, the company talked briefly with a representative of the Small Business Administration

about the possibility of a loan. It appeared to company management, however, that such a loan might impose unreasonable restrictions and reduce the flexibility of company management. As a consequence, the company backed away from such a proposal before exploring the prospects in detail. On another occasion, the company had discussed with a major insurance company the prospects for a long-term loan. The timing of this particular request was unfortunate, however. It had coincided with a decline in company net income and thus encountered questions on the part of the insurance company's loan examiner. The company management had not pursued either of these possibilities consistently or aggressively, however.

QUESTIONS

1. Evaluate Rogers' relationship with the local bank and the firm's various financing arrangements with the bank.
2. How does the firm's management of accounts receivable affect financing? Are any changes in receivables policies or practices desirable?
3. Evaluate the firm's net worth financing.
4. Does the firm have a serious need for additional long-term financing? If so, what type of financing should be attempted?

Case E-2

SAGUARO OFFICE SUPPLY AND PRINTING COMPANY *

In January, 1971, the regional office of the Small Business Administration (SBA) in Phoenix, Arizona, received a request

for management counseling from Clark Judd. Judd is the owner of the Saguaro Office Supply and Printing Company which is located in Hoover, a small town approximately 40 miles south of Phoenix. In December, 1968, Judd had obtained an SBA loan of $10,000 to start his business. On the date of his request for management assistance, approximately $7,500 of the loan was still outstanding, and in his request Judd indicated that he was experiencing financial difficulty. He was

* This case was prepared by Professor A. M. Tuberose of Arizona State University.

desperately in need of funds and would probably require an additional loan.

The Phoenix SBA Office assigned the case to Dr. Teague, a professor of finance and a member of the Active Corps of Executives (ACE). ACE is an SBA-sponsored organization made up of successful business executives and professional men and women. Its sole purpose is to provide management assistance to small business firms. It provides service on a voluntary basis and charges no fees, except for reimbursement to the counselor for mileage and subsistence expenses incurred.

Dr. Teague was asked by the SBA office to make an evaluation of the Saguaro situation, including management ability and the potential of the firm. A meeting time was arranged and Dr. Teague, accompanied by a graduate assistant, spent one morning and, at a later date, an afternoon with the Judds at their place of business in Hoover.

Background of the Judds

The Judds are both in their mid-forties and have three teen-age children. Prior to purchasing Saguaro, the Judds had lived in Boston, Massachusetts, and migrated to Hoover via Tucson. They moved to Arizona to escape the hectic big-city life. Their ambition for years had been to find a small promising business in a small town where they could properly raise their children.

Prior to the westward migration, Judd has been employed as a printer for approximately 20 years by a Boston newspaper. From time to time, Mrs. Judd had also worked as a saleslady in department stores. When they arrived in Tucson, Clark Judd had little difficulty finding a job. Within one week he was working at his old trade for the *Tucson News* at a salary of $180 weekly. In the meantime, they were on the lookout for the type of business opportunity they could acquire for a small down payment and which they could manage themselves.

Promising Business Outlook

Six months after their arrival in Arizona, the Judds heard from a friend that the Saguaro Office Supply Company was for sale. It appeared to be the perfect opportunity. Judd could do job printing, such as advertising handbills, school programs, business cards, invitations, etc. His wife could mind the store and do the necessary record keeping. On further investigation they were more convinced that this was a very good opportunity. The town of Hoover was just the size they would like to settle in. A new trailer home assembly plant had recently been completed; a nationally known manufacturer of men's shirts and underwear operated a large plant in the town; and, nearby in Casa Grande, a junior college had recently opened its doors.

The general economic outlook was good in Hoover and the potential for Saguaro appeared very promising, but there was one drawback. Saguaro had been owned and operated as an adjunct to the local newspaper, *The Sentinel*. Sale of the business would only be made with the restriction that the new owners would not engage in job printing which would be in competition with *The Sentinel*. However, the new owners could take orders for printing jobs which would be filled by *The Sentinel*.

In September, 1968, the Judds agreed to the sales terms and purchased the Saguaro Office Supply and Printing Company for $5,000, which was their entire savings. The purchase included store fixtures and inventory. The store fixtures had an estimated value of $3,000, and the inventory had a book value of $5,000. The inventory was shopworn and fly-specked; it was actually worth closer to $2,000. Shortly after the purchase was consummated, the Judds applied for and received an SBA loan for $10,000. This loan was used for additional inventory and other working capital.

The business is located on the main crossroad of the highway that runs through the town and is adjacent to a T. G. and Y. Department Store, a large cut-rate drugstore, and other stores that form the shopping center of the town. The location is excellent for walk-in trade, but the competition is very keen. Many of the items stocked by Saguaro, such as writing instruments, greeting cards, stationery,

Sales per Product Line
January, 1971

	Amount in Dollars	Percentage of Total Sales
Office supplies	$1,465	60
Art supplies	287	12
Gifts	219	9
Wedding invitations & printing	176	7
Cards	117	5
Hobby kits	114	5
Furniture	49	1
Stationery	37	1
	$2,464	100

Exhibit 1

etc., are also carried by the surrounding stores.

From the outset the Judds realized that the nature of their acquired business was more that of a specialty greeting card and stationery store than a wholesale office supply house, although 60 percent of sales were from office supplies sold in small quantities (see Exhibit 1).

Current Business Situation

It has been two years that the Judds have been in business in Hoover. During this time many changes have occurred that have contributed to a lower level of sales than that which had been forecast by the optimistic Judds. The economic outlook that was so promising two years ago has dimmed. The mobile home assembly plant closed its doors in June of 1969 because of the shortage of skilled labor at reasonable wages. The shirt and underwear factory has also shut down. Over the past two years, the surrounding countryside has experienced a severe drought which drastically reduced the income of farmers and cattlemen in the area.

Clark Judd had anticipated that the opening of the junior college would boost sales of school supplies, typewriters, and books. Despite a rather large amount of advertising in the high school, junior college, and the local newspapers, there had been an insignificant change in sales volume. The owners of Saguaro believe that

the primary reason that they have not been able to increase the sales level is price competition. They cannot compete with the prices charged at the book stores in the schools. They made a concentrated effort to win over the office supply business in the town, but found that they could not meet the low prices of the large distributors from Tucson and Phoenix. Because of its volume purchases, the T. G. and Y. store is able to underprice Saguaro on items from pencils to typewriters.

Saguaro's Financial Picture

The Judds strive for a 50 percent mark-up on sales, but because of competitive pressures they are forced to reduce their margin on some items rather than have their goods become shopworn. They have not hesitated to take on new lines of goods that appeared to have promise. When space travel captured the imagination of most people, the Judds took on a line of working rocket model kits. These sold very well and were profitable until the competition offered these same items at much lower prices. They had the same experience with model racing cars and match box racers.

The business is operated by Mr. and Mrs. Judd alone. Clark Judd works an average of 50 hours per week. A good portion of his time is spent in promotion of sales of letterhead stationery and minor services and repairs of office equipment. Mrs. Judd averages approximately 40 hours weekly.

Saguaro Office Supply and Printing Company
Sales Record

Year	Month	Art Kits	Office Supplies	Invitations & Printing	Cards	Stationery	Hobby Kits	Gifts
1969	Jan.	253	1,815	47	109	68	955	42
	Feb.	256	1,460	39	219	43	365	105
	March	264	1,265	252	230	35	507	80
	April	268	1,136	57	220	36	233	72
	May	168	1,339	110	332	48	673	143
	June	179	1,370	43	200	38	552	140
	July	165	1,142	176	139	42	74	99
	Aug.	186	1,046	16	122	21	406	123
	Sept.	145	1,392	102	179	19	110	66
	Oct.	209	1,666	97	183	27	301	130
	Nov.	154	1,115	202	333	42	213	123
	Dec.	288	1,906	8	704	75	601	577
TOTAL 1969		2,535	16,652	1,149	2,970	494	4,990	1,700
1970	Jan.	205	1,862	65	180	50	79	146
	Feb.	215	1,848	112	201	22	119	165
	March	228	1,493	59	172	27	138	101
	April	242	1,602	71	475	16	98	91
	May	176	1,420	53	195	37	167	199
	June	206	1,786	35	106	23	120	125
	July	130	999	55	91	21	60	103
	Aug.	327	1,123	23	71	15	75	103
	Sept.	191	1,224	100	82	14	116	72
	Oct.	255	1,347	19	133	20	123	63
	Nov.	205	1,146	267	119	14	156	168
	Dec.	254	1,751	298	495	37	406	664
TOTAL 1970		2,634	17,601	1,157	2,320	296	1,657	2,000

Exhibit 2

Saguaro Office Supply and Printing Company
Balance Sheet as of December 31, 1969

ASSETS
Cash on hand	$ 1,182.99	
Accounts receivable	2,846.51	
Inventory	10,588.12	
Total Current Assets		$14,617.62
Furniture & fixtures	$3,185.00	
Delivery equipment	1,165.57	
Less reserve for depreciation	(1,453.88)	
Total Fixed Assets		2,896.69
Refundable deposits	$ 60.00	
Prepaid insurance	325.10	
Total Other Assets		385.10
TOTAL ASSETS		$17,899.41

LIABILITIES AND CAPITAL
Accounts payable	$7,090.93	
Notes payable—SBA	1,452.00	
Notes payable—truck	375.84	
Total Current Liabilities		$8,918.77
Noncurrent note payable—SBA	$7,910.90	
Noncurrent note payable—truck	425.23	
Total Noncurrent Liabilities		8,336.13
Total Liabilities		$17,254.90
Capital Account		644.51
TOTAL LIABILITIES AND CAPITAL		$17,899.41

Reconciliation of Capital Account:
Capital 1/1/69	($1,155.78)	
Net profit	6,391.17	
	$5,235.39	
Less withdrawals	4,590.88	
Capital 12/31/69	$ 644.51	

Exhibit 3

She is the record-keeper and sales clerk. If she were not available, another person would be required to do this work. For their labors the Judds have been drawing approximately $650 a month from the business for living expenses.

The records of the business are very informally maintained. In the past, no effort has been made to determine profitability from month to month (see Exhibit 2 on page 411). Once a year, a local accountant is engaged to prepare financial statements, determine the profit for the year, and prepare the income tax return (see Exhibits 3, 4, 5, and 6). From conversations with the Judds, it is apparent that the financial statements do not reflect the true condition of the firm. For example, a $700 consolidated loan to pay trade creditors was outstanding at the end of 1970. This loan carried an effective rate of interest of 35 percent. Another $1,000 loan was outstanding to the United Bank with an effective rate of interest of 10 percent. Neither of these loans, which were outstanding on December 31, 1970, are shown on the balance sheet (see Exhibit 5 on page 414).

In 1970 the liquidity position of the firm had deteriorated to the point that Saguaro could not meet maturing obligations to trade creditors. The consolidated loan from the Pacific Finance Corporation, payable for $700, was a result of the inability of Saguaro to pay its suppliers. Trade creditors insisted on payment and made the necessary arrangements with Pacific Finance.

Saguaro Office Supply and Printing Company
Profit and Loss Statement for 1969

Gross receipts		$31,059.70
Inventory 1/1/69	$10,324.50	
Purchases	16,970.99	
Total merchandise available	$27,295.49	
Inventory 12/31/69	10,588.12	
Cost of sales		16,707.37
Gross profit		$14,352.33
Expense:		
Rent	$ 1,803.00	
Operating supplies	487.69	
Advertising	416.79	
Delivery expense	1,064.01	
Interest and bank charges	407.08	
Outside services	521.15	
Office expense	96.60	
Taxes	1,031.60	
Freight	87.93	
Utilities	702.52	
Insurance	424.90	
Repairs	42.31	
Legal fees	15.00	
Dues	12.00	
Depreciation	848.58	
Total Expense		7,961.16
Net profit		$ 6,391.17

Exhibit 4

The Judds evidenced reluctance to disclose information regarding the severity of the shortage of funds. They believed that the illiquidity of the firm was due to the unavailability of trade credit. For the past six months, suppliers have demanded cash on delivery of all purchases. When merchandise is sold, funds are immediately earmarked for the replenishment of inventory.

The Saguaro owners are aware of their financial problems, but they feel that an additional loan of $5,000 would see them through the difficult times they are experiencing. An additional loan would permit them to bring all current debts up to date. This would then permit them to again receive favorable credit terms of 30 to 90 days on many items stocked.

Dr. Teague was provided with the financial statements and sales records for the years 1969 and 1970. He informed the Judds that, after a thorough analysis of the records, he would make his recommendations to the SBA. He also stated

that he would provide the Judds with a copy of the report, plus any suggestions or recommended courses of action they might take to alleviate the situation. On leaving, Dr. Teague carefully neglected to collect the agreed traveling expenses of 15 cents per mile.

QUESTIONS

1. Analyze the financial statements of the firm and determine its profitability. What are the meaningful ratios in evaluating its profitability?
2. Analyze the financial condition of this firm. What are the meaningful ratios in evaluating the financial condition?
3. Compute an approximation of the break-even point for Saguaro based on the margin (percentage) and costs in 1969. What would the sales level have to be in 1970 to break even, based on 1970 costs and margin?
4. What is the basic problem of this firm?
5. What action should be taken?

Saguaro Office Supply and Printing Company
Balance Sheet as of December 31, 1970

ASSETS

Cash	$ 92.15	
Inventory	10,218.75	
Accounts receivable	1,626.29	
Total Current Assets		$11,937.19
Store equipment and fixtures	$ 3,185.00	
Delivery equipment	1,165.57	
Less reserve for depreciation	(1,416.26)	
Total Fixed Assets		2,934.31
Refundable deposits	$ 60.00	
Prepaid insurance	325.10	
Total Other Assets		385.10
TOTAL ASSETS		$15,256.60

LIABILITIES AND CAPITAL

Accounts payable	$ 5,382.14	
Note payable—SBA	1,452.00	
Note payable—truck	125.28	
Total Current Liabilities		$ 6,959.42
Noncurrent liabilities		7,142.75
Total Liabilities		$14,102.17
Capital account, 1/1/70	$ 644.51	
Net profit	3,052.49	
	$ 3,697.00	
Drawing	2,542.57	1,154.43
TOTAL LIABILITIES AND CAPITAL		$15,256.60

Exhibit 5

Saguaro Office Supply and Printing Company
Profit and Loss Statement for 1970

Cash receipts		$32,813.35
Less cost of sales		21,577.01
Gross profit		$11,236.34
Depreciation	$ 922.96	
Rent	1,956.00	
Supplies	460.51	
Express and freight	91.46	
Bank charges	647.34	
Interest expense	743.20	
Sales taxes	863.22	
City taxes	74.00	
Dues and subscriptions	23.27	
Truck expense	551.91	
Advertising	306.01	
Repairs and maintenance	192.86	
Utilities	872.64	
Insurance	478.47	
Total expense		8,183.85
Net profit		$ 3,052.49

Exhibit 6

Case E-3

AIR COMFORT, INCORPORATED *

Joe Harris, President of Air Comfort, Incorporated, cast a rueful eye over the cost estimate that he would use as the basis for his bid on the Joy Building job tomorrow. It was already 7 p.m., the time he was due home each evening, and everyone else in the shop had gone. Stan, his right-hand man, had prepared the estimate and Joe had lots of confidence in it. Still, it was possible to leave something out on a job as big as this ($40,000 to $50,000), and it would take 20 "average jobs" to reach this volume. As he wearily jammed the estimate in his briefcase to carry home, he triggered some basic reflections on Air Comfort, *his* company, and his position. He flipped the lights out, secured the front door, and was soon in the scattered late traffic on his way home. His musings continued.

He had started Air Comfort three years ago when an "exclusive franchise" opportunity to be the Graff Company's representative in Metro had come his way. Graff is one of the big three in air conditioning and heating in the United States, and with the trend for air conditioning in homes, stores, offices, and public buildings, such a franchise has considerable potential. This had seemed particularly true in Middle Atlantic Metro with an urban population approaching three million people. Well, it had worked out, but what a sweat! Joe had always worked for large corporations after earning two degrees in mechanical engineering. His engineering training had made it easy for him to grasp the basics and a lot of the subtleties of air conditioning and heating. This same training had been a drawback in accepting some of the business situations that were now forced on him by

trade practices, competition, and less-than-scrupulous general contractors with whom he did business.

Graff's equipment was good, and the Graff Company had proved to be a reliable business partner by guaranteeing some modest bank loans from time to time. Their sales promotion literature was also good, but this was provided at cost beyond a certain free minimum so that direct mail campaigns were costly to conduct.

Air Comfort's Present Situation

Air Comfort was occupying its second home, a splendid 6,000 sq. ft. plant leased for five years and providing plenty of space for office, shops, storage, and garaging of three of the seven trucks. The work force had settled back from the summer rush to 12 reliable people: Joe, the president and jack-of-all-trades; Stan, outside salesman and chief estimator; Mary, the bookkeeper; Helen, the all-around clerk; a refrigeration foreman and three men; and a sheet metal foreman and three men.

Joe reflected on the overall aspects of his business. The results for 1969 had been as follows:

	% of Sales	% Gross Margin *
Residential contracts for add-ons, conversions, replacements, etc.	45	30
Commercial contracts for general contractors on new buildings, houses, etc.	30	30
Service calls on both residential and commercial installations	25	40

* Gross margin is sales less all direct costs; it consists of all overhead expenses plus income taxes and profit.

He had taken no vacation and had drawn a salary below what he had been

* This case was prepared by Professor P. S. Shane of George Washington University.

making in the aerospace industry three years earlier. However, he valued the psychic income and/or potential income of an entrepreneur. But how much?

As he sees it, the problem is one of increasing business volume at a reasonable cost for getting the new volume. The new facilities will accommodate up to a 100 percent increase in volume. Employees could be added. The overhead expenses, which were $75,000 last year, need not increase very much with a larger volume so that the business could then move beyond the critical size and start to return its potential profits.

Joe realized that his situation was critical. He had expanded his business and was faced with a declining economy. His cash flow position was deteriorating. He had to come up with a "second effort" sales plan to hold his position and avoid a savage retrenchment. He knew that an unsuccessful sales plan would push him back, dissipate his present team's capability, and destroy his business momentum. Where could the new volume be obtained economically?

Outline of Sales Plan

1. *Residential contracts*—Use of direct mail, neatly painted trucks with phone numbers, word-of-mouth, etc. Junk mailings cost 12 cents each for postage and material. A one-shot 2½" by 5" advertisement in the local newpapers costs $200. The industry rule-of-thumb was that a line lead in season cost $40 of advertising money. These jobs were all Air Comfort's design and were of two types:

a. *Add-ons*—The average job was $1,200; capture rate, 35 percent; average gross margin, 32 percent. The market was highly seasonal and responded to advertising in season. Pay results were good.

b. *New houses*—The average job was $1,800; capture rate, 10 percent; average gross margin, 25 percent. The market was not particularly susceptible to advertising, but a busy builder who was "using you" was valuable. Pay results were slow.

2. *Commercial contracts*—Bidding jobs to general contractors had been low in productivity. Add-ons to Air Comfort's design had been okay, but new construction to a general contractor's plans and specifications had been tricky. The two types of jobs were:

a. *Add-ons*—The average job was $8,000; capture rate, 25 percent; average gross margin, 33 percent. The market consisted of small stores, churches, restaurants, small office buildings, etc. This market was not particularly seasonal, but it was hard to find. There was high risk because of conflict of operating requirements with Air Comfort's schedules and hidden features in old buildings. Pay results were okay.

b. *New buildings* (to plans and specifications by others)—The average job was $50,000; capture rate, 10 percent; average gross margin, 25 percent. There was high risk in learning commercial procedures, interpreting specifications, satisfying inspectors, etc., but the complex work offered a challenge for cost control, innovation, and management. The work was year-round, but it caused peaks and valleys for Air Comfort because jobs were so big. Pay results were slow.

3. *Service and repair*—This was highly seasonal and hard to get on a reasonable schedule. The first hot day in spring produced more than could be handled. The work was somewhat risky because of the low level of trouble-shooting skills in the available work force. Service clientele developed slowly, but loyalty was showing up with good repeat business. The average job was about $100 although the gross margin averaged 50 percent.

As Joe drove into the driveway, he had an inspiration. A friend of his was taking a course in systems analysis and had described a tricky card problem that he had learned to work. Why wouldn't systems analysis help plot a course of action for Air Comfort? Joe resolved to drop off some financial data to his friend and seek his advice. The financial statements of Air Comfort are shown in Exhibits 1, 2, and 3. You are the friend.

Air Comfort, Incorporated
Comparative Balance Sheet
March 31

ASSETS	1969	1968
Cash	$ 9,151	$ 2,469
Trade accounts receivable	23,580	14,926
Note receivable	2,866	2,866
Materials and supplies	15,257	3,554
Work in process	23,702	22,440
Depreciable assets (net of accumulated depreciation)	8,545	6,665
Other assets	1,750	928
TOTAL ASSETS	$84,851	$53,848
LIABILITIES AND NET WORTH		
Trade accounts payable	$33,566	$ 7,480
Accrued taxes and payroll	7,705	3,495
Notes payable (bank)	10,000	10,000
Advance billings	13,961	22,037
Total Liabilities	$65,232	$43,012
Common stock	$12,000	$12,000
Retained income (Deficit)	7,619	(1,164)
Stockholders' Equity	$19,619	$10,836
TOTAL LIABILITIES AND NET WORTH	$84,851	$53,848

Exhibit 1

Air Comfort, Incorporated
Comparative Income Statement
For the Year Ending March 31

	1969	1968
Revenues	$275,484	$116,263
Cost of contracts (Schedule A)	188,707	71,820
Gross profit (Loss)	$ 86,777	$ 44,443
Operating expenses (Schedule B)	75,592	42,157
Operating profit (Loss)	$ 11,185	$ 2,286
Other income	416	285
	$ 11,601	$ 2,571
Insurance premium/Officer's life	180	216
Net profit (Loss) before taxes	$ 11,421	$ 2,355
Income taxes	2,638	130
Net profit (Loss) after taxes	$ 8,783	$ 2,225

Exhibit 2

Air Comfort, Incorporated
Schedules to Accompany Income Statement

Schedule A

	1969	1968
Material and equipment	$115,733	$42,684
Labor	57,697	23,872
Subcontracts	13,813	4,401
Other direct costs	1,464	863
Cost of contracts completed	$188,707	$71,820

Schedule B

	1969	1968
Equipment maintenance	$ 5,887	$ 2,714
Payroll taxes	5,741	2,789
Unapplied labor	4,599	2,292
Employee benefits	3,545	1,559
Small tools and supplies	3,421	4,635
Office supplies and maintenance	2,556	1,450
Travel and entertainment	2,166	889
Losses on collection	1,381	—
Total variable operating expenses	$ 29,296	$16,328
Salaries (officer and office)	$ 31,698	$15,664
Rent	3,930	3,600
Insurance	2,838	1,658
Professional services	2,300	825
Depreciation and amortization	2,023	1,668
Advertising	1,544	947
Miscellaneous other expenses	1,058	1,029
Interest	905	438
Total fixed operating expenses	$ 46,296	$25,829
Total operating expenses	$ 75,592	$42,157

Exhibit 3

QUESTIONS

1. Evaluate the success to date of Air Comfort, Incorporated.
2. How does Joe Harris propose to increase company profits? What other alternatives might be available?
3. Examine the cost structure as revealed in the financial statements and consider the implications for profit expansion.
4. What steps do you recommend for improving the profits of Air Comfort, Incorporated?

Case E-4

ARENA
SPORTS SHOP *

Early in 1966, John Blair, a college student, went to work part-time for Don Bishop, who at that time was the sole owner of the Arena Sports Shop. In January of 1967, Bishop's father died and left him another business which required his full attention, thus forcing him to give up the sports shop. A deal was made between Bishop and Blair for Blair to take over the operation and eventual ownership of the sports shop. Blair accepted all the inventory in the shop at that time and agreed to pay Bishop the total dollar amount of the inventory plus a five percent charge on this amount to cover the cost of the money Bishop had tied up at that time.

The shop was situated in a major metropolitan city on the edge of the so-called ghetto area of the city, an area with an extremely high crime rate. The shop itself was situated in an arena owned by the city, and its space was leased from the city on a yearly basis. The sports shop dealt only in hockey equipment and sharpening and repair of skates. As there was ice in the area six months of the year, the business was in operation only during the months of October through March.

The sporting goods business is one in which the obtaining and keeping of franchises is a major factor in a successful operation. Blair managed to get and maintain good relationships with these franchisers through steady volume of sales and prompt payment for goods received.

The year 1967-1968 was an extremely lucrative one for Blair, as he managed to

pay Bishop in full and take the summer off in 1968. However, during the same year the shop was broken into twice —once three weeks before Christmas when the inventory was at its peak, and once in February of 1968. Both robberies however, were covered by insurance with the only loss coming from sales lost because of a lack of stock at Christmas time. Although the shop is well secured at night, the city has no watchman on duty and the arena itself is very easy to enter at any time. Therefore, after entering the building, a person had up to six hours to gain entrance to the shop. These facts came to light upon investigation by the insurance companies who, considering the area of operation, cancelled the insurance protection for the coming year.

Faced with this lack of protection, and unable to personally absorb any financial loss, Blair was forced to keep inventories at a minimum. As a result, one very large account was lost; and in the strongly competitive sporting goods field, it was impossible to replace this dollar volume of sales.

During the year 1968-1969, Blair attempted to contact a suburban arena which was running its own skate shop and tried to interest it in his taking over the responsibilities of this operation. However, as yet, there has been no agreement reached in this area. Also, of importance is the fact that Blair has completed his undergraduate college work and within the next year will finish his postgraduate work.

QUESTIONS

1. Describe the unique features of the risk confronting the Arena Sports Shop.
2. What are the possible solutions to the risk problem? Which is best?
3. What are the weaknesses in this business as a career for John Blair?

* This case was prepared by Professor Joel Corman of Suffolk University.

Case E-5

STEVENS-KERN COMPANY

The deal being offered by the manufacturer's sales representative was impressive, to say the least. Despite his resolution to keep stereo inventory to a minimum, John R. Kern, owner and manager of Stevens-Kern Company, could not resist serious consideration of the proposal.

The Stereo Offer

The price reduction offered was substantial—some 35 to 40 percent off the customary wholesale price. There was no question that the manufacturer intended to move some merchandise with a price slash of this size. Sale of stereos nationally had been slow for some months— a fact that, in Kern's thinking, may have prompted the offer.

If stereos were to be purchased at the sharply reduced price, they could be sold at a correspondingly low price to retail customers. In fact, by also reducing the store's margin slightly, Stevens-Kern could offer its customers a "real buy." The normal and special prices on one of the popular priced models would compare as follows:

	Normal Pricing	Special Offer Pricing
Stevens-Kern's retail price	$289	$174
Wholesale cost to Stevens-Kern	204	128
Gross margin	$ 85	$ 46
Gross margin %	29.4%	26.4%

To operate profitably, Kern knew he had to buy a substantial part of his merchandise at reduced prices. By paying the normal wholesale price for appliances, he could do no more than break even. "If a salesman wants me to listen now," he said, "he'd better have some kind of a deal to offer me." That was what made the present offer hard to turn down. It *could* be a *very* good deal.

Inventory Level

The store's inventory turnover rate was a little lower than ideal. Kern had operated on the principle that it was better to be a little long on inventory than a little short on sales. As he put it, "When I reduce inventory, I reduce sales." Still, he was realistic enough to know that inventory could be excessive, thereby contributing more to expense than profit. His inventory position in stereos at the time was thin, but only six or eight stereos were needed to bring it up to a normal level.

The store's inventory investment (for all types of appliances) exceeded $150,000. Thus, the decision to expand inventory was not to be made lightly. Warehouse space was at a premium, with some overflow inventory being kept in a public warehouse. Insurance costs and taxes added further to the cost of building inventory. Kern recalled that someone had suggested that the cost of maintaining an inventory for just six months might be as high as 15 percent of its value.

The Competitive Situation

Kern knew all too well that his leading competitor, located in the same city, was getting the same offer from the same representative. If the competitor bought, Stevens-Kern should also buy in order to remain competitive. If the competitor passed up the opportunity, on the other

STEREO PRICE LIST

Model	Style	Cost	Proposed Selling Price	List Price
GROUP A (50% of order)				
HR27W	Contemporary	$128.50	$174.00	$289.00
HR37W	Contemporary	150.50	198.00	339.00
HR39L	Colonial	153.00	208.00	299.00
HR51S	Spanish	186.75	258.00	459.00
GROUP B (25% of order)				
HR58F	French Provincial	212.50	300.00	440.00
HR59S	Spanish	222.50	290.00	460.00
HR60L	Colonial	222.50	290.00	460.00
HR94LK	Colonial	175.00	240.00	360.00
HR99FK	French Provincial	230.00	310.00	460.00
GROUP C (25% of order)				
HR72W	Contemporary	286.50	400.00	600.00
HR74L	Colonial	286.50	400.00	600.00
HR75S	Spanish	286.50	400.00	600.00
HR82W	Contemporary	375.00	550.00	850.00
HR98LK	Colonial	196.50	290.00	399.95

Exhibit 1

hand, purchasing could give Stevens-Kern a chance for a competitive advantage.

Unfortunately the offer came during the off-season for stereos. Stereos normally sell best in the fall, while the spring, including March, is typically a low-sales period. The big question was whether a stereo priced at $174 (below its normal wholesale price) would be a "hot" enough item to bring in customers during the off season. If the stereos did not sell well, they might possibly be disposed of in May by offering them at cost during the store's anniversary sale.

Buying Alternatives

One condition of the offer was that any purchase must be made in lots of 30. In other words, Stevens-Kern might buy 30 stereos, 60 stereos, or other multiples of 30. The most conservative course of action was to buy none. This would minimize inventory cost. The only risk would be the loss of a competitive weapon if the competitor bought. The larger purchases would involve correspondingly greater risk but would maximize profit in the event the sale proved to be extremely popular with customers. During the preceding year, the store had sold 160 console stereos, about 60 percent of the sales occurring in the fourth quarter. The first decision, therefore, was whether to buy 0, 30, 60, 90, or 120 stereos.

If Stevens-Kern decided to buy, a second decision as to models would be required. Although the price quoted earlier was the price of a typical stereo, a variety of models were available. The buyer was required to divide his purchases among the three groups, as indicated in Exhibit 1. However, the buyer could choose to take an approximately equal number of each model or to buy in greater depth in some specific models. The question was what type of assortment, if any, could be easily sold.

QUESTIONS

1. Evaluate the inventory-carrying problem of this store. Should the inventory costs receive major attention in a decision of this type?
2. Evaluate the prospects for the type of sale envisioned by Kern.
3. Should Kern accept the offer? If so, how many stereos should be ordered?
4. In the event he accepts the offer, what assortment should be specified?

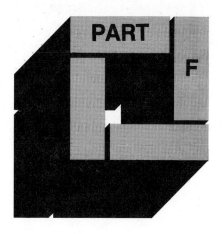

PART

F

Legal and Governmental Controls in Small Business

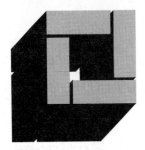

24

Business Law
and the Entrepreneur

Some important areas of the law pertaining to small business have been treated elsewhere in this text. Chapter 9, for example, investigated the application of labor law to small firms. In Chapter 13, the choice of a legal form of organization and the legal steps in initiating a business were discussed. In various other chapters, as well, references are made to pertinent legal questions applicable to a particular subject. In this chapter, first we shall consider certain areas of business law which provide for the orderly conduct of business operations and the just settlement of any disputes that may arise with regard to business dealings. Other legal aspects not necessarily concerned with daily business operations will also be discussed in the latter part of this chapter.

CONTRACTS

Contracts are voluntary agreements between two or more competent parties by which, for a consideration, one party acquires the right to have the other party perform or not perform some lawful act. For a contract to exist, the following requirements must be met:

1. Valid offer and acceptance. The offer to sell at a particular price must be accepted unconditionally by the buyer.
2. Competency of contracting parties. Contracts with parties under legal age or with other legally incompetent parties are typically unenforceable against the incompetent parties.
3. Legal objective. The agreement must not be in conflict with public policy, such as a contract to sell an illegal product or to sell any product at a price established through collusion.
4. Consideration. The seller must receive something of value; a sales contract differs from a gift.
5. Required form. Certain contracts must be in a form specified by law in order to be enforceable. For example, a contract for the sale of real property must be in writing to be enforceable.

Forms of Contract

Contracts may be written or oral. In the case of a written contract, there is little question as to the rights and duties of the parties to the contract. In fact, some types of contracts must be in written form to be enforced. The *statute of frauds* is a state law that requires such transactions as sales of $500 or more, sales of real estate, and contracts extending for more than one year to be in writing.

An oral sales contract may be enforceable if the existence of the contract can be demonstrated in some way. The existence of such an oral sales contract may prove difficult to establish. As a precautionary measure, therefore, the small business should place as many of its sales agreements as possible in writing even though they might be legally binding as oral agreements.

Long-Term Contracts

The small businessman entering into a long-term sales (or purchase) contract should certainly have it checked in advance by his attorney. Fulfillment of such a contract could prove to be financially disastrous. Consider, for example, the problem caused by a recession occurring shortly after negotiating a long-term contract. A small manufacturer might contract (as buyer) for weekly deliveries of 1,000 parts of a given kind at a stated price, covering a 30-month period. Given a severe recession shortly after signing the contract, he would soon be paying much more than the prevailing market price (since price movements tend to follow business cycle movements). He would suffer a considerable loss; the seller would obtain an unearned price profit.

An attorney can eliminate the "price gain-price loss" feature of long-term contracting by inserting a price renegotiation clause operative every time the prices moves up or down by some specified amount—say 4 percent. To back up such a renegotiation clause, the attorney might add another clause terminating the contract if the second party to it refused negotiation or delayed agreement unduly on a new price—for two months or more, perhaps. Or, an "escalator" price clause, automatically adjusting the unit price as of some specified date each month, might be used instead. This would accomplish the same objective as renegotiation. Such legal "hedging" eliminates the prospect of "windfall" gains, but it affords equal protection against excessive price losses. This leaves each contracting party in the position of earning profits through able management and operating efficiency.

Franchising Contracts

The franchising relationship described in Chapter 27 entails a legal contract between the franchiser and franchisee. There are still unsettled legal questions surrounding the use of the franchise. A possible infringement of the Sherman Antitrust Act may occur in the control of dealers by a franchiser. Specifically, the legality of geographical restrictions placed upon dealers is at issue.

In the 1963 White Motor Company case, for example, a divided court refused to declare illegal *per se* geographical restrictions that the truck manufacturer placed upon its dealers. In 1967, the Supreme Court struck down Arnold

Schwinn & Company's rule which prohibited dealers from reselling Schwinn bicycles to nonfranchised dealers, but the Court did not throw out territorial restrictions as such. In 1973, a federal district court struck down two restrictive practices of Holiday Inns, Inc. One of these practices prohibited a Holiday Inns franchisee from holding any interest in a non-Holiday Inns motel. The other practice gave competing franchises a veto power over the granting of new franchises.[1] The Supreme Court's rulings during the course of the next few years may be expected to further reduce the uncertainty that presently exists in this area.

Transfer of Title in Sales Contracts

One of the knotty legal questions involved in a sales transaction is the time of passage of legal title. Ownership does not always accompany physical possession of the goods. Neither does passage of title always occur simultaneously with payment. A customer, for example, may enter a store and arrange for the purchase of a particular type of item. The item is to be delivered later and the customer is to be billed. In such a case, there may easily be a question as to just when the ownership actually passes from seller to buyer. This could become very important to a small merchant if the goods were destroyed by a fire started when the delivery truck was involved in an accident. Thus, the question of who has title to given goods is highly important in the event that these goods are damaged or destroyed. Legally, the risk falls upon the owner or titleholder. Even though the seller has retained possession, the title and the risk may nevertheless have been acquired by the buyer.

Cash Sales. A simple, over-the-counter, cash sale of merchandise is completed with the exchange of money and goods by seller and buyer. If a buyer offers a check in payment, the transfer of title to him is conditional; and the seller retains title until the check is honored when presented to the bank for payment.

Open-Account Sales. If the sale is an open-account sale involving standardized credit terms, the title typically passes at the time of sale rather than the time of payment. In either this or the cash sale, the intention of the parties, to the extent that it is determinable, is the element that controls the timing of passing of title. It is possible, for example, for the passage of title to be delayed by failure to identify the specific item to be purchased. This means that title would not pass prior to selection or identification of the particular product in some way, even though financial arrangements have been completed.

Consignment Sales. A sale on consignment is an arrangement whereby the original owner retains title until the consignee sells the goods to a third person. Title then passes directly to the third party. Pending such a sale, the consignee is a bailee of the goods. Such a consignee is obligated to exercise at least reasonable care for the consigned goods in his possession. His selling price includes his profit margin, and he then remits to the consignor the amount due him.

---

[1] See "Is the Franchise System Legal?" *Business Week* (April 3, 1965), pp. 66-68; "When Bicycle Maker Peddles Alone," *Business Week* (July 1, 1967), pp. 39-40; and "Holiday Inns: Legal Setback for Franchisers," *Business Week* (Sept. 29, 1973), pp. 108-110.

Installment Sales. In installment selling, the seller typically protects himself by arranging for the item that is sold to act as security for the credit. This is done in either of two ways. By a *chattel mortgage*, the seller can pass title on to the buyer but still maintain a claim against the product if the buyer defaults. The other arrangement is known as a *conditional sale*. Under this arrangement the seller continues to hold title until payment is completed. In the event of the buyer's default, therefore, the seller still has title to the goods.

Prevention of and Remedies for Breach of Contract

Although legal action to force specific performance of a contract is not unknown, the courts are generally quite reluctant to rule in this way. As a result, the customary remedy in the breach of a contract is money damages. Competent legal counsel is imperative in preparing for or taking any legal action against the party who commits a breach of contract.

Legal Action by an Unpaid Seller. In many cases, the creditor-seller arranges for certain security devices so that he need not rely exclusively on the credit standing or ability of the debtor to pay. This is true in the case of installment credit provisions for chattel mortgages or conditional sales, as mentioned above. In addition, real estate mortgages serve this same purpose. Another claim against property that is quite important to some types of small businesses is known as the *mechanic's lien*. Materials suppliers or contractors performing repair or construction, for example, would have a lien against the property if the property owner or tenant defaulted in his payments for either materials or construction work. The same would be true of a small firm performing repair work on a machine or piece of equipment.

If the money provided by a security device is inadequate to satisfy the creditor's claim or if no security device exists, the creditor may sue to force payment. If the creditor wins his case, there is a judgment by the court in his favor. If the debtor does not pay, it then becomes necessary to place the execution of the judgment in the hands of the sheriff. The creditor is then paid from the proceeds of the sale of any seized property. During the suit, it is often possible for the creditor to secure an *attachment* to prevent the removal or disposal of property that might be needed to satisfy the claim. Debtor's bank accounts, in particular, are frequently attached thus.

State laws, known as *statutes of limitations*, require creditors to be reasonably prompt in bringing their claims. These are intended to protect debtors from claims in which the evidence is very old and the facts thus more difficult to establish. The length of time specified by these laws varies from one to twenty years. For small creditors, this means that legal action should not be postponed indefinitely if there is any expectation of forcing payment.

Defrauding Creditors. It might be possible for a debtor to defraud a creditor or creditors by the secret sale of an entire business before the creditors could take necessary legal action to collect. To prevent this, the various states have enacted *bulk sales laws* which effectively preclude such action. In general, they provide that any such sale of a business inventory down to the bare walls must be preceded by written notification to the creditors of the business. Otherwise, such bulk sales are fraudulent and void with respect to the creditors.

It is also possible that debtors may seek to avoid their obligations by other conveyances of property to prevent its seizure to satisfy such claims. To protect creditors, such transfers of property are viewed as fraudulent, and creditors are permitted to take a variety of legal actions against fraudulent buyers.

AGENCY RELATIONSHIPS

Small firms are often involved in agency relationships whereby one party, the *agent*, represents another party, the *principal*, in dealing with a third person. Examples of agents are: the manager of a branch office who acts as the agent of the firm, a partner who acts as an agent for the partnership, and real estate agents who represent buyers or sellers.

Agents, however, differ in the scope of their authority. The manager of a branch office is a *general agent*, whereas a real estate agent is a *special agent* with authority to act only in a particular transaction.

Obligations and Liabilities of the Principal

A principal has certain legal obligations to his agent. He must compensate the agent for his services. He must reimburse the agent for payments and expenses incurred by the agent in discharging his duties. And the principal is obligated to indemnify the agent for losses sustained in the execution of his duties.

The principal is liable to a third party for the performance of contracts made by the agent acting within the scope of his authority. A principal is also liable for fraudulent, negligent, and other wrongful acts of his agent executed within the scope of his agency.

Obligations and Liabilities of the Agent

An agent has certain obligations to the principal. In general, he must accept the orders and instructions of the principal, act in good faith, and use prudence and care in the discharge of his agency duties. Moreover, the agent is liable if he exceeds his stipulated authority and causes damage to the third party as a result—unless the principal ratifies his act, whereupon the principal becomes liable.

It is apparent that the powers of agents are such as to make the agency relationship a potentially dangerous one for small firms. For this reason, care should be exercised in selection of agents, and the authority and responsibilities should be clearly stipulated.

NEGOTIABLE INSTRUMENTS

Credit instruments, such as promissory notes, drafts, trade acceptances, and ordinary checks typically possess characteristics that make them negotiable instruments. This means that they can be transferred from one party to another as a substitute for money. When a negotiable instrument is in the possession of an individual known as a *holder in due course*, it is not subject to many of the defenses possible in the case of ordinary contracts. For this reason, the small business firm would wish to secure instruments that are prepared in such a way as to make them negotiable. In general, the requirements for negotiable instruments are as follows:

1. There must be a written, signed, unconditional promise or order to pay.
2. The amount to be paid must be specified.
3. The instrument must provide for payment on demand, at a definite time, or at a determinable time.
4. The instrument must be payable to the bearer or to the order of some person.

If a negotiable instrument is payable on a specific date, it must be presented at a reasonable hour on that date. In the event it is dishonored, the holder of the instrument should take immediate steps to protect himself by formally and immediately notifying any endorsers upon whom he has relied.

The most widely used negotiable instrument is the check. In order to protect the public, the various states have enacted laws making it a criminal offense to pass worthless or "rubber" checks. The law applies to one who draws or negotiates a check knowing there are insufficient funds to pay the check. Even though the law makes forgery a criminal offense, the business firm must still exercise due caution to avoid accepting forged checks.

An open account does not qualify as a negotiable instrument, but it does have a legal standing. It can be assigned to others. It can also be used to support claims in bankruptcy proceedings. Disputes over the amount owed are more likely in the case of this credit arrangement, but traditional methods of doing business may make it difficult or even impossible to substitute negotiable instruments for open accounts. To require a customer to complete a promissory note, for example, would be considered an insult or reflection on the credit standing of buyers in many lines of business.

OCCUPANCY AND REAL ESTATE

A small firm may either lease or own its physical plant or property. Often a particular business needs only a part of the total space available and leases the remainder to another firm. The purchase, sale, and leasing of real estate involve a number of problems causing a need for competent legal counsel.

Ownership of Real Estate

Real property consists of land and buildings and other installations permanently attached to land. It is distinguishable from *personal property* in that the latter is movable in nature. Real estate ownership is the right to possess, use, and dispose of a given piece of real estate.

Ownership of real estate is subject to certain limitations. The public interest, for example, may take precedence over a firm's private ownership interest.

Local governments, in the exercise of police power, engage in city planning and enact zoning ordinances controlling the use of real property located in particular areas. Small firms are directly affected by controls of this nature and should carefully investigate applicable zoning regulations prior to purchase of business sites. Zoning status changes already made may become effective with change of ownership of the property. The right of *eminent domain* represents another governmental limitation on ownership whereby the government can force the sale of privately owned property for such public use as streets or parks.

Certain contractual limitations on real estate ownership may also be created. A mortgage or lease, for example, serves to create certain rights for others in real property. *Easements* may give others rights of ingress and egress (even to running a railroad siding across one's property). Certain restrictions may also be incorporated in deeds, regulating the owner's use of the property. Suppose a small factory operator bought a plot of land having a three-story factory building on it, and moved in—and subsurface oil and mineral rights were held by others. The latter might then take out the oil or minerals, quite legally, causing settlement of the land under the building. The building might then crack down the middle and be adjudged unsafe for tenancy by city building and insurance company inspectors. Where does all this leave the small manufacturer? The moral is to avoid the purchase of property subject to such restrictions. The latter are essentially contractual in nature, representing agreements between the owner (or previous owners) and others.

Legal action may be required at times to prevent infringement or deterioration of one's property rights. Permitting others to possess or use one's property or to erect fences or roads on it may serve to create certain permanent rights. To forestall such action by trespassers or squatters, the property owner must resort to appropriate, timely, preventive legal action.

Transfer of Ownership in Real Property

Ownership interests that constitute real property in a legal sense are known as *estates*. These contrast with other property interests such as those created by a lease. These are different types of estates such as *fee simple estates* and *life estates and remainders*. The fee simple estate constitutes the greatest possible ownership interest in real property.

A conveyance of real property must be in written form to be valid, and legal counsel is desirable to assure transactions that are legally correct and truly represent the desires of the contracting parties. Any transfers of ownership in real property should be recorded in the appropriate public office, a step that assures legal notification to all of the true ownership of the property. Conveyance of an ownership interest in real estate is accomplished by or culminates in the transfer of a deed. The content and form of deeds must meet exacting legal requirements, and the small businessman will do well to have such drawn by a competent attorney.

Leases

A *lease* is an agreement whereby a property owner (the landlord) confers upon a tenant the right of possession and use of real property. Small business firms frequently occupy property on a rental basis or lease real estate to others. For these reasons, the legal aspects of leases are of definite importance to numerous small businesses.

Because of the delay and expense involved in eviction of a non-tenant, there is danger involved in granting possession of property without some type of lease. For this reason, the establishment of some type of tenancy relationship is a desirable precautionary measure. Tenancies may be either definite or indefinite with regard to the time period of the lease. The indefinite lease is illustrated by the *tenancy at will* whereby the lease may be terminated at the volition of either party. Many of these tenancies involve monthly rental payments without any agreement as to a minimum number of months. A few states require the party terminating such a lease to provide some notice of the impending termination. Leases may be either oral or written; according to the laws of most states, however, those for periods longer than one year must be written.

Rent must be either fixed and definite in amount or capable of being determined. As an example of the latter, many small firms operate under leases calling for rental payments based on a percentage of gross sales income.

As a general rule, the tenant is expected to maintain the property and to turn it back at the expiration of the lease in the same condition he received it. Allowance for normal wear would be made, of course. Neither party is required to undertake extensive repairs except as specified in the lease. Any improvements made to the real property belong to the landlord at the expiration of the lease. The lease may provide, however, that fixtures or equipment installed by the tenant may be removed by him.

The tenant is permitted to assign his interest in a lease to another party unless the lease specifies otherwise. In case of an assignment, the original tenant may still be held responsible for rental payments. Similarly, lessees may sublet their property, although leases often contain provisions prohibiting their doing so without written permission from the landlord. The original lessee would generally be liable for rental payments even though he sublet the property.

INSOLVENCY AND BANKRUPTCY

As noted in Chapter 5, business failure is the fate of many small firms. The legal aspects of insolvency and bankruptcy are, thus, pertinent to the many small firms that go through periods of financial distress and failure. In addition, many successful small businesses must understand their legal rights and alternative courses of action with respect to their insolvent customers.

Voluntary Settlements

As a business firm experiences financial difficulty, different warning signs appear. There is a failure to take cash discounts, and payments are postponed beyond their due dates. Lawsuits may be instituted by certain creditors. As of any particular moment, a firm may be in any of many stages of financial health. It may be solvent but not sufficiently liquid to make payments promptly. An excessive investment in inventory, for example, must be converted first into receivables and then into cash before bills can be paid. At the other extreme, a firm may be hopelessly insolvent with liabilities far in excess of assets.

Creditor firms must determine the most appropriate action to take in view of the particular circumstances. In many cases, the forced liquidation of the debtor produces a less desirable settlement than an arrangement permitting continuance of the firm as a going concern. In fact, it is often most logical and least expensive to settle out of court. These out-of-court settlements may be initiated by either the debtor or a group of major creditors. They fall into either of two categories or a combination thereof.

Extensions. An *extension* is an agreement by two or more creditors to postpone payment of a debtor's obligation for some stipulated period of time. This agreement becomes legally binding upon each of the parties to the agreement. The success of such a plan depends upon the "breathing space" given to the debtor, and one of the creditors might wreck the plan if he were permitted to forsake the agreement and press his individual claims. The agreement of each debtor involved in the agreement is considered to be sufficient consideration to the others to make it a binding contract. An extension differs, therefore, from an individual creditor's agreement to postpone payment for a time. Creditors who do not participate in the extension agreement are not bound by its terms. Accordingly, most major creditors must become parties to such an agreement if it is to succeed. Creditors should agree to an extension only if the debtor appears fundamentally honest and the financial problem appears to be temporary in nature.

Composition Settlements. The second type of voluntary settlement is known as a *composition* settlement. Creditors agree to accept a pro rata cash settlement as payment in full. For example, the creditors may accept fifty cents on the dollar in lieu of bankruptcy proceedings which might net even less.

Creditor Arrangements under the Bankruptcy Act

Section XI of the Bankruptcy Act provides for settlements that fall short of bankruptcy. The debtor's business life is spared, and, at the same time, there are elements of compulsion that are not present in purely voluntary settlements. Under this federal law, settlement plans can be adopted without the virtually unanimous agreement of creditors required in voluntary plans.

In developing a plan of settlement under Section XI, the debtor voluntarily initiates action in the court. He proposes a plan—extension, pro rata cash settlement, or some combination—and the court may either appoint a receiver to manage the business or leave it to the debtor's management under court surveillance. There is an investigation of the proposed plan, using auditors and appraisers as technical consultants. Creditors are permitted a voice in negotiations and are allowed to vote on acceptance or rejection of the final plan. If at least half of the creditors holding at least half of the liabilities accept the plan, it is adopted and becomes binding on other creditors as well.

Once the debtor meets all obligations as specified by a court-approved plan, he or she is discharged from other obligations. Further earnings need not be used to pay off other old liabilities. The debtor's advantage in using this plan is the possibility of continuing to operate as a going concern. For the creditors also, there may be a greater return under this arrangement than in forcing liquidation through bankruptcy proceedings.

Bankruptcy Proceedings

A debtor may seek release from liability for debts by voluntarily initiating bankruptcy proceedings. One or more creditors may also petition the court to declare a given debtor bankrupt. This is called *involuntary bankruptcy*. Creditors take this action against a debtor when they believe that fraud is involved or that further operation of the business would only increase their losses. The court grants the petition if it finds that the debtor is unable to pay his debts.

In bankruptcy proceedings, the court recognizes a priority of claims that gives consideration first to secured claims (such as mortgages), then to priority claims (such as wages), and finally to unsecured claims.

Although bankruptcy accomplishes a legal discharge from debts, a moral obligation remains. Furthermore, if a debtor does not "come back" and pay off all legally discharged debts, the bankruptcy will remain a perpetual blot on his credit standing.

OTHER LEGAL ASPECTS

The topics discussed in this section are not concerned with day-to-day business transactions. Nevertheless, they are important legal aspects that an entrepreneur should be familiar with for his own protection.

Trademarks

A *trademark* is a word, figure, or other symbol used to distinguish a product sold by one manufacturer or merchant from the products sold by others. Small manufacturers, in particular, often find it desirable to adopt a particular trademark and to feature it in advertising. Although trademarks may also be used by small merchants, such a practice is typically feasible only for large marketing institutions.

Common law recognizes a property right in the ownership of a trademark. In addition, registration of trademarks is permitted under federal law, a step that generally makes protection easier if infringement is attempted. A trademark registration lasts for 20 years and may be renewed for additional 20-year periods. The different states also have trademark registration laws although it is still the common law that provides the basic protection for the owner of the trademark. Full registration is recommended because the growth of a business firm may eventually make its trademark an extremely valuable asset. Even with proper registration, the user may be considered to have abandoned the trademark if he allows extensive disregard of his mark without seeking legal redress via the courts.

In view of the advertising use of trademarks, a mark's advertising potential is a leading consideration in its selection. In addition, the trademark must be dissimilar to those already in use. Although there is some latitude in defining "similarity," the safest rule is to avoid a trademark involving any likelihood of confusion.

Patents

A *patent* is the registered right of an inventor to make, use, and sell his invention. Items that may be patented include machines and products, improvements on machines and products, and new and original designs. Some small manufacturers have patented items which constitute the major part of their product line. Indeed, some businesses can trace their origin to a patented invention.

A patent attorney should be retained to act for a small business applicant in preparing an application. In addition to attorney's fees, a modest filing fee is required. When obtained, it is good for a period of 17 years and is not renewable except by specific Act of Congress. A patent may be assigned to another party, but such an assignment contract should be in writing for the protection of both parties.

Since improvements may be patented, even a small business firm obtaining an original patent may perpetuate its monopoly control of the device through timely improvements or design changes. The new patent extends the original period of protection for another 17 years. This may, or may not, be in the public interest. Another possibility is that the improvement may be invented by someone other than the holder of the original patent. The inventor of such an improvement cannot manufacture the whole article without paying royalties to the original patent-holder. He must also grant the original holder the right to use the patent improvement.

Suits for patent infringement may be brought, but they are costly and should be avoided if possible. Finding the money and legal talent with which to enforce one's legal rights is one of the major problems of patent protection in small business. Monetary damages and injunctions are available, however, if an infringement can be proved.

Copyrights

A *copyright* is the registered right of an author, composer, designer, or artist to reproduce, publish, and sell books, works of art, and the like, which are the product of the intelligence and skill of that person. The Federal Copyright Law grants such a person copyright protection to prevent the pirating of his creative work by others. Copyrights are granted for 28 years from the date of first publication, and they are renewable for a second 28-year period. A copyright holder can sue a copyright violator for damages.

Libelous Acts

Libel may be defined as printed defamation of one's reputation. Unless proper precautions are taken, there is a danger of including materials in credit correspondence that may be held by the court to be libelous. Even ordinary collection letters to a debtor have in some cases been held to be libelous by virtue of being dictated by a creditor to his stenographer. This was held to constitute "publication" of the statement. Furnishing written credit information to others may similarly subject the writer to charges of libel.

The safest rule to follow in credit correspondence is to stick strictly to the facts. The following tests have been suggested to check messages being sent to debtors:[2]

1. Are the statements true? (If not, obviously they should not be made.)
2. Is the debtor being accused of dishonesty, unfairness, or lack of integrity simply because he has failed to pay his debt? (He might not have the money to pay it.)
3. Is the debtor being accused of unwillingness or refusal to pay the debt simply because payment has not been forthcoming to date?
4. Is the debtor being accused of failure, refusal, or unwillingness to pay, or even of slowness of paying, *all* his debts, or his debts to *others*, where the writer does not have proof of these accusations? (Such accusations, if false, might tend to injure the debtor's credit standing.)

Wills

For the protection of his family and the convenience of the estate administrator, if any, a businessman should execute a will with the aid of a competent attorney. A *will* is a legal document expressing one's wishes concerning the distribution of his property after his death, the administration of the estate, and the guardianship of any minor children. Generally, a will must be in writing and executed in the legally required form to be acceptable to the court.

 Summary

1. A contract must satisfy a number of basic requirements to constitute a legally binding agreement.
2. Long-term contracts for sale or purchase must be drawn in such a way as to avoid commitments that might become financially disastrous. Legal counsel in formulating the contract is essential to assure adequate protection for the small firm.

---

[2] Credit Research Foundation, National Association of Credit Men (ed.), *Credit Management Handbook* (Homewood, Illinois: Richard D. Irwin, Inc., 1958), p. 499.

3. Some of the important features of franchise contracts are those dealing with territories, fees, sales quotas, the right to sell the franchise, and terminations. Uncertainty currently exists as to the legality of some franchise agreements because of possible conflict with the antitrust laws.

4. Passing of title is one of the elements of a sales transaction that may involve legal interpretation. Even oral sales contracts may be binding, and the seller may proceed against a delinquent debtor.

5. From a legal standpoint, there are significant differences among cash sales, open account sales, consignment sales, and installment sales.

6. Various security devices, such as mortgages and mechanic's liens, offer some protection to creditors. The creditor may seek a judgment against a debtor and possibly secure an attachment of the debtor's property. The statute of limitations places limits upon the time allowed for bringing legal action to collect debts. Attempts to defraud creditors may violate the bulk sales law or conflict with laws prohibiting fraudulent conveyances of property.

7. Both the principal and the agent have obligations and liabilities as against each other and third parties.

8. Credit instruments must be carefully drawn and correctly handled to assure their negotiability and collection.

9. Real estate ownership rights are subject to governmental limitations and also to restrictions of a contractual nature. Drawing deeds and transferring ownership of real estate necessitate the use of attorneys. Legal aspects of leases are important to the small firm either as landlord or tenant.

10. Creditors have several alternative courses they may use in dealing with debtors in financial distress. Voluntary settlements require cooperative action on the part of the major creditors. Arrangements permitting continued business life for the debtor are also possible under Section XI of the Bankruptcy Act. Bankruptcy proceedings constitutes a third alternative.

11. Some of the other legal aspects that may affect small firms include trademarks, patents, copyrights, libelous statements, and wills.

Discussion Questions

1. What are the basic requirements for the existence of a contract?

2. Should a franchisee avoid a contract permitting the establishment of other franchises in the same territory? Why or why not?

3. Why should the legality of franchising be questioned?

4. Define the following: (a) Statute of frauds, (b) Mechanic's lien, (c) Attachment, and (d) Statute of limitations.

5. What security devices are

customarily used in installment selling? What is the legal difference between them?

6. Explain the governmental and contractual limitations that may affect the small firm's ownership of real property.

7. Stipulate the lease provisions that would be desirable with regard to repairs and subletting of real estate. Explain the reasons why each of these provisions is desirable.

8. What are the different types of voluntary settlements? Why may they be more desirable than bankruptcy?

9. Why may action under Section XI of the Bankruptcy Act be more desirable than a voluntary settlement?

10. Explain the legal status of a trademark and the steps necessary to protect it.

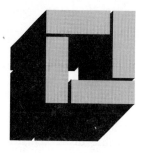

25

Governmental
Regulation
and Taxation

Some familiarity with regulatory laws and rulings of regulatory agencies, as well as with taxation for small business, is a practical necessity. Although familiarity does not qualify managers to make final decisions in many cases, it does enable them to know when they are treading on thin ice and need an attorney or other professional counsel.

FEDERAL REGULATION OF BUSINESS

Federal laws, as well as state laws, have been enacted to regulate business activity for the benefit and protection of both business firms and the general public. Here federal regulations will be discussed within a broad framework of major objectives of public policy. State regulations will be treated in another section of this chapter.

Maintenance of Free Competition

American public policy has long embodied the principle that freedom to enter and engage in business should be guaranteed. This is part of the economic doctrine which emphasizes the importance of free competition as a method of providing maximum values to consumers.

The Sherman and Clayton Acts. Of the various laws intended to maintain a competitive economy, perhaps the best known are the federal antitrust laws—especially the Sherman Antitrust Act of 1890 and the Clayton Act of 1914. Both acts had the objective of promoting free competition through the elimination of artificial restraints of trade. In particular, large-scale collusive action by business firms, to the detriment of the general public, was intended to be eliminated.

It was the oil and other trusts whose growth and power alarmed the public that led Congress to pass the Sherman Act to curb such abuses. Section 1 of this Act states that "every contract, combination . . . or conspiracy in restraint of trade or commerce among the several states . . . is hereby declared to be illegal." Penalties were provided, but court enforcement was another matter. The Supreme Court promulgated the "rule of reason" which materially reduced the impact of the Sherman Act. This act specifically forbade persons or firms engaged in interstate commerce to discriminate in price between purchasers if the effect was substantially to decrease competition.

Although the purpose of these acts and the state antitrust laws is noble, the results leave much to be desired. One would be naive to think that small business need no longer fear the power of oligopolists. The laws prevent some mergers and eliminate some unfair practices, but giant business firms continue to dominate many industries. There has been considerable disagreement concerning the effectiveness and equity in enforcement of these laws.[1]

The Federal Trade Commission Act. In 1914, Congress passed the Federal Trade Commission Act which created the Federal Trade Commission, a body empowered to regulate unfair methods of competition. Thus, this Commission was created in the same session that produced the Clayton Act. It seems evident that Congress wished to establish an agency to maintain surveillance over competitive practices and to prevent unfair acts before legal action became necessary. The regulatory authority of the Commission was extended by the Wheeler-Lea Act of 1938 to provide protection to consumers against "unfair or deceptive acts or practices in commerce."

The effectiveness of the Federal Trade Commission in achieving the purposes of the law has been much debated. Its principal emphasis has been consumer protection (by attacking misleading advertising, for example) rather than regulation of relationships among competing firms. There is a question as to whether greater emphasis should be devoted to this latter area. The Commission has also been accused of neglecting major problem areas by concentrating attention upon relatively insignificant issues. Perhaps some weakness is unavoidable in view of the chronic budgetary and staff deficiencies that have hampered the work of the Commission.

The Robinson-Patman Act. As an amendment to the Clayton Act, the Robinson-Patman Act of 1936 prohibited price discrimination by manufacturers and wholesalers in dealing with other business concerns. In particular, the law is designed to protect independent retailers and wholesalers in their fight against large chains. Quantity discounts may still be offered to large buyers, but the amount of the discounts must be justified economically by the seller on the basis of actual costs. Vendors are also forbidden to grant disproportionate advertising allowances to large retailers. The objective is to prevent unreasonable discounts and other concessions to large purchasers merely because of superior size and bargaining power.

The effectiveness of the Act and its benefit to small business have been much debated.[2] Even those who concede the need for an antidiscrimination law are highly critical of the drafting, administration, and general effectiveness of this law. Small business has been its target as much as its beneficiary. Enforcement provisions have fallen more heavily upon small sellers rather than the large buyers whose behavior prompted enactment of the law.

Even the desirability of some provisions of the Robinson-Patman Act have been debated. One argument holds that a small specialty retailer indirectly

---

[1] For the report of one debate on Capitol Hill by nationally known economists and other public figures, see "Too Big for Antitrust to Handle?" *Business Week* (July 8, 1967), pp. 70-72.

[2] See, for example, "Robinson-Patman: Dodo or Golden Rule," *Business Week* (November 12, 1966), pp. 65-72.

benefits from product advertising by large competitors. For example, large store advertising provides a sense of price legitimacy and greater prestige to the smaller store selling the same products.[3] Consequently, denial of advertising concessions to large retailers may be indirectly harmful to small retailers. Furthermore, those large retailers who are prevented from obtaining advertising concessions may use their strong bargaining strength to obtain other marketing advantages.

While the motivation for such legislation is laudable, therefore, its effectiveness and the desirability of some provisions are unclear. Because the law's protection is inadequate, small business should supplement this legal protection with the most effective competitive strength that is legally possible. Speaking of small retailers, Dickinson commented as follows:

> The only real long-term protection they have under existing legislation is to develop the same power as their larger competitors. Examples of how the small businessman has attained power are the voluntary chains in the food industry and the buying groups in the major appliance business in the New York metropolitan area.[4]

Protection of Consumers

Insofar as freedom of competition is provided by the laws discussed above, consumers will indirectly benefit. This section is concerned more specifically with the direct protection of consumers against some business malpractices.

False Advertising. One of the major activities of the Federal Trade Commission is to expose false advertising and to enforce honesty in advertising. To use legally correct advertising copy, an advertiser must correctly use such terms as "free," "new," "all wool," "homemade," and "handmade." Advertising that offers apparent but unreal "bargains" by pretended reduction from an unused "regular" price is likewise in conflict with the law. These specific examples suggest the forms of misrepresentation that can be used by an advertiser who disregards the truth and the law.

Advertising must not contain statements that are defamatory in nature. For most small businesses, there is little danger of violating this principle as long as they concentrate upon the merits of their own products rather than talk about those of competitors. It can have another application to small business, however, because an advertiser is held liable for statements made by a newscaster or other person on a sponsored radio or television program.

At times, some firms advertise prices in such a way that prospective customers are deceived or misled. Some advertising—particularly of rebuilt appliances—is known as *bait advertising* because the advertiser uses the low price merely to get the prospect into his place of business. He has no intention of selling an article as advertised but intends to talk the customer into a more expensive purchase. Some states have enacted laws to deal specifically with this form of advertising. False claims that prices are "introductory," "special," "wholesale," or "factory" likewise consititute false advertising.

---

[3] For this line of argument, see Roger Dickinson, "The FTC-Large Quality Store Advertising and the Small Retailer," *California Management Review*, Vol. 9 (Summer, 1967), pp. 43-50.

[4] *Ibid.*, pp. 47-48.

Misrepresentation of Products. Examples of misrepresentation of products include the misgrading of goods, adulteration of food products, dispensing of patent medicines as "cure-alls," and improper labeling of clothing. Among the federal laws enacted for the purpose of protecting consumers from these various malicious practices are the Food, Drug, and Cosmetic Act of 1938, the Wool Products Labeling Act of 1939, the Fur Products Labeling Act of 1951, the Federal Flammable Fabrics Act of 1953, the Textile Fiber Products Identification Act of 1958, the Hazardous Substances Labeling Act of 1960, and the Fair Packaging and Labeling Act of 1966.

Unsafe Products. To protect the public against unreasonable risks of injury associated with toys and other consumer products, the federal government enacted the Consumer Product Safety Act in 1972. This act created the Consumer Product Safety Commission to enforce its established goal.[5]

Protection of Investors

To protect the investing public against fraudulent devices and swindles in the sale of stock and bonds, both federal and state laws regulate the issuance and public sale of securities. The federal laws involved are the Securities Act of 1933 and Securities Exchange Act of 1934. The Securities and Exchange Commission, composed of five members, was created to administer the laws. Under this legislation, corporations with securities listed on stock exchanges, or sold in interstate commerce or through the mails, must make annual reports to the Commission and furnish prospectuses and other data when proposing the sale of new securities. The objective is provision of full, honest information to potential investors. Commission regulations prohibit the withholding of material data for personal use by persons "in the know" who might otherwise manipulate the market for personal advantage.

Because of the small amounts involved and the private nature of much of their financing, most small businesses are excluded from extensive regulation under federal law. However, they are subject to state "blue-sky" laws. In general, these require full disclosure of information to the prospective investor in connection with issuance of stocks or bonds. This is accomplished by registration both of the securities and of security salesmen with the appropriate state authorities.

Securities legislation is designed to protect individual investors from deception and fraud at the hands of either large or small business. Legitimate firms have little argument with such regulation and may actually benefit from the conservative practices required by these laws.

Protection of the Public Welfare

In recent years, numerous federal, as well as state and local, ordinances have been enacted to deal with the pollution of both water and air. As explained in Chapter 3, this type of regulation adversely affects some small firms although it may occasionally benefit others.

---

[5] For further information, see "Washington's New Little Giant," *Nation's Business*, Vol. 61, No. 9 (September, 1973), pp. 21-24.

Another form of protection of the public welfare is that found in the regulation of common carriers. The Interstate Commerce Commission Act of 1887 was passed because of both business and public protest of abuses which had entered into public transportation. These included the favoring of one shipper over another by providing freight cars to one and refusing them to others, the provision of secret rebates, and outright discrimination in rates among shippers. Interstate trucks and buses have also been placed under the control of the Interstate Commerce Commission. In fact, the Congress has given the ICC power to regulate all interstate movements of goods, except air transportation and interstate communications via telephone and telegraph.

Some nonrail carriers have alleged that the Commission had attempted to allocate the totality of shipments among carriers. From the standpoint of the public interest, it would seem that some freedom of competition should be allowed (rather than allocating total shipments among carriers). In particular, it would seem that the proposal of equitable rate changes—whether up or down—should be allowed (and even encouraged) and that such rate changes should be approved more promptly.

STATE REGULATION OF BUSINESS

State regulation of competitive businesses varies among the 50 states. What is important to note is that laws and regulations enacted by a state are legal and enforceable as long as they are not in conflict with that state's constitution, the federal constitution, or federal legislation. Some specific areas which are commonly considered by all states to be within the realm of state regulation of business are discussed in this section.

Retail Price Control

In pricing a product or service, an entrepreneur must observe the general minimum price laws applicable to his type of business. The majority of states have *unfair trade practice acts* that specify, for both wholesalers and retailers, minimum prices based upon cost plus some markup percentage. Some of the state laws even cover personal services. Such legislation limits the small firm's opportunity to utilize *loss leaders* in sales promotions.

Fair trade laws in some states permit manufacturers or wholesalers to set minimum resale prices on branded or trademarked merchandise. Among such items are patent medicines, sporting goods, and photographic equipment. Small firms, such as drugstores and discount houses, must observe all minimum prices specified in accordance with state law.

While both unfair trade practice acts and fair trade laws ostensibly aim to eliminate unfair price competition, they are controversial in nature. Unfair trade practice acts prevent a merchant from selling below cost (which is variously defined in the various states), while fair trade price laws permit manufacturers to establish minimum retail prices for particular products. The danger in such laws is their tendency to handicap the efficient businessman who is able to reduce prices because of his efficiency. Thus, in the guise of preservation of free competition, these laws may actually hold a price umbrella over the inefficient, small, marginal business, thus denying freedom of enterprise to the efficient firm and penalizing the public accordingly.

Licensing

State governments restrict entry into numerous professions and types of business by establishing licensing procedures. For example, doctors, barbers, pharmacists, accountants, lawyers, and real estate salesmen are licensed. Not only individuals, but also business firms, must seek entry permits from state officials. Public screening of insurance companies, banks, and public utilities illustrates this type of regulation.

The primary purpose of restricting entry into the types of professions and businesses mentioned above is protection of the public health, safety, and welfare. The public deserves protection from incompetent physicans, bacteria-laden food, and exorbitant charges of public utilities. Although licensing protects the public interest, restriction of entry also tends to restrict the numbers of professionals and firms in such a way as to reduce competition and increase prices paid by customers.

A case of sorts can be made for the regulation of almost any business. However any failure to limit such regulation to the most essential cases erodes the freedom of opportunity to enter business. There is also a difference between licensing that involves a routine application and that which prescribes rigid entry standards and screening procedures. The fact that the impetus for much licensing comes from within the industry suggests the need for careful scrutiny of licensing proposals. Otherwise, we may be merely protecting a private interest and minimizing freedom to enter a field of business.

Other Areas of State Regulation

State regulation of certain types of business activity that affect the public welfare in various directions include the following:

1. Various laws designed to assure efficient, ethical service on the part of the professions and business services.
2. The local licensing of peddlers designed to prevent nuisance approaches by peddlers to individuals on the street or at the doors of their homes.
3. Zoning ordinances in local communities designed to keep stores and factories out of residential communities and to facilitate better city planning.
4. Local building, fire, and sanitation codes.

TAXATION OF SMALL BUSINESS

The primary tax responsibility of a small business firm is to pay all legally required taxes. This necessitates a knowledge of the applicable taxes and dates of payment and the correct determination of amounts payable. In fulfilling this responsibility, the small firm needs expert advisory help. There is the danger of forgetting a tax or overlooking some technicality or deduction.

In paying taxes, the owner-manager is both an agent and a debtor. As an agent, he withholds and pays taxes owed by others. As a debtor, he pays taxes for which he or the firm is directly liable.

Tax-Withholding Obligations of the Entrepreneur

The major tax-withholding obligations of a businessman concern the following taxes:

1. *Income taxes.* Each employee signs a withholding exemption certificate which specifies the number of allowable exemptions he or she decides to take. The amounts withheld from the salaries of employees are passed on to the government periodically by the employer.
2. *Social Security taxes.* An employer is required to deduct a specified amount of each employee's salary towards the payment of Social Security taxes, and this amount is also passed on periodically to the government by the employer.
3. *Sales taxes.* Many state and local governments impose sales taxes. A business firm must collect the stipulated tax and pass it on to the appropriate governmental agency.

Major Taxes Paid by the Entrepreneur

The major taxes for which small firms and owners are directly responsible as debtors are the following:

1. *Income taxes.* The federal income tax paid by a business depends on its earnings and on its legal form of organization. Corporations pay a corporate income tax of 22 percent of all net income, plus a surcharge on taxable income over $25,000. Under certain conditions, a corporation may elect to be taxed as a partnership. In any event, individual owners pay personal income taxes on proprietorship earnings, partnership earnings, corporate salaries, and corporate dividends. Some states and a few cities also impose income taxes.
2. *Federal excise taxes.* Federal excise taxes are imposed on the sale or use of some items and on some occupations. For example, there is a tax on the sale of certain motor fuels, a highway use tax on trucks which use federal highways, and an occupational tax on retail liquor dealers.
3. *Unemployment taxes.* Firms that have four or more employees pay both federal and state unemployment taxes on salaries and wages. The tax rate is usually related to previous unemployment experience.
4. *Local taxes.* Counties, towns, school districts, and other local entities impose various types of taxes. Among these are real estate taxes and personal property taxes. The application of personal property taxes to business inventories provides an incentive for minimizing inventory investment. Business licenses are also taxes even though the owner may not recognize them as such.

Impact of Taxes on Decision Making

The growth of business taxation makes it of increasing importance in business planning. In fact, the diversity of taxes today is such as to affect a wide variety of management decisions.

Impact on Initial Decisions. Taxation should influence decisions regarding the legal form of organization and ownership success. Business executives, including small business entrepreneurs, must also attempt to anticipate the tax impact of any major process, product, or other change before it is put into effect. All tax consequences must be carefully analyzed while the decision is still pending. Ignoring the potential tax results of a particular course of action could lead to operation at a loss.

Impact on Business Location Decisions. Business location decisions, particularly those of small manufacturers, may turn in part upon the tax rates and tax concessions in communities under consideration. It may be possible to make a major tax saving for many years by locating in a community with a favorable tax structure. A compelling example of significant tax concessions is afforded by Puerto Rico, which has bid for American factories by offering substantial tax advantages.

Impact on Financing Decisions. Financing plans likewise involve tax considerations. Many small enterprises are growth enterprises whose primary source of growth capital is that of retained earnings. Any income tax payment reduces the amount of earnings otherwise available for retention in the business. Both the corporation income tax and the personal income tax have this effect, and the substantial size of both taxes makes the financial problem one of considerable magnitude. If the firm seeks outside capital to finance expansion, it encounters the usual difficulties of obtaining funds on reasonable terms and of possibly losing ownership control.

In this connection, it should be noted that income tax rates on individuals (including those operating unincorporated businesses) and on corporations are quite different. The arrangement which would maximize funds for reinvestment would depend upon the size of the business income and the tax bracket of the owner.

In paying the federal income tax, a partner or proprietor uses the regular tax return for individuals. A separate schedule for reporting the profits or loss from business or professional activity is attached to this return. Business net profit is determined by deducting the cost of goods sold and other allowable expenses from the total receipts. It is important to note that net operating losses can be carried back to reduce the taxes of previous years and that gains from sale or exchange of capital assets are taxed at rates that are lower than those on regular income.

Borrowing results in interest charges which are deductible for income tax purposes. In contrast, equity financing permits no deduction from income for the cost of capital. Leasing or buying decisions similarly involve tax considerations because of the differences in allowable expense in computation of taxable income. Even the contributions made for charitable purposes affect income tax payments.

Impact on Inventory Valuation Decisions. Still another example of the impact of taxes is found in the choice among inventory valuation methods, which affect the computation of cost of goods sold and thus affect the amount of taxable net business income. Several valuation methods are approved by the Internal Revenue Service, although a consistent method of valuation must be used year after year.

Impact on Depreciation Methods Used. Another management problem is that concerned with depreciation, for which again there are several approved methods. The present law, for example, permits a choice among alternative rates of depreciation. Acceleration of the depreciation rate, for example, is often attractive to the small firm.

Impact on Dividend Policies. The decision concerning the payment or nonpayment of dividends is also affected by taxes. Owners of small business corporations must pay individual taxes on dividends received. For this reason, the personal tax position of the owners may make undesirable the declaration of dividends by such closely held corporations. Taxes applicable to undistributed earnings similarly affect the decision regarding dividends. Still another tax consideration in dividend policy concerns the payment of cash versus stock or property dividends and the timing of the dividend declarations.

In conclusion, it should be noted that the responsible executive must make a decision not only in the light of tax consequences but also in the light of all factors relevant to that decision. Taxes constitute only one of many pertinent considerations. Even the possibility of conflicting tax consequences must be resolved in reaching a decision.

Possibilities for Tax Savings

Tax savings are possible if one knows the law and all of the permissible tax "loopholes" which it affords. Legal *tax avoidance*, which is in sharp contrast to illegal *tax evasion*, is not immoral and is certainly practical. Above all, the entrepreneur should be honest about tax matters and tax payment—the penalties of dishonesty are all too clear. The small business firm, while relying primarily on tax experts for assistance, may also supplement this assistance by reference to tax articles in periodicals, pamphlets, books, or loose-leaf tax services. The size of the business, of course, will determine the amount which can be spent in the accumulation of such a tax data library as well as the time available for its use.

One example of possible tax avoidance is found in the leasing of equipment on a graduated rental basis by a new small manufacturing firm. The manufacturer avoids the payment of taxes on the equipment if sales do not develop as intended. On the other hand, the purchase money could be borrowed on an intermediate term loan basis from banks, with deductible interest expense, but in this case interest constitutes a fixed charge and might be difficult to pay if sales do not come up to expectations.

In the growth enterprises in particular, where earnings are fully retained, the owner pays only the capital gains tax if he retains his investment for more than six months. Such a substitution of capital gains tax for the much higher income tax can effect substantial savings.

SPECIAL ASSISTANCE TO SMALL BUSINESS

In addition to public policy applying to business generally, some steps have been taken to provide special assistance to small business. Chapter 19, for example, explained the Small Business Administration loan programs and the development and operation of Small Business Investment Companies. Other aspects of special assistance provided by the Small Business Administration are discussed below.

SBA Management and Technical Assistance

When the Small Business Administration was established as a federal agency in 1953, its specific mission was to advise and assist the small business segment of the economy. The policy of Congress was expressed in the Small Business Act in the following words:

It is the declared policy of the Congress that the Government should aid, counsel, assist, and protect insofar as is possible the interests of small-business concerns in order to preserve free competitive enterprise, to insure that a fair proportion of the total purchases for the Government be placed with small-business enterprise, and to maintain and strengthen the overall economy of the Nation.[6]

The provision of management and technical assistance to managers of small firms takes a variety of forms. A series of pamphlets, for example, is published under each of the following titles: (1) *Management Aids for Small Manufacturers*, (2) *Technical Aids for Small Manufacturers*, and (3) *Small Marketers Aids*. In addition, separate publications treat miscellaneous subjects pertinent to small business management. Research studies of small business problems have also been subsidized by grants from the Small Business Administration.

Staff personnel in both Washington and field offices are available for counseling actual or prospective managers of small firms on various management problems. The subjects may range from evaluation of a going concern to analysis of plant location or layout requirements. In some cases, counsel is provided by retired business executives who have volunteered to serve as small business advisers.

Government Procedure and Small Business

Many small firms serve as subcontractors. Both the Department of Defense and the General Services Administration (the largest contract-awarding agencies) provide active encouragement to prime contractors to engage in subcontracting to small firms. As subcontractors, small firms have the problem of learning who the prime contractors are and what component parts are available for subcontracting.

The Small Business Administration works with small firms to help them obtain government contracts. SBA field offices advise small firms as to which agencies buy the products they supply, help them get their names on bidders' lists, and assist them in obtaining drawings and specifications for proposed purchases. The Small Business Administration also publishes a directory which lists goods and services bought by military and civilian agencies and seeks out small companies interested in bidding on purchases on which few small firms have bid in the past.

Set-Aside Programs. Under the "set-aside program," government contracting officers and SBA representatives review purchase orders to select those which may be set aside for exclusive competitive bidding by small firms. Small firms have participated extensively in set-aside programs. This practice is presumably justified by the increasing technological complexity of material produced by federal agencies and the tendency to favor big business by acquiring systems and goods from a single contractor.

Break-Out Contract Programs. In a related program called the "break-out contract program," the procuring agency breaks out suitable portions of a larger contract for competitive bidding by small firms. For example, the

---

[6] *Small Business Administration–What It Is, What It Does* (Washington, D.C.: Small Business Administration, 1954), p. 1.

contract for janitorial services might be broken out of a general contract for housekeeping on a missile installation.

In fiscal year 1972, the federal government spent $43.8 billion on procurement contracts.[7] The small business share was $12.6 billion, up over $1 billion from the preceding year. Although some of this amount was made by subcontracts, $8.7 billion went to small business through prime contracts.

A Desirable Public Policy

Small business deserves the governmental assistance that can make it healthy and productive. The Department of Commerce serves business of all sizes, but many of its activities are particularly useful to big business. Certainly, there should be little objection to an agency, such as the Small Business Administration, which devotes particular attention to small firms, provided its activities are useful to small business and are efficiently performed.

On the other hand, small business cannot rightfully ask for special favors even though the cause of small business is politically popular. When provided equal opportunity to compete, small business must earn its own way. An advantage based upon favoritism is both repugnant to the spirit of free enterprise and dangerously uncertain as a basis for small business success.

Updating Outmoded Business Controls. The whole system of federal, state, and local regulation of business activity has grown like Topsy. That is, many separate congressional and state legislative acts, together with many widely different local ordinances, exist to regulate total business activity. Even some of the laws which originated during wartime have not yet been repealed. The result is a somewhat outmoded set of rules.

Any revision of the rules should recognize the objective of providing fair and full competition, with the minimum of government—which Americans traditionally have believed to be the best government. Furthermore, the central banking philosophy inherent in the Federal Reserve System emphasizes an equally important objective of indirect rather than direct controls.

Achieving fair competition does not necessitate the elimination of natural monopolies or even some which might be considered artificial. The patent, for example, confers a 17-year monopoly upon its owner. The independent businessman would be the first to insist on maintaining his 17-year right to extra profits as the result of his discovery and patent.

It seems reasonable that businessmen, including small entrepreneurs, should speak out in their own defense by attacking outmoded government controls. Some may even wish to enter politics in order to achieve the worthy objective of replacing outmoded controls with a new, unified system of regulations flexibly interpreted to assure fair and full competition and preservation of free enterprise.

Tax Relief for Small Business. It has been noted that the income tax reduces the volume of funds available for business expansion. This reduction of owner capital by taxation occurs regardless of size of the business, but the practical

---

[7] "A Fair Share of Government Contracts," *Nation's Business*, Vol. 61, No. 9 (September, 1973), p. 14.

consequences in limiting expansion are more severe in the case of the small firm. Large companies have easier access to the nation's capital markets and thus are less dependent upon internal financing. For many small businesses, there is no alternative to financing through retained earnings.

Tax reforms that are beneficial to business in general should be helpful to small firms in particular. In other words, tax relief need not be exclusively tailored to assist small firms. Some changes, however, are more directly pertinent to small business. In 1970, the President's Task Force on Improving the Prospect of Small Business urged high priority for these proposals:

1. Permit losses of small businesses to be carried forward for offset against taxable income throughout the first 10 years of a business existence. This would make the tax effect on small business more nearly equal to that on most large companies, which are continually starting new efforts with initial losses too, but usually have taxable income from other sources to obtain an immediate offset. A five-year limitation on loss carry-forwards is too short to permit full offset of losses by some ultimately successful small enterprise.
2. During the first five years of the business's existence, allow deduction from taxable income of modest provisions for a "small business risk reserve." This would help retention of earnings in the early stages to finance receivables and inventories. It is a counterpart to initial and accelerated depreciation allowances where depreciable property is involved. Many small businesses are not capital-intensive but are working capital-intensive. They need this assistance. The reserve deductions could be kept within the Government's fiscal limitations by limiting deductions to a percentage of tax basis receivables and inventories. To avoid abuses, amounts released from these reserves would have to be taxed at ordinary rates.[8]

The main objective of taxation is, or certainly should be, to raise revenue for the support of the government's required activities for promotion of the general welfare of the people. It is emphasized that this should involve fair contributions from all citizens, including business citizens *of all sizes*, to gain revenues for the necessary support of desirable governmental services.

 ## Summary

1. One of the major objectives of public policy is the maintenance of free competition. Legislation varies, however, in terms of its consequences in this area. Although the antitrust laws (including the Sherman Act, Clayton Act, Federal Trade Commission Act, and Robinson-Patman Act) are intended to encourage competition, their general effectiveness has been widely questioned.
2. Other objectives of public policy are protection of consumers, protection of investors, and protection of the public welfare.
3. Some areas of state regulation of business include retail price control and licensing.

---

[8] *Improving the Prospects of Small Business*, The Report of the President's Task Force on Improving the Prospects of Small Business (Washington: U.S. Government Printing Office, 1970), p. 9.

4. Retail price laws ostensibly maintain the competitive system but may in reality have the opposite effect.

5. Growth of business taxation has made it of increasing importance in business planning. The impact of taxes is an essential consideration in many types of decisions.

6. The Small Business Administration was created in 1953 to aid, counsel, and protect the interests of small business organizations.

7. Two areas of special government assistance to small business are (a) management and technical assistance provided through SBA offices, and (b) government procurement (to assure a "fair proportion" of government purchases from small firms).

8. Small business cannot properly ask for special favors even though the cause of small business is politically popular. Desirable public policy, however, may call for updating some business controls and effecting certain changes in tax laws.

Discussion Questions

1. Are any of the stated objectives of public policy opposed to the interests of small business firms?

2. What appears to be the major objective of the following laws or types of legislation: (a) Robinson-Patman Act; (b) fair trade laws; (c) local building codes; and (d) state licensing laws?

3. Does the corporate income tax create any more serious problems for small firms than it does for large corporations?

4. In view of the fact that a small business can operate as a proprietorship or partnership, can it easily avoid any difficulties associated with the corporate income tax?

5. What are the ethical implications involved in taking advantage of "loopholes" in tax laws? Is there a bona fide distinction between "tax avoidance" and "tax evasion"?

6. What management decisions in the small firm would be affected by tax laws?

7. Is there any obvious connection between personal income taxation and small business management?

8. Are the activities of the SBA in helping small business consistent with the philosophy of the free-enterprise system?

9. What is the "set-aside" program in federal procurement? What justification is there for it, if any?

10. It is reported that there are about 60 small firms in the nation which locate competent and responsible drivers for car owners wishing to move their automobiles from one section of the country to another. The Interstate Commerce Commission has required these driver service operations to apply for a Certificate of Convenience and Necessity, which they must have to operate. But these applications have been denied on the ground that rail and motor carriers are able to provide all necessary service. What is your opinion of the fairness of such regulations? Why?

11. A Research and Development Division was created in the Small Business Administration to assist small business in obtaining government contracts for research and development, among other reasons. Does this step appear to be in the public interest?

12. The corporation income tax law provides that income of incorporated firms up to $25,000 be exempted from the 26 percent surtax. Does this provision discriminate in favor of small corporations?

13. The Antitrust Division of the Department of Justice and the Federal Trade Commission have units dealing specifically with small firms and the investigation of their complaints. What is your evaluation of the desirability of such an arrangement?

14. Someone has referred to the "aura of motherhood" which has been placed around small business by politicians. To what does this refer?

15. One writer has called fair trade a "euphemism which interprets price fixing as being fair not only to dealers but to consumers." Is there justification for his view?

16. The federal tax law permits small corporations to be taxed as partnerships if they have no more than ten shareholders. What justification is there for this limitation of ten owners?

Case F-1

PROBLEMS IN BUSINESS LAW

The following incidents have been summarized from official court records.

Workmen's Compensation Law

While on the way to his place of employment, an employee was struck by a train at a railroad crossing and killed. The accident occurred at 7:53 a.m., seven minutes before he was to report for work. He was not on a mission for the employer at the time; gas and maintenance for the automobile were not supplied by the employer. The employee's home was east of the railroad track, and the shop where he was employed was about one quarter mile west of the track. In traveling to the shop, the employee had to cross the tracks. The route he followed on the day he was killed crossed the railroad track, then intersected a main four-lane throughfare, then continued to the shop. This route, used by the public, was not the only route he could have taken. Alternate routes included another of approximately the same distance. At the time he was hired, he was advised by his immediate supervisor of the alternate routes to the shop, although he was not ordered to use any particular course of travel.

The legal question involved a decision as to whether the crossing involved was a means of ingress to or egress from the employer's shop and, therefore, whether the death arose out of and in the course of his employment or whether it was attributable to factors affecting the general public.

QUESTIONS

1. Are hazards off the employer's premises normally the legal responsibility of the employer? Explain.

2. How does a workmen's compensation law affect an employer's liability?

Implied Warranty of Fitness for Human Consumption

Customers have brought suits concerning many different products, claiming the implied warranty of fitness for human consumption by the retailer, manufacturer, or restaurant keeper. The following cases illustrate the nature of such complaints:

1. A customer, while eating a bowl of corn flakes in his home, broke a tooth on a hard, crystal-like object. A chemical analysis showed that it was part of a grain of corn that had been partially crystallized.
2. A customer purchased weiners or sausages in a casing containing pieces of metal.
3. A restaurant customer was injured by swallowing a fragment of chicken bone while eating a chicken pie.
4. A customer was sold a barbecued beef sandwich containing glass.
5. A customer purchased and sustained injury from a jar of prune butter containing a small piece of broken prune pit.

QUESTIONS

1. What is meant by an "implied warranty of fitness for human consumption"?
2. What would seem to be logical reasoning about the business firm's liability in each of these cases?

Liability of Motel Owner

A unit of a motel was rented by the week by a husband whose wife joined him a week later. At the time of renting, the motel proprietor told the renter that the outside porch was shaky. Because the renter's wife was not present at the time, however, this explanation was not given to the wife. Two weeks after the renter's wife arrived, she was crossing the porch to empty some trash when a board gave way beneath her. She fell to the bottom of the steps and sustained injuries. The renters brought suit against the motel owner on the basis of negligence in maintaining

the premises. The motel owner maintained that the renters had been warned of the condition of the porch, but the renter insisted that the explanation had been given only to him personally and not to his wife. Moreover, the motel owner presented evidence that the premises had been recently inspected and that reasonable care had been exercised in maintenance. The renters urged that it was incumbent upon the motel owner to be extremely cautious and careful about such conditions and that mere "reasonable care" was insufficient.

QUESTIONS

1. On what basis might the motel owner argue that he had furnished adequate notification of the property condition?
2. Does it seem likely that courts would require motel owners to exercise "extreme care and caution" in maintenance in contrast to "reasonable care"?

Legal Relationship Between Real Estate Broker and Purchaser

The plaintiff, a prospective real estate purchaser, answered a newspaper ad of the defendant, a registered Florida real estate broker. The plaintiff was shown several properties by the defendant's salesman, including the home of the defendant. At that time, the defendant had an option to buy this home in which he was living, and the plaintiff was told expressly that it was the property of the defendant. A sales agreement was eventually reached concerning this property. The broker exercised his option to buy the property, and the title was then passed to the plaintiff.

The plaintiff subsequently brought suit to recover the profit realized by the broker in the sale of his own home. The plaintiff did not claim that the property was worth less than what she paid; in fact, she admitted that it was worth more. Nor did she complain of any breach of contract by the defendant broker. The plaintiff merely claimed that a confidential relationship existed between her and the defendant as a real estate broker. A breach of this relationship allegedly occurred when the broker realized a profit on the transaction over and above the normal brokerage commission.

QUESTIONS

1. What responsibilities are entailed in a broker's status as an "agent"?
2. Was the "broker" in this case operating as a broker, and did he breach a confidential relationship? Explain.

Case F-2

SAMPSON CLAY PRODUCTS COMPANY *

In 1917 John Barnhart, his brother William, and their cousin, Joseph Stokes, bought the Sampson Clay Products Company, but they continued to be interested primarily in their coal mining and other properties in southern Ohio. Stokes passed away during the 1930s and left his shares (representing 50 percent ownership in Sampson) to his daughter in Cleveland, Ohio. Robert was the only son of John Barnhart, and William was a bachelor. Robert had never wanted to be connected with the coal mining business, and so when he was discharged from the Air Corps in 1946, his father and uncle sold their coal mining interests and took over active management of Sampson.

Robert's father and uncle were killed in October, 1957; Robert thereupon became president of the corporation. Neither estate had been closed by the end of 1958. The shares owned by the Cleveland cousin were purchased and retired by the corporation in 1958, leaving the two estates and Robert's mother as the only stockholders. Neither Robert nor his married sister would own any shares of Sampson until their father's estate was closed, but at that time Robert's wife would also come into the ownership of some shares of the company.

Since the corporation met all the requirements of Subchapter S, it was eligible to elect to have its earnings, whether distributed or retained in the company, taxed to the shareholders rather than to the corporation. Thus the double tax, otherwise incurred by the shareholders on dividends paid by the corporation, would be avoided.

The law stipulated that corporations electing within 90 days of the date of enactment, September 2, 1958, would have 1958 earnings taxed under the provisions of Subchapter S. Beginning with 1959, a corporation can elect only if all shareholders sign their consent during the month immediately preceding or immediately following either January 1 or the beginning of the corporation's fiscal year. Once the owners of the corporation so elect, the election remains in force until terminated as provided in the act.

Robert Barnhart, as the executor of his uncle's estate, and his mother—both in her own name and as the executor of her husband's estate—agreed that the corporation should elect under Subchapter S, and the notice of election was duly filed before December 1, 1958. That unanimous consent remained unchanged throughout 1959. Robert has not regretted this decision, but agreed there were circumstances peculiar to his company that had considerable weight.

Sampson owned one clay pit and leased another. The company was permitted to deduct a depletion allowance of 5 percent of the gross value of the clay dug from

* This case was developed for the Small Business Administration by Indiana University.

these pits. After six years' litigation, the courts decided that depletion should be based on the value of the clay products after they were formed, burned, and graded. Prior to that decision the Internal Revenue Service had maintained that the clay had a market value after it had been graded and screened and that depletion was to be based on that value.

In 1958 Sampson received a tax refund of $108,529, covering six years' excess payment of income taxes due to insufficient depletion allowance deductions plus six percent interest. Added to its cash already on hand, Sampson was able to enter 1959 with almost $200,000 in cash.

Previous to electing to be taxed under the provisions of Subchapter S, dividends had been declared semiannually, payable in June and December. After electing, the shareholders were taxed on total net taxable income of the corporation, whether this income was distributed or not. To place the shareholders in a position to meet the quarterly installments on their personal income tax, the directors voted to distribute all of Sampson's income each quarter. If it had not been for the unusually large amount of cash on hand January 1, 1959, the corporation might have been short of ready funds to meet its obligations during the first quarter when inventory was accumulating seasonally.

The current depletion allowance on clay dug from the pit Sampson owned, as a noncash expense charged against operations, provided a further source of working capital during the year since earnings (after the depletion allowance, of course) were distributed in full.

Sampson Clay Products Company produced approximately 24 million bricks annually, with a sales value of about $760,000. See Exhibits 1 and 2 for financial data for the Sampson company. According to Barnhart, Sampson supplied from 55 to 60 percent of all the face brick used in Columbus, Ohio. The remainder of the Columbus market was divided among eight or ten major competitors and perhaps 50 to 60 other firms who supplied small quantities of special types of face brick.

Barnhart said Sampson's average hourly cost of labor was $1.94, exclusive of fringe benefits. This figure was above the level for the industry in the surrounding area, and consequently the company had attracted and held good workmen. Because of its higher costs, Barnhart stated that Sampson's prices were about $2.00 per thousand bricks higher than the prices quoted by their chief competitors. However, Barnhart added that the high quality of Sampson's bricks, plus its policy of never accepting an order which company officials were not certain could be delivered by the date promised, had enabled Sampson to get a predominant share of the Columbus market. Certain competitors had the reputation, Barnhart said, of delivering perhaps a carload of bricks ordered for some building and then failing to deliver the remaining bricks according to their promised schedules. Delays occasioned by these tactics were very costly to the contractors involved, and they were not likely to specify that maker's brick on later contracts.

Sampson sold through building supply dealers—not directly to contractors. If Sampson had sold directly, Barnhart thought that the company would soon have found itself carrying as much as $150,000 in delinquent accounts.

Barnhart explained another effect of the election decision. Now that the entire cost of any expenditure directly affected profits distributed to shareholders, Barnhart had found that the directors were not as ready to approve increased expenditures as they had been when part of the cost was offset by reduced federal income taxes paid by the corporation. There was a greater tendency to defer replacing equipment (for example, a truck) and to postpone salary increases that formerly would have been granted with little delay.

Barnhart was especially glad that Sampson had entered 1959 with a large cash balance, since he had learned recently that an outlay of no more than $30,000 might result in substantial savings in the company's costs of operation.

The company's plant at Zanesville had 12 beehive brick kilns and 1 tunnel kiln with a continuous conveyor. One day of loading and one and one half days of unloading time had to be allowed for each run through a kiln. Time also had to be allowed for the kilns to cool sufficiently before unloading could commence. With

Sampson Clay Products Company
Balance Sheet, December 31, 1958

ASSETS
Current Assets
Cash $174,520
Trade accounts receivable 27,390
Inventory—lower of FIFO cost or market 90,040
Prepaid insurance and claims 1,370
 Total Current Assets $293,320
Other Assets
Accounts receivable—officers .... $ 26,830
Cash surrender value—officer's life insurance 190
Sundry 50
 Total Other Assets .... $ 27,070
Property, Plant and Equipment
Land—less allowance for depletion .... $ 14,760
Buildings 81,520
Kilns 134,910
Machinery and equipment 228,930
Automobiles and trucks 12,540
Office furniture and fixtures 3,390
                     $476,050
Less allowances for depreciation 342,740
 Net Plant $133,310
TOTAL ASSETS $453,700

LIABILITIES AND NET WORTH
Current Liabilities
Trade accounts payable .... $ 34,350
Salaries and wages, plus taxes thereon 7,980
Other taxes 3,120
Current portion, long term debt 46,000
 Total Current Liabilities .... $ 91,450
Long-Term Debt
Account payable to H. B. Rohleder $115,000
Less amount classified as current 46,000
 Total Long-Term Debt .... $ 69,000
Shareholders' Equity
Common stock—$100 par—authorized, issued, and
 outstanding, 226½ shares .... $ 22,650
Retained earnings 270,600
 Total Shareholders' Equity $293,250
TOTAL LIABILITIES AND NET WORTH $453,700

Exhibit 1

the more modern tunnel kiln, bricks to be fired moved slowly through on a conveyor which operated continuously day and night on a seven-day schedule. About 50 percent of Sampson's production was fired in the tunnel kiln. Mr. Barnhart estimated the labor savings at about 25 percent from this process over the cost of firing in the beehive kilns.

Barnhart stated that the latest esti- mates indicated the construction of another tunnel kiln would cost Sampson $300,000, which was prohibitive for the company. However, he had recently met a Massachusetts brick manufacturer who claimed to be producing 120,000 bricks daily in a tunnel kiln through the use of additional burners and blowers. This output was more than double the daily production of 55,000 bricks in Sampson's

Sampson Clay Products Company
Income Statement

	Year Ended December 31		Percent of Net Sales	
	1958	1957	1958	1957
Net sales	$759,990	$789,790	100.00	100.00
Cost of products sold	651,270	622,820	85.69	78.86
Gross profit on sales	$108,720	$166,970	14.31	21.14
General, selling, and administrative expenses	76,020	89,010	10.00	11.27
Net operating income	$ 32,700	$ 77,960	4.31	9.87
Other income				
Discounts and interest earned	$ 470	$ 470	.06	.06
Scrap sales and sundry	1,100	4,230	.14	.54
Gain on disposal of assets	140	810	.02	.10
Loading fees	13,300	12,150	1.75	1.54
	$ 15,010	$ 17,660	1.97	2.24
	$ 47,710	$ 95,620	6.28	12.11
Other deductions				
Discounts allowed	$ 19,200	$ 20,540	2.53	2.60
Interest expense	310	920	.04	.12
Bad debts	60	3,460	.01	.44
Sundry	700	2,210	.09	.28
	$ 20,270	$ 27,130	2.67	3.44
Income before federal taxes	$ 27,440	$ 68,490	3.61	8.67
Federal taxes on income:				
Provision for the year	$ —0—	$ 18,980	—0—	2.40
NET INCOME	$ 27,440	$ 49,510	3.61	6.27

Exhibit 2

tunnel. The cost of installing the necessary extra blowers and fans was estimated to be between $20,000 and $30,000. The proprietor of the Massachusetts company had told Barnhart that the quality of the bricks was not impaired, and he also said he "could run anybody's clay" through his tunnel kiln. Barnhart had accepted an invitation to personally inspect the Massachusetts operation and expected to do so within a few months.

If what had been claimed was true, Sampson could produce almost its entire requirements in the one tunnel kiln, using the beehive kilns for small lots only—lots which required different firing heats or some other special handling. Should the modification of the tunnel prove success-ful, Barnhart estimated that a labor saving of as much as $70,000 annually might be realized.

QUESTIONS

1. What is the significance of the depletion allowance to the company's decision to be taxed as a partnership? Will it continue to have an important bearing?

2. How does the new method of taxation affect Sampson's investment decisions? Should these tax considerations be permitted to influence important investment decisions as they do?

3. What changes might justify Sampson's reversion to its former tax status as a corporation?

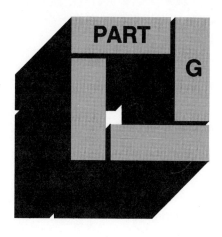

PART

G

Operating Certain Types of Small Business

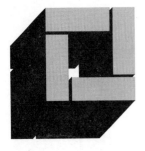

26

Managing a
Retail Store

The practice of merchandising always reacts to changes in the location, income, and living style of customers. In recent years, population shifts and changes in behavior patterns have produced strains in retailing methods used in the past. According to a recent forecasting study, a substantial number of retailers agree that immediate action is required in the following areas:

1. Retailers must revive shrinking profits by the improvement of man/machine systems within the store.
2. They must take advantage of the steady trend toward a service-oriented society by offering more new and profitable services . . . and by differentiating their own store images from those of their competitors. . . .
3. Department store managements must face up to a steady increase in the competition they face from discounters, from revitalized specialty stores, from food and drug chains, and from direct-to-customer warehouse furniture outlets. Increased competition suggests that there will be a reshuffling of the merchandise mix carried in each type of store—with some departments discontinued and others built up—so that stores may eventually classify themselves more by *what* they sell than by *how* they buy it, mark it up, or sell it.[1]

In particular, it has been observed that the growth of chain stores, mail order houses, discount stores, planned shopping centers, department store branches, and other varieties of large-scale retailing has materially reduced the small retailers' market and thereby threatened their future existence. Nevertheless, the small firm still predominates in retailing. To retain supremacy and to prosper in this dynamic field, however, small retailers must capitalize on their natural advantages and effectively manage their operations.

FACTORS THAT SHAPE THE SMALL STORE'S IMAGE

Each store, regardless of size, develops a distinctive personality. The type of personality developed may serve as a competitive weapon in the independent retailer's struggle with chain stores and other large retailers. By their very nature, large retail chains follow a standardized approach to merchandising—a practice that offers advantages but, at the same time, carries the seed of

---

[1] Leo Bogart, "The Future of Retailing," *Harvard Business Review*, Vol. 51, No. 6 (November-December, 1973), p. 16.

weakness. Policies of standardization are based on the principle of the mass product for the mass taste. By concentrating on the average, the mass marketer neglects customers who desire products that differ in some way from the average. By restricting the product line to "best sellers," the mass marketer may fail to provide a reasonable assortment from which customers may choose. By standardizing the selling approach, the mass marketer may eliminate the friendly and helpful service provided by nonstandardized independent retailers. On the other hand, the independent retailer can develop a store personality that is appealing and that sets the independent apart from the chain.

Nature of Merchandise Sold

In shaping a store's distinctive personality, the type of merchandise it sells is a major factor. Stores which sell drugs or hardware differ drastically from those which sell shoes or greeting cards. Even within a general merchandise classification, there is variance in the type of store. For example, some drugstores emphasize prescription service; some feature fountain specialties; and still others become veritable department stores.

Although each store is to some extent different from others, a few stores develop highly distinctive personalities. The Fair Store of Lott, Texas, a small town of less than 1,000 population, has built a reputation as the state's leading retailer of high-quality western wear at moderate prices. In the store, the atmosphere of the Old West is developed by narrow aisles, crowded racks of merchandise, inexpensive fixtures, and informality in operating procedures. Many customers drive hundreds of miles to this store and, at certain times of the year, stand in line on the sidewalk in order to be admitted.

Type of Clientele Developed

Retail establishments also vary with respect to the type of clientele they serve. Perhaps the most obvious distinction is the difference in income levels. Small firms are not limited to low-income clientele by any means. A small men's clothing store may sell expensive, high-quality suits and shirts to discriminating customers in the higher-income brackets. Other clothing stores, in contrast, may sell on the basis of price to customers with more modest incomes.

If the store attempts to serve a high-income market, its fixtures should typically display the elegance and beauty expected by such customers. Polished mahogany and bronze fittings on showcases will lend a richness of atmosphere. Indirect lighting, thick rugs on the floor, and big easy chairs will also make a contribution to the air of luxury. In contrast, a store that caters to lower-income brackets might find luxurious fixtures a handicap in building an atmosphere of low prices. Therefore, such a store should concentrate on simplicity.

Breadth of Personnel Assignments

Although all retail organizations must carry on essentially the same activities, there are basic differences between small stores and larger ones. One is the degree of work specialization. Each employee in a small store typically carries on a number of diverse tasks and often sells a wider range of merchandise than is true of the clerk in the larger retail establishment.

In the small store, the owner himself often does the buying, designs the advertising, and arranges window and counter displays. He is also responsible for credit decisions, collections, bank deposits, and loans. He hires and fires personnel and supervises personnel training. Finally, he evaluates operating results, decides on customer services, supervises selling, signs checks, and plans for cultivation of customer goodwill.

Customer and Community Relations

In any retail store, customer satisfaction is of primary importance. Of course this is true in a general way for almost all types of business. In retailing, however, the service and operating methods of the store become as critical as the merchandise itself in winning customer favor. The customer typically has frequent personal contacts with the physical facilities and personnel of the store. The greeting by the salesperson may be as important as the quality of merchandise in making a sale and earning continued patronage. This situation presents both an opportunity and a hazard for the small firm. If customer satisfaction is taken for granted or slighted in one's concentration upon physical products, the inevitable result is lost business. Without conscious concern about customer satisfaction, this is the natural tendency. On the other hand, the very smallness of a retail firm makes it possible to impress customers with the strong personal interest of the management in their problems. Indeed, it is this quality that has made some small establishments so singularly successful.

As long as the store is essentially a one-man operation, the customer may readily appreciate this attitude of helpfulness and interest. As the firm grows in size, however, it must continue to add personnel. The manager then faces a significant personnel problem in selecting and training employees who will reflect his own interest and aggressiveness in achieving customer satisfaction.

Customer relations are part of, and inseparable from, the small firm's broader area of community relations. Attitudes of the people who live in a community are also the attitudes of a local firm's customers, prospective customers, or ex-customers. The entrepreneur must be sensitive, therefore, in dealing with requests to post announcements of forthcoming events, to contribute to local charities, or to assist in other community projects. Retailers who alienate their neighbors also lose their customers.

Physical Appearance

In Chapter 16 the objectives of a store's internal layout, as well as floor area evaluation, were considered. Here we are concerned with the store's external appearance—which may be attractive and inviting or drab and repelling. What is an appropriate exterior depends upon the type of store and its location, and customers' expectations vary accordingly. They do not expect a salvage house, for example, to present as modern an appearance as a men's clothing shop.

Store identification is made possible by the name or sign on the front of the building. Typically, this shows the name of the proprietor or the company name. Some businesses incorporate distinctive shapes or symbols into their exterior—for example, the picture of a doughnut with the name of the doughnut shop. Neon lights are also widely used to attract attention by illuminating and, in some cases, animating the identifying name or symbol.

Store Fixtures

Recent changes in fixtures have improved the accessibility of merchandise and helped to display it more attractively. At one time, products were shelved behind counters, out of reach and often out of sight of the customer. Modern fixtures not only place many products within reach of the buyer but also practically invite him to pick up and examine them. A customer who walks through a well-managed bookstore finds it difficult to resist the appeal to open some of the books so enticingly displayed.

Adaptability of fixtures is advantageous to the small store. At one time permanent display counters were erected. At present, however, merchants can use movable fixtures which, in turn, have movable shelves or other possibilities for modification. This permits the merchant to make his initial investment in facilities and still remain flexible in meeting seasonal fluctuations, product changes, or other merchandising innovations.

PURCHASING, HANDLING, AND STORING TECHNIQUES

The retailer must discover as accurately as possible what customers want and decide what type of stock to carry on the shelves. First-hand sources that yield potentially valuable information about the products that customers want are inquiries, customer returns and complaints, salespersons' suggestions, and reports of shoppers who shop competing stores. Other sources are manufacturers and wholesalers who often take the initiative by approaching the retailer through catalogs, price lists, direct mail broadsides, other advertising, or by sending a traveling sales representative. Some retailers also take the initiative by making buying trips to central market cities or to trade fairs or shows that feature a type of merchandise of particular interest.

Stock Lists for Staple Goods

The type and amount of paper work necessary for stock control by a retailer depends largely upon the type of merchandise carried. Perishables in a food store, for example, may be controlled visually. The stock of staple goods, on the other hand, should be controlled by other means.

Basic Stock List. One approach to the control of staple goods is the preparation of a basic stock list. This is derived from an analysis of past sales and shows what items have sold profitably. The basic stock list should indicate not only the names of the items to be carried in stock, but also the minimum quantity to be maintained and the quantity to be reordered at any one time. A retailer may create a basic stock list based upon his own past sales experience. However, manufacturers and wholesalers frequently furnish prepared basic stock lists which can be safely followed by the retailer provided that a little discretion is used.

Model Stock List. Since basic stock lists are based upon past experience, they do not suffice for forecasting customer desires for style goods. Hence, a model stock list has been devised to serve this purpose. The model stock list does not list specific items of merchandise because style changes preclude quantity sales in one year on items that were popular the preceding year. Instead, the model stock list specifies the total dollar investment with a breakdown by kinds of merchandise, sizes, and price lines. Manufacturers, wholesalers, and trade associations frequently furnish complete model stock lists to small retailers.

Membership in Voluntaries and Cooperatives

A major source of strength to independent retailers competing with chains and other large business firms is the quasi-integration achieved through voluntaries and cooperatives. The voluntary arrangement involves wholesale firms, e.g., food wholesalers, which sponsor "chains" of independently-owned retailers. Cooperatives, on the other hand, are composed of independent retailers who join together in ownership of a wholesale establishment.

Both of these institutions enable the independent retailer to counter the power of the chain. The buying power of independents is obviously multiplied by this type of concentration. In addition, independents obtain various types of services from the central establishment—promotional aids, modernization assistance, stock control plans, accounting advice, store identification, and so on. The most impressive achievements to date have been in grocery retailing, but the movement has been spreading to fields such as hardware and drugs.

Receiving, Checking, and Marking of Merchandise

Receiving involves taking physical possession of the merchandise ordered by the retailer. The receiving operation starts when the goods are delivered by the common carrier. In the very small store, receiving typically takes place at the alley entrance. Before accepting custody, the retailer should make a rough check as to the quantity and condition of the goods received.

Checking includes the matching of the goods with the invoice or purchase order and verification of the proper quantity and grade of merchandise. Shipping cartons should be opened to determine the precise quantity and condition of their contents.

Marking consists of placing tags or other markings on the cases or items of merchandise to identify them and to assist salespeople and stock clerks in selling and storing. In the case of many small stores, both the sales price and the coded cost price are marked on the tag. Other identifying and price data will also be of assistance when physical inventory is taken. If the date of receipt is included, the retailer will know which items of merchandise are the most likely candidates for markdowns. Thus, while marking of merchandise increases operating expenses, it serves an important purpose.

Storing of Reserve Stocks

The maintenance of a stock room for housing reserve stocks of merchandise makes it possible for the sales floor itself to be uncluttered in appearance. Its use also means that a salesperson may quickly replenish display stock. With a stock room, just enough merchandise is displayed on the sales floor to allow the customer a proper assortment from which to choose.

Some stores do not require written requisitions to release items from stock. For example, written requests would be unlikely in a shoe store. However, somewhat larger stores require requisitioning of items from the stock room before they can be taken to the sales floor. This is intended to facilitate merchandise control.

SELLING TECHNIQUES

In Chapter 17 the general subject of selling was discussed. In this chapter we stress a few of the unique features associated with selling goods at the retail level.

Cooperative Advertising and Sales Promotion

Affiliated retailers (either voluntary or cooperative) participate in the advertising programs of their wholesale organizations. In fact, well-designed advertising programs provide a major benefit of such affiliation, and advertising that stresses the common name creates a national or regional image for the local retail member.

Suppliers often cooperate also with retailers in local advertising of the manufacturer's products. For example, an appliance manufacturer may offer to pay half the cost of local newspaper advertisements for these appliances. The advertisements are prepared by the manufacturer, with blanks for the name of the store, and the manufacturer may also supply related materials for counter displays. Assuming that the products have a good reputation, cooperative advertising of this nature is generally good business for the small retailer. This is true both because it costs less and because the ads are "quality" ads.

A small retail store may also cooperate profitably with other local retail establishments in advertising. Group newspaper advertising by all stores located in a particular shopping area is common practice. This may extend to such practices as Christmas decorations for the area, employment of a community Santa Claus, and the like.

Personal Salesmanship

Aside from self-service departments or stores, most retailers must conclude a sale by means of personal salesmanship. Newspaper advertising or a window display may bring a customer into the store, but these are ordinarily insufficient to complete a sale. There is little doubt in any customer's mind as to the need for good selling. Customers become impatient with poor service. Competing stores have much the same merchandise, and customers feel that the salesperson should display an interest in them and an ability to help solve their buying problems.

Salesperson's Qualifications. Good retail salesmanship begins with a friendly greeting and a courteous attempt to determine the customer's needs.

The small store often sparkles at this point by virtue of an ability to call customers by name and to express a personal interest in the customer. In addition, the customer wants a salesperson who knows the merchandise and can point up the benefits of buying it. Moreover, some customers want to be helped in selecting the particular item that will exactly fit their needs. No customer, however, wants to be high-pressured into reaching a decision. Tact, patience, and understanding must underlie the salesperson's efforts to help the customer. Finally, the salesperson should close the transaction courteously and effectively, expressing the store's appreciation for the customer's patronage.

Such requirements mean that management must make an effective effort to attract suitable persons to work as salespersons. Management can get only the quality of salesmanship for which it pays; its sales volume will reflect its efforts to select conscientious, skilled, friendly sales personnel. Once salespeople are hired, management must train them so that they will have the necessary skill and product knowledge to point out to customers the strong points of the company's merchandise. A salesperson selling power tools, for example, must be able both to tell and demonstrate how they are operated.

Suggestion Selling. Although the principle of suggestion selling is well known, it is not widely practiced. The salesperson who has sold a particular item can tactfully suggest related items which the customer may need. For example, a customer who has purchased a barbecue grill might also buy such accessories as an electric fire starter, a hand or power spit, wire cooking baskets, meat thermometer, fire rake and fire tongs, apron, chef's hat, can openers, hamburger molds, lawn table and chairs, and the like. Similarly, the salesperson can suggest to the buyer of a power lawn mower the purchase of a gasoline storage can, funnel, and oil can—or even an electric lawn edger. Suggestion selling may also take the form of increasing the amount of the sale by pointing out advantages of higher quality items—a practice known as "trading up" the customer—by explaining savings realized by purchasing in larger quantities and by suggesting special bargains currently featured by the store. Suggestion selling must be so tactful and helpful in nature that it will not be construed by the customer as high-pressure selling.

Use of Premiums and Trading Stamps

Small retailers sometimes use consumer premiums as customer traffic builders and sales stimulators. Some service stations, for example, offer free car wash coupons with "fill-ups," and appliance stores give away records with the purchases of record players. To be effective, premiums offered to customers must have a wide appeal and must provide a real value.

Trading stamps are important because of the fact that over half of the families in the United States are accumulating one kind or another. Whether trading stamps are desirable for a particular retailer, however, depends upon the retailer's circumstances and his competition. If trading stamps are used, the small retailer should adopt a trading stamp that is used by other local establishments. This is necessary in order for the customer to have sufficient incentive to save them.

The major advantage of giving stamps is found in their stimulation of increased sales. Many customers feel that there is no cost in the form of higher prices, and some customers who recognize a possible cost enjoy the painless method of saving for luxury items. For the trading stamps to be profitable, therefore, the retailer must have some idle capacity and must be able to stimulate more sales by using the stamps.

Among the disadvantages in the use of trading stamps is the direct cost involved in purchasing them. Since the retailer offers them to all customers, they constitute an additional cost of maintaining existing business as well as a cost associated with the increased sales. There is the possibility that sales volume may not go up enough to offset this cost. It is also difficult to discontinue the issuance of trading stamps at a later date. Though not impossible, it may easily result in the loss of customers who will transfer their purchases to stores that continue to use trading stamps. As an example, in 1967 a large group of service stations discontinued trading stamps simultaneously, coupled with advertising the fact that this meant lower expenses and lower prices. Most of these stations resumed the issuance of stamps within three weeks and continued their use until the energy shortage of 1973-1974 created a seller's market, whereupon they again discontinued the issuance of stamps.

Conducting Special Sales

The typical retailer stages special sales on a storewide basis from time to time. They may be clearance sales, reduction-of-inventory sales, anniversary or holiday sales, back-to-school sales, and so on. If they are to boost sales volume, which is their obvious purpose, special sales must be well advertised. Because advertising costs money, it cannot be too long continued, and the special sale itself is virtually limited to being a two-day or three-day affair. It should be accompanied by in-the-store sales promotions of a special kind as well.

If special sales are to have any significance to customers, the merchant must not conduct them too frequently or continue them too long. The hardware store which had its windows covered for 14 months and made a going-out-of-business announcement is a case in point. This is an obvious hoax which could only hurt the store's customer relations. The consumer is intelligent enough to know that a store could not long continue a special sale at reduced prices even though it had made a special purchase of bargain merchandise.

Use of Automatic Vending Machines

Not too long ago, selling by automatic vending machines was limited to candy bars, cigarettes, and soft drinks. Today almost any product can be sold from these machines, providing that the package is of a standard size. Some machines of European make even handle packages of various shapes. Of course, nationally advertised brand merchandise is more likely to sell from automatic machines than unbranded, unknown products.

One of the major advantages of having automatic vending machines is the instant availability of the merchandise, which permits selling during hours that a store is normally closed if the machine is located outside the store. Another advantage is the elimination of personal selling expenses—a significant factor in the case of small, low-priced items.

Extending Customer Services

Customer services provided by small retailers include delivery service, credit, clothing alterations, gift wrapping, repair service, off-street parking, merchandise returns, and issuance of warranties. Some small retailers—for example, grocery stores—have distinguished themselves from their larger competitors by their willingness to accept telephone orders. Numerous other services are also offered by particular firms; a list of all customer services would be a long one indeed. One hardware dealer lends paint brushes and rollers for use in homes. A barbershop supplies reading materials, radio, and, occasionally, television entertainment for its customers' benefit. Other illustrations will occur to the reader. While a retailer can occasionally charge for special services, traditionally most services are rendered free.

In view of the fact that customers are buying a combination of merchandise and services, the latter are of vital importance in winning continued customer patronage. Customers' desires vary with respect to services. To obtain a lower price, some are willing to purchase from a discount house which refuses credit, delivery, and many other services. Others will expect many free services, including the cashing of checks, with or without a purchase. The retailer must analyze the significance of particular services to his customers and to potential customers. Services do cost money and are justified only on the basis of customer goodwill and patronage.

If a given service is not provided, the retailer may acquaint customers with the reasons and perhaps advertise the fact that prices are correspondingly lower. For example, the retailer's savings realized from refusing delivery service may be passed on to customers in the form of lower prices. Nevertheless, most small retailers find it desirable to offer the services that customers of the store expect and are accustomed to getting in similar stores. In some cases, they can be provided at nominal cost.

This whole area of customer services, however, needs a reexamination for the future. According to the study mentioned earlier in this chapter,

> Seven out of ten merchants believe that, by the end of the 1980s, 20% of the sales volume of general merchandise stores will be generated by new, personalized customer services made possible by new information technology and visual display techniques.
>
> New services may indeed represent potential new profits for retailers, but there is a question as to what the customer can legitimately expect in the way of traditional, merchandise-related store services.
>
> Three out of four retailers believe that by the early 1980s significantly more consumers will be willing to pay a higher markup in order to get more personal service and a wider assortment of unique and individualized merchandise. Retailers say this change in consumer expectations will require each store to define its special niche more carefully.[2]

Self-Service Merchandising

Some years ago supermarkets pioneered the idea of self-service, with a corresponding reduction of personal selling effort and expense. Most customers today accept the notion of self-service. They are willing to look for the marked

---

[2] Bogart, *op. cit.*, p. 32.

prices. They like to save time in shopping. They also enjoy the freedom of choice unhampered by the presence of sales personnel.

Self-service is peculiarly appropriate to the marketing of staple goods. With such merchandise, customers basically help themselves and do not require explanations and assistance from sales personnel. In the case of less standardized and more complex items—for example, expensive cameras—personal selling is still necessary. Many items once thought to require personal selling, however, are now sold successfully via self-service.

Other types of products require protection, and this makes it difficult to use modern, open-shelf displays. One example is the jewelry store, with its high-value, small-bulk items—such as watches and diamond rings—which must be displayed in glassed-in display counters. Similarly, prescription areas of drugstores, which contain valuable drug supplies, must be closed to customers.

From the standpoint of cost reduction, the principal advantage lies in the reduction of sales salaries. Elimination of clerk aisles and conversion to open-faced display counters combine to utilize more efficiently the space in the store. In effect, this reduces the rent and tax expenses. The savings thus possible often make the cost of the changeover a profitable investment.

PROBLEMS OF RETAILERS IN DOWNTOWN AREAS

In many cities, downtown merchants must contend with at least two major problems: the availability of parking space for shoppers and the general appearance of downtown stores.

The Parking Problem

To a degree, the parking problem exists in every sizable community. One woman expressed the attitude of many when she said, "I expect free parking within a block of where I'm going." Another individual, perhaps not too untypical, drove around a downtown shopping area for 35 minutes one Saturday morning looking for a place to park so that he could make a five-minute stop at a bank. Eventually he pulled into a service station, told the attendant to fill the gasoline tank, and took off on the run for the bank.

For the small merchant in the downtown area, the answer is not necessarily to relocate in a suburban shopping center. The downtown area of any city typically remains its principal shopping district. Some stores may cooperate to arrange with parking lots for free service to customers. In some cases, groups of merchants operate parking lots or parking garages.

The General Appearance of Downtown Areas

Many store fronts and interiors in the downtown shopping areas often need remodeling and repainting. Display windows may be too small and may present an out-of-date appearance. If merchants appreciate the problem presented by the run-down, shabby appearance of a downtown section, something can be done about it. There are possibilities of redecoration of the store, installation of automatically operated doors, and change to modern fluorescent lighting of the store interior.

Although some shoppers may refuse to go downtown to purchase staple merchandise, many will travel to the downtown area for style goods and other shopping items. Downtown merchants can work with the city government or with the local chamber of commerce to modify the downtown area so as to make it more attractive to customers. One of the encouraging recent experiments is the development of malls in the downtown section. These are areas, formerly central streets, which are closed to automobile traffic. Some even have trees and fountains with running water. The use of a mall creates a different atmosphere in the downtown area, a greater air of leisure, and a greater ease and speed of movement for pedestrian customers. Certainly, the use of one-way streets and the clearing of residential and obsolete buildings within the downtown area are useful steps to improve its appearance and to find space for parking.

The small retailer in the downtown area will prosper only as other stores in the area also prosper. For this reason, the small retailer should actively cooperate in the efforts of downtown merchants and the local chamber of commerce to overcome obsolescence and unattractiveness of the downtown shopping area.

 Summary

1. Small-scale retailing has a number of important characteristics. Small stores, for example, often develop distinctive images or personalities that distinguish them from other, particularly larger, firms. An image of this type can serve as a powerful weapon in their competition with big firms. The work of their employees is typically less specialized. Customer relations and satisfaction are also of critical importance in their success.

2. What is an appropriate exterior for a retail store depends upon its type and location. Store fixtures have changed markedly in the direction of more attractively displaying merchandise and making it more easily available. Physical facilities, including fixtures, should be consistent with the store's personality.

3. Basic stock lists and model stock lists are aids used in buying merchandise for resale. The retailer may detect customer desires through customer inquiries, customer complaints, salespersons' suggestions, observation of competitors' offerings, and contacts with suppliers.

4. Many small retailers have greatly strengthened their position in buying and have obtained management assistance by affiliating with voluntary wholesalers and retail cooperatives.

5. After taking physical possession of incoming merchandise, the retailer checks it with the invoice or purchase order and marks it for sale. It is then placed on display in the store or held in a stock room.

6. Cooperative retail advertising arrangements with wholesalers and manufacturers are often possible.

7. Effective personal selling is a vital part of the sales program. Personal acquaintance with customers provides a potential advantage for small stores.

8. Sales promotional devices and approaches include premiums, trading stamps, and special sales.

9. Selling of standardized items through automatic vending machines is growing in

importance. One of its key advantages is the reduction of selling cost it makes possible.

10. Delivery service, credit, clothing alterations, and gift wrapping illustrate the many types of services that may be offered to customers. What is a necessary or desirable service depends upon the type of store and the practice of competitors.

11. Self-service selling is particularly appropriate in the marketing of staple merchandise. Its principal advantages are the more efficient utilization of labor and reduction of selling cost.

12. Two major problems of retailers located in downtown areas are the provision of ample customer parking space and the generally shabby downtown appearance of many cities. Cooperation of downtown merchants and participation in chamber of commerce activities may provide some solutions to these problems.

 Discussion Questions

1. A small grocery store is situated three blocks from a shopping center containing a large supermarket. The small store offers delivery service twice daily but prices its products somewhat higher than the supermarket. What are your recommendations concerning cost cutting by discontinuing deliveries with corresponding price reductions to provide stronger competition to the supermarket?

2. What is the principal advantage a small retail establishment has over larger competitors? Does this apply equally in retailing men's clothing, groceries, drug items, automobiles, farm implements, and tires?

3. Do all types of retail stores have some kind of "personality"? What goes to make up a store's "personality"?

4. For what types of retail stores is the factor of external appearance most significant?

5. One rule of thumb suggests that modernization should be carried out at least every ten years. Is this a guide that checks out with your observations of retail stores?

6. How important does modernization seem for drugstores? Shoe stores? Antique shops? Restaurants?

7. Are physical facilities any more important to small retail stores than they were 30 to 40 years ago?

8. In what ways are modern store fixtures superior to those which were used in the past?

9. What are basic stock lists and model stock lists? Should they be used in all small retail establishments in order to maintain effective control over stock?

10. How can a small retailer be sure that he is offering the merchandise that his customers want?

11. What characteristics distinguish effective from poor personal selling?

12. What are the arguments for and against the use of trading stamps? What is necessary in order for them to increase the profit of the firm using them?

13. What limitations do you see in self-service selling by small stores? For what kinds of retail establishments does it appear most desirable?

14. What can the small downtown retailer do about the trend toward suburban shopping? Can he do anything by himself, or is collective action necessary?

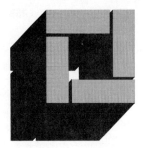

27

Managing a
Franchise

Franchising has helped thousands of Americans to become owners of their own businesses. During the last few decades, in fact, there has been a veritable boom in this type of business. However, even though many franchised firms have succeeded, each new franchising opportunity must be carefully evaluated. Both franchising in general and franchising opportunities in particular have weaknesses, as well as advantages, for prospective entrepreneurs.

SCOPE AND DEVELOPMENT OF FRANCHISING

A *franchise* is a legal agreement by which a franchisee agrees to conduct a business in accordance with certain methods and terms specified by the franchisor. The franchisee owns his own business, hires his own employees, and assumes operating responsibilities. In effect, franchising is a system of distribution in which the franchisee contracts to distribute or sell goods or services in a given area.

Nature of Franchise Arrangements

The independently-owned business operating on a franchise basis appears to be part of a large chain. It typically uses a company name and other symbols or facilities that identify it with the broader business of the franchisor. The franchisee is normally required to maintain some specified quality level of performance and to follow standardized operating procedures. Of course, there is also the required payment of franchise fees and/or purchase of inventory and supplies from the franchisor.

The franchise involves a continuing relationship. It is more than a license or privilege to do business. The franchisor provides some package of professional training and guidance and often supplies goods at wholesale prices. In addition, the franchisor frequently provides financial assistance. In any event, the franchise arrangement provides for a more or less continuous interchange between the two parties.

Early Franchising

One of the first franchise arrangements was concluded in 1898 when an independent dealer was licensed to sell electric and steam automobiles. In the early part of this century, other types of franchising were primarily associated with the sale of automobiles, soft drinks, and gasoline. Today almost every type of product and service is marketed through franchised outlets. Nevertheless, automobile dealerships and gasoline service stations continue to be the most important franchises in terms of volume. Together they account for substantially more than 70 percent of the sales volume of franchised businesses.

The Franchise Boom

The post-World War II franchise boom was based on the expansion of the franchising principle into many different types of businesses. Some of these are franchised motels, beauty parlors, equipment renting outlets, bookkeeping and tax services, variety stores, drug stores, brake and muffler repair shops, dry cleaning services, employment agencies, laundromats, and car rental services. In addition, there has been a great expansion of franchised food service outlets that sell ice cream, hamburgers, pizza, root beer, fried chicken, doughnuts, and other food products. No doubt some of this increase is explained by the increased income and mobility of the population, as well as by the promotion of brand names associated with many of these products.

The franchise boom may be illustrated by the growth of McDonald's, one of the sensationally successful food service franchisors. The first two units of the McDonald's chain opened in 1955 and grossed $235,000, and this hamburger chain expanded so rapidly that it grossed more than $1 billion in 1972.[1] The McDonald's franchises have been sufficiently lucrative that there are numerous applicants waiting for them. The individual who acquires a McDonald's franchise must have about $150,000, one half of which is put up before he opens for business. However, the average annual revenue of a McDonald's store is $500,000, which is several times the average for all drive-in restaurants. Generally, a McDonald's franchisee is expected to pay back his investment in three to five years. New franchisees go through a ten-day training course at McDonald's "Hamburger University," and it is their claim that not one McDonald outlet has ever lost money.

Franchising in the Seventies

The expansion of franchised business has continued at a rapid pace into the 1970s. Between 1971 and 1973, franchised sales increased by an estimated 21 percent.[2] The rate of expansion has varied, however, among the various business areas. For example, the growth rate in newer franchising areas, such as recreation, entertainment, campgrounds, and educational services, has been higher than that of traditional lines. The present size of the franchising industry is indicated by the estimates presented in Table 27-1.

---

[1] "McDonald's Makes Franchising Sizzle," *Business Week*, June 15, 1968, pp. 102-107, and "The Burger That Conquered the Country," *Time*, September 17, 1973, pp. 84-92.

[2] *Franchising in the Economy: 1971-1973* (Washington: U.S. Department of Commerce, 1972), p. vii. Also see Charles L. Vaughn, *Franchising: Its Nature, Scope, Advantages, and Development* (Lexington: D.C. Heath & Co., 1974), for an excellent survey of franchising, including its early history and recent expansion.

Table 27-1
ESTIMATED SIZE OF SELECTED KINDS OF FRANCHISING: 1973

Kinds of Business	Sales (In $1,000s)	Number of Establishments
Automobile and truck dealers	$ 87,743,000	32,953
Gasoline service stations	32,860,000	220,000
Retailing (nonfood)	7,819,267	51,271
Fast foods restaurants (all types)	7,295,905	35,658
Soft drink bottlers	5,634,000	2,750
Automotive products and services	4,065,032	38,564
Hotels and motels	3,284,509	5,219
TOTAL OF ALL FRANCHISING *	156,062,463	466,049

* The totals of franchising sales and number of establishments exceed the totals for the kinds of business shown above because the tabulation excludes many other kinds of franchised businesses.

Source: *Franchising in the Economy: 1971-1973* (Washington: U.S. Department of Commerce, 1972), Table 3.

Table 27-1 indicates clearly that the two traditional lines of franchising—automobiles and gasoline—are still by far the most important with 56 percent and 21 percent, respectively, of total franchising sales. One view of the importance of franchising is given by relating franchising to total retail sales. Franchising sales in retailing (and franchising is important in wholesaling as well as in retailing) amounted to almost 30 percent of total retailing sales in 1973.[3] By 1973, the total number of establishments in all types of franchising was estimated at 466,049. In view of the almost one-half million franchises now in operation, it is clear that franchising occupies an important position in the American economy.

ADVANTAGES OF FRANCHISING

To one who has never owned and managed a business of his own, perhaps the most important advantage of franchising lies in the training and guidance provided by the franchisor. Other advantages that will be discussed below are: customer appeal of the brand name, financial assistance provided by the franchisor, and a proven pattern of successful operation.

Training and Guidance

The importance of the training and guidance received from the franchisor is underlined by the glaring weakness in managerial ability of small entrepreneurs generally. In Chapter 5 it was noted that deficiencies in management account for the large majority of business failures. To the extent that this weakness can be overcome, therefore, the training program offered by the franchisor constitutes a major benefit.

---

[3] *Ibid.,* p. ix.

The value and effectiveness of training is evident from the records of business failure. Some organizations, such as McDonald's and Kentucky Fried Chicken, claim that they have never experienced a failure. There appears to be little question that the failure rate for small enterprises in general is much higher than for franchised businesses in particular. Some claims have been made that the ratio of failure between all business firms and franchises may be as high as 8 to 1 or even 10 to 1. Operating as a franchisee, however, in no way guarantees success. A particular franchisor may offer unsatisfactory training, or the franchisee may fail to apply the training or fail for some other reason.

Initial Training. Training by the franchisor often begins with an initial period of a few days or a few weeks at a central training school or at another established location. As noted earlier, McDonald's franchisees spend three weeks at "Hamburger U" before starting their own businesses. Initial training programs typically cover not only the specific operating procedures to be used by the business but also deal with broader topics such as record keeping, inventory control, insurance, and human relations. The Mister Donut franchise requires an initial training course of eight weeks, including such topics as doughnut making, accounting and controls, advertising and merchandising, scheduling of labor and production, purchasing, and so on. The nature of the product and the type of business naturally affects the amount and type of training that is required in the franchised business. In most cases, training constitutes a potent advantage of the franchising system and permits individuals whose background of training and education is deficient to start businesses of their own and succeed.

Continuing Guidance. Initial training is ordinarily supplemented with subsequent continued training and guidance. This may involve refresher courses and/or training by a traveling representative who visits the franchisee's business from time to time. The franchisee may also receive manuals and other printed materials that provide guidance in his business. Guidance shades into control, and it may be difficult to distinguish the two in particular cases. The franchisor normally places a considerable emphasis upon observing strict controls. However, much of the continued training goes far beyond the application of controls.

Customer Appeal of Brand Name

The entrepreneur who enters a franchising agreement acquires the right to use a nationally advertised trademark or brand name. This serves to identify the local enterprise with the widely recognized product or service. As an example, travelers often recognize a restaurant or motel because of its name, type of roof, or some other feature. They may, for example, turn into a Denny's Restaurant, a Kentucky Fired Chicken outlet, or a Holiday Inn Motel because of their previous experience and the knowledge that they can depend upon the food and service that these outlets provide.

The value of product identification differs with the type of product or service and the extent to which it has received extensive promotion. The value of the name is maintained by continued advertising and promotion. This is also one of the considerations in the franchisor's insistence upon observance of standardized methods of operation and performance standards. If some franchisees were allowed to operate at substandard levels, they could easily destroy the customer's confidence in the entire system.

Financial Assistance

By teaming up with a national franchised organization, the independent businessman also has the possibility of obtaining financial assistance. The costs of starting a new business are often high and the prospective entrepreneur's sources of capital quite limited. His standing as a prospective borrower is likewise weakest at this point.

If the franchisor considers an applicant to be a suitable prospect with a high probability of success, he frequently extends a helping hand financially. The franchise seldom is required to pay the complete cost of establishing the organization. In addition, he is normally given a payment schedule that can be met through successful operation. The franchisor may also permit him to delay payments for products or supplies obtained from the parent organization, thus increasing his working capital.

> Among a few franchise companies, if you express a genuine desire to establish yourself as a franchisee with a particular parent company with whom you really wish to be associated, the fact that you do not have enough capital may mean little to the franchisor. If you are the "right man" for the franchisor and can prove to him that you are sincere, that you have good character and credit references, that you are not merely interested in making money—but in achieving status and independence as a franchised member of the parent company's organization—you need not be too concerned with financing.[4]

Association with a well established franchisor may also enhance the local businessman's credit standing with his own bank. The reputation of the national organization and the managerial and financial controls that are followed as a result of the franchise agreement serve to recommend the firm to a banker. In addition, a franchisor will frequently co-sign notes with a local bank, thus guaranteeing the franchisee's borrowing.

Proven Products and Methods

The franchisor offers the independent businessman a proven pattern of successful operation. His product or service is known and accepted. Customers will readily buy McDonald's hamburgers, Baskin-Robbins ice cream, and Texaco gasoline, because they know these products and their reputation.

Likewise the franchisor has developed and tested methods of operation. He supplies standard operating manuals and procedures that have permitted other entrepreneurs to operate successfully. In addition, he provides counsel and expertise based upon extensive experience. In selecting a location, for example, a franchisor may utilize market research techniques that would seldom be followed by an inexperienced local businessman.

---

[4] Robert M. Dias and Stanley I. Gurnick, *Franchising: The Investor's Complete Handbook* (New York: Hastings House, 1969), p. 52.

The existence of proven products and methods does not prove, of course, that a franchised business will succeed. What appears to be a satisfactory location, for example, may turn out to be inferior, or the franchisee may lack ambition or perseverance. However, the fact that a franchisor can show a record of successful operation proves that the system can work and has worked elsewhere.

In the absence of well-standardized operating methods, the independent businessman is often inclined to do what comes naturally and throw effective management to the wind. Recall, for example, the tendency of small businessmen to disregard financial records and careful financial control. A careful observation of operating methods that have proven successful elsewhere, therefore, should strengthen the new franchisee and offer some assurance of success.

DISADVANTAGES OF FRANCHISING

Among the disadvantages of franchising to the franchisee are the payment of various franchise fees, a diminution of independence, and unsatisfactory training programs promised by unscrupulous promoters.

Costs of Franchising

Fees of various types must be paid to the franchisor. If the local entrepreneur could earn the same income independently, he would otherwise save the amount of these fees. However, this is not a valid objection if the franchisor provides the benefits previously described. In that case, the franchisee is merely paying for the advantages of his relationship with the franchisor. And this may be a good investment indeed.

Loss of Absolute Independence

Any franchisee also surrenders a considerable share of his independence when he signs a franchise agreement. Frequently he has left salaried employment for entrepreneurship because he disliked working under the direct supervision and control of others. By entering into a franchise relationship, he may find that he has simply substituted a different pattern of close control over his endeavors. Even though regulation of his activities may be helpful in assuring success, it may be unpleasant to the entrepreneur who cherishes independence. In addition, some franchise contracts may go to extremes and cover unimportant details or specify practices that are more important in helping others in the chain than in helping local operation. As an operator of a franchised business, the entrepreneur occupies the position of a semi-independent businessman.

Unsatisfactory Training Programs

While some franchise systems have developed excellent training programs, this is by no means universal. Some unscrupulous promoters promise satisfactory training. The following account illustrates the unfortunate consequences of a franchise arrangement which lacked a properly organized training program:

John Smith worked nearly 10 years with the same company before a magazine advertisement caught his eye. The ad read: "Be your own boss. Earn a living in the profitable carpeting business. No previous experience is necessary. We'll teach you all the ropes."

John talked it over with his wife and decided to take the big step into self-employment.

John sent in the clipping and in turn was invited for an interview by the company. After a red carpet tour of the city, franchisor-paid, and an elaborate slide presentation at the franchisor's "Executive Offices," John could hardly wait to get home and start selling carpets. He signed the franchise agreement, which did not mention training, assured by the soothing tone of the company vice-president's words. "Don't worry about a thing," he said. "We'll teach and train you in every aspect of carpet merchandising at one of our best outlets." John returned home after investing the required $8,000 and revamped his personal affairs—and waited for the franchisor's call to report for training. Finally, the call came in the form of a "Do-It-Yourself" book on carpet installation and merchandising. Having signed leases, ordered merchandise, and invested $8,000, he could do little but try it on his own. Even with the help of a fairly experienced "carpeting man" he was in deep trouble within 3 months. After a few more weeks, John was approached by a company representative. "Look Mr. Jones, let's face it. The carpet business is not for you. Our company is prepared to make you an offer of $4,700 for your franchise." John, bewildered and frightened at the prospects of bankruptcy, accepted the offer—a considerable loss from his original $8,000 investment.[5]

EVALUATING FRANCHISE OPPORTUNITIES

As a first step in evaluation, the prospective franchisee must locate the most suitable opportunities. With the proliferation of franchising in recent years, this task is more difficult. Sources of franchise opportunities are not always obvious. To take this first step, the prospective franchisee needs to know where to look.

Sources of Franchising Opportunities

Advertising in newspapers and trade publications is one source of information readily available to anyone.[6] In any issue of a publication such as *The Wall Street Journal*, numerous franchise opportunities are advertised.

A more authorative and inclusive listing of franchise offers may be found in specialized publications. *The Franchise Annual* is a directory of national franchising firms published by Rogers Sherwood, 333 North Michigan Avenue, Chicago, Illinois 60601. This directory lists over 1,000 companies with addresses and descriptions of each business. In addition, Mr. Sherwood issues a monthly report, entitled *National Franchise Reports*, which provides information on franchise opportunities and on the exhibitions and trade shows held by franchisors in various cities from time to time.

In recent years, franchise consultants have appeared and now offer their services to individuals in seeking and evaluating franchise opportunites. As in

---

[5] *Ibid.*, pp. 73-74.

[6] For an excellent discussion of sources of information, see *ibid.*, Chapter 3.

choosing any type of consultant, the prospective franchisee needs to select a reputable, rather than a fly-by-night, consultant. This is not always easy in view of the newness of this consulting field.

Information concerning franchise opportunities may also be obtained from the franchisors themselves. In following up advertisements, the prospect typically receives literature concerning franchise opportunities. In evaluating this or any other information concerning the franchise, he needs to beware of advertising claims that are misleading or that promise more than is warranted.

The Need for Investigation

The nature of the commitment required in franchising justifies a careful investigation inasmuch as a franchised business venture typically involves a substantial investment, possibly many thousands of dollars. Furthermore, the business relationship is one that may be expected to continue over a period of years. Nowhere is it more important to investigate before investing.

Ordinarily, the investigation process is a two-way effort. The franchisor wishes to investigate the franchisee, and the franchisee obviously wishes to evaluate the franchisor and the type of opportunity he offers. Time is required for this type of investigation. One should be skeptical of a franchisor who is overly hurried or who pressures a franchisee to sign at once without allowing for proper investigation.

Franchising Frauds. Every industry has its share of shady operations, and franchising is no exception. Unscrupulous fast-back artists offer a wide variety of fraudulent schemes to attract the investment of unsuspecting individuals. The franchisor in such cases is merely interested in obtaining the capital investment of the franchisee and not in a continuing relationship. The growth of the franchising industry and the substantial opportunities in legitimate franchising create an opportunity for illegitimate operators who attempt to fleece the public. The careless investor may easily lose his money in such "opportunities" even through the culprit may later be brought to justice.

As one example of the fraudulent operator, a national marketing firm in Tulsa, Oklahoma, took more than $400,000 from some 400 investors.[7] The promoters in this case held an exclusive distribution agreement with a legitimate company for the sale of a cleaning solvent. The promoters used newspapers, TV, and radio ads in Dallas and Tulsa. Prospective investors were offered free dinners and told that each distributor would be provided with retail outlets and consumer markets from which he would receive a percentage of all sales. Sales brochures stated that those "getting in on the ground floor of a big money-making enterprise" would receive extra "dividends" by inviting friends and relatives to become members of the same program. An investment of $1,350 presumably would produce a $15,000 yearly income potential. An investor's funds would be refunded at the end of 90 days if the investor was not completely satisfied. The promoter never obtained retail outlets for the cleaner, and no effort was made to warehouse the cleaner. The real intent of the promoter was to sell worthless franchises. The 400 victims included a carpenter without sales experience who mortgaged his furniture to invest $1,200. A couple in their twenties took $23,000 from a trust fund, and a railroad worker bought a

---

[7] *Ibid.,* pp. 99-100.

distributorship for $7,200. The president and officers of the firm received up to ten years in prison, but this did not restore the investments of the victims.

The possibility of such fraudulent schemes requires alertness on the part of prospective investors. In particular, they should be sensitive to exaggerated advertising claims and to fast talkers who insist that they must sign on the dotted line immediately. Only careful investigation of the company and the product can distinguish between such fraudulent operators and legitimate franchising opportunities. It would certainly include visits to, and discussions with, other franchisees operating in the same field.

Pattern for Investigation. If an investigation is to be systematic and thorough, a logical pattern for the investigation is necessary. The following questions have been devised to permit an appraisal of various facets of a franchising opportunity. Careful attention to this list of questions should enable the prospective investor to avoid both marginal opportunities and fraudulent schemes.[8]

The Company

1. Does the company have a solid business reputation and credit rating?
2. How long has the firm been in operation?
3. Has it a reputation for honesty and fair dealing among those who currently hold a franchise?
4. Will the firm assist you with:
   a. A management training program?
   b. An employee training program?
   c. A public relations program?
   d. Capital?
   e. Credit?
   f. Merchandising ideas?
5. Will the firm assist you in finding a good location for your new business?
6. Is the franchising firm adequately financed so that it can carry out its stated plan of financial assistance and expansion?
7. Has the franchisor shown you any certified figures indicating exact net profits of one or more going operations which you have personally checked yourself? (If potential earnings are exaggerated, watch out!)
8. Is the franchisor a one-man company or a corporation with an experienced management trained in depth (so that there would always be an experienced man at its head)?
9. Exactly what can the franchisor do for you that you cannot do for yourself?

The Product

1. Is it in production and currently available?
2. How long has it been on the market?
3. Where is it sold: what states, cities, stores?
4. Is it priced competitively?
5. Is it packaged attractively?
6. How does it stand up in use?
7. Is it a one-shot or a repeat item?
8. Is it easy and safe to use?

---

[8] This list of questions is taken from Dias and Gurnick, *op. cit.*, pp. 38-41.

9. Is it a staple, a fad, a luxury item?
10. Is it an all-year seller or a seasonal one?
11. Is it patented?
12. Does the franchisor manufacture it or merely distribute it?
13. Do product and package comply with all applicable laws?
14. How well does it sell elsewhere?
15. Would you buy it on the open market on its merits?
16. Is it a real product with basic and beneficial qualities, or just a mixture of ordinary raw materials?
17. Will the product or service be in greater demand, about the same, or less in demand five years from now?
18. Is the product manufactured under certain quality standards?
19. How do these standards compare to other similar products on the market?
20. Must the product be purchased exclusively from the franchisor? A designated supplier? If so, are the prices competitive?

The Territory

1. Has the franchise company many available territories?
2. Is the territory completely, accurately, and understandably defined?
3. Is "exclusive representation" thoroughly spelled out and protected?
4. Does the franchisor guarantee a new holder against any infringement of his territorial rights?
5. Is the territory large enough to provide an adequate sales potential?
6. Is the territory subject to any seasonal fluctuations in income?
7. Is the territory above or below statewide average per capita income?
8. Is the territory increasing or decreasing in population?
9. Does competition appear to be unusually well entrenched in the territory? Non-franchise firms? Franchise firms?
10. What is the history of any former franchisees or dealers in the territory?
11. How are nearby franchisees doing?
12. Does the franchise company choose the dealer's location or okay his choice?
13. How does the company settle on a location?
14. Does the company lease or sublease premises to its dealers? What are your costs?

The Contract

1. Does the contract cover all aspects of the agreement?
2. Does it really benefit both parties or just the franchisor?
3. What are the conditions for obtaining a franchise?
4. Under what conditions will the franchise be lost?
5. Is a certain size and type of operation specified?
6. Is there an additional fixed payment each year?
7. Is there a percent of gross sales payment?
8. Must a certain amount of merchandise be purchased?
9. Is there an annual sales quota and can you lose the franchise if it is not met?
10. Can the franchisee return merchandise for credit?
11. Can the franchisee engage in other business activities?
12. Does the contract give you an exclusive territory for the length of the franchise or can the franchisor sell a second or third franchise in your territory?
13. Did your lawyer approve the franchise contract after he studied it paragraph by paragraph?
14. Under what terms may you sell the business to whomever you please at whatever price you may be able to obtain?

15. How can you terminate your agreement if you are not happy for some reason?
16. What period does the franchise agreement cover? Is it renewable? And for how long?
17. Can the franchisor sell the franchise out from under you?
18. Is your territory protected?
19. Is the franchise fee worth it? What exactly is the fee for? If the fee includes the cost of equipment or supplies, is it reasonable?
20. Are royalty or other financing charges exorbitantly out of proportion to sales volume?
21. Are your operations subject to interstate commerce regulations?
22. Have you asked your lawyer for advice on how to meet your legal responsibilities? Your accountant?

Continuing Assistance

1. Does the franchisor provide continuing assistance?
2. Is there training for franchisees and key employees?
3. Does the franchisor select store locations?
4. Does he handle lease arrangements?
5. Does he design store layouts and displays?
6. Does he select opening inventory?
7. Does he provide inventory control methods?
8. Does he provide market surveys?
9. Does he help analyze financial statements?
10. Does he provide purchasing guides?
11. Does he help finance equipment?
12. Does he make direct loans to qualified individuals?
13. Does he actively promote the product or service?
14. How and where is the product being advertised?
15. What advertising aids does he provide?
16. What is the franchisee's share of advertising costs?
17. Are certain franchisees given preferential treatment with regard to pricing and directed purchases?

Examination of the Franchise Contract

The basic features of the relationship between the franchisor and the franchisee are embodied in the franchise contract. This is typically a complex document, often running to several pages in length. Because of its extreme importance in furnishing the legal basis for the franchised business, no franchise contract should ever be signed without legal counsel. In fact, many reputable franchisors insist that the franchisee have legal counsel before signing the agreement.

One of the most important features of the contract is the provision relating to termination and transfer of the franchise. Some franchisors have been accused of devising agreements that permit arbitrary cancellation. It is reasonable, of course, that a franchisor should have legal protection in the event a franchisee fails in a substantial way to obtain a satisfactory level of operation or to maintain satisfactory quality standards. However, it is important to avoid contract provisions that contain overly-strict cancellation policies. Similarly, it is important that the rights of the franchisee to sell the business be clearly stipulated. If the franchisor can restrict the sale of the business to a third party, he is in a position to assume ownership of the business at an unreasonable price. The franchisee is likewise concerned with the provisions that guarantee his right to renewal of the franchise after he has built up the business to a successful operating level.

Among the many other items to be examined in any franchise contract are the fees that are involved, the territorial limits of the franchise, training provisions, and restrictions upon purchase of materials. The contract typically spells out many features that are concerned with the control of operations, including performance standards, quota clauses, prohibitions against sale of competing lines, price requirements, record keeping requirements, and necessary hours and days of operation.

A long and involved contract may properly serve the mutual interests of both franchisor and franchisee. For the franchisee, it is what the contract clauses say that is important. It is desirable that all mutual obligations be spelled out as specifically as possible. It is also important that these provisions be reasonable from the standpoint of the franchisee. To be sure that they are reasonable, he must not only investigate the franchise opportunity personally but should avail himself of necessary counsel.

Use of Outside Counsel

The selection of a lawyer by a prospective entrepreneur was recommended in Chapter 13. This is important in any business but extremely important in the case of a franchised business operation. In any franchise negotiations, the attorney should be consulted before the contract is signed. This person is useful in anticipating trouble and in noting objectionable features of the franchise contract.

In addition to consulting with an attorney, an investor should use as many other sources of help as possible. In particular, he should discuss the franchise proposal with his banker, going over it in as much detail as possible. Likewise, he should obtain the services of a professional accounting firm and have them examine the proposal in some detail. Franchisors often supply a statement showing projected sales, operating expenses, and net income. The accountant can assist the prospective franchisee in evaluating the quality of these estimates and discovering projections which may be unlikely to occur.

THE FUTURE OF FRANCHISING

In the recent rapid expansion of the franchising industry, many small business investors were hurt. Some of the ventures simply lacked a sound economic base. They were not opportunities in the strict sense of the word. In other cases, investors were victimized by fraudulent operators. Many franchisees feel they have been treated unfairly by franchising companies. Automobile dealers, for example, have in recent years expressed various complaints against the major automobile producers. Famous celebrities also allowed their names to be used in franchised businesses, sometimes with little attention to the business itself. The whole arrangement conveyed the impression of a scheme to take the small businessman's investment.

Because of these facts and developments, many questions have been raised concerning the franchising industry. As might be expected, Congress has entered into these investigations. For example, the Committee on Small Business of the United States Senate has conducted hearings concerning the impact of franchising on small business.[9] Although the abuses in franchising clearly justify some measure of skepticism and public scrutiny, the undesirable aspects should not be allowed to obscure the positive values in franchising.

National Association of Franchised Businessmen

The interests of franchisees led to the development in 1969 of a national organization, the National Association of Franchised Businessmen. This development represented an attempt of those in the franchising field to deal with its problems and pitfalls. Whereas investors formerly faced these problems individually, this organization provided a voluntary association for consolidating their efforts.

The association is a nonprofit organization providing services of information and consultation to franchisees. Membership in the association entitles the franchisee to literature on the topic, informative letters and reports, an evaluation service, meetings and seminars on franchising, and representation before governmental agencies.

Franchising—The Last Frontier

Franchising has been called the last frontier for American business. This statement is based upon the many thousands of business opportunities that have become available to independent businessmen in the years of the franchising boom. Franchising has undoubtedly enabled many individuals to enter business who would otherwise never have escaped the necessity of hired employment. Thus, franchising has contributed to the development of many successful, small businesses.

In order for franchising to have a continuing, positive impact upon the small business segment of the economy, it is important that abuses in franchising be eliminated. In any new and growing field, there are practices that deserve examination, and some type of control—either self-control or legislative control—becomes desirable. Legitimate franchising has contributed to the strength of small business in past years and should, assuming proper restraint, continue to provide thousands of small business opportunities.

 ## Summary

1. Franchising is a system of distribution in which the franchisee agrees to distribute or sell specified goods or services in a particular area. The local business is independently owned but appears to function as part of a large chain.
2. In the first part of the present century, franchising was used most extensively in the marketing of gasoline, automobiles, and soft drinks. The "franchise boom" of recent decades has sent its expansion into a large variety of businesses, particularly various types of food service.

---

[9] See U.S. Congress, Senate Hearings Before the Subcommittee on Urban and Rural Economic Development of the Select Committee on Small Business, *The Impact of Franchising on Small Business,* 91st Congress, 2d Session, 1970.

3. Franchising occupies an important position in the present economy. In 1972, sales of franchised businesses represented about 30 percent of total retail sales.
4. Advantages of the franchising arrangement for the franchisee include the following: training and guidance provided by the franchisor; use of the franchisor's name, trademark, or other identification; financial assistance; and use of tested, successful products and business methods.
5. The disadvantages of franchising to the franchisee are the costs involved and the loss of control that is necessary in meeting the standards of the franchisor.
6. The prospective franchisee should make a careful and thorough investigation before investing to avoid business opportunities that are marginal at best and also to avoid fraudulent schemes that are advanced by unscrupulous promoters.
7. The basic features of the franchise arrangement are embodied in a contract. This contract deserves careful evaluation by a professionally qualified analyst.
8. The prospective franchisee should obtain necessary outside counsel prior to entering any franchise agreement. Particularly, he should consult with an attorney, an accountant, and a banker. Other sources of help include franchise consultants and the National Association of Franchised Businessmen.
9. Because of franchise frauds and inequities in some franchise agreements, franchising has developed a tarnished image. Public concern with franchising has prompted Congressional investigation to determine the need for legislative action.
10. The National Association of Franchised Businessmen permits the use of collective action in dealing with the problems of what has become a major industry.
11. Franchising has been called "the last frontier" of American business. Although some promoters have given franchising a bad name, the many ethical and sound franchising companies continue to offer opportunities for thousands of independent businessmen.

 ## Discussion Questions

1. Franchising presumably creates opportunities for small business. Can a franchisee accurately be called an independent businessman?
2. Briefly recount the historical development of franchising.
3. How important is franchising in the present economy?
4. Explain the contribution inherent in the franchisor's training program? Is this important? Why?
5. Enumerate the other advantages of a franchising arrangement.
6. Does the amount of initial investment required constitute a serious disadvantage to franchising? Are many worthy, would-be entrepreneurs prevented from starting their own business due to this factor?
7. Evaluate "loss of control" as a disadvantage of franchising.
8. How may one discover franchise opportunities when interested in starting in business for himself?
9. Should the prospective franchisee investigate prior to investment of his funds? In what areas? To what degree?
10. The typical franchise contract is a rather complex document. Is this desirable? Are there weaknesses in franchise contracts? If so, what are the usual ones?
11. What are the so-called franchise frauds?
12. What is the National Association of Franchised Businessmen? What benefits derive from membership therein?
13. Evaluate the statement that franchising is the last frontier in American business.

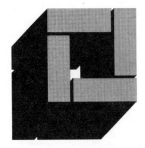

28

Managing a
Service Firm

More than one million business enterprises in the United States are classified as belonging to the service trades.[1] As noted in Chapter 1, the service trades constitute a business area in which small firms are the backbone of the industry. In fact, large firms simply make no attempt to enter many of the service fields. It is the purpose of this chapter to examine some of the operating problems and practices of this multitude of small establishments.

CHARACTERISTICS OF THE SERVICE TRADES

Although most sectors of the economy have experienced growth in absolute terms, they differ markedly in their relative rates of growth. The service sector has shown rapid growth both in absolute terms and in its share of total employment. As income levels have risen and as farm population has declined, services have become increasingly more important.

Table 28-1 reveals the national trend toward a service-employment economy. During the 1960s, the United States became the first nation in history to have over one half of its total employment outside the agriculture and industry sectors—that is, not involved in production of food, automobiles, houses, or other tangible goods.[2] The service firms treated in this chapter account for a substantial portion of the country's nonagricultural and nonindustrial employment. As indicted in Table 28-1, professional, personal, business, and repair services had almost 10 percent of total employment in 1965. Growth of this area is particularly significant to small business because of the predominance of small firms in the service trades.

Labor-Intensive Sector of the Economy

Rapid growth in volume does not guarantee rapid growth in productivity. Although the service sector has expanded, its productivity growth rate has

---

[1] See the *Census of Business, 1967*. Census of Business data do not include medical and health services, legal services, educational services, nonprofit organizations, and certain other specifically excluded services.

[2] Victor R. Fuchs, *The Service Economy* (New York: National Bureau of Economic Research, 1968), p. 1.

Table 28-1
**SHARE OF TOTAL PERSONS EMPLOYED IN PROFESSIONAL, PERSONAL,
BUSINESS, AND REPAIR SERVICES**

Year	Percent
1929	7.3
1937	7.6
1947	8.3
1956	7.8
1965	9.4

Source: Victor R. Fuchs, *The Service Economy* (New York: National Bureau of Economic Research, 1968), p. 19.

lagged somewhat. This reflects the fact that the service sector is a labor intensive sector in contrast to manufacturing. In mass-production industries, the efficiency of labor can be improved by the addition of machinery. In the services, increased productivity requires better performance by personnel. Also, improvement in the quality of service personnel may have lagged behind that of industry in recent years.[3] During the recent years of full employment, service industries have substituted unskilled workers for scarce skilled personnel and have employed workers of marginal quality.

These economic facts underlie the necessity of professional management in service firms. Continuing improvements in the service industry's productivity will call for managers who can skillfully plan, organize, direct, and control their operations.

Diversity of Types of Services

An outstanding characteristic of the "service trades" is their extreme variety. Every reader can name dozens of examples. Among firms representative of this field are barbershops, beauty shops, automobile repair shops, electrical appliance shops, and motels. Even the more specialized repair shops—such as radio and television repair firms and radiator repair firms—are found almost everywhere. The service trades also include many less regularly patronized types of businesses such as taxidermists, gunsmiths, locksmiths, armature rewinding shops, automobile racetracks, riding academies, diaper laundries, shoeshine parlors, telephone answering services, interior decorators, pest exterminators, and private detective agencies.

It may be noted that these diverse types of service firms provide service for one's house, automobile and other personal property, and person. In other words, there are building services, repair services, personal services, and professional services. Although most firms provide services to ultimate

---

[3] *Ibid.*, pp. 60-71.

consumers, a substantial number of them provide services to other business firms. These include advertising agencies, credit bureaus, collection agencies, management consulting firms, employment agencies, blueprint services, etc.

Numerical Predominance

Table 28-2 identifies service fields containing large numbers of establishments. It is apparent from these data that beauty shops, barbershops, and automobile repair shops exist in abundance—with more than 100,000 establishments in each of these categories. All of the other fields show many thousands of firms each, and the list itself is not exhaustive.

Table 28-2
NUMBER OF ESTABLISHMENTS IN SELECTED SERVICE TRADES, 1967

Kind of Business	No. of Establishments
Business services including news syndicates, private employment agencies, management consultants, equipment rental concerns, collection agencies, duplicating service companies, etc.	211,835
Beauty shops	179,209
Automobile repair shops	139,243
Barbershops	112,497
Motels, hotels, tourist courts	65,579
Services to dwellings and other buildings	33,822
Radio and television repair shops	33,063
Bands, orchestras, entertainers, producers	27,698
Photographic studios	26,558
Funeral service, crematories	20,191
Reupholstery, furniture repair	19,418
Shoe repair, shoeshine, and hat cleaning shops	16,270
Bowling, billiards, pool	15,497
Trailer parks	12,437
Motion picture theaters	12,187

Source: *U.S. Census of Business, 1967.*

Sheer numbers invest service firms and their management practices with great significance for individuals, for the business community, and for society as a whole. This significance exists primarily because of a need for the services, but, in part, it also attaches to the service firm's contribution to employment, payrolls, sales of other types of business, and taxes.

One way of assessing the relative importance of the various types of service trades is to examine the distribution of receipts within this sector. As shown in Table 28-3, receipts of the miscellaneous business services group are substantially greater than those of the other major service groups. As stated above, these services include advertising, credit investigation, management consulting, and so on.

Personal services, which include beauty shops, barber shops, laundries, photographic studios, and other businesses of this type, are the second most important group in terms of total receipts. It should be noted that this tabulation of services excludes medical, educational, and governmental services, among others.

Table 28-3
RECEIPTS OF SELECTED SERVICES, 1967

Type of Service	Millions of Dollars	Percent of Total Receipts
Miscellaneous business services	22,595	37.3
Personal services	11,750	19.4
Hotels and motels	7,039	11.6
Auto repair and other auto services	7,028	11.6
Recreational services (except motion pictures)	4,827	8.0
Miscellaneous repair services	3,827	6.3
Motion pictures	3,476	5.7

Source: *U.S. Census of Business, 1967.*

Diversity of Operating Problems

Operating problems confronting management in the various service fields appear, on the surface, to be quite different. Planning and scheduling of work, for example, constitute quite different functions in motels, radio and television repair shops, motion picture theaters, and photography studios. Similarly, advertising media used by pest exterminators or baby-sitting services would hardly be appropriate for advertising agencies or management consultants. It is not the function or objective that differs; rather, it is the means used to achieve the ends that vary so widely.

Deficiency in Management Ability

Perhaps the most consistent characteristic of the service trades is the inferior quality of management. Managerial inefficiency prevails in tens, or even hundreds, of thousands of small service firms. Many are marginal or unprofitable businesses, struggling to survive from day to day and month to month. At best, they earn only a pittance for their owners. The reason for their condition is at once apparent to one who examines their operations. They "run," but it is an exaggeration to say that they are "managed." Poor management is far from universal in the service trades, but there is room for substantial improvement in the management of most small service establishments.

It seems probable that much of this deficiency in management ability results from the inexperience and inadequate education of the entrepreneur. Entry into many of the service trades is extremely simple. The proverbial shoestring provides enough capital to launch many types of service establishments. It is not enough to know a trade, however. Formal education is desirable and some study of business administration is most helpful. Prior management experience also contributes to the efficiency and success of a service establishment.

In some cases, society regulates the entry of individuals into given service trades. Barbers and certified public accountants, for example, must be licensed. Regulation is intended to assure the existence of technical skill or knowledge, however, and not the extent of management ability. Of course, restriction of practice to qualified persons is more common in the profession.

Specialization of Services

An outstanding feature of service establishments is found in their customary concentration on one area, or a very few related areas, of service. Barbers limit their services to haircutting and such closely related services as shaves and shampoos. Pest exterminators restrict their "warfare" to rodents, termites, roaches, ants, and other insects. Automobile repair agencies specialize on repair of automobiles. Piano teachers typically teach only students of the piano. Swimming pools and theaters, likewise, perform the unique entertainment function for which they are designed.

Within given service areas, there may also be specialization of labor. Consider the hair stylists and manicurists in some beauty shops. In a theater, there is the movie projection room operator, usher, and ticket seller. The same work specialization exists for maids in hotels, for lifeguards at swimming pools, for "ironers" of shirts in laundries, and for body or brake specialists in automobile garages.

A final type of specialization to be noted is that of concentration on a particular class or type of customer. Among business services, for example, some private employment agencies restrict their service to placement of executive and professional personnel. Another such example is found in truck leasing organizations that service only those businesses operating fleets of trucks. In the automobile and repair service area, many parking lots exclude trucks by limiting their service to privately owned passenger cars. And, while some hotels and motels welcome convention guests, others avoid conventions on their premises, considering it unprofitable business.

Overlapping of Functions with Retailers

Service establishments exist to perform a service, while retailers exist primarily to sell goods. Nevertheless, some overlapping of functions exists in these two areas. Consider barbers who sell hair tonic and electrical vibrators—or radio and television repair shops that sell tubes and antennas. Automobile repair shops sell parts, while swimming pool operators serve hamburgers, hot dogs, and soft drinks. In most of these cases, the sale of goods is incidental to the service function. In other cases, however, the retailing operation becomes a major part of the business. Motels and hotels, for example, serve food in a coffee shop or dining room, and this food service may attract a substantial number of nonresident guests.

By virtue of retail selling activities, service firms compete with retail organizations. On the other hand, retailers compete with service firms by adding services to their retail operations. Automobile dealers, for example, operate repair service units. Ostensibly, these exist to stock parts and make repairs on automobiles sold by the dealer, but they are open to all comers and frequently service competing makes of cars. Although retail sales of new and used cars is the main line of business, competition with automobile repair shops constitutes a significant sideline. As another example, a retailer of pianos and other musical instruments offers 12 weeks of free lessons with purchase of an instrument. Thus, the line between retailers and service firms is rather blurred and indistinct.

In passing, it may be well to note that both retailers and service firms offer certain free customer services as sales-boosting devices. The department store's gift wrapping, delivery service, and credit extension typify the retailer's services. An example of free service by service agencies is provided by barbershops that provide radio or television entertainment for customers and furnish magazines for them to read. Many laundries and cleaning establishments also perform pickup and delivery service at the customer's home or business.

Such overlapping of sales and service functions makes some types of establishments difficult to classify. The Census of Business *does* put all establishments in one classification or another, which means that some of its decisions are necessarily arbitrary. An example is the gasoline service station, which is classified as a retailing organization by the Census of Business. While its main business may be selling gasoline, tires, mufflers, oil filters, oil, anti-freeze, windshield wiper blades, and other parts, it also performs such revenue-producing services as changing oil, performing "grease" jobs, car washing, fixing flat tires, waxing and polishing, and making minor repairs. In some gasoline stations, such services produce more revenue and profit than the goods sold.

CUSTOMER RELATIONS

Each firm in the service category is by definition a *service* business. It exists in order to render some specific service to individuals or to business firms. Any products made or sold are merely incidental to its primary objective of customer service.

Need for Prompt, Efficient Service

Customers judge a service business by the promptness and quality of its service. Nothing is more annoying to the customer than to wait for a promised repairman who fails to come at the appointed time. For example, a pest extermination service which postponed its service three times was told on the fourth occasion not to bother—a competitor was already doing the job.

Given reasonably prompt service, it is the firm which renders the best service that prospers and grows. Service is *all* that a service firm has to sell. If its service is substandard, there is no real hope for enterprise survival and success.

In terms of specific service fields, a barbershop must provide good haircuts with a minimum of waiting by customers. The television repair shop must repair a television set so that it "stays repaired" for at least a normal interval of time. A photography studio must produce a reasonably good (if not flattering!) likeness of one who sits for a portrait. It is this service principle that must be the "heartbeat" of every service establishment.

Need of a Permanent Clientele

Service establishments need regular customers. In fact, a service firm prospers because satisfied customers keep coming back. The prompt, efficient service mentioned above is a major factor in building repeat business. To illustrate, one automobile owner had his car in the garage for minor repairs for several weeks in a row. When he chanced to mention his run of bad luck to a friend, the friend suggested he try another repairman. The new garage repaired his car in minutes, and months elapsed before further repairs were needed. It was the new garage, naturally, that received his future business.

Other devices may be used to augment the service itself in building a permanent clientele. Consider the bowling establishments that organize and promote bowling leagues. Membership on a team competing for first place in an organized league makes it harder to "skip" one's bowling night.

It might seem difficult for motels to build up a permanent clientele since they provide housing service only for transients. But consider the possibilities in building a permanent patronage for a "chain" or "association" of motels, independently operated but cooperating in name and in advertising, with the privilege of association extended only to those who met exacting standards. Knowing the type of service guaranteed by the association name tends to make the traveler a permanent customer of the various association members.

Personalized Character of the Relationship

The satisfied customer who keeps coming back frequently insists on the services of a given individual. For example, some men change barbershops every time a favorite barber changes employment. Furthermore, some ladies also demand the services of a particular hair stylist who may be one of several employees in a beauty shop. A close personal relationship is most typical in the case of personal service. Actually, no one may be indispensable for rendition of a service, but many people develop strong preferences that must be recognized by a service firm. It is certainly true that many personal service firms are composed of individuals each of whom attracts and holds a loyal following.

Rising Customer Expectations

In recent years, consumer interests have received widespread attention. If the consumer is not king, he is, nevertheless, vastly more critical and powerful than he was a few years ago. Much of the consumer criticism has been directed against manufacturers—automobile manufacturers, for example, who allegedly have produced unsafe cars.

Service firms are not immune, however, and face the same type of rising expectations. Weak service that might have been tolerated a few years earlier is no longer acceptable. The consumer voice is today being heard in government, and the cause of the consumer is politically popular. Some states have started licensing TV repairmen and auto repair shops. Congress has conducted hearings on the auto repair industry. Elimination of fraud and provision of efficient service are imperative if small service firms are to prosper and to avoid further governmental regulation.

LOCATION, PHYSICAL FACILITIES, AND LAYOUT

A distinction might be made between two groups of service firms on the basis of their locational requirements. One group would consist of those service firms whose location is of prime importance from the standpoint of customer convenience. The other group would include service establishments whose locations are a matter of indifference to customers. Of course, many firms might fall between these two groups, but the use of these categories may provide a helpful basis for thinking about their locational problems.

Critical Locations from Customers' Standpoint

The first group of service businesses—those whose locations are of importance to customers—includes firms visited personally by customers. Even within this group, a difference exists in the amount of effort that will be expended by the customer to seek out a particular firm. Convenience is often the customer's major concern. Customers patronize the business that requires the least effort. A motel, for example, must be located near the highway so that it will be easily accessible to the motorist. A highway relocation would be fatal because most customers would never make the effort to seek out the "hidden" motel if any competition existed. The same reasoning would apply to most cleaning and pressing shops operating on a cash-and-carry basis. In the case of automobile repair shops, the customer's less frequent visits make location somewhat less critical. The automobile owner generally expects to go out of his way, although even here there are definite limits to the extent of inconvenience he will accept.

In the case of some services—particularly personal services—the customer is willing to seek out the service firm in spite of a relatively inconvenient location. Music students, particularly those beyond the beginner level, will exert considerable effort to visit the studio of an accomplished musician.

Locations of Less Importance to Customers

The second group of service firms—those whose locations matter very little to customers—include firms that are never visited by customers. Most television and radio repair shops fall in this category as customer requests for service usually originate by telephone. In this case the work typically is performed on the premises of the customer. Other firms that come to the customer to perform service include window washing services, lawn caretakers, and management consultants.

Building and Space Requirements

The place where the service is rendered is also a major factor that affects the amount of space and type of housing needed by a service business. Some services, such as pest extermination, are performed on the premises of the customer. When this is the case, the service firm may need little more than storage and office facilities.

Many service firms, however, perform the required work on their own premises. In this case, there is a further distinction between those visited by the customer and those which the customer never sees. Individuals seeking work, for example, present themselves as applicants at private employment agencies. Similarly, the customer goes to the barbershop or beauty shop, the studio of the music teacher, the automobile repair shop, the theater, the motel, and the photography studio. In contrast, a commercial linen service sends trucks to business offices and barbershops to pick up linens to be laundered.

Elaborate facilities are not needed by service firms to which the customer never comes. They can be located in low-rent areas or elsewhere so long as they can be reached by telephone. Nor is external appearance of the building of major importance in this case. Finally, no reception room for greeting customers and receiving work is required. The reverse is ordinarily true when the customer comes to the service firm. Reception rooms must be neat and clean, and comfortable chairs, together with papers and magazines, may be desirable if customers have to wait for service. Furthermore, the exterior and internal appearance of facilities must be attractive and appropriate to the given type of business.

Equipment and Other Facilities

The facilities required depend upon the type of service rendered and the place the service is performed—that is, at the service firm or at the home or business establishment of the customer. These considerations lead to an extreme variety in the physical facilities of different types of service firms. Consider the bowling alley with automatic pinsetting machines and facilities for serving food and soft drinks. Consider also the specialized equipment required in any garage that performs major automobile repair jobs. Ski lifts are required at mountain resorts for the uphill ride. Motels must provide beds, chairs, desks, dressers, luggage racks, rugs, televisions sets, telephones, bathroom facilities, linens, and shower curtains. Car and truck rental agencies must make huge outlays for late model cars and trucks.

Layout of Facilities

In layout, as in other features of the business, service firms display extreme variety. The general nature of the service being performed establishes some broad limits regarding layout. A swimming pool, for example, requires some type of pool of water. But many other factors or considerations are also applicable. In some types of service businesses, traditional layouts are widely accepted and used by almost all firms. In others, efficiency of operation is the controlling principle in decisions regarding layout. Still other firms give primary consideration to customer convenience and comfort in determining layout. And, of course, various combinations of these factors are involved in layout of many kinds of service organizations.

The private employment agency provides an example of a business that blends considerations of operating efficiency and customer comfort in its layout. A waiting room is generally provided, with a receptionist's desk and a number of chairs for applicants. In addition, it is desirable to have interviewing offices contain a desk and chairs for interviewer and interviewee. These are usually glass enclosed or solid walled to help put the job seeker at ease and to assure privacy. If the employment office were large enough, there might also be a private office for the manager, along with a "business" office.

A barbershop utilizes a simple, highly standardized arrangement with barber chairs in line and a row of chairs for waiting customers. This arrangement provides both working efficiency and customer comfort. The layout problem is so uniform that few variations are found.

In the entertainment field, the business must provide a layout that attracts the customer and provides satisfaction and enjoyment to him. This factor of customer satisfaction is highly significant.

OPERATING METHODS

A truism applicable to the operating methods of all service firms is that they differ with the type of service performed and the location of its performance. This fundamental fact leads to a tremendous diversity in their operating methods.

Advertising and Sales Promotion

Service firms differ greatly in the regularity, media, and type of advertising and sales promotion that they use. Movie theaters, for example, advertise regularly by newspapers, by previews of coming movies on their own screens, and by posters and neon signs at the front of the theater. They occasionally use television "spot" announcements also. Bowling alleys use exterior neon signs and, in some cases, television "spot" ads, together with some newspaper advertising. They receive publicity through reports of bowling league standings and results of competition. Both also typically use the yellow pages of the telephone book.

Motels—a different type of service agency—advertise on large billboard type signs alongside the major highways for 50 miles or more in all directions. Independent motels associated with an "accrediting" chain see that advertising brochures are placed on chests or desks in each motel room. Liberal use is made of flashing neon signs. Motels are also typically listed in the yellow pages of the phone book.

Other service firms display varied advertising programs. In most types of service firms, however, indirect "sales promotion" through good service is one of the best promotional devices for building the business. The satisfied customer returns and also tells others. One automobile repair shop is constantly busy even though repair jobs are frequently postponed a few days. An advance appointment is often necessary in the absence of an emergency condition. This excellent patronage results from its record of economical, dependable repair service. Aside from a small ad in the yellow pages, word-of-mouth advertising is its only form of advertising.

Personal Selling

The service trades generally rely less upon personal selling than is true of retailing, wholesaling, and manufacturing. This is an oversimplification, however, because the different types of service establishments actually vary a great deal in the extent to which they utilize personal selling. It may be convenient to think of the different service trades as falling within one of the following categories:

1. *Personal selling: near zero.* Here the customer has already decided to buy when he makes his first contact with the service firm. A radio and television repair shop, for example, receives a telephone call asking for a serviceman to call and repair a television set.
2. *Personal selling: used to upgrade a purchase.* Although the customer has decided to buy in this case, the amount and nature of the purchase may be somewhat indefinite. A beauty shop operator, for example, may suggest a manicure or special hair rinse to the customer whose objective was merely a hair set.
3. *Personal selling: needed to make the original sale.* In this category, the customer is not committed to buying at the time of original contact with the service firm. For example, a tourist may stop to "look over" a motel. In selling the service, it is up to the motel desk clerk to show the rooms, quote rates, answer questions, and explain available services.

Personal selling increases in importance as one goes from the first category to the third category. Admittedly, the classification made above is somewhat arbitrary. For example, the owner of a cleaning shop might sit back and neglect personal selling entirely, suffering the erroneous impression that he is limited to the first category. Another cleaner, in contrast, might have route men engage in door-to-door solicitation to secure new business.

Some factors that might minimize the need for personal selling by a service firm are (1) the type of advertising it undertakes, whether formal or furnished free by satisfied customers, and (2) the ease of its accessibility, whether by telephone or in person.

Limited Use of Credit

Years ago, service establishments operated on a cash-and-carry basis. Today this practice is far from universal in the service trades, and the use of credit is increasing. Electrical appliance repair firms, automobile repair shops, employment agencies, and bookkeeping services are examples of service firms that extend credit. Credit extension, however, is often a sign of preferred customer treatment—even in such firms.

Barbershops, cleaners, laundries, shoe repair shops, photography studios, parking lots, theaters, swimming pools, bowling alleys, and motels are typical of firms that expect cash payment. Service firms which operate on a cash basis differ only in regard to the time for collecting payment, whether it takes place before or after performance of the service. Theaters, for example, collect prior to providing service, whereas barbershops and cleaners collect after performing the service.

Some reasons for the limited use of credit include the relatively small amounts involved and the intangible nature of the service. A service contrasts sharply with a tangible product (such as an automobile) that may be repossessed if the customer fails to pay his debt.

Purchasing and Inventory Control

Original purchasing problems are primarily those of a financial nature, although the entrepreneur must locate sources of supply for both equipment and materials used in rendering the service to the customer. A related problem is the proper time scheduling of equipment replacement. It may wear out or become obsolete before the expiration of its normal service life. If so, it must be replaced. If competitors acquire better or more efficient equipment, the firm cannot compete on the basis of price or customer appeal. For example, furniture that becomes "dated" makes a motel unattractive to customers.

Most service firms have few problems in the areas of storeskeeping and inventory control of materials and supplies. The service process is the basic part of the business, and materials and supplies are typically incidental to this process. Consider, for example, the small inventory requirements of barbershops, private employment agencies, motels, bowling alleys, photography studios, orchestras, and detective agencies. There are a few exceptions to this general condition, of course. Automobile garages and radio and television repair shops have a major problem in stocking and controlling repair parts.[4]

Another, more serious type of inventory control problem for many service firms has to do with the control of work in process. A shoe repair shop may be required to identify and control hundreds of pairs of shoes belonging to different customers. A laundry must control hundreds of bundles of laundry—each typically containing dozens of different items—belonging to different customers. A photography studio developing film for individuals must keep track of hundreds or thousands of rolls of film coming from different people. The large numbers of separate items of low value make this a somewhat difficult task that requires systematic procedures appropriate to the type of business and involving a minimum of red tape.

Control of Work Flow

Work scheduling is imperative in any service business, even as in the factory, mine, or store. It is essential for proper control of labor cost—a major cost factor in most service firms—and for customer satisfaction. The work load must be predetermined in a motel, for example, so that the right number of porters, maids, and office personnel will be on the job at all times. Maids can start even before checkout time, cleaning rooms evacuated by guests who leave early. A porter, other than during rush hours, may be used in cleaning and chlorinating the swimming pool, "policing" the grounds or making minor repairs.

Other types of service firms may have a work-scheduling task similar to that of manufacturers. Laundries, cleaning establishments, shoe repair shops, and duplicating services constitute examples of such firms.

The automobile repair shop, similarly, faces the problem of daily work planning and scheduling on a job order basis. Particular repair jobs are scheduled for particular mechanics in such a way as to assure completion of the work by the end of the day. Some garages use elaborate control boards for this purpose; others use completely informal methods of scheduling. Regardless of the procedure used, inefficient scheduling is likely to lead to serious problems in terms of customer dissatisfaction or unreasonably high wage costs.

The service firm should not overlook possibilities for improving work flow and overall performance inherent in the use of methods studies and

---

[4] Some automobile dealers have used TV spot ads stating that parts out of stock would be located by a computer system and obtained immediately, thus reducing their control problem on spare parts.

mechanization. Efficient handling and processing methods are a necessary supplement to effective, up-to-date equipment for proper expense control.

SPECIAL PROBLEMS OF PROFESSIONAL PEOPLE

Although the professions are excluded from the service trades section of the economy by the Census of Business, they exist to perform a professional service. Hence, they merit brief mention in this chapter. In the professional group, perhaps the most important are the doctors, dentists, certified public accountants, lawyers, veterinarians, and optometrists.

Importance of Ethical Practice

For professional individuals, what has been said earlier about specialization of function and good customer relations remains true. However, the importance of ethical practice is never elsewhere stressed more than by doctors, lawyers, and certified public accountants. In fact, a code of ethics is a distinguishing characteristic of the professions. Patients and clients know that theirs is a confidential relationship.

Restricted Advertising

Professional men have characteristic, specialized operating techniques. However, advertising by them is severely restricted. They may make brief announcements in newspapers on the formation of new firms or the transfer of offices to new locations. They may also be listed in telephone directories or make use of answering services. But sales promotion or active personal solicitation of trade by professional individuals is considered unethical.

 Summary

1. The service sector of the economy, which includes the small service firms treated in this chapter, has been growing more rapidly than the industrial and agricultural sectors. However, productivity in the service trades has increased more slowly than in some other areas.
2. The service trades, as classified by the Census of Business, include a great variety of services, with each type of service firm specializing typically in one area of customer service. The great number of service firms of each kind make service firm operation of considerable significance.
3. The management problems faced by service entrepreneurs are extremely diverse. The managers, on the other hand, are often of inferior quality.
4. There is considerable overlapping in the functions of service businesses and retailers. Retailers compete in the performance of some services; likewise, some service firms sell replacement parts and other items.
5. Good customer relations are of prime importance in the service trades. The basis for developing and retaining good customer relations is prompt, efficient service.

6. Consumer interests are receiving greater attention in recent years. This has involved increased government regulation and a more critical viewpoint on the part of customers.

7. The extent of customer interest in location is one factor in determining the location of any service firm. Customer convenience is particularly important for the firm to which the customer goes in person to have the service performed; it should be readily accessible to him and have plenty of parking space.

8. Space requirements, type of building, and kinds and arrangement of facilities are all dependent upon the type of service and upon whether the customer comes to the firm for service or it brings the service to him.

9. Operating techniques in management of service firms vary with the type of service and the locus of its performance. Service firms advertise much or little, and personal selling is employed in varying degrees. The use of credit appears to be increasing.

10. Work must be properly time scheduled and work flow properly controlled. Moreover, purchasing and inventory control are important to some service firms.

11. Professional men are not classified as service trade members in the Census of Business. Nevertheless, they exist to render a highly specialized service. Efficient service and ethical conduct are essential to good client relations.

Discussion Questions

1. How does the growth of services compare with the growth of the total economy? What accounts for this?

2. What makes it more difficult for service firms to increase productivity than for manufacturing firms to do so?

3. What factors account for the inferior quality of management that is prevalent in the service trades?

4. Does it seem likely that the quality of management would be fairly uniform throughout the service trades? What might account for differences?

5. Is the overlapping of functions between service firms and retailers an indication of an unfair encroachment of one upon the other's territory?

6. What is the relative importance of promptness and efficiency of service in achieving customer satisfaction?

7. How can a television and radio repair shop develop a permanent clientele? Is the same true for a car-wash establishment?

8. In what way might the personalized character of the customer relationship constitute a problem of the service firm?

9. What is the relationship between customer convenience and service firm location?

10. Is it possible for the equipment of a service firm to become obsolete and thus make it difficult to remain competitive? Illustrate.

11. What variation is there among service firms in their need for personal selling?

12. What accounts for the infrequent use of credit by service firms?

13. What is the nature of a service firm's inventory problem?

14. What are the distinctive features in the operating methods of professional individuals?

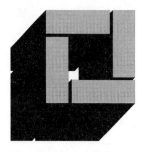

29

Managing a Small Manufacturing Plant

Attention is focused in this chapter on production operations as conducted in small manufacturing plants. More specifically, it considers production planning and control, plant maintenance, quality control, methods engineering, and industrial research.

PRODUCTION PLANNING AND CONTROL

Production planning and control is intended to secure the orderly sequential flow of products through the plant at a rate commensurate with scheduled deliveries to customers. To attain this objective, it is essential that work stoppages be avoided, production bottlenecks eliminated, and machines and manpower utilized efficiently.

Factors That Affect the Production Control System

The production control system is greatly affected by the nature of the product. Control is hardest to achieve for complex products, such as automobiles, with their thousands of component parts. In contrast, controlling the output of simple products—such as doughnuts or denim trousers—is quite easy and requires much less managerial effort.

Another factor that affects the difficulty of production control is found in the type of manufacturing. Small plant operations may be either intermittent or continuous in character, with orders processed either to replenish stock or to fill specific customers' orders. At one extreme is job-lot production of various unstandardized products—as in a small machine shop. In contrast, other firms engage in continuous processing of just a few standardized products. Dairies and soft drink bottling plants exemplify such continuous-process operations.

The Effect of Smallness on Production Control

Simple, informal procedures for controlling work flows are frequently used in small plants. Since systems and procedures are only the means to an end, this may be a virtue. If a process is simple and the output small, a factory manager can keep things moving smoothly with a minimum of paper work. Simple forms suffice. Personal observation may be all that is needed. However, if the informality derives from ignorance of proper controls or a dislike of systematic procedures, the plant in question may suffer from a lack of control. There comes a time in the growth of any manufacturing organization when formalized techniques must be adopted for the sake of processing efficiency.

Work Stoppages

Production control is expected to facilitate the flow of work through a plant. It should avoid or minimize production delays. Delays do not "just happen"; there is always a cause. Among the major causes are the following:

1. Shortages of key materials or parts.
2. Issue of bad parts or materials for processing.
3. Machine breakdowns.
4. Lack of tools, dies, jigs, fixtures, or gages.
5. Production planning errors.

This list is not exhaustive. For example, short work stoppages occur when workers become ill or are injured while at work. Unplanned delays occur also when workers go AWOL, confer with supervisors, talk unnecessarily with other workers, or evacuate the plant for a previously unannounced fire drill.

Steps in a Formal Production Control System

The control system of a small manufacturing plant includes all of the following steps: planning and routing, scheduling and dispatching, and supervising.

Planning and Routing. In small factories, the first step toward production control is the determination, in advance, of the basic manufacturing data needed. The important items of basic manufacturing data are the following:

1. The kinds of raw materials and parts required.
2. The number of parts and units of material of each kind required per unit of finished product.
3. The best sequence of labor operations for making each of the products manufactured.
4. The number of machines and operators needed on each labor operation.
5. The number and kinds of tooling items required to set up each machine properly.
6. The standard output rate of each machine.

Before considering how such data are utilized, a quick look is required at the broad types of manufacturing. At one extreme is the plant producing lot by lot, with work moving slowly and intermittently; at the other extreme is the continuous-processing plant. And in between are plants producing goods lot by lot, with lots moving quickly through the process.

Job-Lot Processing. The first extreme involves job-lot processing. Lots move both intermittently and slowly, so that the basic manufacturing data are needed two to three months ahead of the start of the production season to which the data apply. The data permit preparation of a bill of materials (listing raw materials, consumption standards, and related information) and a route list (showing the sequence of labor operations). Each is separately drawn up for each product to be regularly manufactured. Having the data in advance of actual production also lets management make any necessary changes in plant layout, hire (or transfer) and train workers needed, and buy any new tooling items required—all prior to the beginning of the production season in question.

Continuous Processing. The continuous-processing plant is at the other extreme. It makes highly standardized products for which advance planning may be even more essential. This is because some of the production planning must then be incorporated into the process. The plant layout, for example, governs the routing of the work; the preliminary analysis of material, equipment, tooling, and personnel requirements must also be just right. Once the process is set up and operations on the seasonal run of product have begun, any changes are both difficult and infrequent. This is because of the serious loss of output and high cost involved.

Made-to-Order Processing. For the in-between shop which processes work to customers' specifications, we have a still different situation. The basic manufacturing data must be obtained anew—or again verified for continuing applicability—after receipt of the customer's order and before it is put in process. Similarly, the order of work must be determined, the materials and parts analyzed and obtained, the personnel transfers accomplished, and any special jigs, fixtures, and tools, if needed only for this one order, must also be preplanned. All of this is done, however, after receipt of the customer's order.

Scheduling and Dispatching.
After a process is planned and set up, it must be scheduled by time periods, as well as by departments, machines, and individuals.

The Gantt Chart. For a lot that will be in process for several days, it is possible to use visual control boards or charts to reflect both work assignments and the progress of work toward completion. One such control, the *Gantt chart*, vertically lists all of the shop operations and machines in sequence (see Figure 29-1). Its horizontal dimension is a time scale showing days and hours. The chart starts when work begins on a designated day, with a light black line projected to the right from zero, which shows the number of standard hours of work already assigned to each machine. As the work progresses, lot completions are indicated by entry of a heavy black line above the first one. New lots are assigned to the machines that are least loaded at the time. Their load lines are then extended to the right to reflect the correct new number of assigned standard hours of work.

Current status of lots in process can be shown by moving a colored pointer across the horizontal time scale at fifteen minute intervals (so the chart always shows the approximate correct time). When the entrepreneur or plant manager inspects the chart at any time, he can easily compare work load and progress to date. This shows him which workers are ahead of schedule, which are just on schedule, and which are behind in their work. He can then arrange for overtime or take other corrective action.

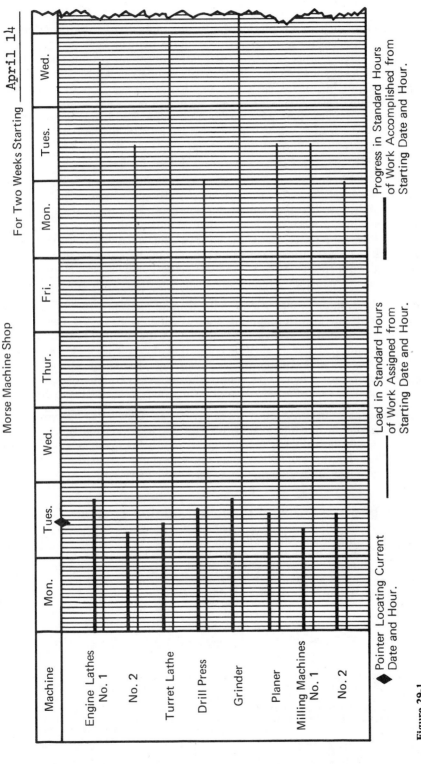

Figure 29-1
GANTT LOAD & PROGRESS CHART

Block Control. In between job-lot shops and those that utilize continuous-process manufacturing are shops that require control devices adapted to their quick-moving processes. One such in-between, compromise scheduling system is that known as *block control*. Approximately equal amounts of each product are put in process each day, divided into equal lots of a standard number of units each. Colored tags are stapled on each day's boxes of work, with blue for Monday, pink for Tuesday, and so on. Red tags indicate "rush" orders. All workers on a given labor operation must process lots carrying the oldest colored tags until all those comprising the given block are finished. Only then may anyone start work on the following day's block. Thus, the oldest work, by days at least, is cleared first on each labor operation.[1]

Continuous Process Flow Control. Continuous processing is done in a minority of small plants. It involves synchronization of outputs of each part and subassembly line to assure a steady flow of finished products off the final assembly line. Line times are deducted from the scheduled delivery time in order to set the proper times for issuing the various materials requisitions, tool orders, and work tickets. Such continuous-process flow control is far simpler and involves less paperwork than any job-shop, order-control system.

Control in Automated Plants. An automated small plant provides the ultimate in terms of simplicity of production control—after a maximum preplanning effort. About all that is needed is knowledge of the input-output rate of the transfer machines. Materials must be regularly fed into these machines. If they function properly and continously, as planned, production schedules and shipping promises will be met. Of course, the accurate preplanning and tooling of the process—prior to the start of processing—may take months of effort.

Supervising. Production control is effective when the work in process is kept moving. Keeping it moving on schedule is a major responsibility of the shop foreman. Hence, he is the key man in the shop. If his performance is poor, the firm may lose thousands of dollars annually. Therefore, the small manufacturer should regularly evaluate the quality of his shop supervisors.

Advantages of a Formal Production Control System

The use of a formal production control system provides certain advantages. First, both work scheduling and delivery promises are more realistic. Next, since the system cares for routine matters, the entrepreneur and his foremen are relieved of part of the burden of planning and control. Again, a balanced, time-scheduled flow of work through the plant reduces the number of machine setups needed and improves control over the tools, jigs, and fixtures set up on the various machines. The shop also is less cluttered and, as a result, more efficient. Moreover, the amount of work currently in process and the money tied

---

[1] Block control is supplemented by use of a daily production clearance list. In sequence, this shows the numbers of all lots put in process. The last operator in a department interlines the numbers, one by one, as he completes the corresponding lots. The foreman inspects the clearance lists every half hour to determine which lots on the oldest lists are still in his department. He then finds these delayed lots, puts a red tag on each such lot to give it priority on all operations, and has it "rushed" back up to schedule. The clearance list assures the proper functioning of the block system through prompt identification of delayed lots and follow-up action.

up in it are both minimized as the result of a time-scheduled, controlled flow of work. The net result is a lower unit cost of production.

Sales Volume and Production Control

The volume of sales may be so great that it forces production at plant capacity. The plant then makes what it can when it can. The planning, volume, and timing of production all are limited by the shop's capacity to produce. Capacity may be enlarged, when financially feasible to do so, if long-term, high-volume sales are expected.

Typically, however, the sales demand can be satisfied with production at less than capacity. The budgeted annual production, derived from the sales forecast and sales budget, is allocated to months and, within months, to weeks and days. Equipment, materials, and personnel requirements are geared to the production schedules.

Stock Level and Production Control

Control based on sales forecasting has an alternative in stock level control, which is illustrated in Figure 29-2. For each kind of product, orders are issued to maintain predetermined levels of finished goods inventory. In some small plants, both sales forecast control and stock level control are used effectively.

PLANT MAINTENANCE

Since machine breakdowns are a major cause of work stoppage, mainte-nance is vitally important in small factories. Plant maintenance includes repair of broken or malfunctioning equipment, lubrication and inspection of equip-ment, and replacement of worn parts. It also includes janitorial service and other routine maintenance activities. Its objective is to keep production facilities in operating condition.

Types of Maintenance

Plant maintenance activities fall into two categories. The first is *corrective maintenance*, which includes both the major and minor repairs necessary to restore a facility to good condition. The second category, *preventive maintenance*, includes the inspections and other activities intended to prevent breakdowns. A small plant can ill afford to neglect preventive maintenance since its disregard results in wasteful emergency repairs. The proper balance between corrective and preventive maintenance depends, among other factors, upon the relative importance of the facilities. If a machine is highly critical to the overall operation, it should be inspected and serviced regularly to preclude costly breakdowns.

Major repairs correct costly breakdowns of machines, handling equipment, or other facilities. Minor repairs, in contrast, are completed easily, quickly, and economically. The regular occurrence of these lesser breakdowns makes the volume of such repair work reasonably predictable; many small plants employ one or two machinists to handle such work. Major repairs, however, are

THE MODEL HEEL PLANT

Weekly Inventory, Cutting & Packing,
and Stock Level Report

Heel Style	Standard Stock Level (in Pairs)	Starting Inventory (in Pairs)	Pairs Cut	Pairs Packed & Shipped	Ending Inventory (in Pairs)
Cuban					
200*	800	607	800	810	597
210**	800	880	800	711	969
220	1,200	1,250	1,700	1,750	1,200
230	1,000	1,020	1,500	1,550	970
250*	2,000	1,864	3,100	3,500	1,464
	5,800	5,621	7,900	8,321	5,200
Low Louis					
350	1,000	1,000	1,400	1,400	1,000
360**	1,200	1,225	1,600	1,500	1,325
	2,200	2,225	3,000	2,900	2,325
Grand Total	8,000	7,846	10,900	11,221	7,525

Key:

* Inventory decrease; sales increase; increase next week's pairs cut to restore proper stock level

** Inventory increase; sales decrease; decrease next week's pairs cut to restore proper stock level

Notes:

1. Pairs cut weekly are equally distributed by days for each heel style. For each style of heel, production quantities of the various sizes are determined in accordance with a "standard size run."

2. If uptrends or downtrends in sales become well defined, then the stock levels themselves require appropriate adjustment, which might occasion sharp increases or decreases in weekly cuttings in the next week's schedule.

Figure 29-2
STOCK LEVEL CONTROL

unpredictable as to time of occurrence, repair time involved, loss of output to expect, and likely idleness cost. In small plants, it may be desirable to contract with electrical and other repair services for major repairs. Of course, very small plants often use production people on maintenance work, contracting out all work beyond their capability.

Scheduling Preventive Maintenance

Preventive maintenance need not involve elaborate controls. Some cleaning and lubrication will be done as a matter of course. Moreover, machine tenders and foremen may detect incipient failures and ask for preventive maintenance. This is like an owner who takes his automobile to a garage for checkup and repair when he hears an unusual noise—or notes some other abnormality.

For preventive maintenance to work well, however, more systematic procedures are needed. The manufacturer may keep records on each piece of equipment, showing cost, acquisition date, periods of use and storage, depreciation scheduled and taken, and frequency of preventive maintenance inspections. On any given day, the machinist is handed the set of cards covering that day's required inspections. He inspects each item of equipment, makes necessary notations on the cards concerned, and replaces overly worn parts.

Good Housekeeping

Although orderliness and plant size are not necessarily related, small factories frequently ignore good housekeeping. A quick tour of several randomly selected plants would demonstrate this fact. Aisles are cluttered, walls need painting, windows are dirty, waste material is visible under machines, and unprocessed materials are stacked haphazardly here and there.

Disregard for good housekeeping practices reflects itself in a plant's production record. Good workmanship and high output are hard to achieve in an ill-kept plant. Good housekeeping, on the other hand, facilitates production control, saves time in looking for tools, and keeps floor areas safe and free for production work.

QUALITY CONTROL

Most consumers view quality subjectively as a single variable ranging from very bad to very good. The manufacturer knows, however, that there is a set of objectively measurable physical variables—such as length or diameter—which *together* determine how good or bad a product is. To approach perfection on even one variable is very costly. To make a product inferior to that of competitors, however, means that they will get the business. Thus, a product must be good enough so that it will be competitive, yet it must not be prohibitively expensive.

In order to produce typically good products, a consistently low ratio of defectives is required so that good lots regularly reach final inspection. The entrepreneur should receive daily reports on the ratio of defective products in the plant and in the individual producing departments.

Objectives of a Quality Control Program

The goal of a quality control program is both remedial and preventive. Inspection is an essential part of such a program. Final inspectors are supposed to sort out all defective items. Final inspection, thus, is remedial in nature. The preventive objective, in contrast, is achieved by in-process inspections that reveal the causes of the defectives. This makes possible a prompt restoration of a good process and prevents the production of too many defectives.

Traditional Quality Control Techniques

Management has traditionally employed a number of approaches to quality control. Inspection is the most important of these, and it is discussed below.

Inspection. Inspection consists of scrutiny of a part or product to determine whether it is good or bad. In making the necessary objective measurements, an inspector typically uses gages or other instruments to evaluate the important quality variables. Effective control requires that the inspector be trained in the proper use of gages. The inspector, furthermore, has to be honest, objective, and capable of resisting pressures from shop personnel for passing borderline cases.

Inspection Instruments. Inspection instruments must be suited to the inspection task. All suitable instruments should be evaluated before they are purchased.

Inspection Standards. Design tolerances constitute the inspection standards used in manufacturing. Tolerances are set for every important quality variable. Tolerances are the limits of variation allowable above and below the desired dimension on the given quality variable. As set by the manufacturer, tolerances must satisfy the requirements which customers will impose on finished products. An inspector will pass as being good only those items whose measurements fall inside the tolerance limits.

Points of Inspection. In planning an inspection system, one must decide just where to inspect. Traditionally, inspection occurs in the receiving room to check on the condition and quantity of materials received from suppliers. Inspection is also customary at critical processing points—for example, *before* operations which would conceal existing defects, or *after* operations which produce an excessive amount of defectives. Clearance inspection is another point of customary inspection. Departmental clearance inspection precedes the transfer of lots from one department to the next and avoids passing defectives on for further costly processing. Final inspection of finished products is even more important. And, of course, it is necessary to inspect gages, machines and handling equipment, tooling to be set up on machines, boilers, electrical installations, and other facilities.

Quantity to Inspect. In the past, manufacturers inspected each item in every lot processed. This is called 100 percent inspection. Supposedly it assures the elimination of all bad materials in process and all defective products prior to shipment to customers. Such goals are seldom reached, however. Nevertheless, the traditional approach to quality improvement has been to increase the number of 100 percent inspections.

Inspection Errors. Inspectors often make honest errors in judgment. For example, the inspector is given scrap, good-item, and rework-item barrels. A reinspection of lots that have been 100 percent inspected will show that inspectors err by placing good items in the scrap barrel, bad items in the good-item barrel, and so on. Perfect inspection probably is unattainable.

Reduction of Inspection Costs. To reduce cost, the manufacturer must be alert to possibilities for further mechanization of inspection. This may take the form of handling or tipping devices to facilitate handling of lots, or items, by the inspector. Or, inspection gages may be built into processing machines. An example is a thickness gage installed in a machine processing strip rubber. This gage consists of a see-through window on which two black lines are drawn to indicate the tolerance limits. The flow of rubber can be viewed intermittently by the operator to see if the thickness is within the tolerance limits.

Reduction of inspection and its cost may also be achieved by using automatic machines, which require first-piece inspection only. After the first pieces are found good, the setup is approved and the production run is started. The operator then rechecks periodically—perhaps every 500th item. So long as the setup remains satisfactory, as demonstrated by these periodic checks, the run continues without other inspection.

Other Traditional Quality Control Techniques. Some other traditional techniques are the following:

1. A "quality man" is given blanket authority to stop processing anywhere in the plant to correct quality lapses. He spends his time going here and there in the plant checking on quality.
2. A quality bonus is paid to supervisors as a spur to keeping subordinates quality conscious.
3. Daily and weekly waste reports are used to inform foremen and employees as to the extent and causes of defective products.
4. Weekly reports showing amount and cost of rework are issued also. These, like the waste reports, should be discussed promptly with the shop foremen, and, by them, with their operators.

Statistical Quality Control Techniques

Modern managers use the laws of probability to control quality. Two potent tools are available: quality control charts and scientifically designed sampling acceptance inspection plans.

Quality Control Charts. There are two types of quality control charts. These are variables control charts and attributes charts.

Variables Control Charts. Variable charts depend on variables inspection, which for each item of product involves a precision measurement of the given quality variable. As few as five items per sample are enough to let variables control charts distinguish efficiently between a controlled process and one out of control.

For control by variables, two charts are needed (see Figures 29-3A and 29-3B). These are called $\overline{X}$ and R charts. The former controls the process average measurement for the given quality variable, and the latter controls the process variation among individual measurements. The sample average—used to estimate the unknown process average measurement—is obtained by dividing the sum of a set of measurements by the number of measurements. It is symbolized by $\overline{X}$. The sample range, symbolized by R, is the difference between largest and smallest measurements for the given sample. It is used to estimate the unknown process variation.

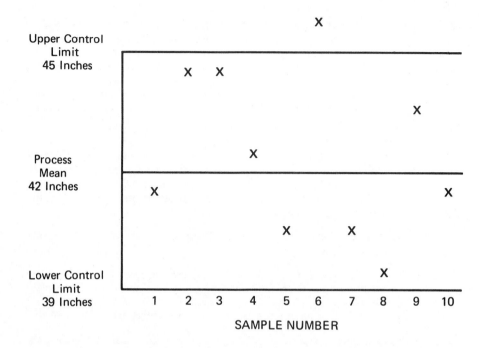

The variable being controlled here is the average length of the lumber squares. Each of the ten consecutive samples contains sixteen items, and it is the average length of the sixteen items in each sample which is plotted on the chart. In this illustration, the process is "out of control" twice. Consecutive samples 2 and 3, for example, are in the *top* sixth of the control chart—an event that would normally occur by chance less than once in 1,932 times. Trouble is therefore evident even though both sample averages are inside the upper control limit. Sample 6 also is above the upper control limit, and the process average, or quality level, is again "out of control" at that point.

Figure 29-3A
X̄ CHART
Average Length of Sixteen 2″ × 2″ Lumber Squares in Each Random Sample Bundle

Variables control charting properly starts with a test of the process set of measurements. If the process is normal, or nearly so, normal curve probabilities apply for interpretation of sampling results. The process is also assured of a stable variation pattern, with individual variations from the process average measurement predictable within a narrow range.

Once a normal process is assured, the enterpreneur takes 25 random samples of five items each and computes the average and range of each sample. Then, central line values for his control charts are obtained from these data, using standard formulas.[2] The X̄ chart central line value is the average measurement produced by the given process. The R chart central line value is the average

---

[2] The formulas for computing $\overline{\overline{X}}$ as central line value for the X̄ chart and $\overline{R}$ as central line value for the R chart (in which k is the number of samples) are the following:

$$\overline{\overline{X}} = \frac{\Sigma \overline{X}}{k}$$

$$\overline{R} = \frac{\Sigma R}{k}$$

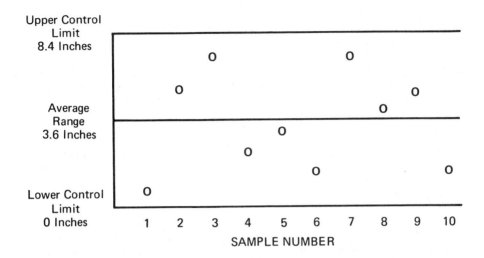

The range of lengths within each of the ten consecutive samples is entered on the chart above. This range is the difference in length between the longest and shortest items in the sample bundle. In this series of samples, the process is consistently within established control limits and so distributed as to indicate an "in control" state for process variation.

Figure 29-3B
R CHART
Range of Lengths of Sixteen 2″ × 2″ Lumber Squares in Each Random Sample Bundle

range for the process. On both charts, the control limits are placed three standard deviations (of the average or range) above and below the central line values—except that on an R chart, a negative-valued lower control limit is replaced by zero. Almost all the sample averages and ranges obtainable by random sampling will fall inside such control limits. In fact, if chance governs the random sampling of a normal process, 99.73 percent of all the sample averages will be inside. For the range, the percentage is not quite so high, but more than 99 percent should fall inside the control limits in this case also.[3]

---

[3] In the case of the $\overline{X}$ chart, the formulas for the three standard deviation control limits are the following:

$$\text{UCL}_{\overline{X}} = \overline{\overline{X}} + 3\sigma_{\overline{X}} = \overline{\overline{X}} + A_2\overline{R}$$

$$\text{LCL}_{\overline{X}} = \overline{\overline{X}} - 3\sigma_{\overline{X}} = \overline{\overline{X}} - A_2\overline{R}$$

In the case of the R chart, the formulas for the three standard deviation control limits are the following:

$$\text{UCL}_R = \overline{R} + 3\sigma_R = D_4\overline{R}$$

$$\text{LCL}_R = \overline{R} - 3\sigma_R = D_3\overline{R} \qquad \text{(which does not exist if } D_3\overline{R} < 0)$$

In both sets of formulas, UCL stands for "upper control limit" and LCL signifies "lower control limit."

A_2, D_3, and D_4 factors are tabulated in all standard quality control books; each of these factors varies in value numerically with n, the random sample size. Hence, the purchase of a book on statistical quality control will make these quality factors available to any small manufacturer.

Inspection of the respective formulas will make it clear that $A_2\overline{R}$ yields the numerical value of three standard errors of the mean and that D_3 and D_4 are multipliers times the average value of the range which directly yield three standard deviation control limits for the R chart. This statement should clarify their meaning and use.

In $\overline{X}$ and R charting, hourly random samples are taken. Hence, such charts promptly tell the manufacturer whether the process has gone out of control—or is still in control—for the quality variable charted. So long as a process is normal and in control at a satisfactory level, the charts will typically show an in-control status for the process. But if assignable causes of quality change enter a process, the charts will signal their advent. Such a signal is very likely on the first sample taken after their advent. There are five definite signals of lack of control commonly given by SQC charts. These are the following:

1. A point across either control limit.
2. Two straight points in either the top sixth or bottom sixth of the control chart.
3. A trend run of points upward or downward.
4. An extreme run of points above or below the central line.
5. A cycle run of points.

All five point clearly to onset of quality trouble on the $\overline{X}$ chart. However, on an R chart, the lack of control signal evidences significant quality improvement instead when (1) a point is across the lower control limit, (2) two straight points lie in the bottom sixth of the chart, (3) a trend run downward occurs, or (4) an extreme run occurs below the central line. When $\overline{X}$ and R charts signal lack of control, processing should stop at once pending an investigation aimed at finding the assignable cause. When found, if trouble was signaled, it should be eliminated by formal corrective action before processing is resumed. If quality improvement was signaled, however, the identified cause should be formally retained in the process. In this way, the manufacturer either keeps, or promptly restores, a satisfactorily low process ratio defective.

Management gains significantly from the use of $\overline{X}$ and R charts in the following ways:

1. A good process is promptly restored after detection of onset of quality trouble. Thus, the ratio defective of the process stays low and is relatively constant. And this, in turn, means that consistently good lots go regularly to final inspection.
2. Maintenance of separate $\overline{X}$ and R charts on each machine in a process will evaluate process capability for holding tight tolerances. In turn, this permits the making of more effective work assignments.
3. $\overline{X}$ and R charts constitute a permanent record, so long as they are retained, of process quality over the period of time charted.
4. Maintenance of a low ratio defective means that the amount and cost of both scrap and rework are greatly reduced.
5. The charts have a telling impact on the quality-mindedness of the work force—when charts are mounted by the machines concerned and findings are regularly discussed with their operators.

Attributes Charts. In contrast to variables control charts, attributes charts that control the ratio defective require very large samples for diagnostic accuracy approaching that of the variables charts. These attributes charts depend on attributes inspection, which involves only a decision that an item is good or bad. Other attributes charts control the number of defects per measuring unit of product, which may be a piece of silverware, a ream of paper, or six inches of randomly chosen photographic film, among other possibilities. Such charts use either large or small samples efficiently, but their usefulness is limited. Of the two, variables charts are more efficient, less costly, and more widely used.

Scientific Sampling Inspection Plans. Scientific sampling inspection plans are of the same two basic types—namely, attributes plans and variables plans. Variables plans use smaller inspection samples, but a separate sample is needed for testing each critical quality variable. This often makes their overall cost greater than that for attributes plans. Accordingly, variables plans are less widely used in industry and will not be discussed further.

Attributes plans themselves fall into two categories—namely, for lot-by-lot processing and continuous processing. Continuous process inspection operates under fixed rules which alternate 100 percent and sample inspection in accordance with inspection results. Such plans are little used in small plants, which typically are job-lot factories. Hence, we shall consider only the lot-by-lot sampling inspection plans. There are three kinds of these—namely, single, double, and sequential plans. It is possible to design plans of the three kinds that are statistically equivalent (in the sense that they provide essentially identical quality assurance). However, even though the average amount of inspection per lot is greatest for single sampling plans, it is single sampling that is most widely used in small job-lot plants—perhaps because it is best understood by the inspectors and shop foremen. Their extensive use dictates our consideration of single sampling plans only.

Single Sampling Plans for Attributes. Given effective use of $\overline{X}$ and R charts, the process ratio defective stays low, so that very good lots are regularly delivered to final inspection. This makes possible the efficient use, in turn, of scientific sampling inspection plans, with the result that amount and cost of final inspection are much lower than for 100 percent inspection. This is accomplished without impairing in any way the quality assurance afforded either manufacturer or customer. And this is how management benefits from using sampling inspection plans.

In establishing a single sampling plan, decisions must be made concerning the lot size, sample size, and maximum number of defectives in the sample that will pass the lot without further inspection. These three quantities are symbolized respectively by N, n, and c. Their determination involves two risks. The first, commonly called the consumer's risk, is the risk that bad lots will be wrongly accepted as being good. If this happens, lots containing too many defectives go to the consumer (or to subsequent processing operations). The second risk, known generally as the producer's risk, is that good lots may be incorrectly rejected by the inspector. This would cause unnecessary inspection cost since rejected lots are 100 percent inspected. The entrepreneur considering sampling plans can find one satisfying his requirements with respect to both these risks.[4]

A single sampling plan is easy for an inspector to use. If his n-item random sample has fewer than c + 1 defectives, he accepts the lot. If it has more than c

---

[4] The consumer's risk is symbolized by β; the producer's risk is symbolized by α. These are specified by the manufacturer. Associated with each of them is a value of the lot ratio defective. p_1 is the value of the lot ratio defective corresponding to the producer's risk; p_2 is the value of the lot ratio defective corresponding to the consumer's risk. p_1 and p_2 must also be specified numerically by the manufacturer.

Lots whose ratios defective range from 0 to p_1 are management-defined "good" lots. Lots whose ratios defective range from p_2 to 1 are management-defined "bad" lots. Incidentally, if p = 1, the lot in question contains no good items at all—such a lot is highly unlikely to occur in any plant at any time.

α, β, p_1, and p_2 comprise the values underlying specification of a sampling plan. Such a specification for a single sampling plan for attributes makes possible an evaluation of N, n, and c.

defectives, he rejects the lot—and then, by S.O.P., inspects all remaining items in the lot. However, some plants do not do this for incoming materials but instead ship back the whole lot to the supplier. At final inspection, every defective found by the inspector in either inspection is replaced by a good item, so that lots shipped should contain N good items.

Accuracy of Acceptance Judgments. The manufacturer needs to know the average accuracy of decisions to accept and reject lots. All plans will accept perfect lots and reject lots that are totally bad. Between these extremes, however, sampling plans vary in their ability to accept good and reject bad lots. A yardstick is needed to evaluate the quality assurance inherent in a sampling plan.

Such a yardstick is provided by an operating characteristic (OC) curve. This portrays the relative effectiveness of a sampling plan in dealing with lots of varying quality, by displaying the acceptance (and rejection) probabilities of lots of varying quality. Thus, by examining its OC curve, the small manufacturer can discover the efficiency of a sampling plan.[5]

Figure 29-4 shows that the lot acceptance probability increases with the quality of the lots submitted for inspection. It should be noted that this is the curve for a particular sampling plan. Other plans would have differently shaped OC curves. The OC curve shows also that good lots are almost always accepted and bad lots almost always rejected. Thus, it efficiently pictures the quality assurance the plan provides.

Ratio Defective in Lot Shipped to Customers. A second look at the quality assurance provided by a sampling plan is afforded by the concept of "average outgoing quality"—which is analyzed by the use of an average outgoing quality (AOQ) curve (see Figure 29-5).[6]

The ratio defective in a lot prior to inspection is related to its ratio defective after inspection. The inspected lot is ready for shipment to a customer (or transfer to the next processing department). Its ratio defective may be thought of as the "outgoing quality." If incoming quality is perfect, outgoing quality is also perfect, of course. But, even for incoming quality that is very bad, outgoing quality is quite good, on the average, as Figure 29-5 demonstrates. This is true because bad lots are ordinarily rejected by the sampling inspection and 100 percent inspected, so that all defectives are found and replaced by good items.

---

[5] The probability of acceptance corresponding to any given lot ratio defective, p, is given by the

formula: $P_a = \sum_{r=0}^{r \lessgtr c} \dfrac{(_{Np}C_r)\,(_{Nq}C_{n-r})}{_{N}C_r}$

Worked for various p's, each larger than the one before, one obtains enough P_a's to plot an OC curve and visualize a plan's effectiveness.

[6] The AOQ corresponding to any incoming quality (measured by the ratio defective in lots coming to inspection) is computed by the following formulas:

$AOQ = (p)\,(P_a)$ (if c = 0)

$AOQ = \dfrac{N-n}{N}\,(p)\,(P_a)$ (if c > 0)

Worked out for various increasing values of p, one obtains enough AOQ-values to plot (and visualize the meaning of) the AOQ curve. It will be recalled that this relates outgoing quality to incoming quality.

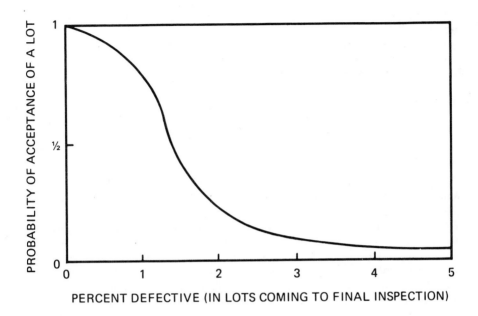

Figure 29-4
OPERATING CHARACTERISTIC (OC) CURVE
Single Sampling Plan

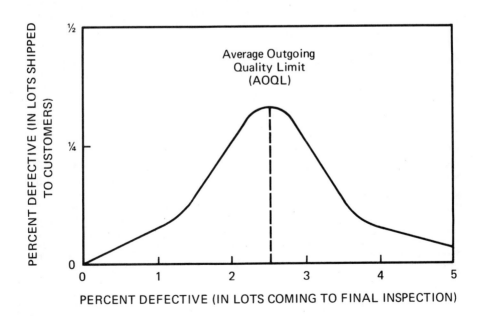

Figure 29-5
AVERAGE OUTGOING QUALITY CURVE
Single Sampling Plan

Accordingly, it is only the outgoing quality for incoming lots neither very good nor bad that is not sure of being high. Their outgoing quality reaches a maximum for a given sampling plan at some point between the extremes of quality; this maximum prevails on the average over a period of time.[7] It is called the average outgoing quality limit (or AOQL). This may be a fraction of one percent and is unlikely ever to exceed three percent. Its precise value varies somewhat from one single sampling plan to another.

In theory, though not always in practice, 100 percent inspection results in shipment of perfect lots. For properly designed single sampling plans, on the average over a period of time, one knows that lots shipped cannot have a ratio defective greater than the AOQL. Accordingly, an AOQ chart provides a second picture of the quality assurance provided by a single sampling plan.

Amount and Cost of Inspection. A third chart may be prepared to show the amount and cost of inspection likely for a given single sampling plan. Figure 29-6 presents two curves—the ASN curve, showing the amount of sampling inspection per lot, and the $\overline{\text{TI}}$ curve, depicting the average total inspection per lot, for lots of various qualities. Obviously, cost varies directly with amount of inspection, so that cost curves need not be plotted. Standard formulas are available for computing the values corresponding to the various possible ratios defective, p, in lots coming to final inspection.[8] $\overline{\text{TI}}$, the average total number of items inspected per lot, may be compared—for each value of p—with $\dfrac{N}{1-p}$, the amount of inspection required per lot in plants using 100 percent inspection. Such comparisons measure the reduction in the average amount of total inspection per lot. On the average, this reduction is substantial, being greatest for very good lots. It varies with incoming lot quality and is small for very bad lots. This is because at least 90 percent of such lots are typically rejected—and 100 percent inspected.

Selection of Sampling Inspection Plan. Investigation of the quality assurance and amount of inspection inherent in various sampling plans permits an intelligent selection of the plan to be used. It also lets one comprehend the value and limitations of such plans.

A manufacturer could design his own single sampling plan, or he may hire a consulting statistician to do it for him. There are also several published books of sampling plans, readily available, from which an appropriate choice of plan may be made. Published plans secure for management the benefits of sampling inspection—reduction in amount and cost of inspection, coupled with high quality assurance.

---

[7] Individual lots shipped may, at any time, be either better or worse than an AOQL lot. But, in theory, over a period of time, the ratio defective for lots shipped will average the AOQL, at most. To achieve even this high an average ratio defective shipped, all lots coming to final inspection would have to have p_{AOQL} as their ratio defective—that is, the p perpendicularly under the AOQL on the AOQ curve. Hence, *in practice*, the average ratio defective for all lots shipped over a period of time will be less than the AOQL, as many p's $\leq P_{AOQL}$ are certain to occur.

[8] These formulas are the following: $\text{ASN} = n$

$$\overline{\text{TI}} = \frac{n + (1 - P_a)(N - n)}{1 - p}$$

These formulas presume immediate 100 percent inspection for any rejected lot, with *all* defectives noted replaced by items which have themselves already passed final inspection.

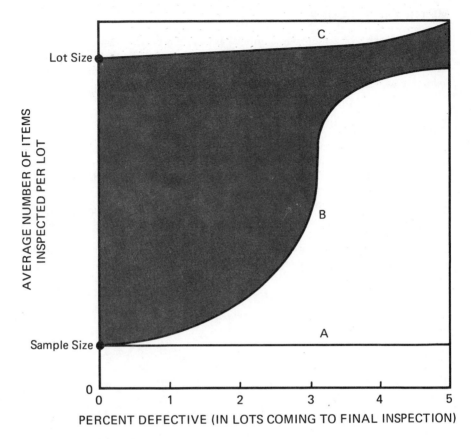

Legend:
A = Average amount of sampling inspection per lot
B = Average amount of inspection per lot, using
single sampling inspection plan
C = Number of items inspected, using 100% inspection
per lot

The sample size is the same regardless of the quality of material coming to inspection, a fact which explains the horizontal line measuring average amount of sampling inspection per lot.

As quality decreases, however, an increasing number of lots will be rejected by the inspectors. Each rejected lot must then be inspected in detail. Thus, with decreasing quality, the average total number of items inspected per lot rises.

The line measuring the average number of items inspected per lot when 100 percent inspection is used also rises with decreasing quality. This is because of the need to replace defectives found by inspectors with items which are good (which have already passed inspection at an earlier time).

It should be noted also that the amount of inspection and cost of inspection will tend to increase, or decrease, together. Thus, the shaded area on the chart, which indicates the difference in amount of inspection required for 100 percent inspection and for inspection done under the given single sampling plan, reflects the savings both in amount and cost of inspection (resulting from use of the single sampling plan).

Figure 29-6
AMOUNT OF INSPECTION REQUIRED
Single Sampling Plan

METHODS ENGINEERING

The objective of a methods engineer is to find a better, easier, and cheaper way of doing work. The currently used method is never ideal. Methods studies critically analyze the work of an operator, department, or plant—with the objective of reducing waste and assuring efficient operating methods.

Manager's Role in Methods Engineering

The manager of a small firm may have to act as his own methods engineer. If so, it is obvious that he must believe in a work simplification program and in the possibility of improvement in his own shop. Given such an attitude, he will undertake methods improvements, which will reward him with reduced costs. And his attitude should stimulate all members of his organization to seek improvements, in turn, since some of his efforts will turn out well. Success is always imitated.

The manager need not master the technical tools of the professional specialist, but he must develop a questioning attitude. He should ask himself such questions as the following:

1. Is the right machine being used?
2. Can one employee operate two or more machines?
3. Can automatic feeders or ejectors be utilized?
4. Can power tools replace hand tools?
5. Can the jigs and fixtures be improved?
6. Is the operator's motion sequence effective?
7. Is the workplace properly arranged?

Once a manager realizes the benefits of work simplification, he can indoctrinate his supervisors and key workers. Through them, he can reach his entire work force and succeed in his work simplification efforts. All employees should be encouraged to think creatively about work. Otherwise, they will continue to accept the *status quo*.

Improvements involve changes, which often are resisted by those affected. However, properly motivated workers will go along with methods changes.

Standards and Standardization

A standard is a yardstick measuring performance or cost. It is set by custom or by management authority. Standards serve as the basis for comparing actual with expected results. They are of many types. Products have tolerances as quality standards. Design standards specify component parts whose tolerances assure interchangeability. Material standards specify form, composition, and surface finish of the raw materials to be processed. Performance standards cover output, motion sequences, and materials consumption. Process standards deal with operating methods and plant and workplace layout. There are even standards for equipment and working conditions.

The specific types of standards needed must be determined and properly set. If put in writing, standards avoid future misinterpretation or unintended alteration. In repetitive work especially, written standard instructions are needed to guide machine tenders.

Work Simplification

Work simplification includes an analysis of an entire operation as well as specific motions of individuals doing repetitive work. The first of these is called operations analysis, while the latter is known as motion study. The goal of both is finding the movement sequence demanding the least physical effort and shortest execution time.

Operations Analysis. Operations analysis may be done in any small plant. For example, any process is helped by locating a storeroom so as to minimize materials handling. Analysis of overall operations is a good first step toward greater operating efficiency; it encompasses standardization of equipment and tooling, plant layout, and working conditions. Individual jobs may be studied next. Even for nonrepetitive work, certain job features, such as workplace layout, may still be improved. If the work is repetitive, formal motion studies can assure use of an optimum motion sequence. If a trained analyst is available, motion pictures may be made and submitted to micromotion analysis.

Motion Study. The small manufacturer who engages in work simplification should also know the laws of motion economy (see Figures 29-7 and 29-8). These have been variously stated by different authorities. Among these laws, usually, are statements such as the following:

1. If both hands start and stop their motion at the same time and are never idle during a work cycle, maximum performance is approached.
2. If motions are made simultaneously in opposite directions over similar paths, automaticity and rhythm develop naturally, and less fatigue is experienced.
3. The method requiring the fewest motions generally is the best for performance of a given task.
4. When motions are confined to the lowest practical classification, maximum performance and minimum fatigue are approached. By lowest classification is meant the physical classes of motions—motions involving the fingers, hands, forearms, and trunk.

A knowledge of these and other laws of motion economy will suggest various job improvements. For example, materials and tools should be located within an operator's "normal reach" working area—that is, so placed as not to require movement of the trunk and, if possible, of the extended arm.

Most small entrepreneurs find it impractical to take motion pictures for micromotion analysis in a well-equipped laboratory. But this does not rule out motion study in small plants. As noted earlier, it is possible to study overall operations and break down work cycles on a common sense basis. Moreover, experienced operators usually are highly capable and often discover short cuts on their jobs. Hence, the suggestions of workers should be solicited, utilized, and rewarded.

When methods for a particular task have been improved and standardized, the operators should be carefully trained in the new procedure. This training should continue until all operators use the new motion sequence or method automatically.

Time Study. Time study is analysis of a labor operation to find the time required for completing a unit of work. This is used to set output rates on repetitive labor operations. Such scientifically set work standards have several

MOTIONS OF THE ARMS SHOULD BE MADE
SIMULTANEOUSLY IN OPPOSITE DIRECTION
AND FOLLOW SYMMETRICAL PATHS.

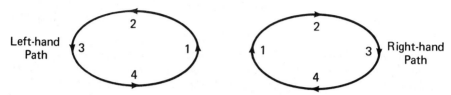

TYPE 1: Numbers indicate corresponding positions
for the two hands, sequentially, at different times.

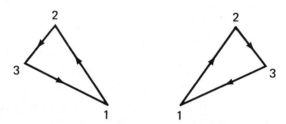

TYPE 2: Numbers indicate corresponding positions
for the two hands, sequentially, at different times.

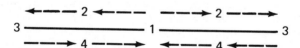

TYPE 3: Numbers indicate corresponding positions
for the two hands, sequentially, at different times.

Figure 29-7
GRAPHIC ILLUSTRATION OF A LAW OF MOTION ECONOMY

uses. They facilitate the scheduling and controlling of production and the predetermination of the number of machines and operators needed to meet the production schedule. They also make possible the use of incentive wage plans under which pay depends directly upon output achieved.

Moreover, making time studies leads to improved layout, mechanization of materials handling, proper location of machine controls, installation of automatic safety devices, and improvements in product design. Thus, time study works hand in hand with the work simplification program already discussed. Theoretically, motion study should precede time study, but, in practice, they are bound to overlap somewhat.

Time study procedures are not inherently complex, but many small plants lack the services of a specialist and find it impractical to make much use of time

Old Method

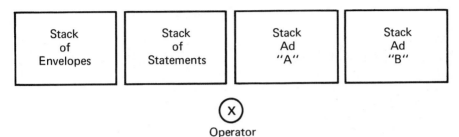

1. With right hand, first picks up Ad "A" and then Ad "B." At the same time, left hand picks up statement.
2. Using both hands, folds statement and places both circulars inside statement.
3. Holds statement in right hand while picking up envelope with left hand.
4. Stuffs envelope and stacks at back of table.

New Method: Two-deck pigeonholes (upper deck recessed back 2 inches)

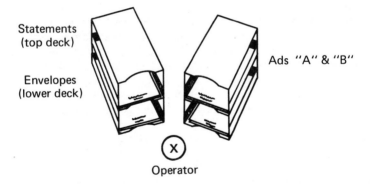

1. Reaches simultaneously to both top pigeonholes and pulls one item from each side part way out.
2. Continuing to hold items from top pigeonholes with two fingers of each hand, pulls one item from each bottom pigeonhole.
3. Brings hands together, dropping envelope directly in front, combining the items, inserting in envelope, and stacking at back of table.

Explanation: A clerical employee stuffs envelopes with customer's monthly statement and two advertising circulars. In the old method, both hands are moving in the same direction. Note the *symmetrical* patterns required by the new method, which saves time, effort, and money.

Figure 29-8
MOTION ECONOMY IN CLERICAL WORK

study. However, numerous small plants, especially those with highly repetitive and simple operations—manufacturers of clothing, for example—have employed time study engineers.

Methods-Time Measurement. Methods-time measurement is an alternative to ordinary time study. It uses a catalog of all the possible work motions, which lists the standard times for all such motions. These were determined by prior time study (in the shop or in a laboratory). The analyst must determine specific job motions, such as reach, move, turn, grasp, position, and disengage. He considers the operations necessary for processing a given product and determines the basic motions required on each operation. He then looks up the corresponding time standards. Properly combined, these yield the output rate. The whole process of setting rates in this way may require less than an hour.

A major criticism of this method is that it takes no account of special conditions in the shop. The accuracy of output rates so determined is surprising, however, even though set prior to the start of production. This makes it possible for job order shops, such as a machine shop manufacturing to customer's order, to use methods-time measurement where ordinary time study would be highly impractical.

Work Sampling. Work sampling, as originated in England by L. H. C. Tippett some 40 years ago, involved random observations of an operation to discover its ratio of downtime. The observations taken over a period of time were totaled and made the basis of estimates of ratios of time spent on each type of activity and of downtime.

Work sampling has several advantages. One is that operators do not ordinarily resent observation by a passer-by, so that honest results are highly likely. Again, over a period of time, the observer gets more information in this way than would be possible by use of other methods. But work sampling also has its limitations. It does not reveal the causes of delays observed; additional studies are needed to make this determination. Furthermore, work sampling provides little operating detail and makes no direct contribution to methods improvement.

In addition to provision of downtime ratios, work sampling is useful for studying rates of personnel utilization. A knowledge of what each office clerk actually does during working hours could lead to a reassignment of duties to utilize individual skills more efficiently. If a supervisor is used as observer, he will become even more aware of the work flow problems faced.

Although alternative sampling procedures are available, for work sampling studies it is best to take simple random samples. Every minute in the work day—for all days included in the study—then has an equal, independent chance of being selected as an observation time. Random observations tend to eliminate observer bias, which could otherwise be a potent source of error in the final results.

Waste Control. Methods engineering and work simplification cannot be considered complete until sources of waste have been identified and waste control procedures successfully inaugurated. Among the more important sources of waste are pilferage from the stock room; poor materials cutting; failures to return excess materials to the storeroom; poor buying; and use of inefficient, or even obsolete, equipment and tooling. There are some legitimate (necessary) wastes, such as sawdust in a woodworking process, though even these may be reclaimed in some cases as by-products. The emphasis, however, is upon controllable wastes.

The idleness of skilled workers and expensive equipment and tooling is a significant form of waste. The small industrialist should compute his machine and manpower utilization rates for all labor operations and should take appropriate steps to correct low utilization rates.

The problem of materials yield provides another example of possible waste control. Consumption standards (amounts of materials required per finished product unit) can be set. For key operations, this standard amount can be compared with actual usage. Such a comparison, if excessive usage is indicated, makes it possible to take appropriate steps for improving the actual yield. If good materials are issued for processing, a knowledge of the actual-to-standard consumption ratio is helpful for evaluating the worker. A materials yield report, prepared both for vendors and operators, could guide the entrepreneur in future buying and serve as basis for bonus payments to workers with high yields.

INDUSTRIAL RESEARCH

Industrial research in small factories is typically aimed at improvement of manufacturing methods, processes, and products. Much of the pure research, the goal of which is expansion of the frontiers of knowledge, is left to large industry, universities, and the government. In spite of this fact, as noted in Chapter 2, many product innovations originate with individuals or small firms.

Some small manufacturers believe any research is too expensive to be undertaken by small firms. This belief is vulnerable on two counts. First, it is technically possible to do some types of research in small plants. Second, it is vitally necessary for most small firms to engage in research to remain competitive. Other firms regularly bring out new products which challenge a given firm's existing products. The latter firm's products must then be upgraded to meet that challenge.

Research is too often equated with experimentation conducted in an expensively equipped laboratory. All it really requires, however, is a questioning attitude, which seeks to improve existing methods and products. Thousands of small plant managers have this attitude.

Nevertheless, research poses two real problems for a small firm. It consumes both money and management time. If it is unproductive, any research is too costly. If it is properly productive, however, the expense involved is outweighed by the cost savings from the improvements achieved.

The problem of lack of management time is not so easily solved. But there are answers, such as the following:

1. Use of individual members of university faculties as consultants.[9]
2. Use of university research bureaus for consummation of research projects.[10]

---

[9] A management professor made motion-time studies and set up a new materials handling system for a large city laundry which had found itself short of space and confronted by rising operating costs. A statistics professor helped with the isolation of the most important variables in a manufacturing process (with respect to quality). Later, he helped install quality control charts and sampling inspection plans at the given plant.

[10] A university's bureau of business research studied the industrial location potential of a medium-size city.

3. Referral of research problems to private research agencies.[11]
4. Participation, through membership, in the research program of the trade association serving the given industry.

Most small manufacturers cannot afford to employ a research scientist or engineer. But they can assign special responsibility for keeping abreast of research in the firm's areas of interest to the technically most proficient member of the organization. He should then review the current trade literature, attend professional and technical conferences, and contact suppliers who do research and development work. He might also check on old, but still useful, inventions which have been thrown open for use by the general public. Then, he could explore the possibilities for reclamation of waste materials (such as metals from waste dumps) or for recycling of already used materials. Finally, there is the possibility of finding substitute raw materials for those materials currently used which are scarce. Given time to fulfill this responsibility, such an individual's contribution could be impressive.

 ## Summary

1. The goal of production planning and control is the orderly, time-scheduled flow of work through a plant. This promotes customer satisfaction (through punctuality of deliveries) and operating efficiency (by minimizing work stoppages). Work stoppages occur due to materials shortages, machine breakdowns, lack of tools, and planning errors, among other causes.
2. To control production of complex products involving many component parts is very difficult; to control the processing of simple products is itself simple. The nature of the manufacturing process also affects the method and the difficulty of control.
3. Production control often is handled informally by small firms. This may be a virtue. More formal procedures become necessary, however, as production operations grow in volume and complexity.
4. Production planning and control involve planning and routing, scheduling and dispatching, and supervising.
5. Plant maintenance includes equipment repair, preventive maintenance, and plant housekeeping. Effective control of preventive maintenance requires systematic procedures to assure periodic attention to key facilities so as to keep them always serviceable.
6. Product quality involves a set of physical variables such as length and diameter. Quality control programs may be either preventive or remedial in character; to supplement inspection, firms have traditionally used tools such as quality bonuses and waste reports.

---

[11] Southwest Research Institute of San Antonio, Texas, is one example. It has counterparts in the other sections of the country.

7. Planning for inspection requires decisions concerning inspection instruments to be used, processing and other points at which inspection is needed, amount of inspection per lot, and inspection standards to be applied. The system must also make possible the control of quality cost.

8. The major statistical tool for process quality control is the control chart. This takes two forms—variables and attributes. $\bar{X}$ and R charts, the variables charts commonly used, are highly efficient. Attributes charts include p and c charts; these are somewhat less effective and less widely used.

9. Management benefits in many ways from the use of SQC techniques. The most important benefits include (a) ability to maintain a consistently good process, (b) reduction of scrap and rework, (c) enhanced quality-mindedness of shopworkers, and (d) decrease in amount and cost of inspection (without impairment of quality assurance).

10. Of the three kinds of attributes sampling inspection plans available for use in job-lot factories, the single sampling plan is efficient and most often used. Such a plan makes it possible to avoid 100 percent inspection while preserving a high level of quality assurance. Small continuous processors use continuous sampling plans.

11. Methods study seeks to find a better, safer, cheaper way of doing work. It is described by such titles as "methods engineering" and "work simplification."

12. Standards are criteria for measuring and controlling cost, quality, performance, and work practices.

13. Work simplification includes both operations analysis and motion study. It may involve human engineering, workplace layout, and the laws of motion economy.

14. Time study determines output standards that can be used in scheduling production and administering incentive wage programs.

15. Work sampling studies a process (or worker) through random sampling observations. It measures downtime on production machines and evaluates activity-to-total-time ratios for the various work activities undertaken by a given individual.

16. Control of waste caused by any of a large number of possible factors is an essential part of methods study.

17. Although industrial research is difficult for a small firm, some efforts of this type are possible through the use of an imaginative approach.

18. Some small firms have solved the problem of industrial research by employing consultants, contracting out research projects to private research institutes, and taking part in trade association research programs.

19. Assigning someone special responsibility to keep the firm abreast of current research developments can also be helpful in the small industrial concern. The "someone" should be the technically most proficient person in the organization.

Discussion Questions

1. What are the proper objectives of production planning and control in a small manufacturing establishment?

2. Is production control solely a manufacturer's problem? If not, how should control procedures differ in the following types of

businesses: (a) a furniture factory with 125 employees; (b) a laundry employing 40 persons; (c) a cash-and-carry wholesale-grocery firm serving a local market; (d) a small city supermarket (locally owned); (e) a fairly good-sized restaurant?

3. What specific contributions to control of production may properly be expected of the shop supervisor?

4. Classify and evaluate the several kinds of plant maintenance required in a manufacturing firm.

5. Machine breakdowns during use constitute preventive maintenance failures. Why should these always be investigated promptly? What should be the outcomes of such investigations? Are cost considerations or lost production of paramount importance in such situations? Why?

6. What contributions, if any, are made by good plant housekeeping to each of the following: (a) level of shop morale; (b) accident control; (c) product quality?

7. Why is it that even with 100 percent inspection of products a manufacturer cannot prevent the occasional shipment of a few defectives?

8. What inspections are essential in any manufacturing organization? Where? Why?

9. To what degree is quality the responsibility of all members of a factory organization? Explain.

10. Enumerate the three most important management benefits inherent in effective use of SQC methods. State why each is important.

11. State and explain the specification of an attributes single sampling acceptance inspec-

tion plan. Explain also how its inherent quality assurance may be demonstrated.

12. Are methods improvement and work simplification really feasible in small firms such as the following (each located in a city of 35,000 population): (a) a job printing shop; (b) a toy factory; (c) a dry cleaning shop; (d) a TV sales and service agency? If so, how and under what governing conditions?

13. Under what circumstances may a small factory owner safely guaranteee time-study-based piece rates against change? When and how may such guaranteed rates be changed after they have been put into effect?

14. Why must standards and standardization precede motion studies in factories and offices if the results are to be effective?

15. Are waste control and cost reduction drives properly continuing or intermittent in character? Why?

16. How essential is industrial research for a small manufacturer? Specifically, what percentage, if any, of his sales dollar should be allocated to research aimed at methods and process improvement?

17. What outside help is available to small firms conducting industrial research? Evaluate each agency suggested as to efficiency and cost.

18. How much industrial research typically can be undertaken successfully by a small factory owner and his employees? Are there any technical skill or other limitations on the amount of successful, "within-the-firm" research that can be done? Discuss fully.

Case G-1

BELL SUPERMARKET

History of the Business

In 1948, W. J. Bell moved to a small city of 8,000 and bought out an independent food store. Previously, he had operated grocery stores in two other cities, having opened his first store 10 years earlier at the age of 20. The purchased store was heavily involved in selling on credit, and Bell's first move was to go into a strict cash sales operation—the first of its kind in the city.

Bell's motto was "Low Prices Every Day," and he emphasized friendly, efficient service, high quality merchandise, and reasonable prices. His competitors were old line stores who did not welcome the strong competition. Several innovations helped him to get established and increase sales volume. For example, Bell Supermarket was the first store in the city to feature advertised weekend specials. Bell was also one of the first stores in that area of the state to give trading stamps. By 1958, his store had become the number one food store in the city.

By 1958, the store had also outgrown the original downtown location. A modern, 10,000-square-foot store was erected at the east edge of the city—the direction of city growth. Shortly after this move, Gulfway, a regional food chain, opened the first real chain store in the city. This competition was of great concern to Bell, but he continued to follow his basic business philosophy and to operate even more efficiently. As a result, Bell Supermarket continued to show yearly progress in sales and profits.

Recent Developments In Bell Supermarket

In the late 1960s, Bell sold a 25 percent interest in the business to his brother and another 25 percent interest to his son, David. David had recently been graduated from college, and he became an active partner in the business. For many years

the store had been recognized as one of the leading independent food store operations in that section of the state.

As of 1967, the city's population had grown to 14,000, and Bell Supermarket was located in the newest section of the city. Residents in the area were predominantly in the middle to high income brackets. However, there was also a substantial amount of lower income trade.

Bell affiliated with one of the nation's largest independent wholesalers in 1967. This made possible the use of many private labels and permitted more effective competition. The wholesaler also provided advertising themes and promotions to member stores. Examples were promotions featuring china, art reproductions, record albums, and stainless steel mixing bowls. These promotions served as good stimulants for increasing sales volume. Customers were inclined to say, "There's always something going on at Bell's!"

Local Market Structure in 1967

The Gulfway chain store was located at the edge of the downtown section and catered primarily to customers in middle to lower income brackets. However, they also had some middle to upper income trade and were Bell's major competitor.

Bell's strongest independent competitor was Morgan Food Store—which was also the strongest independent when Bell came in 1948. Morgan Food Store had also moved to the east edge of the city but still had a problem of limited parking space. Its major appeal was the credit offered to customers and goodwill which had been built up through years of service. This business had dwindled in recent years, however.

The pricing structure could be described as very healthy. There was no excess of large food stores, and a "reasonable" markup was possible. There was competition, but it was not fierce.

Beginning of Discount Store Competition

In 1968, a new type of competition entered the city with the opening of a discount store. Kelly Discount Center, a 20,000-square-foot operation, carried not only a complete line of nonfood items but also a wide line of grocery items—dry groceries as well as fresh meats, dairy products, produce, and frozen foods. The store was franchised, and the owner operated two other Kelly Discount Centers in a large city some 80 miles away.

When Kelly Discount Center opened for business, they dropped prices drastically, especially in staple items. They featured many "deep-cut" loss leaders, seemingly using the food operation as a drawing card for their more profitable lines.

Competitive Developments

Gulfway made it apparent immediately that it did not intend to be undersold—even by a discount house that gave no stamps and provided no carry-out service. Week-long specials, rather than weekend specials, became the rule. Competition became intense, and everyday shelf items were lowered to near cost or below.

J. A. Morgan, owner of Morgan Food Store, died in 1968, shortly after the opening of the discount store. A young man with chain store management experience purchased the store from the Morgan estate. He immediately eliminated both credit and stamps and tried to start a discount type of operation himself.

Loss leaders became more prevalent. The Gulfway chain not only met the discount prices but even attempted to undersell. They also increased their advertising—more newspaper advertising, handbills, and some radio commercials. Morgan likewise stayed in the thick of the price competition.

Bell's Dilemma

The arrival of the discounter marked the beginning of a disturbing period for Bell Supermarket. The relatively calm situation that had prevailed for several years was suddenly shattered. Their sales volume quickly declined about 20 percent.

The Bells reacted, as might be expected, by lowering prices. As they saw prices cut to profitless levels, however, they questioned the wisdom of such extreme competition. Part of the question was the type of store they should try to be. They wondered whether Bell Supermarket could continue to project an image that distinguished it from the discounter. At times, it seemed that the price war made price cutting the only effective weapon in attracting business.

QUESTIONS

1. What has been the basis of Bell's successful operation and growth in the past?
2. What are its greatest sources of strength in the current period of intense competition?
3. Which store would be likely to suffer the most from the opening of the discount store? Why?
4. What general course of action should be followed by Bell Supermarket during the next few months?

Case G-2

LARAMIE OIL COMPANY *

In January, 1970, Don Currie, vice president in charge of domestic

automotive gasoline distribution for the Laramie Oil Company, was considering what action he should take with regard to the company's 14,800 franchised and lessee-operated service stations. A number of developments that indicated discontent among franchisees and lessees had recently occurred. Although he was unsure as to what extent these developments indicated real widespread dis-

---

* This case was prepared by Thomas C. Kinnear under the direction of Professor C. Merle Crawford of The University of Michigan.

content, Don Currie was wondering what might be causing the discontent and what action he should take at the present time.

Company Background

The Laramie Oil Company was a fully integrated petroleum company with operations in 21 countries. In 1968, domestic sales for Laramie were $4.23 billion and net income was $312.6 million. The Laramie product line included automotive gasoline, aviation fuels, distillates, lubricants, and assorted agricultural and industrial chemicals. Sales of automotive gasoline and related products accounted for 52 percent of revenues earned and 64 percent of net profit. Laramie ranked tenth in *Fortune's* 500 companies in sales and twelfth in profits.

Both the international and domestic American head offices were situated in New York City. Don Currie's office was located in the domestic head office building. As distribution vice president, Don Currie had responsibility for the overall maintenance of a strong network of retail outlets. This responsibility involved the setting of policies concerning lease terms, the selection of dealers, the training of dealers, the motivation of dealers, the dismissal of dealers, and any other factors involving the maintenance of dealer morale and overall effectiveness.

Don Currie described his objective as distribution vice president as follows:

"We've done a great deal of research to determine why gasoline purchasers use one brand of gasoline or another. In almost every instance, the consumer's perception of the gasoline retail outlet was a very significant determinant in brand selection. It appears that we're halfway to first base if we can keep our outlets modern and clean, plus provide the service that the consumer desires. By service, I mean more than just good, fast, competent pump-island work. Service includes having outlets open when consumers need them, and making sure that outlets handle our national promotions. There is nothing more

irritating to a customer who expects to receive a glass or coupon to find that the station he happens to be in isn't participating in the national promotion. That is one of the best ways to lose customers for good.

Our whole retail distribution policy is directed toward providing a consistent type of physical outlet and service from one end of the country to the other. That's how gasoline is sold."

Implementation of Distribution Policies

Don Currie's control over the implementation of his department's policies was quite indirect.

A general manager in each of six geographical divisions had responsibility for all marketing activities in his division, including retail distribution. Each division had a distribution manager whose responsibilities included the day-to-day implementation of corporate policies in regard to service station operations. The division distribution manager reported directly to the division general manager. The corporate and divisional distribution managers did, however, maintain informal contact with each other. Each divisional distribution manager had a number of district sales managers reporting directly to him. Direct contact with service station operators was maintained by company sales representatives each of whom reported to a district sales manager. The sales representative was the final link in the chain of implementation between Don Currie's office and the service station operator. (See Exhibit 1 for a partial organization chart.)

Types of Service Stations

Laramie Oil Company distributed its automotive products through three types of service stations:

1. Company-Operated. These stations were owned or leased by Laramie Oil who hired the service station personnel to operate them on a straight salary basis. Laramie controlled the retail price and all other aspects of all products sold through

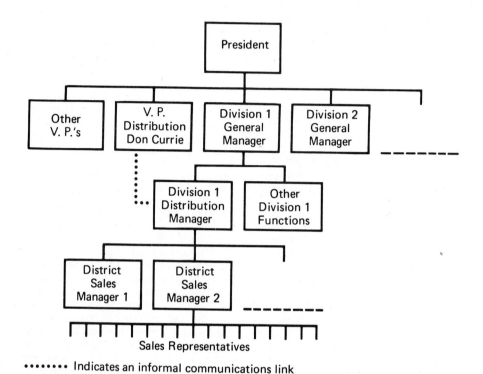

•••••••• Indicates an informal communications link

Exhibit 1
LARAMIE OIL COMPANY PARTIAL ORGANIZATION CHART

these stations. About 200 of Laramie's 15,000 stations were operated in this manner.

2. Franchised Dealers. The station site and all physical facilities of franchised dealer operations were owned by the dealers themselves. Laramie did, however, provide financing, so that an individual dealer could commence operation by putting up as little as $2,000. The company, or local financial institutions, held mortgages on the land and physical facilities. About 6,000 outlets were in this category.

3. Lessee-Operated. Lessee operators were dealers who leased their service stations from Laramie Oil. The stations, in these cases, continued to be owned by Laramie Oil. The lessee purchased petroleum products from Laramie but

was free to set his own operating policies as related to such things as hours, prices, brands of accessories carried, etc. The lessee's cost price of gasoline was based on a "tank wagon price" which included all taxes and delivery charges to the lessee's station. Typical lessee operators were charged per gallon as follows:

Transport price (ex tax)	$0.1330
Plus: State and federal taxes	0.1700
Transport price (including tax)	$0.3030
Plus: Jobber margin	.0345
Tank wagon price	$0.3375
Plus: Rent paid to Laramie	.0315
Lessee's margin	.0500
Retail price	$0.4190

The cost price of gasoline to franchised dealers closely approximated the lessee cost arrangement, except that rent charges were not included. For most franchisees, interest charges on their mortgages tended to make up this cost difference.

A Closer Look at Two Lessee Dealers

1. Jerry Williamson's Laramie Service Station, Dearborn, Michigan. Jerry Williamson's service station was located at one of the main intersections in the Detroit suburb of Dearborn. His customers were drawn mainly from local residents and commuters who drove through Dearborn on their way to and from their work in Detroit. Williamson was a class A automobile mechanic who had worked for a Ford dealership for eight years before becoming a Laramie dealer in 1959. He had put up $7,500 of his own money to obtain the right to be the Laramie lessee for his Dearborn location. Most of the $7,500 had been used to finance product inventories and tools, while some had been used to physically upgrade the station.

Williamson did a large automobile repair business. Over the years he had built up an excellent reputation among the residents of Dearborn for providing competent and reliable repair service. As a result of this business and his good location for attracting gasoline customers, he did an annual sales volume of slightly over $225,000. His profit statement for 1968 is presented in Exhibit 2 on page 530.

Williamson took great pride in the fact that he had been able to build a very successful business operation. He thought of himself as being a part of the community through his memberships in the Lion's Club and the Chamber of Commerce. In the latter organization he had risen to the position of vice president and was looking forward to being president at some time.

When he was asked if there were any negative aspects to being a Laramie dealer, Williamson replied as follows:

"Well . . . not really; it's tough to complain a lot when you're making $15,000 a year. The only thing I really have to complain about is that Laramie pressures me to buy most of my repair parts and accessories from its own supply company or from company-approved jobbers. I think I could get slightly better margins from other jobbers, as the company takes a percentage rake-off from the approved jobbers. However, it's really a small complaint when you consider all the pluses that Laramie gives. Over all, I'm extremely pleased."

2. Fred Shaw's Laramie Service Station, Detroit, Michigan. Fred Shaw's service station was located in an industrial section of Detroit, with most of his customers being people who worked in the plants in the surrounding area. Prior to becoming the lessee of his current station, Shaw had worked as an employee in a suburban Laramie station. He had always wanted to be in business for himself and whenever he heard that a station was available, he would approach the sales representative involved to see if he could obtain the station. Most of the stations had required too much capital, but finally he was able to obtain his current station by putting up $2,500 for the required inventories.

Although managing his station required long hours for Shaw, he preferred it to a very great extent over working for another dealer. It was in a very real sense to him the fulfillment of his dream of being his own boss.

Due to the nature of the surrounding environment, Shaw's station was quiet most of the day except when the shifts changed, and then it was extremely busy. This constant changing "from feast to famine" made proper staffing extremely difficult and required long hours to cover all shift changes.

Shaw's station was not as productive in either gasoline sales or repair service as was Jerry Williamson's. As a result, his 1968 sales volume was just under $75,000. Exhibit 2 also presents his 1968 profit statement.

Hank Homes was the Laramie sales representative in Shaw's district, and on one of his weekly visits recently he asked Fred to take part in a special china

	Jerry Williamson	Fred Shaw
Sales	100.00%	100.00%
Cost of goods sold	75.36	75.24
Gross profit	24.64	24.76
Expenses:		
Labor for outside work	.46	.29
Supplies	.75	.79
Wages (excluding owner)	8.38	8.69
Repairs and maintenance	.34	.24
Advertising	.79	.93
Delivery	.41	.42
Bad debts	.02	.02
Administrative	.38	.35
Miscellaneous	.96	.72
Rent	2.60	2.00
Insurance	.47	.46
Utilities	.96	1.00
Taxes	.74	.66
Interest	.10	.11
Depreciation	.60	.65
TOTAL EXPENSES	17.96	17.33
Net Profit	6.68	7.43
Inventory Turnover x 1 year	17.26	12.88

Exhibit 2
PERCENTAGE PROFIT STATEMENTS FOR 1968
JERRY WILLIAMSON'S AND FRED SHAW'S SERVICE STATIONS

give-away promotion. Part of the conversation between the two men went as follows:

Hank: This looks to me to be one of the best promotions the company has ever put together. They're going to put about $2 million in advertising behind it. You should draw a pile of customers.

Fred: Come on, Hank, the type of customer who buys from my outlet isn't interested in English bone china. It may be fine for other outlets, but I don't want in on this one.

Hank: I disagree, Fred. I'm sure you'd do well with it. Why don't you let me sign you up? I think you'd be pleased with the results. We pretested this in Chicago and it went well. Think about it for a few minutes while we discuss a few other things.

It looks to me as if your station could use a new coat of paint this spring. If we let it go any longer it will chase customers away.

Fred: I don't think I can afford to put out for the paint right now, Hank. You know what a problem I'm having making ends meet here.

Hank: Well, maybe I can help you out on that score. If I work on them at the regional office, they might let me absorb part or even all of the expense for you . . . Think about the china promotion, Fred, and I'll drop back tomorrow.

Franchisee and Lessee Discontent

The dealer comments enumerated below were taken from meetings of several Laramie retail dealer associations in various parts of the United States.

Laramie retail dealer associations were groups of Laramie dealers who had gotten together on their own for such purposes as the discussion of mutual problems, the collective purchasing of products from independent suppliers, and the undertaking of various social activities. Not all Laramie dealers belonged to associations, and the strength and activity level of associations varied greatly.

Lessee 1: "The company claims that we can set our own prices, but that . . . sales rep comes into my place and tells me I can't sell at more than a four cent mark-up. I can hardly scrape from one week to the next at that rate . . . I know for sure he'll drop my lease if I don't set these prices. Our dealer association has had economists do studies that showed that on the average it takes a gross profit margin of nine cents a gallon to operate profitably. Margins today run from about three cents to eight cents with the average at about five and a half cents. That's just not enough."

Lessee 2: "What really bugs me is those stupid games and contests I have to put up with. They advertise them like mad on TV, so I have to carry them or the customers start screaming . . . I don't get any more business with them—all the oil companies are running some game or another—all they do is add to my costs. It's really frustrating."

Lessee 3: "I couldn't be more satisfied. I make a really good living. If some of you guys stopped complaining and started working, you could do the same."

Lessee 4: "You know I'd really like to close my place down at night . . . the only reason I'm open nights is because the sales rep said he wouldn't renew my lease if I didn't keep his hours—imagine that, I've worked for Laramie for 15 years as a dealer and they'd drop me just like that. I can't afford to lose my station, but I'm losing money by staying open."

Lessee 5: "The company is more interested in their gallonage than our profits, and those one-sided leases let them dictate what we'll charge and what products we'll sell. They also use the lease to ride herd on our prices."

Lessee 6: "I had hoped the Supreme Court rulings that prevented them from forcing their TBA (tires, batteries, and accessories) brands on us would have helped; all it's done is make their methods more subtle."

Franchisee 1: "I thought when I put up my bucks I was going to be in business for myself—fat chance—that sales rep is in my place all the time suggesting what hours to work, how to work, what price to set. . . . If I object, he starts talking about revoking my franchise. I know the Laramie name draws customers, but some of his suggestions are unreasonable."

Comments of Sales Representatives (SR)

The following comments were taken from individual interviews with selected sales representatives:

SR 1: "Sure, I set hours and prices and procedures; if I didn't, some of those dolts would be out of business tomorrow."

SR 2: "To get the volume out of my territory that the district manager demands, I have to pressure the dealers. Talking about the lease is always effective. However, I've never actually threatened any of my dealers with the loss of their lease."

SR 3: "If you're honest and friendly with your dealers and show them what they will gain from following what you suggest, then you don't have to threaten them to get cooperation."

SR 4: "You can bet your life I'm out pushing our TBA line to dealers. That right hasn't been taken away from us. However, that doesn't mean we're going to club them over the head if they don't."

Comments by Don Currie

(Made before a Congressional Committee) "It isn't our policy to require dealers to maintain company-directed hours or prices. The whole idea is that the dealer has the right to establish his own hours and prices."

"I'd fire any sales representative found pressuring dealers on matters like prices or hours or contests."

"It seems to me that what we have here is a situation completely analogous to the normal arrangement between landlord and tenant. We have up to $200,000 invested in large stations, and if the dealers are mismanaging them we have a right and a duty to protect our investment."

The Legal Background

(TBA Rulings) In 1965 the Supreme Court of the United States ruled that the Atlantic Refining Company could not require its dealers to carry an exclusive TBA line for which Atlantic got a commission from manufacturers on retail sales. In 1966, the Court ruled that Texaco and Shell could not force their dealers to sell their own private brand products on an exclusive basis. Both rulings indicate that an oil company cannot force service station dealers to carry designated brands exclusively.

Short-Term Leases

The majority of service station dealers operate on a one-year lease. Many dealers have complained that this allows the oil companies to exert undue pressure on them. To date, the courts have not ruled against oil company leasing policies. In December, 1969, the Third Circuit Court of Appeals rejected a dealer suit against Gulf Oil. This suit alleged that the use of one-year leases by Gulf gave the company leverage over retail prices and TBA brands carried, and that this was in violation of the Sherman Act. The court ruled that it could not state that the use of one-year leases was "inherently violative of the antitrust laws."

In September, 1969, the New York State Supreme Court ruled against a dealer's suit against the Mobil Oil Company. In this instance Mobil had refused to renew his three-year lease, not because the contract had been violated but because it wanted to convert the location to a diagnostic center. The court ruled that "stability of contract obligations must not be undermined by judicial sympathy."

Possible Legislation

The current prospects for legislation are unclear. A "Fairness in Franchising Act" introduced by Michigan Senator Philip Hart has been waiting for four years to clear the Antitrust Subcommittee. At its inception this bill made franchisers liable for reparations to franchisees whose contracts were broken without good reason or not renewed upon expiration. However, the bill has been softened by the subcommittee. It now reads that contracts and leases cannot be terminated unless terms are violated and that 90 days' notice must be given to franchisees.

The likelihood that the Act will ever clear the subcommittee and what form it will take, if it does clear, both remain uncertain.

Developments in November, 1969

A number of developments that concerned Don Currie took place in November, 1969.

1. A group of dealers in Chicago filed a suit against Laramie, alleging that Laramie violates the antitrust laws by using short-term leases to intimidate the dealers into following suggested retail prices. No decision had been handed down yet by the court.

2. A Laramie Marketing Research Staff report indicated that the turnover rate among Laramie dealers had increased significantly in the last few years. This problem of dealer turnover was common throughout the oil industry. Estimates indicated that approximately one third of all service stations in the United States change management every year. The Laramie turnover rate was below the national average, but was still very high. This high turnover was considered to be a very serious problem by Don Currie.

Also disturbing was the fact that a significant number of long-service Laramie dealers had left to join cut-rate chains who guaranteed station managers at least $1,500 income per month.

3. The Automotive Retailer Trade Association, which included Laramie dealers, had persuaded the Federal Trade Commission (FTC) to control service station games of chance.

4. Local Dealer Associations, which represented dealers for all manufacturers, had helped bring about FTC investigations in New England, California, and Colorado over alleged price and product coercion.

QUESTIONS

1. What appeared to be the principal causes of dealer discontent?
2. How do the views of Laramie Oil Company and its dealers differ on these matters?
3. Evaluate the use of short-term leases and franchises. Are these devices being used as coercive devices?
4. What action should Don Currie take?
5. What insights about franchising and small business opportunities did you get from this case?

Case G-3

ALPHA CLEANING COMPANY *

Tim Black ran a small repair shop for several years after his graduation from high school. Tim worked hard, and his shop had been quite successful. He was an ambitious, willing worker and anxious to increase his earning power. Accordingly, he was pleased when he was contacted by Mr. Alpha, of the Alpha Cleaning Company, a firm specializing in franchising a home cleaning service.

After lengthy negotiations with Mr. Alpha, Tim decided to accept an Alpha Cleaning franchise in a territory near his home. The territory which he accepted had been operated by the previous franchisee at a loss. Nevertheless, Tim was convinced that he would be able to make a go of it with hard work and the assistance of his contacts in the area. Tim paid $40,000 for the franchise package, which consisted mainly of cleaning equipment and supplies. He rented a small shop which he used as a base of operation and as a warehouse for his equipment and supplies.

Within six months, Tim's business was making a profit. His previous repair experience, his contacts in the town, plus the assistance given him by Mr. Alpha, combined to make the business a success. During the next five years, Tim's business grew considerably. He increased the amount of space at his shop and hired additional employees to help him run the business. His profits increased accordingly to over $20,000 a year.

Quite early in the relationship, Tim became somewhat irritated by Mr. Alpha's constant inferences that his success was due primarily to the advantages offered by the Alpha Cleaning Company's franchise package. Tim felt that the service package was good, but the success of his business was due primarily to the effort he had put into it and to several innovations which he had introduced. One of these was the source of direct conflict with Mr. Alpha. Specifically, Tim had continued to offer some repair services to the various homes he visited to provide the cleaning service. These extra repair jobs were particularly important to Tim in the beginning when the cleaning service was not yet profitable. Mr. Alpha, on the other hand, was concerned that Tim was not putting full time and energy into the cleaning service.

* Taken from *Partners for Profit: A Study of Franchising* (New York: American Management Association, 1966), pp. 109-111.

He pointed out that the contract specifically called for Tim's full-time efforts in the cleaning business. Though he was not convinced of the reasonableness of Mr. Alpha's stand, Tim finally agreed to drop the extra repair services.

Shortly after Tim agreed to discontinue repair services, he became displeased over what he considered to be a lack of advertising support in his local area. According to his contract, he was required to contribute 2 percent of his gross revenue, or approximately $7,000 a year, to an advertising fund. When he investigated the advertising provision more thoroughly, he discovered that Mr. Alpha was using the fund primarily to attract new franchises, rather than to advertise the cleaning service locally. When confronted with this fact, Mr. Alpha pointed out that, technically, the contract provided for the use of the money in this way. Furthermore, Mr. Alpha assured Tim that additional franchises would increase the advertising funds which, in turn, would be used for more aggressive and effective advertising campaigns. Though Tim was not convinced of the legality of Mr. Alpha's action, he was so involved in his business that he did not wish to take the time to pursue the matter further.

As time passed, Tim became increasingly dissatisfied with his franchise arrangement. Contacts with Mr. Alpha became progressively more difficult. The advertising program and promotions became points of issue with Tim because he felt that he was being forced to do things which were unnecessary for his business. He became more upset when he realized that he was paying what he estimated to be a 50 percent markup on the cleaning supplies which he was obligated to purchase in bulk from the Alpha Cleaning Company. As he understood it, the cleaning supplies, which were purchased in bulk by Alpha, were marked up a nominal 10 percent. This charge was supposedly necessary to offset the purchase and handling costs incurred by the Alpha Company. When confronted with the markup issue, Mr. Alpha responded that the markups were, in fact, nominal and that the quality of the cleaning supplies could not be duplicated as reasonably elsewhere.

By this time, the relationship between Tim and Mr. Alpha had degenerated to an open break. In his anger, Tim contacted other Alpha franchisees in the surrounding area and discussed his various gripes with them. He tried, with moderate success, to organize their support against what he considered to be coercion by the Alpha Company. In a further attempt to express his anger, Tim reduced the price of the cleaning services in his area and advertised this fact in the local newspapers. As a result, the profitability of his operation was lowered to near the breakeven point, which substantially reduced the flow of profits to the Alpha Company. When Mr. Alpha threatened legal action to make Tim meet the original prices, Tim responded with a suit charging restraint of trade and claiming triple damages. After nine months of legal maneuvering and expenditures in excess of $15,000 by Tim and $35,000 by Mr. Alpha, they were still at odds awaiting a decision by the courts. In short, *everyone lost*.

QUESTIONS

1. If legally permissible, should Tim Black provide home repair services in addition to standard cleaning services?
2. If granted complete freedom, how could Tim Black most effectively advertise with the $7,000 being currently contributed to the franchisor's advertising fund?
3. What loss to the franchisor has occurred as a result of conflict with the franchisee?
4. What have been the adverse effects of the conflict upon the franchisee?

Case G-4

WOOD MANUFACTURING COMPANY

The Wood Manufacturing Company is located in Grand Prairie, Texas. It manufactures wood heels for ladies' shoes, having contracts with a number of leading ladies' shoe manufacturers, including Lone Star Shoes, Inc., of Dallas, Texas. The firm employs 188 men (plus a dozen young lady clerks in its general offices). The Wood Manufacturing Company has just contracted also to supply all heels needed by the new Solar Shoe Co., Inc., of Fort Worth, Texas, during its first six months of operations. This contract is renewable for the following six months with a guarantee of an average requirement by Solar Shoe of 4,500 pairs of heels a day. This new contract will force The Wood Manufacturing Company to increase its number of employees to 270 within six months and to purchase new equipment. Turning lathes, for shaping the rear contours of heels, in particular, will have to be increased to 17 from the 12 now operated. The management expects organization changes together with possible changes in processing methods and materials handling system.

Plant Relayout

Some two months after the signing of the Solar Shoe Co., Inc., contract, the management had decided upon, and completed, the relayout of the plain wood heel room (which actually manufactures the heels). Other departments—including lumber room, receiving room, supply room, machine shop, stock room, shipping room, and general offices—retained their former layouts. The turning lathe operators vigorously objected to the placement of their machines, which were turned so that the operators faced the west wall. This consisted of an almost solid bank of floor-to-ceiling windows, each twenty feet high. The plant was not

air-conditioned, so that these windows were opened wide in the Texas summertime, which meant that the turning lathe operators faced the sun from 1:00 to 5:00 p.m. daily. The union complaint, just received, includes a veiled strike threat. The company expended $50,000 in accomplishing the relayout.

Inspection Continuance vs. New Grooving Machines

Management has talked with Popp Machine Tool Co. of Boston, Massachusetts, about the possibility of the latter's designing and building new grooving machines to do the rough shaping of the fronts of the heels. Three new, heavy-duty groovers (costing $30,000 as per design and cost estimates approved by both companies) would do the labor operation now requiring four groovers (purchased 12 years ago and now outmoded and fully depreciated by The Wood Manufacturing Company). Use of the new groovers would also make possible the elimination of the plain wood inspection operation, now done on all heels made, because of the smooth cut which would be possible with the new machines. However, the new turning lathes cost $275,000 and other new equipment, already contracted for, will cost $33,800. Management can settle with Popp Machine Tool Co. by paying the design engineering costs (some $8,800), or it can contract for the three new groovers (at a total cost, installed, of $90,000). If the purchase is consummated, one grooving machine operator and two inspectors would need other jobs—or would have to be laid off.

Gifts to Officers

On December 23, the purchasing agent of The Wood Manufacturing Company, Guy E. Hayes, Jr., received a pen-and-pencil desk set (valued at $100) as a Christmas gift from the Warman Lumber Co., major supplier of the plank and lumber squares which constitute the principal raw material of The Wood Manufacturing Company. Hayes has consulted with top executives as to the propriety of his keeping this gift, expressing to them a fear that the thought of the gift might influence the objectivity of his purchasing decisions in the future. He was told that the company did not have any established policy governing acceptance of gifts of any kind from business suppliers or from customers (whether by buyers or by other officers of the concern).

Workplace Arrangement and Materials Handling

The sand-wheels used for sand-smooth, backlining, and breast sanding of the heels manufactured by The Wood Manufacturing Company stand 45 inches above the floor, which is of uncovered concrete. The stop-start switch must be pulled up to start and pushed down to stop the rotation of the sand-wheel. It rotates at 1,300 r.p.m. But the stop-start switch is located six inches from the floor on the left front of the machine, with a heavy 3½ foot leather belt, moving at high speed when the sand-wheel is in operation, between the operator and the stop-start switch. The operator sits on a table made in the firm's own machine shop, in front of the sand-wheel. On his left is a tray of 60 pairs of heels from which he lifts a few at a time for actual sanding, with the tray sitting on a table like that on which the sander himself sits. On the sander's right is another such table, with a tray, originally empty, into which he "flips" the sanded heels one by one as they are finished. Between the right-hand table and that on which the operator is seated is a six-inch space, through which the sander must pass to get into working position from the outside or to get out from in front of the sand-wheel in case of need. When the emery paper burns through, the wheel continues to rotate at 1,300 r.p.m., and the sander is hit by the loose end of the emery paper at each revolution of the wheel (until and unless the operator can get out of the way). He must get out from in front of the wheel, in this case, and circumnavigate tables and machine (the latter half way only) to reach the stop-start switch to stop the rotation of the wheel. When the machine is stopped, the operator travels back around machine and

tables, returns to the front of the wheel, disengages it, and changes the emery paper. Once more he circles the tables and machine to restart it and then returns to start operations once again.

The back-sanders also have to walk 20 feet to the supply room door to get new racks of heels for sanding, with 60 pairs of heels in each tray, and seven trays per rack. The racks stand 5½ feet high; they have unaligned steel wheels (two inches in diameter) at the foot of each of the rack's four corner posts. The racks usually require best efforts of two sanders to move into position between them. Then, the sanders remove the homemade trays from the racks, one by one, for sanding of the heels. When all seven trays have been sanded, two breast sanders come and push the racks to their sand-wheels, in turn. After the full rack is both back-sanded and breast-sanded, the latter sanders must push it, two being typically required to do the job once again, to the shipping room. This is a distance of some 35 feet.

QUESTIONS

1. What should now be done in respect to the union grievance of the turning lathe operators? Why? Does this reflect on the efficiency of the plant relayout? If so, how, and why?

2. Would you advise paying Popp Machine Tool Co. the $8,800, thus foregoing purchase of the new groovers? Why? To what degree, if any, would the decision depend upon finding jobs to which to transfer the displaced employees? Discuss.

3. Is the company attempting too much expansion all at once? Discuss (including a forecast of the managerial organization changes likely as a result of the expansion).

4. Should the company adopt a policy on gifts to company executives? Why? Should Hayes return the Christmas gift to Warman Lumber Co.? Why?

5. What improvements in workplace arrangements and materials handling system do you recommend? Discuss. (Remember the need for low product cost and operating efficiency and the importance attaching to any commitment of fixed capital).

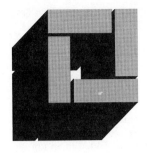

COMPREHENSIVE CASE

Cabot Brothers Manufacturing Company*

Cabot Brothers Manufacturing Company is a New England firm whose facilities are located in Boston, Massachusetts. It is a close family corporation, the sole stockholders being the three Cabot brothers—Bruce, Marvin, and Lyman. The company can trace its humble beginnings back to 1946 when the brothers pooled their resources to go into the heating duct business. This venture stopped before it started due to a shortage of sheet metal. As time went on, the brothers tried their hands at the cement block business and also attempted to market a home brake press they had built. They had some success in this latter venture, but the brothers wanted something more enduring.

It was at this time that they came upon an inventor who had a rotary mower idea for sale. Impressed with its possibilities, they contracted to use his basic design and started production.

During their first years in business, the brothers worked long hours in the plant as machinists, welders, assemblers, and painters. They were their own designers, accountants, engineers, and salesmen.

As Cabot Brothers' mowers found acceptance among farmers and large industrial users, sales volume grew from year to year beyond the brothers' expectations. In the five-year period from 1964 through 1968, sales had risen from $708,198 to a high of $7,357,000. At present, the company has a work force of 80 employees working under five foremen in nine departments, and manufacturing facilities covering several acres.

Management

The executive group is composed of Bruce Cabot, President and Treasurer; Lyman Cabot, Production Head; Marvin Cabot, Vice President; Vincent Goodwin, Controller; and Malcome Lusk, Sales Manager. The brothers consider themselves equal and thus there are no formal management lines between them.

Bruce and Marvin got along well together, but Lyman was usually at odds with them. There were constant arguments among the three men concerning various facets of company operations and procedures. Marvin was a follower and usually sided with Bruce on major issues. When Lyman did not get his way, he usually became quite obstinate and would not speak to his brothers for days on end.

In the course of a business meeting among the company executives, the topic of raw material purchasing came up. Lyman, as Production Head for the company, was in charge of raw material purchases. During the discussion, Bruce made note that while checking some recent purchase vouchers and inventory levels he had noticed that Lyman, in an effort to get a 10 percent discount, had purchased a two-year supply of toggle gears. Bruce suggested to Lyman that his policy of trying to obtain quantity discounts indicated a penny-wise and dollar foolish attitude since the company had tied up needed money unnecessarily for a two-year period.

* This case was prepared by Professor Joel Corman of Suffolk University.

Lyman stated that he had recently read a report that indicated an upcoming steel strike which economists felt would result in higher steel costs. Based on this information, Lyman had made the purchase. Lyman went on to say that production was his specialty and that, being an equal partner, his decisions should not be questioned and torn apart. "After all, I'm interested in the success of this company just as much as you are and thus I do those things which I feel are in the best interests of the firm." With this, Lyman's voice rose and he became quite excited stating that, if Bruce and Marvin were interested in pushing him out of the business, they would have a fight on their hands. The meeting ended in an uproar with Lyman walking out, slamming the door behind him. A few days later, observers noted that the brothers were back on speaking terms and all seemed forgiven.

Product Line

As noted earlier, Cabot Brothers Manufacturing is involved in the production of mowers. It caters to farmers and large industrial firms. Distribution is achieved through 26 distributors of farm equipment who in turn sell the products to farm implement dealers. Nine of these, located in the North Central, North East, and Southern part of the country, do 70 percent of the business. The only area where the company deals directly with individual dealers is in Montana. Mower sales are highly seasonal. The company depends on its largest sales volume during the spring and summer months. In the autumn, sales begin to fall off and during the midwinter months they virtually cease. This seasonal problem results in a two-month close down of operations each year. It is during this period that the brothers take their annual vacations.

Marketing

In its early years of operation, the company was represented by three salesmen who concentrated their efforts in the states of Indiana, Illinois, and Iowa as these were considered real farm-belt states which offered high sales potential. The company, however, experienced trouble in controlling these salesmen and was constantly involved in arguments over commission rates.

To alleviate this problem, Malcome Lusk was hired as sales manager. Shortly after taking over his duties, Lusk came to the conclusion that the company could get a wider coverage of its product by deleting its present sales force and shifting over to a distributor system. He defended his idea not only by stressing better coverage but also by pointing out to his principals that the mower business was so seasonal that it did not support a salesman from November 11 to April 1, a period of roughly five months. The brothers were not happy with their sales force and agreed that Lusk might have a sound idea.

At present, the company has no sales personnel. It sells its mowers through 26 distributors who, as mentioned earlier, cover a large portion of the North Central, North East, and Southern part of the country. These distributors in turn sell to farm implement dealers and the choice of dealers is left to the distributors. Lusk has no idea of how many dealers actually sell Cabot Mowers.

Malcome Lusk calls on the distributors fairly often. Sales meetings are held for the dealers at the distributors' places of business, and the distributors' men make periodic visits to the company plant to see the equipment and operate it for training purposes. The company advertises in magazines specifically oriented towards the farm and industry.

Credit Policy

Cabot Brothers' distributors receive a discount of 40 percent off list, and an additional 2 percent discount is offered to induce cash payment. Both Vincent Goodwin, the Controller, and Malcome Lusk, the Sales Manager, pass on credit. Collection letters are written by Goodwin and sent to Lusk for review before being mailed to the customer. Credit procedures vary for each account.

Production

With reference to the 85-man working force, 35 were considered skilled; the others ranged from semiskilled to unskilled. Of the three brothers, Lyman, as Production Head, was constantly in contact with the workers. Lyman was often very rude to employees, especially if a mistake had been made. He tended to make arbitrary decisions and often showed partiality toward one worker over another. He even went so far as to make intimate friendships with favored workers.

For some time the brothers had been trying without success to increase their output of mowers. During 1966 and 1967, the men had been turning out exactly 16 completed mowers a day. In 1968 the company made extensive improvements in the production operations. Power hoists had replaced hand lifting, jigs were refined, there was a minimum of precision fitting, and the finished mowers were hung on a conveyor belt which carried them away.

When the improvements in methods had been completed, Lyman timed the operation and set a rate of 18 mowers a day. Nevertheless, output remained at 16.

Even more of a problem was the fact that these improvements had done away with the need for 12 men. However, a check of records revealed that these men had not only been retained, but that two additional employees had been hired. Still output remained at 16. This situation was not only disheartening production-wise, but resulted in rising production costs. As a result, the company found it necessary to raise its selling prices.

During the latter part of 1967, the company was subjected to a secret attempt at unionization by the employees themselves. The attempt was unsuccessful because the brothers discovered it and fired the ringleaders before the situation got out of hand. After the unionization attempt, Bruce decided to establish a shop committee which would meet with him to discuss any topic bothering the workers, and he promised to do his best to correct any gross injustices or legitimate complaints. The workers had not responded well to this suggestion.

QUESTIONS

1. Evaluate the seriousness of family conflicts in this firm.
2. What major problems, if any, exist in the following areas: (a) product line? (b) marketing? (c) credit policy? (d) production?
3. List in the order of their priority the problems calling for management action and defend your ranking.
4. Present and justify solutions for each problem indicated in the preceding question.

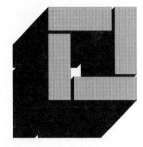

APPENDIX A

Checklist for Going into Business*

Thinking of starting a business? Ask yourself these questions.

You want to own and manage your own business. It's a good idea—provided you know what it takes and have what it takes.

Starting a business is risky at best. But your chances of making it go will be better if you understand the problems you'll meet and work out as many of them as you can before you start.

Here are some questions to help you think through what you need to know and do. Check each question if the answer is YES. Where the answer is NO, you have some work to do.

BEFORE YOU START

How About YOU?

Are you the kind of person who can get a business started and make it go? (Before you answer this question, use Worksheet 1 on pages 544-545.) _____

Think about *why* you want to own your own business. Do you want to badly enough to keep you working long hours without knowing how much money you'll end up with? _____

Have you worked in a business like the one you want to start? _____

Have you worked for someone else as a foreman or manager? _____

Have you had any business training in school? _____

Have you saved any money? _____

How About the Money?

Do you know how much money you will need to get your business started? (Use Worksheets 2 and 3 on pages 546 and 548 to figure this out.) _____

Have you counted up how much money of your own you can put into the business? _____

Do you know how much credit you can get from your suppliers—the people you will buy from? _____

Do you know where you can borrow the rest of the money you need to start your business? _____

* From *Small Marketers Aid No. 71* (Washington, D.C.: Small Business Administration, Revised August, 1970).

Have you figured out what net income per year you expect to get from the business? Count your salary and your profit on the money you put into the business? _____

Can you live on less than this so that you can use some of it to help your business grow? _____

Have you talked to a banker about your plans? _____

How About a Partner?

If you need a partner with money or know-how that you don't have, do you know someone who will fit—someone you can get along with? _____

Do you know the good and bad points about going it alone, having a partner, and incorporating your business? _____

Have you talked to a lawyer about it? _____

How About Your Customers?

Do most businesses in your community seem to be doing well? _____

Have you tried to find out whether stores like the one you want to open are doing well in your community and in the rest of the country? _____

Do you know what kind of people will want to buy what you plan to sell? _____

Do people like that live in the area where you want to open your store? _____

Do they need a store like yours? _____

If not, have you thought about opening a different kind of store or going to another neighborhood? _____

GETTING STARTED

Your Building

Have you found a good building for your store? _____

Will you have enough room when your business gets bigger? _____

Can you fix the building the way you want it without spending too much money? _____

Can people get to it easily from parking spaces, bus stops, or their homes? _____

Have you had a lawyer check the lease and zoning? _____

Equipment and Supplies

Do you know just what equipment and supplies you need and how much they will cost? (Worksheet 3 and the lists you made for it should show this.) _____

Can you save some money by buying secondhand equipment? _____

Your Merchandise

Have you decided what things you will sell? _____

Do you know how much or how many of each you will buy to open your store with? _____

Have you found suppliers who will sell you what you need at a good price? _____

Have you compared the prices and credit terms of different suppliers? _____

Your Records

Have you planned a system of records that will keep track of your income and expenses, what you owe other people, and what other people owe you? _____

Have you worked out a way to keep track of your inventory so that you will always have enough on hand for your customers but not more than you can sell? _____

Have you figured out how to keep your payroll records and take care of tax reports and payments? _____

Do you know what financial statements you should prepare? _____

Do you know how to use these financial statements? _____

Do you know an accountant who will help you with your records and financial statements? _____

Your Store and the Law

Do you know what licenses and permits you need? _____

Do you know what business laws you have to obey? _____

Do you know a lawyer you can go to for advice and for help with legal papers? _____

Protecting Your Store

Have you made plans for protecting your store against thefts of all kinds—shoplifting, robbery, burglary, employee stealing? _____

Have you talked with an insurance agent about what kinds of insurance you need? _____

Buying a Business Someone Else Has Started

Have you made a list of what you like and don't like about buying a business someone else has started? _____

Are you sure you know the real reason why the owner wants to sell his business? _____

Have you compared the cost of buying the business with the cost of starting a new business? _____

Is the stock up to date and in good condition? _____

Is the building in good condition? _____

Will the owner of the building transfer the lease to you? _____

Have you talked with other businessmen in the area to see what they think of the business? _____

Have you talked with the company's suppliers? _____

Have you talked with a lawyer about it? _____

MAKING IT GO

Advertising

Have you decided how you will advertise? (Newspapers —posters—handbills—radio —by mail?) _____

Do you know where to get help with your ads? _____

Have you watched what other stores do to get people to buy? _____

The Prices You Charge

Do you know how to figure what you should charge for each item you sell? _____

Do you know what other stores like yours charge? _____

Buying

Do you have a plan for finding out what your customers want? _____

Will your plan for keeping track of your inventory tell you when it is time to order more and how much to order? _____

Do you plan to buy most of your stock from a few suppliers rather than a little from many, so that those you buy from will want to help you succeed? _____

Selling

Have you decided whether you will have salesclerks or self-service? _____

Do you know how to get customers to buy? _____

Have you thought about why you like to buy from some salesmen while others turn you off? _____

Your Employees

If you need to hire someone to help you, do you know where to look? _____

Do you know what kind of person you need? _____

Do you know how much to pay? _____

Do you have a plan for training your employees? _____

Credit for Your Customers

Have you decided whether to let your customers buy on credit? _____

Do you know the good and bad points about joining a credit card plan? _____

Can you tell a deadbeat from a good credit customer? _____

A FEW EXTRA QUESTIONS

Have you figured out whether you could make more money working for someone else? _____

Does your family go along with your plan to start a business of your own? _____

Do you know where to find out about new ideas and new products? _____

Do you have a work plan for yourself and your employees? _____

Have you gone to the nearest Small Business Administration office for help with your plans? _____

If you have answered all these questions carefully, you've done some hard work and serious thinking.

That's good. But you have probably found some things you still need to know more about or do something about.

Do all you can for yourself, but don't hesitate to ask for help from people who can tell you what you need to know. Remember, running a business takes guts! You've got to be able to decide what you need and then go after it.

Good luck!

WORKSHEET NO. 1

Under each question, check the answer that says what you feel or comes closest to it. Be honest with yourself.

Are you a self-starter?

- ☐ I do things on my own. Nobody has to tell me to get going.
- ☐ If someone gets me started, I keep going all right.
- ☐ Easy does it, man. I don't put myself out until I have to.

How do you feel about other people?

- ☐ I like people. I can get along with just about anybody.
- ☐ I have plenty of friends—I don't need anyone else.
- ☐ Most people bug me.

Can you lead others?

- ☐ I can get most people to go along when I start something.
- ☐ I can give the orders if someone tells me what we should do.
- ☐ I let someone else get things moving. Then I go along if I feel like it.

Can you take responsibility?

- ☐ I like to take charge of things and see them through.
- ☐ I'll take over if I have to, but I'd rather let someone else be responsible.
- ☐ There's always some eager beaver around wanting to show how smart he is. I say let him.

How good an organizer are you?

- ☐ I like to have a plan before I start. I'm usually the one to get things lined up when the gang wants to do something.

☐ I do all right unless things get too goofed up. Then I cop out.

☐ You get all set and then something comes along and blows the whole bag. So I just take things as they come.

How good a worker are you?

☐ I can keep going as long as I need to. I don't mind working hard for something I want.

☐ I'll work hard for a while, but when I've had enough, that's it, man!

☐ I can't see that hard work gets you anywhere.

Can you make decisions?

☐ I can make up my mind in a hurry if I have to. It usually turns out O.K., too.

☐ I can if I have plenty of time. If I have to make up my mind fast, I think later I should have decided the other way.

☐ I don't like to be the one who has to decide things. I'd probably blow it.

Can people trust what you say?

☐ You bet they can. I don't say things I don't mean.

☐ I try to be on the level most of the time, but sometimes I just say what's easiest.

☐ What's the sweat if the other fellow doesn't know the difference?

Can you stick with it?

☐ If I make up my mind to do something, I don't let *anything* stop me.

☐ I usually finish what I start—if it doesn't get fouled up.

☐ If it doesn't go right away, I turn off. Why beat your brains out?

How good is your health?

☐ Man, I *never* run down!

☐ I have enough energy for most things I want to do.

☐ I run out of juice sooner than most of my friends seem to.

Now count the checks you made.

How many checks are there beside the *first* answer to each question?   _____

How many checks are there beside the *second* answer to each question?   _____

How many checks are there beside the *third* answer to each question?   _____

If most of your checks are beside the first answers, you probably have what it takes to run a business. If not, you're likely to have more trouble than you can handle by yourself. Better find a partner who is strong on the points you're weak on. If many checks are beside the third answer, not even a good partner will be able to shore you up.

Now go back and answer the first question on page 540.

WORKSHEET NO. 2

Estimated Monthly Expenses

Item	Your estimate of monthly expenses based on sales of $_____ per year	Your estimate of how much cash you need to start your business (See column 3.)	What to put in column 2 (These figures are typical for one kind of business, you will have to decide how many months to allow for in your business.)
	Column 1	Column 2	Column 3
Salary of owner-manager	$	$	2 times column 1
All other salaries and wages			3 times column 1
Rent			3 times column 1
Advertising			3 times column 1
Delivery expense			3 times column 1
Supplies			3 times column 1
Telephone and telegraph			3 times column 1
Other utilities			3 times column 1
Insurance			Payment required by insurance company
Taxes, including Social Security			4 times column 1
Interest			3 times column 1
Maintenance			3 times column 1

Legal and other professional fees		3 times column 1
Miscellaneous		3 times column 1
Starting Costs You Only Have To Pay Once		Leave column 2 blank
Fixtures and equipment		Fill in Worksheet on page 548 and put the total here
Decorating and remodeling		Talk it over with a contractor
Installation of fixtures and equipment		Talk to suppliers from whom you buy these
Starting inventory		Suppliers will probably help you estimate this
Deposits with public utilities		Find out from utilities companies
Legal and other professional fees		Lawyer, accountant, and so on
Licenses and permits		Find out from city offices what you have to have
Advertising and promotion for opening		Estimate what you'll use
Accounts receivable		What you need to buy more stock until credit customers pay
Cash		For unexpected expenses or losses, special purchases, etc.
Other		Make a separate list and enter total
TOTAL ESTIMATED CASH YOU NEED TO START WITH	$	Add up all the numbers in column 2

WORKSHEET NO. 3

List of Furniture, Fixtures, and Equipment

Leave out or add items to suit your business. Use separate sheets to list exactly what you need for each of the items below.	If you plan to pay cash in full, enter the full amount below and in the last column.	If you are going to pay by installments, fill out the columns below. Enter in the last column your down payment plus at least one installment.			Estimate of the cash you need for furniture, fixtures, and equipment.
		Price	Down payment	Amount of each installment	
Counters	$	$	$	$	$
Storage shelves, cabinets					
Display stands, shelves, tables					
Cash register					
Safe					
Window display fixtures					
Special lighting					
Outside sign					
Delivery equipment if needed					

TOTAL FURNITURE, FIXTURES, AND EQUIPMENT (Enter this figure also in Worksheet 2 under "Starting Costs You Only Have To Pay Once," page 547.) $

INDEX